CITY POLITICS
PRIVATE POWER
AND PUBLIC POLICY

Third Edition

DENNIS R. JUDD
University of Chicago at Illinois

TODD SWANSTROM
State University of New York–Albany

Longman

New York   San Francisco   Boston
London   Toronto   Sydney   Tokyo   Singapore   Madrid
Mexico City   Munich   Paris   Cape Town   Hong Kong   Montreal

Publisher: *Priscilla McGeehon*
Acquisitions Editor: *Eric Stano*
Marketing Manager: *Megan Galvin-Fak*
Production Manager: *Mark Naccarelli*
Project Coordination, Text Design, and Electronic Page Makeup: *Nesbitt Graphics, Inc.*
Cover Design Manager: *Wendy Ann Fredericks*
Cover Designer: *Nancy Sabato*
Cover Illustration: *© Daniel Glavez/Corbis*
Manufacturing Buyer: *Roy Pickering*
Printer and Binder: *The Maple-Vail Book Manufacturing Group*
Cover Printer: *John P. Pow*

Library of Congress Cataloging-in-Publication Data

Judd, Dennis R.
    City politics: private power and public policy / Dennis R. Judd,
Todd Swanstrom.— 3rd ed.
        p.   cm.
    Includes bibliographical references and index.
    ISBN 0-321-05269-2
    1. Municipal government—United States. 2. Urban policy—United States. 3. United
States—Economic policy. 4. Sociology, Urban—United States.   I. Swanstrom, Todd.
II. Title.

JS331 .J78 2002
320.8′5′0973—dc21   00-052057

Please visit our website at http://www.ablongman.com

ISBN 0-321-05269-2

1 2 3 4 5 6 7 8 9 10—MA—04 03 02 01

CONTENTS

Preface   ix

CHAPTER 1   THE POLITICS OF AMERICAN CITIES:
            AN INTRODUCTION   1

            The Culture of Privatism   1
            The Expanding Responsibilities of City Governments   3
            The Complex Task of Governance   5
            The Politics of Choice   8
            The Politics of Secession   10

PART I   CONTESTED TERRAIN:
            POLITICAL CONFLICT IN THE CITIES   13

CHAPTER 2   THE PRIVATE CITY AND LOCAL DEMOCRACY:
            THE POLITICAL LEGACY OF THE NINETEENTH
            CENTURY   15

            National Development and the Cities   15
            The Urbanization of America   16
            The Competition for Urban Growth   18
            The Breakdown of Community: Industrialization   24
            The Breakdown of Community: Transportation   27
            The Breakdown of Community: Immigration   30
            Social Darwinism and the Ideology of Success   35
            The Increasing Importance of Municipal Services   37
            The Fight for Control of City Governments   42
            The Political Isolation of the Cities   44

CHAPTER 3   PARTY MACHINES AND POLITICAL
            ENTREPRENEURS   52

            Machines and Machine-Style Politics   52
            The Origins of Machine Politics   53

James Pendergast: A Political Entrepreneur in Action   57
Did Machines Centralize Power and "Get the Job Done"?   59
Were Machines Vehicles of Upward Mobility?   63
Did the Machines Help the Immigrants Assimilate?   65
The Social Reform Alternative   67
Machine Politics in Today's Cities   71

CHAPTER 4   THE STRUGGLE FOR POLITICAL CONTROL:
THE REFORM LEGACY   78

The Motive for Reform   78
The Reform Environment   80
The Campaigns Against Machine Rule   82
"Efficiency and Economy" in Municipal Affairs   91
The Business Model   94
Commission and Manager Government   96
The Bias of Municipal Reform   99
Did Reform Kill the Machines?   101
The Reform Legacy and the Politics of Representation   103

CHAPTER 5   THE NEW DEAL COALITION AND THE CITIES   110

The Changing Political Balance   110
The Political Isolation of the Cities   111
The New Urban Consciousness   114
The Urban Wing of the Democratic Party   116
The Depression and the Cities   117
The Cities in the Intergovernmental System   123
The Cities in National Politics   128

PART II   THE CITY IN NATIONAL POLITICS   133

CHAPTER 6   THE RISE OF THE DIVIDED METROPOLIS   135

The Roots of the Urban Crisis   135

◆ The Central Cities   138
The Great Migration: From the Farm to the City   138
The New Immigrants   145
Concentrated Poverty   152

◆ The Suburbs   157
The Railroad and Streetcar Suburbs: 1815–1918   158
The First Automobile Suburbs: 1918–1945   160
The Bedroom Suburbs: 1946–1965   162
The Enclave Suburbs: 1965–Present   166
The Great Divide   169

CHAPTER 7   NATIONAL POLICY AND THE DIVIDED METROPOLIS   177

National Policies and Urban Development   177
Housing, Slums, and Racial Segregation   178
The Struggle over Public Housing   182
Urban Renewal and Its Problems   185
The Urban Renewal Steamroller   188
Public Housing: Urban Renewal's Stepchild   191
The Legacy of Inner-City Programs   194
National Policy and the Suburbs   195
The Weak Policies of the Post–Civil Rights Era   200
The Suburban Bias in National Transportation Policies   202
The Contradictory Effects of National Urban Policy   206

CHAPTER 8   THE RISE AND FALL OF NATIONAL URBAN POLICY   214

The Politics of National Urban Policy   214
The Federal Role Under Two Democratic Presidents   215
    The Great Society Programs: Between Image and Reality   220
    The Backlash Against Urban Programs   222
The Decentralization of Urban Programs   224
    *Streamlining Government: The Housing and
        Community Development Act*   227
President Carter and the Decline of Urban Policy   231
The Reagan/Bush Urban Policy: Survival of the Fittest   235
    Urban Enterprise Zones   240
Urban Policy in the Clinton Era   242
The Waning Political Influence of Cities   246

CHAPTER 9   THE RISE OF THE SUNBELT CITIES   257

The Concept of the Sunbelt   257
The Rise of the Sunbelt   260
The Changing Political Balance   265
Why the Sunbelt Boomed   267
Regional Conflict: Sunbelt Versus Frostbelt   271
The Changing Politics of Sunbelt Cities   272
The Reaction Against Uncontrolled Growth   273
The Changing Electorate   276
The Future of Urban Politics in the Sunbelt   277

PART III   URBAN POLITICS AND THE FRACTURING
OF THE AMERICAN POLITICAL COMMUNITY   283

CHAPTER 10   THE POLITICS OF SECESSION: THE SUBURBS   285

The Governmental Fragmentation of America's Urban Areas   285
The Motive to Separate from the Cities   287

The Entrepreneurial Shaping of Suburbia   290
  Selling the American Dream   294
  Enforcing Segregation   295
Suburban Governments and Zoning   298
The National Challenge to Exclusionary Zoning   302
New Jersey's Challenge to Exclusionary Zoning   305
The Costs of Exclusion   308

CHAPTER 11   URBAN SPRAWL AND THE GOVERNANCE OF
             METROPOLITAN REGIONS   316

Post-Suburbia   316
The Growing Concerns About Sprawl   317
The Consequences of Sprawl   320
Smart Growth   323
The New Urbanism   328
Reforming Metropolitan Governance   331
Whither Sprawl?   336

CHAPTER 12   FISCAL CRISIS AND THE PROBLEMS OF
             GOVERNANCE   340

The Roots of the Urban Fiscal Crisis   340
City Expenditures   341
City Revenues   349
Municipal Bonds   353
The Ratings Game   356
A Useful Comparison: New York and Chicago   358
The Political Sources of Urban Fiscal Stress   364

CHAPTER 13   REVITALIZING THE CITIES: THE GROWTH
             IMPERATIVE   370

An Urban Renaissance   370
Why Cities Pursue Growth   372
The Changing Economic Fortunes of the Central Cities   375
The Corporate Center Strategy: The Baltimore Example   378
The Development of Urban Tourism   382
  Convention Centers   382
  Sports Stadiums   386
  Festival Malls and Urban Entertainment Centers   389
  Casino Gaming   391
The New Downtown Economies   394

CHAPTER 14   THE CHALLENGE OF URBAN GOVERNANCE   400

The Delicate Task of Governance   400
Urban Liberalism and the Dilemmas of Coalition Politics   402
  The Rewards of Political Incorporation   405

Urban Populism: The Rise of the Neighborhood Organizing
Movement 411
From Protest to Politics 415
Neighborhood Nonprofits and City Politics 419
Urban Conservativism 422
Finding a Consensus 427

CHAPTER 15 THE FRAGMENTED SOCIETY 433

The Rise of Urban Enclaves 433
Are Cities Obsolete? 435
The Urban Future 436

Index 439

PREFACE

This third edition of *City Politics* has been comprehensively revised to make it relevant to the issues of the new millennium. New research has been incorporated throughout the book so that it may serve as a scholarly reference work—as it has in the past—as well as a textbook accessible to students at all levels. *City Politics* should be useful to advanced scholars and graduate students as well as students taking their first courses in urban politics, urban sociology, urban planning, urban geography, or urban history. It is not easy to write a book intended to accomplish such diverse goals. To do so, we not only attempt to synthesize the findings in the vast secondary literature of urban politics; we also rely on our own original research. To make the complex scholarship of the field accessible to students, we build the book around a clear, coherent narrative. As far as possible, each chapter picks up where the previous one left off, so that the reader can gain an understanding of how urban politics have unfolded for the more than two hundred years of the nation's history.

As in the previous editions of this text, the thread that knits the book together is spun from the premise that the politics of cities and metropolitan areas can be understood as a complex interaction among the institutions, actors, and resources of both the public and the private spheres. Urban life would hardly be possible without the public sector. Governments are vested with the capacity to represent the collective needs and aspirations of citizens. But in the United States, governments operate within strict boundaries delimited, on the one hand, by democratic processes, and on the other, by a culture that tends to favor private activity and the marketplace over collective action. A bewildering array of private institutions—defense contractors, large corporations, banks, insurance companies, retailers, real estate companies, and so on—make critical decisions that determine the well-being of urban communities. Because of this, any comprehensive account of city politics must show how public and private institutions interact to make cities both governable and economically viable.

The politics of cities cannot be understood without keeping in mind that cities have evolved within a larger metropolitan and national context. For more than one hundred years, a national population movement has been relocating people from the urban core to the suburbs. Suburbanization has profoundly affected the central cities and has also helped shape national politics and political issues. In the nineteenth century, some of the nation's most contentious political issues revolved around westward expansion and the growth of the cities. For decades, Americans moved west. Images of the frontier sustained an anti-urban national culture. At the same time, immigrants streamed into the cities. In the twentieth century, the older central cities continued to attract a disproportionate share of new immigrants and of minorities living in poverty, while at the same time the suburbs developed as separate political jurisdictions made up predominantly of white, more affluent families. The westward movement seemed to continue. In the last half century, millions of Americans have left the so-called Frostbelt for Florida, Texas, California, and other places in the Sunbelt. Deep political divisions have arisen as a result of these demographic changes. Within urban areas, racial and ethnic tensions have nurtured a politics of secession; affluent Americans have moved away from minorities and the recent immigrants into protected enclaves. Older cities have often been pitted against suburbs, suburbs compete with one another, and the Frostbelt has often battled the Sunbelt.

To weave these elements into a single narrative, we show that city politics in the United States can be understood as involving: (1) a national culture of privatism, (2) a growth imperative at the local level, (3) a logic of governance arising from democratic norms, and (4) a politics of secession within metropolitan regions.

1. *A culture of privatism:* More than from any other source, the American political tradition is derived from Thomas Jefferson's injunction that the best government is that which governs least. The limited government ideal was founded on the assumption that freedom would be preserved not primarily through activities of government, but through its absence. Considering how strong this cultural imperative has been, it might seem strange that, over time, the responsibilities of governments at all levels in the United States have expanded remarkably. Sometimes, this expansion has taken place as a result of bitter struggles between those who believe that governments should protect collective interests, and those who believe the market can provide. Just as often, however—and perhaps usually, in the case of local governments—the public sphere has expanded to promote and support economic growth.

2. *A politics of growth:* City governments are under constant pressure to attract investors who can provide economic opportunities for city residents and boost the local tax base. Without investment, cities soon find themselves in a fiscal bind, forced to either cut services or raise taxes. Without local prosperity, businesses and residents look elsewhere, and if sufficiently dissatisfied, they move. For these reasons, business and investors with mobile resources can make claims on cities that are difficult for public officials and voters to resist, even if they want to. In the nineteenth century, this imperative was expressed in the railroad wars from the 1850s and beyond, when cities went heavily into debt buying railroad stock and providing terminal facilities and land to railroad companies, all with an eye to promoting local prosperity. In

the late twentieth century, this imperative has become expressed in the intense competition among cities for professional sports teams, convention centers, corporate office towers, and similar undertakings.

3. *A logic of governance:* At the same time that city officials must satisfy investors, they must also satisfy voters. Under city charters, political authority flows from the voters, who elect the mayor and other public officials. To assemble a winning electoral coalition, politicians must spread the benefits of city government broadly enough to gain a minimum level of satisfaction from a variety of political interests and groups. If enough people begin to feel that their interests or needs are ignored, two things may happen: other politicians may step into the fray and depose those in office, or unrest and even violence may erupt as an expression of pent-up grievances. This is the fundamental logic of governance in a democratic polity, as urban history reveals. In the late nineteenth century, immigrant politicians came to power by appealing to feelings of ethnic solidarity among the Irish and other groups. Likewise, late in the twentieth century, African-American and Latino mayors were elected because their constituents felt that their needs were being ignored.

4. A *politics of secession:* Throughout American history, the urban population has tended to sort itself out into neighborhoods of different class, racial, and ethnic characteristics. At the end of the twentieth century, these divisions have become institutionalized in independent and often competing political jurisdictions. Urban areas have become fragmented into enclaves that divide rich from poor, minority from white, immigrant from "native." Such fragmentation has undermined processes of political accommodation and compromise. The politics of secession occurred when municipalities first adopted zoning laws in the early years of the twentieth century. Its latest expression is found in gated communities, with their guarded gates and privatized governments.

The culture of privatism, the imperative of growth, the logic of governance, and the politics of secession are constant elements that recur throughout America's urban history. These four forces generate the tensions that make the study of urban politics so interesting. Urban leaders in all historical periods have tried to promote local economic prosperity, but they have had to do so within the context of a culture that is distrustful of government, democratic processes with many claimants, and often against a background of intense racial, ethnic, and social divisions and animosities. Truly, American cities have been the crucibles in which many of the nation's most difficult political conflicts have converged.

Scholars and students will find their own research opportunities enriched by several new features incorporated into this edition:

- Comprehensive revisions of all chapters in order to achieve thematic clarity and incorporate recent research;
- The incorporation of preliminary estimates and data from the 2000 census, and updated statistics from other sources as well;

- A new chapter on urban sprawl and the remedies commonly promoted to alleviate its worst effects. In this chapter we show that Smart Growth, the New Urbanism, and Metropolitan Reform all are made politically difficult because of the politics of privatism, the imperative of growth, the logic of governance, and the politics of secession. In a nutshell, the growing national concern about sprawl has come up against a resistance to comprehensive planning, the tendency of every jurisdiction to fight for its share of investment, a deep attachment to small government, and an unwillingness to join in regional solutions to urban problems;
- A revised analysis of the evolution of national urban policy, with a complete account of the urban policies of the Clinton Administration;
- Expanded material on suburban enclaves, including gated communities;
- An updated account of urban fiscal conditions;
- A revised discussion of tourism as an important component of central city revitalization;
- A new concluding chapter that focuses on the problems that cities and regions face at the beginning of the twenty-first century.

We are pleased to be able to thank, in print, the following reviewers who made insightful comments and suggestions:

Yvette Alex-Assensoh at Indiana University; Susan E. Clarke at University of Colorado; Joseph R. Marbach at Seton Hall University; Melissa Marschall at University of Illinois at Chicago; David J. Olson at University of Washington; Michael Rich at Emory University; Nadia Rubaii-Barrett at New Mexico State University; Alan Saltzstein at CSU-Fullerton; Mara Sidney at Rutgers University-Newark; and Jon R. Taylor at University of St. Thomas. These scholars did their best to help us refine our themes and bring the latest research to bear. Eric Stano, our editor at Longman Publishers, helped keep the book on track. We thank him for his support and guidance.

Dennis R. Judd

Todd Swanstrom

THE POLITICS OF AMERICAN CITIES: AN INTRODUCTION

THE CULTURE OF PRIVATISM

City politics in the United States arises from the intersection of governmental power and private resources. At both the national and local levels, governments in twentieth-century America have vastly increased their responsibilities. Even so, the growth of the public sector has not eclipsed the authority of private institutions to make many of the society's most critical decisions involving jobs, land use, and investment. City governments (indeed, governments at all levels) can influence, but they do not control, the voluntary actions and decisions that, taken together, determine the material well-being, the social character, and the quality of life of an urban community.

Throughout our national history, cities have been conceived more in economic than in cultural, social, and political terms. Founded originally as centers of trade and commerce, America's cities and towns came into being as places where people could make money. This was true for the oldest colonial cities and for cities on the frontier. The movement west across the continent placed towns at the leading edge of territorial expansion:

> America was settled as a long, thin line of urban places, scattering outward and westward from the Atlantic seaboard. The popular imagination has it that farmers came first and villages later. The historian's truth is that villages and towns came first, pulling farmers along to settle the land around and between urban settlements.[1]

Each town was its own capitalist system in miniature, held together by the independent actions of individuals in search of profit and fortune. The restless search for wealth encouraged the formation of what urban historian Sam Bass Warner called a "culture of privatism." In using this term, Warner was referring to a set of cultural values stressing individual efforts and aspirations over collective or public purposes: "[the] local politics of American cities have depended for their actors, and for a good deal of their subject matter, on the changing focus of men's

1

private economic activities."[2] In a culture of privatism, the goal of local government was to maximize the opportunities for individual economic advancement.

The culture of privatism has made the American pattern of urban development unique. Like American cities, the great cities of Europe, Asia, and elsewhere evolved as places of commerce and trade. Very much in contrast to the cities of the United States, however, they also evolved as centers of religious, military, cultural, and political authority. Before the modern nation-state, there was the city-state, "owing no fealty to any other sovereign, temporal or spiritual, outside its own territory."[3] The English writer Charles Dickens wrote, "The city . . . as it appears throughout all ages and in all lands, [is] the symbol and carrier of civilization. . . . it is an institutional centre, the seat of the institutions of the society which it represents. It is a seat of religion, of culture and social contact, and of political and administrative organization; . . . it is the seat of commerce and transport."[4]

Rome, the historic capital of Italy, has been occupied since about 1500 B.C. When workers excavated the city's subway system after World War II, they uncovered, layer by layer, traces of the city's history reaching far into the past.[5] By the sixth century B.C. Rome had established political control over the central Roman province and was beginning to assert authority over other parts of the Italian peninsula. In the next few centuries it became the political and administrative center of a vast empire, reaching the height of its grandeur in the first and early second centuries A.D., when its population exceeded one million people. Even as the empire weakened and finally dissolved, the city continued to exert enormous cultural and religious influence around the globe as the seat of the Roman Catholic Church.

Like Rome, London has also presided over a global empire. The Romans founded the city they called Londinium as an administrative outpost at the far reaches of their empire. It experienced rapid growth in the sixteenth and seventeenth centuries, and subsequently became the industrial, commercial, and political capital of the British Empire. The Crown, Parliament, the Royal Navy, and vast governmental bureaucracies clustered together in London to manage an empire that circled the globe.

Paris is older than London. Sitting in the center of a huge basin drained by the Seine, it has been a center of trade and commerce for more than 2,000 years and has also emerged as a center of religion, culture, and political power. From the time that it was designated a capital in Roman times until the present, no city in France has challenged its preeminence. Indeed, probably no other city in the world, not even Rome, so completely defines and dominates the national culture of its country.

Urban development in the United States took an utterly different course. Despite its status as a global center of finance and corporate power, even New York cannot be compared to the ancient cities of the world. New York began as a Dutch colonial settlement in 1609, becoming a city, known as New Amsterdam, in 1625. By the time of the American Revolution its population was just over 50,000, making it, by far, the largest city on the eastern seaboard. Throughout the nineteenth and twentieth centuries, it remained the nation's greatest financial and commercial city. It is important to note, however, that New York never exerted political or administrative authority on behalf of a central government, and it was never the seat of religious authority—no city could be in a nation that had explicitly divorced religion from state power. In 1790 Congress designated Washington, D.C., as the new nation's capital, making it one of the few cities in the world to be planned solely as a national capital. Almost all the states followed that first example; indeed most of them took great care to locate their state capitals "downstate" or "upstate," well away from the major cities.

In other parts of the world, cities have had long histories as the carriers of power, culture, and civilization. By contrast, in the United States the primary and sometimes the only purpose of cities was practical. They were places of economic opportunity, or they were nothing. The French philosopher Jean-Paul Sartre observed, "For [Europeans] a city is, above all, a past; to [Americans] it is mainly a future; everything they like in the city is everything it has not yet become and everything it can be."[6] Like so many Europeans before him, Sartre was startled by the chaos and squalor of American cities, the relative absence of monumental architecture and orderly development. He recognized the cause of this difference when he said, "The American city, originally, [was] a camp in the desert. People from far away, attracted by a mine, a petroleum field or fertile land, arrived one day and settled as quickly as possible in a clearing, near a river."[7] Though containing a bit of poetic license, Sartre's version captures the essence of American city building.

Lacking a long cultural, social, and political history, valued for little more than their economic utility, cities in the United States have generally been regarded with distrust and as threats to, rather than the seats of, civilization. The habit of equating cities with corrupt political power and with a breakdown of social morals is as old as the nation. Thomas Jefferson wrote, "I view great cities as pestilential to the morals, the health, and the liberties of man." He even thought that democracy could not withstand the growth of cities: "I think our governments will remain virtuous for many centuries as long as they are chiefly agricultural; and this will be as long as there shall be vacant lands in any part of America. When they get piled upon one another in large cities as in Europe, they will become corrupt as in Europe."[8] More recently, John V. Lindsay, a former mayor of New York, observed that "in the American psychology, the city has been a basically suspect institution."[9]

THE EXPANDING RESPONSIBILITIES OF CITY GOVERNMENTS

Despite the persistence of an antiurban cultural tradition, the United States has become one of the most urbanized countries in the world. The basic reason is simple: Cities are engines of economic growth. Early American cities, usually located on rivers or seacoasts, were centers of exchange where the agricultural surplus could be traded for manufactured goods. Without towns, farmers would have remained at subsistence levels, unable to adopt new technologies or to accumulate wealth. National economic growth was promoted through penetration into unsettled land, and exploitation of the land and resources found there was made possible by the constantly expanding network of cities, towns, and villages.

Over time, American cities were transformed from centers of trade to centers of production. The economic transformation brought about by the factory system in the nineteenth century depended on cities. Energy, raw materials, and labor converged at the wharves, factories, and the downtowns of cities, and these cities sent forth to the world an amazing variety of goods such as finished steel, farm implements, prepackaged meat, and clothes. Cities still play that role. Today, it is in the largest cities that businesses have the best chance of assembling teams of computer experts, corporate lawyers, fashion models and fashion designers, and advertising executives. It is not surprising that the fashion industry is centered in midtown Manhattan and a dynamic concentration of small businesses specializing in the new media of linked computers such as the Internet has emerged in lower Manhattan.

It is tempting to think that the economic vitality that makes cities work occurs through market forces, that somehow cities become trade centers in one era and locations for computers and media in another solely because entrepreneurs happen to locate in one city, but not another, for their own unpredictable reasons. Actually, this has never been the case. Ironically, an important reason why the public powers of American cities expanded was that local entrepreneurs wanted some protection from the vicissitudes of the marketplace. As we discuss in Chapter 2, the founders of cities and the business elites who made their money in them recognized that in order to ensure their mutual success, they had to take steps to promote their city or region. In nineteenth-century America, boosters went to some pains to advertise their city's natural advantages—a harbor or strategic location on a river, for example, or proximity to rich farming and mining areas. They boasted about local culture—music societies, libraries, and universities. And they went further than boasting; they used the powers of city governments to promote local prosperity. These entrepreneurs were aware that they were participating in a race that some cities would win and others would lose. As the city went, so went their own prospects. Municipalities were corporations that could be used to help finance crucial transportation connections. After the 1850s, cities aggressively bought railroad stocks, made loan guarantees to railroad companies, and gave away land in their efforts to become linked to a growing network of rail lines. Many cities spent so much money in these efforts that they were dragged into financial ruin when a national depression hit in the early 1870s.

Today—as we discuss in Chapter 13—civic elites still use the powers and resources of cities to promote local (and their own) prosperity; indeed, at times and for some cities, it appears that all politics revolves around such efforts. Cities float bonds to build new sports stadiums. They offer tax abatements and hand out subsidies to encourage the construction of enclosed malls. They run convention and tourism bureaus, repair fountains, plant flowers, restore historic buildings, and intensify crime control in areas used by tourists. In these and countless other ways cities today use their public powers and resources to promote local economic prosperity.

Besides promoting economic development, urban leaders have expanded the public powers and responsibilities of cities over time in an attempt to solve the social and physical problems of the urban environment. As cities grew, sometimes exploding within a few years from small settlements to densely packed industrial cities teeming with immigrants, the consequences of unrestrained private activity became impossible to ignore. Individuals saw that they were powerless to correct or to escape from collective problems such as crime, fire, and disease. As urban problems grew worse, municipal governments assumed increasingly complex responsibilities—to supply water and dispose of wastes, to fight fire and crime, to build and maintain streets and bridges. The expansion of the public sector was fueled by recurring crises that threatened not only the health and welfare of urban residents but also local economic vitality.

Industrial cities began to expand their responsibilities significantly not only in response to crises threatening the health and welfare of urban residents, but also because some conditions that had seemed tolerable and inevitable (from muddy streets and polluted water to open sewers) came to be regarded as unacceptable. Much of the infrastructure and many of the municipal responsibilities of American cities date from the half-century of city growth following the Civil War. Municipal governments provided a range of new and expanded services administered by full-time employees. They built parks, adopted building codes, and paved streets. They wrote health and sanitation codes. They granted franchises and licenses for telephone, gas, and electrical service, and public transportation.

Cities today provide a remarkable array of services. They build and maintain a public infrastructure—roads, bridges, sewer lines, sewage treatment plants, water mains, parks, zoos, hospitals, and sometimes even universities. They provide police and fire protection. They collect garbage (or pay someone who does). They run public health services that inspect restaurants, vaccinate children, and test for the HIV (AIDS) virus. Through city zoning ordinances, they influence the location of homes, factories, office buildings, restaurants, and parking lots. Through local building codes, they regulate such matters as plumbing, wiring, building materials, the height of structures, and architectural styles. Cities poison rats and sometimes try to scare away pigeons. These public activities and more are essential to the safety and well-being of all city residents. Without them, life in most cities would quickly become not only dangerous but intolerable.

THE COMPLEX TASK OF GOVERNANCE

Although American cities often seem preoccupied with promoting prosperity, they are not plutocracies, with political power simply handed over to wealthy elites. American city governments are run according to rules that reflect a long tradition of local democracy that cuts against the grain of the culture of privatism.[10] Alongside individual rights are the rights of cities to self-rule based on democratic principles.[11] In order to be elected mayor or a member of the city council, politicians must appeal to voters. City charters and the formal rules of city politics emphasize votes, not money.

Until the mid-nineteenth century, political authority was held mostly by men of social standing or wealth. In the cities, "leadership fell to those who exercised economic leadership. All leadership, political, social, economic, tended to collect in the same set of hands."[12] Business owners, professionals, and aristocrats ran municipal affairs without challenge, deriving their authority from their social standing within the informal communities that composed the cities. However, as cities grew in size and complexity, formal mechanisms of governance slowly replaced community norms. Gradually, politics became a full-time occupation for professional politicians who learned to mobilize the mass electorate. When forced to compete in the electoral arena, members of the business, professional, and social elites often won elections, but after the Civil War they were increasingly replaced by politicians from working-class backgrounds (see Chapter 3). In appealing for immigrants' votes, these politicians had a significant advantage, for they were drawn from the ranks of the ethnic groups that were streaming into the industrial cities. By the end of the nineteenth century machine-style politics became the subject of a momentous political struggle. In Chapter 4 we describe the strategies employed by civic elites and upper-middle-class elements to loosen the grip of the machines and reduce the influence of immigrant voters.

The leaders of the municipal reform movement—one of the most influential reform movements in American history—argued that city government should be run just like a business; experts and administrators, they said, should replace politicians. In their view the major objectives of city government should be to keep taxes as low as possible and to provide municipal services cheaply and efficiently. Such a definition of a city's purpose certainly seems plausible, but it is a restricted view of what urban government is about because it ignores the complex task of *governance.* City governments are mechanisms for arbitrating among the groups and factions that make up the local polity, a task that is as difficult today as it ever was in the past (a topic we take up in Chapter 14). Democratic procedures invest those who govern with the legitimacy to act in the name of citizens collectively. Governmental authority springs from the right to "make and apply decisions that are binding upon any and all segments of society."[13] City officials can preserve their claim to authority only as long as they seem sufficiently responsive to a large enough proportion of the urban population. Just as the currency of the economic marketplace is money, votes are the currency of the political system. In a democratic system, politicians must spread the rewards of public policies around in order to construct governing coalitions. If only a few benefit from the activities of government, opposition will arise, and political leaders may find themselves replaced.

Democratic procedures impose a *political logic* that forces public leaders to build broad coalitions of support. To keep these coalitions intact, politicians must provide as many services as possible in order to please a sufficient number of voters and to maximize their chances of getting reelected. Yet, the fiscal resources of local government are limited, and some groups are bound to receive more benefits than others. For example, middle-class residents may bridle at the idea of providing free health care, housing assistance, and college tuition to the disadvantaged; equally, they often resent the subsidies used to support sports stadiums, convention centers, and other civic projects. When local governments begin spending enough to cause taxes to rise significantly, businesses and middle-class homeowners may revolt, or move away.

Because investors and businesses are generally free to locate wherever they please—they can, if they wish, move from a central city to a nearby suburb, from one suburb to another, or from one metropolitan area to another—cities must compete with one another. Politicians, therefore, are forced to follow an *economic logic* requiring them to adopt policies acceptable to businesses and investors. Normally, this means keeping tax rates acceptably low while providing an adequate level of services and amenities. In most cases, it also means that a city will actively promote investment in various ways. Nothing enhances a politician's prospects quite so much as local prosperity, whether or not the city's public policies had anything to do with it.

The problem is that economic growth does not benefit everyone—in an urban economy a rising tide does *not* lift all boats. For renters and low-income residents, for example, a booming economy with rising land values may put affordable housing out of reach. Growth in the downtown corporate and financial sector may create a lot of high-paying jobs for educated (and mostly suburban) professionals but leave many central-city residents unemployed. A downtown that encroaches on nearby neighborhoods may benefit the businesses located in the new office towers but compromise the quality of life for nearby residents. Many analysts have noted a pattern in the costs and benefits of urban growth. Recently, cities have frequently subsidized corporate investment in downtown offices, upscale shopping, and tourism and entertainment. However, the best jobs in the downtown service economy often have been taken mostly by suburban commuters, and the big projects that have driven cities into debt have not always delivered the promised benefits.

Throughout the 1980s, cities tried to regenerate their local economies by lowering taxes and offering subsidies to business investors. In cities all across the country, gleaming office towers, luxury hotels, and enclosed malls sprang up. At the same time, cities slashed spending for housing, schools, and other public services and amenities. Partially as a result, downtown prosperity existed side by side with growing numbers of homeless people, decaying neighborhoods, and deteriorating parks, bridges, and roads. For a time, economic logic, the idea that cities should primarily promote growth, seemed to overwhelm other concerns, such as the well-being of neighborhoods or the health and welfare of ordinary citizens.

Social issues took on renewed urgency in 1992, in the wake of the riots that broke out in Los Angeles that spring. The riots served as a reminder that issues connected to race, ethnicity, and poverty could not be ignored. As we discuss in Chapter 6, in recent decades American cities have had to absorb millions of immigrants from the Caribbean, Mexico, Latin America, and Asia. Urban governance has become a delicate task of keeping a precarious social peace. Thus, politicians often find themselves caught in a tug-of-war between a political logic that tempts them to finance and support policies that will improve the lives of as many people as possible, and an economic logic that forces them to acknowledge that business is the first and most important interest group in city politics.[14] How city politicians juggle the often conflicting economic and political imperatives is a central theme of this book.

The choices available to local political leaders are strictly limited by the environment within which cities are situated. Cities do not exist in isolation. They are located within a complex intergovernmental system, and they are subject to economic forces beyond their control. For a time in the nation's history, cities derived considerable benefit from the political alliances that urban politicians forged with Democrats in Congress and the White House. As we discuss in Chapter 5, cities came of age politically during the 1930s, when the urban electorate became pivotal partners in President Franklin Delano Roosevelt's New Deal coalition.

After World War II, several national initiatives influenced urban development, but as we point out in Chapter 7, these programs were deeply flawed. Public housing and urban renewal were meant to help the cities, but their effects were often more negative than positive. Federally insured loans for homeowners and a federally subsidized freeway system accelerated a massive middle-class flight from the central cities to the suburbs. The sorry history of misguided national policies goes right up to the present, as we detail in Chapter 8.

In addition to governmental policies, economic changes made things difficult for the central cities. The transformation of the global and national economies—especially the loss of manufacturing employment in favor of service-sector jobs since the mid-1970s—reverberated throughout urban communities. In the 1970s and 1980s, older industrial cities tried to cope with high unemployment and population losses, while Sunbelt cities, as we discuss in Chapter 9, were confronted with both the benefits and the infrastructure costs associated with rapid population growth. Reductions in urban social programs and the replacement of higher-wage industrial-sector jobs by minimum-wage service-sector jobs created the phenomenon of divided cities; in urban areas everywhere, pockets of poverty expanded, and so did affluent neighborhoods. Though crime rates began to drop in the latter half of the 1990s, drug use, gang violence and other problems associated with poverty continued as the mainstay stories on the nightly news. In Chapter 12, we show that cities have not had the fiscal capacity to address the root causes of any of these problems, though they have been expected to deal with the consequences.

THE POLITICS OF CHOICE

It may seem as if the external forces impinging on cities leave them with little room to maneuver in deciding among policy options. In fact, however, even in depressed cities choices are available. There is no "one best way" to pursue prosperity, and the choices a particular city makes among alternative policies reflect its history and size, the composition of its population, the nature of its economy, and the region within which it is located—even the creativeness of its leadership. Cities that appear to face similar problems often respond to the challenges that confront them in very different ways.

The cities located at the core of older metropolitan areas share a distinctive history, politics, and political culture. Many of them were once governed by party machines that prospered by mobilizing ethnic voters. During the nineteenth century, these cities attracted waves of foreign immigrants, and in the twentieth century they served as magnets for blacks streaming out of the South, for Mexicans escaping violence and poverty in their own country, and white families fleeing grinding poverty in Appalachia and elsewhere. Over the past three decades, they have attracted new waves of immigrants from Latin America, the Caribbean, and Asia. As a result, the politics of these cities always have involved ethnic, racial, and neighborhood issues.

As we detail in Chapter 9, until the 1970s the politics of most cities of the South and Southwest was tightly controlled by business elites, who kept taxes as low as possible and provided a minimal level of public services and infrastructure. For most of its history, for example, Houston was run by a white-male business group that met in private to make policy and slate candidates for public office. In the 1970s, Kathy Whitmire won the mayor's office, backed by an electoral coalition of middle-class whites, Latinos, blacks, gays, and feminists. In other Sunbelt cities Latinos and blacks have come to power. The opening of the political process in those cities reflects the fact that the Sunbelt cities have become more diverse. They are, in other words, becoming more like the older cities of the Frostbelt.

The politics of suburbs and smaller cities and towns is different from the politics of larger cities. Their politics are often rather simple, especially if the population is homogeneous. Frequently, a few "insiders" exercise tightfisted control over local elections and the day-to-day running of the suburb or town. In the smallest towns and cities, there may be no full-time politicians or administrators at all, and a small group of citizens—usually business owners and professionals—in effect takes turns holding public office. In small cities and suburbs political issues are likely to be defined narrowly, typically focusing on the preservation of real estate values, the quality of police services, the character of the schools, and little else.[15] Even so, in recent years suburbs and smaller cities have been urbanizing, that is, they have begun to exhibit many of the problems of the big cities. And their politics have been changing as well.

Scholars have employed the concept of urban regimes to describe the political coalitions that govern cities. This concept is based on the recognition that local politics involves more than what government does; it involves the coordination of public power and private resources. Because business institutions control access to investment and jobs, they tend to enjoy a special status. In most cities, they wield enormous influence over politicians and public policies, with other organized interests playing a lesser role. When political scientist Clarence Stone wrote about politics in Atlanta, he observed, "What makes governance in Atlanta effective is not the formal machinery of government but rather the informal partnership between city hall and the downtown business elite. This informal partnership and the way it operates constitutes the city's regime; it is the same means through which major policy decisions are made."[16] In Stone's account, the "regime" in Atlanta has involved a long-time, continuing, cooperative relationship between a succession of mayors and the city's business elite.

But the political structure in other cities is not necessarily similar to Atlanta's. In some cities power may be dispersed quite broadly. San Francisco, for instance, has long had a politics of "hyperpluralism" in which the city's multitude of racial, ethnic, and ideological groups fight it out.[17] As a result, it has been difficult for a stable regime to emerge; instead, groups that oppose the centralized exercise of power have constituted themselves into an "anti-regime" that tends to fragment decision-making.[18] In Pittsburgh, the political center of gravity has been located in the nonprofit sector for several decades, and in Chicago, though business exerts overwhelming influence (as elsewhere, ultimately), the Democratic party machine acts as the main political broker and deal-maker.[19] A broadly comparative book that investigates the variations among regimes in cities would be a worthwhile undertaking, but we do not believe it would be easily integrated into a textbook. Therefore, we do not rely on the regime concept in this book, though we do adopt the idea that urban politics is centered in the informal alliances between public officials and private-sector institutions and individuals.

THE POLITICS OF SECESSION

A complete narrative of urban politics in America cannot rely solely on an analysis of the politics *within* cities. It must also take into account the relationships *between* the many political jurisdictions that make up urban areas. Especially in the United States, most metropolitan areas are composed of an incredible number of separate governments. Because of this extreme pattern of fragmentation, citizens who possess the necessary resources can choose to move from one jurisdiction to another instead of engaging in the messy process of political bargaining and compromise. Escape is an option that is often exercised.

Because America is a land of immigrants, it has sometimes been said that Americans have a tendency to pick up and move whenever they feel dissatisfied. First there was the move to America, and then—or so goes the standard narrative—there was the move to the frontier. The story of westward expansion fills the history books, but there was another important movement as well. In nineteenth-century cities, the wealthy and the middle-class began a restless flight from the densely crowded neighborhoods close to the waterfront. The development of new forms of transportation, first the streetcar and then the automobile, enabled the well-to-do to move further and further from the inconvenience and problems of the city. As we discuss in Chapter 10, in the last few decades an increasing proportion of affluent urban dwellers have withdrawn into defended enclaves made up of people much like themselves. This politics of secession became the defining feature of urban America in the twentieth century.

Geographical avoidance behavior is common in cities throughout the world. What makes it especially significant in the American context is that the affluent can in effect secede from political responsibility simply by moving. In the late nineteenth century, people who migrated to the urban fringe formed separate suburban governments. This process has continued all through the twentieth century, so that now metropolitan areas are composed of literally hundreds of separate governmental jurisdictions. There is, however, a pattern to this arrangement. Typically, older central cities are encircled by a ring of autonomous suburban governments and edge cities, and, almost always, a high proportion of affluent white families reside in the suburbs.

By 1992, there were 86,692 local governments in the United States, including 19,296 municipalities. The fastest growing component of local government in the United States is special districts—authorities set up with taxing and spending powers to serve special purposes, such as running toll bridges or building sewer systems. Many of the services previously supplied by city governments are now provided by special districts, which are run more like private corporations than governments.[20] These districts are so numerous and they overlap so haphazardly that most surburbanites know nothing about them, at least until the tax bill arrives.

Such fragmentation makes it difficult to solve regional problems that confront all urban residents. Urban sprawl, for example, has become a pressing issue. In Chapter 11 we demonstrate that sprawl has brought not only a monumental gridlock to many urban areas, but also is implicated in the decline of the urban core, high levels of air pollution, the loss of agricultural land and open space, and the degradation of the social and esthetic environment of the suburbs. Without some form of metropolitan cooperation, it is difficult to see how sprawl will be reigned in.

The politics of secession undermines the politics of bargaining and compromise that makes governance possible. When people become sorted out into separate enclaves that mirror racial, ethnic, and class divisions, they become fearful of others and susceptible to stereotypes. The politics of secession accentuates racial and class differences. Those who lack the resources to move to exclusive suburbs or gated communities are forced to live in jurisdictions where the needs are great but the resources to treat them are meager. Urban politics in the United States involves a struggle between separate places as much as a struggle between groups and individuals within places. Accordingly, a politics of accommodation, negotiation, and compromise has become substantially replaced by a politics of separation, segregation, and confrontation.

NOTES

1. Lawrence J. R. Herson and John M. Bolland, *The Urban Web: Politics, Policy, and Theory* (Chicago: Nelson-Hall, 1990), p. 43.
2. Sam Bass Warner, Jr., *The Private City: Philadelphia in Three Periods of Its Growth* (Philadelphia: University of Pennsylvania Press, 1968), p. 4.

3. Frederic Harrison, quoted in James A. Clapp, *The City: A Dictionary of Quotable Thoughts on Cities and Urban Life* (New Brunswick, N.J.: Center for Urban Policy Research, Rutgers University, 1984).

4. Quoted in ibid., p. 66.

5. Fellini's film *Roma* opens with scenes of a subway excavation that results in a dramatic archeological discovery.

6. Quoted in Clapp, *The City,* p. 210.

7. Ibid.

8. Quoted in ibid., pp. 128–129.

9. Quoted in ibid., p. 148.

10. Robert Bellah, et al., *Habits of the Heart: Individualism and Commitment in American Life* (Berkeley: University of California Press, 1985).

11. For a theoretical analysis of the popular democratic theory of American local government, see Anwar Syed, *The Political Theory of Local Government* (New York: Random House, 1966).

12. Herson and Bolland, *The Urban Web,* p. 46.

13. Eric Nordlinger, *On the Autonomy of the Democratic State* (Cambridge, Mass.: Harvard University Press, 1981).

14. Todd Swanstrom, "Semisovereign Cities: The Politics of Urban Development," *Polity* 21, no. 1 (Fall 1988): 83–110.

15. Robert C. Wood, *Suburbia: Its People and Their Politics* (Boston: Houghton Mifflin, 1958).

16. Clarence N. Stone, *Regime Politics: Governing Atlanta, 1946–1988* (Lawrence: University Press of Kansas, 1989), p. 3.

17. Frederick Wirt, *Power in the City: Decision Making in San Franscisco.* (Berkeley: University of California Press, 1974).

18. Richard Edward DeLeon, *Left Coast City: Progressive Politics in San Franscisco, 1975–1991* (Lawrence, Kans.: University Press of Kansas, 1992).

19. Barbara Ferman, *Challenging the Growth Machine: Neighborhood Politics in Chicago and Pittsburgh* (Lawrence, Kans.: University Press of Kansas, 1996).

20. Nancy Burns, *The Formation of American Local Governments: Private Values in Public Institutions* (New York: Oxford University Press, 1994).

CONTESTED TERRAIN: POLITICAL CONFLICT IN THE CITIES

2

THE PRIVATE CITY AND LOCAL DEMOCRACY: THE POLITICAL LEGACY OF THE NINETEENTH CENTURY

NATIONAL DEVELOPMENT AND THE CITIES

When the Constitution was ratified in 1789, the cities of the new nation were scattered along the coastline of a vast, mostly unexplored continent. Only five of these cities exceeded 10,000 in population. Over the course of the next century the nation's social and economic development went hand in hand with the growth of cities. By the beginning of the twentieth century, a culture that had defined its character by reference to rural life and a western frontier had become urban and industrial.

Urbanization occurred at such an incredible pace and scale that it generated nearly irresolvable political and social tensions. The symbols and the reality of the industrial age—belching smokestacks, wave after wave of foreign immigrants, social disorder, and racial and ethnic strife—all were concentrated in the cities. The cities and the people who lived within them became the symbols of vast, disruptive economic and cultural changes. A distrust and fear of the cities became an enduring feature of American culture. The antiurban attitudes formed in an earlier time have proved to be resilient, as America's love affair with urban sprawl amply illustrates.

The new industrial economy required a steady supply of cheap and plentiful labor. A flood of foreign immigration began to surge into the country in the 1840s and it did not ebb until Congress passed legislation to curb it, in the 1920s. Most of the immigrants settled in crowded urban neighborhoods close to the factories. Right from the start there were tensions between the newcomers and those who thought of themselves (mistakenly) as native Americans. Cultural and religious conflict became an everyday occurrence, and sometimes it escalated into violence. Successive waves of immigrants—poor, often illiterate, unfamiliar with the language and customs of their new country, and unaccustomed to city life—struggled to cope with miserable conditions in overcrowded slums.

Those who had come to America earlier generally viewed the most recently arrived as not only inferior but as threatening and morally deficient.

The basic outlines of this historical narrative are relevant to the contemporary American city because in recent decades the cities once again became associated with images of poverty, crime, racial conflict, social disorder, and moral decline.[1] By the 1980s a backlash against immigrants began to take the form of legislation to curb immigration and reduce social spending on illegal immigrants, and laws requiring "English only" instruction in the schools. "Underclass" neighborhoods were targeted for intensified law enforcement. As in the past, immigrants and the poor served as lightning rods for people's fears. Throughout much of the nineteenth century, the cultural representation of cities was remarkably similar to current media images of inner-city minority neighborhoods. To understand urban politics in the United States today, there is no better place to start than the cities of the past.

THE URBANIZATION OF AMERICA

In the 100 years between 1800 and 1900, cities of the Western industrializing nations grew at a pace unprecedented in history. In 1800 London was the only city in the world to approach one million in population.[2] Paris ranked second among European cities with a population of 547,000. Just over 60,000 people lived in New York, which was the largest city in America by far. By 1900, eleven Western cities had topped the million-person mark; London had 6,586,000, Paris 2,714,000,[3] and New York 3,437,000. In England and Wales, the percentage of the population living in towns[4] and cities increased from 25 percent to 77 percent in the nineteenth century. Commenting on the growth of cities in 1895, the *Atlantic Monthly* noted: "The great fact in . . . social development . . . at the close of the nineteenth century is the tendency all over the world to concentrate in great cities. This tendency is seen everywhere."[5]

The experience in the United States was similar. As shown by the data in Table 2.1, from the first national census of 1790 to the census of 1920, the urban population (defined by the census bureau as people living in cities and towns of 2,500 or more) increased in most decades more than twice as fast as the U.S. population as a whole. The only significant exception to this trend showed up between 1810 and 1820, when homesteaders and farmers streamed across the Appalachian Mountains to settle the old Northwest (now western Pennsylvania, Ohio, and Indiana). But in subsequent decades, even the expanding frontier could not absorb enough people to keep America from becoming urban.

As late as the census of 1840, only one American in ten lived in cities and towns of 2,500 or more. In that decade, however, cities began growing at breakneck speed. Millions of Irish and German immigrants began pouring into the cities, and at the same time a steady migration from farms to cities began to transform the United States irretrievably into an urban nation. Foreign immi-

TABLE 2.1 THE PACE OF URBANIZATION IN THE UNITED STATES, 1790–1920

Year	Total Population	Percent Increase over Preceding Census	Urban Population	Percent Increase over Preceding Population	Percent of Total Population Urban	Rural
1790	3,929,214	—	201,655	—	5.1	94.9
1800	5,308,483	35.1	322,371	59.9	6.1	93.9
1810	7,239,881	36.4	525,459	63.0	7.3	92.7
1820	9,638,453	33.1	693,255	31.9	7.2	92.8
1830	12,866,020	33.5	1,127,247	62.6	8.8	91.2
1840	17,069,453	32.7	1,845,055	63.7	10.8	89.2
1850	23,191,876	35.9	3,543,716	92.1	15.3	84.7
1860	31,443,321	35.6	6,216,518	75.4	19.8	80.2
1870	39,818,449	26.6	9,902,361	59.3	25.7	74.3
1880	50,155,783	26.0	14,129,735	42.7	28.2	71.8
1890	62,947,714	25.5	22,106,265	56.5	35.1	64.9
1900	75,994,575	20.7	30,214,832	36.7	39.6	60.4
1910	91,972,266	21.0	42,064,001	39.2	45.6	54.4
1920	105,710,620	14.9	54,253,280	29.0	51.2	48.8

Source: U.S. Department of Commerce, Bureau of the Census, *Historical Statistics of the United States, Colonial Times to 1970*, pt. 1, Bicentennial ed. (Washington, D.C.: U.S. Government Printing Office, 1975), p. 8; U.S. Department of Commerce, Bureau of the Census, *1970 Census of Population*, vol. 1, *Characteristics of the Population*, pt. 1 (Washington, D.C.: U.S. Government Printing Office, 1973), p. 42.

grants and rural migrants were lured to the cities by the promise of jobs. By 1860, the census bureau classified almost 20 percent of the American population as urban and by century's end, the urban proportion had doubled again to almost 40 percent. When the 1920 census was taken, 51.2 percent—more than half—of the American people lived in urban places. In less than a century the United States had become urban.

Because of their importance as financial and commercial (and later as industrial) centers, the old cities on the eastern seaboard benefited from national development. New York maintained its supremacy as the hub of finance and trade. Its continued status as the nation's premier city was assured in 1825, the year that the Erie Canal was completed. The canal linked the city directly to the Great Lakes, turning New York into a giant funnel gathering the resources of a vast continent into a worldwide trading system. After the Civil War it consolidated its status when it became a great manufacturing city. Huge numbers of immigrants passed through New York, and many of them settled there. From a population of 369,000 in 1840, New York exploded to over 3.4 million by 1900. By 1920 it had become a leading global center of finance, trade, and manufacturing, and its population exceeded 5.6 million.

Despite its incredible growth, New York's share of the nation's urban population fell steadily throughout the nineteenth century. Hundreds of new towns
and cities sprang up as the nation expanded westward, and these cities grew as
fast or faster than did New York—though none ever reached its size. In 1800, 18
percent of the nation's urban population (almost one out of five) was concentrated in New York, but by 1890 this proportion had fallen to 7 percent.[6] New
York remained the largest city, but as the century progressed other cities assumed prominent places in a truly national urban network (see Table 2.2). As
the continent filled in, interior towns popped up like mushrooms. One of the
oldest, St. Louis (the old French settlement where Lewis and Clark outfitted
their expedition in 1805), increased its population tenfold in only twenty years,
growing from only 16,000 people in 1840 to over 160,000 by the census of 1860.
In the same twenty years, Chicago grew from a swampy frontier village of 4,500
to a city of more than 112,000, and by 1920 Chicago's population had soared to
2.7 million people. Smaller urban settlements dotted the landscape between the
larger cities. In 1840 only twenty-five cities in the United States could claim
10,000 people or more, but by the turn of the century 465 cities had grown to that
size, or larger.[7]

Until at least the middle of the nineteenth century, the settlements that
sprung up along the leading edge of westward movement and that gradually
filled in the interior served as trading and distribution centers. It did not take
long until an urban hierarchy began to emerge. Cities located along rivers and
waterways, such as St. Louis, New Orleans, Chicago, and Cincinnati, got a head
start as major trading centers, transferring goods through the Great Lakes or the
inland river system to the eastern seaboard cities, or directly to Europe. The civic
leaders of every city thought that their city was destined for greatness.

After midcentury the railroad network powerfully shaped the urban pattern. A growing web of rail lines tied the older port cities with the cities and
towns springing up along the new rail lines. The biggest cities sat atop the urban
hierarchy. They prospered because they attracted huge volumes of capital investment and cheap immigrant labor. Second-tier cities had more specialized
economies, and they served as transfer points to the larger urban centers. The
bottom of the hierarchy was composed of the multitude of small towns that
transferred agricultural and extractive resources from the countryside to distribution points in the larger cities. Without such an urban hierarchy, the nation
could not have opened its frontier.

THE COMPETITION FOR URBAN GROWTH

For much of the nineteenth century, the interurban competition for economic
growth supplied the main dynamic in urban politics. The fortunes of individual
cities were only partially determined by locational advantages—what might be
called "place luck." Instead, transportation connections—turnpikes, canals, and

	New York City[b]	Percent Increase	Chicago	Percent Increase	Philadelphia	Percent Increase	St. Louis	Percent Increase	Boston	Percent Increase	Percent Increase in U.S. Population
1820	137,388		—		63,802		4,598		43,298		
1830	220,471	60.5	—		80,462	26.1	5,847	27.1	61,392	41.8	33.5
1840	369,305	67.5	4,470		93,665	16.4	16,469	181.7	93,383	52.1	32.7
1850	660,803	78.9	29,963	570.3	121,376	29.6	77,860	372.8	136,881	46.6	35.9
1860	1,183,148	79.1	112,172	274.4	565,529	365.9	160,773	106.5	177,840	29.9	35.6
1870	1,546,293	30.7	298,977	166.5	674,022	19.2	310,864	93.4	250,526	40.9	26.6
1880	2,061,191	33.3	503,185	68.3	847,170	25.7	350,522	12.8	362,839	44.8	26.0
1890	2,507,474	21.7	1,099,850	118.6	1,046,964	23.6	451,770	28.9	448,477	23.6	25.5
1900	3,437,202	37.1	1,698,575	54.4	1,293,697	23.6	575,000	27.3	560,892	25.1	20.7
1910	4,766,883	38.7	2,185,283	28.7	1,549,008	19.7	687,029	19.5	670,585	19.6	21.0
1920	5,620,048	17.9	2,701,705	23.6	1,823,779	17.7	772,897	12.5	748,060	11.6	14.9

[a]These five cities were ranked as the five largest in the 1910 census.
[b]Using the consolidated borough boundaries of 1898.

Source: Glen E. Holt, personal files; U.S. Department of Commerce, Bureau of the Census, *The Growth of Metropolitan Districts in the United States: 1900–1940,* by Warren S. Thompson (Washington, D.C.: U.S. Government Printing Office, 1947); Blake McKelvey, *American Urbanization: A Comparative History* (Glenview, Ill.: Scott-Foresman, 1973), pp. 24, 37, 73.

especially railroads—determined a city's destiny. Good links to the national transportation network could instantly secure a city's place by expanding its reach into a surrounding hinterland and tying it into national and or even international trade networks. Because such connections were so important, city governments provided expensive subsidies to the railroads in the form of free land and terminal facilities and stock purchases. The logic was simple: Rising real estate values were expected to provide more than enough additional revenues to pay off the debts. This logic did not always pan out, but any city that failed to make the effort to secure good railroad links would surely die on the vine.

Thus, rather than depending on luck and circumstance, civic leaders tried to shape patterns of trade and economic development. Local entrepreneurs were keenly aware that they were involved in a competition in which some cities would grow while others would stagnate or even die. Railroad building intensified the competition. Before the railroads, commercial quantities of corn could be transported by wagon only 125 miles and wheat, 250 miles.[8] Beyond that distance, agricultural land was almost worthless for anything except subsistence farming because there was no way to get crops to market. Railroads opened up huge areas of farmland to commercial agriculture, which not only allowed the countryside to fill in but also resulted in soaring land values and population growth for the cities that could capture the increased trade in agricultural goods. The entrepreneurial motive for city building ignited a "struggle for primacy and power" in which "like imperial states, cities carved out extensive dependencies, extended their influence over the economic and political life of the hinterland, and fought with contending places over strategic trade routes."[9]

The building of the Erie Canal demonstrated that individual cities could gain substantial control over their own destinies. In 1817, after being prodded by the civic elite of New York City, the New York State legislature authorized money for the construction of a 364-mile waterway to connect the Hudson River with Lake Erie. When the canal opened in 1825, it became possible to ship huge volumes of agricultural and extractive goods from the continental interior through the Great Lakes to Buffalo, down the canal, and on to the port at New York, where they could be distributed along the eastern seaboard, used in factories, or shipped to Europe. Many producers and shippers abandoned the long, circuitous, and hazardous journey down the Ohio, Missouri, and Mississippi rivers to the port at New Orleans. New York's direct connection to the heartland via the canal quickly vaulted it past all the other eastern seaboard cities in population and volume of trade. By 1860, 62 percent of the nation's foreign trade passed through New York's harbor.[10]

The lesson was not lost on entrepreneurs elsewhere. Urban leaders lobbied their state capitals for financial assistance to build canals. Pennsylvania, Maryland, Virginia, North Carolina, and South Carolina financed canal projects designed to cut through the Appalachians. Between 1824 and 1840 more than 3,000 miles of canals were constructed, most of them run by state governments.[11] About 30 percent of the costs were raised through private sources, but the capacity of the states to sell bonds was essential for these expensive undertakings.[12]

Canal building was so expensive, the engineering so complicated, and the natural barriers often so formidable that most cities could not hope to build them unless state legislatures helped out. The railroads changed all that. In the first decades of the century, for the river towns like St. Louis, Pittsburgh, Cincinnati, and New Orleans, the steamboat had been "an enchanter's wand transforming an almost raw countryside of scattered farms and towns into a settled region of cultivated landscapes and burgeoning cities."[13] In the 1850s and in subsequent decades, the railroads became the new enchanter's wand. The rail lines became the new rivers of commerce, capable of carrying huge volumes at amazing speed over long distances. A rail connection carried the promise of economic prosperity for a city. The railroads guaranteed that America's frontier would eventually vanish and that a network of cities, towns, and villages would spread over the entire continent.

In 1840 only 2,800 miles of track existed, most of it in the urban East. No connection reached even as far west as Pittsburgh. The early steam locomotives were hazardous contraptions, blowing up with a regularity that provoked opposition to their use in urban areas. Lacking the capital to take on bigger projects, railway companies built short lines. Because each company used its own particular gauge (width between the rails), at the end of each line, goods had to be unloaded from one company's cars and put onto cars that fit the next company's rails. Even so, the early rail system was vastly superior to the only alternative, horse-drawn wooden wagons.

Rail lines were built at astonishing speed, and by the 1880s standard gauge sizes made the system much more efficient. The rail network expanded from 9,021 miles of track in 1850 to 258,784 miles by the turn of the century.[14] In 1857 the newly consolidated Pennsylvania Railroad first connected Pittsburgh to Chicago. Three years later, eleven trunk lines ended in Chicago, and twenty branch and feeder lines passed through it, making the city the nation's largest rail center terminus. By 1869 and amidst great ceremony, the symbolic Golden Spike was driven at Promontory Point, Utah. It completed the first cross-continental route by joining the Union Pacific line originating on the east coast to the Central Pacific line starting in San Francisco. Within a few years the outline of the modern rail system was almost complete, a spider's web with strands reaching into every section of the country.

The United States laid more miles of track more quickly than any other nation in the world. The main reason for this rapid growth was the huge public subsidies that were pumped into railroad building. Relying strictly on private investment, the railroads would have expanded much more slowly than they did. Until the 1890s, most private corporations lacked the ability to raise the huge amounts of capital that would later become routine for them. Public subsidies helped to make the railroads "America's first big business,"[15] thus rendering the popular image of the nineteenth century as the age of laissez-faire capitalism utterly false.[16]

In the Pacific Railways Acts of 1862 and 1864, the federal government gave massive amounts of land to railroads, which the companies sold to raise capital. The most generous subsidies, however, were provided by cities. Treasury secretary Albert Gallatin's 1808 plan for a federal system of transportation improvements had failed to gain congressional approval because of regional rivalries.[17] Following President Andrew Jackson's veto of the Maysville Turnpike bill in

1830, transportation became viewed mainly as a state responsibility. States rushed into the vacuum and began feverishly subsidizing canals and railroads. The Panic of 1837 caused many states to lose money on their railroad investments, causing what one historian called a "revulsion against internal improvements."[18] In the 1840s many states wrote prohibitions against loaning money or buying stock in private corporations. Facing state prohibitions, railroad promoters quickly shifted their efforts to the local level. Like an escalating arms race, cities offered higher and higher subsidies to obtain railroad connections.

The anarchic competition imposed many costs, including overbuilding and redundancies that resulted in bond defaults and bankruptcies. Up to 1861, 25 to 30 percent of all direct investment in railroad building was supplied by state and local governments. The cities were the biggest spenders; they contributed an estimated $300 million in railroad subsidies, while the states spent $229 million and the federal government $65 million.[19] Both the states and the federal government provided huge indirect subsidies in the form of land grants, however, which the railroads then converted to cash by selling the land to settlers. Indeed, in the post–Civil War period the railroads owned so much land that they sent agents to the Scandinavian countries, Germany, and elsewhere to recruit immigrants who could buy and settle it. Partly because the railroads recruited heavily there (and also because of persistent hardships in their homeland), one-sixth of all Swedish citizens left for the United States in the last half of the century.

Railroad entrepreneurs became adept at playing cities off against one another to secure the most lucrative subsidies. By the 1850s, cities along the eastern seaboard were floating bond issues so that they could invest in stock subscriptions, clear rights-of-way, and build terminal facilities—actions intended to entice railroads to build a line through their city. The competition quickly spread west. In the 1860s, the business leaders of Kansas City, Kansas, sold bond issues to private investors, gave the proceeds to a railroad company, and persuaded Congress to approve a federal land grant to a railroad company. As a result of its success in this venture, Kansas City prospered while its nearby rival Leavenworth stagnated (today, Leavenworth is known mainly for its federal prison).[20] Denver's board of trade raised $280,000 to finance a 100-mile spur line to obtain access to the intercontinental track that ran through Cheyenne, Wyoming.[21] Some of Denver's businesses had already moved to Cheyenne in the expectation that its position astride the intercontinental line would make it the premier city of the Rocky Mountain West. The convergence of rail lines from all directions into Denver, however, secured its status as the dominant city of the Rocky Mountain region.

No city benefited from railroad building as dramatically as did Chicago, whose phenomenal growth was founded on its access to agricultural and extractive products gathered from a vast region. Corn and grain, cattle and hogs, iron ore and coal poured into Chicago through the Great Lakes and over the rails. The city became a center for steel making, the manufacturing of agricultural implements, tools, and machines, slaughtering and meat packing, and trade. By 1870 Chicago eclipsed St. Louis as the Midwest's premier city, a feat accomplished partly through the success of its local business community in securing railroad links. Chicago built its first railroad in 1852 and then helped finance feeder lines into the city. The city also invested in grain elevators, warehouses, switching yards, and stockyards. In contrast, St. Louis's business community held fast to a faith that the steamboats would be enough to guarantee the city's continued prosperity. By the time St. Louis began seeking rail connections, Chicago's advantage was overwhelming. Although Chicago also enjoyed the considerable advantage of being located on the Great Lakes and it was closer to the great farming regions of the Midwest than St. Louis, its actions clearly gave it more of an edge over St. Louis than its locational advantage alone would have conferred.

For many years there was little conflict over the question of whether cities should go into debt to secure rail connections. When asked to vote for bond subscriptions and other subsidies, most urban voters supported railroad subsidy schemes. As long as everyone's attention was riveted on external threats to local prosperity, a politics of consensus tended to develop around the schemes to subsidize local prosperity: "Developmental policy was almost wholly a product of consensus-building among groups of merchant elites to support particular canal, turnpike, rail and other projects in response to merchant elites in nearby communities."[22] From 1866 to 1873, the legislatures of twenty-nine states granted over 800 authorizations for aid by local governments to railroad projects.[23] A study of governmental aid to railroads in New York found that no community ever voted against subscribing to railroad stock.[24] The votes were usually so lopsided as to be a foregone conclusion.[25]

For many cities the fight for rail connections brought prosperity, but just as often the overheated competition brought disaster. Railroad promoters played one town against another in search of better subsidies (a process akin to the competition today among state and local governments for footloose businesses and sports franchises). Unplanned redundancy and overbuilding, to say nothing of outright thievery and swindling by promoters, left many cities with little to show for their financial sacrifices. The competition among cities was often so fierce that they bid up the subsidies beyond what was economically rational; cities incurred huge debts on a hope and a promise. In New York State, for example, 50 towns bypassed by a major railroad joined in a $5.7 million stock subscription to the New York and Oswego Railroad. Zigzagging across the state to link the towns, the railroad went bankrupt shortly after completing the line in 1873 because the areas it served had too few people and products to sustain a healthy business. Most of the investments made by the towns were wiped out, with taxpayers left holding the bag.[26]

Then, as now, promoters exaggerated the positive effects to be expected from public subsidies, predicting rapid town growth, rising real estate values, and overflowing municipal treasuries. Profits on railroad stocks, they often promised, would eliminate the need for local taxes altogether. For most cities, however, "the direct effect on government finances was on the whole unfavorable."[27] Too many cities bought railroad stock that went bust, or the railroads brought far less prosperity than promised.

Many cities that had heavily invested in speculative railroad ventures found themselves dragged into fiscal crises. Although some cities defaulted on railroad debts in the 1860s, during the three-year depression that began in 1873 (which was itself partially brought on by the overbuilding of railroads and the over-valuing of railroad stock and local real estate), hundreds of towns and cities were forced into default. In 1873 an astounding $100 million to $150 million of municipal debt was involved in railroad bond defaults—one-fifth of all the municipal debt in the nation.[28]

Municipal bond railroad defaults and revelations of political corruption associated with railroad building affected politics at all levels. Citizens rebelled against paying back Eastern financiers for municipal railroad bonds that had become worthless. In some cases the railroads had not even been built. When federal marshals came to towns to collect the debts, they were sometimes run off by shotgun-wielding mobs. Cries of debt repudiation filled the air, and some cities and states did manage to repudiate their debts.[29] From 1864 to 1888 the most common type of case before the U.S. Supreme Court involved railroad bonds.[30] Especially after 1872, many states adopted restrictions on local debt and limited the aid that could be given to private corporations.[31]

Financial and political abuses by railroad barons fueled a populist rebellion against big business that shook the national political system in the late nineteenth century.[32] In many smaller cities consensus dissolved into conflict. In larger cities, however, the bonds of community had already become frayed. The twin processes of industrialization and immigration fragmented the cities into separate social, ethnic, and racial enclaves. Increasingly, the diverse groups clashed with one another for political control of the city.

THE BREAKDOWN OF COMMUNITY: INDUSTRIALIZATION

A statistical portrait of the frenetic growth of cities in the nineteenth century cannot adequately convey the social and political turmoil brought about by urbanization. In both Europe and the United States, urbanization on this scale was historic. Never before in world history had cities grown so large or so fast, and never before had such a high proportion of the population lived in cities. The urban historian Eric Lampard has said that "the period c. A.D. 1750–1850 [is] one of the crucial disjunctions in the history of human society. Whatever constraints had hitherto checked or moderated the growth and re-distribution of population were suddenly relaxed."[33] In the United States the economic and technological changes brought about by industrialization signaled an abrupt break from the past. Cities changed from relatively compact communities held together by informal community norms to sprawling industrial cities characterized by social stratification and segregation, constant population change, and social and political conflict.

Before the age of industry and the railroad, trading cities sprung up along navigable waterways and harbors. The lifeblood of these merchant-run cities flowed along the waterfront. Wharves and docks, warehouses, clerks' offices, banks, newspapers and printing establishments, taverns and breweries, and private homes all clustered close to the harbor or riverfront. Urban historians have labeled the mercantile city "the walking city," because the area of urban settlement was bounded by the distance that the inhabitants could walk within an hour or two. Typically, the city spread out about two miles from the center, but the area of dense settlement was only a few blocks deep. The cost and inconvenience of hauling goods on horse-drawn wooden wagons guaranteed that cities would remain compact. For the same reason, settlements without access to water transportation could not amount to much. In the first decade of the nineteenth century, a ton of goods could be shipped all the way from Europe for the same amount that it cost to haul it nine miles over inland roads.[34] Inland cities without waterfronts could not conceivably compete with port and river cities as centers of trade.

The political systems of the merchant cities slowly became more democratic in the first decades of the nineteenth century. Property qualifications for voting began to be eased after 1776 and by 1850 almost all free white males were eligible to vote.[35] Until the 1820s, almost all mayors were appointed by governors or city councils. Beginning with Boston and St. Louis in 1822, charter revisions gradually transformed the office into a popularly elected post, and by 1840 this practice had become nearly universal.[36] The secret ballot and the private polling booth became the norm.[37]

Though democratic practices and norms began to spread, extreme social and economic inequality undermined their full implementation. The economy of the merchant cities revolved around trade and commerce: the importation and distribution of European goods; the regulation of docks and farmers' markets; the financing and insuring of ships and goods; the printing of accounting ledgers, handbills, and newspapers. Educated aristocrats, importers, bankers, wholesalers, and shopkeepers were among a city's most prominent citizens. A notch down in the social hierarchy were the craftworkers and artisans engaged in services and small manufacturing: shoemakers, hatters, bakers, carpenters, blacksmiths, potters, butchers, wheelwrights, saddle and harness makers, and boatwrights. At the bottom were sailors, domestic workers, servants, and the unskilled workers who moved goods from docks to warehouses. Overall, in colonial New England the inequality in wealth was about the same as in the slave-holding South.[38] At the time of the Revolution, about three out of four white persons in Pennsylvania, Maryland, and Virginia had come to America as indentured servants, and most of them remained at the bottom of the social hierarchy.[39]

The rigidly enforced class relationships were generally accepted by people at both ends of the spectrum. The small size of the merchant cities (so called because social, economic, and political affairs were dominated by the merchant class) moderated the effects of inequality by fostering "a sense of community identification similar to that of traditional societies."[40] Production was located mostly in small shops typically run by skilled artisans who employed one or two apprentices who often lived on the premises. A close relationship and interdependence between employer and employee was common. People of all classes often lived within the same neighborhoods. Workers clustered together in shanties or back alleys, still within shouting distance of the better homes of wealthy merchants. In his study of colonial Philadelphia, Sam Bass Warner found that various occupational groups were highly segregated in 1774, but it was a proximate segregation: "It was the unity of everyday life, from tavern, to street, to workplace, to housing which held the town together in the eighteenth century."[41]

Class conflict was moderated by this proximity as well as a sense that everyone's welfare depended on the commercial success of the city. The merchant elites expected to run the city's affairs, and they did. With few exceptions they acceded to the mayor's office and dominated city councils without opposition.[42] Consistent with their view that the scope of local government should be limited, they spent very little on the poor or on public services for public health, sanitation, parks, and libraries. In 1810 prosperous New York City spent only $1 per capita on all public services combined.[43]

In the second half of the nineteenth century, the dislocations of rapid industrialization and urbanization transformed city politics. In 1850 not much more than 10 percent of all workers were engaged in manufacturing, and they produced less than 20 percent of the nation's economic output. But by 1870 industrial production exceeded the commercial and agricultural sectors in value added to the economy, and by the turn of the century manufacturing accounted for more than both sectors combined.[44]

Especially in the larger cities, extreme class inequalities increased social tensions. The rapid growth of big corporations spawned a class of industrial magnates who flaunted their wealth by building mansions and estates, throwing lavish parties, and constructing monuments to themselves.[45] The number of poor people in the cities multiplied, prompting the rich to found charitable societies to deal with the "dangerous classes." Between these extremes, the number of people in middle-class occupations soared. Between 1870 and 1910, the number of clerical workers, salespersons, government employees, technicians, and salaried professionals multiplied 7.5 times, from 756,000 to 5,609,000.[46]

Industrialization removed economic production from small shops and homes and put it in factories. Before the Civil War, manufacturing establishments rarely employed more than 50 workers, and even in large cities they ranged between 8 and 20 workers. In 1832, for example, the average-sized manufacturing establishment in Boston employed 8.5 workers.[47] In the years following the Civil War, manufacturing firms grew quickly in size. In agricultural implements and machinery, the number of employees per establishment increased from 7.5 in 1860 to 79 in 1910. In malt liquor breweries, the number of workers increased from 5 to 39, and in iron and steel establishments, from 54 to 426.[48]

Capital became concentrated in large firms. Limited-risk corporations[49] were relatively rare before the Civil War, but by the turn of the century, there were 40,000 such firms, and though they amounted to only one-tenth of all business firms, they produced 60 percent of value in manufacturing.[50] (Such corporations raised capital by selling stocks to investors who risked their investment, but not their personal assets if the company failed.) In 1896, twelve firms were valued over $10 million; by 1903 there were fifty firms worth over $50 million.[51] Several giant corporations were formed between 1896 and 1905, including U.S. Steel, International Harvester, General Electric, and American Telephone and Telegraph.

In the small shops of the mercantile cities, relations between the owner and his workers tended to be highly personal and informal. Within limits, artisans and craftworkers chose their working hours and manner of production. By contrast, in the factories relationships between capitalists and workers were impersonal, hierarchical, and rigid. Most workers did not even know the owner of the business that employed them. Machine-tooled, standardized parts replaced handcrafted goods. Standardized production began in 1798, when Eli Whitney designed a musket that was built and repaired with interchangeable parts. Before long standardized components made it possible to make a variety of goods rapidly and cheaply, so that clocks, sewing machines, and farm machinery (for example) soon were assembled by factory workers rather than by craftsmen. Huge military orders during the Civil War led to mass-produced shoes and clothing. As a result of these new processes, work became regimented and closely monitored. Factory methods of production required specialized, repetitive work and a rigid distinction between management and workers.

THE BREAKDOWN OF COMMUNITY: TRANSPORTATION

Throughout the nineteenth century, city residents tried to escape the noise, congestion, and filth of the waterfront. A series of transportation improvements—most of them the products of the technological advances made possible by industrialization—allowed the cities to spread over larger areas. Class differences increasingly became expressed in segregated residential patterns. Immigrant working-class tenement slums crowded close to the downtown business districts or in bottomlands near the docks and factories. Middle-class neighborhoods tended to be located away from the crowded center. The wealthy claimed such exclusive areas as Park Avenue in New York and Beacon Hill in Boston, or lived on newly developed suburban estates.

When the omnibus was introduced to the streets of New York City in 1828, it represented a genuine breakthrough in urban transportation. The way that people commuted to work had changed little for hundreds of years. The wealthy owned or rented carriages; everyone else walked or, rarely, rode a horse. From the 1830s until the Civil War, dozens of omnibuses careened down the streets of all the major cities. Basically an enlarged version of the long-distance stagecoach, the omnibus was pulled by a team of two to four horses and typically carried up to a dozen people. Omnibuses were crowded and uncomfortable, cold in the winter, hot in the summer, and slow, barely moving faster than a person could walk. The coaches swayed and lurched over cobblestones and rutted unpaved streets.[52] A newspaper of the time complained that "during certain periods of the day or evening and always during inclement weather, passengers are packed in these vehicles, without regard to comfort or even decency."[53]

Nevertheless, those who could afford the fares—merchants, traders, lawyers, artisans, managers, junior partners—crowded into these crude conveyances. The omnibus ran on a fixed schedule and route, and picked up and dropped off passengers at frequent intervals. The fixed fare, typically a nickel, was a small fraction of the cost of renting a hackney coach. The omnibus was thus more convenient and less expensive than any alternative mode of traveling except walking. By encouraging in some urban residents the "riding habit,"[54] the omnibus signaled the beginning of the end of the walking city. For the first time the workplace could be located at some distance from the home. American cities began to take on their present form, the center being abandoned by the affluent classes. The omnibus, the first mass transportation device used in American cities, facilitated a process of spatial segregation and differentiation that is still occurring in urban areas.

Other transportation innovations exerted a similar impact. Steam railroad lines, for example, were constructed in Boston in the late 1830s and in several other large cities over the next twenty years. Steam engines were suited for constant speed rather than for frequent stops and starts, they were expensive to build and operate, and they were fearfully loud and prone to blowing up. They did not therefore compete with omnibuses on crowded urban streets but instead facilitated the commute from the area of dense settlement in the city center to smaller towns and villages a few miles away. The 40- to 75-cent fares were out of reach of all but the wealthy (the average laborer made about $1.00 a day; sometimes skilled workers made as much as $2.00 a day).[55] Even so, by 1848 one-fifth of Boston's businessmen commuted daily by steam railway[56] (though in other cities the proportion was much lower).

After 1852, with the development of a steel rail that could be laid level with the surface of the street, horse-drawn streetcars quickly replaced the omnibuses on main thoroughfares. Because they were pulled on rails rather than over potholed streets, the horsecars were able to carry twice as many passengers and travel almost twice as fast as the omnibuses. The lower cost of the horsecars "contributed to the development of the world's first integrated transportation systems."[57] In the bigger cities the lines radiated out from the center like spokes on a wheel. Because horsecars could travel 6 to 8 miles in an hour, middle-class residential settlements spread as many miles and more from the city center. In addition the horsecar lines sometimes extended well beyond built-up areas, serving hospitals, parks, cemeteries, and independent villages.[58] Wherever they reached, land speculators and builders bought up property in the usually realistic expectation that development would follow and real estate would escalate.

In 1888 Frank Julian Sprague revolutionized urban transit when he installed the first electric streetcar system in Richmond, Virginia.[59] The motive force driving the electric streetcar came from a wheeled carriage that rode atop an overhead cable. This device trolled along the wires, pulling the car as it went. The "troller" gave the trolley car its name.[60]

Trolley cars had so many advantages over horsecars that despite the expense of installing overhead wires, traction companies and cities rushed to install them. In 1890, 60 percent of the nation's streetcars were still pulled by horses. Twelve years later the figure was less than 1 percent.[61] Trolleys traveled almost twice as fast as horsecars. Areas 6 to 8 miles from the city center could now be reached in half an hour, making it possible for people to live 10 miles or more from work. (The rule of thumb, then as now, was that most people were willing to commute up to an hour, but not much more.) And electric streetcars were infinitely cleaner than the horsecars they replaced. City residents had always complained about "an atmosphere heavy with the odors of death and decay and animal filth and steaming nastiness."[62] The trolley allowed cities to permanently remove thousands of horses, together with their tons of manure, from the streets.

The horse-drawn streetcars and then the electric trolleys facilitated a segmentation of activities within the cities. Until the 1870s, crowded financial and retailing districts were located close by and even mixed in with warehouses and factories.[63] In the last third of the nineteenth century, distinct downtown shopping and financial districts became separated from industrial and warehouse areas. The middle class developed a new shopping habit, riding the streetcars downtown to shop in the new chain and department stores. The first chain retail company, the Great Atlantic and Pacific Tea Company, was organized in 1864, and in the 1870s the A&P stores expanded to several cities. Frank W. Woolworth opened his five-and-dime store in Lancaster, Pennsylvania, in 1879, and by the 1880s Woolworth's became a familiar marquee in downtown areas.[64] The middle-class habit of shopping in downtown stores for major purchases persisted right up until the end of the 1950s, by which time the streetcar system had been largely dismantled in most cities.

While distinct residential and business zones developed within the cities, new residential communities proliferated just beyond city boundaries. Between 1890 and 1910, the nation experienced its first suburban boom. In most large metropolitan areas suburbs grew almost as fast as the central cities in the 1890s and often faster than the cities after the turn of the century. Chicago's population grew by 29 percent between 1900 and 1910, but the population of its suburbs increased by 88 percent. In the St. Louis, Philadelphia, Boston, Pittsburgh, and New York urban areas, the suburbs also grew at a faster pace than did the central cities.[65]

Segregation on this scale changed most people's conception of community. If the term had once evoked images of a diverse assortment of people rubbing shoulders in their daily lives, it now came to mean a collection of people who were similar. The poor began to inhabit different neighborhoods than the middle class, who became, in turn, separated from the wealthy. The Irish, Italians, and Jews likewise claimed their own turf. From the industrial city to the present time, urban politics has often been animated by the conflicts between communities segregated in just this way.

THE BREAKDOWN OF COMMUNITY: IMMIGRATION

Industrialization set off waves of foreign immigration and a restless internal population movement that eventually destroyed the informal and complex urban community of the mercantile era. The industrial economy depended on a constantly expanding pool of cheap labor. Millions of foreign immigrants were pushed out of their homelands by war, civil unrest, and hardship and pulled to American shores to find work. They worked on the railroads, in meat packing, in steel making, in coal and lead mining, and in factories of every kind. Simultaneously, an unprecedented migration from farm to city was set in motion. Between 1830 and 1896, developments in farm machinery cut in half the average time and labor required to produce agricultural crops. During this period, for example, the time required to harvest wheat was reduced by 95 percent and labor costs for farming fell by one-fifth.[66] The new machinery drove up the capital investment required for starting and running a farm, which forced a rising number of people to leave the land. Unemployed farm laborers and young people streamed into the cities.

Between 1820 and 1919, 33.5 million foreign immigrants arrived on American shores (see Table 2.3). Almost three-fourths of them, 24 million in all, settled in the cities. By 1870, more than half the population of at least twenty American cities were foreign-born or children of parents who had immigrated (see Table 2.4). The census of 1920 showed that almost half (48 percent) of the nation's entire urban population were first- or second-generation immigrants,[67] a result of the fact that in just the two decades between 1900 and 1920, 14.5 million immigrants entered the country.[68] The immigrant flood would have continued had Congress not enacted restrictive immigration laws in 1921 and 1924.

Immigrants passed through the port cities of the eastern seaboard, and many of them stayed in those cities and contributed to their phenomenal growth. From midcentury on, increasing numbers fanned out to the growing cities in the interior, went on to mining camps, or joined railroad construction gangs. Most of the immigrants, however, settled in cities. In 1920 more than 80 percent of the Italians, Irish, Russian, and Polish immigrants were urban, as were 75 percent of the immigrants from the United Kingdom.[69] A lesser proportion of German immigrants, about two-thirds, lived in towns and cities, reflecting the fact that in the middle decades of the century many of them had settled in rural areas of the Midwest. A smaller proportion of the Scandinavians settled in urban places than any other group. Many of them were lured into immigration by railroad agents sent to the Scandinavian countries in search of buyers for land secured through government land grants. Enough Scandinavians settled in rural areas in Wisconsin, Minnesota, the Dakotas, and throughout the Midwest that only 55 percent were classified as urban in the census of 1920.

Sixty percent of all the European immigrants between 1820 and 1919 flowed through New York harbor. Between the turn of the century and World War I, approximately two-thirds of all U.S.-bound immigrants were processed through New York's Ellis Island, making it (together with the Statue of Liberty) an en-

TABLE 2.3   DECENNIAL IMMIGRATION TO THE UNITED STATES, 1820–1919

	1820–1829	1830–1839	1840–1849	1850–1859	1860–1869	1870–1879	1880–1889	1890–1899	1900–1909	1910–1919
Total in millions	0.1	0.5	1.4	2.7	2.1	2.7	5.2	3.7	8.2	6.3
Percentage of total from:										
Ireland	40.2	31.7	46.0	36.9	24.4	15.4	12.8	11.0	4.2	2.6
Germany	4.5	23.2	27.0	34.8	35.2	27.4	27.5	15.7	4.0	2.7
United Kingdom	19.5	13.8	15.3	13.5	14.9	21.1	15.5	8.9	5.7	5.8
Scandinavia	0.2	0.4	0.9	0.9	5.5	7.6	12.7	10.5	5.9	3.8
Canada	1.8	2.2	2.4	2.2	4.9	11.8	9.4	0.1	1.5	11.2
Russia					0.2	1.3	3.5	12.2	18.3	17.4
Austria-Hungary					0.2	2.2	6.0	14.5	24.4	18.2
Italy					0.5	1.7	5.1	16.3	23.5	19.4

Source: From N. Carpenter, "Immigrants and Their Children," *U.S. Bureau of the Census Monograph,* no. 7 (Washington, D.C.: U.S. Government Printing Office, 1927), pp. 324–325.

PROPORTION OF IMMIGRANT POPULATION IN CITIES OF 500,000 OR MORE, 1870 AND 1910

		Percent Foreign-born	Percent Foreign-born or Native-born with at Least One Foreign Parent[a]
New York	1870	44.4	80.0
	1910	40.4	78.6
Chicago	1870	48.3	87.0
	1910	35.7	77.5
Philadelphia	1870	28.4	51.1
	1910	24.7	56.8
St. Louis	1870	36.1	65.0
	1910	18.3	54.2
Boston	1870	35.1	63.2
	1910	35.9	74.2
Cleveland	1870	41.8	75.3
	1910	34.9	74.8
Baltimore	1870	21.1	38.0
	1910	13.8	37.9
Pittsburgh	1870	32.3	58.2
	1910	26.3	62.2
Mean for all 8 cities (each counted equally)	1870	40.0	72.0
	1910	32.0	72.3

[a]Native-born with foreign parents is unavailable in the 1870 census. The figures for 1870 are estimated by adding 80 percent to the number of foreign-born. In all cases, this should yield a safely conservative estimate.

Source: U.S. Department of the Interior, Superintendent of Census, *The Ninth Census* (June 1, 1870), vol. 1, *Population and Social Statistics* (Washington, D.C.: U.S. Government Printing Office, 1872), p. 386; U.S. Department of Commerce, Bureau of the Census, *Thirteenth Census of the United States Taken in the Year 1910*, vol. 1, *Population 1910* (Washington, D.C.: U.S. Government Printing Office, 1913), p. 178.

during symbol of America's immigrant history. Though clustered in large numbers in a few northeastern and midwestern cities, immigrants spread out to all the cities that supplied industrial jobs. As shown in Table 2.4, by 1870 immigrants made up 40 percent, and immigrants and their American-born children accounted for at least 72 percent, of the populations of eight cities of more than 500,000 people. In New York City, first- and second-generation immigrants made up almost 80 percent of the population. In Chicago an astounding 87 percent of the population was composed of the foreign-born and their American-born children. And the immigrants kept coming. Despite a huge migration from rural areas to the cities in the latter years of the nineteenth century, by 1910 the proportion of first- and second-generation foreign-born in most cities was about the same as it had been forty years before (see Table 2.4). By the census of 1920, just before Congress passed legislation restricting immigration, 58 percent of the population of all cities with over 100,000 people was first- or second-generation immigrant.[70]

The ethnic composition of the immigrant tide changed substantially over the decades. The data in Table 2.3 show that in the 1840s and 1850s the Irish and Germans made up more than 70 percent of all immigrants. By the 1880s, however, their proportion had fallen to 40 percent, and after the turn of the century they accounted for only about 8 percent of all immigrants. Likewise, immigration from the United Kingdom declined decade by decade, then plummeted after the turn of the century.

After the depression of 1873–1879, immigration reached floodtide proportions. It doubled from 2.7 million in the 1870s to 5.2 million in the 1880s. After falling slightly because of a major depression in the 1890s, the number of immigrants in the first decade of the twentieth century soared to the highest level in American history, to over 8 million. In the 1890s, Jews from Russia and Austria-Hungary, together with Catholics from Italy, made up 42 percent of immigrants, and their proportion of all immigrants rose to more than 60 percent from 1900 to 1920.

The Irish and then the Germans set off the first big surge of nineteenth-century immigration. Famine and disease pushed the Irish to American cities. Irish peasants subsisted primarily on potatoes and vegetables grown on tiny, rocky plots of ground and in strips of soil along the roads, the only usable land not claimed by English landlords. When a potato blight swept through Europe in the 1840s, its effects were more devastating in Ireland than elsewhere. Between 1845 and the mid-1850s, up to a fourth of Ireland's peasants starved to death. Many of the survivors streamed into Liverpool and bought or bartered passage on ships heading for America.

As soon as they arrived, the Irish encountered intense hostility. Irish workers could rarely read or claim a skilled occupation. They took menial, temporary, low-paying jobs—moving goods on the waterfront, building streets and roads, working in slaughterhouses and packinghouses. Because of their poverty and their religion and perhaps their peasant origins as well, they became etched in the public mind as dangerous, alcoholic, criminal, and dirty. Anti-Catholic and anti-Irish riots broke out from time to time. Irish churches, taverns, and neighborhoods were attacked by mobs whipped up by a rhetoric that spoke of "an invasion of venomous reptiles . . . , long-haired, wild-eyed, bad-smelling, atheistic, reckless foreign wretches."[71] Protestant Yankees were in a position to hire, promote, and fire. Even as late as the 1920s, want ads in Boston frequently added "Protestant" as a qualification for employment.[72] The Irish clustered on the lowest rungs of the social and economic ladder well into the twentieth century.

The Germans encountered far less antipathy. A large proportion of German immigrants were wealthy or from middle-class origins. They were escaping war and political turmoil, not poverty and starvation. They brought with them music and literary societies and a commitment to formal education. Although the Germans nominally faced a greater language barrier than did the Irish, the Irish brogue—and even more, the widely used Gaelic—sounded just as foreign to American ears as did the German language.

Important variations existed among the different immigrant groups as they strove to catch up to the native Yankee Protestants. In late nineteenth-century Boston, for example, an immigrant "pecking order favored some groups over others."[73] The Irish and Italians competed for the lowest wages and lowest-skill jobs. Only blacks were below them. German and recent British immigrants frequently entered middle-class occupations right away. A few with exceptional education or a needed skill achieved real success quickly. The Russian and Eastern European Jews, who came in the 1890s and later, placed emphasis on formal education and business. Though discrimination kept them out of corporations and larger business enterprises, they occupied their own niche as jobbers, middlemen, and shopkeepers.

The various immigrant groups crowded into densely packed communities near the waterfront and factories. In the 1840s and 1850s, real estate speculators and landlords shoehorned them into deteriorated houses and into attics and basements, into unused warehouses and factories. Housing was so scarce and rents so high that a large proportion of property owners made money by renting extra space in their own living quarters.[74] Narrow, three- and four-story buildings divided into tiny living quarters sprung up in alleyways and on back lots. On vacant lots and behind and between buildings, immigrants crowded into sheds and shanties.

In New York as early as the 1850s and in other cities somewhat later, the first tenement districts began to spread. With the middle class beginning to leave the city center, it became cost-efficient to raze older structures and replace them with buildings designed to crowd as many people as possible into the available space. The tenement—the name given to any low-cost multiple-family rental building—became a universal symbol for urban slums. Indeed, by the twentieth century multistory buildings of any kind came to represent city living and the suburbs became identified with free-standing houses and low-density subdivisions. The "dumbbell"—so named because of two twenty-eight-inch-wide air shafts that provided the only light and air to the interior rooms—became the most notorious tenement structure. Based on an award-winning 1879 design, the dumbbell maximized economic return but not ventilation and sanitation. Tenants on the upper floors would pitch their garbage down the shafts where it was left to rot. On each floor, located next to the foul air shafts, were one or two public toilets and a sink. By 1893, 70 percent of the population of New York City lived in tenements, most of them dumbbells.[75]

The dense clustering of immigrants into slum districts led native-born Protestants to conclude that the immigrants were dangerous and morally deficient. In spite of the obvious problems caused by overcrowding, however, the clustering of the various immigrant groups into separate communities was crucially important for assimilating them into city life. For some groups ethnic traditions and social and religious practices smoothed the transition to city life in America. Thus, although the Lower East Side of Manhattan became the most densely crowded residential district in any American city during the 1890s, its disease, death, crime, and alcoholism rates remained extremely low. The customs and lifestyles of the Eastern European Jews who settled there accounted for this anomaly. Jewish families insisted on personal cleanliness and careful preparation of food. By 1897, over half of New York's bathhouses were Jewish.[76] Jewish children were imbued with the idea that education was the sure road to success. Orthodox Jews did not tolerate heavy drinking, and suicide and crime were virtually nonexistent among Jewish youth.

In contrast, rates of crime, alcoholism, and disease ran high in the Irish wards. The Irish tended to be the hardest hit by the periodic epidemics that swept through the cities. The Irish populations were virtually decimated, for example, by the yellow fever epidemics that swept Memphis in 1873 and 1878. No other group suffered as much.[77]

SOCIAL DARWINISM AND THE IDEOLOGY OF SUCCESS

All city residents, whether native-born or immigrant, rich or poor, were subjected to the dislocations arising from the frenetic pace of urban growth. For most city residents in the latter half of the nineteenth century, the conditions of urban life ranged from squalid to barely tolerable. Epidemics sometimes swept through the cities. Streets turned to seas of mud in winter and to dust bowls in summer, and in every season they were littered with refuse and piles of steaming horse manure. A Swedish novelist commented that Chicago in 1850 (when it still had only 30,000 people) was "one of the most miserable and ugly cities," where people had come "to trade, to make money, and not to live."[78]

Urban residents complained about the conditions of daily life, but there was no guiding philosophy about what municipal governments should do to improve things. The American Revolution was fought to throw off an oppressive imperial power. As a consequence, all governments became defined as threats to individual liberty. Alongside the suspicion of government was a tradition of privatism—the idea that progress came through individual, not collective, endeavors. As a consequence, though urban leaders could persuade their fellow citizens to use local government to support schemes to promote the local economy, it was much more difficult to persuade them to tax themselves to support municipal services.

In the compact mercantile cities, most services were provided by volunteers. Volunteer night watchmen, for instance, tried to enforce the law; even in big cities, full-time, paid, uniformed police forces were rare until the mid-nineteenth century. Volunteer fire gangs answered the fire alarm. Individual property owners swept the streets and collected refuse. Even when city life became increasingly unpleasant, city residents were reluctant to acknowledge that municipal government might do better than the community's volunteer efforts.

After the Civil War, the cultural tradition of limited government and individualism inherited from the revolutionary period was given a new interpretation. Increasingly, individual liberty became measured by a singular standard: material success. Social Darwinism provided the logic and the language needed to transform this principle into a public philosophy. In 1859, Charles Darwin proposed a revolutionary theory of "natural selection." In *The Origin of Species,* he theorized that the "struggle for existence" weeded out the weakest individuals and species. Those unable to adapt to changing conditions in nature died out, resulting in the "survival of the fittest."

The Darwinist idea provided a convenient justification for the adverse consequences of industrialization (unemployment, poverty, starvation), a rationale by which the more prosperous could "reconcile their fellows to some of the hardships of life and to prevail upon them not to support hasty and ill-considered reforms."[79] The Social Darwinists suggested that society, like nature, provided a competitive environment in which the fittest survived if no one intervened to save the weak. They argued that any measures designed to mitigate the effects of capitalism could only upset the natural social processes that resulted in progress for the human species. The Social Darwinists "suggested that all attempts to reform social processes were efforts to remedy the irremediable, that they interfered with the wisdom of nature, that they could lead only to degeneration."[80] They maintained that any attempts to help the weak individuals of society would endanger the welfare of all. "Let it be understood," wrote the influential American Social Darwinist William Graham Sumner, "that we cannot go outside of this alternative: liberty, inequality, survival of the fittest; not—liberty, equality, survival of the unfittest."[81] The Social Darwinists argued that in society, wealth was the indicator of superior work and virtue, and therefore a healthy society required both success and failure. In the words of John D. Rockefeller, "The growth of large business is merely the survival of the fittest. . . . The American Beauty Rose can be produced in all its splendor and fragrance which bring cheer to its beholder only by sacrificing the early buds which grow up around it."[82] Obviously, Rockeller considered himself to be an American Beauty Rose.

The premises of Social Darwinism were soon incorporated into a "success" literature that became wildly popular between the 1860s and the turn of the century. Dozens of books extolled the virtues of hard work, thrift, moral habits, discipline, and cleanliness as the main ingredients leading to the attainment of wealth. The titles of some of the bestsellers are revealing. P. T. Barnum published *The Art of Money Getting* in 1882 and two years later followed it with *How I Made Millions. The Secret of Success* (1881), *How to Succeed* (1882), *The Royal Road to Wealth* (1882), *Success in Life* (1885), and *Danger Signals: The Enemies of Youth from the Business Man's Standpoint* (1885) were other popular books. Poverty was widely acclaimed as a great teacher of virtue; rural life was promoted as the teacher of moral habits and industry. By playing on the twin themes of poverty and rural beginnings, the literature offered hope of success to anyone who worked hard enough. A Unitarian minister, Horatio Alger, stitched these themes together into a winning literary formula. From his first book, *Ragged Dick,* and continuing through 106 more by 1904 (though the last books were written by other writers using his name), his rags-to-riches stories told of a poor boy who, through perseverance, hard work, honesty, religious probity and a little luck, achieves moderate financial success.

The success literature flooded the schools. *McGuffey's Readers,* the main primer used in the schools from the 1830s through the 1890s, were full of stories and poems based on success themes. A philosophy that romanticized individual progress and denigrated public measures to ameliorate life's travails could obviously be applied to mean that all governments, including city governments, should do as little as possible.

THE INCREASING IMPORTANCE OF MUNICIPAL SERVICES

Even in a political atmosphere that denigrated collective undertakings, the responsibilities of municipal governments vastly increased in the latter half of the nineteenth century. In New York City, for example, per capita city expenditures increased from $6.53 in 1850 to $27.31 in 1900.[83] During this half-century, cities spent more money and employed more people than either the state governments or the national government. When governmental spending was catalogued for the first time in the federal census of governments in 1902, it was found that local governments accounted for half of all governmental expenditures in the United States.[84]

There were at least three reasons why city governments took on new public responsibilities. First, new public services were provided in cases when urban residents of all classes felt threatened by imminent catastrophe or crisis. Second, local boosters assumed the lead in organizing public services when the absence of such services threatened local economic vitality. And third, by the late nineteenth century the growing middle class became intolerant of urban conditions that had previously been considered normal or inevitable.

In the absence of a positive philosophy about the responsibilities of government, urban services had always tended to be minimal. Essential as they were to basic health, water systems, for instance, were chronically inadequate. In the early nineteenth century most city residents got their water from wells, and these were often contaminated by waste. As a result, outbreaks of contagious diseases occurred with regularity. In the summer of 1793, 10 percent of Philadelphia's population died from yellow fever.[85] The city's economy came to a standstill, and a third of the population and virtually all wealthy families fled for the summer months. Outbreaks of yellow fever or cholera occurred in Philadelphia, Baltimore, and New Haven in 1793; in New York City, Baltimore, and Norfolk, Virginia, in 1795; and in Newburyport, Massachusetts, Boston, and Charleston, South Carolina, the next year.[86] Nearly a dozen cities were hit in 1797; three-fourths of Philadelphia's population fled and 4,000 people died (about 7 percent of the population).[87]

The threat of contagion prompted cities to invest in waterworks, drain swamps, and regulate the keeping of animals and the dumping of refuse. Philadelphia was goaded by its epidemics to construct the first municipal waterworks in the nation's history. Begun in 1799 and operational by 1801, it piped water to the city from the upper Schuylkill River. Philadelphia's system was constantly improved by the merchant elites that ran the Watering Committee. By the 1840s, however, these elites began to withdraw from political activities, partly because competition for political office had become more intense. Without their guiding hand on the committee, the water supply system became less and less adequate.[88] Only slowly did the city take over the responsibilities of the Watering Committee.

New municipal services tended to lag behind the need for them because they always constituted a minimal response to a crisis; "municipal authorities, loath to increase taxes, usually shouldered new responsibilities only at the prod of grim necessity."[89] Devastating outbreaks of yellow fever, typhoid, and cholera periodically made their rounds, especially in the inland cities such as New Orleans and Memphis that lagged farthest behind in providing uncontaminated water. Several urban water systems were built in the 1850s, and by the Civil War seventy towns had waterworks, owned by eighty different private companies.[90] Most people, however, had to fetch the water from street hydrants and hand pumps. Only wealthy people who could afford to pay for the service had water piped into their homes. In 1860, about one-tenth of Boston's residents had access to a bathtub and only five percent of the homes had indoor water closets.[91]

Urban water supplies were polluted by human and animal waste. Sewage was generally not drained away from the cities but instead was collected in huge community cesspools, which had to be dug out frequently. Even when sewer pipes carried waste away from the city, that was not necessarily the end of it. Serious typhoid epidemics broke out in the cities along the Merrimac River in Massachusetts in the 1880s because residents were drinking water polluted by cities located upstream. Because of Boston's habit of dumping wastes directly into it, by 1877 Boston Harbor had become "one vast cesspool."[92] Until the 1920s, crowded residential districts were dotted with outdoor privies, and water bearing a burden of horse manure and other refuse flowed in open gutters along the edges of the streets. There were so many sources of contamination that only those cities that piped their water from isolated watersheds far away from urban settlement could avoid a contaminated water supply.

Ultimately, the water supply problem could be solved only through the development of adequate technology. Even Philadelphia's relatively sophisticated system delivered its water with only the heaviest silt filtered out.[93] Pumps frequently failed; in the winter pipes froze. People found dirt, insects, and even small fish in their water. During the first decade of the twentieth century, when modern filtration techniques were developed, death rates in New York, Boston, Philadelphia, and New Orleans were cut by one-fifth.[94]

Epidemics also prompted cities to build sewers. In 1823 Boston began installing the nation's first sanitary sewers. Other large cities followed suit, but slowly. By 1857 New York City, at that point nearing the million-person mark in population, provided sewers under only one-fourth of its streets, and most of these were storm rather than sanitary sewers.[95] Taxpayers resisted the high cost of laying underground pipes and installing costly pumps. Though most of the big cities had constructed sewers by the 1870s, these were usually paid for by the property owners who subscribed, leaving vast areas, always the neighborhoods inhabited by the poor, without service.

In response to crisis, cities also began to finance and organize professional police forces. In the merchant cities of the early nineteenth century, social control had been based on face-to-face relations within the household and the community. Most cities remained "a community in which every citizen was closely bound to other members of the community by familial, recreational, economic, and social ties. The social hierarchy was clear; a series of institutions supported that hierarchy; and the community was so compact that it was difficult to escape the vigilance of the dominant class."[96] Until at least midcentury, the law was enforced in most cities by night watches and constables.

As cities grew in size and complexity, it became clear that informal community norms could not keep the peace. The constant influx of new immigrants provoked high levels of ethnic conflict, pushed up crime rates, and broke apart the bonds of community. In the 1830s and 1840s, rioting directed against Irish immigrants and free blacks broke out regularly in Philadelphia. Almost all cities experienced rising levels of violence. In frontier cities the connection between rapid population growth and social instability was especially apparent. In the early years more than half the residents of San Francisco, St. Louis, and New Orleans were transients. A constant stream of river men, wagoners, and traders moved in and out of these cities. Saloons proliferated; gambling and prostitution flourished. Violent crimes became such a fact of everyday life in San Francisco in the gold rush years of the 1850s that merchants funded vigilante committees. The vigilantes soon organized their own crime rings and became almost as dangerous as the criminals they were supposed to catch.[97]

In 1845 Boston became the first city to provide uniforms for its officers. The same year, when its population numbered more than 400,000, New York replaced its force of part-time policemen with full-time officers. The police went about the jobs in streetclothes, completely untrained and without supervision.[98] Eight years later the city's police finally received uniforms and some modest training. Until the late 1830s, Philadelphia relied on posses, militia, and night watches to enforce the law. They worked part-time and did not wear uniforms.[99]

New York's police forces were in constant turmoil for many years. There was considerable resistance to the idea of creating a professional police force because the two political parties that contended for power in the city considered the police an important source of patronage jobs. Following the 1857 mayoral election, the new mayor fired everyone on the police force and installed officers loyal to his own party. The former police officers refused to quit their jobs, and so for several months the city had two competing police forces. In June of that year a full-scale riot broke out between the two groups.[100] Similar confusion repeated itself again in 1868, when the newly elected Democratic governor removed all of the city's police commissioners because they were Republicans. The commissioners refused to vacate their offices. Finally, the state legislature resolved the dispute by assuming the power to appoint the police commissioners.

These events illustrate why it took so long to build modern, fully profession-alized police forces. Many people feared that, as a quasi-military organization, the police might be used by one political faction against another. This fear was well founded. At least until the mid-twentieth century, police departments were prolific sources of patronage jobs, and their political loyalties and political debts, as well as their ethnic prejudices, often affected their work. And even today po-lice are often accused of a biased enforcement of the law.

If it seems that crisis goaded governing elites into organizing and financing municipal services, this fact still begs an important question: What provoked a sense of crisis? Objective conditions, however dire, may be adjusted to, may be considered normal, or may seem beyond anyone's control. In the nineteenth century, urban leaders perceived that a crisis had arrived when the economic vi-tality and very existence of the cities they lived in seemed threatened. On the whole, civic elites and business leaders preferred to support public services rather than to abandon the city.

Once provided, urban services became institutionalized; they quickly seemed normal and routine. This was especially the case with services such as water sys-tems and fire departments that required the construction of permanent infrastruc-ture and investment in expensive equipment. In this way the responsibilities of city governments grew step by step. In the early nineteenth century, when con-fronted with a new problem, the cities' merchants, landowners, and other civic leaders would typically organize a committee to decide what to do. Over time such informal arrangements gave way to services provided by full-time, paid em-ployees. This is exactly what happened with Philadelphia's waterworks. At first the Watering Committee raised money through private donations and individual subscriptions to the water service. Prominent merchants led the committee until 1837.[101] But in subsequent decades, the system expanded until it provided water to all citizens, and it became necessary to impose taxes to support it.

The origins of modern bureaucracies can be found in the breakdown of in-formal community and recognition of the inadequacy of the informal committee system. Part-time politicians could not organize and supervise complex urban services. Increasingly, during the latter half of the nineteenth century, city ser-vices were provided by paid employees of city governments who were orga-nized into bureaucratic hierarchies. As the scope of municipal services broad-ened, the number of paid city employees multiplied. Where volunteers once joined firehouse gangs and scavengers picked garbage off the streets, salaried, full-time employees took their place.

Milwaukee's volunteer fire department gave way to paid professionals in the 1850s, when new steam pumps proved too complicated for volunteers to maintain and operate.[102] Public works employees were hired to maintain the streets when it became too difficult to find volunteers for the task. In the same decade, the provision of health services became too complex for volunteers when the Milwaukee city council required vaccination for smallpox and when it provided funds to build a sewer system. Gradually, the day-to-day administra-tion of services was put in the hands of salaried employees: "Politics became a

full-time business and professionals moved in to make careers of public office."[103]

In the last three decades of the nineteenth century, a growing middle class
began to demand integrated water and sewer systems,[104] and by the 1890s
there was popular pressure to improve services of all kinds. From 1840 to the
1870s, assistance to railroads had been the largest single cause of municipal
debt. In striking contrast, during the last thirty years of the century, the cities
went into debt mainly to finance the expansion of new services and to build
infrastructure.[105] Compared to the merchant elites who had previously dominated city governments, the working-class professional politicians who ran
urban machines had few qualms about increasing taxes to pay for city services. In fact, city contracts and patronage jobs provided the glue that held local political machines together. Cities ran up debts at a feverish pace to finance improved water systems, sewers, paved streets, parks, and other
improvements.[106] Because of rising standards of public health, new technologies, even when very expensive, were quickly adopted. The creation of integrated sewerage systems is instructive. Systems of separate sanitary and
storm sewers were not completed in most cities until late in the nineteenth
century. Laying sewer pipe was a huge public works project for any city. Nevertheless, the number of miles of sewer pipe laid increased fourfold from 1890
to 1909.[107]

By the late nineteenth century, American cities, in general, provided more
and better services than did European cities, with more miles of sewer and water
mains, more miles of paved streets, more street lamps, better mass transportation,
and more fire departments with better equipment.[108] Urban residents in the
United States used more than twice as much water per capita as their counterparts in England, and many times more than city dwellers in Germany.[109] This
was no doubt due to the fact that flush toilets and bathtubs were far more widespread in American cities.[110] The building of integrated sewer systems and the
adoption of new water filtration technology dramatically reduced typhoid mortality rates.[111]

The cities also vastly expanded public health efforts. Using the new science
of bacteriology, health inspectors examined children in schools, checked buildings for ventilation and faulty plumbing, and inspected food and milk.[112] Death
rates fell sharply in the big cities, by 20 percent or more in New York, Chicago,
Cleveland, Buffalo, and other cities in the 1890s[113] and just as sharply again in
the first decade of the twentieth century.[114]

In many ways, the late nineteenth century was the golden age of American
city building. Investing heavily in basic urban infrastructure, city governments
placed themselves at the cutting edge of technology, building such engineering
marvels as the Brooklyn Bridge and New York's Croton aqueduct system. The
Parks Movement and the City Beautiful Movement, both supported by urban
elites and the middle class, swept the country, resulting in new and improved
parks, ponds, formal gardens, bandstands, ball fields, broad tree-lined avenues,
ornate public buildings, and other amenities. Urban residents came to expect a

level of municipal services that was previously unheard of. The squalor of the nineteenth-century American city began to yield to the relative safety, cleanliness, and health of the twentieth-century city.

THE FIGHT FOR CONTROL OF CITY GOVERNMENTS

The new responsibilities being taken on by cities tended to be administered piecemeal—a water board added here, a health commission there, perhaps a police commission and a harbor board next. The precedent for the board system can be found in the committee system of the merchant city. For example, when a water system was needed, the merchant elite that controlled the mayor's office and board of aldermen would organize a committee to build the system; an epidemic would prompt them to create a health board. Over time each service expanded according to its own logic. City governments evolved in chaotic fashion; no one would even have been able to obtain an organization chart to make sense of it.

The increasing disorganization of city government was a perfect recipe for corruption. Typically, a city was governed by a board of aldermen or a city council, with each representing a separate ward. No one could easily coordinate their efforts. A politics of tradeoffs, logrolling, and partisan wrangling could, and often did, result in a free-for-all, with each alderman looking for a way to trade his vote for some material consideration. Individual aldermen often sold their votes to paving contractors, restaurant or brothel owners, or utility companies in exchange for contracts, licenses, and franchises. Aldermen also got in the habit of filling the multitude of independent committees, boards, and commissions with their political cronies, who also took bribes when the opportunity arose.

The widespread graft and corruption incensed civic and business elites and middle- and upper-class voters. Their remedy was to approach state legislators with requests for charter reform or for special legislation designed to curtail the powers held by aldermanic councils. Over the last three decades of the nineteenth century, city councils lost more and more of their authority. State legislatures intervened to take budgetary and supervisory authority from elected councils and to give these powers to mayors or to full-time boards and commissions that were independent of aldermen. In the 1870s and 1880s, state legislative committees assumed financial or administrative control of the police departments of Detroit, Baltimore, Boston, St. Louis, Kansas City, and New York. Fights for political control within cities often ended up in the state house. Reformers, citizens' committees, party leaders, and mayors all became accustomed to trying to persuade legislatures to pass special legislation favoring their cause. Legislatures became, in effect, referees among the contending interests that were trying to control city politics.

Legislative interference took many forms and sprang from a variety of motives. In 1869, the boss of New York City's machine, William Marcy Tweed, paid $600,000 in bribes to state legislators to get a new city charter passed.[115] Two years later (and, ironically, just before Tweed was arrested for bribery), the legislature helped Tweed consolidate his control over the city's budget by creating the Board of Estimate and Apportionment. The board, composed of the mayor, comptroller, the president of the Department of Taxes and Assessments, and the president of the Board of Aldermen, was required to submit the city's budget to the aldermen for review but could then make its own decisions.[116] Two years later, despite a series of trials involving Tweed and his cronies, the legislature passed still another charter giving the mayor, rather than the Board of Aldermen, the authority to appoint department heads.[117]

In cities elsewhere the story was similar. In 1891 the Indiana legislature gave the city controller of Indianapolis the authority to draft the budget; the council could lower but could not increase appropriations. New charters also gave the mayors of Cleveland and Indianapolis the authority to remove executive officials, a feature that was also adopted in new charters approved in other states: New Orleans in 1896 and Baltimore in 1898.[118] In most states mayors gained the right to veto legislation. Budget authority passed out of the hands of municipal legislators and into the hands of comptrollers or independent boards. In 1892 New York's legislature mandated a Board of Estimate and Apportionment, modeled on New York City's, for all cities over 50,000 in population. In other states commissions or boards were created to take over functions such as public parks, education, libraries, health, and public works.

Why were state legislators so eager to give more powers to mayors and to special boards and commissions? Whereas aldermen and city councilors came from and represented neighborhoods, the members of boards and commissions often were "bastions of the city's elite."[119] They were businessmen, bankers, lawyers, and other men of professional and social standing. The men of wealth and social prestige, who had deserted electoral politics in the industrial city, now found a new niche. They refused to run for office against the new breed of immigrant saloonkeepers and party loyalists. Instead, they were appointed by governors, legislative committees, and mayors to sit on boards and commissions. These boards were "protected from popular control, insulated from the undue influence of the city's aldermen, and dominated by those perched proudly on the top rung of the urban social ladder."[120]

In contrast to the aldermen, mayors tended to come from prominent, even upper-class, backgrounds. Rather than running for election in only one ward, they were required to win citywide elections, and thus they were forced to appeal to a broad cross-section of the urban electorate. Campaigns covering an entire city were expensive, and in the late nineteenth century candidates for mayor paid most of their own campaign costs.[121] What was an advantage, even a requirement, for an alderman—to come from the neighborhood, meet people in saloons and beer halls, speak the language of immigrants, accentuate ethnic identity, be one of the people—became a liability for someone running for citywide office. In the first years of the twentieth century (as we discuss in the next chapter), party machines were able to centralize power, and machine mayors were able to win elections even without personal wealth and social standing. In late nineteenth-century America, however, the powers of city government were up for grabs. The immigrants, by virtue of their numbers, were able to elect their representatives to boards of aldermen. Middle- and upper-class elites, by being able to persuade state legislatures to amend city charters and vest more authority in mayors and administrators, were nevertheless able to keep their grip on important levers of power.

According to the urban historian Jon Teaford, this arrangement amounted to an "unheralded triumph" because it allowed city governments in the late nineteenth century to accomplish two difficult but essential tasks. The first task, democratic governance, required public officials to broker among the various interests that contended for power within the cities. Without formal representation in politics, immigrants would never have considered city governments legitimate, and the level of social turmoil in cities would probably have been higher than it was.

The second task of city government required the competent administration of the panoply of services and amenities provided by modern cities. An acceptable level of services would have been almost impossible without the development of institutions of professional management. This occurred through boards and commissions that were able to operate, at least to some degree, independently from immediate political pressures. There was a price to be paid, however, for the evolution of an independent cadre of urban bureaucrats: Local democracy was substantially compromised.

THE POLITICAL ISOLATION OF THE CITIES

If upper- and middle-class urban residents often thought that city governments were corrupt, people in rural America thought that cities, in general, were entirely beyond redemption. Until the mid-nineteenth century, cities were largely ignored by state legislatures. As long as cities were ruled by patricians and business leaders, they were allowed to run their affairs without interference. This laissez-faire attitude gave way when rural interests became convinced that the industrial cities, and even the whole nation, might soon be governed by immigrants and Catholics.

State and federal court decisions consistently upheld the powers of the states to interfere in city affairs. In 1819, in the Dartmouth College case, the U.S. Supreme Court held that cities were created by the states and that their charters could therefore be amended or rescinded at will. (By contrast, private corporations were protected from interference by the constitutional provision against "impairing the obligation of contract.")[122] Prior to the Civil War, basically because state legislatures tended to ignore them, cities retained a great deal of local autonomy. In 1868, however, the chief justice of the Iowa Supreme Court, John F. Dillon, handed down a highly influential decision. In language destined to become quoted in books on municipal law, Judge Dillon declared that states could rightfully exert total control over their cities:

Municipal corporations owe their origin to, and derive their powers and rights wholly from, the legislature. It breathes into them the breath of life without which they cannot exist. As it creates so it may destroy. . . . Unless there is some constitutional limitation on the right, the legislature might, by a single act, if we can suppose it capable of so great a folly and so great a wrong, sweep from existence all of the municipal corporations of the state, and the corporations could not prevent it. . . . They are, so to phrase it, the mere tenants at will of the legislature.[123]

Dillon's historical analysis was actually wrong. During the colonial period, local governments had been self-organized. Since they had existed before the states and the constitution, they were not simply legal creations of the states. Because it does not mention cities, the Constitution did not change this fact. In his classic work *Democracy in America* (1835), Alexis de Tocqueville emphasized that local governments in the United States were sovereign, and he compared them to independent nations: "Municipal independence is . . . a natural consequence of the principle of the sovereignty of the people in the United States: all the American republics recognize it more or less."[124] Even after Dillon's rule, many articles, books and court rulings made the case for the autonomy of local governments.[125]

In the long run, however, "Dillon's rule," as it came to be known, won out in the courts. Most judges agreed with Dillon that state control over cities was needed to ensure that cities could not interfere too much in the private economic realm. Dillon was motivated by the fact that cities had been so active in providing subsidies to railroads—and he reasoned that if they could help private corporations so directly, they could regulate them as well. Dillon's missionary zeal was also fired by a conviction that cities were governed by riffraff: "men the best fitted by their intelligence, business experience, capacity and moral character, for local governors and counsellors are not always, it is feared—it might be added, are not generally—chosen."[126] His solution was for state governments and courts to supervise cities and strictly limit their powers. In 1872 Dillon published his *Treatise on the Law of Municipal Corporations*. Originally 800 pages long, by the time the fifth edition was published in 1911, it had grown to five thick volumes.[127] It became the bible on municipal law. By 1924 William Munro, the author of a leading textbook, *The Government of American Cities*, wrote that Dillon's rule was "so well recognized that it is not nowadays open to question."[128]

Inspired by a similar distrust of cities—or, rather, of immigrant voters—state legislators took steps to ensure that no matter how fast and big cities grew, their representatives to the state house would never be able to gain a majority of the votes in state legislatures. Most rural legislators would probably have agreed with a delegate to the New York state constitutional convention of 1894, who said, "the average citizen in the rural district is superior in intelligence, superior in morality, superior in self-government to the average citizen of the great cities."[129] A distrust of cities was hardly new. Decades earlier, Maine's constitutional convention of 1819 had established a ceiling on the number of representatives who could represent towns in the state legislature. In 1845 the Louisiana legislature limited New Orleans to 12.5 percent of the state's senators and 10 percent of the state's assemblymen. (The population of New Orleans then accounted for 20 percent of the state's total.[130]) By the end of the century, every state had ensured that no matter how large the cities became, representatives from rural legislative districts would continue to hold a controlling majority in state legislatures.

It mattered very much who controlled state legislatures. By the end of the nineteenth century, more people lived in the cities of some states than lived outside them. If their influence in state legislatures had grown in step with their populations, cities would have been able to secure state financial support for the expansion of city services. In fact, however, cities received practically no help at all. If urban voters had been able to gain more influence in state politics and in state governments, they also could have asserted a political voice in national politics. Rural elites firmly controlled the party caucuses that nominated governors, members of congress, senators, and presidents. Immigrants and labor unions had no effective means of influencing governmental policies at the state or national levels. The underrepresentation of the cities resulted in indifference to the problems faced by big cities in state legislatures, governors' offices, Congress, and the White House. Traffic congestion, slum housing, orphaned children, contagious diseases, poverty—none of these problems interested rural and small-town legislators or a Congress and president beholden to state party leaders who answered to rural constituents.

Underrepresentation of cities throughout the federal system had profound and enduring consequences, for it allowed governmental leaders at all levels to wash their hands of the devastating effects of industrialization and urbanization. In the late nineteenth century, powerful populist movements pushed for the recognition of the right of labor unions to organize. In the first twenty years of the twentieth century, reformers lobbied state legislatures to adopt universal health insurance, workers' compensation, and relief programs for widows, children, and the elderly. A groundswell of opposition to child labor swept the country; nevertheless, the federal government did not adopt child labor legislation until 1916, and it was struck down by the Supreme Court two years later.[131] Partially because urban residents had so little political voice, these and other reforms were delayed until the New Deal of the 1930s, and some reforms, such as national health care, have never been adopted.

The federal courts finally moved against legislative malapportionment in the 1960s, more than forty years after the 1920 census showed that a majority of Americans lived in urban places. In *Baker v. Carr* (1962) a group of Knoxville, Tennessee, residents challenged the fact that the Tennessee legislature had not been reapportioned since 1901.[132] Their lawyers argued that citizens living in urban areas were being deprived of "equal protection of the law," as guaranteed by the Fourteenth Amendment to the U.S. Constitution. The important court decision that decided this case, as well as others, came on June 15, 1964, when the U.S. Supreme Court, in *Reynolds v. Sims*, ruled that state legislative apportionments must follow a "one man–one vote" principle.[133] Within a few years, for the first time in the nation's history, state legislative and congressional districts were apportioned to give city residents equal representation.

The "one man, one vote" remedy came too late: By the time it was adopted, cities were losing population to the suburbs. The nation's political power was shifting to the suburbs and to the Sunbelt. If cities had gained equal representation in state legislatures and in Congress decades earlier, the influence of urban voters would have virtually guaranteed that they could have secured from the federal government as well as from many states funding for such urban priorities as mass transit, public housing, urban revitalization, and community health programs. The support for cities would have been similar to the support provided by many European countries. But the American political system was structured to reduce such influence—a circumstance that arose because the people who lived in the cities of America had long been regarded as "strangers in the land."[134]

NOTES

1. Robert A. Beauregard, *Voices of Decline: The Postwar Fate of U.S. Cities* (New York: Blackwell, 1993).
2. London proper had 957,000, but the greater London area had 1,117,000 people.
3. Brian R. Mitchell, *European Historical Statistics, 1750–1970* (New York: Columbia University Press, 1975), p. 76.
4. Defined as settlements with at least 5,000 population.
5. "The Inevitability of City Growth," reprinted from *Atlantic Monthly*, April 1985, in *City Life, 1865–1900: Views of Urban America*, ed. Ann Cook, Marilyn Gittell, and Herb Mack (New York: Praeger, 1973), p. 17.
6. Eric H. Monkkonen, *America Becomes Urban: The Development of U.S. Cities and Towns, 1780–1980* (Berkeley: University of California Press, 1988), p. 78.
7. U.S. Department of Commerce, Bureau of the Census, *Historical Statistics of the United States, Colonial Times to 1970*, pt. 1, Bicentennial ed. (Washington, D.C.: Government Printing Office, 1975), p. 11.
8. D. Philip Locklin, *Economics of Transportation*, 7th ed. (Homewood, Ill.: Irwin, 1972).
9. Richard C. Wade, *The Urban Frontier: Pioneer Life in Early Pittsburgh, Cincinnati, Lexington, Louisville, and St. Louis* (Chicago: University of Chicago Press, 1959), p. 103.
10. David M. Gordon, "Class Struggle and the Stages of American Urban Development," in *The Rise of the Sunbelt Cities*, ed. David C. Perry and Alfred J. Watkins (Beverly Hills, Calif.: Sage, 1977), p. 64.
11. George Rogers Taylor, *The Transportation Revolution, 1815–1860* (New York: Holt, Rinehart and Winston, 1951), p. 52.
12. Carter Goodrich, *Government Promotion of American Canals and Railroads, 1800–1890* (New York: Columbia University Press, 1960), pp. 266–267.
13. Wade, *The Urban Frontier*, p. 70.
14. *Historical Statistics of the United States, Colonial Times to 1970*, pt. 2, pp. 728, 731.
15. Alfred D. Chandler, *The Railroads: The Nation's First Big Business* (New York: Harcourt Brace Jovanovich, 1965).
16. Henry W. Broude, "The Role of the State in American Economic Development, 1820–1890," *United States Economic History: Selected Readings*, ed. H. N. Scheiber (New York: Knopf, 1964).
17. Paul Kantor, *The Dependent City Revisited: The Political Economy of Urban Development and Social Policy* (Boulder, Colo.: Westview, 1995), p. 24.
18. Carter Goodrich, "The Revulsion Against Internal Improvements," *Journal of Economic History* 10, no. 2 (November 1950): 145–169.
19. David Chalmers, *Neither Socialism Nor Monopoly* (Philadelphia: Lippincott, 1976), p. 4.

20. Blake McKelvey, *American Urbanization: A Comparative History* (Glenview, Ill.: Scott, Foresman, 1973), pp. 25–26.
21. Ibid.
22. Paul Kantor with Stephen David, *The Dependent City: The Changing Political Economy of Urban America* (Glenview, Ill.: Scott, Foresman, 1987), pp. 499–500.
23. Goodrich, *Government Promotion*, p. 241. Goodrich estimates that until 1860 local governments provided 29 percent of total public subsidies (p. 268). The proportion of local contributions increased significantly after the Civil War. In his study of New York from 1826 to 1875, Harry Pierce concludes that three-quarters of the subsidy came from local governments and one-quarter from the state. See Harry H. Pierce, *The Railroads of New York: A Study of Government Aid, 1826–1875* (Cambridge, Mass.: Harvard University Press, 1953).
24. Ibid.
25. In 1849, for example, the voters of Cleveland approved a $100,000 subscription to stock in the Cleveland and Pittsburgh Railroad by a vote of 1,157 to 27. Despite the enthusiasm of the voters, the stock never paid any dividends and eventually sold at far below par. Charles C. Williamson, *The Finances of Cleveland* (New York: Columbia University Press, 1907), pp. 218–220.
26. Goodrich, *Government Promotion*, p. 42.
27. Ibid., p. 272. One study gave the following figures for New York: "Only 52 of the 297 municipalities that bought stock in a railroad disposed of their securities at par or better, 162 held stock with no market value." (Pierce, *The Railroads of New York*), p. 273.
28. A. M. Hillhouse, *Municipal Bonds: A Century of Experience* (Englewood Cliffs, N.J.: Prentice-Hall, 1936), p. 39.
29. Goodrich, *Government Promotion*, pp. 268–271. Repudiation goes beyond default, which is simply a failure to pay the debt on time. Repudiation declares an unwillingness to ever repay the debt.
30. Alberta M. Sbragia, *Debt Wish: Entrepreneurial Cities, U.S. Federalism and Economic Development* (Pittsburgh: University of Pittsburgh Press, 1996), p. 91.
31. Goodrich, "Revulsion Against Internal Improvements"; see also Sbragia, *Debt Wish*, chap. 5.
32. Lawrence Goodwyn, *The Populist Movement* (New York: Oxford University Press, 1978).
33. Eric Lampard, "Historical Aspects of Urbanization," in *The Study of Urbanization*, ed. Philip M. Hauser and Leo F. Schnore (New York: Wiley, 1965), p. 523.
34. Allan R. Pred, *The Spatial Dynamics of Urban-Industrial Growth, 1800–1914* (Cambridge, Mass.: M.I.T. Press, 1966), p. 103.
35. Donald S. Lutz, *Popular Consent and Popular Control: Whig Political Theory in the Early State Constitutions* (Baton Rouge: Louisiana State University Press, 1980), p. 105; Advisory Commission on Intergovernmental Relations, *Citizen Participation in the American Federal System* (Washington, D.C.: U.S. Government Printing Office, 1979), p. 41.
36. William Bennett Munro, *Municipal Government and Administration* (New York: Macmillan, 1923), p. 94.
37. Lee Benson, *The Concept of Jacksonian Democracy* (Princeton, N.J.: Princeton University Press, 1961).
38. Edwin J. Perkins, *The Economy of Colonial America* (New York: Columbia University Press, 1980), p. 157.
39. Philip Foner, *History of the Labor Movement in the United States* (New York: International, 1975), pp. 13–18.
40. Howard P. Chudacoff, *The Evolution of American Urban Society* (Englewood Cliffs, N.J.: Prentice-Hall, 1975), p. 26.
41. Sam Bass Warner, Jr., *The Private City: Philadelphia in Three Periods of Its Growth* (Philadelphia: University of Pennsylvania Press, 1968), p. 21.
42. Kantor, *The Dependent City*, p. 22.
43. Ibid., p. 33.

44. Pred, *The Spatial Dynamics*, p. 16.
45. The skyscraper boom on Fifth Avenue between 1900 and 1915 was largely fueled by the desire of rich individuals to outdo one another in pretentious architecture. See Seymour I. Toll, *Zoned American* (New York: Grossman, 1969), chap. 2.
46. Samuel P. Hays, *The Response to Industrialism, 1885–1914* (Chicago: University of Chicago Press, 1957), p. 73.
47. Ibid., p. 170.
48. Ibid., pp. 68–69.
49. Chartered by the states, limited-risk corporations allowed the selling of shares to investors whose liability in case of corporate failure was limited to their direct investment. In partnerships the partners were liable for all debts incurred by the company, and these could easily exceed the partners' own assets. The corporate form of business organization thus made it easier to raise capital, for investors risked less than in other forms of business investment.
50. U.S. Department of the Interior, Census Office, *Census Reports of 1900*, vol. 7, Manufacturers, pt. 1: "United States by Industries" (Washington, D.C.: U.S. Government Printing Office, 1902), pp. 503–509.
51. William Miller, "American Historians and the Business Elite," *Journal of Economic History* 9 (1949): 184–208.
52. Kenneth Jackson, *Crabgrass Frontier: The Suburbanization of the United States* (New York: Oxford University Press, 1985), p. 35.
53. George Rogers Taylor, "Building an Intra-Urban Transportation System," in *The Urbanization of America: An Historical Anthology*, ed. Allen M. Wakstein (Boston: Houghton Mifflin, 1970), p. 137.
54. Glen E. Holt, "The Changing Perception of Urban Pathology: An Essay on the Development of Mass Transit in the United States," in *Cities in American History*, ed. Kenneth T. Jackson and Stanley K. Schultz (New York: Knopf, 1972), p. 327.
55. Taylor, "Building an Intra-Urban Transportation System," p. 139.
56. C. G. Kennedy, "Commuter Services in the Boston Area, 1835–1860," *Business History Review* 26 (1962): 277–287.
57. Jackson, *Crabgrass Frontier*, p. 41.
58. David Ward, *Cities and Immigrants: A Geography of Change in Nineteenth-Century America* (New York: Oxford University, Press, 1971), p. 4.
59. Jackson, *Crabgrass Frontier*, p. 108.
60. Ibid.
61. Gary A. Tobin, "Suburbanization and the Development of Motor Transportation: Transportation and Technology and the Suburbanization Process," in *The Changing Face of the Suburbs*, ed. Barry Schwartz (Chicago: University of Chicago Press, 1975), p. 99.
62. "The Smell of Cincinnati," *Enquirer* (Richmond, Va.), November 15, 1874, in *City Life*, ed. Cook, Gittell and Mack, p. 143.
63. Ward, *Cities and Immigrants*, chap. 3.
64. Blake McKelvey, *The Urbanization of America, 1860–1915* (New Brunswick, N.J.: Rutgers University Press, 1963), p. 54.
65. U.S. Bureau of the Census, *The Growth of Metropolitan Districts in the United States: 1900–1940*, by Warren S. Thompson (Washington, D.C.: U.S. Government Printing office, 1947).
66. Hays, *The Response to Industrialism*, p. 14.
67. Ward, *Cities and Immigrants*, p. 52.
68. Thomas Monroe Pitkin, *Keepers of the Gate: A History of Ellis Island* (New York: New York University Press, 1975), p. ix.
69. Ward, *Cities and Immigrants*, p. 56.
70. Ibid., p. 52.
71. John Higham, *Strangers in the Land: Patterns of American Nativism, 1860–1925* (New Brunswick, N.J.: Rutgers University Press, 1955), pp. 54–55.

72. Stephen Thernstrom, *The Other Bostonians: Poverty and Progress in the American Metropolis, 1880–1970* (Cambridge, Mass.: Harvard University Press, 1973), p. 160.

73. Ibid.

74. Charles N. Glaab and A. Theodore Brown, *A History of Urban America* (New York: Macmillan, 1967), p. 160.

75. Gwendolyn Wright, *Building the American Dream: A Social History of Housing in America* (Cambridge, Mass.: MIT Press, 1983), p. 123.

76. Moses Rischin, *The Promised City, New York's Jews, 1870–1914* (Cambridge, Mass.: Harvard University Press, 1962), p. 87.

77. Gerald M. Caters, Jr., "Yellow Fever in Memphis in the 1870s," in *The City in American Life, From Colonial Times to the Present,* ed. Paul Kramer and Frederick L. Holborn (New York: Capricorn Books, 1970), pp. 180–185.

78. Glaab and Brown, *A History of Urban America,* p. 86.

79. Richard Hofstadter, *Social Darwinism in American Thought,* rev. ed. (New York: Braziller, 1955), p. 5.

80. Ibid., p. 7.

81. Quoted in Robert Green McCloskey, *American Conservatism in the Age of Enterprise, 1865–1910* (New York: HarperCollins, 1951), p. 49.

82. Quoted in Ralph Nader, Mark Green and Joel Seligman, *Taming the Giant Corporation* (New York: Norton, 1976), p. 44.

83. Glaab and Brown, *A History of Urban America,* p. 180.

84. Terrence J. MacDonald and Sally K. Ward, eds., *The Politics of Urban Fiscal Policy* (Beverly Hills, Calif.: Sage, 1984), p. 14.

85. Nelson M. Blake, *Water for the Cities: A History of the Urban Water Supply Problem in the United States* (Syracuse, N.Y.: Syracuse University Press, 1956), p. 6.

86. Ibid., pp. 102–103.

87. Ibid., p. 6.

88. Warner, *The Private City,* pp. 107–109.

89. Arthur N. Schlesinger, "A Panoramic View: The City in American Life," in *The City in American Life,* ed. Kramer and Holborn, p. 23.

90. McKelvey, *The Urbanization of America,* p. 13.

91. Edgar W. Martin, *The Standard of Living in 1860* (Chicago: University of Chicago Press, 1942), pp. 44–47, 89–112.

92. McKelvey, *The Urbanization of America,* p. 90.

93. McKelvey, *The Urbanization of America,* p. 13.

94. Ibid., p. 90.

95. McKelvey, *American Urbanization,* p. 44.

96. Stephen Thernstrom, *Poverty and Progress: Social Mobility in a Nineteenth-Century City* (Cambridge, Mass.: Harvard University Press, 1964), p. 39.

97. Fred M. Wirt, *Power in the City* (Berkeley: University of California Press, 1974), p. 110.

98. James F. Richardson, "To Control the City: The New York Police in Historical Perspective," in *Cities in American History,* ed. Kenneth T. Jackson and Stanley K. Schultz (New York: Knopf, 1972), pp. 272–289.

99. Warner, *The Private City,* chap. 7.

100. Richardson, "To Control the City," p. 278.

101. Warner, *The Private City.*

102. Bayrd Still, *Milwaukee: The History of a City* (Madison: State Historical Society of Wisconsin, 1984), chap. 10.

103. Warner, *The Private City,* p. 86.

104. Sbragia, *Debt Wish,* p. 76.

105. Ibid.

106. Ibid.

107. Ibid.
108. Jon Teaford, *The Unheralded Triumph: City Government in America, 1870–1900* (Baltimore: Johns Hopkins University Press, 1984), chap. 8.
109. Ibid., p. 222.
110. Ibid., p. 221.
111. Stanley K. Schultz, *Constructing Urban Culture: American Cities and City Planning, 1800–1920* (Philadelphia: Temple University Press, 1989), p. 174.
112. Teaford, *The Unheralded Triumph*, p. 247.
113. Ibid., p. 246.
114. McKelvey, *The Urbanization of America*, p. 90.
115. Alexander Callow, Jr., *The Tweed Ring* (New York: Oxford University Press, 1966).
116. Teaford, *The Unheralded Triumph*, p. 17.
117. Ibid., p. 18.
118. Ibid., p. 45.
119. Ibid., p. 68.
120. Ibid., p. 76.
121. Ibid., p. 47.
122. See *Dartmouth College v. Woodward,* 4 Wheat. 518 (1819).
123. *City of Clinton v. Cedar Rapids and Missouri River Railroad Co.,* 24 Iowa 455–475 (1868).
124. Alexis de Tocqueville, *Democracy in America,* vol. 1 (New York: Shocken Books, 1961), p. 60.
125. For citations, see Gerald Frug, "The City as a Legal Concept," *Harvard Law Review* 93, no. 6 (April 1980), 1113–1117.
126. Schultz, *Constructing Urban Culture,* p. 73.
127. Ibid., p. 69.
128. William Munro, *The Government of the American Cities,* 3rd ed. (New York: Macmillan, 1924), p. 53.
129. Mark I. Gelfand, *A Nation of Cities: The Federal Government and Urban America, 1933–1965* (New York: Oxford University Press, 1975), p. 11.
130. Ibid., p. 11.
131. *Hammer v. Dagenhart et al.,* 247 U.S. 251 (1918).
132. *Baker v. Carr,* 369 U.S. 189 (1962).
133. *Reynolds v. Sims,* 377 U.S. 533 (1964). "One man–one vote" was the term used in the court's decision.
134. Higham, *Strangers in the Land.*

C H A P T E R

3

PARTY MACHINES AND
POLITICAL ENTREPRENEURS

MACHINES AND MACHINE-STYLE POLITICS

The image of the rotund, cigar-smoking machine politician handing out buckets of coal to poor widows and cutting deals in smoke-filled rooms is part of the lore of American urban politics. Though machine-style politics exists throughout the world, the city-based party machine that appealed for votes strictly on the basis of ethnic solidarity and individual service to constituents was unique to the United States. Americans have long been ambivalent about the machines. President Theodore Roosevelt caught this mood when he observed in his autobiography, "A leader is necessary; but his opponents always call him a boss. An organization is necessary; but the men in opposition always call it a machine."[1]

Defining political machines is difficult because they differ so much in organization and style. A suburban political organization may be run by a small clique of well-dressed "suits"—a stark contrast to the usual image of machine politicians, but we can still label it a "machine" if it is a stable organization that depends primarily or entirely on material incentives to build and maintain political support. Such incentives may come in many forms: a patronage job, a government contract, a zoning variance, a fixed parking ticket, an expedited business license. A political organization that extensively and regularly uses such material incentives to maintain support engages in what we call machine-style politics.

However, something more than machine-style politics is needed if we are to apply the term "machine" to a political organization.[2] A machine is a hierarchical organization controlled by a single leader, a "boss," or by a well-organized clique. Many cities, suburbs, and rural counties are run by factional machine-style politics, with various politicians having their own bases of support. In some local governments a hierarchical structure centralizes power into one or a few hands. A full-fledged political machine is characterized by both machine-style politics and a well-defined hierarchy.

At some time in the past, most of America's big industrial cities had machine-style politics. From 1870 to 1945, seven of the nation's cities with populations of more than 500,000 had no machine politics at all, but twenty-three of them did. Seventeen of them had boss rule and a disciplined, hierarchical party organization at some point in their history.[3] In most cities that had party machines, factional machine-style politics existed for some time before machines emerged. With only two or three exceptions in the big cities, the classic machines flowered in the first few years of the twentieth century. Boss rule peaked sometime in the late 1920s and early 1930s. In 1932, the year that Democratic candidate Franklin D. Roosevelt won the presidency, ten of America's thirty biggest cities were ruled by machine bosses. Today, the urban political machine is pretty much extinct. The death of Chicago boss Richard J. Daley in 1976 marked the end of the era of big-city machines.[4]

Despite the demise of the machines, any comprehensive narrative of American urban politics must take them into account. First, machine-style politics is still common in American politics, even if the disciplined party organizations are gone. Second, the reformers who fought the machines put into place a complex set of electoral rules and institutions that still comprise the rules of the game for urban politics today. The reform legacy can only be appreciated by examining the object of the reformers' wrath. Third, it is useful to consider whether machine-style governance might help to deliver important benefits to ethnic and racial groups in today's cities.[5]

THE ORIGINS OF MACHINE POLITICS

The rise of the machines was made possible by the confluence of two factors: the emergence of a mass electorate, and industrialization.[6] When the Constitution was ratified in 1789, only about 5 percent of adult white males were eligible to vote, but by the presidential election of 1840, 80 percent of adult white males went to the polls, the highest rate in any major democracy.[7] The spread of universal male suffrage coincided with the explosive growth of cities. From the 1830s to the 1920s, more than 30 million immigrants came to the United States, most of them pouring into the cities. As soon as they were citizens, if they were male, they could vote. A new breed of enterprising politician took advantage of this circumstance.

The mass electorate could be mobilized on the basis of feelings of ethnic solidarity and the promise of material rewards. Politicians who managed to gain control of local government commanded important resources that could be distributed to loyal supporters. Between 1870 and 1900, municipal workforces grew even faster than the population of cities.[8] During this period, local governments spent more money than either state governments or the federal government.[9] The growing resources of city governments provided machine politicians with the glue they needed to piece together local party organizations.

Because they lived in the immigrant wards, machine politicians were able to forge personal relationships with voters. In most large American cities, a "friends and neighbors" or "local followings" style of politics prospered for a time. Working-class immigrants were able to enter politics by taking advantage of their extensive social networks. Pub owners, in particular, often took the opportunity to go into politics. Saloons were central to the day-to-day life in working-class wards and, more than any other institutions, they served as neighborhood centers. Especially in the Irish neighborhoods, pub owners were often considered to be reliable sources of information and advice. There was an astonishingly large number of them in the cities. In 1915, there was a saloon for every 515 residents in New York, and the number was greater in Chicago, with a saloon for every 335 persons, and in San Francisco, with a saloon for every 218 residents.[10] In working-class districts the ratio in most cities was at least one pub for every fifty males.[11] In late nineteenth-century Chicago, half the city's total population entered a saloon every day.[12] A large proportion of machine politicians got their start as pub owners. Of New York City's twenty-four aldermen in 1890, eleven were pub owners. Pub owners made up a third of Milwaukee's city councilmen in 1902 and a third of Detroit's aldermen at the turn of the century.[13]

Party machines combined two apparently contradictory qualities: the absence of formal rules, and a disciplined organization. Precinct captains, who were responsible for getting out the vote in each election district, knew each voter personally, often as a friend and neighbor. To secure a following at this level, a politician had to be known not only as a person involved in politics, but as someone who participated in local community life. At the same time, machine politicians climbed the political ladder only if they could put together coalitions with other politicians.

Most machine politicians had backgrounds and personalities that offended silk-stocking elements. Schooled in rough-and-tumble political competition, they often were men of incredible energy, hot tempers, and inflated egos. At the least, they loved what they were doing; they felt no alienation from politics. Far from being a part-time avocation, as it had been for the merchant elites of the preindustrial cities, politics was everything the machine politicians knew and did—it was their social life, their profession, their first love. They pursued political power, not social standing.[14] George Washington Plunkitt, a sachem in the Tammany Hall organization in New York, advised against what he called the "dangers of the dress suit in politics." "Live like your neighbors," Plunkitt admonished aspiring politicians, "even if you have the means to live better. Make the poorest man in your district feel that he is your equal, or even a bit superior to you."[15]

Successful political machines were able to unite the various politicians, each with their followings, into a disciplined hierarchical organization. This structure was once described by Frank Hague, the Jersey City boss, to columnist Joseph Alsop: "He [Hague] was talking in the dining room of one of the local hotels. He took the squares on the tablecloth to illustrate precincts and wards, tracing them out with his finger, and he explained the feudal system of American politics, whereby the precinct captain is governed by a ward lieutenant, the lieutenant by a ward leader, and each ward leader by the boss."[16]

As shown in Figure 3.1, precincts and precinct captains constituted the foundation of the machine organization. The precinct captain was responsible for delivering the vote for the party's slate. In the typical precinct there were 400 to 600 voters, making it possible for precinct captains to know most of their voters by name. Thirty to forty precincts were generally included within a ward. The captains of the precincts were chosen by and worked for the wards alderman. The alderman served as the chair of the ward's party committee, unless he selected a committeeman to supervise the precinct captains on his behalf. Finally, the ward leaders reported to the machine boss, who was usually but not always the mayor.

The whole structure was held together because everyone gained by cooperating in what was, in essence, a "system of organized bribery."[17] Bosses and individual aldermen had at their disposal patronage jobs in police, fire, sanitation,

FIGURE 3.1 **The Organization of Machine Politics**

Precinct Captains

►The organization of local political machines, or parties, parallels the formal structures of government but is also separate from them. Like the mayor, the party leader or boss controls the entire city, or perhaps county. The alderman represents a ward in the city council or board of aldermen. The alderman may or may not serve as ward leader of the party. Each ward consists of many precincts or election districts. Precinct captains are responsible for delivering the vote in their precinct.

In principle, power flows from the bottom up: precinct captains elect the ward leaders, and the ward leaders elect the party boss. In fact, power flows from the top.

and streets departments—and sometimes even in private industry. Construction projects, such as levee construction or road building, could give a boss control over hundreds of permanent and temporary jobs. The best jobs went to party workers who performed well. Precinct captains usually held low-level jobs arranged through the machine, perhaps serving as supervisors on street crews. Ward committeemen generally were rewarded with higher-paying administrative positions in city government. Aldermen and other elected officials typically owned lucrative insurance companies, ran their own construction firms, or owned saloons. The most menial jobs were passed along to some of the loyal voters who turned out faithfully on election day.

An understanding of the patronage ladder can be gained by examining the machine of Richard J. Daley, mayor of Chicago from the mid-1950s until his death in 1976. In the early 1970s, the Cook County Central Committee had about 30,000 positions available for distribution. Most of these jobs were unskilled; 8,000 were available through Chicago's departments and commissions, including street cleaners, park supervisors, and the like.[18] The jobs ranged from $3,600-a-year elevator operators and $6,000-a-year stenographers to $25,000-a-year department directors. Individual ward committeemen controlled as many as 2,000 jobs. (Richard Daley had begun his career as committeeman of his ward.) There were (and still are) fifty wards in the city of Chicago, with an average of 500 to 600 jobs available in each of them.[19]

The number of jobs available for distribution by individual precinct captains and ward committeemen was determined by the election-day result. A precinct captain in Chicago was expected to know all the voters in the precinct and to be known by them. "When a man is given a precinct, it is his to cover, and it is up to him to produce for the party. If he cannot produce for the party, he cannot expect to be rewarded by the party. 'Let's put it this way,' [one alderman said] 'if your boss has a salesman who can't deliver, who can't sell his product, wouldn't he put in someone else who can?'"[20]

Alderman Vito Marzullo was a successful salesman for the Chicago organization. Every week he scheduled a formal audience with his constituents. Flanked on each side by a precinct captain, he heard their complaints:

> A precinct captain ushered in a black husband and wife. "We got a letter here from the city," the man said. "They want to charge us twenty dollars for rodent control in our building." "Give me the letter, I'll look into it," Marzullo replied. The captain spoke up. "Your daughter didn't vote on November fifth. Look into it. The alderman is running again in February. Any help we can get, we can use."[21]

In the course of hearing his constituents, Marzullo exclaimed, "Some of those liberal independents in the city council, they can't get a dog out of a dog pound with a ten-dollar bill. Who's next?" Marzullo then arranged to have a traffic ticket fixed, agreed to recommend someone for a job at an electric company, refused to donate money to the Illinois Right to Life Committee ("Nothing doing. . . . I don't want to get into any of those controversies. People for it and people against it."), agreed to try to find a job for an unemployed truck driver, gave $50 to a welfare mother. Responding to several more requests, he offered to "see what I can do."[22]

During the Daley years, the Chicago machine was structured like a political pyramid. Committeemen and the aldermen directed the captains of the precincts within their wards; in turn they reported to the Cook County Central Committee. Although most of the city machines at the turn of the century were similarly organized, some were directed from the top with an iron hand, as in Daley's Chicago, while others were little more than loose confederations of politicians. However tightly run the individual machines might be, they all showed these qualities: They were rooted in neighborhoods and they were held together by a combination of material incentives and ethnic and community attachments.

JAMES PENDERGAST: A POLITICAL ENTREPRENEUR IN ACTION

The career of a machine politician, James Pendergast of Kansas City, Missouri, illustrates the process and structure of machine politics.[23] Pendergast possessed two qualities that facilitated his rise through the organization: access to material resources and an engaging personality. At a critical juncture Pendergast became a pub owner and was thus in a position to meet and help people in his ward. This was the basis of a network of "friendship," but it was a friendship built on a combination of material assistance and Pendergast's personality and place in the community. But it is doubtful that the material rewards Pendergast had at his disposal would have been sufficient, by themselves, to buy the loyalty needed for a political career.

In 1876, Pendergast, an Irishman with a short, thick neck and massive arms and shoulders, moved to Kansas City. Just 20 years old and with only a few dollars in his pocket, he rented a room in the West Bottoms ward, an industrial section on the floodplain of the Missouri River. The residents of West Bottoms worked in the meat packinghouses, machine shops, railroad yards, factories, and warehouses of the area. Blacks, Irish, Germans, and rural migrants lived in crowded four- and five-story tenements and tiny shanties. Overlooking this squalid area of dirt streets and open sewers was Quality Hill, from which the wealthy elite presided over the town. Pendergast held jobs in the packinghouses and in an iron foundry until 1881, when he used racetrack winnings to buy a hotel and a saloon. He named the saloon Climax, after his lucky horse.

Three factors contributed to Pendergast's success in First Ward (West Bottoms) politics. First, he was Irish, like the majority of his constituents. Second, most of the politicians of the First Ward made their money from gambling, prostitution, and liquor, and Pendergast's new business made him a member of this group. Third, as a successful saloonkeeper, Pendergast was in a position to meet the people of his ward. By staying out of factional fights within his ward's Democratic party and simultaneously making himself a trusted friend of politicians and ward residents, he soon found himself being promoted for an alderman's seat, which he won in 1892.

During his first term Pendergast established himself as a champion of the working class, by successfully fighting against salary reductions for firefighters, securing a city park in the West Bottoms, and opposing an attempt to move a fire station out of the ward. He won support from reform elements by favoring lower telephone rates and by proposing an improved garbage collection system. Within his ward, he served his constituency. On payday he cashed payroll checks and settled credit agreements; he posted bonds for men who had been arrested for gambling. His generosity cost money, but his business flourished: "Men learned that he had an interest in humanity outside of business and that he could be trusted, and they returned the favor by patronizing his saloon and giving him their confidence."[24] Thus, Pendergast's politics and his everyday life became one and the same. It even seemed that politics was merely an extension of his personality, rather than a calculated activity:

> He had a big heart, was charitable and liberal, . . . no deserving man, woman or child that appealed to "Jim" Pendergast went away empty handed, and this is saying a great deal, as he was continually giving aid and help to the poor and unfortunate. . . . Grocers, butchers, bakers and coal men had unlimited orders to see that there was no suffering among the poor of the West Bottoms, and to send the bills to "Jim" Pendergast.[25]

By building on his solid support in the West Bottoms, Pendergast extended his influence into other areas of the city. In 1892, he opened another saloon in the Second Ward in the North End. In that saloon he employed twenty-two men to run gambling tables, and in his West Bottoms ward he continued to employ a large gambling staff. Gambling operated on a large scale in Kansas City. Opening his own operations in the North End enabled Pendergast to form alliances with the politicians of that ward, and he soon became as influential in the Second Ward as he was in the First. He was able to secure police protection for gambling and liquor operations by paying off individual police officers and by influencing the choice of a police chief in 1895.

Pendergast's political influence began to spread, especially when he extended the legendary generosity he had long shown to his West Bottoms constituents to the politicians and citizens of the Second Ward:

> The North Siders went to Pendergast for more than jobs. They went to him when they were in trouble and needed someone to soften the stern hand of justice. Many of them got fuel and other supplies from his precinct captains when they were down and out. Others ate his turkey and trimmings at the free Christmas dinners, . . . beginning with fifty guests and growing into the hundreds as the number of drifters increased year after year.[26]

Because he could count on the voters of two wards (and thus name the alderman representing the Second Ward), Pendergast was able to forge alliances with other politicians. In 1900, he ran the city's Democratic party convention and selected a mayoral candidate whom he could control. After the election, the mayor gave Pendergast control over hundreds of patronage jobs. He appointed his brother, Tom, to the position of superintendent of streets. More than 200 men were employed by the streets department, which placed orders for gravel and cement from suppliers and contractors loyal to the machine. Positions in the fire department also became available to Pendergast. One of Pendergast's men was appointed as the city's deputy license inspector, an important job because saloons and other business establishments needed licenses to operate. Finally, and perhaps most important of all, by 1902 Pendergast had named 123 of the 173 patrolmen on the police force. Thus he leveraged his ability to control politics in two wards into alliances with men who benefited from knowing him. He soon became Kansas City's most powerful politician.

Like the party machines in other cities, the Pendergast machine operated on the basis of mutually beneficial relationships. The boss distributed material rewards and expected loyalty in return. Some machine politicians made this relationship explicit, but the most effective ones never had to. After helping their constituents with problems such as paying the rent or dealing with the police, a machine politician could advise them to "vote your conscience." A politician could get a lot of mileage out of only a modest amount of help; the word spread. Pendergast expressed this principle in this way: "I've been called a boss. All there is to it is having friends, doing things for people, and then later on they'll do things for you."[27] Pendergast's ward always elected him by at least a 3-to-1 margin, and without discernible vote fraud. It never occurred to him that he would need to steal an election.

Machine politicians like Pendergast were supreme pragmatists. Pendergast went out of his way to ascertain the needs of his constituents. This was not true of all political machines. Though all machines provided something to their supporters, a great many of them delivered less than the James Pendergast story might suggest. Several scholars have agreed that machines fulfilled several positive functions for their constituents and for cities. The Pendergast story can be used to support three claims often made on behalf of machines, namely, that they (1) centralized power and "got the job done"; (2) served as vehicles of upward mobility for immigrants; and (3) helped assimilate the immigrants into American life. In the next three sections we examine a broad array of evidence to see if these claims have merit.

DID MACHINES CENTRALIZE POWER AND "GET THE JOB DONE"?

It has often been asserted that political machines arose in the late nineteenth century to fill a void left by the absence of effective local governments. City governments were characterized by an extreme, often chaotic division of responsibilities among a multitude of separate officials, boards, and departments. The mayor generally wielded little authority. The city council or board of aldermen typically controlled the budget and made most decisions. Day-to-day administrative responsibilities were generally assumed by committees whose members were appointed by the city council, or sometimes by the mayor, state legislature, governor and other state or local officials. When committee or board members were elected by the voters, a long list of names on the ballot made it impossible to know anything about the candidates (like today, when judges are elected). Edward Sait wrote in 1933 that "when the people or particular groups among them demanded positive action, no one had adequate authority to act. The machine provided an antidote."[28] Parallel to the official governmental structure, the argument goes, machines built a centralized, extralegal structure that was able to consolidate power in order to accomplish tasks that local governments neglected.

If it were true that machines arose mainly because municipal government was so disorganized and inefficient that a party organization filled the vacuum, then we would expect to find that machines prospered best in those cities where governments were the most fragmented. This is not the case, however. In the big cities, municipal reformers achieved their aims of concentrating more power in the hands of mayors and civil service administrators in the late nineteenth century and early twentieth centuries. Centralized party machines emerged at about the same time that the institutions of local government were being reformed.[29]

It turns out that it was easier to build disciplined organizations where local government had been streamlined and reformed than where government was fragmented and chaotic. In 1913, for example, reformers in Jersey City, New Jersey persuaded the voters to fuse legislative and executive functions into one five-member commission. When the machine mayor, Frank Hague, was able to gain control of the city commission, he was able to accomplish something he had not been able to do before: consolidate his power over a faction-ridden Democratic party and become the uncontested boss of Jersey City.[30]

No doubt in some instances machines succeeded in consolidating power in circumstances where official governmental institutions could not do it, but more often machine politicians turned reforms to their own advantage. In either case, it is important to ask an essential question: What did the machines use their power for?

In the late nineteenth and early twentieth centuries, all big cities spent huge gobs of money on infrastructure—they paved streets, installed water and sewer lines, laid trolley tracks, strung electric power lines, built public harbors, and constructed parks and public buildings. A study of cities from 1890 to 1940 found that there was no difference between machine and nonmachine cities in the overall level of public expenditures.[31] Even cities with factionalized politics, such as Los Angeles, were able to make huge investments in infrastructure.[32] The centralization of the machines may not have been necessary to "get the job done." The political support for reducing disease rates through better water and sewer services, for better roads and public transit, for new public utilities and better parks was sufficiently strong that these services were bound to expand, however badly the government of a city was organized.[33] In any case, most urban infrastructure was built through specialized bureaucracies, not by party politics.

Often enough, corruption canceled out any benefits that might have accrued from the informal centralization of power. Corruption could make the price of "getting the job done" astonishingly high. Probably the most notoriously corrupt machine in American history was led by William Marcy "Boss" Tweed, who ran the infamous Tweed Ring in New York City from 1868 to 1871. In three years Tweed diverted $30 million to $100 million of public funds to himself and his cronies. Under his regime, the machine's traditional "take" of 10 percent on construction contracts ratcheted upward. A courthouse project originally estimated to cost $250,000 ended up costing taxpayers $14 million. At least 90 percent of this cost overrun went to pay payoffs, bribes, and fake contracts.[34] Tweed's rule has been called the politics of "rapacious individualism" because everyone in the machine seemed to be after personal wealth. Because Tweed was not able to count on the loyalty of his fellow politicians, he was forced to buy it directly, and therefore his authority was fragile and short-lived.[35] From 1869 to 1870, the city's debt increased from $36 to $97 million. By 1871, when Tweed was arrested, the city was bankrupt.

Machines bosses frequently resorted to corruption to build and maintain their organizations. During the machine era, the major types of graft in American cities involved the handing out of lucrative franchises, the setting of highly profitable utility rates, authority over the city's police power (involving tavern and liquor regulations, gambling, and prostitution), and the control of public works (construction and maintenance, including roads, public buildings, and parks).

Control over the police force was a central feature of Abraham Reuf's regime, which ruled San Francisco just after the turn of the century.[36] Soon after his handpicked candidate for mayor entered city hall in October 1901 (Reuf himself was an attorney who never held public office), Reuf let it be known that the city's laws against prostitution would be strictly enforced. He advised the brothel owners that it would be wise to have an attorney—himself—who could effectively represent their interests. The owners agreed to pay him a fourth of their profits, half of which Reuf shared with the mayor. This arrangement allowed the brothels to continue their operations without fear of prosecution. Reuf also "advised" saloons in the red-light district to pay premium prices for a low-quality whiskey supplied by one of Reuf's legal clients. In return the saloon owners were protected from police raids.

In 1905, for an annual retainer of $5,000, Reuf became the attorney for the French Restaurant Keeper's Association of San Francisco. The restaurant owners had decided to retain Reuf after a decision by the city's police commissioners to revoke the liquor license of one of their establishments. On behalf of his new clients, Reuf persuaded the mayor to remove one of the commissioners and replace him with someone sympathetic to the owners, thus ensuring renewal for all of the restaurants' liquor licenses.

Illicit business owners commonly forged alliances with machine politicians. This kind of relationship benefitted both parties: The businesses were free to operate without having to worry about the law, and the politicians could count on a steady flow of bribes. In the prohibition era of the 1920s, several machines flourished by selling police protection to speakeasies and bootleggers.

The urban machines made life easier for some legitimate enterprises as well. Government authorities routinely made important decisions affecting businesses. Like other growing cities of the late nineteenth century, San Francisco invested huge resources in a variety of new municipal services, and businessmen competed viciously for the contracts. The mayor, the city council, or a utilities commission could, in a single stroke of a pen, enrich one business owner and impoverish others by awarding a contract to build electric trolley lines, install streetlights, supply gas, or install telephones. The temptation to make decisions secretly in smoky rooms was overwhelming. The chairman of the public utilities committee of the San Francisco Board of Supervisors reminded a group of businessmen in January 1906:

> It must be borne in mind that without the city fathers there can be no public service corporations. The street cars cannot run, lights cannot be furnished, telephones cannot exist. And all the public service corporations want to understand that we, the city fathers, enjoy the best of health and that we are not in business for our health. The question at this banquet board is: "How much money is in it for us?"[37]

There seemed to be plenty of money for everyone. When two telephone companies submitted competing bids to supply service to the citizens of San Francisco, Reuf collected a $1,200 monthly "attorney's fee" from one company while secretly accepting a $125,000 bribe from the other. Reuf persuaded the Board of Supervisors to award the contract to the company that paid the biggest bribes. Keeping $63,000 for himself, he distributed the remainder of the $125,000 to the individual supervisors, using a loyalty test: $6,000 each to those who had received no independent bribes (showing they were not trying to compete with Reuf), $3,500 to those voting correctly despite bribes to do the opposite, and nothing to those who would not cooperate.

Reuf's position as the power behind the mayor's throne ended when he was indicted and tried for corruption. His downfall was precipitated by too much success. After seeing how lucrative politics in the city could be, other members of the city administration struck out on their own in search of bribes, and before long the feeding frenzy attracted attention.

Although most machines were less reckless than Reuf's, virtually all of them took graft. The temptation was overwhelming. The machines governed the cities during a period of explosive growth in population, services, and construction. Even if the politicians tried to be honest, business tycoons eager to expand their empires were eager to spread their money around to get what they wanted. They found it convenient to work with bosses who could make decisions expeditiously behind the scenes. Big business paid bigger bribes than anyone else. As a result, companies were able to negotiate monopoly contracts on favorable terms. The franchises typically were granted for periods of fifty to a hundred years, and some specified no terminal dates at all.[38] In the 1880s and 1890s, national financial syndicates made millions of dollars by gaining control of street railway franchises. In 1890 there were thirty-nine street railway companies in Philadelphia, nineteen in New York City, twenty-four in Pittsburgh, nineteen in St. Louis, and sixteen in San Francisco.[39] By the turn of the century, only one or two major street railway companies operated in most cities.

It needs to be said that then, as now, corruption was hardly unique to machine governments. In any case, the extent and style of corruption varied from one machine to the next, as did the apparent benefits. During the 1930s, Boss George Cox was credited with bringing "positive and moderate reform government to Cincinnati."[40] In the years when Richard J. Daley was boss, Chicago was known as "the city that works." Daley was popular with voters because they felt that he was responsible for the efficient delivery of city services, and there is no evidence he ever took money for himself.[41]

WERE MACHINES VEHICLES OF UPWARD MOBILITY?

An influential scholar has argued that the machines succeeded partly because they provided "alternative channels of social mobility for those otherwise excluded from the more conventional avenues of 'advancement.'"[42] In the nineteenth century many employers refused to hire the Irish; "Irish need not apply" was written on many an employment notice. Local politics was "like a rope dangling down the formidable slope of the socioeconomic system" which poor immigrants could use to pull themselves up.[43]

There is ample evidence to support the thesis that machines aided the upward mobility of immigrants. Though surely not a typical example, politics was pivotal to the rise of the Kennedy clan in Boston from poverty to wealth and national power. President Kennedy's grandfather on his mother's side, John "Honey Fitz" Fitzgerald, rose from ward heeler to become mayor of Boston. Kennedy's grandfather on his father's side was a respected ward politician and saloonkeeper, whose contacts helped the early career of JFK's millionaire father, Joseph P. Kennedy, who made a fortune in bootleg liquor.[44]

The thesis that the machines aided the upward mobility of immigrants is based on the notion that machines operated in a highly competitive environment and had to work tirelessly to incorporate new groups of voters into their coalitions by offering them jobs and other favors. In their early years, machine politicians typically worked hard to attract voters so that they could gain access to the patronage jobs in city government.[45] Once they had built a winning coalition, however, machine politicians often became complacent. They continued to reward their loyal supporters but stopped reaching out to new groups.

Most of the big city machines built in the nineteenth century were dominated by Irish politicians, and they stayed that way a long time. In a study of six machines, Steven Erie concluded that they were consistently biased in favor of Irish constituents. Machine leaders "turned their backs on later-arriving immigrants."[46] Between 1900 and 1930, for example, the machines in New York City, Jersey City, and Albany, New York, added nearly 100,000 municipal jobs. Close to two-thirds of the new jobs went to the Irish, even though they made up only about one-third of the population in these cities. The Irish were especially careful to maintain their control over police forces. As late as 1970, for instance, 65 percent of police officers in Albany were of Irish descent, even though no more than 25 percent of the city's population could trace their ancestry to Ireland.[47]

Later-arriving immigrants to American cities found themselves shut out of the benefits of machine rule. In New York City, Jews and Italians were excluded by the Irish-dominated machine called Tammany Hall. Though Jews and Italians represented 43 percent of New York's population in the 1920s, only 15 percent of the city's aldermen and assemblymen were Jewish and only 3 percent were Italian in 1921.[48] Fiorello LaGuardia, who was elected mayor in 1933, was able to smash the Tammany machine by assembling a coalition of disgruntled Jews, Italians, and other excluded groups. LaGuardia was a master at ethnic politics, perhaps because, "half Jewish and half Italian, married first to a Catholic and then to a Lutheran of German descent, himself a Mason and an Episcopalian, he was practically a balanced ticket all by himself."[49]

It goes without saying that blacks were also excluded by the Irish machines. In some cities "submachines" run by black bosses eventually were built, but they were subordinate in every way to the white machine bosses.[50] In Chicago, William Dawson, who was a congressman from 1942 until his death in 1970, ran a submachine in the South Side ghetto, but he was kept on a short leash by white politicians. Dawson reliably delivered huge pluralities for machine candidates from the black wards, but black voters received relatively little in return.[51] Throughout Chicago's history, weak and inexperienced black politicians who accepted a devil's bargain were recruited into the machine: in exchange for a few favors they delivered the vote, and kept a more militant black leadership from emerging.[52] The legacy of such practices was still apparent in the Daley years. Though blacks made up 40 percent of Chicago's population in 1970, they held only 20 percent of the government jobs in the city, and most of those jobs were the least desirable.[53] A study of a typical ward in Chicago in the 1970s found that the machine consistently overrewarded middle-class voters and underrewarded loyal lower-class voters.[54] As in New York City, the Chicago machine was finally challenged by disaffected groups: In 1983 a charismatic black politician, Harold Washington, assembled a coalition of poor people, blacks, Hispanics, and white liberals to defeat the machine's mayoral candidate.[55] But the victory was short-lived. After Washington suffered an unexpected heart attack in his office in 1987, Richard M. Daley, Jr., won the next mayor's race, by successfully reassembling the remnants of his father's organization and adding new pieces to it.

Considering the pressures that machine politicians faced, their tendency toward "ethnic particularism" was understandable.[56] The more ethnic groups there were in a machine's coalition, the greater the interethnic squabbles over the distribution of patronage and the thinner the distribution of rewards. As a consequence, "Once minimal winning coalitions had been constructed, the machines had little incentive to naturalize, register, and mobilize the votes of later ethnic arrivals."[57] For entrenched machines, expanding the electoral base past the coalition needed for winning just complicated things.

Even for the Irish, the machines did not generally provide many opportunities for upward mobility. Though city governments grew rapidly in the late nineteenth century, the number of public jobs was pitifully small compared to the jobs available in the private economy. In 1900 Tammany's vaunted patronage army made up 5 percent of New York City's workforce. It is true that from 1900 to 1920 local governments grew so fast that public employment accounted for 20 percent of all urban job growth.[58] But for most people, including the immigrants, private industry still provided the best opportunities for upward mobility.

Though for decades the Irish laid claim to a disproportionate share of the jobs in city government, it took a long time for them to catch up to other ethnic groups. Scandinavians, Germans, and Jews, for example, participated relatively little in machine politics; yet they assimilated into the American middle class faster than the Irish, who achieved economic parity with these groups only in the 1960s and 1970s. Ironically, the preoccupation of the Irish with public-sector employment may have slowed their entry into middle-class occupations. Most patronage jobs were blue-collar and they were distributed not to further the upward mobility of immigrants, but to maintain machine organizations. Especially at the bottom of the patronage ladder, jobs were deliberately kept low-paying in order to maximize the number that politicians could distribute.

DID THE MACHINES HELP THE IMMIGRANTS ASSIMILATE?

Though the machines did not appreciably contribute to the economic success or upward mobility of their constituents, they nevertheless were instrumental in assimilating millions of impoverished immigrants into a culture that was generally fearful of and hostile to every new immigrant group. The machines helped to create a sense of community and belonging for the immigrants. Machine organizations organized picnics, patriotic gatherings (always Fourth of July celebrations), baseball teams, choirs, and youth clubs. Machines were important community institutions, the Democratic Club being a place where men played cards and checkers or just talked.[59]

With the material resources at their disposal already devoted to their core constituency, machine politicians learned to satisfy immigrants that arrived later with largely symbolic benefits. In New York City, Tammany leader "Big Tim" Sullivan, an Irishman, ruled the Lower East Side even though as early as 1910 it was 85 percent Jewish and Italian. He retained the loyalty of his constituents by doing favors:

> He and his Irish lieutenants distributed coal, food, and rent money to needy Jews and Italians on the Lower East Side. Tammany's police department opened up station houses as temporary shelters for the homeless. Sullivan expedited business licenses for ethnic shopkeepers and pushcart peddlers. He shamelessly "recognized" the new immigrants with symbolic gestures and donned a yarmulke to solicit Jewish votes. Sullivan solicited Italian votes by sponsoring legislation to make Columbus Day a holiday.[60]

Many immigrants felt like outsiders in the dominant Protestant and middle-class culture of the United States. One of the secrets of the machines' appeal was that they tolerated the immigrants' "strange" practices and defended them from the dominant culture.[61] This was a benefit that machine politicians could deliver at little cost. Though working-class communities in American cities were not economically independent, they were, to a remarkable degree, socially independent. Immigrants built their own churches, mutual aid societies, and clubs for drinking and gambling. Machine politicians supported such activities because they could use them for campaigning and political organizing.[62]

Machine politicians appealed to and were supported by the immigrant voters because they represented the possibility of success in this strange new country. Almost all machine politicians came from lower-class, immigrant origins. One study of twenty bosses found that fifteen were first- or second-generation immigrants, thirteen had never finished grammar school, and most had gone into politics at a young age, serving as messenger or detail boys at rallies and meetings.[63] Machine leaders, therefore, become symbols of success. Immigrants may not have read the Horatio Alger stories, but in machine bosses they could see men who had risen out of poverty. Aspiring politicians often accepted this interpretation of themselves, too; they viewed themselves as examples of what could be done with hard work and a little luck along the way. These real-world symbols of upward mobility were sources of pride and hope for the masses of immigrants who were living and working under incredibly difficult conditions. However, symbol exceeded substance, especially for later-arriving southern and eastern European immigrants. Irish politicians would shrewdly pick a handful of men from other immigrant groups and place them on the ballot to demonstrate their generosity. Meanwhile, the bread-and-butter patronage stayed home.

The immigrants paid a big price for assimilation on these terms. Machines never attempted to address the collective aspirations of ethnic groups. The immigrants were encouraged to "cast their ballots on the basis of ethnicity rather than policy considerations."[64] Immigrants gave their votes to party politicians not as an act of consciousness about group goals but because it was easy to do and there were rarely plausible alternatives. The vote was a minimal commitment by the immigrant but a sufficient one for the machine. Commensurate with the level of commitment, constituents could hardly expect miracles in return.

The operating principles and structures of the urban machines ensured that the politicians who ran them would steer clear of ideological battles. To deal with constituents' requests effectively, machine politicians had to learn the art of manipulating power within the framework of the existing political system. A special premium was placed on effective pragmatism, the ability to pull strings to get things done. Idealism was scorned. If a constituent came to complain about a building inspector, the politician's job was to make things nice with the inspector. Changing the building code was irrelevant and even counter-productive, because it might reduce the need for the politician's services.

Machines were hostile to political movements that tried to reform the system because such movements threatened their control of the immigrant vote. Until the 1930s, most machines vigorously opposed labor unions. In the first years of the twentieth century, Irish machine politicians ordered the police to attack labor organizers in Lawrence, Massachusetts, and in New York City.[65] In Pittsburgh's 1919 steel strike, the machine likewise ordered police to harass strikers.[66] After Franklin D. Roosevelt's landslide victory in the presidential election of 1932 some of the big city machines formed alliances with the moderate trade unions, but the relationship was never easy to maintain. The machines expected the unions to respect their turf by focusing mainly on state and national politics and on labor-business relations.

On balance, the immigrants' potential as a political force was stunted by the machines. Working-class immigrants desperately needed reforms such as widows' pensions, better working conditions, laws regulating hours and wages (especially for women and children), and workers' compensation. On occasion machine politicians supported these reforms, as well as the regulation of utilities, the legal recognition of labor unions, and the regulation of insurance companies.[67] This kind of selective and often half-hearted support for some reform measures did not exactly transform machine politicians into crusading reformers. Machine politicians were willing to offer support for selected pieces of reform legislation at the state level if it made them look good, but they never became active advocates of reform. Machine politicians could be quite capricious, for immediate political circumstances always took precedence over principle.

Machine politicians rarely considered how things could be changed. They often referred to reformers as "goody-goodies" or "goo-goos," who presumably were in politics for a few thrills. ("Goo-goo" was derived from "good government," often the reformers' rallying cry.) Much of this disdain was rooted in the social differences between upper-class reformers and the lower-class, less educated immigrant politicians. The result was an excessive respect for the pragmatic fix.

THE SOCIAL REFORM ALTERNATIVE

Defenders of political machines have argued that there were few alternatives to the machines' style of politics, that in the face of the vast economic and political resources held by corporations and wealthy elites, machine politicians milked the system on behalf of their constituents as effectively as they could, and that to criticize them is to engage in utopian fantasizing.

But practical alternatives were available. In the first two decades of the twentieth century, social reformers won elections in cities all across the country. The social reformers were intent on improving the quality of life for immigrants and workers, and they campaigned for support from both working-class immigrant and middle-class voters.[68] Mayors Tom L. Johnson of Cleveland, Ohio (1901–1909), Samuel "Golden Rule" Jones of Toledo, Ohio (1897–1903), and Brand Whitlock of Toledo (1906–1913) all won election by fighting against high streetcar and utility rates and for fair taxation and better social services. Their campaigns became models for like-minded reformers elsewhere. Reform-oriented mayors in Jersey City, Philadelphia, and Cincinnati, for example, attempted to raise more municipal revenue by raising taxes for businesses and wealthy property owners and by renegotiating streetcar and utility franchises. Machine politicians and the business community bitterly fought reform in these cities, just as they had a few years earlier in Cleveland and Toledo.[69]

Hazen S. Pingree, who served as Detroit's mayor from 1890 to 1898, showed the enormous possibilities of reform. Born in Maine to a poor farmer and itinerant cobbler, Pingree did not seem destined to become a political reformer. After fighting in the Civil War, Pingree moved to Detroit where he worked as a leather cutter in a shoe factory. By saving his meager earnings he was able, with the help of a partner, to purchase the outdated factory. Modernizing the machinery and shrewdly adjusting production to meet changing styles in footwear, in a short time Pingree became independently wealthy. He was picked as the Republican candidate for mayor in 1889, largely because he was the only member of the exclusive Michigan Club who could be persuaded by its members to run. The conservative businessmen who controlled Republican politics trusted him, as a member of the club, to advocate a program of low taxes and a minimal number of municipal services. In any case, few of them imagined he would win, and they had grown used to working with the Irish-dominated Democratic machine.

But unlike the typical business candidate, Pingree campaigned in the ethnic wards, and in fact kicked off his campaign by drinking red-eye whiskey in an Irish saloon. Pingree was a big hit with German and Polish voters, who had long been ignored by the Irish politicians. He called attention to the corruption of the machine and advocated an eight-hour workday for city employees. His willingness to seek the ethnic vote was the foundation on which he built his subsequent political success.

Pingree's programs, and the strategies he used to implement them, reveal how much could have been accomplished in other cities. When Pingree took over city hall, Detroit had one of the worst street systems in the nation. Many of the streets were made of wooden blocks, which would catch fire in the summer and sink into the mire in the winter. The paved streets were pocked with ruts and potholes. Pingree quickly realized that collusion between paving contractors and machine politicians was at the heart of the street problem. He launched an aggressive campaign against this arrangement, appealing to his business supporters by pointing out that the prosperity of the city depended on good streets. His insistent efforts led the city council to adopt strict paving specifications for the city, and as a result, by 1895 Detroit had one of the best street systems in the country.

It was not long before Pingree came to recognize that the local business establishment was as much a problem as was the machine. He challenged the high fare charged for a ferry ride across the Detroit River to Belle Isle Park. The company dropped its rate from 10 cents to 5 cents after the mayor threatened to revoke its franchise or put into operation a municipal ferry service. In a related action, Pingree found that private companies had located along the Detroit River waterfront, often on municipal property, which choked off public access to water and recreation. He soon opened up waterfront areas for public use.

Above all, it was Pingree's fight with the Detroit City Railway Company that turned him into a true social reformer willing to use public authority to limit private power when it benefited the city as a whole. At a time when streetcar companies in other cities were converting from horses to electric power, Detroit's company refused to make the change. In April 1891, the company's employees went on strike, presenting a perfect opportunity for Pingree to begin a battle for modernization and lower fares.

The three-day strike culminated in a riot in which workers and citizens tore up the tracks, stoned the streetcars, and drove off the horses. Pingree ignored the company's request to call in the state militia and instead took the position that privately owned public services were "the chief source of corruption in city governments."[70] Pingree's stance initiated a protracted, bitter fight to regulate the streetcars. This conflict vaulted him to national prominence.

Many business leaders had supported the strike, feeling that the street railway was so badly run that it was hurting local business. The business community was mainly interested in more reliable service, but Pingree pressed further, pressing for lower fares and municipal ownership. Such a position ran afoul of business leaders when the company passed into the hands of a wealthy eastern entrepreneur. The new owner's first action was to pack the company's board of directors with prominent business leaders from Detroit. The company then demanded that the city negotiate a more favorable franchise. Pingree countered with a lawsuit meant to terminate the existing company in favor of municipal ownership. At that point, his former colleagues lost their patience with Pingree. The company bought Pingree's own attorney away from him and proceeded to offer bribes to city council members, including a $75,000 bribe to Pingree himself. The Preston National Bank dropped Pingree from its board of directors; he lost his family pew in the Baptist church; he and his friends were shunned in public. For Pingree, the lesson he learned in all this was that business supported reform only on its own terms. He also began to form an analysis about what was wrong with America's cities.

In 1891 Pingree began attacking the tax privileges of the city's corporations. The railroad, he observed, owned more than one-fifth of the property value in the city but paid no taxes at all because of the tax-free status granted to it by the state legislature. Shipping companies, docks and warehouses, and other businesses escaped local taxation by claiming that their principal places of business existed outside the city. The city's biggest employer, the Michigan-Peninsula Car Company, paid only nominal taxes. In questioning these privileges, Pingree was confronting the combined wealth and power of the city's business elite. Although he was unsuccessful in equalizing the tax burden, Pingree was able to modify some of its worst features, especially the practice of assessing, for tax purposes, real estate owned by wealthy people at rates far below value. Pingree earned the special enmity of the city's elite by successfully campaigning for a personal property tax on home furnishings, art objects, and other luxury items.

On April 1, 1895, Detroit began operating a municipal electric plant to supply power for its streetlights. This ended a five-year running battle between Pingree and the private lighting company. Pingree had used two issues to win his battle. His main argument against the private control of electricity was that it cost too much. Pingree gathered voluminous information to show that Detroit's service was more expensive and less reliable than in other cities. Despite the merits of his case he would have lost, but a scandal tipped the scales in his favor. In April 1892, Pingree walked into a city council meeting waving a roll of bills and dramatically accused the Detroit Electric Light and Power Company of bribing council members. The mayor had been sure to pack the room with his working-class supporters. With Pingree's followers whipped into a dangerous mood, the council members hastily capitulated.

Pingree used similar tactics in his fights with the gas and telephone interests. To force the Detroit Gas Company to lower its rates for natural gas, he initiated a campaign to inform the public about the high price of Detroit's gas. When his attempt to force lower prices stalled in the courts, he got the public works board to deny permits to excavate streets for the purpose of laying gas lines. When the gas company attempted to excavate anyway, Pingree saw to it that the owners were arrested. "Possession is a great point," argued Pingree. "Let them get their gas systems connected and then they could float their $8,000,000 of stock in New York City and become too powerful for the city to control. Detroit would be helpless in the hands of corporations as never before in her history."[71]

Pingree continued his battle, encouraging users not to pay their gas bills. As public resistance against the Detroit Gas Company mounted, investors' confidence in the company plummeted, initiating a plunge in the company's stock values. Even after Southern Pacific Railroad magnate Samuel Huntington became the company's principal investor, stock prices continued to fall, and Huntington negotiated an agreement to lower the price of gas from $1.50 a cubic foot to $0.80.

In his fourth term, Pingree took on the Bell Telephone Company. Again, the issue was high prices and inadequate service. This time he helped organize a competing phone company that charged less than half Bell's rate. The new Detroit Telephone Company soon attracted twice as many customers as Bell. In response, Bell initiated a rate war and began to improve its equipment and service. By 1900, when Michigan Bell bought out Detroit Telephone, Detroit had the lowest telephone rates and the most extensive residential use of any large city in America.

No other mayor accomplished such a broad program of social reform. During his last two terms, Pingree traveled around the country making speeches and gathering information. He wrote prolifically. He inspired reformers elsewhere, and his national prominence helped him bring reform to his own city. After winning four terms as the mayor of Detroit, Pingree went on to serve two terms as the governor of Michigan, where he continued to fight for reform.

Pingree recognized the necessity of building a broad-based political coalition. He so assiduously courted ethnic voters that by his fourth term he had even won the dependable Irish away from the Democratic machine. In effect, Pingree pieced together his own machine, filling patronage jobs with his own supporters and firing his opponents. However, "he absolutely refused to tolerate dishonesty or theft."[72] Unlike Detroit's machine politicians, who regularly exploited ethnic hostilities to win votes in their wards, Pingree tried to unify working-class Poles, Germans, Irish, and the middle class. In short, he was aware that to accomplish reform it was necessary to "recruit a coalition of power sufficient for his purpose."[73] A great many political machines had likewise constructed powerful electoral coalitions but these usually favored one group, and the politicians who built them were more interested in furthering their own careers than in helping their constituents by fighting for reform.

MACHINE POLITICS IN TODAY'S CITIES

Cities are once again magnets for millions of immigrants and minorities. In this context an intriguing question arises: Would recent immigrants and ethnic and racial minorities benefit if they were able to build political machines much like those that ruled one hundred years ago?

The urban machines brokered a deal in which poor immigrants and economic elites each gave up something and got something in return. Business elites ceded control over local governments to working-class ethnic politicians who controlled armies of patronage workers, supported in part by income from bribes and contributions paid by the wealthy. In return, machine politicians essentially promised to leave business alone. The compromise involved a recognition of distinct spheres of influence—a sharp separation between the market and the public sphere. This compromise was important in managing the tension between capitalism, with its attendant inequalities, and popular democracy.[74]

In the end, political machines and their ethnic supporters gave up a great deal and got little in return. Rather than passing out favors and low-paying jobs, machine politicians could have emulated Pingree by attacking the practices that inflated the cost of urban services and infrastructure. They could have forged alliances with labor unions to pursue programs designed to modify dangerous working conditions, long hours, child labor, and low pay. Instead, the machines discouraged the immigrants from organizing around their common interests.

There is reason to believe that today's city residents can expect even less from machines. The machines prospered in rapidly growing industrial cities that required massive expenditures on roads, bridges, sewers, streetcar systems, schools, and parks.[75] The resulting government jobs, contracts, and franchises were traded for the political support necessary to maintain the party organizations. Like the industrial city a century ago, contemporary cities still hold large numbers of needy people. A potential electoral base exists to support machine organizations.

But it would be extremely difficult for today's politicians to assemble the patronage and other material rewards necessary to build and maintain machine organizations. City services have been bureaucratized and merit employment systems have been put in place so that patronage can no longer be regularly delivered on the basis of personal or political relationships. Even in the city of Chicago when it was ruled by the Daley machine, decisions on the distribution of city services relied heavily on "technical-rational criteria" that were "largely devoid of explicit political content."[76]

The urban machines that lasted beyond the 1920s relied heavily on intergovernmental political relationships and federal aid for their survival.[77] After the New Deal, many machines skillfully used federal programs to expand their resource base.[78] Those days are past. After the late 1970s the federal government sharply cut grants to cities. Adding to their fiscal problems, central cities have generally been in a period of population and fiscal contraction. The exodus of industry and the middle class to the suburbs has deprived the cities of critical tax sources and borrowing power.[79]

All this does not necessarily mean that the political control of cities is "a hollow prize."[80] For example, there are important policies that minority mayors can implement to advance the interests of their constituents. For example, affirmative action hiring and city residency requirements for city jobs favor city minority residents over nonminority workers who live in the suburbs—and who often take the lion's share of central city jobs. Minority contractor set-asides help to ensure that a percentage of jobs on public projects go to minorities.[81] City agencies can be made to be more sensitive to poor and minority constituents. When Harold Washington served as Chicago's mayor from 1983 to 1987, capital improvement programs were put in place in neighborhoods; special loan programs provided capital for businesses owned by minorities and women; the city made a commitment to purchase 25 percent of its services from minority-owned and women-owned businesses; and job training programs were funded for unemployed people.[82]

City governments make decisions and command resources critical to the well-being of city residents. City politics, however, will not likely proceed again on the basis of simple tradeoffs and favors exchanged for the vote. The Chicago machine, led by Richard M. Daley—the son of a legendary machine boss, Richard J. Daley—may be the only party machine left operating today in a big city. The way that it operates illustrates how much politics has changed over the course of a century. The younger Daley has been able to revive the machine by adapting to the new realities. Although the Daley organization still calls upon precinct captains to manage their precincts and to deliver the vote, and although the aldermen routinely rubberstamp the mayor's decisions, patronage is no longer what it used to be. Court decrees from the 1980s ended most blue-collar patronage jobs. A new kind of "white-collar" patronage is now distributed, to lawyers, brokers, financial consultants, advertising and public relations firms, and lobbyists. Reflecting the shape of a new globalized economy, the most important source of campaign contributions come from the financial services sector, the construction industry (including its unions), law firms, the tourism and hospitality sector, and downtown corporations.[83] Campaign contributions from aldermen and other politicians and governmental employees loyal to the mayor amount to less than 2 percent of Daley's financial support. The big volumes of money required for Daley's campaigns go mainly to media advertising aimed more toward higher-income voters who have moved into gentrified neighborhoods than for grass-roots activities. The lesson from all this is that modern machines, even where they exist, are not likely to be oriented to ethnic voters, or to a politics of immediate material rewards.

NOTES

1. As quoted in Edward McChesney Sait, "Political Machines," in *Encyclopedia of the Social Sciences*, ed. Edwin R. A. Seligman (New York: Macmillan, 1933), p. 657. We will use the terms "machine" and "boss," but in doing so we are not implying any moral judgment.
2. Raymond Wolfinger, "Why Political Machines Have Not Withered Away and Other Revisionist Thoughts," in *Readings in Urban Politics: Past, Present, and Future*, ed. Harlan Hahn and Charles H. Levine (New York: Longman, 1984), p. 79. Wolfinger makes the distinction that we draw here between machine politics and a centralized machine. See also Roger W. Lotchin, "Power and Policy: American City Politics Between the Two World Wars," in *Ethnics, Machines and the American Urban Future*, ed. Scott Greer (Cambridge, Mass.: Schenkman, 1981), p. 9.
3. M. Craig Brown and Charles N. Halaby, "Machine Politics in America, 1870–1945," *Journal of Interdisciplinary History* 17, no. 3 (Winter 1987): 598. In order to qualify as a dominant political machine, a machine-style party had to control both the executive and the legislative branches of the city for an uninterrupted series of three elections.
4. One of the last classic machines, the O'Connell machine in Albany, New York, has finally lost its grip. See Todd Swanstrom and Sharon Ward, "Albany's O'Connell Organization: The Survival of an Entrenched Machine" (paper delivered at the American Political Science Association Convention, Chicago, September 1987).
5. For the definitive treatment of this question, see Steven P. Erie, *Rainbow's End: Irish-Americans and the Dilemmas of Urban Machine Politics, 1840–1985* (Berkeley: University of California Press, 1988). President Lyndon Johnson's National Advisory Commission on Civil Disorders linked the 1960s urban riots to the "demise of the historic urban political machines." *Report of the National Advisory Commission on Civil Disorders* (New York: Bantam Books, 1968), p. 287.
6. Amy Bridges, *A City in the Republic* (Cambridge, England: Cambridge University Press, 1984), p. 8.
7. William N. Chambers, "Party Development and the American Mainstream," in *The American Party System: Stages of Political Development*, 2d ed., ed. William Nisbet Chambers and Walter Dean Burnham (New York: Oxford University Press, 1975), p. 12.
8. Alan DiGaetano, "The Rise and Development of Urban Political Machines," *Urban Affairs Quarterly* 24, no. 2 (December 1988): 247, table 3. For more information on the expansion of city governments in the late nineteenth century, see Jon C. Teaford, *The Unheralded Triumph: City Government in America, 1870–1900* (Baltimore: Johns Hopkins University Press, 1984); Eric H. Monkkonen, *America Becomes Urban: The Development of U.S. Cities and Towns, 1780–1980* (Berkeley: University of California Press, 1988).
9. Terrence J. McDonald and Sally K. Ward, "Introduction," in *The Politics of Urban Fiscal Policy*, ed. Terrence J. McDonald and Sally K. Ward (Beverly Hills, Calif.: Sage, 1984), p. 14.
10. Jon M. Kingsdale, "The 'Poor Man's Club': Social Functions of the Urban Working-Class Saloon," in *The Making of Urban America*, ed. Raymond A. Mohl (Wilmington, Del.: Scholarly Resources, 1988), p. 123.
11. Ibid.
12. Ibid.

13. Ibid., p. 130.
14. "He [the boss] does not seek social honor; the 'professional' is despised in 'respectable society.' He seeks power alone, power as a source of money, but also power for power's sake." Max Weber, "Politics as a Vocation," in *From Max Weber: Essays in Sociology*, ed. H. H. Gerth and C. Wright Mills (New York: Oxford University Press, 1946), p. 109.
15. William L. Riordan, *Plunkitt of Tammany Hall* (New York: Dutton, 1963), p. 50.
16. Dayton McKean, *The Boss* (Boston: Houghton Mifflin, 1940), p. 132.
17. Edward C. Banfield and James Q. Wilson, *City Politics* (New York: Vintage Books, 1963), p. 125.
18. Milton Rakove, *Don't Make No Waves . . . Don't Back No Losers: An Insider's Analysis of the Daley Machine* (Bloomington: Indiana University Press, 1975). The following material on Daley's machine is drawn from Rakove.
19. Ibid., pp. 114–115.
20. Ibid., p. 115.
21. Ibid., p. 120.
22. Ibid., p. 122.
23. The information presented here on the Pendergast machine comes from Lyle W. Dorsett, *The Pendergast Machine* (New York: Oxford University Press, 1968). Only direct quotations from Dorsett are cited by page in subsequent notes.
24. Ibid., p. 14.
25. Ibid., p. 21.
26. Ibid., p. 41.
27. Ibid., p. 26.
28. Sait, "Political Machines," p. 658. See also Robert M. Merton, *Social Theory and Social Structure* (New York: Free Press, 1949), pp. 126–127. For decades Merton's functional analysis of political machines was widely accepted, but it has been seriously challenged in recent years. See Erie, *Rainbow's End*; DiGaetano, "The Rise and Development of Urban Political Machines"; M. Craig Brown and Charles N. Halaby, "Functional Sociology, Urban History, and the Urban Political Machine: The Outlines and Foundations of Machine Politics, 1870–1945" (Albany: Department of Sociology, State University of New York at Albany, n.d.).
29. DiGaetano, "The Rise and Development of Urban Political Machines," pp. 257–262. See also M. Craig Brown and Charles N. Halaby, "Bosses, Reform, and the Socioeconomic Bases of Urban Expenditure, 1890–1940," in *The Politics of Urban Fiscal Policy*, ed. Terrence S. McDonald and Sally K. Ward (Beverley Hills, Calif.: Sage), p. 90.
30. DiGaetano, "The Rise and Development of Urban Political Machines," p. 261. Urban politics is often portrayed as a "morality play" in which reformers are pitted against machine politicians. In fact, machines often used reforms to consolidate their power and put reformers on the ballot in order to legitimate their rule. On the other side, reformers often created their own type of political machines. For a critique of the dichotomy between bosses and reformers, see David P. Thelen, "Urban Politics: Beyond Bosses and Reformers," *Reviews in American History* 7 (September 1979): 406–412. For an example of a reformer who created a new type of political machine, see Robert Caro's masterful biography of Robert Moses, *The Power Broker: Robert Moses and the Fall of New York* (New York: Vintage Books, 1974).
31. M. Craig Brown and Charles N. Halaby, "Bosses, Reform and the Socioeconomic Bases of Urban Expenditure, 1890–1940," p. 87. Interestingly, the authors found that machine cities, after reform—such as the establishment of a city manager form of government—spent more than other cities, p. 89.
32. Lotchin, "Power and Policy," p. 11.
33. Stanley K. Schultz, *Constructing Urban Culture: American Cities and City Planning, 1800–1920* (Philadelphia: Temple University Press, 1989).

34. There are many sources of information on the Tweed Ring. The two books used here are Alexander Callow, Jr., *The Tweed Ring* (New York: Oxford University Press, 1966), and Seymour J. Mandelbaum, *Boss Tweed's New York* (New York: Wiley, 1965). For a provocative, yet ultimately unpersuasive, defense of Tweed, see Leo Hershkowitz, *Tweed's New York: Another Look* (Garden City, N.Y.: Anchor Books, 1977).

35. Martin Shefter, "The Emergence of the Political Machine: An Alternative View," in *Theoretical Perspectives on Urban Politics*, ed. Willis D. Hawley et al. (Englewood Cliffs, N.J.: Prentice-Hall, 1976), p. 21.

36. The information presented here on Abraham Reuf's machine is taken from Walter Bean, *Boss Reuf's San Francisco* (Berkeley: University of California Press, 1952; reprinted 1972). Only direct quotations from Bean are cited by page in subsequent notes.

37. Ibid., pp. 93–94.

38. Paul Kantor, with Stephen David, *The Dependent City: The Changing Political Economy of Urban America* (Glenview, Ill.: Scott Foresman, 1988), p. 104.

39. Ernest S. Griffith, *A History of American City Government: The Conspicuous Failure, 1870–1900* (New York: Praeger, 1974), p. 183.

40. Zane Miller, *The Urbanization of Modern America: A Brief History* (New York: Harcourt Brace Jovanovich, 1973), p. 121.

41. Ester R. Fuchs and Robert Y. Shapiro, "Government Performance as a Basis for Machine Support," *Urban Affairs Quarterly* 18, no. 4 (June 1983): 537–550.

42. Merton, *Social Theory and Social Structure*, p. 130.

43. Robert A. Dahl, *Who Governs? Democracy and Power in an American City* (New Haven, Conn.: Yale University Press, 1961), p. 34.

44. See Doris Kearns Goodwin, *The Fitzgeralds and the Kennedys: An American Saga* (New York: Simon and Schuster, 1987).

45. The discussion of mobilizing versus entrenched machines relies heavily on Erie's "life cycle" theory of political machines in *Rainbow's End.*

46. Erie, *Rainbow's End*, p. 69.

47. Terry Nichols Clark, "The Irish Ethic and the Spirit of Patronage," *Ethnicity* 2 (1975): 341–342.

48. Martin Shefter, "Political Incorporation and the Extrusion of the Left: Party Politics and Social Forces in New York City," in *Studies in American Political Development*, vol. 1, ed. Karen Orren and Stephen Skowronek (New Haven, Conn.: Yale University Press, 1986), p. 55.

49. Caro, *The Power Broker*, p. 354.

50. For a useful review of the relationships between African Americans and political machines, see Hanes Walton, Jr., *Black Politics: A Theoretical and Structural Analysis* (Philadelphia: Lippincott, 1972), chap. 4.

51. William J. Grimshaw, *Bitter Fruit: Black Politics and the Chicago Machine, 1931–1991* (Chicago: University of Chicago Press, 1992).

52. Ibid.

53. Erie, *Rainbow's End*, p. 165.

54. Thomas M. Guterbock, *Machine Politics in Transition: Party and Community in Chicago* (Chicago: University of Chicago Press, 1980).

55. See Paul Kleppner, *Chicago Divided: The Making of a Black Mayor* (DeKalb: Northern Illinois University Press, 1985).

56. Michael Johnston, "Patrons and Clients, Jobs and Machines: A Case Study of the Uses of Patronage," *American Political Science Review* 73, no. 2 (June 1979): 385–398.

57. Erie, *Rainbow's End*, p. 218.

58. Ibid., pp. 48, 242.

59. For a discussion of the role of political clubs in the evolution of Tammany Hall, see Shefter, "The Emergence of the Political Machine," p. 35.

60. Erie, *Rainbow's End*, pp. 102–103.

61. Kenneth D. Wald argues that ethnics supported machines not so much in response to socioeconomic disadvantage but out of an awareness of their social marginality and in the belief that machines would defend them from external pressures; see his "The Electoral Base of Political Machines: A Deviant Case Analysis," *Urban Affairs Quarterly* 16, no. 1 (September 1980), pp. 3–29.

62. It would be misleading to say that such practices simply reflected the desires of poor immigrants. Irish family life was disrupted by the easy availability of illicit entertainment. Catholic priests and a significant proportion of the immigrant population opposed vice activities.

63. Harold Zink, *City Bosses in the United States* (Durham, N.C.: Duke University Press, 1930).

64. Wolfinger, "Why Political Machines Have Not Withered Away," p. 70.

65. Allan Rosenbaum, "Machine Politics: Class Interest and the Urban Poor," paper delivered at the annual meeting of the American Political Science Association (September 4–8, 1973), pp. 25–26.

66. Ibid., p. 26.

67. John D. Buenker, *Urban Liberalism and Progressive Reform* (New York: Scribner, 1973). Joseph J. Huthmacher also provides evidence of machine legislators' support for reform; see his "Urban Liberalism and the Age of Reform," *Mississippi Valley Historical Review* 44 (September 1962): 231–241.

68. For the distinction between social and structural reformers, see Melvin G. Holli, *Reform in Detroit: Hazen S. Pingree and Urban Politics* (New York: Oxford University Press, 1969), chap. 8. We discuss the social reformers in this chapter; in the next chapter we discuss the structural reformers.

69. Martin J. Schiesl, *The Politics of Efficiency: Municipal Administration and Reform in America, 1880–1920* (Berkeley: University of California Press, 1977), pp. 80 ff.

70. Quoted in Holli, *Reform in Detroit*, p. 42.

71. Quoted in ibid., p. 92.

72. Ibid., p. 195.

73. Peter Marris and Martin Rein, *Dilemmas of Social Reform* (New York: Atherton Press, 1967), p. 7.

74. Kantor, *The Dependent City*, pp. 117–118. Machine politicians appealed to voters on the basis of where they lived (their ethnic identification), not on the basis of where they worked (their class identification). Thus machine politics confirmed the "city trenches" that have divided the American political landscape into community politics and workplace politics and blunted political action by the working class. See Ira Katznelson, *City Trenches: Urban Politics and the Patterning of Class in the United States* (New York: Pantheon, 1981).

75. See James C. Scott, "Corruption, Machine Politics, and Political Change," *American Political Science Review* 63 (December 1969): 1142–1158; Clarence N. Stone, Robert K. Whelan, and William J. Murin, *Urban Policy and Politics in a Bureaucratic Age*, 2nd ed. (Englewood Cliffs, N.J.: Prentice-Hall, 1986), chap. 7.

76. Kenneth R. Mladenka, "The Urban Bureaucracy and the Chicago Political Machine: Who Gets What and the Limits to Political Control," in *Readings in Urban Politics: Past, Present, and Future*, ed. Harlan Hahn and Charles H. Levine (New York: Longman, 1984), p. 114. A later study of Chicago found that the local party structure did influence the provision of one service: building code enforcement. See Bryan D. Jones, "Party and Bureaucracy: The Influence of Intermediary Groups on Urban Public Service Delivery," *American Political Science Review* 75, no. 3 (September 1981), pp. 688–700.

77. Erie, *Rainbow's End.*

78. By ending the dependence of the urban poor on political machines for favors, many argued that the rise of the New Deal welfare state undermined political machines. See Rexford Tugwell, *The Brain Trust* (New York: Viking, 1968), pp. 366–371. Historical research has shown, however, that many machines were able to use the welfare state to strengthen their organizations. See Bruce M. Stave, *The New Deal and the Last Hurrah: Pittsburgh Ma-*

chine Politics (Pittsburgh: University of Pittsburgh Press, 1970); Lyle W. Dorsett, *Franklin D. Roosevelt and the City Bosses* (Port Washington, N.Y.: Kennikat Press, 1977); Wolfinger, "Why Political Machines Have Not Withered Away" pp. 85–88; Erie, *Rainbow's End.*

79. Lotchin, "Power and Policy," p. 17.

80. H. Paul Friesema, "Black Control of Central Cities: The Hollow Prize," *Journal of the American Institute of Planners* 35 (March 1969), p. 75.

81. Melvin G. Holli and Paul M. Green, *Bashing Chicago Traditions: Harold Washington's Last Campaign* (Grand Rapids, Mich.: Eerdmans, 1989), p. 120.

82. Dennis R. Judd and Randy L. Ready, "Entrepreneurial Cities and the New Policies of Economic Development," in *Reagan and the Cities,* ed. George E. Peterson and Carol W. Lewis (Washington, D.C.: Urban Institute Press, 1986), pp. 232–233.

83. Dick Simpson, *Rogues, Rebels, and Rubber Stamps: The Politics of the Chicago City Council, 1863 to the Present* (Boulder, CO: Westview Press, 2001).

4

THE STRUGGLE FOR POLITICAL CONTROL: THE REFORM LEGACY

THE MOTIVE FOR REFORM

In 1902 George Washington Plunkitt of Tammany Hall pontificated that reformers "were mornin' glories—looked lovely in the mornin' and withered up in a short time, while the regular machines went on flourishin' forever, like fine old oaks."[1] At the time Plunkitt delivered himself of that poetic homily, he was essentially correct. Through the last quarter of the nineteenth century, reform movements sprang up in cities all across the country. The reformers aimed to dismantle the party organizations that thrived on immigrant votes, but these movements tended to be short-lived, exactly as Plunkitt observed. Reformers were often successful in persuading state legislatures to take budgeting and the administration of some services out of the hands of aldermen and city councils and put them under the control of boards dominated by a "better class" of people. They were not able, however, to undercut the electoral influence of the immigrants. Aldermen elected from individual wards still decided such matters as streetcar and utility franchises, construction contracts, and overall tax policy. Plenty of patronage jobs and money, the stuff of machine politics, were bound up in these decisions.

To many middle- and upper-class Americans, cities seemed to be in the hands of criminals who plundered the public for their own personal gain. Although reformers in Cleveland, New York, Chicago, and other cities sometimes did throw machine politicians out of office and succeeded in getting some of them prosecuted in the courts for corruption, the offending politicians were easily replaced by men just like themselves. Commenting on this fact of life, Englishman James Bryce expressed the view that "the government of cities is the one conspicuous failure of the United States."[2] Many middle- and upper-class voters shared his opinion. As stated at the time in a pro-reform textbook on municipal government:

The privilege seeker has pervaded our political life. For his own profit he has willfully befouled the sources of political power. Politics, which should offer a career inspiring to the noblest thoughts and calling for the most patriotic efforts of which man is capable, he has . . . transformed into a series of sordid transactions between those who buy and those who sell governmental action.[3]

The widespread concern about political corruption in the cities was closely connected to a growing fear of foreign immigrants—the so-called Great Unwashed. The reaction against immigrants had been building for a long time. As early as 1851, for example, an issue of the *Massachusetts Teacher* asked:

The constantly increasing influx of foreigners . . . continues to be a cause of serious alarm to the most intelligent of our people. What will be the ultimate effect of this vast and unexampled immigration . . . ? Will it, like the muddy Missouri, as it pours its waters into the clear Mississippi and contaminates the whole united mass, spread ignorance and vice, crime and disease, through our native population?[4]

Protestants descended from the older immigrant groups were scandalized when they observed the Irish and German immigrants drinking beer on Sundays and by lurid newspaper accounts of prostitution, gambling, and public drunkenness in the immigrant wards. Protestant moralists secured city and state statutes abolishing prostitution, gambling, and Sunday liquor sales. To teach immigrant children middle-class versions of dress, speech, manners, and discipline, reformers passed laws requiring school attendance and raised the upper age limit for mandatory schooling. Truant officers were hired to search for wayward youth.

The vicious reaction against immigrants further aggravated class, racial, and religious tensions. Immigrants were compared to the Goths and Vandals who invaded Europe in the second century A.D. In his book, *Our Country*, the Reverend Josiah Strong accused the immigrants of defiling the Sabbath, spreading illiteracy and crime, and corrupting American culture and morals. Gathered into the cities, he said the immigrants provided "a very paradise for demagogues" who ruled by manipulating the "appetites and prejudices" of the rabble.[5]

The spatial segregation of social classes within the cities exacerbated middle- and upper-class fears about the immigrants. By the turn of the century, all large cities contained overcrowded immigrant ghettos near the waterfronts and factories, with middle- and upper-class neighborhoods located further out from the urban center. Jobs were still concentrated in downtown districts, so the more affluent city residents could hardly escape seeing, on their way to work and to shop, the drab tenements, dirty streets, and littered alleys where the immigrants lived.

Most reformers were members of the upper class or exceptionally well-educated members of the middle class. The reforms they advocated were designed to enhance the influence of the "better classes" and to undercut the immigrants' electoral influence in city politics. Where they were successful, they fundamentally changed the way local political systems operated. As we show in this chapter, we still live with many of the effects of their reforms.

THE REFORM ENVIRONMENT

The municipal reform movement was energized by the social reform impulse that swept the country in the first decades of the twentieth century. Several developments ushered in the so-called Progressive Era. Excesses of wealth existed side by side with the grinding poverty of the immigrant wards. Newly developed mass media brought a heightened awareness about these conditions to upper-class and educated middle-class readers. By the turn of the century, falling paper prices and technical advances in rapid printing made it possible to produce high-quality mass-circulation newspapers and magazines. During the 1890s, newspaper circulation doubled and then tripled. A multitude of new periodicals appeared. All that was required to develop a mass audience was a way to popularize the press. "Muckraking" was such a technique. Crusading journalists investigated and reported "inside stories" exposing organized vice and the corruption of the urban machines. They also wrote about pervasive corruption in the national government, big business, the stock market, and the drug and meat packing industries.

Beginning with its September 1902 issue, *McClure's* magazine printed a series of seven articles by Lincoln Steffens, telling lurid stories of municipal corruption in the nation's big cities. In October, *McClure's* carried an article by Ida Tarbell exposing corporate corruption and profiteering by John D. Rockefeller's Standard Oil Company. The stories were an instant success, revealing an insatiable appetite in the public for sensational accounts of wrongdoing in business and government. A new mass circulation formula was discovered. Over the next few years *Munsey's, Everybody's, Success, Collier's, Saturday Evening Post, Ladies' Home Journal, Hampton's, Pearson's, Cosmopolitan,* and dozens of daily newspapers carried stories that appealed to the popular feeling that political, economic, and social institutions had become corrupted. Big business was accused of producing unsafe and shoddy goods, fixing prices, and crushing competition. There were exposés of fraudulent practices in banking; heart-rending accounts of women and children working at long, tedious, and dangerous jobs in factories and sweatshops; stories about urban poverty, prostitution, white slavery, and business-government collusion to protect vice.

An outpouring of popular books played on the same themes. Steffens collected his *McClure's* articles together into a best-selling book, *The Shame of the Cities,* published in 1904. Other popular titles included *The Greatest Trust in the World,* an exposé of price-fixing and collusion in the steel industry; *The Story of Life Insurance;* and *The Treason of the Senate,* which detailed systematic bribery of U.S. senators. Several important novelists entered the field. In *An American Tragedy* Theodore Dreiser stood Horatio Alger on his head by describing the corrupting influence of greed on a self-made small-town boy. Dreiser's *Sister Carrie* and David Graham Phillip's *Susan Lenox* both played on the theme of how the impersonal forces of urban life victimized young women. In *The Financier* Dreiser's theme was the ruthless drive for power and wealth, using the Chicago streetcar magnate Charles Yerkes as his model. Upton Sinclair's *The Jungle* dealt with a Lithuanian immigrant's fight to survive in a corrupt and chaotic Chicago.

Beaten down by destitution and poverty, eventually his wife becomes a prostitute, his children die, and he becomes a socialist revolutionary. By vividly portraying the nauseating conditions in Chicago's meatpacking industry (with rats, feces, and spoiled meat being swept into sausage vats, for example), Sinclair catalyzed a national crusade that resulted in congressional legislation creating the U.S. Food and Drug Administration in 1905. The literature produced by the "muckrakers"—an epithet applied to them in 1906 by President Theodore Roosevelt, referring to a character in John Bunyan's 1645 book *Pilgrim's Progress* who was too busy raking muck to look up and see the stars—was influential in building popular interest in reform. Although investigations by reform organizations were often dull and unexciting to the average citizen, the muckrakers' stories provided a feeling of drama and urgency.

In this environment a multitude of organizations sprang up to regulate business practices, improve working conditions, impose standards on the professions, and reform government. Business leaders organized the National Civic Federation in 1900. By advocating workers' compensation and other minor social insurance schemes, the founders of the federation hoped to undermine more militant demands being put forth by union organizers.[6] The National Child Labor Committee was organized in 1904 to fight for child labor legislation. In 1910 the National Housing Association brought together housing reform groups from many cities to agitate for building codes. A large number of public officials' associations and municipal research bureaus came into existence specifically to promote municipal reform: the National Association of Port Authorities, the Municipal Finance Officers Association, the American Association of Park Superintendents, the Conference of City Managers, the National Short Ballot Association. Groups such as these multiplied.

Though government corruption had provoked campaigns to "throw the rascals out" in a few cities during the 1870s and 1880s, the issues had usually been local and the remedies specific to an immediate situation. Several developments in the 1890s transformed reform into a national movement aimed at promoting change in local government structures. In response to widespread government corruption, citizens' groups sprang up all across the country to agitate for improved public services and honesty in government. The problems faced by the reformers varied little from one city to another. Like-minded reformers from different cities soon began to exchange advice and information about their efforts. These informational networks subsequently led to the formation of national reform organizations.

In 1894 delegates to the First Annual Conference for Good City Government met in Philadelphia to found the first national municipal reform organization, the National Municipal League. The delegates to the conference were united in the belief that democratic institutions in the cities had been corrupted by machine politicians and their immigrant constituents. There was, however, little agreement about the measures that could be taken to change this condition. "We are not unlike patients assembled in a hospital," one of the participants put it, "examining together and describing to each other our sore places."[7] After the formation of the National Municipal League, the nationalization of reform proceeded quickly. Within two years there were 180 local chapters affiliated with the league and, by the turn of the century, all large cities had member organizations. In their yearly meetings reformers from all over the country got a chance to compare notes. By its November 1899 meeting, the members of the National Municipal League reached agreement on a model municipal charter containing the elements making up the reformers' ideal of "good government." The charter was meant to serve as a blueprint for bringing fundamental change to local government.

To abolish the machines, the model charter recommended that ward elections be abandoned in favor of at-large elections, so that all city councilors would represent the entire city rather than each alderman or councilor representing a single ward. It also recommended that nonpartisan elections replace the party label on election ballots. It urged reformers to fight for civil service appointment procedures, so that party officials would not be able to use public jobs for patronage. The league also said that local elections should be held in different years than national and state elections, so that the national political parties would find it more difficult to influence local affairs.[8]

All of these measures were designed to undermine the basic foundation of machine politics: the political party. But in addition to eliminating the machines, the reformers wanted to reorganize local government. The league's model charter recommended that a small, unicameral city council replace the bicameral councils then existing in most cities (many city governments had been modeled on the national government, with its two legislative chambers). In addition, it encouraged reformers to lobby for new city charters that would give the mayor the power to appoint top administrators and to veto legislation. The assumption behind this reform—which they called "strong mayor government"—was that with authority centralized in the hands of the mayor, voters would be able to hold the mayor accountable for the city's overall governance. At the same time, the reformers thought that this change might help end the style of politics in which city councilors or aldermen made deals with one another behind the scenes. Finally, the league urged city reformers to seek so-called "home rule" charters from their state legislatures, reasoning that this reform would free cities from state party leaders and reduce meddling by state legislatures in local affairs.

To get their preferred reforms accepted, the municipal reformers shared a conviction that it was their responsibility to educate and instruct the public about the principle of what they called "good government." They placed their faith in rule by educated, upper- and middle-class Americans and, increasingly, in administration by trained administrators and professionals. In this way, the municipal reform movement began to build a style of government by bureaucracy that many Americans complain about today.

THE CAMPAIGNS AGAINST MACHINE RULE

The urban machines and their immigrant constituents were the reformers' principal targets. In their zeal to undermine the machines, some reformers went so far as to question the wisdom of universal suffrage, using the argument that immigrants were too ignorant and illiterate to vote intelligently. There was quite a lot of support for this view among the reform ranks. The Tilden Commission, appointed by the New York legislature to investigate the Tweed Ring scandals in New York City, recommended in 1878 that suffrage be restricted to those who owned property.[9] The commission's report was reprinted in an 1899 issue of *Municipal Affairs*, the National Municipal League's magazine, and was read with approval by those reformers who shared the view that an ignorant electorate accounted for the city's problems. The rationale for disenfranchising the immigrants was stated by the first president of Cornell University, Andrew D. White, who wrote in an 1890 issue of *Forum* that:

> A city is a corporation; . . . as a city it has nothing whatever to do with general political interests. . . . The questions in a city are not political questions. . . . The work of a city being the creation and control of the city property, it should logically be managed as a piece of property by those who have created it, who have a title to it, or a real substantial part in it, . . . [and not by] a crowd of illiterate peasants, freshly raked in from the Irish bogs, or Bohemian mines, or Italian robber nests.[10]

Although taking the vote away from the immigrants appealed to some reformers, it was hardly feasible to attempt such a drastic remedy. To wage an all-out campaign on this issue would surely have invited a negative reaction even from groups that supported reform causes. From the constitutional period until the Jacksonian voting reforms of the 1820s and 1830s, most states had restricted the vote to owners of property. The abolishment of these restrictions had been hailed as a triumph for popular democracy. It seemed unlikely that property qualifications could ever again be attached to the vote. The 1912 charter of Phoenix, Arizona, restricted voting in municipal elections to taxpayers, but the state courts invalidated this restriction as unconstitutional.[11] Even before Phoenix's attempt, it was clear that the reformers would have to find less direct methods to reduce the influence of immigrant voters.

Most reformers did not oppose voting participation by the immigrants per se. They were convinced that the real problem with elections was that they were run in a corrupt fashion by machine politicians who victimized their immigrant constituents. On this score they were not entirely wrong: Without doubt, municipal elections were chaotic and corrupt. Local elections were virtually free-for-all affairs, conducted in the absence of well-established rules and regulations. Because the political parties were considered private organizations, their nominating procedures were not regulated at all. To select candidates for public office, political parties held city conventions or ward caucuses according to their own changeable rules, often on short notice and at locations known only to insiders. It was not unusual for caucuses to be held in the backrooms of saloons owned by ward bosses. According to one scholar,

> This was the period of massive voting frauds. In the elections of 1868 and 1872, 8 percent more people voted in New York state than were registered. In 1910, when the New York City vote was challenged and recounted, half of the votes were found to be fraudulent. In New Jersey, the stuffing of ballot boxes was so common that the state legislature replaced the wooden boxes with glass ballot jars. In Pennsylvania and Michigan, gangs of thugs moved from polling place to polling place beating up

the opposition and voting at will. Fictitious and repeat voters, false counting, and stuffed ballot boxes were such regular features of city elections that voting statistics from this period are suspect.[12]

A Philadelphia politician once boasted that the signers of the Declaration of Independence were machine loyalists: "'These men,' he said, 'the fathers of American liberty, voted down here once.' 'And,' he added with a sly grin, 'they vote here yet.'"[13]

Politicians sometimes completed the ballot for voters or accompanied them into the voting booth. "Farmer Jones," a member of the Chicago machine in the 1890s, revealed to an inquiring reformer how he guaranteed voter loyalty:

> [The reformer asked,] "When you got the polling stations in your hands, what did you do?"
> "Voted our men, of course."
> "And the negroes, how did they vote?"
> "They voted as they ought to have voted. They had to."
> ". . . how could you compel those people to vote against their will?"
> "They understood, and besides," said he, "there was not a man voted in that booth that I did not know how he voted before he put the paper in the judges' hands."[14]

Buying the vote was the most direct and effective means of guaranteeing election-day results. The 1896 election in the First Ward of Chicago was conducted thusly:

> The bars were open all night and the brothels were jammed. By ten o'clock the next morning, though, the saloons were shut down, not in concession to the reformers, but because many of the bartenders and owners were needed to staff the First Ward field organization. The Bath, Hinky Dink and their aides ran busily from polling place to polling place, silver bulging in their pockets into which they dug frequently and deeply. The effort was not in vain, and the outcome was gratifying.[15]

Not content with mere fraud, machine politicians sometimes resorted to intimidation and violence. Tom Pendergast, who inherited the Kansas City Democratic organization after his brother Jim died, regularly resorted to a mixture of fraud and coercion. In the summer of 1914, Pendergast's organization "used money, repeat voters, and toughs to produce North Side majorities" to gain approval of a proposed railway franchise.[16] Machine workers distributed liquor and money in black and Italian neighborhoods. They "paid men to vote under assumed names; and election judges who questioned some of those dragged off the streets and out of flop houses to vote were intimidated and abused, both verbally and physically."[17] On election day in 1934, four persons were killed by thugs. Two years later, an attempted assassination and massive voter fraud led to an investigation that eventually resulted in 259 convictions for election fraud and criminal behavior.

The Chicago ward boss John Powers intimidated voters and told business owners that they would lose their business licenses unless they supported him in his 1898 campaign for alderman.[18] "Hinky Dink" Kenna and "Bathhouse John" Coughlin of Chicago's First Ward defended their loyal constituents but routinely harassed opponents. During the 1920s, organized crime and machine politics in Chicago became closely connected. Gangland "hits" were visited on meddling politicians who stood outside the inner circle of men controlling and protecting illegal liquor, speakeasies, prostitution, and gambling.

Ed Crump, the boss of Memphis, Tennessee, won his first mayoral election in 1909 by watching the polls himself. He personally interfered with the use of marked ballots by a machine he was opposing, in one case by hitting a voter in the face.[19] In Pittsburgh's state and city elections of 1933, the Democrats and Republicans—both rightly fearing fraud by the other party—mobilized opposing armies of poll watchers. The state police were called in to keep the peace, and lawyers and judges stood by to provide quick court action.[20]

In the late 1890s reformers introduced several measures to reduce election fraud. The key reforms included the following:

- *Voter registration and literacy requirements.* These requirements reduced repeat voting and stopped the practice of importing voters for an election. By 1920, almost all states had imposed registration laws.
- *Australian ballot.* This was a ballot that could be marked only by the voter and cast in secrecy. Before its introduction in the 1880s, ballots were printed by the parties and often marked and placed in a ballot box in front of observers. They were even handed already marked to voters. Use of the Australian ballot became universal after the turn of the century.
- *Nonpartisan elections.* Reformers fought hard to remove party labels of any kind from many state, and most municipal, election ballots. Where they succeeded, voters had only one clue as to how they should vote: the printed name of the individual candidate.

Though these reforms helped to clean up elections, they also had the effect of reducing voting participation by immigrants and less educated voters. Twenty-five percent of the white males of voting age in the United States in 1900 were first-generation immigrants, and two-thirds of them had come from non–English-speaking countries. In the cities the proportion of foreign-born immigrants was much higher—typically more than two-thirds of the voters in the big cities. Illiterate voters often asked for help in reading and filling out the ballot, or they even cast a premarked one. When they showed up at the polling place, no one questioned their right to vote. After reforms were adopted, they had to register to vote in writing, often months before an election. And when they went to the polling station, they now faced an election judge, a secret voting booth, and a printed ballot they could not read. Machine politicians were frequently able to get around the problems of the secret ballot by controlling polling places, but these actions exposed them to the possibility of criminal prosecution.

Large numbers of voters were effectively disenfranchised by reforms adopted in the cities of the South and Southwest. Because those cities lacked machine organizations, precinct captains and ward committeemen did not help voters to register or look over a sample ballot. In the South there was an explicitly racist motive for adopting the Australian ballot, as made clear by a Democratic campaign song popular in Arkansas in 1892:

The Australian Ballot works like a charm,
It makes them think and scratch,
And when a Negro gets a ballot
He has certainly got his match.

Illiteracy among southern white males varied between 8 percent and 19 percent; for black males it varied between 39 percent and 61 percent. Thus because a voter had to read it and fill it out without assistance, the Australian ballot drastically reduced voting by both blacks and poor whites. Some states also imposed poll taxes and literacy tests to make sure that blacks could not vote. When such measures did not work well enough in deterring blacks from voting, Ku Klux Klan violence was brought to bear.

By 1905 voter registration laws had been placed on the books in most of the states.[21] From 1905 to 1920, states and localities set up election boards, made it illegal to vote more than once, and tried to define the legitimate uses of campaign funds. Although enforcement of these laws was uneven, especially in the cities—the machines continued to control prosecutors and the courts in many places—the existence of new laws provided the basis for investigations and prosecutions when the middle- and upper-class public became disturbed about corruption.

Once electoral reform was adopted, the reformers focused their attention on the machine organizations. It was obvious that machine politicians derived their strength from the ethnic neighborhoods and that the machines greatly benefited from the immigrants' ability to identify a party label on the election ballot. By voting a straight-party ticket, the voter did not have to read the candidates' names. To make it harder for the voters to support machine candidates in this way, the reformers fought hard for two reforms—nonpartisan ballots and at-large elections.

Municipal reformers agreed that party labels encouraged bloc voting and blind loyalty to a political organization. They wanted a more "rational," educated voter who could "accumulate and carry in his head the brief list of personal preferences and do without the guidance of party names and symbols on the ballot."[22] The reformers asserted that it was the responsibility of citizens to educate themselves and to vote for the best candidates strictly on their merits, not on the basis of party loyalty or ethnic solidarity.

The proposal to remove the party label from election ballots reflected the reformers' conviction that an overall public interest overrode the preferences of particular ethnic groups or political factions. Reformers generally agreed that the public interest could be defined by one singular standard: Public services should be provided as cheaply and efficiently as possible. Just as business firms produce a product as cheaply and efficiently as possible, cities should—and could—do the same. Party symbols created the impression that there were political differences when, according to the reformers, everyone had the same fundamental interest. Voters were supposed to ask only one question: Which candidate was most qualified to help the city provide services at lowest cost? Brand Whitlock, the famous reform mayor of Toledo, Ohio, observed:

It seems almost incredible now that men's minds were ever so clouded, strange that they did not earlier discover how absurd was a system which, in order to enable them the more readily to subjugate themselves, actually printed little woodcuts of birds—roosters and eagles—at the heads of the tickets, so that they might the more easily and readily recognize their masters and deliver their suffrages over to them.[23]

Just as the reformers intended, the nonpartisan ballot made it harder for immigrants to vote as a bloc. Reading their alderman's printed name could be hard for illiterate voters. Recognizing the party symbol on the ballot was infinitely easier than reading the names of candidates.

Nonpartisan elections favored educated voters, and it made it harder for working-class candidates as well. The party organization supplied campaign money and workers and freed working-class candidates from the necessity of holding a normal job, which would have denied them time to participate in politics. Few politicians in the cities could have started or stayed in politics without a party organization's help. Party organizations pooled resources and built cooperative relationships among politicians; without them, people of wealth and social standing tended to hold an overwhelming advantage. This result was, in fact, the objective of the nonpartisanship crusade—to make politics once again a calling appropriate to the educated and cultured classes.[24]

The proposal to replace wards with at-large elections was designed to break the link between neighborhoods and machine politicians. Andrew White complained that "wards largely controlled by thieves and robbers can send thieves and robbers" into public office, and "the vote of a single tenement house, managed by a professional politician, will neutralize the vote of an entire street of well-to-do citizens."[25] The remedy was to require every candidate for the city council or board of aldermen to seek the votes of all city residents. By constituting the entire city as the one and only election district, no particular neighborhood or ethnic group could elect a candidate. Gone would be the politics of tradeoffs, logrolling, and compromise among legislators representing their own neighborhoods, ethnic groups, and wards. "Special interest" politics would supposedly give way to "public interest" politics. To the reformers, honest politics was virtually impossible as long as elections were decided by wards:

> For decades the election of councils by wards had superimposed a network of search for parochial favors, of units devoted to partisan spoils, and of catering to ethnic groups that time and again had either defeated comprehensive city programs or loaded them with irrelevant spoils and ill-conceived ward projects. The ward and precinct were the heart of machine control, and the councils so elected were usually also infested with corruption, however acceptable the councilors may have been to the voters of their wards.[26]

Small wards potentially gave even relatively small ethnic and racial groups leverage at the ballot box. Lithuanians, for example, might be able to send a Lithuanian alderman to the city council, even if they constituted a tiny proportion of a city's total population. Small wards multiplied the points of access through which groups and individuals could influence public officials. City-wide, at-large elections exerted an opposite effect. If the city is one big electoral district, candidates representing ethnic and racial groups clustered in specific neighborhoods are handicapped; in order to be elected they are forced to appeal to a variety of other groups distributed over many neighborhoods. Because campaigns covering a city are costly and time-consuming, wealthier candidates have a built-in advantage. In such a system, personal wealth and social status become the ingredients of political success. These effects were well known to reformers, which explains why the National Municipal League's model city charter of 1899 recommended at-large elections and nonpartisan ballots. Every subsequent model charter of the League contained these two features, and over the years the League compiled annual statistics to track the adoption of these reforms across the nation.

Civil service hiring systems constituted the last big plank in the reform platform. Reformers considered civil service to be crucial because it was aimed at the machines' practice of rewarding loyal supporters with patronage jobs. Under civil service reform, written and oral civil service examinations were to become the sole basis for hiring municipal employees, and a system of tenure and seniority was supposed to make employees safe from political firings. Without patronage, the machine would quickly whither away.

Within the first two decades of the twentieth century, nonpartisan, at-large elections and civil service reforms were implemented in cities from coast to coast. Reformers were least successful in the big industrial cities with large numbers of immigrant voters. In smaller cities, however, and in the newer cities in the West and Southwest, working-class voters tended to be outnumbered, discouraged from voting, or divided along ethnic lines. As a consequence, when reform proposals were put before the voters, they usually passed. Though there was widespread recognition that some reforms effectively disenfranchised the immigrant and working-class electorate, the aggressive campaigns sponsored by the National Municipal League persuaded local voters to pass reform measures. When local electorates balked, the reformers were able to bypass them altogether in some states by persuading state legislatures to abolish ward elections and require nonpartisan elections, civil service, and other reforms for all cities in the state.

Campaigns to adopt nonpartisan, at-large elections and civil service were energized by a melodramatic rhetoric that recounted lurid episodes of corruption. Such stories could just as well, and often were, imported from cities hundreds of miles away. In this fashion reformers were able to persuade voters to adopt reform in cities where machines had never existed. Reformers constantly made machines into a bogeyman that was hiding just around the corner, ready to pounce at the first opportunity. [27] In smaller towns and cities, where machines did not exist, reform was sold as a way to streamline government and make it efficient. The residents of smaller cities viewed government as, at best, a necessary evil that should provide such essential public services as water, sewage disposal, streets, and perhaps libraries and community centers. "Consensus" politics—which tended to exclude the ethnic and racial minorities that might be present—characterized politics in small towns then as it often does now.

The electoral rules preferred by the municipal reformers are much in evidence in contemporary cities. Before 1910 nonpartisan elections were almost unknown. By 1929 they were utilized in 57 percent of the cities with populations of more than 30,000. [28] By the 1960s many states required their cities to use nonpartisan elections; these included Minnesota, California, Alaska, and most of the western states. In ten more states nonpartisan ballots were used in 90 percent or more of the cities (the exceptions usually being cities above a specified size). In the West, 94 percent of cities used nonpartisan elections. The eastern seaboard was the only region of the country where more cities used partisan than nonpartisan elections. Among the nation's cities with over 500,000 people today, 85 percent use partisan elections. Reforms generally go together; most cities with nonpartisan elections use at-large rather than district or ward elections.

Reformed electoral systems were originally designed to reduce influence by working-class ethnic voters, and there is plenty of evidence that reform accomplished its intended purpose. Before the adoption of nonpartisan and at-large elections, working-class candidates, many of them socialists, were elected to city offices in dozens of cities. [29] At-large elections made it much more difficult for these kinds of candidates to win. In the 1909 elections in Dayton, Ohio, socialists elected two aldermen and three assessors from wards. Because they only received 25 percent of the citywide vote, without the ward system these candidates could not have won. Before the 1913 election, Dayton implemented citywide elections and abolished ward boundaries. In 1913, the socialists received 35 percent of the popular vote and, in 1917, 44 percent, but because all candidates were elected at-large, in neither year were the socialists able to elect a single candidate. Similarly, in 1911, Pittsburgh adopted at-large elections, with the result that upper-class business leaders and professionals pushed lower- and middle-class groups out of their previous places on the city council and the school board.[30]

St. Louis provides an excellent example of these two electoral systems at work. The members of the city's Board of Aldermen are placed in office through partisan elections in each of the city's twenty-eight wards (see Figure 4.1). In a city that was 41 percent African American by 1970, race had become a contested terrain. Because of St. Louis's ward system, ten blacks were elected to the city's Board of Aldermen in the 1977 municipal elections (and eleven by 1996). All of them represented predominantly African American wards located in the northern half of the city. On the other hand, all of the eighteen majority-white wards elected white aldermen. (As in many cities, alderman is an official term in the St. Louis city charter and does not refer exclusively to males.)

Because all school board candidates must run at-large, the composition of the school board was entirely different. In the 1977 election, in a city where 70 percent of the public school enrollment was African American, not a single black candidate was elected to the school board. All five of the seats on the ballot went to white, middle-class candidates because the three African-American candidates were rejected by white voters.

The St. Louis case illustrates the effects of at-large elections on racial and ethnic minorities. In the late 1970s the highly concentrated African-American minority was excluded from effective participation in the governing of the local schools, even though more than two-thirds of the students in the city school system were African American. The ward representation used to elect aldermen, in contrast, ensured that blacks would be represented in city hall.

The combination of nonpartisan and at-large elections was adopted in virtually all cities throughout the Southwest. Partially as a result, a style of politics

FIGURE 4.1   **Racial Composition of Municipal Wards in the City
of St. Louis, 1977**

0–5% African American

10–30% African American

70–100% African American

evolved that was tilted heavily in favor of business elites. Most cities provide a
very minimal level of services to citizens, but they are extremely active in promoting economic development. "Frugality, efficiency, and professionalism in
public administration" have always been the themes guiding government in
southwestern cities, but frugality has rarely been applied to what business has
wanted government to do.[31] For decades, legions of bureaucrats and professionals have found employment in special districts and authorities devoted to developing land, providing water, dredging harbors, supplying electricity, and lobby-

ing the federal government so that business could grow.[32] Until the 1960s candidates for public office tended to be selected by business groups. In effect, these groups constituted a kind of political machine that controlled the political realm. Turnout for elections tended to be low—much lower, in fact, than for elections in the industrial cities of the North.[33] This state of affairs began to change in the 1960s only when civil rights and neighborhood groups mobilized in several Sunbelt cities to challenge the business-dominated regimes (a subject we discuss in some detail in Chapter 9).

"EFFICIENCY AND ECONOMY" IN MUNICIPAL AFFAIRS

In the early years of the municipal reform movement, "efficiency and economy" became the code words for good government. When Theodore Roosevelt addressed the delegates to the First Annual Conference for Good City Government in 1894, he urged them to go beyond their moral outrage at the way things were being run to find ways of streamlining and improving government: "There are two gospels I always want to preach to reformers. . . . The first is the gospel of morality; the next is the gospel of efficiency. . . . I don't think I have to tell you to be upright, but I do think I have to tell you to be practical and efficient."[34] Actually, it is doubtful that the reformers needed such advice. Municipal reformers were hard at work searching for some guidelines that would show them how to govern cities. If they succeeded at "kicking the rascals out," they needed to know what to do with their inheritance.

By the late 1890s, the municipal reformers managed to develop a theory of governance. The reformers held that there was a public interest that could be defined objectively and that, if implemented, would benefit all citizens equally. As they defined it, the public interest could be satisfied by observing four sacred principles: (1) there must be strict budgetary controls to ensure that taxes would be kept as low as possible and public services would be delivered at the lowest possible cost; (2) the day-to-day administration of city government should be strictly separated from "politics"; (3) experts with training, experience, and ability should run city services; and (4) government should be run like a business and the principles of scientific management, then being applied in business organizations, should also be applied to government.

The reformers derived their ideas about how to run government from the scientific management movement that swept the country in the first two decades of the twentieth century. As businesses became larger, accountants, engineers, and corporate managers were busily inventing the structure of the modern corporation. If science could invent efficient machines, it was thought, then surely it could also discover how to make workers more efficient. What emerged from this search for efficiency was a quasi-military model for business organizations.

In 1911 Frederick Winslow Taylor became world famous with the publication of his book *The Principles of Scientific Management*.[35] Basically, Taylor wanted to apply military discipline and hierarchy to the factory. He said that the movements of individual workers could be studied in order to discover how to organize work tasks to achieve the maximum output with a minimum expenditure of each worker's energy. Taylor promised that his efficiency principles would bring progress, prosperity, and happiness to society by increasing material wealth to all. By applying the new science of management, Taylor said, it would be possible to achieve harmony and cooperation between owners and workers because both had the same interest in maximizing output. There was even a spiritual side; principles of efficiency would allow each man to develop "his greatest efficiency and prosperity."[36] The essence of the Taylor catechism was that "In the past, the man has been first; in the future the system must be first."[37]

Taylor and his disciples spread an urgent message: "Soldiering" (slow work) and inefficiency should be stamped out both at work and at home. Popular magazines featured articles on efficient housework—describing, for instance, how a housewife could sequence her daily chores and arrange appliances and furniture so as to minimize wasted movement while doing household work. The efficiency movement quickly achieved the status of a secular religion; its gospel of progress through efficiency swept the country.

To its advocates, scientific management seemed to be a bloodless revolution, a perfect solution to hostile employer-worker relations, disastrous economic panics, and poverty and want. Efficiency societies sprang up in cities all over the country, and efficiency experts were in demand as speakers.[38] Taylor's disciples invaded the factories to implement the gospel of efficiency. They also applied the principles of scientific management to the governmental realm. Efficiency and scientific management—"business methods"—soon became the model for municipal reform. The appropriateness of efficiency principles to government seemed obvious to the reformers: "The rising prestige of technicians in industry and the increasing demand for new public works and municipal services strengthened the desire for more technical efficiency in local government."[39]

In 1912, Henry Brueré, the first director of the privately funded New York Bureau of Municipal Research, published a book applying efficiency principles to municipal management.[40] Brueré took the position that much of the mismanagement in New York City "formerly attributed to official corruption and to popular indifference was really due to official and popular ignorance of . . . orderly and scientific procedures."[41] What these procedures amounted to were elaborate accounting and reporting devices designed to codify the responsibilities of city officials, the actions taken by them to carry out their duties, the costs of equipment and personnel, and other details. Brueré invented a scoring system so that the efficiency of various cities could allegedly be rated and compared. Cities were to be rated on the basis of such questions as: "Is a record kept of all city property?" "How often are the treasurer's books audited?" "Twenty questions on the protection of milk supply." "Is the location of houses of prostitution known and recorded?"[42] In all, Brueré and his aides used a list of 1,300 standardized questions to rate cities from the "worst governed" to the "best."

In 1913 Brueré was given the opportunity to make New York City efficient. In November of that year, John Purroy Mitchell, one of Brueré's closest confidants, was elected New York's mayor. Mitchell appointed Brueré to the office of city chamberlain (the mayor's policy adviser). Brueré immediately launched an attack on Tammany Hall's patronage system. He managed to push through the first large civil service system in the nation. It was explicitly designed as a Taylorite approach to municipal reform.

Brueré assigned the task of designing the details of the civil service system to Robert Moses, a young staff member at the New York Bureau of Municipal Research. Moses carried out his assignment with the enthusiasm of a Taylorite zealot. He proposed a system in which all municipal employees would be closely and constantly observed at work by trained efficiency experts who would rate each worker's efficiency according to an elaborate mathematical formula. Various functions and responsibilities of each employee were codified and "given a precise mathematical grade. These grades would . . . be used as a basis for salary increase and promotion."[43] To implement his system, Moses instructed his assistants to draw up rating forms, which he then distributed to supervisors. The idea was that each day the supervisors would hand a scorecard to each employee with the employee's mathematical rating. City workers would be paid, promoted, or fired on the basis of the ratings.

Such a system, if implemented, would have fallen of its own weight. There was no way to ensure objective ratings. The amount of time required to rate employees would have resulted in a truly enormous civil service administrative staff. Instead of spending the prodigious amounts of money required to hire hundreds of specially trained supervisors, Moses tried to rely on the existing city employees. The 50,000 city employees steadfastly refused to use the reporting forms. They objected that the system was hopelessly time-consuming and unwieldy—and arbitrary and capricious to boot.

The civil service reform attempted during Mitchell's mayoral tenure illuminates the values, assumptions, and foibles of the municipal reformers. As Taylor had put it, "The natural laziness in men is serious, but by far the greatest evil from which both workmen and employers are suffering is the systematic soldiering which is almost universal."[44] Reformers were taking on the formidable task of remaking human beings. Such an ambition could only be based on a distrust of people as they were. The human element was lacking. Mayor Mitchell, while trying to reorganize city departments and implement civil service procedures, tried to reduce all "unnecessary" programs and expenditures. He instituted cutbacks in school expenditures, asked teachers to work without salaries in the summers, tried to close down special schools for the retarded, and reduced park and recreational expenditures.[45]

New York's civil service proposals proved too draconian even for most reformers. Suitably modified, however, the reform agenda made sense. There was little doubt that more careful administration and well-trained city workers could save money and result in better service besides. Cities across the country adopted a modified version of efficiency principles through civil service systems. Not only the cities but the federal government and the states entered the field. President Taft appointed a Commission on Economy and Efficiency, and President Wilson later created the Bureau of Efficiency. Between 1911 and 1917, sixteen states established efficiency commissions. These commissions generally recommended streamlining of budgeting procedures, centralizing more power in the governor, consolidating state agencies, and civil service reform.[46]

THE BUSINESS MODEL

With efficiency and scientific management supplying the rationale, it was predictable that the organization of municipal government would be compared with the structure of private business. Reformers pointed out that municipal governments, unlike business firms, were not organized to maximize efficiency. A history of reform sympathetic with this view described the problem in these terms: "The reformers, who tried to get good men into office, found . . . that, even if they elected a mayor or council, they were intolerably handicapped by the existing systems of municipal government. [Due to] the principles of separation of powers and of checks and balances . . . there was no single elective official or governing body that could be held responsible for effecting reform."[47] Reformers claimed that the "weak mayor" form of government, which existed in most cities, left too much authority in the hands of a multitude of politicians— aldermen or councilors—as well as specialized boards and commissions. No one person could be held accountable for overall governmental policy. The reformers used organizational charts like the one shown in Figure 4.2 to demonstrate this fact.

It was supposed that businesses, in contrast, operated efficiently because there was clear separation between policy-making, which was located in a board

FIGURE 4.2   **Weak Mayor Government**

of directors, and day-to-day administration, which was left in the hands of professional executive officers. Applied to cities, this model would still leave policy-making to elected officials, who represented their constituents, just as a board of directors in a business presumably represents the interests of the stockholders. The policies, however, would be implemented by administrators, the equivalent of the professional executive officers, applying "scientific" principles of cost accounting and personnel management.

The business model required a strong executive with sufficient power to run the company. Applying this principle to city government, reformers sought charter reforms to reduce the number of elected officials and to expand the mayor's power to appoint most city officials and to veto legislation passed by the council. The mayor would preside at the top of a hierarchical chain of command with clear lines of authority and accountability. As recommended by the National Municipal League in 1899, the "weak mayor" was to be replaced by a "strong mayor" form of government, as represented in Figure 4.3. The league's model city charter also recommended a small city council of five to nine members elected at-large, together with a strong mayor with broad appointive and veto powers. In the first decade of the twentieth century, municipal research bureaus began to design organization charts in order to promote governmental reorganization along these lines.

Now that the reformers felt confident that they knew what to do if they gained control of cities, they attempted to persuade state legislatures to grant them broad "home rule" charters. In contrast to the latter decades of the nineteenth century, when municipal reformers often went to state legislatures to request special legislation to bypass elected officials, they now wanted cities to possess full authority to set their own tax rates and decide how and where to

FIGURE 4.3 **Strong Mayor Government**

provide services. They argued that trained administrators should replace elected and appointed boards and commissions. At its state constitutional convention in 1875, Missouri became the first state to write a general home rule charter for its cities, though the legislature retained control of St. Louis's police budget. Ultimate legal power was still held by the state, but Missouri's cities would not have to seek approval for their every action, as long as they stayed within their broad charter powers. Cities could hire new sanitation workers and firefighters, for example, or build a new street without consulting the legislature. The general charter spelled out the range of services to be provided, not such details as salary levels, the location of firehouses and streets, and the number of city employees. The home rule movement, pushed hard by the National Municipal League and other organizations, was quite successful. By 1925, fourteen states had granted home rule charters to their cities, and today virtually all cities are governed by such charters.

COMMISSION AND MANAGER GOVERNMENT

Galveston, Texas, set up the first municipal government derived explicitly from the business model. In 1894 Galveston's business and professional leaders organized a campaign to elect business leaders to the city government. The following year a coalition of city council members and business leaders secured a charter amendment from the Texas legislature that replaced ward with at-large elections, but the reform did not result in the sweeping changes its sponsors had hoped for. Over the next few years, some business leaders were elected to the city council, but they continued to be outvoted by a nonbusiness faction.[48]

An emergency provided the pretext for business and corporate leaders to decisively assert themselves. On September 8, 1900, hurricane-driven waves breached the seawall protecting Galveston, and the inrushing sea washed over the town, killing 6,000 of the town's 37,000 residents. Half of the property in the city was destroyed. To rebuild the city, prominent business leaders organized the Deepwater Committee and set out to gain control of local government. If "a municipality is largely a business corporation,"[49] as reformers maintained, it follows that it should be run as such, with the voters being viewed as stockholders and a board of directors responsible to the stockholders. On this principle, the Deepwater Committee drafted an outline of a commission form of government and asked the state legislature to approve it. It was promptly enacted.

The Galveston Plan created a five-member commission that exercised the legislative powers previously assigned to the city council and also the administrative authority normally assigned to professional supervisors. Each of the commissioners headed a separate department of government. Such a concentration of authority seemed appropriate in an emergency. Initially, the commission was even given jurisdiction over criminal and civil law enforcement in the city, though this power was subsequently struck down by a state court. Even without this power, however, the commission exercised sweeping authority. Behind the leadership of five aggressive businessmen, Galveston initiated a vigorous re-building program and in the process reduced its debts and restored and improved public services.

The success of Galveston's commission form of government captured national attention. Commission government spread like wildfire. Its appeal was obvious: It seemed to streamline government; it held the potential for attracting business and civic leaders back into active government service; and it was a straightforward plan around which reformers could rally in challenging machine politics and the urban party bosses. Galveston's performance so impressed business leaders in other Texas cities that they pressed the Texas legislature to allow them to install commission government. By 1907, seven major cities in the state had imitated Galveston's charter, including Houston, Dallas, and Fort Worth.

In 1908, voters in Des Moines, Iowa, approved a charter that became a model for reformers around the country. Besides a five-member commission, Des Moines adopted the initiative, referendum, and recall; nonpartisan and at-large elections; and a civil service system. This package of items, labeled the Des Moines Plan by reformers, caught on rapidly. Commission government was adopted by 23 cities in 1909 and by 66 cities in 1910.[50] By September 1915 at least 465 cities were governed by a commission, and by 1920 about 20 percent of all cities with populations of more than 5,000 had adopted it.[51] During these years, a few states made commission government compulsory for their cities, and in most states it became an option for cities that wanted to adopt it.

Reformers promoted the Des Moines Plan as a cure-all, sure to bring less taxation, more efficient public services, and a "better class of men" to government. In city after city it was promoted as a means of making government more businesslike. Accordingly, chambers of commerce and other organized business groups became the strongest backers. The Commercial Club succeeded in pushing through Des Moines's new charter in 1907, though, interestingly, the first commissioners voted into office represented a working-class slate—much to the dismay of the business group.[52] In Pennsylvania the Pittsburgh Chamber of Commerce organized a statewide convention of business organizations with the purpose of persuading the state legislature to require cities above a minimum size to adopt commission government. The coalition of bankers, merchants, and manufacturers secured the legislation in 1913.[53] The pattern was similar elsewhere: Business leaders were trying to transform government into a businesslike operation.

Commission government was not, however, without its problems. To its critics, its worst feature was that it did not fit the business model faithfully enough. A commission was not truly like a board of directors because commissioners engaged in both policymaking and administration. Because each of the commissioners headed a separate department, leadership was fragmented, with the commissioners often refusing to cooperate with one another. Sometimes they built their own personal empires by adroitly handing out jobs and contracts. It was hard for the mayor to prevent such practices because all the commissioners were "first among equals." This feature was the chief complaint of the secretary of the National Short Ballot Association, Richard S. Childs. Noting that commission government was "an accident, not a plan" (referring to the Galveston emergency that brought it into being), he addressed the problem of having five coequal executives: "The theory that the commission as a whole controlled its members in their departmental activities became neglected—the commission could not discipline a recalcitrant member."[54] Commonly, Childs asserted, commissioners would ignore one another's performance ("You attend to your department and quit criticizing mine") or exchange favors and support ("I'll vote for your appropriation if you'll vote for mine").[55] It sometimes seemed like a replay of machine politics.

Municipal reformers responded to these complaints with still another idea. This time they wanted to place all administrative authority in the hands of a single appointed, trained administrator—a city manager. According to this plan, the mayor and the city council would be responsible for making policy, but a professional city manager specifically trained for the job would be responsible for coordinating all administrative functions: "The reform leaders realized that technical ability could not be expected of elected officials, and they hoped that a strong mayor could appoint trained technicians and administrators as department heads."[56] The city manager was to supervise day-to-day administration, thus bringing to local government administrative unity, expertise, clear accountability, and formal training in management.[57]

This time the reformers intended to get the business model right. In 1913 the National Municipal League issued a report (written by Childs) recommending that commission government be abandoned in favor of the city manager plan. Only six years later, in 1919, the League amended its model charter to recommend city manager government. Because of its persuasive logic and "pure" business analogy, the city manager structure quickly replaced commission government. By the 1920s the commission form was regarded as a failed experiment.

Between 1908 and 1912, several midwestern cities hired city managers. The idea caught on in earnest when Dayton, Ohio, changed its city charter, though the ward system remained. As in Galveston, an emergency served as the catalyst for a new government form. In 1913 John H. Patterson, president of the National Cash Register Company, persuaded the Dayton Chamber of Commerce to draft a new city charter. The chamber established the Bureau of Municipal Research to promote the idea, and the Committee of One Hundred, a group funded by the business community, sponsored a slate of candidates for city office who were pledged to changing the city charter. By organizing a well-run campaign ward by ward, the business slate put several Republican candidates on the city council, but they still were outnumbered by Democratic machine politicians. Charter reform seemed to be stymied. Two months later, however, the Miami River flooded the town, and the municipal government was slow in organizing emergency services. Patterson turned his factory into a shelter for flood victims. Overnight, he became the town's leading citizen. When requested by local business leaders, the state governor appointed Patterson to head a new charter reform commission. The commission successfully persuaded the voters to adopt its recommended charter.[58]

The results were spectacular. The new government improved public services, retired most of the city debt, instituted new budget-making procedures, enforced a uniform eight-hour day for city employees, and established civil service. The Dayton Plan soon became the nation's most popular "good reform" reform model. Though rarely instituted in the big industrial cities, it became common in smaller cities around the country. In the five years before 1918, 87 cities adopted manager charters, and 153 did so between 1918 and 1923. During the next five years, 84 more cities were added to the list. [59]

The commission and then the manager plans become popular because they seemed able to fulfill the reformers' desires to find an objective, nonpolitical, efficient way to run government. Analogies to business organizations almost always supplied the principal supporting arguments for reform. The *Dallas News* promoted the manager plan in 1930 by asking, "Why not run Dallas itself on a business schedule by business methods under businessmen? . . . The city manager plan is after all only a business management plan. The city manager is the executive of a corporation under a board of directors. Dallas is the corporation. It is as simple as that. Vote for it."[60]

THE BIAS OF MUNICIPAL REFORM

The commission and manager movements succeeded in gaining support from the middle- and upper-class voters not only because they promised to save taxpayers' money but also because they placed political handicaps in the way of the Great Unwashed. Reform was inspired by class antagonisms. Changes in electoral rules and in the structure of city government were designed to undercut the electoral influence of the working class and the immigrants. A historian summarized the class differences between reformers and the ethnic constituents of the machines in this way:

> There were differences in nationality or religion that intensified their social and political disagreements; . . . and each of them [the local reform movements] established the city manager plan through a concerted effort, organized by commercial or reform organizations, to take the city government away from the politicians, to give it to businessmen, and to make it conform to business ideals and standards.[61]

The change to manager government resulted in "the election of men who had never before taken part in municipal affairs and who had promised to end politics in the business of city government."[62]

Studies of the social class backgrounds of reformers have revealed a uniformly upper-class bias. Studies of the origins of reform movements show that business and upper-class elements normally championed reform, while lower- and working-class groups usually opposed it. For example, the New York City

Bureau of Municipal Research, founded in 1906, was initially financed by Andrew Carnegie and John D. Rockefeller.[63] The U.S. Chamber of Commerce provided office space and paid the executive secretary of the City Managers Association for several years.[64] Civic clubs and voters' leagues generally contained names from elite social directories. Professional people involved in reform tended to be the most prestigious members of their professions, and many of them came from the upper class.

The historian George Mowry has traced the backgrounds of more than 400 prominent reformers of the Progressive Era, and his data show that most were upper class.[65] Many of the prominent reformers were wealthy industrialists, including names like McCormack, du Pont, Pinchot, Morgenthau, and Dodge. Most had a college education in a day when this fact marked a select social strata. Even more striking, most of the women and social workers had gone to college. In a sample of 400 reformers, a majority were lawyers and almost one-fifth were newspaper editors or publishers. Most of the remainder were engaged in business, medicine, real estate, or banking. Most of them were native-born Americans of British ancestry, Protestant, and urban. Other studies confirm this profile. A California sample of forty-seven reformers found that fourteen of them were engaged in banking, real estate, or business; seventeen in law; and fourteen in journalism.[66] In Baltimore the reform group was overwhelmingly white, Anglo-Saxon, Protestant, university-graduated, and engaged in professional practice or business. Studies in Ohio, Chicago, Pittsburgh, and Kansas City reported similar findings.[67] In cities where people of professional occupations were less active in reform, business organizations filled the vacuum.[68] This was particularly the case in Dallas, Des Moines, Pittsburgh, and several other cities.[69] The expectation that new forms of government would result in the election of a "better" class of citizens, meaning businessmen or their favored candidates, was usually fulfilled, and this fact explains why business leaders were at the forefront of the municipal reform movement.[70]

Machine politicians, socialists, and trade unionists generally opposed reform plans because they correctly perceived that centralized electoral systems and decision-making processes would make it more difficult for working-class candidates to win public office.[71] Because immigrants accounted for a disproportionate share of the working class and poor within cities, both class and ethnicity were important factors determining attitudes toward reform—though there is evidence that ethnicity was even more important than class in determining voting patterns.[72] In the big cities, coalitions of immigrants and working-class groups generally successfully opposed key features of the reform agenda. In smaller cities, however, especially when the immigrants and working-class groups made up a minority of the electorate, they could not effectively resist reform. In Oakland, California, socialists polled nearly 50 percent of the vote in the 1911 city elections.[73] With the vociferous assistance of the *Oakland Tribune*, local business leaders then led a successful reform movement to secure commission, at-large, nonpartisan government. Running at-large, the socialists were unable to win any seats on the commission in the next city elections. Still not satisfied, the business coalition mounted a successful campaign in 1928 to replace the commission with a council-manager government.[74] The manager was much easier to control than were the elected commissioners. In 1938 the chamber of commerce in Jackson, Michigan, persuaded voters to approve a council-manager charter with at-large elections. After the charter was adopted, the new slate of candidates sponsored by the chamber swept into office. The new mayor and council members celebrated with a reception in the Masonic hall (the Masons were an anti-Catholic organization) and, once in power, dismissed most of the Roman Catholic city employees.[75]

By putting business leaders in charge of local government, reformers were able to ensure that cities would not try to take on social responsibilities. The contrast to the "social reformers," such as Hazen Pingree in Detroit, is striking. Social reformers like Pingree wanted to restructure tax burdens so that wealthy property owners and businesses would pay their fair share, secure lower public utility rates, and provide recreation, public health and jobs programs to less privileged people. A delegate to the 1913 meeting of the League of Kansas Municipalities, after listening to his colleagues orate about the necessity of treating the city as a business, protested that "a city is more than a business corporation" and that "good health is more important than a low tax rate."[76] The vast social chasm dividing municipal reformers from the rest of the urban populace, however, made such utterances anathema to most reformers. In most cities, the structural reformer, who was interested mainly in kicking out working-class politicians, won the day.

DID REFORM KILL THE MACHINES?

It has often been assumed that the party machines died out because the reformers were successful in changing the rules of the game under which local politics was conducted. A large number of machines had short lives, only a decade or so, before they went into slow decline or machine politicians suddenly lost their grip on elective offices. Between 1909 and 1918, machines fell apart in Dayton, Ohio; Detroit and Grand Rapids, Michigan; Los Angeles; Portland, Oregon; Milwaukee; Minneapolis; San Francisco; and Seattle. In each case a variety of reforms was put through; in each case, civil service systems changed hiring rules.[77] Most of the machines that survived this era of reform died by the mid-1950s, if not before, including New York's Tammany Hall. By World War II, it would have been impossible to find a city left completely untouched by reform: Voter registration was universal and civil service hiring was nearly so; at-large, nonpartisan elections were used in most cities. Even in the big industrial cities, where reform was generally less successful, election rules were at least partially reformed. Boston, New Orleans, and Pittsburgh had switched to at-large elections; Memphis and Detroit had adopted both at-large and nonpartisan elections. Denver, New Orleans, Philadelphia, Cleveland, and Pittsburgh also became nonpartisan before World War II.[78]

Nevertheless, these reforms did not lead inexorably to the demise of the machines, and, therefore, they did not immediately or invariably restructure politics so that ethnic voters lost influence: "The adoption of structural reform was not sufficient to eliminate or preclude the appearance of machine politics."[79] Machines were often adept at adjusting to the new rules and institutions. In fifteen cities they actually seem to have been helped by the reformers' centralization of power in the hands of mayors or city managers.[80] The reformers accomplished their goal of making someone accountable to voters, but the voters did not always use their power as the reformers hoped. After the adoption of city manager government in Cleveland in the 1920s, the city's machine was able to appoint a party hack as manager because it still controlled the city council, which was elected by wards.[81] Richard J. Daley built his powerful machine in Chicago, beginning with his election in 1953, despite the fact that the city's elections were nonpartisan and the vast majority of its employees were civil service.

The machines died, in most cases, because they were unable to adapt to large-scale population and economic transformations. Two developments were particularly important. First, the immigrant base of the machines began to erode. After the turn of the century Irish and German immigration dropped sharply; the bulk of new immigrants came from Italy and Eastern Europe. The Irish and, secondarily, the Germans had been the mainstay groups for most machines, and, as their numbers declined, machines found that their support gradually eroded. In Boston, for example, the Irish and Germans accounted for 32 percent of ethnics in 1890, but only 20 percent by 1930; in New York City, their share of the total ethnic population fell even more.[82] In New York City, Fiorello LaGuardia put together a coalition of Italian and Jewish voters to defeat Tammany Hall's candidate in 1933. James Michael Curley, Boston's longtime boss lasted longer than most other bosses but was finally defeated for reelection in 1949.[83]

The second devastating blow to the machines occurred when their immigrant constituents began to move up the economic ladder. As the immigrants joined the ranks of the middle class, the petty favors and patronage offered by the machines carried less weight, both in material and symbolic terms. After World War II, the immigrants and the children of immigrants joined the mass movement to the suburbs. Precinct captains saw their constituents moving out of the city, and sometimes they moved, too. Machines were not generally successful in reaching out to immigrants or to blacks and poor whites who moved into the cities during and after World War II.[84]

After the war, a new generation of politicians came to power by mobilizing the business community, labor, and the middle class behind programs of urban revitalization. In this cause they were helped by the federal government, which supplied the funds for public housing and slum clearance (we discuss these programs in Chapter 7). Richard Daley rebuilt the Chicago machine by adding the middle class, business, and African-Americans to the machine's base in the old immigrant neighborhoods. Daley aggressively sought federal funds for the city. Few machine leaders in other cities, however, had the vision or the political ability to follow his example.

THE REFORM LEGACY AND THE POLITICS OF REPRESENTATION

Interest in local election rules has been rekindled over the past two decades because of clear evidence that at-large elections frequently result in the underrepresentation of racial and ethnic minorities. The social science research showing this relationship has been consistent and persuasive.[85] In 1982, over the strenuous objections of the Reagan Administration, Congress amended the 1965 voting rights act to make it easier for minorities to challenge local election practices. Congress passed the amendments, contained in Section 2 of the new act, in explicit reaction to a 1980 U.S. Supreme Court decision that required litigants to demonstrate an intent to discriminate before an election rule could be declared invalid.[86] In Section 2, Congress specified that challenges to local election rules could meet a much easier standard than before: They would be considered illegal if they merely had the effect of underrepresenting minorities in elected positions.

On June 30, 1986, the Supreme Court handed down a landmark decision, *Thornburg v. Gingles*, interpreting the 1982 amendments.[87] This case came to the Court after the U.S. Justice Department brought suit against the state of North Carolina, arguing that several multimember state legislative districts in North Carolina violated the voting rights of blacks, since in those districts white candidates invariably won all seats. The Court ordered North Carolina to create single-member districts and laid down some standards for deciding when at-large and multimember district systems would be considered suspect: (1) when litigants could show that it would be possible to create at least one single-member electoral district that would give a minority group an electoral majority; (2) when it could also be demonstrated that the minority group seeking more representation was politically cohesive; and (3) when it could be shown that whites had previously voted as a bloc to prevent minority candidates from being elected.[88]

At-large and some district systems have since been successfully challenged throughout the United States. In 1986, after finding that at-large elections made it impossible for African-American candidates to win, a federal court ordered several Alabama counties to institute single-member districts for electing county commissioners.[89] In a 1987 lawsuit filed against the city of Springfield, Illinois, a federal judge ordered the city to expand the number of electoral districts from five to ten. Since only 10.8 percent of the city's population was African American, the expansion to ten districts was necessary if any one of them was to contain a majority of black voters.[90] (Interestingly, a different federal judge did not require this solution in a similar suit against the Springfield Park District.[91]) In the same year, the city of Danville, Illinois, expanded its city council to fourteen members elected from seven wards, after a federal judge threw out its previous system, in which a three-member commission and a mayor were all elected at-large.[92]

The extensive litigation arising from the 1982 amendments to the Voting Rights Act produced an extraordinary amount of conflict and confusion about local election rules. All through the 1980s and into the 1990s numerous court decisions called into question the electoral systems of hundreds of cities, counties, townships, and special districts. To preempt court action, some local governments voluntarily redrew district and ward boundaries so as to facilitate minority representation. Frequently, this required devising districts with tortuously meandering boundaries.[93] The attempt to redraw boundaries, however, is not a solution available to every city and may, in fact, be available only to those whose minority populations live in rather segregated circumstances rather than in several distinct but unconnected neighborhoods. In a series of decisions beginning in 1993, the U.S. Supreme Court has invalidated congressional district boundaries that do not meet standards of "compactness, contiguity, and respect for political subdivisions."[94] Though the courts seem to be enforcing this standard quite strictly, it does not necessarily signal an end to all redistricting meant to achieve representation by particular racial or ethnic groups.[95] One way to meet the court's standards would be to increase the number of legislative districts to ensure that even somewhat small neighborhoods containing a large proportion of minorities would make up most of a compact legislative district. For several years it was unclear whether there was some upper limit to the number of districts that a local government might have to draw to achieve the equitable representation of minorities. By 1987, however, it seemed likely (despite the city of Springfield case) that, under normal circumstances, the number of districts already existing would be left alone.[96]

Another question that arose was whether the minority population or the voting-age minority population would be counted in the districts drawn to give minorities better representation. Most courts decided that a majority voting-age population was required.[97] Could two or more minority groups be combined to constitute a district if the combined minorities would make up the majority of voters in a district? Only, the courts have said, if it could be shown that the groups were politically cohesive—and research makes it clear, for example, that blacks and Latinos do not generally vote similarly.[98]

The principle that electoral districts should always be drawn so as to maximize the representation of ethnic and racial minorities reverberated through all levels of the American political system. In 1991 minority representation was at the forefront of the political infighting over congressional reapportionment required as a result of the decennial census of 1990. In that year, there were thirty-seven blacks and Latinos in Congress. As a result of redistricting in 1992, 19 additional blacks and Latinos were elected to Congress. In Texas the Democrats, who made up a majority of the state legislature, took on the task of creating one black-majority congressional district in Dallas and two Latino-majority districts in Houston and San Antonio. A similar process took place in several other states as well.

In June 1991 the Supreme Court ruled that judicial elections in Louisiana and Texas violated the 1982 voting rights act because at large election districts diluted the electoral strength of minorities. A flurry of lawsuits followed that challenged election procedures for state and local judges. Traditionally, nearly all state and local judges have been elected at-large, and this perhaps explains why, as of 1985, only 3.8 percent of judges in state courts were black and only 1.2 percent were Latino.[99]

The multitude of court challenges resulted in an ongoing revolution in local electoral practices. In 1981, 66.5 percent of cities used at-large election systems. By 1986, a space of only five years, the proportion had fallen to 60.4 percent.[100] This revolution was energized by research demonstrating that changing from at-large to district elections did, as anticipated, improve the representation of blacks and Latinos.[101] Cities all across the country came under pressure to redraw existing ward and district boundaries. In 1991, for example, African-American leaders in St. Louis threatened to go to court to force a redrawing of the city's wards. At the time, eleven of the twenty-eight aldermen were African American, but a new ward map would have made it mathematically possible to give half of the wards a majority of African-American voters.[102]

After the period of municipal reform that we have discussed in this chapter, it took more than half a century for questions about representation and local democracy to resurface as a political issue. The years since the Voting Rights Act of 1965 may be properly regarded, therefore, as the first reform period since the Progressive Era to focus specifically on local electoral politics. It is interesting that this latter period of reform has focused on undoing some of the reforms adopted in an earlier time.

NOTES

1. William L. Riordon, *Plunkitt of Tammany Hall* (New York: Dutton, 1963), p. 17.
2. James Bryce, *The American Commonwealth*, 3rd ed., vol. 1 (New York: Macmillan, 1924), p. 642.
3. H. E. Deming, *The Government of American Cities: A Program of Democracy* (London and New York: Putnam, 1909), p. 194.
4. Quoted in Michael B. Katz, *School Reform: Past and Present* (Boston: Little, Brown, 1971), p. 169.
5. Josiah Strong, *Our Country*, ed. Jurgen Herbst (Cambridge, Mass.: Belknap Press, Harvard University Press, 1963; first published in 1886), p. 55.
6. James Weinstein, *The Corporate Ideal in the Liberal State, 1900–1918* (Boston: Beacon Press, 1968).
7. Melvin G. Holli, "Urban Reform in the Progressive Era," in *The Progressive Era*, ed. Louis L. Gould (Syracuse, N.Y.: Syracuse University Press, 1974), p. 137.
8. Frank Mann Stewart, *A Half Century of Municipal Reform: The History of the National Municipal League* (Berkeley: University of California Press, 1950), chap. 1.
9. Samuel Haber, *Efficiency and Uplift: Scientific Management in the Progressive Era, 1890–1920* (Chicago: University of Chicago Press, 1964), p. 99.
10. Andrew D. White, "City Affairs Are Not Political," originally titled "The Government of American Cities," *Forum*, December 1890, pp. 213–216; reprinted in Dennis Judd and Paul

Kantor, eds., *The Politics of Urban America* 2nd ed. (New York: Addison Wesley Longman, 2002).

11. Amy Bridges, "Winning the West to Municipal Reform," *Urban Affairs Quarterly* 27, no. 4 (June 1992), p. 511.

12. Arthur T. Hadley, *The Empty Polling Booth* (Englewood Cliffs, N.J.: Prentice-Hall, 1978), p. 61.

13. Alexander B. Callow, Jr., ed., *The City Boss in America* (New York: Oxford University Press, 1976), p. 158.

14. William T. Stead, *If Christ Came to Chicago* (Chicago: Laird and Lee, 1894), pp. 56–57.

15. Lloyd Wendt and Herman Kogan, *Bosses in Lusty Chicago* (Bloomington: Indiana University Press, 1967), p. 169.

16. Lyle W. Dorsett, *The Pendergast Machine* (New York: Oxford University Press, 1968), p. 59.

17. Ibid., p. 60.

18. Allan F. Davis, *Spearheads for Reform* (New York: Oxford University Press, 1967), pp. 156–162.

19. William D. Miller, *Mr. Crump of Memphis* (Baton Rouge: Louisiana State University Press, 1964), p. 74.

20. Bruce M. Stave, *The New Deal and the Last Hurrah: Pittsburgh Machine Politics* (Pittsburgh: University of Pittsburgh Press, 1970), p. 77.

21. Ernest S. Griffith, *A History of American City Government, 1900–1920* (New York: Praeger, 1974), p. 71.

22. Richard S. Childs, *Civic Victories: The Story of an Unfinished Revolution* (New York: Harper and Brothers, 1952), p. 299. In this passage Childs was referring to the short ballot reform in conjunction with nonpartisanship. The short ballot reformers felt that there should be fewer elected officials so that voters would not be confused and elected officials would be held accountable to voters.

23. Edward C. Banfield, ed., *Urban Government: A Reader in Administration and Politics* (New York: Free Press, 1969), p. 275. Selection from Brand Whitlock, *Forty Years of It*, preface by Allen White (New York and London: Appleton, 1925; first published 1914).

24. Haber, *Efficiency and Uplift*, pp. 99–101.

25. White, "City Affairs Are Not Political."

26. Griffith, *A History of American City Government*, p. 130.

27. Amy Bridges, *Morning Glories: Municipal Reform in the Southwest* (Princeton, N.J.: Princeton University Press, 1997), chap. 8.

28. Willis D. Hawley, *Nonpartisan Elections and the Case for Party Politics* (New York: Wiley, 1973), p. 14. Subsequent information on the use of nonpartisan elections is from Hawley, pp. 15–18.

29. Weinstein, *The Corporate Ideal*, p. 109. Subsequent information on the Dayton election is from Weinstein.

30. Samuel P. Hays, "The Politics of Reform in Municipal Government in the Progressive Era," in *Social Change and Urban Politics: Readings*, ed. Daniel N. Gordon (Englewood Cliffs, N.J.: Prentice-Hall, 1973), pp. 107–127.

31. Bridges, *Morning Glories*, p. 146.

32. Ibid., chap. 7.

33. Ibid., pp. 144–145.

34. Quoted in Holli, "Urban Reform in the Progressive Era," p. 144.

35. Frederick Winslow Taylor, *The Principles of Scientific Management* (New York: Harper and Brothers, 1919; first published 1911).

36. Ibid., p. 140.

37. Ibid., p. 7.

38. Haber, *Efficiency and Uplift*, p. 56.

39. Harold A. Stone, Don K. Price, and Kathryn H. Stone, *City Manager Government in the United States: A Review After Twenty-five Years* (Chicago: Public Administration Service, 1940), p. 5.

40. Henry Brueré, *The New City Government: A Discussion of Municipal Administration Based on a Survey of Ten Commission-Governed Cities* (Englewood Cliffs, N.J.: Prentice-Hall, 1912).

41. Ibid., p. v.

42. Ibid., pp. 27–29.

43. Robert A. Caro, *The Power Broker: Robert Moses and the Fall of New York* (New York: Oxford University Press, 1969), p. 75.

44. Taylor, *The Principles of Scientific Management,* p. 20.

45. Melvin B. Holli, *Reform in Detroit: Hazen S. Pingree and Urban Politics* (New York: Oxford University Press, 1969), p. 167.

46. Haber, *Efficiency and Uplift,* p. 115.

47. Stone, Price, and Stone, *City Manager Government,* p. 4.

48. Martin J. Schiesl, *The Politics of Municipal Reform: Municipal Administration and Reform in America, 1880–1920* (Berkeley: University of California Press, 1977), pp. 134–135.

49. Quoted in Weinstein, *The Corporate Ideal,* p. 96.

50. Clinton R. Woodruff, ed., *City Government by Commission* (Englewood Cliffs, N.J.: Prentice-Hall, 1911), pp. 293–294.

51. Childs, *Civic Victories,* p. 138.

52. Hays, "The Politics of Reform," p. 116.

53. Weinstein, *The Corporate Ideal,* p. 99.

54. Childs, *Civic Victories,* p. 137.

55. Ibid.

56. Stone, Price, and Stone, *City Manager Government,* p. 5.

57. Griffith, *A History of American City Government,* p. 167.

58. Ibid., p. 166; Schiesl, *The Politics of Municipal Reform,* pp. 175–176.

59. Weinstein, *The Corporate Ideal,* pp. 115–116.

60. Quoted in Stone, Price, and Stone, *City Manager Government,* p. 27.

61. Ibid., p. 37.

62. Ibid., p. 43.

63. Hays, "The Politics of Reform," p. 111.

64. Griffith, *A History of American City Government,* p. 167.

65. Mowry, *The Era of Theodore Roosevelt, 1900–1912* (New York: Harper and Row, 1958), p. 86. Mowry claims the reformers represented the "solid middle class," but his own data belie this classification.

66. Griffith, *A History of American City Government,* p. 21. Subsequent information on studies of reform is from Griffith.

67. Though most historians have labeled the reformers middle class, research uniformly documents upper-class occupations, incomes, and educational status. It defies common sense to think that middle-class people would have had the time or the personal resources to participate in politics as active reformers. Middle-class bank clerks, accountants, small business owners, sales clerks, schoolteachers, small-town lawyers, and college professors normally worked sixty-hour weeks. Their salaries were little above that of working-class skilled laborers. If college educated (and most were not), their degrees were usually granted by small, unprestigious private colleges or state schools. Then as now, only a small percentage of the middle class participated in politics at any level. Much of the problem with the historians' labeling is that they have rarely provided careful definitions of social class. Often the term middle class seems to cover everyone except immigrant unskilled laborers.

68. Hays, "The Politics of Reform," p. 111.

69. Ibid.; Weinstein, *The Corporate Ideal,* pp. 99–103.

70. Weinstein, *The Corporate Ideal,* pp. 103–105; Stone, Price, and Stone, *City Manager Government,* pp. 32–50.

71. Weinstein, *The Corporate Ideal,* pp. 106–109.

72. Kenneth Finegold, *Experts and Politicians: Reform Challenges to Machine Politics in New York, Cleveland, and Chicago* (Princeton, N.J.: Princeton University Press, 1995), p. 175.

73. Edward C. Hays, *Power Structure and Urban Policy: Who Rules in Oakland?* (New York: Mc-Graw-Hill, 1972), p. 11.
74. Ibid., pp. 13–14.
75. Stone, Price, and Stone, *City Manager Government*, pp. 35–36. Several other case studies in this book reveal a similar bias.
76. Quoted in Weinstein, *The Corporate Ideal*, pp. 106, 107.
77. Alan DiGaetano, "Urban Political Reform: Did It Kill the Machine?" *Journal of Urban History*, 18, No.1 (November 1991), pp. 37–67.
78. Ibid.
79. Ibid.
80. Ibid.
81. Ibid.
82. Ibid.
83. Ibid.
84. Steven P. Erie, *Rainbow's End: Irish-Americans and the Dilemmas of Urban Machine Politics, 1840–1985* (Berkeley: University of California Press, 1988).
85. Robert L. Lineberry and Edmond P. Fowler, "Reformism and Public Policies in American Cities," *American Political Science Review* 61 (September 1967); Chandler Davidson and George Korbel, "At-Large Elections and Minority Group Representation: A Re-examination of Historical and Contemporary Evidence," *Journal of Politics* 43 (November 1981): 982–1005; Jerry L. Polinard, Robert D. Wrinkle, and Thomàs Longoria, Jr., "The Impact of District Elections on the Mexican American Community: The Electoral Perspective," *Social Science Quarterly* 71, no. 3 (September 1991): 608–614; Richard L. Engstrom and Michael D. McDonald, "The Effect of At-Large Versus District Elections on Racial Representation in U.S. Municipalities," in *Electoral Laws and Their Political Consequences*, eds. Bernard Grofman and Arend Liphart (New York: Agathon, 1986), pp. 203–225; W. E. Lyons and Malcolm E. Jewell, "Minority Representation and the Drawing of City Council Districts," *Urban Affairs Quarterly* 23 (1988): 432–447; Delbert Taebel, "Minority Representation on City Councils: The Impact of Structure on Blacks and Hispanics," *Social Science Quarterly* 59 (1982): 729–736; Jeffrey S. Zax, "Election Methods, Black and Hispanic City Council Membership," *Social Science Quarterly* 71 (1990), pp. 339–355.
86. *City of Mobile v. Bolden*, 446 U.S. 55 (1980).
87. *Thornburg v. Gingles*, 106 S.Ct. 2752 (1986).
88. C. Robert Heath, "*Thornburg v. Gingles:* The Unresolved Issues," *National Civic Review* 79, no. 1 (January–February 1990): 50–71.
89. *Dillard v. Crenshaw County*, 649 F.Supp. at 289 (C.O. Ala. 1986).
90. *McNeal v. Springfield*, 658 F.Supp. at 1015, 1022 (C.D. Ill. 1987).
91. *McNeal v. Springfield Park District*, 851 F.2d at 937 (7th Cir. 1988).
92. *Derrickson v. City of Danville*, 87–2007 (C.D. Ill. 1987).
93. Joseph F. Zimmerman, "Alternative Local Electoral Systems," *National Civic Review* 79, no. 1 (January–February 1990): 23–36.
94. The quotation is from *Shaw v. Reno* 509 U.S. 630 (1993), commonly known as Shaw I. Other cases are *Miller v. Johnson*, 63 U.S.L.W. 4726 (1995); *Shaw v. Hunt*, 64 U.S.L.W. 4437 (known as Shaw II), *King vs. Illinois Board of Elections*, 65 U.S.L.W. 3353 (1996); *Abrams v. Johnson*, 65 U.S.L.W. 4478.
95. Carmen Cirincione, Thomas Darling, and Timothy O'Rourke, "Does the Supreme Court Have It Right?" Paper delivered at the 1997 Annual Meeting of the American Political Science Association, Washington, D.C., August 28–31, 1997.
96. Heath, "*Thornburg v. Gingles*," pp. 51–53.
97. Ibid., pp. 54–55.
98. Ibid., pp. 55–59; Charles S. Bullock III, "Symbolics or Substance: A Critique of the At-Large Election Controversy," *State and Local Government Review* 21, no. 3 (Fall 1989): 91–99.

99. Scott Armstrong, "Minorities Seek More Clout on the Bench," *Christian Science Monitor,* October 1, 1991, pp. 1, 2.
100. International City Management Association, *Baseline Data Report: Municipal Election Processes: The Impact on Minority Representation* 19, no. 6 (November–December 1987): 3–4.
101. Ibid., pp. 6–9; Polinard, Wrinkle, and Longoria, "The Impact of District Elections," pp. 608–614.
102. Tim O'Neil, "Blacks Want Half of City's Wards in Redistricting," *St. Louis Post Dispatch,* June 8, 1991, p. 3A.

CHAPTER 5

THE NEW DEAL COALITION AND THE CITIES

THE CHANGING POLITICAL BALANCE

In 1912 a Harvard political scientist wrote that "before many years have passed, the urban population of the United States will have gained numerical mastery."[1] His judgment was based on a simple calculation of demographic change. Though an increasing number of people were beginning to move from the cities to the suburbs in the early years of the twentieth century, the volume of migration to the cities still vastly exceeded the population growth in the suburbs.[2] In the thirty years from 1890 to 1920, more than 18 million immigrants poured into America's cities. These new urban immigrants came mainly from Italy, Poland, Russia, Greece, and Eastern Europe. They were overwhelmingly Roman Catholic and Jewish. They made up the preponderance of the workforces in the iron and steel, meatpacking, mining, and textile industries. Few spoke English, and many were illiterate even in their own language. To so-called native Americans (who were themselves simply the descendants of earlier immigrants), the immigrants and the cities they poured into seemed on the brink of overwhelming the nation's politics and culture. The distrust of cities became amplified into a political reaction against immigrants and their cultures.

The nativist reaction ultimately failed to keep the cities and the people who lived within them from gaining a voice in national politics. In the election of 1928 the ethnic groups clustered in the inner-city immigrant wards began to identify with the national Democratic party. In that year, the Democrats selected an Irish Catholic from New York City, Alfred E. Smith, as their presidential nominee. With Franklin D. Roosevelt's landslide victory in the presidential election of 1932, voters in the industrial cities became crucial to the electoral prospects of the Democratic party. For the first time in the nation's history, the politicians representing urban voters began to wield influence in national politics. Attention to the problems of the cities was guaranteed when both of the national political parties began to win or lose elections on the basis of urban votes.[3] From the Roosevelt presidency until its decline and collapse by the 1980s, the New Deal coalition, which relied on loyal Democratic voters in the South as well as on ethnics, blue-collar workers, and blacks in the industrial cities in the North, provided the foundation for the Democratic party's electoral success in Congress and in presidential elections. Modern American liberalism, as expressed in the New Deal programs of the 1930s and the Great Society programs of the 1960s, can be traced to the pivotal position of city electorates in national politics.

THE POLITICAL ISOLATION OF THE CITIES

Before the 1930s, neither the Republicans nor the Democrats had ever paid much attention to the cities. The national party organizations did not care much about urban voters because they had not had to. Following the Civil War, each of the parties appealed to distinct sectional interests. The Republicans, the triumphant party of Abraham Lincoln, emerged from the war as the dominant national party controlling Congress and the presidency. Between 1860 and 1928, the Republicans won fourteen of eighteen presidential contests and controlled both houses of Congress the majority of the time. Representing eastern finance, industry, and commerce, they enacted high tariffs on foreign imports, gave land to the railroads for westward expansion, and financed canal and river improvements. Republicans opposed taxes on business, encouraged private exploitation (mineral, grazing, homesteading) of federal lands in the West, used troops to quell strikes, and generally promoted a laissez-faire ideology protecting business from regulation.

The Republican party encompassed other political interests as well. It was popular in the middle- and working-class electorates in the North because of the outcome of the Civil War and because it presided during a period of general economic expansion tied closely to frontier development and industrial growth. In the prairie states and in the West, "cattle barons, lumber kings, the mineral exploiters, the land speculators, and the humble homesteaders"[4] identified their prospects with the party. By identifying with the ideas of competitive individualism, the Republicans appealed to all those elements that hankered after the "main chance": "Thanks to a deep-rooted American ideology of individual enterprise, even the small farmers generally remained faithful to the party. . . . They, too, were entrepreneurs, after a fashion."[5] The Republicans' business philosophy fit well with the post–Civil War climate that stressed the exploitation of natural resources and the glorification of unfettered individual enterprise.

In the years after the Civil War, the Democrats became the party of protest. Southerners joined with a loose coalition of groups opposed to economic domination by eastern banks and corporations, the railroads, and "big money." The worst problem with the Democrats' coalition was its instability, for its major issues arose from the insecurities of small farmers about credit and prices, the bitterness of the South, and the tension between business and labor. The party prospered during hard times but lost support when the economy improved. Its only secure base was in the South, where the Republican party—the party of Lincoln—was virtually absent.

In the presidential race of 1896, near the end of a three-year economic depression, the Democrats campaigned on a program advocating government intervention to protect the common man against the "money interests" symbolized by the industrial magnates Andrew Mellon, Andrew Carnegie, James Fisk, and J. P. Morgan. With William Jennings Bryan of Nebraska as its presidential candidate, the party advocated lower tariffs as a means of forcing industrial enterprises to compete with foreign producers by reducing prices. Bryan called for a paper currency backed by silver as well as by gold. Such a move would have increased the amount of money in circulation, thus inducing inflation and helping heavily indebted small business owners and farmers. The Democrats also proposed a graduated federal income tax, government takeover of land grants previously ceded to railroads, and public ownership of telegraphs and telephones. The Democrats lost the election mainly because these positions failed to appeal to workers in the cities, who felt that high tariffs protected their jobs.

Between the elections of 1896 and 1932, several issues helped broaden the electoral base of the Democratic party. In 1900 Bryan was once again the Democratic nominee. This time he fashioned an appeal specifically designed to build support among the urban working class. He assailed trusts and monopolies, claiming that they were crowding out smaller businesses and entrepreneurs. He urged the direct election of senators, opposed government injunctions against strikes, and advocated the creation of a Department of Labor. Bryan saw the possibility of forging a coalition between western farmers, southerners, and industrial labor against big business's control of the nation's money supply, credit, and economic policies. The American Federation of Labor (AFL) endorsed Bryan when he again ran as the Democrats' choice in 1908.

In 1912 the Democrats won the presidency for the first time in the twentieth century. President Woodrow Wilson immediately pushed a distinctively Democratic legislative agenda. The Underwood-Simmons Act lowered tariffs for the first time since 1857 and put wool, lumber, paper, wood pulp, steel rails, and sugar on a free trade list. The prices of these commodities quickly dropped. A graduated income tax was adopted, which shifted federal revenues from reliance on excise taxes and tariffs, which consumers paid in higher prices, to direct taxation on earnings. The Federal Reserve Act of 1913 reformed the banking system. It spread the money supply more evenly across the nation by establishing a dozen regional banks to receive federal deposits, and it increased the money supply by the issuance of notes that did not have to be backed by full value in gold reserves. The Clayton Act and the Federal Trade Act outlawed some unfair business practices (such as price fixing), established boards for voluntary mediation between management and labor, created an eight-hour workday for railroad workers, and provided federal administrative assistance to states and companies to set up workers' compensation programs. The Federal Farm Loan Act extended a very limited amount of credit to farmers. Additionally, the Wilson administration sponsored child labor laws and laws to limit women's work hours, exempted labor unions from antitrust legislation, and encouraged employers to negotiate with organized labor.

Despite these programs, ethnic voters in the cities did not immediately rally to the Democratic banner. About half of the urban party machines were Republican, but whatever their party affiliation, machine leaders had little connection to the national or even the state party organizations. In most states, party leaders came out of the governor's mansion and state legislature, and these tended to be dominated by rural, not city, interests. Machine politicians had gotten into politics through their local precincts and wards and they paid little attention to national candidates and issues. Theirs was a politics of ethnicity and tradeoffs, not of abstract political issues. The machines were strictly local organizations, a product of the segregation of ethnic voters from the rest of American society.

There was little pay or respect for urban ethnic politicians who were elected to the state legislature. It was often a kiss of political death to be sent away to small, conservative upstate or downstate towns like Albany, New York, or Springfield, Illinois, away from friends, family, and the local community. When Tammany Hall sent Al Smith to the state legislature at the age of thirty, he had scarcely been outside New York City. He felt exiled:

> Al Smith went to Albany unprepared to be legislator—or even to sleep away from home. . . . [O]vercome by the intricacies of the legislative process, he sat day after day in the high-ceilinged chamber in silence.
>
> As he sat there staring down at the desk, a page boy would deposit another pile of bills on it. The wording was difficult enough for the expert. It might have been designed to mock a man whose schooling had ended in the eighth grade, who had never liked to read even the simple books of childhood, who, he had once said, had in his entire life read only one book cover to cover: *The Life of John L. Sullivan*.[6]

Before Al Smith, no Tammany politician had ever done much in Albany.

Urban ethnic voters, too, were motivated by their personal loyalties and by their pocketbooks more than by political issues. When precinct captains took them to the polls, they voted for the local party organization, not for a cause. What in their background would excite them about national issues and candidates—tariff policy, child labor legislation, William Jennings Bryan, Woodrow Wilson? The upshot was that although many cities were dominated by powerful party machines, the leaders of these organizations and their loyal constituents had only occasionally become important in gubernatorial contests and had hardly figured at all in presidential elections.

Though President Wilson sponsored several programs in response to demands made by labor unions during World War I and though Bryan had campaigned for a Labor Department and for laws against strike injunctions in the presidential elections of 1896 and 1900, the national Democratic party had not transformed itself into anything resembling an urban working-class party. Far from it. Its center of gravity was still found in the South and on the farm. When the urban wing of the party began to grow in strength, a potentially devastating split developed between the cities and the party's southern wing. By the 1920s, the party was bitterly divided.

THE NEW URBAN CONSCIOUSNESS

The cleavages within the Democratic party mirrored the urban-rural conflicts that obsessed the nation. Rural Democrats feared that the urban wing of their party might someday command a voting majority. A similar concern preyed on the minds of native Protestants. What would happen to political and religious traditions if the barbarous hordes from Europe took over? The ever-present nineteenth-century nervousness about the "strangers in the land" escalated into a national phobia in the twentieth century. The rise of the cities in national politics began when nativist Protestant elements launched a national assault on the city machines and their immigrant constituents. In doing so, they created issues that an urban electorate could easily understand.

Prohibition constituted a direct assault on the cities. Proposed to the states by Congress in 1917 and ratified in 1919, the Eighteenth Amendment prohibited the sale, use, and distribution of alcoholic beverages. Small-town Methodists and Baptists—joined in their crusade by upper- and middle-class Protestants in the cities and in the new suburbs—hoped to reduce poverty, improve workers' efficiency and family life, and end immorality and crime by forcing the immigrants to abstain from alcohol. Prohibition became the most compelling political issue of the 1920s, for it represented a frontal assault upon the cultural values and customs of the immigrants:

> [Drinking] was associated with the saloonkeepers who ran the city machines and who used the votes of the whiskey-loving immigrant . . . with the German brewers and their "disloyal" compatriots who drank beer and ale. . . . The cities, which resisted the idea that "thou shalt not" was the fundamental precept of living, were always hostile to prohibition. The prohibitionists, in turn, regarded the city as their chief enemy, and prohibitionism and a pervasive antiurbanism went hand-in-hand.[7]

To rural and urban Protestants, the sins of liquor were indistinguishable from the sins of the immigrants. Southern and western newspapers reflexively connected crime, national origin, and liquor. When it was not legitimate to attack foreigners directly, it was easy to attack them through the surrogate liquor issue, allowing "prohibition partisans to talk about morality when in reality they were worried about cultural dominance and political supremacy."[8]

Prohibition was intimately connected to religious conflict. To Protestant Americans, the Roman Catholic church was evil incarnate. It signified ostentatious authority—the robes, the ceremony, and the architecture of Catholic cathedrals bespeaking a menace to the simplicity and informality of small-town life. Like the right-wing groups of the 1950s obsessed by the specter of an international Communist conspiracy poised to subvert American politics, religious fundamentalists of the early twentieth century were convinced that the Roman Catholic Church was intent on subverting civil authority around the world.

Feeding on such fears, the Ku Klux Klan attracted millions of members. Revived in Atlanta in 1915, for a few years the Klan enjoyed spectacular growth in both the North and the South. Klan membership skyrocketed in California, Oregon, Indiana, Illinois, Ohio, Oklahoma, Texas, Arkansas, and throughout the South. At its peak in 1924, 40 percent of the Klan's membership resided in Ohio, Indiana, and Illinois. Half of its membership was located in cities of more than 50,000, with chapters of hundreds of members in such cities as Chicago, Detroit, Indianapolis, Pittsburgh, Baltimore, and Buffalo.[9] The Klan was a powerful political force until at least the mid-1920s. It helped elect a member of the Senate; governors in Georgia, Alabama, Oregon, and California; and seventy-five members of the House of Representatives.

Though the Klan found its strongest support among lower-middle-class fundamentalist Christians, its basic message reached a broad audience. In 1916, Madison Grant, curator of New York City's Museum of National History, published a book entitled *The Passing of the Great Race,* in which he worried that Aryans might someday be overwhelmed by dark-skinned races. His book was elevated to the status of a scientific work, along with Lothrop Stoddard's *The Rising Tide of Color Against the White World-Supremacy* (1921).

Congress responded to the rising xenophobia with the Emergency Quota Act of 1921 and the National Origins Act of 1924. Both laws drew support from a broad range of groups made up of intellectuals, labor leaders, southerners, western farmers, and many others. The Emergency Quota Act reaffirmed the total exclusion of Orientals and established a national origins quota of 3 percent of each nationality's proportion of the U.S. population as recorded in the 1910 census. The law succeeded in cutting immigration from 805,228 in 1920 to 309,556 in 1921–1922.[10] The National Origins Act further reduced the origins quota to 2 percent and established the 1890 census as the baseline for calculating the quota. By changing the baseline census used for calculating the percentage, Congress was able to sharply reduce the quotas for those nationality groups that had flooded into the country after 1890. Italian immigration was reduced by 90 percent; British and Irish immigration, by contrast, declined by just 19 percent.[11] The total number of immigrants fell drastically, from 357,803 in 1923–1924 to 164,667 in 1924–1925.

In debates on these two bills, members of Congress reviled the foreign-born of the cities in language not unlike that found in Ku Klux Klan pamphlets. This assault helped make immigrants aware of how deeply national politics could affect them and in the 1920s they began to express their new awareness. Before long it became apparent that they "were not going to support candidates who wanted them to stop drinking, Protestantize their schools, or tell them as often as possible that they were inferior."[12]

THE URBAN WING OF THE DEMOCRATIC PARTY

The prosperity of the 1920s came as a serious blow to the Democratic party because the party's coalition had long been held together mainly with the glue of shared grievances. The party was composed of an unlikely combination of eastern and northern urban ethnics; western farmers and prohibitionists; and southern, dry, Klan-saturated religious fundamentalists. The fragility of this coalition was revealed by the 1924 Democratic convention, held in Madison Square Garden in New York City. The Democrats treated the first radio audience of a national convention to a futile 103-ballot marathon. The galleries booed the speeches of southerners and westerners, especially when William Jennings Bryan asked the convention to reject a proposed resolution condemning the Ku Klux Klan by name. The resolution to condemn the Klan brought forth such heated oratory that police were brought onto the convention floor in case a free-for-all broke out. Delegates shouted and cursed at one another. When the final vote on the resolution to condemn the Klan was taken, it lost by one vote, 542 $\frac{3}{20}$ to 541 $\frac{3}{20}$. Demands for a recount were drowned out when the band struck up "Marching Through Georgia." After sixteen days, the convention finally nominated a presidential candidate neither the rural nor the urban delegates wanted.

The delegates from the towns and farms of the South and West were disoriented and frightened by the crowds and the din of New York City. They found New Yorkers unfriendly and rude, and the city seemed all too easy to get lost in. Delegates who "wandered downtown to Fourteenth Street to gawk at Tammany Hall with its ancient Indian above the door reacted as if they expected to see an ogre come popping out. Almost all delegates were dismayed by the New York traffic, the noise and hustle."[13] Their antagonisms toward the city were reaffirmed every day the convention dragged on through the muggy July heat. Small-town reporters filled their hometown newspapers with vivid accounts of the horrors of the city.[14]

Despite these divisions, only four years later the Democrats nominated Al Smith, the four-term governor of New York, for the presidency. Smith projected everything that was anathema to the city haters. He was a self-made Catholic graduate of Tammany Hall. He said "foist" instead of "first" and wore a brown derby, which only accentuated his bulbous nose and ruddy complexion. He proudly reminisced about his past: swimming in the East River and working at the Fulton Fish Market as an errand boy. Considering the divisive conflicts within the party, how could he have been nominated? Once he had been nominated, why did the party not simply come apart?

The southern and western factions had little choice but to stay within the fold. In spite of their differences, the Democrats had come to share, however crudely, a class interest. The party had symbolically become—mostly by default because the Republicans took a pro-business stand—the "little man's" party. Those who opposed Republican policies could never hope to have a voice in national presidential politics unless they aligned with the Democrats.

The time was ripe for compromise. Few Democrats thought that Smith could win, but no candidate was available who was capable of bridging the gap between the disparate factions. In addition, Smith had acquired broad political support. As the four-term governor of New York, he had gained national prominence as a progressive governor who had created state parks and beaches, sponsored workers' safety legislation, and financed public improvements throughout the state. He had reorganized state government, making New York the model for progressives who believed in efficiency principles. Admired by progressives for his record as governor and supported by Democratic organizations with ethnic constituencies, his nomination could be denied by rural delegates, but only at the cost of another fiasco like 1924—multiple ballots and a guaranteed loss for the presidential nominee. There was even reason to believe that Smith might have a chance. In his victorious gubernatorial run in 1924, he had received 100,000 more votes than the losing Democratic presidential ticket in New York.

In 1928, the Democrats gave the nomination to Al Smith. Though he lost the election, his candidacy marked the beginning of the party's political ascendancy in the big cities. The election of 1928 marked a significant change in the attitude of the urban masses. Both in 1920 and 1924, the twelve largest cities in the United States had, taken together, given a decisive majority to the Republicans; now the tables were turned, and the Democrats came out ahead. As later elections were to prove, this marked the beginning of a long-term urban trend.[15]

For the Roman Catholic ethnics in the cities, Smith's campaign sharpened their perception of the national issues of Prohibition, ethnicity, and religion. Smith campaigned with his brown derby and his theme song, "The Sidewalks of New York." Protestants shuddered at the idea of a Catholic in the White House. Smith's equivocal stand on Prohibition made drink the main issue of the campaign. Blue-blood upper-class Protestants found him beneath them. The campaign highlighted the issues of race, religion, culture, and social class so clearly that never again would the ethnics be unmindful of their stake in national politics. The election of 1928 brought a Democratic electoral plurality to the cities of the nation (see Table 5.1). Since then, the major cities have normally voted heavily Democratic, and until the 1980s they were a mainstay of the Democratic party's electoral strength. Al Smith's candidacy broke new ground for a recognition of the role of cities in American politics. What cemented the relationship between the cities and the Democratic party was the Great Depression and Franklin Delano Roosevelt's New Deal.

THE DEPRESSION AND THE CITIES

The Great Depression came as a shock to Americans and to their public leaders. The 1920s had been a decade of prosperity and optimism, especially for the rapidly growing middle class. Business leaders and politicians promoted the idea that the potential for sustained economic growth was limitless. A strong undertow of poverty ran below the surface, in the immigrant slums and on farms alike, but on the surface the signs of prosperity prevailed. It was an age that extolled mass consumption and complacency. The discontents of the industrial order seemed long past.

TABLE 5.1	THE REVOLT OF THE CITY: VOTING IN THE LARGEST TWELVE CITIES
Year	Net Party Plurality
1920	1,540,000 Republican
1924	1,308,000 Republican
1928	210,000 Democratic
1932	1,791,000 Democratic
1936	3,479,000 Democratic
1940	2,112,000 Democratic
1944	2,230,000 Democratic
1948	1,481,000 Democratic

The cities in this table include New York, Chicago, Philadelphia, Pittsburgh, Detroit, Cleveland, Baltimore, St. Louis, Boston, San Francisco, Milwaukee, and Los Angeles.

Source: Reprinted from the table on page 49 in *The Future of American Politics,* 3rd Revised Edition by Samuel Lubell. © 1951, 1952, 1956, 1965 by Samuel Lubell. Reprinted by permission of Harper & Row, Publishers, Inc.

The symbolic beginning of the Great Depression occurred on October 24, 1929. On that day—Black Thursday—disorder, panic, and confusion reigned on the New York Stock Exchange. Stock prices virtually collapsed. For several months prices had sagged, then risen, then sagged again, with each trough lower than the previous and each peak less convincing. When the bottom fell out, "the Market . . . degenerated into a wild, mad scramble to sell, . . . the Market . . . surrendered to blind, relentless fear."[16] In one morning, eleven well-known speculators committed suicide. From Wall Street the economic catastrophe rippled outward, with consequences that would fundamentally reshape American politics.

Over the next three years the nation sank steadily deeper into economic stagnation. In the spring of 1929, the unemployment rate stood at 3.2 percent. Within a few months, the number of unemployed exceeded 4 million, representing 8.7 percent of the labor force.[17] By 1932, 23.6 percent of all workers—more than 12 million workers in all—could not find jobs. In the depths of the depression, during the spring of 1933, the number of unemployed reached 13 million workers, fully 25 percent of the labor force.[18]

The depression dragged on for a decade. Unemployment levels remained above 20 percent in both 1934 and 1935 and dropped below 15 percent only in 1937. Most of those who managed to find work made less than before. From 1929 to 1933, the average income of workers fell by 42.5 percent.[19] Weekly wages dropped from an average of $28 in 1929 to $17 by 1934, and workers faced the ever-present threat of layoffs. Many jobs were reduced from full-time to part-time status, and employers cut wages and hours to meet payrolls. For example, the payroll of the nation's largest steel company, U.S. Steel, was cut in half from 1929 to 1933, and in 1933 it had no full-time workers at all.[20] Steel mills operated at only 12 percent of capacity by 1932.[21]

The productive capacity of business seemed irreparably damaged. In the three years following the stock market collapse, national income fell by 44.5 percent. By the summer of 1932, stocks had fallen 83 percent below their value in September 1929.[22] By the end of 1932, 5,096 commercial banks had failed. Farm income declined from $7 billion in 1929 to $2.5 billion in 1932.[23] For many farmers whose incomes had been sharply dropping throughout the 1920s, the depression was the final blow.

The statistics only hinted at the extent of human suffering. Between 1 million and 2 million men rode the rails and gathered in hobo jungles or camped in thickets and railroad cars. Others lived in "Hoovervilles," clusters of cardboard, scrap wood, and scrap metal shacks in empty lots and city parks. Those who had been chronically poor in the 1920s were now hungry and destitute. They stood in bread lines, ate from garbage cans, or went begging from door to door. One-quarter of all homeowners lost their homes in 1932, and more than 1,000 mortgages a day were foreclosed in the first half of 1933.[24] By March 1933, when Franklin D. Roosevelt was inaugurated as president, 9 million savings accounts had been lost.[25]

Never before had the nation faced such an economic catastrophe, nor was there a tradition of federal government assistance for the unemployed and destitute.[26] Unemployment and poverty were certainly not new. In the period from 1897 to 1926 unemployment levels in four major industries fluctuated around the 10 percent level,[27] and poverty was a chronic condition of industrialization and immigration. What made this depression unique was its depth, persistence, and broad reach. In earlier depressions, including the panics of the 1870s and 1890s, production and employment declined much less severely and the recovery began within a year or two.[28] The depression of the 1930s lasted for over a decade, it touched all classes, and its effects were felt by rich and poor alike. The measure of the crisis of the 1930s was not just unemployment and poverty, but the breakdown of economic institutions.

No one knew how to respond. President Herbert Hoover firmly resisted intervention by the federal government and instead launched two national drives to encourage private relief. Late in 1930, he appointed the President's Emergency Committee for Employment. Its main task was to encourage state and local committees to expedite public construction and to coordinate the public and private giving of relief. In August 1931, he formed the President's Organization on Unemployment Relief, whose job was to help organize private unemployment committees in states and communities.

Despite Hoover's undying opposition to federal intervention, two major programs were funded during his administration. First, the Federal Home Loan Bank Act supplied capital advances to a small number of mortgage institutions so that they could forbear rather than foreclose on mortgages in default. A few banks were saved by this program. Second, the Emergency Relief and Construction Act extended $300 million in loans to state and local governments so that they could continue to provide relief to indigent people.

Hoover was hardly alone in opposing an expanded federal role. Until 1932, most governors took a "we'll do it ourselves" attitude toward solving unemployment and its associated problems.[29] Two governors refused to work with the President's Organization on Unemployment Relief, even though federal funds were not involved.[30] The officials of financially strapped local governments were also skeptical of federal aid. In July 1931 the socialist mayor of Milwaukee wrote to the mayors of the largest one hundred cities asking them to come to a conference with the purpose of requesting a national relief program. He got no response at all from several of the major cities, and several mayors criticized the idea on the premise that federal aid would constitute "an invasion of community rights."[31]

In the 1932 campaign, the Democrats accused Hoover of doing too much rather than too little. Their nominee, Franklin Delano Roosevelt, promised to balance the budget while accusing Hoover of having presided over "the greatest spending administration in peace times in all our history."[32] It was apparent that the weight of the past lay heavily on both political parties. Against a cultural tradition that extolled individualism and free enterprise, there was great reluctance to expand the powers of government—especially the federal government—to meet the crisis. Nevertheless, when Roosevelt was inaugurated on March 4, 1933, he set in motion a concentrated period of reform that vastly increased the powers of the federal government in areas of business regulation, farm policy, and social insurance. Why did Roosevelt break so thoroughly from tradition?

Roosevelt's change of heart was motivated by the overwhelming sense of crisis that ushered him into the White House. Between his election in November and his inauguration in March, the nation passed through the worst months of the depression. The economy teetered on the brink of complete collapse. In February 1933 some of the nation's biggest banks failed; "People stood in long queues with satchels and paper bags to take gold and currency away from the banks to store in mattresses and old shoe boxes. It seemed safer to put your life's savings in the attic than to trust the financial institutions in the country."[33] Roosevelt wondered if there would be anything left to salvage by the time he assumed office. By inauguration day, thirty-eight states had closed their banks, and on that day the governors of New York and Illinois closed the nation's biggest banks.[34] The New York Stock Exchange stopped trading. The Kansas City and Chicago Boards of Trade closed their doors; "In the once-busy grain pits of Chicago, in the canyons of Wall Street, all was silent."[35]

It was also one of the harshest winters on record. In desperation, people overran relief offices and rioted at bank closings. Relief marchers invaded state legislative chambers. Farmers tried to stop foreclosure proceedings and blockaded roads. Amid marches, riots, arrests, and jailings, politicians feared a revolution.

The first one hundred days of Roosevelt's administration were characterized by frenetic activity.[36] On March 9th, Roosevelt signed the Emergency Banking Act. The act extended financial assistance to bankers so they could reopen their doors and gave the government authority to reorganize banks and to control bank credit policies. It received a unanimous vote from a panicked Congress, sight unseen. A flurry of legislation followed: the Civilian Conservation Corps (March 31), the Agricultural Adjustment Act and the Federal Emergency Relief Act (May 12), the Tennessee Valley Authority (May 18), the Federal "Truth in Securities" Act (May 27), the Home Owners' Loan Act (June 13), the National Industrial Recovery Act (June 16), and more than a score of other bills.

Most of the legislative onslaught was designed to stimulate, regulate, and stabilize the most important economic institutions of the economy. But the benefits filtered down. After the Emergency Banking Act was passed, depositors gained confidence and redeposited their savings. Under the National Housing Act (adopted in 1934), home buyers could secure long-term mortgages from banks whose loans were guaranteed by the federal government. Foreclosures on farms and homes were sharply reduced when the government, through the Farm Credit Administration and Home Owners' Loan Corporation, agreed to buy up defaulted mortgages. New Deal programs affected many people's lives by salvaging their savings, houses, and farms. Nevertheless, the New Deal's attempts to reform the economy were designed more to bring stability to financial institutions than to fight poverty and destitution. Home lending and farm credit programs primarily helped the nation's important economic institutions and secondarily aided the heavily mortgaged middle class.

The other side of the New Deal included its public works and relief programs, which assisted millions of unemployed and penniless people. These programs vastly broadened the Democratic coalition by bringing into the fold the same elements that had identified with Al Smith. For millions of families the New Deal meant the difference between hunger and having food, between unemployment and finding a job. Between 1933 and 1937 the federal government administered public works programs for several million people and supplied direct relief to millions more. The earliest of the public works programs was the Civilian Conservation Corps (CCC), established on March 31, 1933. In all, more than 2.5 million boys and young men were employed by the CCC. In 1935 alone, 500,000 men were living in CCC camps. They planted trees, built dams, fought fires, stocked fish, built lookout towers, dug ditches and canals, strung telephone lines, and built and improved bridges, roads, and trails. Their contribution to conservation was enormous: The CCC was responsible for more than half of all the forest planted in the United States up to the 1960s.[37]

The Civil Works Administration (CWA) was much larger and broader in scope. Established in November 1933, it employed 4.1 million by the third week of January 1934.[38] In a few months it employed almost a third of the unemployed labor force. Although the CWA lasted for less than a year—Roosevelt ended it in the spring of 1934 because he thought it was too costly—it enabled many families to survive the bitter winter of 1934. The CWA was "immensely popular—with merchants, with local officials, and with workers," and its demise was resisted in Congress.[39] The Public Works Administration (PWA) enjoyed a longer run, and its impact was more lasting. In six years, from 1933 to 1939, the PWA built 70 percent of the new school buildings in the nation and 35 percent of the hospitals and public health facilities.[40]

The Federal Emergency Relief Act (FERA), signed into law on May 12, 1935, was never as popular as public works legislation, for it undercut the cherished principles of work and independence by making relief money directly available to the destitute. Roosevelt himself viewed the Federal Emergency Relief Administration with distaste, thinking that it would sap the moral strength of the poor. Though Roosevelt constantly sought ways to cut its budget and though its benefit levels were extraordinarily low, it was mandated by the want and the civil disorder that prevailed in Roosevelt's first term. In the winter of 1934, 20 million people received FERA funds.[41]

The FERA was treated as an embarrassing necessity. The government's response was understood to be an emergency measure, comparable to helping victims of catastrophes such as floods, earthquakes, and tornadoes. Congressional debate on the FERA received little coverage by the media. When the act was passed on May 9, 1933, the *New York Times* mentioned it on page 3 only in a column listing legislation passed by Congress. When it was signed by President Roosevelt on May 12, it made page 21 of the *Times,* but only in reference to the appointment of the administrator. In a culture that extolled individualism, competition, and hard work, people were ill at ease with the idea of relief.

Franklin Roosevelt often expressed doubts about relief and public works programs. He preferred economic recovery to government spending. But his response to the economic emergency broadened the base of the Democratic party. Public works and relief created a loyal following among middle- and working-class people who were benefited. By the 1936 election, and for decades thereafter, voting in small towns split between the Republicans on the "right" side of the tracks and the working class and poor on the other. The most reliable new Democratic following, however, could be found in the cities. Urban ethnics, especially if they were union members, learned to vote Democratic. The loyalty of black voters to the Republican party was broken by New Deal programs. Before the 1936 election, a prominent black publisher counseled, "My friends, go turn Lincoln's picture to the wall. That debt has been paid in full."[42] In the 1936 election blacks gave Roosevelt 75 percent of their votes.

The Great Depression revolutionized the group composition of the party system in the United States. Both parties became more class-oriented than before. In addition to its traditional base in the South, the Democrats now claimed solid support among workers, blacks, and the poor in the northern cities, where large numbers of the working class and the poor were concentrated. Additionally, so many people benefited through New Deal programs that the electoral coalition supporting the party broadened sufficiently to ensure that the Democrats would become the ascendant national party. In 1936 the Gallup poll found that 59 percent of farmers favored Roosevelt (Agricultural Adjustment Act, Farm Credit Administration, Farm Mortgage Corporation, abolition of the gold standard); 61 percent of white-collar workers (bank regulation, Federal Housing Administration, savings deposit insurance); 80 percent of organized labor (government recognition of collective bargaining, unemployment insurance, work relief); and 68 percent of people under 25 (Civilian Conservation Corps, National Youth Administration). Among lower-income groups, 76 percent favored Roosevelt, compared with 60 percent of the middle class.[43] In contrast, upper-income groups identified overwhelmingly with the Republican party.

THE CITIES IN THE INTERGOVERNMENTAL SYSTEM

The depression years marked a turning point in American politics. Presidential candidates and a large number of Senators and House members knew that they needed to campaign for the votes of people living in cities. To secure the votes of urban ethnics, they supported the New Deal's initiatives. Another development also enhanced the influence of urban political representatives: the forging of a direct relationship between federal policymakers and city governments. Three elements stand out as key factors in this development: (1) the crisis in the cities; (2) the intransigence of the states; and (3) the forging of an alliance among city officials for the purpose of securing a federal response to their problems.

Even before Roosevelt took office, the cities had exhausted their resources. In the 1920s, they had borrowed heavily to finance public improvements and capital construction. They were already seriously in debt when the onset of the depression confronted them with rising unemployment and poverty. Local officials could not avoid seeing the misery and want on their streets. Faced with a manifest emergency, they provided relief funds as rapidly as they could, but it was not enough. Municipal governments simply lacked the financial resources to cope with the emergency.

During the 1920s, counties and municipalities financed a multitude of new public improvement programs. The government activity represented a response to the automobile, to middle-class demands for improved public education, and to public demands for parks and recreational facilities. The auto imposed heavy new costs on local governments. Cities invested in traffic signals, police cars, garbage trucks, school buses, snowplows, roads, and bus and airline terminals. The cities increased spending for education, and built new school buildings, public libraries, and invested heavily in improving parks and recreational facilities.

Local governments made heavier investments in these areas than did either the state or federal governments. During the 1920s, counties and municipalities spent 55 percent to 60 percent of all public funds in the nation, and their total debts mounted to $9 billion.[44] From 1923 to 1927, while the states increased expenditures by 43 percent, spending by the largest 145 cities rose by 79 percent, and cities of 100,000 or more increased their budgets by 82 percent.[45] In these latter cities expenditures for work relief and welfare shot up 391 percent from 1923 to 1932, while the states in this period increased their public welfare budgets by only 63 percent. In the last year of the Hoover Administration, the thirteen cities with populations above 100,000 spent $53 million more than all the states combined for public welfare. Federal grants as a percentage of all public expenditures actually declined from 2 percent to 1.3 percent over the decade of the 1920s.[46] The thirteen biggest cities incurred 50 percent more debt during this period, and many of them were hard-pressed, even at the beginning of the depression, to pay for government services and public improvements.[47]

The depression placed unprecedented responsibilities on city officials at the very time that fiscal resources were drying up. Cities could not expand tax revenues to keep pace with increased responsibilities. Two-thirds of the revenue for city budgets derived from property taxes, and these declined precipitously between 1929 and 1933. As assessments on deteriorating property plummeted, property tax revenues fell by 20 percent during the four-year period.[48] At the same time, the rate of tax delinquency increased from 10 percent to 26 percent in cities of over 50,000 in population.[49] Tax losses resulted in an actual reduction in the budgets of the largest thirteen cities between 1931 and 1933, from $1.8 to $1.6 billion.[50] State-imposed debt limitations did not allow cities to borrow for day-to-day services. Cities were allowed, in principle, to borrow for capital improvements, but this option soon evaporated. By 1932, because of their high debt loads, cities found it impossible to sell long-term bond issues to investors. In 1932 and 1933, many states and municipalities, including Mississippi, Montana, Buffalo, Philadelphia, Cleveland, and Toledo, were unable to market any bond issues at all.[51] Temporary loans with high interest rates replaced long-term notes.

When the cities financed public works programs to help the unemployed, their budgets quickly ran dry. Municipal governments lacked sufficient resources to treat the depression's symptoms, yet many mayors saw this as their principal mission. Detroit's experience revealed the impossibility of the task. In the fall of 1930, Frank Murphy won a surprise victory in a special mayoralty election on a campaign promising unemployment relief.[52] His efforts to provide relief by expanding public jobs and welfare in Detroit attracted national attention. He appointed an unemployment committee, operated an employment bureau, sponsored public works projects, raised private donations for poor relief, and consulted with private firms about rehiring workers. Detroit did more than any other city for its unemployed, but its compassion was costly. With over 40,000 families receiving relief and one-third of the work force unemployed, it was spending $2 million a month for relief in 1931, far more than second-place Boston.[53]

The burden soon brought financial disaster to the city, and by the spring of 1931, Detroit faced municipal bankruptcy. To avoid default on its debts and payroll, Murphy curtailed the city's health and recreational services and slashed the fire and police department budgets. Only an emergency bank loan allowed Murphy to meet the June 1931 payroll, but even this measure was insufficient. Under pressure from the New York banks that held most of Detroit's bonds, Murphy was forced to cut relief expenditures in half during 1932. Thousands of families were dropped from the relief rolls as it became obvious that Detroit could not single-handedly solve the local problems caused by a national depression.

The mayors of other cities were learning the same lesson. Finally, their sense of desperation galvanized them to take action. In the spring of 1932, Murphy invited the mayors of the major cities to a conference. In June representatives from twenty-nine cities met in Detroit with a single purpose in mind. Murphy stated the cities' case succinctly: "We have done everything humanly possible to do, and it has not been enough. The hour is at hand for the federal government to cooperate."[54] New York City's mayor likewise pleaded for assistance:

> The municipal government is the maternal, the intimate side of government; the side with heart. The Federal Government doesn't have to wander through darkened hallways of our hospitals, to witness the pain and suffering there. It doesn't have to stand in the bread lines, but the time has come when it must face the facts and its responsibility.
>
> We of the cities have diagnosed and thus far met the problem; but we have come to the end of our resources. It is now up to the Federal Government to assume its share. We can't cure conditions by ourselves.[55]

The mayors' demands for federal assistance marked a turning point. Historically, there had been no direct relationship between cities and the federal government. Many local officials felt it was illegitimate to ask the federal government for help, and others feared any aid, thinking it might cause their cities to lose their independence. Only a few months before, most of the mayors had declined to attend a similar mayors' conference suggested by the mayor of Milwaukee.[56] Desperation finally brought about a change of heart.

The situation was made worse by the fact that state governments refused to respond to the cities' plight. While municipal governments' expenditures for jobs and relief skyrocketed, the states sharply cut back: "As tax revenues dwindled and unemployment increased, economy in government became a magic word."[57] State officials were more concerned with balancing budgets than with alleviating human suffering. As state tax revenues declined, public works and construction programs were curtailed. Whereas in 1928 the states had spent $1.35 billion for public works projects, mainly in the form of road building, this amount was reduced to $630 million by 1932 and to $290 million for the first eight months of 1933.[58] Because these budget cuts reduced public payrolls, they aggravated the unemployment crisis.

Per capita spending for highways and education fell only slightly from 1927 to 1932,[59] but in some states budgets were cut drastically. Tennessee, for example, failed to provide funds for its rural schools for much of 1931.[60] Beginning in 1932, several states slashed their budgets: Arizona by 35 percent; Texas, Illinois, and Vermont by 25 percent; South Carolina by 33 percent. State educational institutions, especially universities, were hard hit. During 1933, education budgets dropped by 40 percent in Maryland, 53 percent in Wyoming, and more than 30 percent in several other states.[61]

Relief spending by the states went up in the early years of the depression, from $1.00 per capita in 1927 to $3.50 four years later.[62] But the overall amount of welfare spending was small and failed to come close to what was needed. The overall statistics, in any case, masked a tremendous variation among the states.

From mid-1931 to the end of 1932, welfare spending by the states increased from $500,000 to $100 million, but nearly all the money was provided by a few states, principally New York, New Jersey, and Pennsylvania.[63] When the New Deal began, only eight states provided any money at all for relief.[64]

Local officials petitioned the states for help, and their pleas sounded increasingly desperate as the depression wore on.[65] Except for the very few states that provided relief payments to the unemployed, no response was forthcoming. The states' indifference prompted the mayors of Michigan's cities, led by Frank Murphy, to issue an appeal for federal assistance. Their fears that such aid would compromise local autonomy were overcome by the corruption and conservatism of their state's government.[66]

State governments were slow to respond to the needs of their cities because their legislatures were controlled by rural representatives. In state after state, legislative districts were drawn up to ensure that rural counties would outvote cities in the state legislative chambers. In Georgia, each county was represented equally in the legislature, regardless of its population.[67] Louisiana likewise provided that each parish would have at least one representative in the state senate and house. Rhode Island applied this standard to each town.[68] Without exception, all the states made sure that representatives from rural areas would continue to hold legislative majorities, no matter how much a state's population became concentrated in the cities.

There were important political stakes in this pattern of underrepresentation. If cities were allowed to gain majorities in legislatures because of their growing populations, political alignments and party structures would fundamentally change. Incumbent rural legislators would lose their positions, and a shift in legislative power would inevitably result in new governmental policies. The persistent underrepresentation of urban areas resulted in indifference to urban problems. Traffic congestion, slums, inadequate park space, and smoke pollution did not interest rural and small-town legislators. Governors, too, tended to be insensitive to urban problems. Governors' and legislators' national conferences studiously ignored the depression. At the 1930 governors' conference in Salt Lake City, for example, the major topics of discussion included such topics as the essentials of a model state constitution, the need for constitutional revisions, constitutional versus legislative home rule for cities, and the extent of legislative control of city governments.[69] The 1931 conference likewise ignored the economic crisis. In the face of such indifference, the cities had nowhere to go but to the federal government.

Urban leaders could not necessarily expect favorable action from the federal government, either. Conditions in many rural areas were even worse than in the cities. There was grinding poverty in the Appalachian region and throughout the South; families lived in one-room hovels, children walked around with distended bellies caused by malnutrition, and some parents could not afford to clothe their children to send them to school. A drought from the Midwest to the Rockies turned much of the plains into a vast dust bowl; in the winter of 1934, New England's snow turned red from the huge billowing clouds of dust blowing from Texas, Kansas, and Oklahoma. Families left the ravaged land by the thousands; the experiences of those heading for California provided the grist for John Steinbeck's novel, *The Grapes of Wrath*.

Not only was there compelling need in rural areas, but Roosevelt and his advisers distrusted city politics and culture. For example, Roosevelt's first public works program, the Civilian Conservation Corps, was based on his feeling that the moral character of unemployed youth in the cities would be improved by living in the country.[70] Roosevelt felt "small love for the city."[71] One of the president's closest advisers confessed that "since my graduate-school days, I have always been able to excite myself more about the wrongs of farmers than those of urban workers."[72] In its first two years, the New Deal accomplished a comprehensive farm policy of guaranteed price supports, crop allotments to reduce supplies and increase prices, and federally guaranteed mortgages. By contrast, it produced its first program specifically for the cities, the Wagner-Steagall Housing Act, in 1937, and that program provided slum clearance and public housing on a very limited scale.

Despite the initial indifference to the plight of the cities, city officials were able to forge close relationships with politicians and administrators in Washington, D.C. The New Deal's first relief and recovery programs were administered through the states, but federal programs were later enacted that put local officials in charge. The three major public works programs—the Public Works Administration, Civilian Works Administration, and the Works Progress Administration—were administered by federal officials in cooperation with both state and local officials. The Federal Emergency Relief funds were channeled through the states, but local relief agencies actually administered the funds. In several cities such as New York, Pittsburgh, and Kansas City, local Democratic party organizations found that the new federal resources allowed them to rebuild machines that had almost fallen apart.[73] Local officials found themselves testifying to congressional committees about programs that affected the cities. By 1934, a southern mayor observed: "Mayors are a familiar sight in Washington these days. Whether we like it or not, the destinies of our cities are clearly tied in with national politics."[74]

The New Deal transformed American politics. Local officials learned to petition the federal government for help. This learning process took two forms. First, it became legitimate to seek federal assistance. Second, local officials formed an enduring urban lobby organized specifically to represent cities in the federal system. It was the coming of age for cities in American national politics. Through the United States Conference of Mayors (USCM), formed in 1932, mayors met annually to discuss their mutual problems. The USCM financed a permanent office in Washington to lobby for urban programs. Together with the International City Management Association, the National Municipal League, the American Municipal League, and other organizations representing local public officials, cities developed the capacity to lobby federal administrators, Congress, and the White House. In subsequent decades, these organizations began to wield significant influence in Washington.

THE CITIES IN NATIONAL POLITICS

By the mid-1930s, the nation had completed one political cycle and entered another. For the century and a half since the nation's founding, the conflict between rural America and the cities steadily worsened. Overall, the cities seemed to be the losers. Cities had little or no influence in state houses and in Washington, and it seemed unlikely that this situation would change. State legislatures were careful to apportion seats in their legislatures to guarantee rural control. Cities were the losers in a cultural sense as well. Urban and rural nativists launched repeated attacks on the immigrants' religious traditions and social customs. Though ethnic community life and the party machines provided some buffer against the attacks, racism and xenophobia ran rampant.

The Great Depression expanded the reach of the federal government. For the first time, federal agencies were granted powers to regulate the economy and to assist citizens during times of need. Urban working-class people were benefited by labor legislation such as Section 7a of the National Industrial Recovery Act and the Wagner Labor Act, which implemented workers' compensation, factory regulations, and the right of workers to organize unions. Craft and industrial unions became important participants in the New Deal coalition.

Urban working-class whites and the black electorate became important to the northern wing of the Democratic party. Though it was a long way from their collective vote to Congress and the White House, the potential for political influence was obvious, and it soon was felt. Prohibition was repealed in 1933. Even in the 1930s, long before civil rights legislation was possible, the Roosevelt Administration took steps to ensure that blacks received a few appointments to federal posts and a share of the benefits from job and relief programs.

The first urban programs also were passed. Through the 1937 Housing Act, the federal government undertook slum clearance and built public housing. In the late 1930s, federal policymakers expressed a concern about urban problems. The National Resources Committee, composed of federal administrators and experts appointed by the president, published a report in 1937 entitled *Our Cities: Their Role in the National Economy*.[75] The committee asserted that slums and urban blight threatened a hoped-for economic recovery and recommended federal action to improve the economic performance of cities. In 1941 the National Resources Planning Board prepared a report entitled *Action for Cities: A Guide for Community Planning*. The report recommended that cities devise local plans to combat blight and that the federal government provide assistance for this purpose.[76] In 1944 a federally assisted highways bill was enacted; unlike previous highway legislation, this time the cities got their fair share of construction money. Five years later, in 1949, Congress passed a massive program to build public housing and clear slums in the inner cities.

The cities' new position in the federal system was only partially assured when they learned to vote Democratic. It was further enhanced when city officials became convinced that they could rightfully lobby for their interests in Washington. It is true that between 1953 and 1961, when a Republican president,

Dwight Eisenhower, served in the White House, urban interests were able to push through only one significant new program, the Interstate Highway Act of 1956, and only because nonurban interests wanted it too. From 1959 to 1961, President Eisenhower even eliminated public housing requests from the federal budget. After the election of John F. Kennedy in 1960, however, the urban lobby groups found a receptive environment, and as we show in Chapter 8, it did not take long for them to exploit it.

NOTES

1. W. B. Munro, *The Government of American Cities* (New York: Macmillan, 1913), p. 27.
2. For a discussion of suburbanization before World War II, see Chapter 6.
3. Francis E. Rourke, "Urbanism and the National Party Organizations," *Western Political Quarterly* 18 (March 1965): 150.
4. Wilfred E. Binkley, *American Political Parties: Their Natural History* (New York: Knopf, 1943), p. 285.
5. Ibid., pp. 285–286.
6. Robert A. Caro, *The Power Broker: Robert Moses and the Fall of New York* (New York: Knopf, 1974), pp. 118–119. John L. Sullivan was a well-known boxing champion.
7. William E. Leuchtenburg, *The Perils of Prosperity, 1914–1932* (Chicago: University of Chicago Press, 1958), pp. 213–214.
8. Robert K. Murray, *The 103rd Ballot: Democrats and the Disaster in Madison Square Garden* (New York: Harper and Row, 1976), p. 9.
9. Kenneth T. Jackson, *The Ku Klux Klan in the City, 1915–1930* (New York: Oxford University Press, 1967).
10. Murray, *The 103rd Ballot*, p. 7.
11. Ibid.
12. Kenneth Finegold, *Experts and Politicians: Reform Challenges to Machine Politics in New York, Cleveland, and Chicago* (Princeton, N.J.: Princeton University Press, 1995), p. 174.
13. Ibid., p. 103.
14. For good accounts of the 1924 convention, see Murray, *The 103rd Ballot*; Edmund A. Moore, *A Catholic Runs for President: The Campaign of 1928* (New York: Ronald Press, 1956); Arthur M. Schlesinger, Jr., *The Crisis of the Old Order, 1919–1933* (Boston: Houghton Mifflin, 1956).
15. John D. Hicks, *Republican Ascendancy, 1921–1933* (New York: Harper, 1960), p. 212.
16. John Kenneth Galbraith, *The Great Crash, 1929*, rev. ed. (Boston: Houghton Mifflin, 1979; first published 1961), p. 99.
17. Lester V. Chandler, *America's Greatest Depression, 1929–1941* (New York: HarperCollins, 1970), p. 5.
18. Ibid.
19. Ibid., p. 35.
20. William E. Leuchtenburg, *Franklin D. Roosevelt and the New Deal, 1932–1940* (New York: Harper and Row, 1963), p. 19.
21. Ibid., p. 1.
22. Chandler, *America's Greatest Depression*, p. 19.
23. Ibid., p. 57.
24. Arthur M. Schlesinger, Jr., *The Coming of the New Deal* (Boston: Houghton Mifflin, 1957), p. 3.
25. Leuchtenburg, *Franklin D. Roosevelt*, p. 18.

26. Most relief was given by local public and private agencies. Though many states had programs for relief to designated categories of people—dependent children, the blind, and the disabled—few of these were actually funded.

27. Arthur E. Burns and Edward A. Williams, *Federal Work, Security, and Relief Programs* (New York: Da Capo Press, 1971), pp. 1–2; first published as *Research Monograph 24* (Washington, D.C.: Works Progress Administration, Division of Social Research, 1941).

28. James T. Patterson, *The New Deal and the States: Federalism in Transition* (Princeton, N.J.: Princeton University Press, 1969), p. 30.

29. Ibid., p. 15.

30. Ibid.

31. Mark I. Gelfand, *A Nation of Cities: The Federal Government and Urban America, 1933–1965,* Urban Life in America Series (New York: Oxford University Press, 1975), p. 35.

32. Leuchtenburg, *Franklin D. Roosevelt*, p. 11.

33. Ibid., p. 39.

34. Ibid.

35. Ibid., p. 40.

36. For a thorough account of New Deal programs, see Burns and Williams, *Federal Work.*

37. Leuchtenburg, *Franklin D. Roosevelt*, p. 174.

38. Burns and Williams, *Federal Work*, pp. 29–36.

39. Leuchtenburg, *Franklin D. Roosevelt*, pp. 122–123.

40. Ibid., p. 133.

41. Josephine Chapin Brown, *Public Relief, 1929–1939* (New York: Holt, Rinehart and Winston, 1940), p. 249.

42. Quoted in Binkley, *American Political Parties*, p. 284.

43. Ibid., pp. 380–381.

44. Patterson, *The New Deal and the States*, p. 26.

45. Calculated from James A. Maxwell, *Federal Grants and the Business Cycle* (New York: National Bureau of Economic Research, 1952), p. 23, table 7.

46. Ibid.

47. Gelfand, *A Nation of Cities*, p. 49.

48. U.S. Department of Commerce, Bureau of the Census, *Historical Statistics on State and Local Government Revenues, 1902–1953* (Washington, D.C.: Government Printing Office, 1955), p. 12.

49. Maxwell, *Federal Grants and the Business Cycle*, p. 27, table 11.

50. Ibid., p. 24, table 8.

51. Ibid., p. 29.

52. Gelfand, *A Nation of Cities*, p. 31.

53. Ibid., p. 32.

54. Ibid., p. 36.

55. Ibid.

56. Ibid., p. 34.

57. Patterson, *The New Deal and the States*, p. 39.

58. Ibid., p. 40.

59. Ibid.

60. Ibid., p. 44.

61. Ibid., p. 47.

62. Ibid., p. 40.

63. Brown, *Public Relief*, pp. 72–96.

64. Ibid.

65. George C. S. Benson, *The New Centralization: A Study in Intergovernmental Relationships in the United States* (New York: Holt, Rinehart and Winston, 1941), pp. 104–105.

66. Gelfand, *A Nation of Cities*, p. 34.

67. Robert G. Dixon, Jr., *Democratic Representation: Reapportionment in Law and Politics* (New York: Oxford University Press, 1968), p. 174.

68. Ibid., pp. 71–75, 80, 86–87.

69. Patterson, *The New Deal and the States*, p. 45.

70. Leuchtenburg, *Franklin D. Roosevelt*, p. 52.

71. Ibid., p. 136.

72. Guy Rexford Tugwell, quoted in ibid., p. 35.

73. Finegold, *Experts and Politicians*, p. 12; Bruce M. Stave, *The New Deal and the Last Hurrah: Pittsburgh Machine Politics* (Pittsburgh: University of Pittsburgh Press, 1970); Lyle W. Dorsett, *Franklin D. Roosevelt and the City Bosses* (Port Washington, N.Y.: Kennikat, 1977); Dorsett, *The Pendergast Machine* (New York: Oxford University Press, 1968).

74. Quoted in Gelfand, *A Nation of Cities*, p. 66.

75. U.S. Department of the Interior, National Resources Committee, Urbanism Committee, *Our Cities: Their Role in the National Economy* (Washington, D.C.: Government Printing Office, 1937).

76. Philip J. Funigiello, "City Planning in World War II: The Experience of the National Resources Planning Board," *Social Science Quarterly* 53 (June 1972): 91–104.

PART II

THE CITY IN NATIONAL POLITICS

CHAPTER
6

THE RISE OF THE DIVIDED METROPOLIS

THE ROOTS OF THE URBAN CRISIS

In the nineteenth century, cities were often viewed as dangerous outposts within American civilization, the places where foreign immigrants clustered together into densely packed ethnic communities. All through the twentieth century as well, the cities continued to serve as magnets for people escaping oppression and poverty and searching for jobs and opportunity. Before and again after the Great Depression, blacks left the South by the millions and poured into the cities of the North, Mexicans moved into cities of the Southwest, and poverty-stricken white families fled depressed rural areas. After 1965, when Congress relaxed the nation's immigration laws, foreign immigration reached volumes not experienced since the early years of the century. All these movements brought in their wake racial and ethnic tensions.

If in the nineteenth century the urban and the rural could be regarded as the nation's great cultural divide, in the twentieth century the city-suburban divide became a defining feature of America's political consciousness. At the same time that new racial and ethnic groups continued to pour into the cities, white families fled the cities for the suburbs. The movements into and out of the cities created a deep social and cultural divide. Americans became accustomed to thinking in dichotomies—city/suburban, black/white, ghetto/subdivision, poor/affluent—and these habits of thought consistently cast cities in a dismal light.[1] By the 1970s a nightly menu of lurid stories of murder, mayhem, and drugs became the way that local news stations kept their ratings up. For suburbanites, crime became a signifier of the inner city and the people who lived there.[2]

The Great Divide that has separated the cities from the suburbs began to open as early as the 1920s, and by the end of the 1950s it had become a yawning chasm. In the aftermath of the Great Depression and World War II, the cities were beset with serious economic and social crises. In the many years since the prosperity of the 1920s, the physical condition of inner-city business districts and residential neighborhoods had deteriorated. The problems of cities went far beyond the quality of housing and physical infrastructure, however. Even before the suburban boom of the 1950s it was obvious that a long-term dual migration was reshaping urban areas. Put simply, impoverished blacks, Latinos, and white families were moving into the cities, and affluent white families were moving out.

Three periods of migration and immigration created the crisis of segregation, race, and poverty that characterized America's cities in the twentieth century (see Table 6.1).[3] The first wave crested in the two decades before the Great Depression. Between 1910 and 1930, 700,000 Mexicans moved into Texas, New Mexico, Arizona, and California, and more than 1 million blacks left the southern states for Chicago, Detroit, Cleveland, New York City, Pittsburgh, Philadelphia, and other cities of the industrial Midwest and Northeast. The second, bigger wave washed over the cities during World War II and did not ebb until the late 1960s. From 1940 to 1970 up to 5 million blacks and 700,000 Mexicans moved into America's inner cities. During this same period, more than a million and a half impoverished whites also streamed into the cities, though their migration received little attention. The third wave began with the reform of the immigration laws in 1965, which resulted in a massive influx of foreign immigrants to the cities, mostly from Asia and Central and South America.

White flight from the cities to the suburbs reached flood-tide proportions after World War II. In the 1950s and 1960s middle- and upper-income white families left such cities as St. Louis, Pittsburgh, Chicago, and Boston in significant numbers. At the same time large numbers of city-bound migrants continued to arrive. Year by year, the numbers of minorities and poor in the cities increased, and at the same time suburban subdivisions multiplied, seemingly without end.

A series of presidential commissions gave expression to the rising concern that the extreme racial segregation between cities and suburbs had developed into a national urban crisis. The National Commission on Urban Problems (1958), the National Commission on Civil Disorders (1967; called the Kerner Commission after its chairman, Illinois Governor Otto B. Kerner), the President's Task Force on Suburban Problems (1967), President Nixon's Commission on Population Growth and the American Future (1972), and a great number of state and city task forces decried the segregation of the poor, the aged, and the nonwhite in central cities. In 1967 the Kerner Commission warned of "two nations, one black, one white—separate and unequal."[4] It might just as well have said "two nations: one city, one suburban."

The divide between the racial and ethnic groups living in central cities and the affluent whites living in the suburbs is at the heart of some of the most enduring and divisive issues of American politics. Even if population movements had slowed down after the 1960s, racial and ethnic tensions would remain. In fact, however, since the mid-1960s the United States has been experiencing one of the heaviest periods of immigration in the nation's history. Asians and

TABLE 6.1   RURAL TO URBAN MIGRANT STREAMS IN TWENTIETH-CENTURY AMERICA

Migrant Group	Principal Migration Period	Approximate Number of Migrants[a]	Origin	Destination
Appalachian whites	1940–1970	1,600,000	Southern Appalachian Mountains (Kentucky and West Virginia)	North central states
Mexicans	1910–1930	700,000	*Mesa Central* primarily, also *Mesa Del Norte*	Texas and southwestern states
	1950–1970	700,000[b]	*Mesa Central* primarily, also *Mesa Del Norte*	Texas and California
Blacks	1910–1930	1,250,000[b]	Mississippi delta, black belt, Atlantic coastal plain	Illinois, Ohio, Michigan, New York, and Pennsylvania
	1940–1970	5,000,000[b]	Mississippi delta, black belt, Atlantic coastal plain	Cities everywhere

[a]These figures are approximate. The data for the Mexican migration, for example, are obscured by contract labor, two-way migration, and illegal entrants.

[b]U.S. Bureau of the Census, *Historical Statistics of the United States: Colonial Times to 1970* (Washington, D.C.: Government Printing Office). In Greenberg's original table, he lists 1 million blacks, 1910–1930, and 3.5 million blacks, 1940–1965.

Source: Adapted from Stanley B. Greenberg, *Politics and Poverty: Modernization and Response in Five Poor Neighborhoods* (New York: Wiley, 1974), p. 19.

Latinos now constitute a substantial and growing proportion of the residents of America's cities. The political consequences of this development have been far-reaching. For decades the urban crisis was defined as the segregation between blacks in the central cities and whites in the suburbs. What is different now is that metropolitan areas have become fractured along several ethnic and racial dimensions; and the problems once associated mainly with the central cities have spread to the suburbs.

In this chapter, we trace the origins of America's Great Divide by discussing the evolution of the central cities in the twentieth century, and then profiling the growth of the suburbs. We present both developments in a single chapter in order to emphasize the point that the evolution of cities and suburbs is best understood as an interdependent process. It is important to keep in mind that this chapter should be read as history, but not necessarily as prologue. For reasons explored in the remainder of this book, the chasm that opened in the twentieth century between America's cities and suburbs may be slowly closing because the tensions of urban society are spilling beyond the old boundaries.

◆ THE CENTRAL CITIES ◆

THE GREAT MIGRATION: FROM THE FARM TO THE CITY

For a century, the ethnic and racial conflicts that have played out in America's urban areas have been important features of its national politics. Issues of race became central themes in presidential campaigns from 1964 through 2000, and race, ethnicity, and immigration are sure to remain as enduring issues in the twenty-first century. Though the particular issues connected to race and ethnicity have changed over time, their roots are deep; they have had a century to grow and evolve. America's twentieth-century urban experience provided a rich, nurturing soil.

Between 1910 and 1926 Mexicans were driven into the southwestern states by the bloody and protracted violence of the Mexican Revolution. Although the revolution released millions of peasants from their feudal relationship with landholders, it left many of them without the means to sustain an independent livelihood. Bloody confrontations between the Mexican government and landowners drove the newly liberated peasants into Texas, Arizona, and California. During World War II and its aftermath, employment opportunities in the southwestern states induced still more Mexicans to cross the border. By 1970, 5.5 million Mexican Americans lived in the American Southwest, the great majority in towns and cities.[5] Latino immigrants from several other Latin American countries streamed into the southwestern states in even larger numbers in the 1980s and 1990s, pushed by political repression and poverty and pulled by the availability of jobs.

The decline of the coal industry in the southern Appalachian Mountains and the Cumberland plateau of Virginia, West Virginia, and Kentucky prompted a massive movement of desperately poor rural white families from the 1930s to the 1960s. The exodus reached such proportions after World War II that some counties in Appalachia were almost depopulated in just a few years. In his moving book, *Night Comes to the Cumberlands,* Harry Caudill describes the grinding poverty that forced families and entire communities to pick up and leave their marginal farm plots and shabby towns. Many of the families that were forced to leave could trace their roots in Appalachia several generations back. An entire genre of country music—bluegrass—was inspired by the homesickness for the hills and hollows left behind. In the 1950s alone, a quarter of the population deserted the Cumberland plateau, settling in cities and towns of Kentucky, Tennessee, Maryland, Virginia, and the industrial belt of the upper Midwest.[6] Joining them were a steady stream of impoverished white families who were leaving the border areas of southern Illinois, Kentucky, and Arkansas. Regardless of where they actually came from, the new migrants were derisively called Hoosiers, Oakies, and Arkies. Like the epithets flung at African Americans, such labels were a way of keeping them apart.

African Americans initiated one of the most momentous population movements of the twentieth century, and perhaps of any time. The waves of migration from the southern states to northern cities that lasted for more than sixty years constituted "one of the largest and most rapid mass internal movements of people in history—perhaps the greatest not caused by the immediate threat of execution or starvation."[7] From 1910 to 1920, 450,000 blacks moved out of the South, followed by another 750,000 in the 1920s.[8] In the twenty years between 1910 and 1930, about one million blacks—one-tenth of all blacks living in the South—moved to cities in the Northeast and Midwest. In only twenty years, the black population living outside the South shot up by 134 percent, and the proportion of the nation's black population residing in the South dropped from 89 percent to 79 percent.[9] The northward movement was slowed by the depression of the 1930s, but it gained even more momentum during and after World War II. Between 1940 and 1970 an estimated 5 million blacks left the South.

Like the European immigrants who preceded them, African Americans were pushed by crisis and pulled by opportunity. Poverty and unemployment in the South provided the push; jobs in the North were the pull. Beginning in southern Texas in the late 1890s and sweeping eastward through Georgia by 1921, boll weevil infestations wiped out cotton crops, forcing black sharecroppers off the land. During the same period, an abrupt decline in European immigration occasioned by World War I, combined with the rapid expansion of armaments industries, produced labor shortages in the northern industrial cities.

Almost all the African Americans leaving the South left poverty-stricken rural areas and settled into densely packed neighborhoods in northern cities. Only 10 percent of the nation's African Americans lived in cities of 100,000 or more in 1910. This percentage increased to 16 percent in 1920 and to 24 percent by 1930.[10] The biggest cities lured most of the migrants. The proportion of blacks living in cities smaller than 100,000 declined from 1910 to 1930, but the proportion increased substantially in cities of over 100,000.[11] Thus the Great Migration, as it came to be labeled by historians, had two principal components: Blacks were becoming northern and they were becoming urban. In several of the largest cities, black populations multiplied by a factor of three or more in the two decades from 1910 to 1930 (see Table 6.2).

African Americans made up more than 2 percent of the population in only a handful of northern cities in 1910. By 1930, however, they accounted for 18 percent of the population of Gary, Indiana, and in East St. Louis, Illinois, with its stockyards, rail yards, and heavy industry, blacks were 16 percent of the population. In big cities, percentages by 1930 ranged from almost 5 percent in New York City to just over 11 percent in St. Louis and Philadelphia (these proportions had roughly doubled in twenty years). African Americans became concentrated in well-defined ghettos. In north Harlem in New York City, about one-third (36 percent) of the population was black in 1920, but this proportion increased to 81 percent by the time the 1930 census was taken.[12]

There were many reasons for the migration to northern cities, but the basic factors were employment opportunities in the North, the grinding poverty of southern agricultural life, and dissatisfaction with the racial caste system in the South. The North was a "promised land" that offered an escape from the violent racism of the South and the opportunity for economic advancement. With the onset of the Great Depression of the 1930s, which brought mass destitution and unemployment to northern cities as well as to the South, the migration from the farms to the cities slowed abruptly and did not pick up again until after World War II.

Southern blacks began to stream North as a means of escaping the shackles of the southern system of race relations. The migration northward had already commenced when, in May 1917, the publisher of the *Chicago Defender* launched "The Great Northern Drive" to persuade blacks to move. Founded in 1905, by

TABLE 6.2	GROWTH OF BLACK POPULATION IN SEVERAL CITIES, 1910–1930					
					Percent of Total Population	
City	1910	1920	1930	Percent Increase 1910–1930	1910	1930
New York	91,709	152,467	327,706	257.3	1.9	4.7
Chicago	44,103	109,458	233,903	429.3	2.0	6.9
Philadelphia	84,459	134,229	219,599	160.0	5.5	11.3
St. Louis	43,960	69,854	93,580	112.9	6.4	11.4
Cleveland	8,448	34,451	71,889	751.0	1.5	8.0

Source: U.S. Bureau of the Census, *Negroes in the United States, 1920–1932* (Washington, D.C.: Government Printing Office, 1935), p. 55.

World War I the *Defender* already had reached a circulation of 100,000, and it was read avidly by blacks throughout the South. The *Defender*'s editorials exhorted blacks to come north to the land of opportunity, where they could find employment and, if not equality, at least an escape from harassment and violence. Its columns of job advertisements added substance to the "promised land" vision. At the same time, the *Defender* attacked conditions in the South. Lynchings and incidents of discrimination were regularly highlighted in lurid detail. Moving out of the South was portrayed as a way to advance the cause of racial equality for all blacks.[13]

The *Defender* was only one of many voices encouraging blacks to leave the South. Those who had already moved wrote letters to relatives and friends describing their new life in glowing terms. Despite pervasive job and housing discrimination in the North, they found conditions preferable to what they had left behind. Throughout the South, blacks lived under a cloud of terror. From 1882 to 1930, there were 1,663 lynchings in the states of the Cotton Belt alone—Alabama, Georgia, Louisiana, Mississippi, and South Carolina. During the same period, 1,299 blacks were legally executed.[14] The legal systems of the southern states were so completely rigged that the difference between lynching and legalized murder by police and the courts was not much more than a technicality. Blacks who failed to obey the racial caste system, even inadvertently, could expect immediate retribution in the form of beatings or worse. Failing to step off the sidewalk, forgetting to say "sir" or "ma'am," or looking a white person in the eye could be cause for violent retribution.

The opportunities for leaving such conditions improved in proportion to the labor shortages in northern factories. After war broke out in Europe in 1914, factory owners found themselves with lucrative armaments contracts but with too few workers. They sent labor agents into the South with free train tickets in hand, which could be exchanged for a labor agreement. By the spring of 1916, the Great Migration began in earnest.

Southern white employers and planters took steps to prevent the exodus of their cheap labor. Magazines, newspapers, and business organizations decried the movement, as in this October 5, 1916, editorial in the Memphis *Commercial Appeal:*

> The enormous demand for labor and the changing conditions brought about by the boll weevil in certain parts of the South have caused an exodus of negroes which may be serious. Great colonies of negroes have gone north to work in factories, in packing houses and on the railroads. . . .
>
> The South needs every able-bodied negro that is now south of the line, and every negro who remains south of the line will in the end do better than he will do in the North. . . .
>
> The negroes who are in the South should be encouraged to remain there, and those white people who are in the boll weevil territory should make every sacrifice to keep their negro labor until there can be adjustments to the new and quickly prosperous conditions that will later exist.[15]

States and communities went to considerable lengths to discourage migration. Jacksonville, Florida, passed an ordinance in 1916 levying heavy fines on unlicensed labor agents from the North. Macon, Georgia, made it impossible for labor agents to get licenses and then outlawed unlicensed agents. The mayor of Atlanta talked to blacks about how "dreadfully cold" the northern winters were.[16] In some communities, police were sent to railroad stations to harass blacks near the stations, keep them from boarding trains, or even drive them off the trains.

But the promised land beckoned, and the exodus continued. What the new arrivals found was opportunity—but not equal opportunity—and persistent discrimination. Whenever blacks attempted to move into white neighborhoods, they were harassed or violently assaulted. In the workplace they were the last hired and the first fired. They were kept in the most menial occupations. Job opportunities were limited not only by employers but even more so by labor unions, which generally prohibited blacks from membership. Because the North was more heavily unionized than the South, there were actually fewer opportunities in some occupations, especially for skilled laborers.[17] In both union and nonunion shops, white workers often refused to work alongside blacks. To avoid trouble, employers assigned blacks to the least desirable jobs.

Blacks found it difficult to adjust to urban life. Hardly any of them had previously lived in a city. Many had never even participated directly in the cash economy. Sharecroppers had often worked under contracts that contained provisions that they buy only from the planters' stores and then with scrip and credit rather than cash. Some of them had never seen U.S. currency. As was the case with previous immigrant groups, they were often cheated and overcharged.

These conditions, when amplified by the intense segregation into dilapidated, overcrowded ghettos, led to astonishing levels of social pathology. The arrest rate for blacks in Detroit in 1926 was four times that for whites. Blacks constituted 31 percent of the nation's prison population in 1923, though they made up only 9 percent of the total population. The death rate in Harlem between 1923 and 1927 was 42 percent higher than in New York City as a whole, despite the fact that Harlem's population was much younger than the overall city population. Harlem's infant mortality rate was 111 per 1,000 births, compared with the city's rate of 64 per 1,000. Tuberculosis, heart disease, and other illnesses also far exceeded the rates for the city's general population.[18]

Blacks moving into northern cities were often surprised when they encountered hostility, racism, and discrimination as bad as in the South. Restaurants and stores refused to serve them, though discrimination was not practiced quite as universally as in the South. Banks typically refused them loans. Cemeteries, parks, bathing beaches, and other facilities were put off limits or divided into "white" and "colored" sections. Many dentists, doctors, and hospitals refused to treat blacks. Worse, the violence that had plagued them in the South followed them everywhere they went. On July 2, 1917, 39 blacks and 5 whites died in a race riot in East St. Louis, Illinois.[19] In the infamous "Red Summer" of 1919, more than 20 cities experienced race riots, all of them involving attacks by white mobs against blacks. Chicago's riot of that summer started when a young black man inadvertently swam across the strip of water separating the beach designated "For Coloreds Only" from the beach reserved for whites only. A white crowd stoned the boy to death and then terrorized blacks throughout the city for days. From July 1, 1917, to March 1, 1921, Chicago experienced 58 racial bomb-ings.[20] Unemployed blacks were forced out of Buffalo by city police in 1920. That same year, in perhaps the worst mass-murder of blacks in U.S. history, more than 300 blacks were killed by white mobs in Tulsa, Oklahoma—an incident covered up for almost eighty years.[21] In 1925 blacks who attempted to move into white neighborhoods in Detroit were terrorized by cross burnings, vandalism, and mob violence.

In all cities, restrictive covenants were attached to property deeds to keep blacks from buying into white neighborhoods. Deeds with these restrictions were filed in the office of the county clerk or the register of deeds and were en-forced by the courts. Chicago, with more than eleven square miles covered by restricted deeds in 1944, was typical of northern cities.[22] Neighborhood im-provement associations were formed in new subdivisions and, by legal prosecu-tion and social persuasion, forced homeowners to accept and abide by racial re-strictive covenants.

Though the migration to the North slowed to a crawl during the Great De-pression, the movement gained momentum again during and after World War II. As before, factory jobs pulled blacks into northern cities, and conditions in the South provided a push. The mechanization of southern agriculture, in particular the widespread adoption of the mechanized cotton picker, threw hundreds of thousands of sharecroppers and farm laborers out of work. From Texas, Louisiana, and Arkansas, blacks streamed into cities of the West, especially to California; from the middle South, they moved to St. Louis, Chicago, Detroit, Cleveland, and other cities of the Midwest; and from Mississippi and eastward in the Deep South, they moved to Washington, D.C., New York, Boston, and other cities in the East. In 1940, 77 percent of the nation's blacks still lived in the southern states (compared with 87 percent in 1910). By 1950, only 60 percent lived in the South, and in the next two decades the South's share declined to 56 percent (1960) and to 53 percent (1970).[23] Nearly all the northward-bound mi-grants ended up in cities. By the 1970 census, 90 percent of all the blacks who lived outside metropolitan areas in the United States were located in the South. (In the 1970s, a reverse migration of blacks back to the South began. The num-bers have gradually increased, reaching 369,000 between 1990 and 1995. Eighty percent have located in urban areas.)[24]

A movement of this magnitude would have created a crisis under any con-ditions, since most of the migrants were of rural origin and predictably found the adjustment to city life difficult. But the crisis was made worse by the same factors that had plagued earlier black migrants: housing and job discrimination, racism, and extreme segregation. All of the problems faced by northern blacks in the 1920s still existed after World War II. Further, whites were leaving the cities by the millions every year, seeking their own "promised land"—the suburbs. While blacks were flooding into the cities, whites were moving out. Table 6.3 shows that racial segregation between cities and suburbs had become pro-nounced by 1950 and worsened over the following decades.

For most of the twelve cities shown in Table 6.3, the highest rates of growth in the black population occurred in the two decades from 1950 to 1970. White

TABLE 6.3 PERCENTAGE OF BLACKS IN CENTRAL CITIES AND SUBURBAN RINGS IN TWELVE SELECTED SMSAS, 1940–1990

	Central City						Suburban Ring					
	1940	1950	1960	1970	1980	1990	1940	1950	1960	1970	1980	1990[a]
All 12 SMSAs	9.0	13.7	21.4	30.8	32.6	32.9	3.9	4.4	4.4	6.0	7.4[b]	8.7[b]
New York	6.4	9.8	14.7	23.4	25.2	28.7	4.6	4.5	4.8	6.4	6.8[b]	11.0[b]
Los Angeles–Long Beach	6.0	9.8	15.3	21.2	16.4	14.0	2.3	2.7	4.1	7.4	9.6	6.7
Chicago	8.3	14.1	23.6	34.4	39.8	39.1	2.2	2.9	3.1	4.1	5.6	8.7
Philadelphia	13.1	18.3	26.7	34.4	37.8	39.9	6.6	6.6	0.3	7.1	8.1	10.8
Detroit	9.3	16.4	29.2	44.0	63.1	75.7	2.9	5.0	3.8	4.0	4.2	5.4
San Francisco–Oakland	4.9	11.8	21.1	32.7	24.1	22.1	3.6	6.8	6.8	9.4	6.5	5.7
Boston	3.3	12.3	9.8	18.2	22.4	25.6	0.9	0.8	1.0	1.6	1.6	2.9
Pittsburgh	9.3	18.0	16.8	27.0	24.0	25.8	3.6	3.5	3.4	3.6	4.0	4.5
St. Louis	13.4	5.3	28.8	41.3	45.6	47.5	6.7	7.3	6.3	7.7	10.6	11.0
Washington, D.C.	28.5	35.4	54.8	72.3	76.6	65.8	13.7	8.7	6.4	9.1	16.7	19.4
Cleveland	9.7	16.3	28.9	39.0	43.8	46.6	0.9	0.8	0.8	1.1	7.1	9.1
Baltimore	19.4	23.8	35.0	47.0	54.8	59.2	11.9	10.2	6.9	6.2	9.1	11.0

[a]Except for St. Louis, Baltimore, and Washington, D.C., figures for 1990 refer to the Consolidated Metropolitan Statistical Areas (CMSAs) that are not strictly comparable to earlier years. See U.S. Bureau of the Census, *Statistical Abstract of the United States, 1991*, 111th ed. (Washington, D.C.: Government Printing Office, 1991), tables 37, 38, and 40.

[b]This figure includes data from the Nassau-Suffolk SMSA, which was deleted from the New York City SMSA in 1971. They are included to maintain comparability across time periods.

Source: Adapted from Leo F. Schnore, Carolyn D. André, and Harry Sharp, "Black Suburbanization, 1930–1970," in *The Changing Face of the Suburbs*, ed. Barry Schwartz (Chicago: University of Chicago Press, 1976), p. 80. Reprinted by permission. The figures here were transposed to yield data on black percentages; 1980 data from U.S. Bureau of the Census, *Census of the Population, 1980*, suppl. reports, *Standard Metropolitan Statistical Areas and Standard Consolidated Statistical Areas* (Washington, D.C.: Government Printing Office, 1981) p. 3, table 1.

families stayed in the cities until the suburban housing boom following the Korean War. By the census of 1970, blacks accounted for more than 72 percent of the population of Washington, D.C., 47 percent in Cleveland, and more than 41 percent in St. Louis. Blacks moved to the surburbs in significant numbers in the 1970s, 1980s, and 1990s,[25] but the suburbs remained overwhelmingly white. Within the central cities, most of the population increases among blacks after 1970 could be traced to natural increase rather than to migration. Their proportions rose only modestly in most cities and actually fell sharply in Washington, D.C., reflecting the middle-class gentrification of poor neighborhoods and the immigration of Asians, Latinos, and other groups. Thus the black population of the twelve cities shown in Table 6.3 barely increased from 1980 to 1990, from 30.8 percent to 32.6 percent.

THE NEW IMMIGRANTS

The number of immigrants entering the United States has increased steadily since 1950, and during this period the sources of immigration have shifted from Europe to Asia, Latin America, and the Caribbean. As shown in Table 6.4, in the 1950s, 57 percent of immigrants originated from Europe, 22.5 percent came from the Western Hemisphere south of the United States, and 6 percent came from Asia. From 1991 to 1996, by contrast, only 14 percent came from Europe, while 49 percent originated from Western Hemisphere countries and 32 percent from Asia. In the 1990s, the proportion of immigrants from Asia dropped somewhat from the levels sustained in the previous two decades, but immigration from south of the United States increased sharply. Immigration from Europe also rose somewhat when families from the formerly Communist countries of eastern Europe began to migrate, their numbers bolstered by Bosnians fleeing civil war.

Few people realize that the 1980s was the second largest decade of legal immigration in American history, exceeded only by the immigrant flood tide from 1900 to 1910. The proportion of immigrants in the population was far less than in the late nineteenth and early twentieth centuries, but a larger number of immigrants lived in the United States by 1990—17 million—than in any previous period in the nation's history.[26] In addition, by 1990 an estimated 2.5 to 4 million illegal aliens resided in the United States.[27]

The immigration laws in effect from the 1920s to the mid-1960s reflected fears that foreigners might overwhelm the country. The National Origins Immigration Act of 1924 allowed 2 percent of the base population of the foreign-born nationality groups to immigrate into the United States, as recorded in the census of 1890. This quota accomplished its intended goal of drastically reducing immigration by all groups except those from northern Europe. Immigration by Slavs, Jews, Italians, Greeks, and other supposedly "inferior" peoples, most of whom entered the country after 1890, was cut by more than 90 percent.

By the 1960s, such a blatantly biased (and racist) formula became difficult to justify. In the Hart-Cellar Act of 1965, Congress essentially put immigrants from

TABLE 6.4 IMMIGRANTS, BY PLACE OF ORIGIN, 1951–1996

Year	Percent of Total Immigration					Total Number (Thousands)
	Europe	Asia[a]	Canada	Other Western Hemisphere[b]	All Other[c]	
1951–1960	57.2	6.1	10.9	22.5	3.1	2,515.5
1961–1970	36.9	13.2	8.6	38.9	2.3	3,321.7
1971–1980	18.1	35.9	2.6	40.4	3.1	4,493.3
1981–1990	9.6	38.4	1.6	47.2	3.2	7,338.1
1991–1996	14.2	31.6	1.5	48.7	4.0	6,146.3

[a]Cambodia, China, Taiwan, Hong Kong, India, Iran, Israel, Japan, Korea, Philippines, Thailand, Vienam, and "other Asia."

[b]Mexico, Caribbean, Central America, South America.

[c]Africa, Australia, New Zealand.

Source: U.S. Department of Justice, Immigration and Naturalization Service, *Statistical Yearbook of the Immigration and Naturalization Service, 1989* (Washington, D.C.: Government Printing Office, 1990), pp. 2–5; and U.S. Census Bureau, The Official Statistics, *Statistical Abstracts of the United States,* 1998, Sept. 25, 1998.

all countries on an equal footing and granted a high priority to family reunification. Expanded by special provisions for political refugees from socialist and communist countries, the volume of immigration soared well beyond expectations, and the ethnic composition of the immigrants changed rapidly. After the 1960s, between 80 and 85 percent of the new immigrants to the United States came from the Caribbean, Central and South America, and Asia, with Asians accounting for about 46 percent of the total.[28]

Recent immigrants have tended to settle in the central cities of major metropolitan areas, usually moving into neighborhoods already occupied by members of their own ethnic group, a process called chain migration. In 1987 less than 7 percent of legal immigrants settled in nonurban areas, and more than half of them moved into just ten metropolitan areas in the United States. Figure 6.1

FIGURE 6.1   **Immigrant Flows to Seven U.S. Cities, 1994**

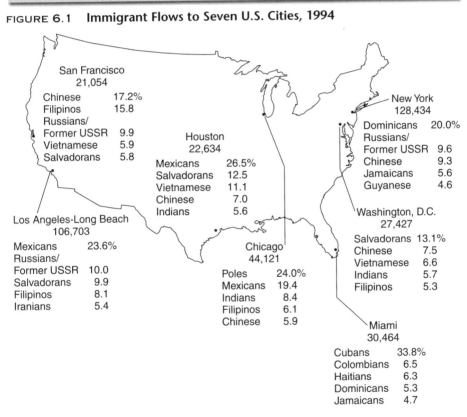

San Francisco
21,054

Chinese	17.2%
Filipinos	15.8
Russians/ Former USSR	9.9
Vietnamese	5.9
Salvadorans	5.8

New York
128,434

Dominicans	20.0%
Russians/ Former USSR	9.6
Chinese	9.3
Jamaicans	5.6
Guyanese	4.6

Houston
22,634

Mexicans	26.5%
Salvadorans	12.5
Vietnamese	11.1
Chinese	7.0
Indians	5.6

Los Angeles-Long Beach
106,703

Mexicans	23.6%
Russians/ Former USSR	10.0
Salvadorans	9.9
Filipinos	8.1
Iranians	5.4

Chicago
44,121

Poles	24.0%
Mexicans	19.4
Indians	8.4
Filipinos	6.1
Chinese	5.9

Washington, D.C.
27,427

Salvadorans	13.1%
Chinese	7.5
Vietnamese	6.6
Indians	5.7
Filipinos	5.3

Miami
30,464

Cubans	33.8%
Colombians	6.5
Haitians	6.3
Dominicans	5.3
Jamaicans	4.7

► Composition of legally admitted immigrant flows to seven major metropolitan destinations, 1993.

Notes: (1) "Chinese" includes migrants from mainland China only. (2) Orange County, just south of Los Angeles, was the sixth-largest metropolitan area of immigrant destination in 1993.
Source: Alejandro Portes and Rubén G. Rumbaut, *Immigrant America: A Portrait,* 2nd ed. (Berkeley: University of California Press, 1996), p. 36.

shows that the racial and ethnic composition of the immigration flow differs considerably from one urban area to another. In San Francisco, Asians from many countries accounted for the largest proportion of immigrants in 1993. Most of the new immigrants to Miami in the same year, however, came from the Caribbean and Latin America; more than one-third came from Cuba alone. Mexican immigrants led the list in Los Angeles and Houston; immigrants from the Dominican Republic were the most numerous in New York City, while Washington, D.C. attracted large number of Salvadorans. Interestingly, Poles led all groups in Chicago, followed in numbers by Mexicans. In large part these patterns reflect the fact that immigrants tend to go to cities where communities of their own ethnic group already reside.

In 1998 about 69 percent of the nation's 26 million Latinos lived in five southwestern states, plus Florida. California, with 10.1 million Latinos in 1998, had 33 percent of the nation's Latino population; the second state, Texas, with 5.8 million Latinos, had 19 percent.[29] Approximately 80 percent of the Latinos in the southwestern states came originally from Mexico, compared to 60 percent for the United States as a whole. Recent immigrant flows are likely to change that situation rapidly. More Latino immigrants have been moving to New York City, Chicago, Washington, D.C., and other cities outside of the Southwest,; thus, they are sure to spread out more evenly across the country in the next few years.

In the early 1990s, most Latinos lived in metropolitan areas: about 80 percent of Mexicans and more than 98 percent of Puerto Ricans, Cubans, and South and Central Americans. As shown in Table 6.5, Latinos constituted about one-third of the population of eight large cities of the Sunbelt in 1990, but the proportions varied considerably, from 62.5 percent for Miami, to 15 percent in Tampa-St. Petersburg. In the Dallas-Fort Worth, Houston-Galveston-Brazoria, and Miami-Fort Lauderdale metropolitan areas, Latinos made up one-sixth or more of the population. To understand the political implications of these figures, it is important to note that Latinos and blacks now compete vigorously for political power and for jobs. As shown in Table 6.5, African Americans account for an average of 16 percent of the population of the eight Sunbelt cities shown. Over the next few years, it is certain that the politics of these cities will reflect either antagonisms between blacks and Latinos, or the emergence of political cooperation. The alliances that do emerge may be strained, however, by the fact that the Latino population is increasing at a much faster rate than non-Latino whites and African Americans, and some researchers predict that Latinos will equal African Americans in national population by the year 2003. By the end of this century they are certain to become the dominant ethnic group in a large number of cities of the Sunbelt.

In the 1980s Asian-Americans were the fastest-growing ethnic group, with the metropolitan areas of Los Angeles, San Francisco, and New York having the largest Asian communities. The number of immigrants coming from Asia in the 1980s almost equaled the number from all countries of the Western Hemisphere south of the U.S. border. There is evidence, however, that in the 1990s Asian immigration has slowed down while Latino immigration has increased.[30] The new immigrant communities are often quite complex in social and economic

TABLE 6.5

BLACK AND HISPANIC POPULATION IN SELECTED SUNBELT CITIES AND METROPOLITAN AREAS, 1990

Metropolitan Area	Percent Black in Largest Central City	Percent Hispanic in Largest Central City	Percent Black in Metropolitan Area	Percent Hispanic in Metropolitan Area	Percent Minorities[a] in Central Cities
Los Angeles-Anaheim-Riverside (CMSA)	14.0	39.9	8.5	32.9	64.2
San Diego (MSA)	9.4	20.7	6.4	20.4	42.5
Phoenix	5.2	20.0	3.5	16.3	28.8
Dallas-Fort Worth (CMSA)	29.5	20.9	14.3	13.4	53.1
Houston-Galveston-Brazoria	28.1	27.6	17.9	20.8	60.1
Miami-Fort Lauderdale (CMSA)	27.4	62.5	18.5	33.3	90.7
Tampa-St. Petersburg-Clearwater (MSA)	25.0	15.0	9.0	6.7	41.7
Denver-Boulder (CMSA)	12.8	23.0	5.3	12.2	39.4
San Antonio (MSA)	7.0	55.6	6.8	47.6	64.1
Mean for eight cities	16.3	33.2	8.0	24.1	56.3

[a]Includes Asians, Pacific Islanders, American Indians, Eskimos, and Aleuts.

Source: U.S. Bureau of the Census, Statistical Abstract of the United States, 1991, 111th ed. (Washington, D.C.: Government Printing Office, 1991), tables 37, 38, and 40.

characteristics, and in this sense they are not unlike the immigrant communities of a century ago. Though there are areas where only the poorest immigrants live, there are also economically diverse neighborhoods that are made up of immigrants of various backgrounds and occupations.

Immigration is changing the face of urban America. In some ways the ethnic enclaves in many American cities seem little different from their counterparts in the immigrants' countries of origin. Koreatown in Los Angeles is a thriving enclave of immigrant businesses that advertise their wares in brightly colored signs in both English words and Korean characters. Walking along Calle Ocho (S.W. 8th Street) in Miami, the heart of "Little Havana," there is the ever-present smell of Cuban-style coffee and cigars. Bolsa Avenue in Westminster (Orange County), California, called the Vietnamese capital of America, is lined with restaurants selling Asian food. In New York City, Manhattan's Chinatown grew so fast that it burst its seams and spread across the East River into Flushing in the borough of Queens. This new Chinatown bustles with Asian tourists and has become famous for its variety of Chinese restaurants.

The economic well-being of each immigrant group is closely related to the conditions faced by the group before the move to the United States. Adverse economic conditions and political repression have pushed most of the new immigrants to American shores. Economic opportunity in the United States exerted the necessary "pull." The minimum wage in the United States, for example, is approximately six times the prevailing wage in Mexico, where wages are higher than in most other Latin American countries.[31] Though many immigrants work in poorly paid jobs, quite a few come into the country to work in professional and technical occupations. Indeed, the proportion of immigrants with professional and technical backgrounds who work in this country consistently exceeds the average for U.S. workers as a whole.[32]

For the most part, Asian immigrants have done well, quickly achieving educational credentials and succeeding at small businesses.[33] Latinos, as a group, have not fared as well, falling well below the general U.S. population on all indicators of economic well-being. Their median family income in 1995 ($22,860) was only 61.5 percent of the $37,178 median income for the non-Hispanic white families. Latinos lagged far behind on educational attainment: More than 82 percent of all non-Hispanic whites had completed high school in 1995, compared with 53 percent of Hispanics; only 9 percent of Hispanics had earned a college degree.[34] The relative lack of educational qualifications, plus a measure of discrimination, have meant that Latinos have also occupied lower rungs on the job ladder. Even though Hispanics held 8.9 percent of all jobs in 1995, they held just 4.4 percent of managerial and professional jobs.[35] Only a small minority of people of Hispanic descent have entered the middle class in income, education, and occupational status. African Americans are even more disadvantaged. Despite the fact that they have, as a group, a higher level of educational attainment than Hispanics, they have lower family incomes and higher unemployment rates. Since the early 1970s, neither African Americans nor Hispanics have made significant gains in comparison with non-Hispanic whites. In 1969 black median income was 61 percent of white median income (up from 52 percent in 1959). By 1995 black families were making only 60 percent as much as whites. The ratio of Hispanic income to non-Hispanic white income actually worsened, dropping from 71 percent to 65 percent between 1972 and 1989, and to 60.5 percent in 1995.[36]

Tensions have escalated in recent years among Asians, Latinos, and African Americans. Riots erupted in black neighborhoods in Cuban-dominated Miami four times during the 1980s, beginning with the Liberty City disorders in May 1980. Each of the riots was associated with the killing of a black man by Latino or non-Latino white police officers.[37] Rioting erupted in Washington, D.C., when a black female police officer attempted to arrest some Latino men and when a Salvadoran immigrant was shot by police. Ethnic tensions reached a breaking point in Brooklyn in 1991–1992, culminating in a boycott by the African-American community of a Korean greengrocer and violent street confrontations between African Americans and Hasidic Jews. In the 1992 Los Angeles riots, 30 percent of the approximately 4,000 businesses destroyed were Latino-owned,[38] but Korean-owned businesses were especially singled out by looters and arsonists.[39]

Illegal immigration has intensified the competition for jobs among African Americans and the new immigrants. Undocumented aliens, whose numbers peaked in 1986 at three to five million, are willing to take (or are coerced) into taking jobs paying less than the minimum wage, and they often end up in sweatshops working under abysmal conditions. Frequently led across the border by professional smugglers, called "coyotes" for their predatory habits, illegal aliens remain at the bottom of U.S. society. Because they live in constant fear of detection by the Immigration and Naturalization Service (INS), they are in no position to bargain with employers.

To deal with the problem of illegal immigrants, Congress enacted the Immigration Reform and Control Act (IRCA) in 1986, which established stiff penalties for employers who knowingly hire illegal aliens. At the same time, the law made it possible for illegals who had already entered the country to achieve citizenship by registering with the INS. After passage of the IRCA, approximately 2.5 million formerly illegal aliens attained legal status by 1990,[40] and the INS stepped up efforts to find employers who violated the law. One of the unintended effects of the 1986 reform is that many employers began to discriminate against anyone who looked or sounded like they came from anywhere south of the U.S. border.[41]

In 1990 Congress again reformed the immigration laws, an act that increased the number of legal immigrants allowed into the country by 40 percent. The law more than doubled the number of visas granted to immigrants with job skills needed in the United States, and it allowed the highest percentage of European-origin groups into the country since Hart-Cellar.[42] In the mid-1990s the United States was admitting more legal immigrants than all the rest of the nations of the world combined.[43] Immigration issues were important in the presidential election of 1996 and continue to be particularly divisive in California. Under the Personal Responsibility Act of 1996 that reformed welfare, legal immigrants were denied welfare benefits, including food stamps and Medicaid, a provision that was, however, rescinded in 1997. In the years ahead, immigration will continue to reshape America's urban areas, and urban politics will as a result continue to revolve around issues of race and ethnicity.

CONCENTRATED POVERTY

Just as they did in the nineteenth century, massive population movements in this century have brought in their wake social dislocations and political tensions. American cities have continued to house a disproportionate share of the nation's poor. At the same time that the cities have had to absorb millions of new immigrants, they have also had to deal with the effects of concentrated poverty. The problems of the urban poor are magnified by the fact that they live in neighborhoods that have been abandoned by the middle and working classes. More and more, the poor live apart from everyone else. In 1959 more than half of the nation's poor lived in rural areas and 27 percent lived in central cities.[44] Accordingly, a leading book published in 1963 devoted far more space to the problems of rural than to urban poverty.[45] By the census of 1990, however, the situation had changed considerably: 43 percent of the nation's poor lived in central cities and 28 percent lived in the suburbs. Since most of the suburban poor were concentrated into inner-ring suburbs contiguous to central city poverty areas, this meant that about 60 percent of poor people were concentrated in areas in or near the urban core.[46]

Within central cities a large proportion of the poor live in neighborhoods in which almost everyone is poor, and such areas of poverty have been spreading rapidly for some time. According to the 1970 census, 27 percent of the census tracts in the 100 largest cities in the country were classified as "poverty" tracts, areas where at least 20 percent of the residents were poor. Of these, 6 percent were classified as "extreme poverty" tracts in which at least 40 percent of residents were poor. By 1990 the percentage of poverty tracts had increased to 39 percent of all census tracts in these cities, and the proportion of extreme poverty tracts had more than doubled, to 13.7 percent.[47]

The intensified segregation of the poor interacts with the segregation of minorities and recent immigrants to create a hypersegregation of the minority poor.[48] An analysis of sixty metropolitan areas found that the degree of residential segregation changed little between 1970 and 1980, with blacks being twice as segregated as Latinos and Asians.[49] In the 1980s the segregation of blacks was reduced slightly in most metropolitan areas, and blacks continued to move to the suburbs.[50] At the same time, however, the concentration of poor blacks into poverty census tracts intensified.[51] When the 1990 census was taken, 71 percent of low-income, black, central city residents lived in poverty neighborhoods, compared with only 40 percent of low-income, white, central city residents.[52] Low-income whites can often escape the ghetto and move into working-class or even middle-class neighborhoods, but low-income blacks find it very difficult to find affordable housing outside racially segregated areas.

The concentration of poverty has important consequences. The spatial segregation of the minority poor intensifies racial tensions and animosities. The spread of ghettos and the problems associated with them creates the perception that entire areas are hostile, dangerous, and off-limits. Such areas provide the media images of poverty, and they also become part of the everyday awareness of anyone living in a metropolitan area: "How big an area of the city do you consider off-limits? How far out of your way will you drive not to go through a dangerous area?"[53]

Within poverty neighborhoods, the consequences of concentrated poverty multiply quickly. Sociologist William Julius Wilson used the term "underclass" to refer to people who not only were concentrated into poverty areas but also exhibited a range of behaviors defined as negative and dysfunctional. The media, politicians, and social scientists quickly appropriated the term, using it to refer loosely to a constellation of behaviors or conditions, including being poor and living in the inner city, being chronically unemployed, on welfare, homeless, residing in a single-parent family (especially with illegitimate children), having a criminal record, or using drugs (especially crack cocaine)."[54] Though this list clearly includes behaviors that might be exhibited throughout society or by poor people regardless of where they live, the term was normally used to refer to African Americans exclusively. Sometimes the underclass was defined so broadly that it included blacks not living in poverty areas at all but who allegedly exhibited a single characteristic (such as unemployment or single parenthood) that was thought of as "underclass." Basically, the underclass concept became a way of speaking about race without actually admitting that race was the topic of conversation.[55]

Perhaps because the underclass concept has been used so loosely and inaccurately, most scholars have now abandoned it, though it continues to be used, almost as a slang term, by the popular media. Wilson also stopped using the term and began instead to refer to the harmful effects that result from concentrating the poor together as "concentration effects" when discussing the high incidence of unemployment, high rates of family breakdown, poor health, substance abuse, deteriorating housing, homelessness, and crime in some poverty neighborhoods.[56] More recently, Wilson has called the effects of concentrated poverty "the new urban poverty," and his main focus has turned to the concentration of unemployed males in particular areas: "poor, segregated neighborhoods in which a substantial majority of individual adults are either unemployed or have dropped out of the labor force altogether."[57] According to Wilson, most of the negative social behaviors of blacks who live in the "new urban poverty" can be traced to unemployment.

A substantial proportion of residents in high-poverty urban areas have become disconnected from the economy. In 1980, for example, the unemployment rate in high-poverty areas was 29.6 percent, but this statistic counted only people who were looking for work and could not find it.[58] Wilson found that in fifteen high-poverty black areas in Chicago, just 37 percent of adults held jobs during a typical week in 1990.[59] According to Wilson, persistent joblessness in

Chicago's African-American areas can be traced to a steep decline of manufacturing jobs over the past thirty years. In the past, African Americans held a disproportionate share of blue-collar jobs, and even though their employment in the service sector has risen sharply, full-employment wages have declined by 25 to 30 percent.[60] Even for the available service jobs, educational requirements have gone up, and the arrival of new immigrants has intensified competition for the jobs that do not require a formal education. Finally, a large proportion of desirable jobs are located in the suburbs. Since public transportation is expensive and inconvenient (especially for working parents), it is doubly difficult for those living in inner-city areas to find work.[61] The experience in Chicago would apply to virtually all large urban areas in the United States.

According to Wilson, joblessness is more closely associated with social disorganization than is poverty itself. Without work, a necessary structure for daily life is eroded, and the activities that replace work often undermine family life.[62] Certainly it is easy to show that poverty areas suffer from unusually high levels of violent crime, drug use, family disorganization, poor health, and other problems. It is also the case that people living in such areas have little access to quality schools and services such as child-care centers, family counselors, and treatment programs.

Poverty is closely correlated with family structure. In 1993, families headed by divorced women made only 40 percent as much as households headed by a husband and a wife.[63] Households headed by women who had never been married, however, made only 21 percent as much, and *two-thirds* of all children in such families lived in poverty (compared to one-tenth for married-couple families).[64] Since the mid-1970s, middle-class families have been able to maintain high living standards because there are typically two wage earners. For both the poor and the nonpoor, family income is negatively affected when there is only one female earner. This is because women, on average, make less than men in the same jobs; in addition many of the jobs that are traditionally female are lower paying than the job categories dominated by men. Many women in poverty areas are forced to stay home to take care of their children and to try to make ends meet on welfare. If women manage to find jobs, they usually have to pay for child care, or forgo regular, supervised child care while they are working. In fact, a large proportion of African-American mothers are forced to do just this because of the absence of extended-family networks that might make low-cost child care available.[65] Adolescents in single-parent households are subjected to less supervision, which probably accounts for their higher school dropout rates.[66]

Health and health care in inner-city poverty areas have deteriorated sharply since the late 1970s. Chronic illnesses and contagious diseases are common. The poor lack health insurance and often do not have access to even the most basic health care. In 1990 the United States had among the highest infant mortality rates in the industrialized world.[67] While the overall national rate was about 10 deaths for every 1,000 live births in the late 1980s, the rate for inner-city poverty neighborhoods approached that of Third World countries. In 1988–1989, for example, the infant mortality rate in Central Harlem was 23.4 per 1,000 births, about the same as in Malaysia.[68] The interaction between health and poverty is equally obvious in the case of the AIDS epidemic. AIDS is primarily an urban disease; with only one-eighth of the nation's population, ten metropolitan areas had five-eighths of the nation's caseload in 1988.[69] Within metropolitan areas AIDS has become concentrated in the poorest neighborhoods. Previously in the United States, AIDS was primarily a disease of homosexuals, but by the early 1990s, the disease was spreading most rapidly among poor black and Latino intravenous drug users and their sex partners and offspring. The evidence suggests that a large proportion of future AIDS cases will be concentrated in poor and minority neighborhoods.[70] A hospital in Newark estimated in the early 1990s that 1 in every 46 babies delivered in 1988 was born infected with the AIDS virus.[71]

Substance abuse is still another pervasive problem in poverty neighborhoods. Crack cocaine first appeared on the streets of America's cities in the mid-1980s. Although drug use as a whole is no more prevalent in big cities than in small towns and suburbs, the use of crack cocaine (as opposed to powdered cocaine) remains concentrated in inner cities.[72] Before crack, cocaine was a preferred drug of the rich. Free-based cocaine gave a sharper, more pleasurable rush, but the process was expensive and dangerous—resulting in explosions like the one that hospitalized comedian Richard Pryor in 1987. Crack was developed as a way of producing the intense high of free-based cocaine at a lower cost. Crack is produced by boiling down cocaine into crystals that can be smoked (the name comes from the crackling sound made when it is smoked). In effect, crack was a breakthrough in mass marketing, a stroke of genius: Cocaine, the "champagne" of drugs, was made available at jug wine prices, less than $10 a hit.

Crack began to devastate inner-city poverty neighborhoods in the mid-1980s. The murder rate among young black males tripled between 1984 and 1991, in part because of crack cocaine use.[73] Young men in well-armed gangs fought one another to control the lucrative business, which became "nearly the only high-profit, well-paying economic activity available to them."[74] The connection between crack and violence went beyond the gangs, however. Because crack was so addictive, users would do almost anything to get another fix. Burglary, car theft, and robbery helped to support the habit. Women who became crack addicts often turned to prostitution to support their habit; casual sex in crack houses became a major factor in the AIDS epidemic. By the early 1990s, thousands of babies had been born addicted to crack, costing the nation an estimated $2.5 billion annually.[75]

Violent crime soared in American cities in the late 1980s and early 1990s.[76] In 1990, New York City set a record with 2,262 murders, yet its per capita homicide rate ranked it only slightly above average for the country's twenty-five largest cities.[77] Violent death reached pandemic proportions among young black and Latino males in inner-city areas. Citing the fact that homicide was the leading cause of death for black males aged 15 to 24 in 1990, the federal Centers for Disease Control stated that the casualty rate was approaching that of war. According to a study in the *New England Journal of Medicine,* young men in Harlem, primarily because of high homicide rates, were less likely to survive to the age of 40 than their counterparts in Bangladesh.[78] A survey of schoolchildren in Chicago found that an astonishing 24 percent of them had personally witnessed a murder.[79]

In the 1990s, rates of violent crime went into a steep, and surprising, decline. For the nation as a whole, violent crime per 100,000 persons fell by 17 percent from 1990 to 1997 (after an increase of 20 percent from 1987 to 1990), and the murder rate fell by 28 percent (after a 13 percent increase).[80] The drop in crime was even more dramatic in big cities than elsewhere; homicide rates, for example, fell by 75 percent in New York City from 1990 to 1998 (from more than 2,200 to just over 600).[81] The falling crime rates improved the quality of life for ghetto residents, but did not, of course, change the fact that they still faced inadequate health care, housing, and other problems.

In ghetto areas, dilapidated housing is the most visually striking effect of concentrated poverty. Housing conditions in urban ghettos continue to deteriorate, in large part because the federal government has retreated from low-income housing programs on any meaningful scale. The worst form of housing deprivation, of course, is homelessness. In the 1980s, the number of homeless people multiplied and the composition of the homeless population changed. The homeless are now made up of a broad cross-section: single women with children, temporarily unemployed people of every social, ethnic, and racial group, families, mentally and emotionally impaired people. By the very nature of their condition, the homeless are difficult to count; estimates in the early 1990s varied from a low of 250,000 to 350,000 to as high as three to four million, and the numbers of the homeless were rising year by year.[82] The homeless are concentrated in older central cities, usually near or in downtown areas and in areas that have abandoned or boarded up buildings. As the supply of affordable housing dwindled during the 1980s, many families, an estimated three million families nationwide, were forced to double up.[83]

Though areas of concentrated poverty are located disproportionately in central cities, the older cities are far more complex than a focus on ghettos and slums would suggest. In most cities there are large areas of healthy middle- and working-class neighborhoods, as well as poor neighborhoods that do not fit an underclass stereotype at all. The downtowns and many neighborhoods in most cities have gone through a revival over the last two decades, as evidenced by the renovated waterfronts, new domed stadiums, festival malls, luxury hotels, and office towers. Cities usually house a disproportionate share of the social and cultural assets that are important to metropolitan areas. Normally, the largest and most important downtown office functions are clustered in central cities. These central business districts are essential anchors for metropolitan economies. Cities also provide place identity, an essential feature not only for many businesses but also for tourists. They contain historic districts, revitalized waterfronts, festival malls, convention centers, sports stadiums, symphony and concert halls, museums and zoos, restaurants, and entertainment districts. In addition, cities contain healthy older neighborhoods with significant architectural features that cannot be duplicated in the suburbs. Because booming downtowns and affluent neighborhoods are spreading in many cities, the urban pattern inherited from the twentieth century may be slowly slipping away. If so, it is still too early in the process to make firm predictions.

◆ THE SUBURBS ◆

It is easy to overstate the city-suburban divide—Racial and ethnic tensions, poverty, slums, and crime that have long existed in cities have come also to many suburbs. Nevertheless, in the twentieth century Americans learned to think in dualist images that sharply contrasted the cities with the suburbs. Images of poverty and slums seemed to symbolize the inner cities, while the suburbs tended to evoke images of tranquil subdivisions with cul-de-sacs and expanses of lawn. These images became deeply rooted in the social consciousness of Americans—and they are still constantly nurtured and kept alive by the media. Up to this point, we have considered just one side of the dualist images that have pitted cities against the suburbs. In the second half of this chapter, we look at the Great Divide from another angle by tracing the development of the twentieth-century American suburb. Especially when read together with Chapter 13 (which also deals with central cities), it becomes apparent why images of sick cities and healthy suburbs are often misleading.

The tendency to think of cities negatively and suburbs positively goes back a long way in American culture. This long-standing antiurban bias gained renewed vigor in the twentieth century when millions of white middle- and upper-class households moved out of central cities to low-density, largely single-family subdivisions in the suburbs. In the 1920s, for the first time in the nation's history, suburban populations grew at a faster rate than did the central cities.[84] Decade by decade this trend continued. By the 1970 census, for the first time, more Americans lived in suburbs than lived either in cities or in small towns and rural areas. During the 1980s and 1990s, population continued to sprawl in ever-widening suburban arcs around the core cities.

Suburbanization in the United States has passed through four distinct stages: (1) the railroad and streetcar suburbs, (2) the automobile suburbs, (3) the bedroom suburbs, and (4) the enclave suburbs. During each period, a sorting out process occurred that lowered population densities in urban areas and increased the separation of people of different incomes, family characteristics, and ethnic and racial backgrounds. As the suburbs sprawled further and further from the city, the city-suburban divide became ever more stark—especially in the collective imagination. Even though suburbs varied tremendously in housing conditions, the income, racial and ethnic characteristics of residents, and the competency of their local governments, in the United States the move to the suburbs was always associated with the powerful idea of escaping urban problems and conflicts. In the twenty-first century, the tendency to want to escape from the ills of urban society will probably be expressed as often in fights among suburbs as in conflicts between city and suburb. Still, if the history of suburbanization is any guide, the central cities will remain as symbols of what suburbanites want to escape from for some time to come.

THE RAILROAD AND STREETCAR SUBURBS: 1815–1918

Before the industrial revolution, American cities were compact and population densities were high. Homes were rarely located more than a mile or two from places of work, and almost everyone walked. Outlying areas farther from work and the waterfront were mostly reserved for the lower orders of society.[85] To be sure, the very wealthy sometimes built retreats outside of the cities, but large-scale suburbanization as we know it today, with people living on the outskirts and commuting to jobs, awaited the industrial city. As soon as new forms of transportation made it possible, the upper and upper-middle classes began to escape the congestion of downtown in large numbers.

The American habit of wanting to escape the cities can be traced not only to the conditions in the crowded cities but also to a deeply ingrained antiurban bias that dates to the nation's founding, if not before. Thomas Jefferson is well known for his suspicion of city life. "The mobs of great cities," he wrote, "add just so much to the support of pure government, as sores do to the strength of the human body."[86] In the 1830s and 1840s, the tendency to dislike cities was given specific form by the Romantic movement, which idealized nature and advocated a balance between humanity and nature that was, Romantic writers argued, being destroyed by cities and technology.

Later in the century, the move away from the urban center was also driven by changes in the location of production and in the division of labor within families. In preindustrial cities, most production took place in the home and wives and children often participated in some aspects of the artisan production process. Industrialization brought with it the factory, which massed large numbers of workers under one roof. As work and residence separated, the home gradually became viewed not as a place of production open to outside relations and extended kin but as a haven from the world of work. Especially among the middle and upper classes, the family became the center of emotional life, a sphere controlled by women and set apart from the grime and disorder of the factories and the crowded cities. The emerging cultural ideal situated the family in a single-unit house with a front yard that acted like a moat separating the intimacy of the home from the streets of commerce and competition. Over time, the moat went beyond the front yard, and eventually separated the cities from the suburbs. As one urban historian put it, "The growth of suburbs was to build into the physical environment that division between the feminine/natural/emotional world of family and the masculine/rational/urban world of work."[87]

In 1814 Robert Fulton began the first steam ferry service between Manhattan and Brooklyn, providing a chance for those who could afford it to live apart from the hustle and bustle of Manhattan. Brooklyn thus became the first commuter suburb.[88] The nineteenth century witnessed a succession of transportation improvements that made it possible for people to live farther and farther from the city center: the steam ferry, the omnibus, the commuter railroad, the horsecar, the elevated railroad, the cable car, and the electric trolley.

Railroads were best used for travel between cities and not for commuting, but they did enable a small elite to live in pristine isolation from the problems of industrial society. In a pattern repeated in every stage of urban history, transportation improvements were planned not so much for moving people as for capturing the increased land values that resulted from opening up new suburban land for development. Some railroads lost money on day-to-day operations, but that did not prevent railroad entrepreneurs from amassing fabulous fortunes through suburban land speculation.[89] Commuter tickets on railroads were far too expensive for ordinary workers; thus the railroad suburbs that prospered in the mid-nineteenth century were restricted to the wealthiest classes. In many ways, the early railroad suburbs, like Chestnut Hill outside Philadelphia, Bronxville outside New York, and Forest Park outside Chicago, became the epitome of the suburban ideal. Winding lanes, in contrast to the grid-patterned streets of cities, made these suburbs look like "scattered buildings in a park," the homes integrated with nature, with no hint of the grimy factory on which this suburban wealth was based.[90]

Horse-drawn streetcars became widespread after 1850, providing less expensive transportation for urban residents and expanding the commuting distance for workers up to three miles from downtown.[91] The electric trolley began to revolutionize urban transportation in the 1890s. It was the breakthrough that caused a sudden jump in the rate of suburbanization, and trolleys continued to run until the 1960s, many decades after autos had made their entrance. By tripling the radius of cities, the trolley increased the amount of land that could be developed for residential use by 900 percent. Its introduction was followed by a near frenzy of speculation in land.

Henry E. Huntington was one of the most astute rail entrepreneurs to profit from land speculation. As much as any single person, he was responsible for laying the foundation for the extreme urban sprawl that would come to characterize southern California in the twentieth century. The son of one of the founders of the Southern Pacific Railroad, Huntington failed in his bid to take over that railroad in the 1890s and turned his considerable wealth toward developing a local rail system in the Los Angeles area. In 1901 he formed the Pacific Electric Railway Company. Recognizing that the first few years of intraurban transit were bound to be unprofitable, Huntington bought up huge tracts of land in the western San Gabriel Valley through which his rail lines would be built. When conditions were ripe, he subdivided and sold the land at huge profits. By 1911 he was able to make a deal with the president of the Southern Pacific, which essentially gave him monopoly control over local rail transit in the Los Angeles area. By 1921 his Pacific Electric system was carrying more than 250,000 passengers daily on more than 1,000 miles of track, and Huntington was fabulously wealthy.[92]

With the construction of the streetcar suburbs, suburban growth entered a new phase. Still, no one thought that the suburbs constituted a threat to the cities. Overcrowding, not emptying out, created most of the problems for the industrial cities. Between 1900 and 1920, for example, New York City grew by 2.2 million people, compared to a population increase of just 190,000 in its surrounding area (see Table 6.6). By 1920 New York City's population was 5.6 million people; 379,000 people lived in its suburban ring. In the first three decades of the twentieth century, the vast majority of people living in urban areas still lived in the core cities, even though in several urban areas suburbs grew at a faster rate than did the central cities.

Industrial and manufacturing facilities remained near water and rail transportation links in the city centers. Between 1904 and 1914, St. Louis lost some industry to its suburbs (its share of industrial employment fell from 95 to 90 percent of the area's manufacturing establishments), as did Baltimore (96 to 93 percent) and Philadelphia (91 to 87 percent), but these cities were the exception rather than the rule.[93] The industrial cities overwhelmingly dominated the economies of their urban areas. Men left the suburbs in the morning to commute to their jobs downtown, and at night they returned home. Railroad and streetcar suburbs prospered, but they were still wholly dependent on the central cities.

THE FIRST AUTOMOBILE SUBURBS: 1918–1945

The automobile ultimately came to be regarded as an expression of American values of privacy and individualism. When it was first introduced in the late nineteenth century, it was mainly an expensive plaything for the rich. Henry Ford changed that. In 1908 Ford introduced the Model T, a car for the masses that was dependable and easy to operate. Through the introduction of the moving assembly line in 1913, Ford was able to reduce the cost of a Model T from $950 in 1910 to $290 in 1924. Car ownership skyrocketed. American car production increased from 63,000 automobiles in 1908 to 550,000 by 1914. After World War I, car production really took off, reaching 2.27 million in 1922 and 4.45 million in 1929.[94] The construction of adequate roads lagged seriously behind car ownership, but this problem was eventually solved when automobile owners successfully pressed for massive state and federal funding, mainly through gasoline taxes.

For the rapidly expanding upper-middle class, the automobile provided the opportunity to move to the suburbs. Whereas streetcar suburbs had sprung up along the rail lines like the spokes on a wheel, the automobile made it possible to develop the areas in between. Vast new tracts of land were opened to land speculation and suburban development, and the upper-middle class invested much of its newfound wealth in suburban real estate. Total national wealth doubled in the ten years from 1912 to 1922, and from 1915 to 1925 average hourly wages

TABLE 6.6

METROPOLITAN AREA POPULATION, 1900–1940 (INCREASES IN POPULATION EXPRESSED AS PERCENT GROWTH AND NUMBER OF PEOPLE ADDED)

Districts	1900–1910		1910–1920		1920–1930		1930–1940	
	Central City	Outside Central City	Central City	Outside Central City	Central City	Outside Central City	Central City	Outside Central City
New York City[a]	38.7%	60.9%	17.9%	35.2%	23.3%	67.3%	7.6%	18.2%
Chicago	28.7	87.7	23.4	79.1	24.9	73.9	0.6	10.4
Boston	19.6	23.4	9.0	21.2	4.4	21.2	-1.3	3.1
St. Louis	19.4	90.6	12.5	26.4	6.7	71.3	-0.7	15.7
Cleveland	46.0	46.5	40.1	140.0	11.8	125.8	-2.7	13.0
Los Angeles	206.1	553.3	80.7	107.6	114.7	157.9	21.3	30.1
Mean for all metro districts	33.6	38.2	25.2	32.0	20.9	46.4	4.4	13.6
Non-metro population increase	16.4		9.6		9.5		7.2	
Total U.S. population increase	21.0		14.9		16.1		7.2	

[a]Includes growth of population in New York City proper and in satellite areas of New York State. New Jersey population is excluded.

Source: U.S. Bureau of the Census, *The Growth of Metropolitan Districts in the United States, 1900–1940*, by Warren S. Thompson (Washington, D.C.: Government Printing Office, 1947), especially table 2.

climbed from 32 to 70 cents.[95] The value of residential land and improvements doubled in the 1920s.[96]

In the prosperous decade of the 1920s, suburbs outpaced the cities. Table 6.6 documents this development. In all metropolitan districts in the nation, almost five million people moved to the suburbs in the 1920s, and in the same decade the central cities grew by nearly six million people. However, if the New York and Chicago regions are omitted from the totals, an interesting statistic emerges: The total suburban growth outmatched the cities in all the other metropolitan areas.

The suburban growth spurt did not alarm central-city civic leaders because almost all jobs remained located in and near downtown areas. But there was one ominous but largely overlooked development. The proportion of factory employment in central cities declined in every city of more than 100,000 residents between 1920 and 1930, and this trend was likely to continue because the new assembly line production techniques required lots of land rather than vertical buildings, and this land was in the suburbs. However, all through the affluent 1920s office construction and retailing in central business districts boomed. Almost all white-collar people worked and shopped in the old downtowns. Downtown office space tripled in the 1920s, and employment continued to soar in most central cities.[97]

The Great Depression slowed suburban development, but it even more drastically applied the brake to central city population growth. The depression signaled the twilight of the city-building era. The data in Table 6.6 reveal that Boston, St. Louis, and Cleveland all lost population in the 1930s. So did Philadelphia, Kansas City, and the New Jersey cities—Elizabeth, Paterson, Jersey City, and Newark. San Francisco, which had grown by 27 percent in the 1920s, was no bigger by the census of 1940 than it had been in 1930. A great many small manufacturing cities of New England and the Midwest lost population—Akron and Youngstown, Ohio; Albany, Schenectady, and Troy, New York; Joplin, Missouri; and New Bedford, Massachusetts.

The depression affected the suburbs as well as the cities, since most upper-middle- and middle-class people lacked the means to buy a new suburban home. The growth rate of New York's suburbs fell from 67 percent in the 1920s to only 18 percent in the 1930s. In the same decade Chicago's suburban expansion slowed from 74 percent to 10 percent, Cleveland's from 126 percent to 13 percent, and Los Angeles's from 158 percent to 30 percent. All through the 1930s, the effects of the depression lingered. With the coming of World War II, materials needed for housing construction were commandeered for the war effort. As a result, suburban growth came to a virtual standstill.

THE BEDROOM SUBURBS: 1946–1965

The slowdown in housing construction would have caused a serious housing shortage all by itself, but the postwar baby boom made the situation worse. After reaching a low point during the depression, the birthrate began to rise in 1943 and then took off in the postwar years when 16 million GIs returned to civilian life.[98] By 1947, 6 million families were doubling up with relatives or friends because they could not find a home of their own.[99] The housing industry geared up to meet the demand, pushing single-family housing starts from only 114,000 in 1944 to 1,692,000 by 1950.[100] Virtually all of this new construction took place in the suburbs.

Utilizing mass production methods and sophisticated marketing techniques, big companies began to dominate the housing industry. Big corporations accounted for only 5 percent of all houses built in 1938, but they increased their share of the market to 24 percent by 1949. A decade later, they produced 64 percent of all new homes.[101] These builders concentrated overwhelmingly on the suburbs. Their preferred method was to buy tracts of land on the outskirts of cities and to create whole new communities in a new landscape by bulldozing everything to an even surface and constructing houses quickly using standardized production techniques.

In earlier decades, suburbanization had been mainly an upper- and middle-class phenomenon, but now it filtered down to include working-class families. For most families, owning their own home in the suburbs became a better economic bargain than trying to stay in their old neighborhoods. Federally insured home loans, cheap energy, and new efficient building technologies made it less expensive to build a new house in the suburbs than to rehabilitate a home or rent an apartment in the city. The home ownership rate increased from 43.6 percent in 1940 to 62.9 percent by 1970.[102]

The population of the suburbs exploded. The data in Table 6.7 make it possible to appreciate the magnitude of the population movements in the fifty years between 1940 and 2000. During the 1940s, the core cities grew by just over 6 million people, a 14 percent rate of growth. The suburbs surrounding these cities, by contrast, grew by 9 million people, a 36 percent increase. The suburban growth rate was actually much higher than these statistics suggest because most suburban subdivisions were built after 1946, when wartime conditions finally ended. In the 1950s, central cities grew by an average of 11 percent, but the suburbs that surrounded them grew by 49 percent. In this one decade alone suburban populations increased by 19 million, but the core cities grew by only 6 million. Most of the central city growth, moreover, occurred in midsize and smaller central cities. Most of the big cities in the industrial belt that ran from New England through the Great Lakes states actually lost population. Attempts to reverse this trend by annexing suburbs were prevented by state laws that made such annexation effectively impossible without the approval of the suburbs involved.

Only in the South and the West were cities still booming: Atlanta went from 331,314 people in 1950 to 487,455 by 1960; Phoenix from 106,818 to 439,170 in the same decade. But the suburbs surrounding most of these cities were growing as well. The exceptions were cities like Jacksonville, Florida; Oklahoma City; and Phoenix—and they were exceptions only because they were able to annex new subdivisions before the subdivisions were able to incorporate as separate municipalities.

In the 1960s, the nation's central cities grew on the average by 6 percent, but this statistic hides huge variations. Central cities all across the manufacturing

TABLE 6.7 METROPOLITAN AREA POPULATION, 1940–1990 (INCREASES IN POPULATION EXPRESSED AS PERCENT GROWTH AND NUMBER OF PEOPLE ADDED)

Districts	1940–1950 Central City	1940–1950 Outside Central City	1950–1960 Central City	1950–1960 Outside Central City	1960–1970 Central City	1960–1970 Outside Central City	1970–1980 Central City	1970–1980 Outside Central City	1980–1990 Central City	1980–1990 Outside Central City	1990–2000 Population Change in Central City
Frostbelt											
New York City	5.9%	23.2%	−1.4%	75.0%	1.5%	26.0%	−10.4%	0.4%ᵃ	+3.5%	+0.6%ᵃ	+1.4%
Chicago	6.6	31.2	−2.0	71.5	−5.2	35.3	−10.8	13.6	−7.4	+7.4	+0.6
Boston	4.0	11.5	−13.0	17.7	−8.1	11.3	−12.2	−2.6	+2.0	+3.5	−3.3
St. Louis	5.0	33.8	−12.5	50.8	−17.0	28.5	−27.2	6.3	−12.4	+7.3	−15.8
Cleveland	4.2	41.6	−4.2	67.3	−14.3	27.1	−23.6	0.4	−11.9	+0.0	−0.7
Detroit	13.9	54.8	−9.7	79.3	−9.5	28.5	−20.5	7.8	−14.6	+2.5	−6.1
Pittsburgh	0.8	8.9	−10.7	17.2	−13.9	4.4	−18.5	−2.2	−12.8	−5.8	−9.0
Minneapolis	6.0	76.2	−7.5	115.7	−10.0	55.9	−14.6	20.6	−0.7	+22.8	−4.0
Sunbelt											
Atlanta	9.6	57.8	47.1	33.9	2.0	68.6	−14.1	45.8	−7.3	+42.5	+2.0
Dallas	47.4	73.7	56.4	27.0	24.2	61.8	7.1	47.9	+11.2	+48.5	+6.9
Denver	29.0	73.4	18.8	121.8	4.2	63.7	−4.5	59.9	−5.1	+23.4	+6.9
Phoenix	63.3	86.3	311.1	−0.3	32.4	72.0	30.9	92.1	+24.5	+61.2	+22.5
Los Angeles	31.0	69.8	25.8	66.6	13.6	20.0	5.0	0.7	+17.4	+19.2	+4.2
Miami	44.8	157.2	17.0	161.7	14.8	45.0	3.6	37.1	+3.4	+25.1	+4.2

TABLE 6.7 (Continued)

Districts	1940–1950 Central City	1940–1950 Outside Central City	1950–1960 Central City	1950–1960 Outside Central City	1960–1970 Central City	1960–1970 Outside Central City	1970–1980 Central City	1970–1980 Outside Central City	1980–1990 Central City	1980–1990 Outside Central City
Mean for all SMSAs	14.0	35.9	10.7	48.6	6.4	26.8	0.1	18.2	2.3	12.3
Number added	(6,021,074)	(9,199,931)	(6,251,181)	(19,081,702)	(3,849,814)	(15,974,243)	(80,054)	(15,631,197)	(451,423)	(3,335,814)
Non-metro population increase	6.1		7.1		6.8		15.1		3.9	
Total U.S. population increase	14.5		18.5		13.3		11.4		9.8	

[a] Nassau and Suffolk counties were deleted from the New York City SMSA in 1971. They have been included here for purposes of comparability. The actual Outside Central City figure for the revised New York City SMSA is −1.4%.

Source: U.S. Department of Commerce, Bureau of the Census, *Census of Population, 1950,* vol. 1, *Number of Inhabitants,* pt. 1 (Washington, D.C.: Government Printing Office, 1952), p. 69, table 17; *Census of Population, 1970,* vol. 1, *Characteristics of the Population,* pt. A, p. 180, table 34; *Census of Population, 1980,* suppl. reports, *Standard Metropolitan Statistical Areas and Standard Consolidated Statistical Areas,* p. 2, table B; p. 6, table 1; p. 49, table 3; *State and Metropolitan Areas Data Book, 1991,* table D.

belt suffered massive population losses: St. Louis, for example, lost 17 percent; Cleveland, 14 percent; and Minneapolis, 20 percent. In the same decade the nation's suburbs added 16 million people. Cities in the South and the West continued to grow, some of them (like Phoenix) very rapidly, but a slowdown was evident in the older cities even outside the industrial belt. Denver, for instance, grew by only 4 percent and Atlanta by 2 percent. Both cities, like their counterparts in the northern industrial states, were already ringed by suburbs and therefore they found it hard to annex new housing subdivisions that were springing up beyond their borders.

The suburbs of the 1950s and 1960s were by no means all cut from the same cloth. There were working-class, blue-collar subdivisions, a few isolated areas populated by blacks, and, of course, enclaves of the wealthy. However, most suburban homes of that period were built for white, middle-class families. Individual suburbs tended to be remarkably uniform, with row after endless row of houses that looked as if they had been produced by a cookie cutter. Suburbia came to be portrayed in the popular media as a place of look-alike streets and people, where bored couples with small children spent their free time watching television and picking crabgrass out of their lawns, where the men commuted to office jobs leaving behind frustrated housewives to care for the children in culturally sterile environments. This image of suburbia was captured in three bestselling novels published during the period: *The Man in the Gray Flannel Suit* (1955), *The Crack in the Picture Window* (1956), and *The Split Level Trap* (1960). Though the cultural images of suburbia undoubtedly traded on stereotypes, they struck a responsive chord.[103]

Leaders of central cities were not concerned with the cultural shape of suburbia, but they were increasingly alarmed that the suburbs represented a threat to the vitality and even viability of the central cities. It was not only that the suburbs were growing faster than the cities; they were also pulling affluent white families out of the cities, leaving behind a segregated population made up of blacks, the poor, and other minorities. Increasingly, suburbanization was understood in racial terms; the phrase "white flight" started to be heard, suggesting that suburbanization was motivated in part by racism, a suggestion for which there is abundant evidence.[104] The riots of the mid-1960s heightened the fears connected to race. In 1967, when the National Commission on Civil Disorders called attention to the stark dichotomy between the cities and suburbs, the suburbs had become far removed from life in the central cities. Many people living in the suburbs regarded the inner cities as reservations for blacks, and many blacks had become completely estranged from the rest of America.[105]

THE ENCLAVE SUBURBS: 1965–PRESENT

In recent decades the suburbs have gradually been transformed from wholly dependent satellites of cities, places where people lived but not where they worked, to increasingly self-sufficient enclaves. Though historically suburbanization was primarily a residential movement, at least since 1948 jobs have de-centralized even faster than population.[106] Retailing moved out at a slower pace than did manufacturing and wholesaling because retailing is directly dependent on a nearby critical mass of buyers. By the early 1960s, however, such a critical mass had been established, and before long huge regional shopping malls began to spring up to cater to the shopping and entertainment needs of suburban con-sumers.[107] Suburbanites no longer needed to go downtown, and a historic link between cities and suburbs was severed. Downtown retailing went into a tail-spin from which it has never fully recovered.

The suburbanization of manufacturing employment was made possible by technical innovations that freed factories from a dependence on rail connections. Electrification made single-story plants on suburban land more economical than multistory buildings that housed belt-driven machinery driven by water or steam power. In addition, manufacturers left cities because they viewed them as hotbeds of union organizing and unrest.[108] Through accelerated depreciation of assets, which allowed manufacturers to take tax deductions when they aban-doned inner-city factories, and investment tax credits, which allowed manufac-turers to take tax credits for new plant and equipment, the federal government subsidized the flight of industrial jobs to the suburbs.[109] By 1970, a majority of the manufacturing jobs in metropolitan areas were located in the suburbs.

The service sector was the last to suburbanize. Central business districts of-fered advantages to firms desiring face-to-face relations with clients and benefiting from the concentration of business services in downtowns. Advances in communi-cations, however, made proximity less of an advantage than before. Routine ser-vice employment, the so-called "back office" functions such as copying and secre-tarial services, were the first to leave expensive downtown office space. In 1975, for the first time, the amount of office construction in the suburbs exceeded the vol-ume of office construction in central cities. Higher level and higher paid corporate services, on the other hand, such as legal assistance, corporate consulting, account-ing services, and investment services, continued to locate in the downtowns of large cities, partly for prestige reasons. Although many corporations were still headquartered in central cities, many had moved out to the suburbs, in whole or in part. Some suburbs had developed into Edge Cities, complete with their own office complexes that duplicated many of the characteristics of central business districts.

The effect of these developments was that the suburbs became more inde-pendent of their core cities than in the past. Cross-commuting became common; by 1980, twice as many people commuted from suburb to suburb as commuted from suburb to central city.[110] The historic urban form, in which a city is sur-rounded by dependent suburbs, began to break down and be replaced by the "polynucleated metropolis," characterized by several nodes of concentrated land use (residential, retail, recreational, industrial, service) usually around free-way interchanges and airports. Suburbanization has now progressed to the point that it may be accurate to speak of exurbanization or even counterurban-ization.[111] The urban agglomerations in suburbia have been given a variety of odd and often confusing labels such as "urban villages, technohubs, suburban downtowns, suburban activity centers, major diversified centers, urban cores, galactic city, pepperoni-pizza cities, a city of realms, superburbia, disurb, service cities, perimeter cities, and even peripheral centers."[112] Usually called Edge Cities, what these centers have in common is that they are today springing up as places where jobs, housing, light industry, retail malls, and recreation are concentrated, usually near freeway interchanges or airports.

The data presented earlier in Table 6.7 showed that all through the 1970s and 1980s cities in the area of the country called the "Rustbelt" continued to lose population right to the end of the millenium. Because of their long-term population losses, St. Louis, Pittsburgh, and Minneapolis had become middle-sized cities by the end of the century, with populations ranging from 333,000 (St. Louis) to 353,000 (Minneapolis). All of these cities had topped 600,000 in mid-century. The cities of the Sunbelt, meanwhile, continued to grow, though less rapidly in the 1990s than in previous decades. But in all regions of the country, suburbs grew faster than central cities. By century's end, it was clear that most metropolitan regions had become far more suburban than "urban," if the latter term is used to refer to cities and not to suburbs. The century-long movement to the suburbs had reached a logical conclusion: with a few exceptions, the older cities continued to be "central" mainly because of image and past history. They remained as the biggest cities of their regions, but most of the people living in "St. Louis," for example, only borrowed the name of that historic city.

As more and more people emptied out of the cities, the suburbs became a great deal more diverse than they had been at any time in the past. Condominiums, town houses, and apartment complexes became as common as the single-family subdivisions that had defined suburban life in the 1950s and 1960s. Developers were especially keen to appeal to the fastest growing segments of the American population: young singles and childless couples, and the elderly. As the suburbs became more diverse, they also became "urbanized," in the sense that they began to exhibit the problems long associated with central cities. Just as importantly, suburban families were subject to the same societal changes as families everywhere else. The decline of the traditional nuclear family, for example, affected all income, racial, and ethnic groups. Though a higher proportion of black families in inner-city poverty areas was headed by a single parent, after the 1960s the rate of increase for out-of-wedlock births was greatest among white families. Between 1980 and 1992, out-of wedlock births for whites rose by 94 percent, but by just 9 percent for blacks.[113] Day-care and after-school services were erratically available in the United States, even in affluent suburbs. "Latchkey" children existed in families at all income levels.

Though crack cocaine use had not hit middle-class families as hard as it had poor families in inner cities, by the 1980s, if not before, substance abuse had become a major problem in even the most affluent suburbs, with alcohol, marijuana, and powder cocaine being the drugs of choice. And though crime was clearly higher in central cities, it had been rising faster in many suburban areas than anywhere else.[114] The residents of Green Valley, Nevada, a gated community of more than 20,000 affluent residents on the outskirts of Las Vegas, learned that problems have a habit of following people wherever they go. In the early 1990s a rash of crimes was committed within the community, all by affluent residents, demonstrating that crimes of rape, child molestation, burglary, teenage gang fights, and even murder are not the exclusive province of the poor. Even the president of the Green Valley Community Association was arrested for burglary. One resident commented, "People are coming here from all over the place and bringing their problems with them." [115]

As indicated poignantly by an epidemic of shootings in suburban schools, many of the problems associated with the central cities have sprung up in the suburbs. As a consequence, the city-suburban divide will someday become less important than the divisions pitting suburb against suburb. Such an outcome is unavoidable, given the response of affluent suburbanites who try to escape all problems by moving to defended enclaves, complete with walls, gates, guards, and elaborate security systems. In the 1990s many suburban residential areas became narrowly defined enclaves of like-minded people engaging in "geographical avoidance behavior"; they were trying to sever all contact with central cities and their residents, and even with the residents of nearby neighborhoods.[116]

Some gated communities built in the 1980s and 1990s seem like fortresses built to keep the menacing hordes at bay. The emphasis on security in some of these developments is akin to a state of war. Leisure World, a California retirement community, is surrounded by 6-foot walls topped with barbed wire. Quayside, a planned community in Florida, blends the atmosphere of a Norman Rockwell small town of the 1920s with the latest in high-tech security: Laser beams sweep the perimeter, computers check the coded entry cards of the residents and store exits and entries from the property in a permanent data file, and television cameras continuously monitor the living and recreation areas. Such trappings of security constantly remind the inhabitants that the world beyond their walls is dangerous, so that "'being inside' becomes a powerful symbol for being protected, buttressed, coddled, while 'being outside' evokes exposure, isolation, and vulnerability."[117] In Southern California, fortress enclaves have become a ubiquitous feature of suburban development. In search of high-tech security, architects for the rich "are borrowing design features from overseas embassies and military command posts," building hardened walls, secret passages and doors, and installing a dazzling array of sophisticated electronic surveillance devices.[118] There is such a heavy demand for gated communities in the Los Angeles suburbs that they are quickly replacing all other kinds of development. Enclave suburb against enclave suburb—perhaps this will gradually replace the city-suburban divide.

THE GREAT DIVIDE

On the eve of the twenty-first century, America's urban areas sometimes seem on the verge of fracturing into defended fortresses and enclaves, with central cities competing with suburbs, the suburbs with one another, and private gated communities trying to keep out all who live outside the walls. The tendency to flee from problems rather than to try to confront and solve them has now taken on a momentum of its own. The fear of crime and social disorder drives much of this process. Despite a steadily falling rate of violent crime, the nation's obsession with crime and violence has persisted, and despite all evidence crime continues to be identified mainly with the inner cities and their residents. Local media rely heavily on sensationalized accounts of crime and violence to maintain their ratings. Approximately 20 percent of front page news stories and local news broadcasts focus on violent crime.[119] Live footage of crime scenes is a must for local new stations. The format is extremely standardized. A reporter typically stands at a crime scene in front of a minicam. The talking head soon gives way to a video collage of a bloodstained street or sidewalk, shocked spectators, and perhaps grief-stricken friends and relatives. The reporter often ends his or her monologue with a "running total for the number of murders committed for the year and compares the toll to last year. Like body counts from the war in Vietnam, the numbers are more important for the emotions they arouse than the information they convey."[120]

The sensationalizing of crime and associating it with the inner city has the effect of increasing social and racial tensions. For all but those urban residents that live in crime-infested areas, there is no direct link between crime rates and the fear of crime. Most people do not have personal experiences with violent crime. Crime is highly segregated, especially along racial lines. Most crime committed by young black males, for instance, is directed against other blacks, with attacks against whites—so-called zebra crimes—constituting a much smaller proportion of all crimes. Image and reality are often far apart, however, because the media tend to play up crimes against whites involving blacks, and relatively neglect black-on-black crime. Lurid stories about crime feed fear. Studies have shown that fear of crime is related to the amount of time spent viewing television programs dealing with crime in distant urban settings.[121] Because a local area may not produce a sufficient quantity of sensational crime stories on a daily basis, local news stations often "import" crime stories from other areas to fill in the gaps. People are sensitive to such coverage. Although people express more fear of crime when the stories are about local crimes,[122] newspaper reports that emphasize random and sensational crimes, whatever their origin, increase the fear of crime.[123]

By the late twentieth century the discourse about the inner cities and the urban underclass had become "our . . . national morality play," a performance made up of sensationalized and exaggerated narratives of good and evil.[124] In response to images of violence and disorder, people try to insulate themselves from potential harm: "The more vulnerable we feel, the more we fragment into small living units and working units, or whatever it takes to create the feeling of insulation and safety and home . . ."[125] To the degree that urban residents continue to segregate themselves from one another, the Great Divide will continue to be an apt phrase describing American Society and its cities.

NOTES

1. Robert A. Beauregard, *Voices of Decline: The Postwar Fate of U.S. Cities* (Cambridge, Mass.: Blackwell, 1993).
2. Dennis Judd, "Urban Violence and Enclave Politics: Crime as Text, Race as Subtext," in Seamus Dunn (ed.), *Managing Divided Cities* (Keele, Staffordshire, UK: Ryburn Publishing, Keele University Press, 1994), pp. 160-175.

3. A brief but excellent account of these movements may be found in Stanley B. Greenberg, *Politics and Poverty: Modernization and Response in Five Poor Neighborhoods* (New York: Wiley, 1974), pp. 15–27.

4. *Report of the National Advisory Commission on Civil Disorders* (New York: Bantam Books, 1968), p. 1.

5. See Greenberg, *Politics and Poverty*, pp. 15–27; Leo Grebler, Joan W. Moore, and Ralph C. Guzman, *The Mexican-American People* (New York: Free Press, 1970), p. 113.

6. Harry M. Caudill, *Night Comes to the Cumberlands* (Boston: Little, Brown, 1962).

7. Nicholas Lemann, *The Promised Land: The Great Migration and How It Changed America* (New York: Vintage Books, 1991), p. 6.

8. Stewart E. Tolnay and E. M. Beck, "Rethinking the Role of Racial Violence in the Great Migration," in *Black Exodus: The Great Migration from the American South,* ed. Afrerdteen Harrison (Jackson: University Press of Mississippi, 1991), p. 20.

9. Robert B. Grant, ed., *The Black Man Comes to the City: A Documentary Account from the Great Migration to the Great Depression, 1915–1930* (Chicago: Nelson-Hall, 1972), p. 27; see pp. 16 to 30 for a complete set of statistics on black migration from 1890 to 1930. These data are used throughout this section.

10. Ibid., p. 22.

11. Ibid., p. 23.

12. Winfred P. Nathan, *Health Conditions in North Harlem, 1923–1927,* Social Research Series no. 2 (New York: National Tuberculosis Association, 1932), pp. 44–45, excerpted in Grant, *The Black Man Comes to the City,* pp. 59–61.

13. *Chicago Defender,* reprinted in Grant, *The Black Man Comes to the City,* pp. 31–40.

14. Tolnay and Beck, "Rethinking the Role of Racial Violence," p. 27.

15. *Memphis Commercial Appeal,* October 5, 1916, reprinted in Grant, *The Black Man Comes to the City,* pp. 43–44.

16. *Chicago Defender,* August 12, 1916, reprinted in Grant, *The Black Man Comes to the City,* p. 45.

17. Herbert Northrup, *Organized Labor and the Negro* (New York: Kraus Reprint, 1971).

18. These statistics are from several sources excerpted in Grant, *The Black Man Comes to the City,* pp. 58–61.

19. See Elliott M. Rudwick, *Race Riot at East St. Louis,* July 2, 1917 (Carbondale: Southern Illinois Press, 1964) for a discussion of this event.

20. Chicago Commission on Race Relations, *The Negro in Chicago: A Study of Race Relations and a Race Riot* (Chicago: University of Chicago Press, 1922), p. 122.

21. Tom Kenworthy, "Okla. Starts to Face up to '21 Massacre," *USA Today* (February 18, 2000): 4A.

22. Grant, *The Black Man Comes to the City,* p. 71.

23. U.S. Department of Commerce, Bureau of the Census, *Census of Population 1970: General Social and Economic Characteristics* (Washington, D.C.: Government Printing Office, 1972), pp. 448–449, table 3.

24. Based on unpublished census data reported in Vern E. Smith and Daniel Pederson, "South Toward Home," *Newsweek* (July 14, 1997), pp. 36–38.

25. U.S. Census Bureau, 1990 to 1998 Annual Time Series of Population Estimates by Age, Race, Sex and Hispanic Origin, January 2000 (Website: www.census.gov/population/estimates/countypop.html).

26. "Immigration Reform: Recent Trends and Legislative Responses," *The Urban Institute Policy and Research Report* (Winter/Spring 1991): 12.

27. Rodman D. Griffin, "Illegal Immigration," *CQ Researcher* 2, no. 16 (April 24, 1992): 364.

28. Louis Winnick, *New People in Old Neighborhoods* (New York: Russell Sage Foundation, 1990), p. xvi.

29. U.S. Census Bureau, *1990 to 1998 Annual Time Series of State Population Estimates by Race and Hispanic Origin* (Washington, D.C. Government Printing Office, 1999).

30. U.S. Bureau of the Census, 1990 to 1998 Annual Time Series of Population Estimates by Age, Race, Sex, and Hispanic Origin, January 2000 (Website: www.census.gov/population/estimates/countypop.html).

31. Alejandro Portes and Ruben Rumbaut, *Immigrant America: A Portrait* (Berkeley: University of California Press, 1990), p. 10.

32. Ibid.

33. See Min Zhou, *Chinatown: The Socioeconomic Potential of an Urban Enclave* (Philadelphia: Temple University Press, 1992).

34. U.S. Bureau of the Census, *Statistical Abstract of the United States, 1996* (Washington, D.C.: Government Printing Office, 1996), p. 159. When specifically citing census figures, we employ the term "Hispanic," which is consistent with the term used by the bureau. At all other times we prefer the term "Latino."

35. Ibid., p. 405.

36. U.S. Bureau of the Census, Current Population Reports, P60–193, *Money Income in the United States: 1995* (Washington, D.C., U.S. Government Printing Office, 1996).

37. Christopher L. Warren, John G. Corbett, and John F. Stack, Jr., "Hispanic Ascendancy and Tripartite Politics in Miami," in *Racial Politics in American Cities,* ed. Rufus P. Browning, Dale Rogers Marshall, and David H. Tabb (New York: Longman, 1990), p. 166.

38. Jack Miles, "Blacks vs. Brown," *Atlantic,* October 1992, pp. 41–68. See also Mike Davis, "In L.A., Burning All Illusions," *Nation,* June 1, 1992, pp. 743–746.

39. Tim Rutten, "A New Kind of Riot," *New York Review of Books,* June 11, 1992, pp. 52–54.

40. "Immigration Reform," p. 13.

41. Reported in Charles Kamasaki and Paul Yzaguirre, "Black-Hispanic Tensions: One Perspective" (paper delivered at the Annual Meeting of the American Political Science Association, Washington, D.C., August 29–September 1, 1991), p. 5. See also Stephen Castles and Mark J. Miller, *The Age of Migration: International Population Movements in the Modern World* (New York: Guilford Press, 1993).

42. Robert Pear, "Major Immigration Bill Is Sent to Bush," *New York Times,* October 29, 1990; see also Castles and Miller, *The Age of Migration,* p. 249.

43. Griffin, "Illegal Immigration."

44. The official poverty line is established by the U.S. Department of Health and Human Services (HHS) and is based on the amount of money HHS calculates is required to purchase an "emergency" diet (a diet that provides adequate nutrition) for one person for a year. That amount is multiplied by three to arrive at the income below which an individual is deemed to be at a poverty level. The definition makes the assumption, challenged by virtually all researchers, that all other necessities can be covered by an amount no more than twice the amount spent for food. In 1990, the poverty line for a family of four was set at $12,293.

45. Michael Harrington, *The Other America: Poverty in the United States,* rev. ed. (New York: Macmillan, 1962).

46. U.S. Bureau of the Census, Series P-60, *Current Population Reports* (Washington, D.C.: Government Printing Office, 1991).

47. John Kasarda, "Inner-City Concentrated Poverty and Neighborhood Distress: 1970 to 1990," *Housing Policy Debate* 4, No. 3 (1993): 253–302.

48. Douglas Massey and Nancy Denton, *American Apartheid: Segregation and the Making of the Underclass* (Cambridge, Mass.: Harvard University Press, 1993), pp. 74–78.

49. Douglas S. Massey and Nancy Denton, "Trends in the Residential Segregation of Blacks, Hispanics, and Asians: 1970–1980," *American Sociological Review* 52 (1987): 802–825.

50. John E. Farley, "Racial Housing Segregation in the St. Louis Metropolitan Area, 1990" (paper delivered at the Annual Meeting of the Illinois Sociological Association, Evanston, Ill., October 18, 1991).

51. Ibid.; see also Douglas Massey and Mitchell Eggers, "The Ecology of Inequality: Minorities and the Concentration of Poverty, 1970–1980," *American Journal of Sociology* (March 1990): 1153–1189; Douglas Massey, "American Apartheid: Segregation and the Making of the Underclass," *American Journal of Sociology* (June 1990): 329–357; William Julius Wilson, *The Truly Disadvantaged: The Inner City, the Underclass, and Public Policy* (Chicago: University of Chicago Press, 1987); William Julius Wilson, *When Work Disappears: The World of the New Urban Poor* (New York: Knopf, 1996).

52. William W. Goldsmith and Edward J. Blakely, *Separate Societies: Poverty and Inequality in U.S. Cities* (Philadelphia: Temple University Press, 1992), p. 48.

53. Paul A. Jargowsky, "Ghetto Poverty Among Blacks in the 1980s," *Journal of Policy Analysis and Management* 13 (1993): 288–310.

54. Michaela di Leonardo, "White Lies/Black Myths: Rape, Race, and the Black Underclass," *The Village Voice*, September 22, 1992, p. 31.

55. Norman Fainstein, "Race, Class, and Segregation: Discourses About African Americans," *International Journal of Urban and Regional Research*, 17, No. 3 (1993): 384–403.

56. William Julius Wilson, *The Truly Disadvantaged*.

57. Wilson, *When Work Disappears*, p. 19.

58. Goldsmith and Blakely, *Separate Societies*, pp. 51–52.

59. Wilson, *When Work Disappears*, p. 51.

60. Ibid., p. 31.

61. For further information on the mismatch between the geographic location of inner-city blacks and available jobs, see John Kasarda, "Urban Change and Minority Opportunities," in *The New Urban Reality*, ed. Paul E. Peterson (Washington, D.C., Brookings Institution, 1985), pp. 33–67; John D. Kasarda, "Urban Employment Change and Minority Skills Mismatch," in *Creating Jobs, Creating Workers: Economic Development and Employment in Metropolitan Chicago*, ed. Lawrence B. Joseph (Chicago: Center for Urban Research and Policy Studies, 1990), pp. 65–89.

62. Wilson, *When Work Disappears*, pp. 25–88.

63. Ibid., p. 92.

64. Ibid., p. 93.

65. Ibid., p. 92.

66. Sonia L. Nazario, "High Infant Mortality Is a Persistent Blotch on Health Care in U.S.," *Wall Street Journal*, October 19, 1988, p. 1.

67. Lisa W. Foderaro, "In Harlem, Children Reflect the Ravages U.N. Seeks to Relieve," *New York Times*, September 30, 1990, p. 1.

68. Walter J. Jones and James E. Johnson, "AIDS: The Urban Policymaking Challenge," *Journal of Urban Affairs* 11, No. 1 (1989): 85.

69. *Confronting AIDS: Update 1988* (Washington, D.C.: National Academy Press, 1988), p. 52.

70. Lena Williams, "Inner City Under Siege: Fighting AIDS in Newark," *New York Times*, February 6, 1989, p. 1.

71. Joel A. Devine and James D. Wright, *The Greatest of Evils: Urban Poverty and the American Underclass* (New York: Aldine De Gruyter, 1993), p. 166.

72. Wilson, *When Work Disappears*, p. 21.

73. Devine and Wright, *The Greatest of Evils*, p. 167.

74. "Crack," editorial, *New York Times*, May 29, 1989.

75. Michael deCourcy Hinds, "Number of Killings Soars in Big Cities Across U.S.," *New York Times*, July 18, 1990, p. 1.

76. Robert D. McFadden, "New York Leads Cities in Robbery Rate, but Drops in Murders," *New York Times*, August 11, 1991, p. 1.

77. See James Diego Vigil, *Barrio Gangs: Street Life and Identity in Southern California* (Austin: University of Texas Press, 1988).

78. Ronald Kotulak, "Study Finds Inner-City Kids Live with Violence," *Chicago Tribune*, September 28, 1990, p. 1.

79. Jonathan Kozol, *Rachel and Her Children: Homeless Families in America* (New York: Crown, 1988), p. 9.

80. U.S. Bureau of the Census, *Statistical Abstract of the United States*, table 342, Crimes and Crime Rates, by Type of Offense: 1987 to 1997; U.S. Federal Bureau of Investigation, *Crime in the United States Annual* (Washington, D.C.: Government Printing Office, 1998).

81. Sophie Body-Gendrot, *The Social Control of Cities? A Comparative Perspective* (Malden, Mass. and Oxford, U.K.: Blackwell, 2000), p. 116.

82. Ibid., p. 11.

83. Philip L. Clay, *At Risk of Loss: The Endangered Future of Low-Income Rental Housing Resources* (Washington, D.C.: Neighborhood Reinvestment Corporation, 1987), p. 4.

84. Population growth on the outskirts probably exceeded population growth in the center before the 1920s. However, before 1920, annexation of suburban land by central cities obscured the statistical trend. See John D. Kasarda and George V. Redfearn, "Differential Patterns of City and Suburban Growth in the United States," *Journal of Urban History* 2, No. 1 (November 1975): 53.

85. Kenneth T. Jackson, *Crabgrass Frontier: The Suburbanization of the United States* (New York: Oxford University Press, 1985), chap. 1.

86. Quoted in James A. Clapp, ed., *The City: A Dictionary of Quotable Thoughts on Cities and Urban Life* (New Brunswick, N.J.: Center for Urban Policy Research, Rutgers University, 1984), p. 129.

87. Robert Fishman, *Bourgeois Utopias: The Rise and Fall of Suburbia* (New York: Basic Books, 1987), p. 62. Fishman's account stresses the role of changing cultural values and family life in the rise of suburbs; see also Jackson, *Crabgrass Frontier*, chaps. 3 and 4.

88. Jackson, *Crabgrass Frontier*, pp. 25–30. Robert Fishman dates the first true suburb somewhat earlier, in the 1790s in Clapham and other villages outside London; see Fishman, *Bourgeois Utopias*, p. 53.

89. For accounts of railroad suburbs and land speculation, see Jackson, *Crabgrass Frontier*, chap. 5; Fishman, *Bourgeois Utopias*, chap. 5; Harry C. Binford, *The First Suburbs: Residential Communities on the Boston Periphery, 1815–1860* (Chicago: University of Chicago Press, 1985).

90. The phrase "scattered buildings in a park" is Lewis Mumford's; see his *The City in History: Its Origins, Its Transformations, and Its Prospects* (New York: Harcourt, Brace & World, 1961), p. 489.

91. Peter O. Muller, *Contemporary Suburban America* (Englewood Cliffs, N.J.: Prentice-Hall, 1981), p. 28.

92. Our account of Huntington relies on Robert M. Fogelson, *The Fragmented Metropolis: Los Angeles, 1850–1930* (New York: Cambridge, 1967), pp. 89–92; Jackson, *Crabgrass Frontier*, p. 122; Fishman, *Bourgeois Utopias*, pp. 159–160.

93. Gary A. Tobin, "Suburbanization and the Development of Motor Transportation: Transportation Technology and the Suburbanization Process," in *The Changing Face of the Suburbs*, ed. Barry Schwartz (Chicago: University of Chicago Press, 1976), p. 100. See also U.S. Bureau of the Census, *Industrial Districts: 1905, Manufactures and Population*, Bulletin 101 (Washington, D.C.: Government Printing Office, 1909), pp. 9–80. U.S. Bureau of the Census, *Census of Manufactures: 1914*, vol. 1, *Reports by States with Statistics for Principal Cities and Metropolitan Districts* (Washington, D.C.: Government Printing Office, 1918), pp. 564, 787, 1292.

94. These data are cited in Tobin, "Suburbanization and the Development of Motor Transportation," pp. 102, 103, and are also available in National Industrial Conference Board (NICB), *The Economic Almanac 1956: A Handbook of Useful Facts About Business, Labor and*

Government in the United States and Other Areas (New York: Crowell for the Conference Board, 1956).

95. Tobin, "Suburbanization and the Development of Motor Transportation," pp. 102, 103.

96. Ibid.

97. Jackson, *Crabgrass Frontier*, pp. 174, 184.

98. The birthrate (the number of live births per 1,000 population) increased from 18.4 in 1936 to 26.6 in 1947. U.S. Bureau of the Census, *Historical Statistics of the United States, Colonial Times to 1970*, Bicentennial edition, pt. 2 (Washington, D.C.: Government Printing Office, 1975), p. 49.

99. Jackson, *Crabgrass Frontier*, p. 232.

100. Ibid., p. 233.

101. Checkoway, "Large Builders, Federal Housing Programs, and Postwar Suburbanization," in *Marxism and the Metropolis: New Perspectives in Political Economy*, ed. William K. Tabb and Larry Sawers (New York: Oxford University Press), pp. 155–156.

102. U.S. Bureau of the Census, *Historical Statistics of the United States, Colonial Times to 1970*, Bicentennial edition, pt. 1 (Washington, D.C.: Government Printing Office, 1975), p. 646.

103. For criticisms of the 1950s stereotype of suburbia, see Bennett M. Berger, *Working-Class Suburb: A Study of Auto Workers in Suburbia* (Berkeley: University of California Press, 1968); Herbert J. Gans, *The Levittowners: Ways of Life and Politics in a New Suburban Community* (New York: Pantheon, 1967).

104. Thomas M. Guterbock, "The Push Hypothesis: Minority Presence, Crime, and Urban Deconcentration," in *The Changing Face of the Suburbs*, ed. Barry Schwartz (Chicago: University of Chicago Press, 1976), p. 26.

105. National Advisory Commission on Civil Disorders, *Report of the National Advisory Commission on Civil Disorders* (New York: Bantam Books, 1968), p. 1.

106. James Heilbrun, *Urban Economics and Public Policy*, 2nd ed. (New York: St. Martin's Press, 1981), p. 48.

107. Muller, *Contemporary Suburban America*, p. 123.

108. David M. Gordon, "Capitalist Development and the History of American Cities," in *Marxism and the Metropolis: New Perspectives in Urban Political Economy*, 2nd ed., ed. William K. Tabb and Larry Sawers (New York: Oxford University Press, 1984), p. 41.

109. George E. Peterson, "Federal Tax Policy and Urban Development," in *Central City Economic Development*, ed. Benjamin Chinitz (Cambridge, Mass.: Abt Books, 1979), pp. 67–78.

110. Robert Cevero, "Unlocking Suburban Gridlock," *Journal of the American Planning Association* (Autumn 1986): 389.

111. Brian J. L. Berry, *The Open Housing Question: Race and Housing in Chicago, 1966–1976* (Cambridge, Mass.: Ballinger, 1979).

112. Joel Garreau, *Edge City: Life on the New Frontier* (Garden City, N.Y.: Doubleday, 1991), p. 6.

113. Wilson, *When Work Disappears*, p. 88.

114. Josh Barbanel, "From L. I. Teller Machines to Gas Stations, Suburban Robberies Are on the Rise," *New York Times*, February 18, 1992, p. 1.

115. David Guterson, "No Place Like Home: On the Manicured Streets of a Master-Planned Community," *Harper's*, November 1992, p. 63.

116. Muller, *Contemporary Suburban America*, p. 180.

117. Trevor Boddy, "Underground and Overhead: Building the Analogous City," in *Variations on a Theme Park: The New American City and the End of Public Space*, ed. Michael Sorkin (New York: Noonday Press, 1992), p. 139.

118. Mike Davis, "Fortress Los Angeles: The Militarization of Urban Space," in *Variations on a Theme Park: The New American City and the End of Public Space*, ed. Michael Sorkin (New York: Noonday Press, 1992), p. 173.

119. Margaret T. Gordon and Claudette Guzan Artwick, "Urban Images in the Mass Media" (research proposal, Urban University Research Consortium, June 17, 1991), p. 2.
120. Suro, "Crime and Its Amplified Echoes are Rearranging People's Lives," *The New York Times*, February 9, 1992, p. 1.
121. Heath and J. Petraitis, "Television Viewing and Fear of Crime: Where Is the Mean World?" *Basic and Applied Social Psychology* 8 (1987): 91–92.
122. E. Liska and W. Baccaglini, "Feeling Safe by Comparison: Crime in the Newspapers, A Multi-methodological Investigation," *Journal of Personality and Social Psychology* 47, No. 2 1989: 366.
123. Heath and Petraitis, "Television Viewing and Fear of Crime": 92.
124. Michaela di Leonardo, "White Lies/Black Myths," p. 31.
125. Richard Louv, *America II: The Book That Captures Americans in the Act of Creating the Future* (New York: Penguin Books, 1983), p. 34.

CHAPTER

7

NATIONAL POLICY AND THE DIVIDED METROPOLIS

NATIONAL POLICIES AND URBAN DEVELOPMENT

The antiurban prejudice that has pervaded American culture for so long does not, by itself, explain the extreme racial segregation that has continued to separate cities from suburbs. It is true that the residents of urban areas always have tended to sort themselves out along racial, ethnic, and class lines. In the twentieth century, however, the social preferences of individual homebuyers did not solely prompt the mass movement of affluent white families to the suburbs and the concentration of racial and ethnic minorities into the inner cities. The racial and social class composition of urban areas was not left to personal choice or to the marketplace. Instead, the housing and urban development policies of governments intervened to fundamentally shape the patterns of racial segregation that we see today. Segregation was accomplished by national policies and through policies enforced by local governments. In Chapter 10 we discuss the role of local governments in promoting segregation in the suburbs. In this chapter we show how the housing and urban development policies of the national government were used to enforce racial segregation.

From the 1930s through much of the 1960s, the federal government helped finance a housing boom that was effectively put off limits to blacks. Federal administrators worked hand-in-hand with local developers and financial institutions to enforce restrictive covenants and implement loan policies that kept blacks from buying into suburban neighborhoods. In the cities, nationally funded urban renewal policies were used to clear large tracts of slum properties. The supply of housing available to African-American homebuyers and renters was sharply reduced. Since they were denied access to the suburbs, many low-income blacks were forced into the high-rise public housing projects being constructed through federal funds, and both low-income and middle-class blacks were forced into an intense competition for the older housing left available in urban neighborhoods. Though the federal government began to change policies in the 1960s, the changes came too little and too late. By then the metropolitan pattern of segregation was written in cement.

The extreme racial segregation that characterizes America's urban areas was further encouraged by the federally assisted highway programs, which cut broad swaths through central city neighborhoods all through the 1950s and 1960s—the same decades when the suburbs were booming. Within a brief period, urban areas began to sprawl outward. The patterns of residential segregation that quickly separated the central cities from the suburbs began to differentiate inner-ring suburbs from the newer subdivisions spreading inexorably outward. The irony of the federal government's policies is that all of them were viewed as either benign in their racial impacts, or as positively beneficial to poor and affluent, black and white, alike. In fact, the housing, urban renewal, and highway policies of the federal government helped to create the racially segregated living patterns of today's urban areas.

HOUSING, SLUMS, AND RACIAL SEGREGATION

Taken at face value, the national programs to clear slums and to build low-cost housing in inner cities should have helped impoverished city residents the most. Slum clearance and public housing were always defended as socially beneficial to slum residents. The promise was that instead of living in dilapidated, unsafe properties, the poor would have the opportunity to move into safe and adequate housing constructed by the government. The politics of urban renewal and public housing programs, however, undercut their announced social objectives. For blacks, these programs turned into a cruel hoax. Local politicians and businesses used slum clearance to protect the property values of downtown business districts. Slum clearance became a means of moving blacks from potentially valuable real estate. What made such practices so damaging is that the amount of housing lost to the bulldozer vastly exceeded the number of public housing units ever built. Even worse, public housing projects soon were transformed into high-rise slums that segregated blacks even more than before.

The first positive federal response to the problems of urban America came in 1892, when Congress appropriated $20,000 to investigate slum conditions in cities with populations over 200,000.[1] In his subsequent report to the Congress, the Commissioner of Labor noted, among other observations, that all of the nation's big cities contained block after block of rundown tenement districts that packed immigrants together into often unsafe and unsanitary conditions. The commissioner made much of the fact that these areas had a higher incidence of arrests and saloons than anywhere else in the country.

Federal assistance for the construction of urban housing can be traced to the entry of the United States into World War I. In 1918 Congress authorized direct federal loans to local realty companies.[2] At a cost of $69.3 million, 8 hotels, 19 dormitories, 1,100 apartment units, and approximately 9,000 houses were con-structed to house wartime shipyard workers in 27 cities and towns.[3] Later in the same year, Congress approved the nation's first public housing program, de-signed to accommodate defense plant workers who needed housing near wartime factories. The U.S. Housing Corporation was created to manage the program. In the brief three months of the program's existence, the Housing Cor-poration built about 6,000 single-family dwellings, plus accommodations for 7,200 single men, on 140 project sites scattered around the country.[4] At the con-clusion of the war, all of these federally owned housing units were sold to pri-vate owners and the government removed itself from the housing business.

The next federal intervention into housing came during the Great Depression. Initially, the government's efforts were motivated mainly by the economic condi-tions of the depression, though the social conditions of inner-city slums also elicited concern. However, other reasons were not hard to find. Even after the prosperous twenties, all the nation's cities contained rundown business districts and residential slums. As the depression wore on, the situation deteriorated rapidly: Landlords and owners invested little or no money in repairs and renovation, and the con-struction of new housing slowed to a crawl. The apparent solutions to the problems of housing and slums lay beyond the financial capacity of local governments. The slums that plagued the nation's cities slowly became defined as a national problem, and local officials and business elites who were concerned about deteriorating business and residential districts looked to the national government for help.

In 1932, the last year of Herbert Hoover's presidency, Congress created the Reconstruction Finance Corporation (RFC) and authorized it to extend loans to private developers for the construction of low-income housing in slum areas.[5] Only two projects were actually ever undertaken, with over 98 percent of the money spent in three slum blocks of Manhattan to construct Knickerbocker Vil-lage, with its 1,573 apartments.[6] This program had two contradictory purposes. On the one hand, it was supposed to help revive the construction industry; on the other hand, it was supposed to be a means of increasing the supply of low-income housing in New York. In the case of Knickerbocker Village, the first goal won out. Eighty-two percent of the slum families who initially moved into the apartments were soon forced to move back to the slums they had left because of the escalating rents charged by the owners.[7]

Franklin D. Roosevelt introduced a great number of national programs de-signed to stimulate the economy and end the depression. One of the first of these, the National Industrial Recovery Act of 1933, included a minor provision authorizing "construction, reconstruction, alteration, or repair, under public regulation or control, of low-rent housing and slum clearance projects."[8] The Housing Division of the Public Works Administration (PWA) was charged with implementing this provision. At first the PWA tried to entice private developers into constructing low-income housing by offering them low-interest federal loans. This strategy conformed with one of the major purposes of the program, which was "to deal with the unemployment situation by giving employment to workers . . . [and] to demonstrate to private builders the practicability of large-scale community planning."[9] But contractors and home builders did not find low-interest loans sufficiently attractive, and only seven projects ever met specifications and were approved. As a result, the PWA decided to bypass the housing industry altogether and finance and construct its own federally owned housing. The U.S. Emergency Housing Corporation was created for this purpose in 1933, and it claimed the right of eminent domain to force the sale of slum property for clearance and construction.

Federal court decisions in Kentucky and Michigan stopped federal administrators from using eminent domain to take over slum land for clearance,[10] so they tried another tack. The Emergency Housing Corporation decided to make low-income housing grants to local public housing authorities. Local authorities could be chartered by the states, and previous court cases made it clear that the states could use eminent domain to accomplish a variety of public purposes. With the offer of federal money dangled before them, city officials lobbied their state legislatures to allow them to create local housing authorities to receive the funds. By the end of the PWA public housing program in 1937, twenty-nine states had passed enabling legislation allowing local governments to create and operate local public housing authorities, and forty-six local housing agencies had come into existence.[11] These authorities built almost 22,000 public, low-income housing units in thirty-seven cities.[12]

For all the effort to get the PWA program off the ground, the eventual results were questionable. More low-income units were torn down through slum clearance than were ever built. Local public housing authorities were closely tied to the housing industry in their communities, with the result that a substantial proportion of PWA funds were used to help owners sell slum properties to local housing authorities at inflated prices.[13] These properties were then slated for clearance, even though no new housing units were planned to replace them. In all these respects, the PWA experience provided a warning for the future: Program goals were easily subverted if local communities were allowed to make all of the consequential decisions. Unfortunately, the warning was ignored.

The PWA experience provided the administrative model for future housing programs. It was accepted that if federal grants were made available for public housing in the future, local public housing agencies would become the recipients of the funds and federal agencies would not try to build public housing units themselves. The Public Housing Act of 1937 (also called the Wagner-Steagall Public Housing Act after the names of its legislative sponsors) succeeded the PWA program. The act adopted the principle that housing programs would be implemented through federal grants-in-aid to local housing authorities. Under the legislation, public housing would be built and administered by local agencies, not by the federal government, and private realtors and contractors would handle land sales and construction. Its stated purposes were:

> To provide financial assistance to the states and political subdivisions thereof for the elimination of unsafe and unsanitary housing conditions, for the eradication of slums, for the provision of decent, safe, and sanitary dwellings for families of low income and for the reduction of unemployment and the stimulation of business activity, to create a United States Housing Authority, and for other purposes.[14]

The Public Housing Act of 1937 was "designed to serve the needs of those of low income who otherwise would not be able to afford decent, safe, and sanitary dwellings."[15] However, the absence of substantial profits for realtors, builders, and banks for constructing public housing projects meant that they steadfastly opposed public housing. As far as they were concerned, government-owned housing competed with the private housing market. Its only redeeming virtue was that public housing provided jobs in the construction industry. But this benefit failed to outweigh the unpopularity of providing housing subsidies to the bottom third of the population. As explained by the president of the National Association of Real Estate Boards, the housing industry's philosophy was that low-income housing should become available through a filter-down process:

> Housing should remain a matter of private enterprise and private ownership. It is contrary to the genius of the American people and the ideals they have established that government become landlord to its citizens. There is a sound logic in the continuance of the practice under which those who have the initiative and the will to save acquire better living facilities and yield their former quarters at modest rents to the group below.[16]

Senator Robert F. Wagner of New York, one of the co-sponsors of the 1937 housing bill, defended the legislation by pointing out that it was not intended as a program that would interfere with the private housing market:

> The object of public housing in a nutshell, is not to invade the field of home building for the middle class or the well-to-do which has been the only profitable area for private enterprise in the past. Nor is it even to exclude private enterprise from major participation in a low-cost housing program. It is merely to supplement what private industry will do, by subsidies which will make up the difference between what the poor can afford to pay and what is necessary to assure decent living quarters.[17]

To make sure that middle-class families could not opt out of the private housing market by moving into public housing, the legislation contained specific limitations on the costs and quality of rental units and a restriction that occupancy be strictly limited to low-income families. A requirement was also added that the number of new housing units constructed could not exceed the number of slum dwellings torn down.[18]

The U.S. Housing Administration (USHA) was authorized by the 1937 act to extend low-interest loans to local public housing agencies. The loans could cover up to 100 percent of the cost of financing slum clearance and the construction of low-income housing units. The USHA was also authorized to make grants and annual subsidies to local housing agencies for the operation and maintenance of housing units after they were built. The USHA and its successor agencies, the Federal Public Housing Authority (1942 to 1946) and the Public Housing Administration (1946 to the present), completed a total of 169,451 low-income public housing units under the authority of the 1937 housing act.[19]

World War II was the third national emergency (the others were World War I and the depression) recognized by Congress as requiring the production of publicly built and financed housing. In addition to 50,000 units built during the war through the 1937 housing act authorizations, two million more housing units were provided through temporary and emergency programs to house workers who streamed into cities to take jobs in defense industry plants. Of these, around one million units were privately built with federal financial assistance.[20] Another one million were completed under programs that left ownership in the hands of the federal government. As soon as the war was over, these government-owned units were sold on the private market.

THE STRUGGLE OVER PUBLIC HOUSING

The concerns about inner-city slums that had been expressed during the Great Depression were voiced again following World War II. A broad coalition of interests pressed for congressional action. Local public officials and business leaders were alarmed by the condition of downtown business districts and nearby residential areas. Public housing administrators, labor unions, social workers, and liberal Democrats were concerned about the plight of the poor and argued that slum residents had a moral right to adequate housing. In addition, they said, slums bred disease, crime, and delinquency and were therefore detrimental to the moral fiber and social fabric of the city. It was noted, for example, that though Cleveland's slum areas contained only 3 percent of the city's population, they accounted for 8 percent of the juvenile delinquency arrests and 21.3 percent of the city's murders in 1932.[21] Improving the physical environment of slum residents, it was argued, was a good thing to do not only because it gave poor people immediate aid but also because it would help families and individuals living in the slums to begin improving their lives, thus lowering the level of social disorder.

Realtors, developers, financial institutions, and local business elites had their own reasons for favoring slum clearance. They were not concerned so much about the conditions of life for slum dwellers as for their own real estate investments. Dilapidated commercial and residential areas, they said, threatened the economic vitality of the central cities. They reasoned that falling rents and increasing vacancy rates formed a downward spiral with less and less maintenance in slum areas. The powerful U.S. Savings and Loan League voiced support for the redevelopment of blighted areas: "Our people have studied the problem of slum clearance for some years and agree that it is an appropriate field for public action . . . we think it appropriate for . . . land assembly [to proceed] in the slum areas of our cities."[22] Even the National Association of Real Estate Boards (NAREB) favored urban redevelopment, as long as it was implemented through private developers and involved slum clearance but not public housing.[23] NAREB spearheaded the lobbying against federally subsidized public housing. Although its headquarters were in Chicago, NAREB maintained a well-staffed office in the nation's capital—known as the "Realtors' Washington Office"—from which it exerted pressure on Congress and federal administrators. The executive vice president of the association was Herbert U. Nelson, who was fond of labeling his opponents communists and subversives. Throughout the 1940s, though NAREB and its allies promoted federally subsidized urban redevelopment, the issue remained subordinated to their venomous opposition to public housing programs. This unwavering opposition derived its force from Nelson's ideological stand against the evils of "socialism"—defined as publicly subsidized housing—and was supported by the real estate industry's interest in preventing government competition with private landlords.[24] The association pressed its opposition to public housing all across the country—on Capitol Hill, in state houses, in city halls, and in communities and neighborhoods. Between 1939 and 1949, it was instrumental in stalling congressional legislation. The blind hatred that NAREB held for public housing led it to adamantly oppose the 1949 housing act, even though this legislation also made federal funds available for slum clearance, which NAREB favored.

The U.S. Savings and Loan League was the second most powerful housing industry group. In 1949 the league represented 3,700 associations, which included in their membership most of the nation's savings and loan institutions. These financial institutions issued long-term mortgage loans for the construction and purchase of homes. Although originally established to serve the working class as an alternative to conventional banking institutions, over the years savings and loan institutions acquired a middle- and upper-class bias in their policies. Like the realtors, the savings and loan industry opposed any governmental action that competed with privately owned housing.

The National Association of Home Builders (NAHB), which represented approximately 16,500 companies in 1949, weighed in, and was joined by an array of industry, trade, and financial associations that also opposed public housing, including the U.S. Chamber of Commerce, the Mortgage Bankers Association of America, the Producers Council, the National Economic Council, and the National Association of Retail Lumber Dealers.[25]

Though a broad coalition of groups favored public housing, perhaps the most influential among them was the National Public Housing Conference. Formed during the early years of the depression, this group became a kind of brain trust for public housing policy. It had been largely responsible for the research and staff work that underlay the development of the 1937 housing act. Unlike the real estate lobbies, it was not a federation of local groups, nor was it a mass-based organization. It was an elite group of individuals interested in housing policy, and it included some of the more influential local housing administrators, government officials, and academic experts on housing problems and policies. The Public Housing Conference maintained close connections with the federal government's housing administrators and thus was able to partially offset the housing industry's opposition to public housing.

Organized labor provided decisive support for public housing. The AFL and the CIO both maintained housing committees and participated in the Washington-based Labor Housing Conference. Of all the pro-public housing groups, only the unions carried the substantial political clout attendant to mass-based organizations. Organized labor led the way in criticizing the real estate industry's redevelopment proposals. A booklet of the period published by the United

Auto Workers accused realtors and developers of promoting their own narrow economic interests under the cover of slum clearance:

> Climbing on the "slum clearance" band wagon, they [the real estate and building trade associations] are trying to hoodwink the public into buying city slum areas at a high price and turning such areas over to them at a fraction of such cost to the public. Not a word of "subsidy" here. Not a word of rehousing the families who now live in the slums.[26]

The National Association of Housing Officials (NAHO) also attacked the urban redevelopment proposal advocated by the real estate industry. This group was formed during the depression and was responsible for educating supporters of public housing through its publication, the *Journal of Housing*. Reflecting the basic values that drew the pro-public housing coalition together, NAHO insisted that the social goal of providing adequate housing was far more important than urban economic development itself.

Local government officials and the organizations representing them were interested in federal subsidies in any form, and therefore they lobbied for both slum clearance and public housing. The U.S. Conference of Mayors, the National League of Cities, and the American Municipal Association all lined up behind a program of federally subsidized development. They were instrumental in knitting together a coalition sufficiently broad so that the legislation before Congress would not be sabotaged by the bickering among the various interest groups. Perhaps the best indicator of the unlikely nature of the political alliance that supported the 1949 housing act is to be found in its unofficial title—the Wagner-Ellender-Taft Act. The three senators whose names were identified with the legislation spanned the spectrum of American political philosophy. The conservative Republican presidential aspirant, Robert A. Taft of Ohio, the New Deal big-city liberal, Robert F. Wagner of New York, and the segregationist southern Democrat, Allen J. Ellender of Louisiana, united to see their bill through five rounds of hearings, four years of controversy, three redraftings, and two changes of leadership in Congress.

The housing bill was introduced in the Senate (S. 1592) in 1945 and approved there in April 1946, only to die in the House Banking and Currency Committee—killed by "very potent private lobby groups" opposing public housing.[27] The bill (now S. 866) again passed the Senate in April 1948, despite the fact that as a result of the 1946 elections the Republicans had become the majority party in that chamber. Again, the bill was killed in the House. The general elections of 1948 returned Democratic majorities to both houses of Congress. Finally the Housing Act passed in the spring of 1949. Despite intensive lobbying efforts by the realtors and their allies, the public housing title was retained by a razor-thin five-vote margin, and the entire bill was then passed by a bipartisan majority of northern Democrats, urban Republicans, and a few southern Democrats.[28]

In the Housing Act of 1949, Congress declared a national commitment to rebuild the cities, eliminate slums and blight, and provide decent housing for the nation's citizens. The preamble to the act, titled a "Declaration of National Housing Policy," made a sweeping statement about the need for a housing program:

The general welfare and security of the Nation and the health and living standards of its people require housing production and relating community development sufficient to remedy the serious housing shortage, eliminate substandard and other inadequate housing through the clearance of slums and blighted areas, and the realization as soon as feasible of the goal of a decent home and suitable living environment for every American family.[29]

The housing industry got most of what it wanted in the housing bill, but to get federal subsidies for slum clearance, it was forced to accept public housing. The housing bill received the endorsement of key business, real estate, and housing interests because of the key provisions that allowed local authorities to supervise and profit from redevelopment. Title I of the act empowered the Housing and Home Finance Agency (HHFA) to assist local efforts at blight and slum removal. Through this agency the federal government offered grants-in-aid to help local urban renewal agencies absorb the cost of the "write-down" on land that had been cleared of slum buildings. The write-down was the difference between the local agency's cost of assembling and clearing the site and a negotiated below-market price subsequently paid for the land by private developers.

In addition to the money authorized for the write-down subsidies, HHFA was authorized to extend loans to local urban renewal or public housing agencies for land assembly and site clearance. The act gave private developers preference over local governments in redeveloping the clearance sites. Tenants and slum dwellers displaced by renewal programs were supposed to be supplied with "decent, safe and sanitary dwellings." The redevelopment effort was required to be "predominantly residential" in character. Amendments to the legislation, adopted in 1954, allowed communities to use 10 percent of project funds for nonresidential, commercial revitalization. In 1960 this proportion was raised to 30 percent.

Title III, Low-Rent Public Housing, authorized (but did not appropriate money for) the production of 810,000 government-subsidized housing units over the next six years. This amounted to 10 percent of the estimated national need for new low-cost dwellings. Occupancy preferences were given for veterans and families displaced by Title I (clearance) activities. Per-room and per-unit cost limitations were imposed to prevent "extravagance and unnecessary" amenities. Rent levels and tenant eligibility requirements were regulated to minimize competition with the private housing market and to ensure that public housing benefited only the neediest families.

URBAN RENEWAL AND ITS PROBLEMS

Local political and economic elites were far more concerned about the economic decline of central business districts (CBDs) than they were about slum residents. Business leaders and politicians were convinced that slums were responsible for the steady decline in downtown property values and retail activity. As a consequence, they were interested in slum clearance, but not in low-cost housing for residents displaced by clearance. Right from the beginning low-income housing was sacrificed to commercial development, a sacrifice made possible by the way federal administrators interpreted the legislation. Any renewal project that allocated 51 percent or more of its funds to housing was designated by the federal administrators as a "100 percent housing" project. By applying such elastic definitions or by ignoring guidelines altogether, local authorities were able to allocate as much as two-thirds of their funds for commercial projects, despite the "predominantly residential" language contained in the legislation.

Public housing immediately ran into trouble. In the abstract, housing for low-income people might seem worthwhile, but few local politicians felt they could afford to tolerate it in their own neighborhoods. Site selection was of paramount concern, for example, to Chicago's politicians in the 1950s.[30] The Chicago experience was duplicated in cities across the country. Public housing had failed to develop strong grassroots support in local communities. Quite the opposite. Local chapters of the National Association of Real Estate Boards organized opposition to public housing projects in city after city. In often vitriolic campaigns, the opponents of subsidized housing played on fears that public housing might be used to promote racial integration. Between 1949 and the end of 1952, public housing programs were rejected by referenda, many of them sponsored by local chapters of the National Association of Real Estate Boards, in Akron, Houston, and Los Angeles and in almost forty other cities. Social and political realities at the local level made public housing a volatile issue. Local officials were acutely aware that "there could hardly be many votes to be gained in championing the cause—and perhaps a great many lost."[31]

In contrast, slum clearance and economic redevelopment added up to good politics. Seizing on redevelopment as a way to secure federal funds, enterprising mayors could simultaneously advance their political fortunes and improve the public image of the city. To implement big clearance and redevelopment projects, an alliance had to be forged between the mayor and other local officials on the one hand and the business community on the other. In most cities, the alliance was organized by corporate executives, but there were other crucial participants as well. Real estate and merchant interests in central business districts, metropolitan newspapers, and frequently the construction trades unions lent their support. For many years, this political alliance constituted a "new convergence of power" that completely dominated the politics of most large cities.[32]

By the end of the 1950s, scarcely a large city in the United States lacked an urban renewal coalition. Richard J. Daley, first elected mayor of Chicago in 1953, rebuilt the Democratic machine in that city by aggressively launching the revitalization of Chicago's downtown Loop and lakefront. By contrast, Boston's machine met its demise at the hands of a political coalition dedicated to renewing the city. The candidate selected by the business-sponsored New Boston Committee defeated long-time machine boss James Michael Curley in the 1951 mayoral race, then backed the massive clearance of Boston's Italian West End and the construction of a large governmental center. Ultimately, Boston's renewal program took 10 percent of the city's land area.[33] In 1950, St. Louis's Mayor Joseph Darst received widespread national publicity when his city became the nation's first to secure federal funding for a massive urban renewal program. Raymond Tucker, who replaced him in 1953, was even more aggressive in pushing clearance projects. A former St. Louis mayor recalled that renewal united political and business leaders behind a common cause:

> About a year ago, a group of distinguished citizens of our community were called into the Mayor's office and there charged by Mayor Darst with the responsibility of giving leadership to a program . . . It was suggested that an urban redevelopment corporation be organized. There was much fine publicity on the part of the metropolitan press—they not only gave considerable space but they also subscribed to the extent of better than a quarter of a million dollars to the debentures and stock of that corporation. So, we salute the press on this occasion. I should add that many other fine business institutions, sixty-nine in number, subscribed a total in excess of $2,000,000 toward the capital structure of the corporation. It is a distinguished list. There's the May Department Stores, Stix, Baer and Fuller, Scruggs, Vandervoort and Barney, the Anheuser Busch Company, Ely Walker Company, the Falstaff Company, the First National Bank, . . . and others.[34]

A similar alliance came together in New Haven, Connecticut, where the young Democrat Richard Lee hung his mayoral aspirations and his political future on the prospect of a successful urban redevelopment program. He won the 1952 election and several terms thereafter by leading a broad coalition that sponsored federally funded redevelopment. Lee's political capital derived from an alliance between government officials and local notables, particularly business leaders. It took shape in the formation of the Citizen's Action Committee (CAC), an advisory board required by the federal legislation, which included "businessmen concerned with traffic and retail sales, trade union leaders concerned with employment and local prosperity," and "political liberals concerned with slums, housing, and race relations." This group was characterized by Mayor Lee as the political alliance that ran New Haven. He described it as

> the biggest set of muscles in New Haven. . . . They're muscular because they control wealth, they're muscular because they control industries, represent banks. They're muscular because they head up labor. They're muscular because they represent the intellectual portions of the community. They're muscular because they're articulate, because they're respectable, because of their financial power, and because of the accumulation of prestige they have built up over the years as individuals in all kinds of causes.[35]

The programs financed by the 1949 housing act were perfect vehicles that mayors could use to secure their personal political futures. Mayors and business leaders tended to share the view that the economic fortunes of their cities depended on the health of the central business district. The full-scale flight of the middle class to the suburbs was seriously undermining the economic viability of inner cities. Since the central business district was the center of activity where the local business establishment held heavy real estate and business investments, it was only logical that businesses would seek to protect their investments through revitalization of their immediate environment. The need for political visibility and campaign contributions from wealthy donors ensured that elected officials would favor downtown sites. Those areas were generally the oldest in the cities and were therefore easily designated as officially "blighted," by the local urban renewal authority, the first step in a process that led to condemning and clearing property.

The separate members of the renewal coalition needed one another. Local officials needed investment capital and the public prestige the business community possessed. The business community in turn depended on the resources of the public sector. Governmental authority was a necessary ingredient for a successful redevelopment effort. Public authority was, in the first instance, called on to apply for federal funds through an officially constituted urban renewal agency. The government's power of eminent domain, which allowed it to condemn "blighted" property for a "higher" public use, was critical for land assembly, because individual property owners could not otherwise be compelled to sell. Finally, the unique ability of local renewal agencies to receive the necessary write-down subsidies and loans from the federal government made local officials and agencies indispensable to business leaders who wanted urban redevelopment. "This strange coalition"[36] was thus a mutually reinforcing alliance of formidable power.

THE URBAN RENEWAL STEAMROLLER

As a result of their successful efforts to secure federal backing for urban renewal, the national political coalition that pushed the urban renewal program through Congress "engineered a massive allocation of private and social resources" in the cities.[37] The public funds invested in write-down subsidies and clearance leveraged investments by developers, corporations, and local businesses. By 1968, $35.8 billion had been committed by private institutions in 524 renewal projects.[38] In addition, the huge federal expenditures on the interstate highway program, funded through the National Defense Highway Act of 1956, provided hundreds of thousands of jobs and considerable profits to construction firms building highways through urban neighborhoods.

The clearance of neighborhoods associated with urban renewal and highway building soon ignited resistance and controversy. While business leaders talked glibly about benefiting all the residents of the city through the provision of jobs and increases in revenues, it was painfully apparent that viable neighborhoods were often destroyed in the process. In Boston block after block of well-kept bungalows and row houses, grocery stores, barber shops, bakeries, and taverns—all the elements making up historic, safe, thriving Italian neighborhoods in Boston's West End—were leveled. "Blight" was such a loose term that it could be, and often was, applied even to healthy neighborhoods.[39] Because of this a great deal of community protest was directed at the massive destruction of neighborhoods caused by urban renewal and highway construction projects. According to one scholar, "development issues . . . dominated the neighborhoods" in the 1950s and 1960s in the four cities he studied.[40]

Considering the intensity and frequency of protest, it seems surprising that neighborhoods won so few victories. The reason for this poor record was that the groups that opposed renewal were small and often quite parochial, and divided from one another on the basis of race and ethnicity. Neighborhoods acted as interest groups protecting their own turf. The various neighborhoods were so diverse that it was difficult for them to form stable alliances with one another. As a consequence, the renewal coalition usually outlasted protests originating from a single neighborhood. By astutely selecting renewal and redevelopment sites, urban renewal administrators could pursue a politics of divide and conquer.

Atlanta provides an excellent example of this process. Beginning in 1952, Atlanta's Metropolitan Planning Commission became concerned about the movement of blacks into neighborhoods close to the central business district. In its report of that year, entitled *Up Ahead,* the commission maintained that "from the viewpoint of planning the wise thing is to find outlying areas to be developed for new colored housing." The commission recommended "public policies to reduce existing densities, wipe out blighted areas, improve the racial pattern of population distribution, and make the best possible use of central planned areas."[41] The actual goal, thinly disguised by this verbiage, was to move blacks into areas further from the downtown area, and to secure land near the CBD for redevelopment.

Atlanta's organization of big corporations, the Central Atlanta Improvement Association, backed faithfully by the white-owned newspapers, energetically promoted clearance. Special care was taken to obtain the backing of the Chamber of Commerce, which represented smaller businesses. The Atlanta Real Estate Board was brought on board by promises that renewal would help to maintain segregated housing patterns and that no public housing would be constructed on urban renewal land. Support from some leaders of the black community was obtained by promises to make land available for the construction of black housing subdivisions farther from the CBD and by a commitment to build single-family, owner-occupied housing for blacks, which was to be subsidized by federal funds available under Section 221 of the 1949 housing act. Years after the area was cleared, downtown Atlanta was still undergoing massive clearance and reconstruction, and the historic downtown had been entirely replaced by a huge enclosed mall called the Peachtree Center.

The local renewal coalitions born in the 1950s used their potent political muscle to crush opponents. Though almost any city could be used as an example, San Francisco's single-minded pursuit of downtown renewal is especially revealing.[42] In 1953 the San Francisco Board of Supervisors approved a plan to clear several blocks of land adjacent to the financial district, and south of Market Street. This area, with its market stalls, narrow passageways, and constant bustling activity, concerned business and political leaders, who worried about the impact it might have on the future downtown business district, which they envisioned as an expanding agglomeration of corporate, cultural, and tourist facilities. By the late 1950s, a plan for redevelopment had taken shape. The city planned to build a huge sports arena and convention center on the site, to be named the Yerba Buena Center. It was thought that Yerba Buena would act as a magnet for the expansion of the city's financial center.

It was easy for the mayor and urban renewal administrators to build support for such a concept. San Francisco contained scores of corporate giants, including Standard Oil of California, Southern Pacific, Transamerica Corporation, Levi Strauss, Crown Zellerbach, Del Monte, Pacific Telephone and Telegraph, Bethlehem Steel, and Pacific Gas and Electric. Among the many financial institutions located in downtown San Francisco were Bank of America, Wells Fargo, Crocker National Bank, Bank of California, Aetna Life, John Hancock, and Hartford Insurance. During the 1960s, the buildings that housed these institutions changed San Francisco's skyline. Between 1960 and 1972, twenty-three high rises were constructed in downtown San Francisco.[43]

The director of the San Francisco Redevelopment Agency, M. Justin Herman, became the "chief architect, major spokesman, and operations commander" for the massive renewal project. Under his leadership the redevelopment agency hired several hundred professionals and dozens of consultants and applied for millions of dollars in federal urban renewal subsidies. Herman believed in his mission so zealously that he interpreted any criticism of his project as an attempt by parochial interests to stand in the way of progress. In 1970, he was quoted as saying, "this land is too valuable to permit poor people to park on it."[44] He was cited in a major publication in 1970 as "one of the men responsible for getting urban renewal" renamed "the federal bulldozer" and "negro removal":

> He was absolutely confident that he was doing what the power structure wanted in so far as the poor and the minorities were concerned. That's why San Francisco has mostly luxury housing and business district projects—that's what white, middle-class planners and businessmen envision as ideal urban renewal. . . . Also, with Herman in control, San Francisco's renewal never got slowed down by all this citizen participation business that tormented other cities.[45]

Federal administrators turned a blind eye to the fact that the Yerba Buena Center project was being planned with no thought to building replacement housing for the people who lived in the clearance area. During the summer of 1969, the residents living in the proposed clearance area challenged the project in federal court, arguing that it violated the 1949 Housing Act's requirement that residents in clearance projects be relocated into safe and suitable housing. The judge who heard the case concluded that the secretary of the Department of Housing and Urban Development "had not been provided with any creditable evidence at all" in regard to the redevelopment agency's plan to relocate residents.[46] Temporarily stopped in its tracks, the redevelopment agency eventually agreed to increase the hotel tax in San Francisco in order to finance the construction of low-income housing for tenants who would be displaced by the Yerba Buena Center. Court battles over this plan, however, plus the escalating costs of the Center, eventually doomed it, and it was not built.

Justin Herman's attitudes toward the poor were shared by urban renewal administrators and their allies everywhere. In the core areas of the cities poverty and race were inextricably linked; as a result, most urban renewal programs had racial (or racist) overtones. The blacks who moved to the cities in the twentieth century were housed in the most rundown areas of the inner cities. The oldest and most dilapidated housing was generally located near central business districts, which meant that black populations were frequently displaced by clearance projects. The "black residents of the inner cities [and] black businesses were among the prime victims of federally-sponsored urban renewal programs" referred to as "black removal."[47] The program was appropriately described by critics as "Negro clearance," a phrase that derived from the fact that over three-fourths of the people displaced by urban renewal in the first eight years of the program, and 66 percent of those displaced through 1961, were black.[48] Black tenants were forced into other parts of the city by clearance projects—usually to dilapidated housing in a slightly more distant slum, or to public housing constructed on cleared land still surrounded by slums. Economic and racial barriers left them no other choice but to move to another area much like the slum they left behind: "Given the realities of the low-income housing market . . . it is likely that, for many families, relocation [meant] no more than keeping one step ahead of the bulldozer."[49] Thus a new game was added to the harsh realities of urban life—"musical slums."

Not only were the poor displaced, but they were forced to pay higher rents when the supply of low-rent housing units dwindled. With only 5 percent of the new housing units within the economic reach of low-income families, there was a 90 percent decline in the supply of low-income housing within redevelopment areas during the first ten years of the program's operation.[50] The residents of slum areas who were initially supposed to benefit from the urban renewal program were often the biggest losers. In the first fourteen years of the program's operation, "urban renewal demolished the homes of 177,000 families and another 66,000 single individuals, most of them poor and most of them black."[51] Less than one-fourth of the housing units were replaced, and many of these were too expensive for those who were displaced.[52] Only $34.8 million of the urban renewal funds—less than 1 percent—was used for relocation assistance, placing a disproportionate share of the cost of the program on the slum residents who were forced to move.[53]

PUBLIC HOUSING: URBAN RENEWAL'S STEPCHILD

Public housing was kept in the 1949 housing act because the advocates of urban renewal could not get their program passed without it. It was obvious to even the most ardent opponents of public housing that the families and individuals displaced by clearance would have to find new housing. The 1949 legislation required that people displaced by clearance be given priority in moving into public housing projects. Public housing was reluctantly accepted as a necessary evil by supporters of renewal, but this lukewarm support meant that over the years Congress appropriated far less money for low-cost housing than called for in the original legislation. By the end of 1961, clearance had eliminated 126,000 hous-ing units. The 28,000 new units that replaced them could house less than one-fifth of the 113,000 families and 36,000 individuals who were displaced by clear-ance.[54] Most of the cleared land was slated for commercial uses rather than housing. Public housing accounted for only 6 percent of the construction started and only 1 percent of additional construction planned in urban renewal areas as of April 1, 1961.[55]

Their status as slum dwellers gave blacks "the dubious privilege of eligibil-ity for public housing."[56] Nationwide, nonwhites accounted for 38 percent of all public housing tenants in 1952, but by 1961 this percentage had risen to 46 per-cent. In individual projects segregation was the norm. Whites who were eligible for public housing or who had been victims of slum clearance had housing op-tions in the private market that were unavailable to blacks. Blacks, therefore, tended to take over public housing in the cities by default—the supply of low-income housing units was shrinking—and, as a result of racial discrimination, they were often kept out of many of the neighborhoods that they could afford.

Public housing never got over its stepchild status. In most European coun-tries, housing constructed and administered by governments in the years fol-lowing World War II was available to middle-class families as well as to the poor, and much of this housing was considered as good as or sometimes better than the housing available through the private market. As a consequence, there was widespread political support for a public role in housing.[57] In the United States, by contrast, public housing was regarded essentially as a welfare pro-gram, and therefore it was never politically popular.

Public housing "was born with profound defects, and the hostile environ-ment in which it grew aggravated its congenital ailments."[58] There were three nearly fatal restrictions built into the program. The first, and perhaps most im-portant, problem was that eligibility was restricted to those who could not afford any other kind of housing. The real estate lobby would have tolerated no other policy. The insidious result of such a policy was to concentrate those poor fami-lies together that, for whatever reasons, were unable to improve their circum-stances. Tenants who got jobs and increased their incomes were evicted. Already, in the 1950s, the concentration of families in poverty meant that public housing projects were prone to high levels of violence and juvenile crime. Over the years, public housing tenants were increasingly made up of "broken families, depen-dent families, and welfare families."[59] If the families whose incomes went up had been able to stay in their apartments and pay higher rents, the tendency to wors-ening social pathologies might have been moderated,[60] and the rental income they paid would have helped to make public housing more economically viable.

A second built-in flaw was related to the fact that public housing projects were almost always built on slum land that had been cleared for that purpose; almost never were they built outside ghetto areas or, heaven forbid, in the sub-urbs. This meant that almost all projects were surrounded by slums, and most of these areas were inhabited by blacks. From the beginning, most public housing projects were segregated by explicit policy in all but a few northern states.[61] By the time President John F. Kennedy signed an executive order forbidding the practice in 1962, it could have little practical effect, since by then the overwhelming majority of public housing tenants in large cities were African American anyway. Public housing policy had the perverse effect of reinforcing and intensifying the racial segregation that already existed in the cities.

A third fundamental problem flowed from cost and design restrictions that guaranteed that most of the units would be undesirable. Public housing served as a constant reminder to its tenants and to everyone else that this was a grudging welfare program. To save money on site preparation and construction costs, cities built clusters of high-density, high-rise buildings. The African-American writer James Baldwin might have been describing almost any of these projects when he referred to those in Harlem as "colorless, bleak, high and revolting."[62] Of course, big American and European cities are full of high rises that command steep rents from affluent clientele, but such structures, especially when built cheaply, "were not suitable for poor people with big families."[63] It was difficult for parents to supervise children even when suitable play facilities were available. The architecture was a virtual invitation to vandalism and crime: Elevators were often broken and stuck; laundry rooms were many floors removed from tenants' apartments; dark hallways and stairwells were poorly lighted even when there were bulbs available.

The Cabrini-Green projects north of Chicago's Loop began as two-story brick row houses built to house war workers in World War II. All of the occupants were white. In 1958 these houses were replaced by fifteen high-rise buildings, and another eight were constructed in 1962. These 19-story rectangular monstrosities loomed over the surrounding neighborhoods. Almost all the tenants were black. The same situation existed in New York City, where public housing often rose to more than 20 stories. The Pruitt-Igoe project in St. Louis, completed between 1954 and 1959, was composed of 2,762 apartments in 33 eleven-story buildings on a 57-acre site. By the time the last building was completed, it was already a community scandal.[64] By 1973 it had become an international symbol for the failure of American public housing. In that year, photographs that made *Life* magazine's "The Year in Review" showed the shocking spectacle of one of the buildings imploding from hundreds of charges of carefully placed dynamite. As a monument to a policy failure, the episode could hardly have been more dramatic and fitting: Explosives experts got the opportunity to hone their demolition skills on buildings that had been built, complete with awards to the architectural firm, only fifteen years before.

Perhaps the most unfortunate legacy from this period of public housing is that the "projects" became enduring symbols of racial segregation, crime, and poverty in the inner cities, and as such they obscured the fact that not all public housing was a failure. The two- and three-story town houses constructed in the 1930s were often pleasant places with satisfied tenants. Town house projects built in the 1960s and after were often quite successful—but of course success rarely made the news. The reality is that the high-rise projects projected an enduring image of policy failure.

THE LEGACY OF INNER-CITY PROGRAMS

By the early 1960s, there was widespread opposition to federally assisted urban renewal. Liberal critics viewed urban renewal as a "federally financed gimmick to provide relatively cheap land for a miscellany of profitable, prestigious [private] enterprises."[65] Conservatives were also appalled by the results of the program. At its inception and through its early years, business leaders and politicians expected a miraculous reversal of central city decline. The optimism soon turned into frustration. Redevelopment took too long. By the later 1960s, it took an estimated four years to plan a clearance and renewal project and then an additional six years to complete it. Often, by the time a project was finished, the original plans had long been abandoned.[66] Blighted neighborhoods and slums grew faster than the renewal projects could eliminate them.

In 1965 rent supplement programs were enacted as an alternative to public housing for the poor. Through direct housing aid, the poor would presumably be able to choose their own housing on the private market. The Housing and Urban Development Act of 1968 required that a majority of housing units constructed on redevelopment sites be for low- and moderate-income families.[67] Such tinkering with the urban renewal and public housing programs was designed to provide more benefits for the poor. The improvements, in the end, were modest. Low-income housing continued to be replaced at far less than a one-to-one basis; indeed, only 51 percent of the new units built in urban renewal areas after 1968 were reserved for people of low or moderate incomes.[68]

Both public housing and urban renewal met their effective demise in the 1970s. The inability of either program to slow significantly the decay of the nation's inner cities weakened their bases of support. They had persisted in the face of bitter criticism because everyone felt that something should be done, but there was no agreement on what would work. In 1974 urban renewal was merged into the Community Development Block Grant program. Public housing was allowed to wither away during the Nixon Administration, from 104,000 starts in 1970 to only 19,000 starts by 1974.[69] A few years later, it was essentially abandoned when the Reagan Administration eliminated constructed low-income housing built by the government in favor of programs to subsidize landlords and a few experiments in housing vouchers.

The urban renewal and public housing programs inflamed racial tensions and helped shape contemporary attitudes and stereotypes about African Americans, who were forced to cluster together in densely packed, rundown areas where rents were cheap. Those who could not move far enough often found themselves facing the nightmare of the bulldozer all over again. Families that could qualify for public housing were somewhat better off, but they ended up being segregated from the rest of society even more than before. The intense segregation of blacks in poverty made it seem as if they were different from everyone else, as if somehow their isolation from the rest of urban society was natural or preordained.

By reducing the supply of inner-city housing, clearance projects increased the pressure on neighborhoods at the margins of ghetto areas, an effect that was enforced by policies that kept middle-income blacks from looking for homes in the suburbs. Because they were kept out of all other areas, middle-class blacks could find good housing only on the fringes of the inner-city ghetto. The movement of a black family onto a block inhabited by whites became a symbol of neighborhood decline—and a self-fulfilling prophecy. Realtors eagerly exploited whites' fears by blockbusting likely areas. In a typical scenario, a realtor would sell a home to a black family, then send someone door-to-door or distribute leaflets to spread the word that the neighborhood was about to change. The realtor would then offer to buy property from panicked whites at bargain-basement prices. When white families would begin to move, the realtor would advertise the for-sale properties in neighborhoods occupied by potential black buyers, and sell the homes at inflated prices. In this way the white middle class learned to associate the presence of blacks with residential decline.

Through its Federal Housing Administration and Veterans Administration loan programs, the federal government helped millions of middle-class white families buy a home in the suburbs. If blacks had been given the same opportunity, racial segregation probably would have occurred in the suburbs, but middle-class blacks, like their white counterparts, would have been able to invest in new homes in pleasant surroundings, close to newly constructed schools and the other amenities available in the suburbs. Perhaps most importantly, African Americans would have been able to invest in the future: For white middle-class America in the postwar period, the home became the principal source of capital worth and savings, money that could be invested in a child's education, in a bigger or newer house, or saved for retirement. Most African Americans were denied this crucial means of upward mobility.

NATIONAL POLICY AND THE SUBURBS

The migration of millions of white, middle- and upper-class families from the central cities to low-density suburbs constitutes one of the "great population migrations in American history"[70] (another author used similar words to describe the post–World War II movement of blacks to northern cities). A movement to the suburbs certainly would have occurred in twentieth-century America, with or without governmental policies to hurry the process along. The spilling across city boundaries was a logical extension of the outward push from the urban center that had begun with the nineteenth-century development of the omnibus and the horsecar. However, the suburban movement of the last half-century would have been far slower and more uneven if it had depended on the housing market alone. Without doubt, its pace was quickened, and its shape was substantially determined, by powerful national policies. From the 1930s through the 1960s, suburban development was accelerated by two programs: the Federal Housing Administration (FHA) loans established by the National Housing Act of 1934 and the Veterans Administration (VA) loans made available to returning

GIs by the Serviceman's Readjustment Act of 1944. Millions of Americans were able to purchase their first suburban home because of the liberal financing features of the FHA and VA programs.

Until the depression of the 1930s, the housing market in the United States was an almost perfect expression of laissez-faire economics, with government playing little role in housing provision. The only exceptions were some minimal building codes and fire regulations imposed by a few big cities. All that was changed by the Great Depression. The federal government was prompted to intervene in the nation's housing market because it comprised a significant sector of the national economy. Second only to agriculture as an employer, the housing industry experienced a sudden, devastating retrenchment in the late 1920s. Before the stock market crash of October 1929, 900,000 new housing units were being built each year. In 1934 only one-tenth of this number, 90,000 units, were constructed. Throughout the 1930s, housing starts lagged far behind the demand for new housing.[71] In Chicago, only 131 new housing units were constructed in all of 1933, compared with 18,837 in 1929 and 41,416 in 1926.[72] Across the nation, 63 percent of the workers in the housing industry were unemployed in 1933. The housing problem was exacerbated by foreclosures on mortgages, as millions of families lost their homes and millions more were faced with hardship in meeting their mortgage payments. They looked to the federal government for assistance.

The National Housing Act of 1934 created the Federal Housing Administration (FHA) and the Federal Savings and Loan Insurance Corporation (FSLIC). The FSLIC insured individual accounts up to $5,000 (it has since risen in a series of steps to more than $100,000). It was hoped that such insurance would inspire confidence by potential savers and investors, so that people would put their savings into banks instead of under their mattresses. These savings accounts would enable savings and loan institutions to invest more capital in the floundering housing market.

By far the most important provision of the 1934 housing act is Section 203, the basic home mortgage insurance program under which the bulk of FHA insurance has been written up to the present day. Fully 79 percent of all FHA-insured units from 1934 to 1975, about 9.5 million units representing a face value of more than $109 billion, were insured under Section 203.[73] The purpose of the program was to finance the acquisition of proposed, under construction, or existing one- to four-family units. The housing act provided for FHA insurance of 80 percent of the value of the property. (Through the Housing and Urban Development Act of 1974, this amount subsequently was increased to 97 percent of the first $25,000 and 80 percent of the remaining value, and since then the formula has been changed from time to time.) The low risk involved for the lending institution permits the mortgagee to pay a low down payment, with the remaining principal and interest spread out over a twenty-five or thirty-year period.

Various groups viewed the 1934 Housing Act with totally different goals in mind. Title I of the act provided FHA insurance for loans used for "permanent repairs that add to the basic livability and usefulness of the property."[74] Social welfare liberals saw Title I as a means of eliminating substandard living conditions in the central cities by providing low-interest, low-risk loans. City officials hoped Title I would be a catalyst to entice affluent people to stay within the city limits and remodel their homes rather than move to new homes in the suburbs. Downtown business interests had a different goal in mind; they favored Title I because they thought it could shore up the value of the central business districts. Most banks, savings and loan institutions, realtors, and contractors saw Section 203 as a way to finance new construction beyond the city. In lobbying for the Housing Act, they had agreed to Title I only as a compromise to facilitate quick congressional action.

Despite the impression one could derive from reading the legislation, new construction under FHA came to mean housing outside the cities. Very little money was ever appropriated to finance Title I repairs. Section 203, by contrast, was used to assist millions of people to move to the suburbs in the years after World War II. The VA loans had much the same impact as the FHA. Together with the FHA, the no-down-payment policy of the VA helped increase the federally insured share of the mortgage market from 15 percent in 1945 to 41 percent by 1954.[75]

Table 7.1 shows how much more difficult it was to buy a home before the FHA program. In the 1920s, down payments of 30 to 50 percent were standard, and savings and loan institutions normally allowed a maximum of eleven years for loans to be repaid. Banks were not so generous; six years was the norm, often with a balloon payment due at the end. In the 1960s conventional mortgage loans typically required only 25 percent down and were amortized over a twenty-year period (since then, loans with 10 percent to 20 percent down became the norm, with amortization periods of 30 years). Under the FHA, a home buyer could get a thirty-year mortgage with only 5 percent down and could obtain a much larger loan. The VA allowed banks to finance a mortgage with no down payment at all.

The FHA loan guarantee program exerted a huge influence on the home credit market. Between 1935 and 1974, more than three-fourths of the total FHA insured home mortgages financed new housing.[76] The proportion of all homes that were owner-occupied increased from 43.6 percent in 1940 to 62.9 percent in 1970.[77] Table 7.2 shows how much the FHA and VA programs influenced the housing market. About one-third of all homes purchased in the 1950s were financed through the FHA or VA programs. The proportion of government-financed loans gradually declined after the 1950s, but they remained important to the housing market, especially during economic downturns. By 1972, however, the FHA had helped almost 11 million families become homeowners.[78] In 1984 the FHA-VA share of home loans fell below 10 percent for the first time since World War II, but it later rebounded to 25 percent by 1988, and was still at 15 percent in 1998. The fluctuations closely followed the state of the economy.

Almost all of the new homes bought with FHA-VA loans were built in the suburbs. Throughout the 1940s and 1950s, the FHA exhibited an overwhelming bias in favor of the suburbs; for instance, in its first twelve years it did not insure a single dwelling on Manhattan Island. In part, the FHA's suburban bias reflected a preference for less dense, single-family neighborhoods, as found in the

TABLE 7.1 RELATIVE BURDEN OF LOAN TERMS, 1920s AND 1960s[a]

Decade and Lender	Terms	Percent of Annual Income	
		Down Payment	Annual Payment
1920s			
Savings and loan association	60 percent of house value loaned for 11 years at 7 percent; fully amortized	100	20
Bank or insurance company	50 percent of house value loaned for 5 years at 6 percent; unamortized	125	7.5 plus 125 in 5th year
1960s			
Conventional lender	75 percent of house value loaned for 20 years at 7 percent; fully amortized	62.5	18
FHA	95 percent of house value loaned for 30 years at 7.5 percent; fully amortized	12.5	20

[a]For a house equal to approximately two and one-half times the purchaser's annual salary.

Source: Henry J. Aaron, *Shelter and Subsidies: Who Benefits from Federal Housing Policies*, Studies in Social Economics (Washington, D.C.: Brookings Institution, 1972), p. 77. Copyright © 1972 by the Brookings Institution. Reprinted by permission.

suburbs, over more dense, multiunit neighborhoods, as found in the cities. But the FHA suburban preference went far beyond a simple matter of geography; FHA administrators actively promoted the idea that housing, and therefore neighborhoods, should be racially and ethnically segregated.

FHA mortgage insurance programs depended on private-sector lending institutions, which made the actual loans. From the beginning, the FHA absorbed the values, policies, and goals of the real estate and banking industries.[79] Indeed, the staff of the FHA was drawn from the ranks of those industries, and it was only logical that the FHA's philosophy would parallel theirs. Thus "FHA's interests went no farther than the safety of the mortgage it secured."[80] Mortgages were typically made available only in "economically sound" areas, where depreciating housing values seemed unlikely.

FHA administrators shared the real estate and banking industry's view that racially segregated neighborhoods were the soundest investments. When it issued its underwriting manual to banks in 1938, one of the guidelines instructed loan officers to steer clear of changing or integrated areas:

> Areas surrounding a location are [to be] investigated to determine whether incompatible racial and social groups are present, for the purpose of making a prediction

TABLE 7.2	**USE OF FHA- AND VA-INSURED LOANS IN THE UNITED STATES, 1950–1998**	
Year	Percent of Private Housing Financed Through FHA or VA	Total Number of Single Family Housing Starts (in Thousands)
1950	35	1,952
1955	41	1,646
1960	26	1,274
1965	16	1,510
1970	37	1,434
1975	15	1,160
1980	24	1,292
1984	9	1,750
1988	25	1,488
1995	13	1,354
1998	15	1,617

Source: U.S. Dept. of Commerce, Bureau of the Census, *Statistical Abstract of the United States, 1998* (Washington, D.C.: Government Printing Office, 1998), pp. 723 and 725; and *Current Construction Reports,* Series C20, Housing Starts, Dec. 1998 (Washington, D.C.: Government Printing Office, 1999), p. 7. And Historical Statistics of the United States to 1970, Part 2 (Washington, D.C.: Government Printing Office, 1975) pp. 369, 641.

regarding the probability of the location being invaded by such groups. If a neighborhood is to retain stability, it is necessary that properties shall continue to be occupied by the same social and racial classes. A change in social or racial occupancy generally contributes to instability and a decline in values.[81]

A revealing glimpse into how sensitive FHA administrators were to the issue of race can be gained by reading the language of a 1933 report submitted to the agency by one of its consultants, Homer Hoyt, who was a well-known sociologist and demographer at the time. He offered his view that land values and the racial composition of a neighborhood were closely linked:

If the entrance of a colored family into a white neighborhood causes a general exodus of the white people it is reflected in property values. Except in the case of Negroes and Mexicans, however, these racial and national barriers disappear when the individuals of the foreign nationality groups rise in the economic scale or conform to the American standards of living. . . . While the ranking may be scientifically wrong from the standpoint of inherent racial characteristics, it registers an opinion or prejudice that is reflected in land values; it is the ranking of races and nationalities with respect to their beneficial effect upon land values. Those having the most favorable effect come first in the list and those exerting the most detrimental effect appear last:

1. English, Germans, Scotch, Irish, Scandinavians
2. North Italians
3. Bohemians or Czechoslovakians
4. Poles
5. Lithuanians

6. Greeks
7. Russian Jews of lower class
8. South Italians
9. Negroes
10. Mexicans[82]

FHA administrators advised the developers of residential projects that they should draw up restrictive covenants barring sales to nonwhites before they applied for FHA-insured financing.[83] Through such policies the federal government essentially required that new subdivisions be segregated. Thus, federal policy acted as a powerful instrument to establish the social and racial patterns that emerged in urban America in the post-war years.[84] Between 1946 and 1959, less than 2 percent of all the housing financed with the assistance of federal mortgage insurance was purchased by blacks.[85] In the Miami area, only one black family received FHA backing for a home loan between 1934 and 1949, and there is "evidence that he [the man who secured the loan] was not recognized as a black" at the time the transaction took place.[86]

When the U.S. Supreme Court ruled in 1948 that racial covenants attached to property deeds could not be enforced in courts of law, the FHA was forced to change its policies. In 1950 the FHA revised its underwriting manual so that it no longer openly recommended racial segregation or restrictive covenants. The FHA, however, did nothing to reverse the effects of its previous policies, and took no actions to discourage realtors, developers, or lending institutions from discriminating against blacks. Until the housing act of 1968 it was still legal for realtors and mortgage institutions to discriminate on the basis of race.

THE WEAK POLICIES OF THE POST–CIVIL RIGHTS ERA

The housing and civil rights acts of 1968 and other measures enacted in the 1960s were supposed to reverse decades of discriminatory behavior in the housing industry. Beginning in 1964, President Lyndon Johnson urged Congress to outlaw discrimination in housing. All eyes were focused on the more basic civil rights legislation, however, and in any case, the idea of applying civil rights remedies to housing ran up against the idea that individual property rights ought not be curbed. In both 1966 and 1967 a fair housing bill died in the Senate. Finally, under Title VIII of the Civil Rights Act of 1968,[87] Congress outlawed racial discrimination in housing. Its provisions were quite sweeping, barring discrimination in rentals and sales and in the provision of information about cost and availability, advertising, purchasing, construction and repair, and real estate services and practices. The statute mandated that each of the federal regulatory agencies involved with the real estate industry would take affirmative steps to enforce both the spirit and the letter of the law.[88]

There can be little doubt that the 1968 legislation helped to open up the suburban housing market to African Americans. Between 1970 and 1980, the number of blacks who lived in suburbs grew by almost 50 percent, an increase of 1.8 million persons.[89] One in ten blacks living in the central cities in 1970 moved to the suburbs during this period and the percentage of urban blacks living in the suburbs increased from 16 percent to 21 percent.[90] In the 1980s the trend continued. By the 1990 census, about one-fourth of urban black families lived in the suburbs, while about 85 percent of white families did so.

As is the case with whites, blacks who move to the suburbs tended to have higher incomes than those who stayed behind.[91] Suburbanization doubtlessly has expanded housing choice for blacks, but they in the suburbs have remained about as segregated from whites as they were before.[92] For the most part, suburbanization did not bring about residential integration. Instead, blacks moved mostly into older inner-ring suburbs where white flight had occurred, much as it did previously in central cities.[93] These older suburbs tended to have many of the same problems as the central cities. In general, the suburbs where blacks moved to had lower tax bases, higher debts, poorer municipal services, lower socioeconomic status, and higher population densities than did suburbs that are mostly white.[94]

Most suburban whites continued to have little contact with suburban blacks: In the mid-1980s, 86 percent of suburban whites lived in suburbs with a black population of less than 1 percent.[95] Even those suburbs that were racially mixed tended to be highly segregated internally, and it appeared that racial segregation intensified in the 1980s.[96] Why was the racial segregation characteristic of the cities being replicated in the suburbs? Research indicated that discrimination, not social class or income, determined residential location.[97] Socioeconomic differentials between blacks and whites accounted for less than 15 percent of the segregation among suburbs in 1980.[98] Research conducted in the St. Louis area indicated that in the 1980s, nonracial factors such as housing cost and economic factors seemed to be less important in explaining patterns of residential segregation than in any previous decade,[99] and this pattern appeared to continue into the 1990s.[100]

Despite legislation outlawing it, racial discrimination in housing seems to have continued unabated. An important reason for this is that the enforcement provisions of the 1968 legislation were weak. Rather than being granted positive responsibilities for identifying discrimination, the Department of Housing and Urban Development was limited to receiving complaints initiated by citizens. By thus assuming a passive rather than an active enforcement role, it was easy for HUD to avoid controversy by treating each case as isolated and nonpolitical. For citizens, the time and red tape involved in initiating a complaint was daunting, and thus all through the 1970s the volume of complaints processed by HUD remained quite low. Interestingly, enforcement improved somewhat under a Republican president, Ronald Reagan, when HUD took steps to publicize the remedies available under the 1968 civil rights legislation. Partially as a result, the number of complaints received by HUD rose sharply in the 1980s. Still, most citizens bypassed HUD and state and local civil rights agencies, and went directly to the courts.[101] By focusing on individual remedies rather than on large-scale efforts to enforce compliance, the governmental role in fair housing enforcement remained small and inconsequential.

Other efforts by the federal government to eliminate housing discrimination also benefited blacks, but in small, limited ways. The Equal Credit Opportunity Act of 1974, Mortgage Disclosure Act of 1975, and Community Reinvestment Act of 1977 (CRA)[102] were intended to ensure that blacks received equal consideration for home loans and that banks stopped redlining areas where blacks lived. (Redlining derives its name from the red line drawn on maps to designate neighborhoods considered poor investment risks.) In the past, banks would simply refuse to make home loans in certain areas regardless of the qualifications of individual loan applicants. Since the 1977 legislation, banks have been subjected to repeated protests and a substantial amount of litigation from community groups challenging apparent redlining practices. Rather than engage in extensive litigation and respond to investigations by federal regulators, banks generally have been willing to enter into negotiations with community groups. According to one estimate, by 1991 approximately $18 billion in urban reinvestment commitments had been negotiated in more than seventy cities across the country.[103] Just as it would be premature to conclude that all redlining has stopped, however, it would be inaccurate to assume that all individual loan applications are judged strictly on their merits. A 1992 study by the Federal Reserve Bank of Boston found that minorities were roughly 60 percent more likely to be turned down for a mortgage, even after controlling for thirty-eight factors affecting creditworthiness, such as credit history and total debt.[104]

To break down the patterns of residential segregation that exist in urban areas, the federal government would have to implement housing policies with the strength and effect of the policies that were once used to promote segregation. Such policies would change the principal dynamics of the housing market. Rather than merely regulating lending institutions, for instance, the government could, conceivably, become a primary lender. It could also, in principle, seek reparations and damages from landlords and homeowners who violate antidiscrimination laws. It could challenge local zoning laws that have the effect of maintaining segregated housing patterns (a subject we discuss at length in Chapter 10). No such policies would be politically feasible, but without them it is likely that the effects of decades of national policies that helped create racially segregated neighborhoods will persist.

THE SUBURBAN BIAS IN NATIONAL TRANSPORTATION POLICIES

As we have seen, housing and urban renewal policies sponsored by the federal government have powerfully shaped the racial and socioeconomic segregation that exists in America's urban areas. National transportation policies also encouraged suburban growth and central-city decline. In a few years and at great expense, the U.S. government ensured the triumph of the automobile over mass transit. In doing so, the poor were left stranded in the central cities, ever more distant from suburban jobs, and with few affordable ways to get to them. "Auto-mobility" enabled Americans to implement Henry Ford's solution to urban problems: "We shall solve the problems of the city by leaving the city."[105]

Americans depend on the automobile for urban travel more than people in any other country. Though other advanced industrial nations such as Germany, Britain, and Japan embraced the automobile, they also maintained modern systems of mass transit as workable alternatives. In West Germany, for example, between 1950 and 1974, at the same time that automobile travel increased fifteen times, public transit use more than doubled.[106] In the United States, by contrast, between 1950 and 1977, as the volume of automobile traffic on urban roads more than tripled from 182 to 666 million vehicle miles, urban mass transit ridership declined by over half and it has not rebounded since. Except for New York City and a few other big cities on the east coast, public transit accounts for much less than 10 percent of commuting trips in most metropolitan areas of the United States.[107] Most metropolitan areas in the United States now have a one-dimensional urban transportation system.

In the early period of the automobile, cars were built much faster than highways. Between 1910 and 1920, the number of cars increased 1,600 percent, but the miles of paved roads rose by only 82 percent.[108] Mass production methods reduced the cost of automobiles, but highways were expensive, and there was conflict over who would pay for them. The method of paying for them finally agreed to was a tax on gasoline, and by 1929, all forty-eight states had enacted gasoline taxes (such taxes are still the main source of highway funds in the United States). Over time, the National Highway Users Conference, which is made up of 2,800 lobbying groups, has pressured successfully for the creation of trust funds earmarked for highways.[109] By 1974, forty-six of the fifty states had established highway trust funds, thus guaranteeing a steady source of revenue for highway construction, free from the uncertainties of the political process.[110] In addition, local taxes have paid for the feeder roads and local streets that make car travel so convenient.

Highway subsidies were pushed through by a powerful coalition led by the nation's largest auto, oil, and tire companies. The beginning of this coalition dates to June 28, 1932, when Alfred P. Sloan, Jr., president of General Motors, called together representatives from several companies to form the National Highway Users Conference. The purpose of the conference, which was chaired by Sloan until 1948, was to unite the petroleum-related industries against the railroads and the urban transit companies.

While the conference lobbied for highway legislation, General Motors, Standard Oil of California, and Firestone Tire Company set out to buy up electric streetcar lines and replace them with buses. GM took the lead in this effort in 1932 when it formed the United Cities Motor Transit Company as a subsidiary. United Cities bought up electric streetcar companies, tore up the tracks, replaced the trolleys with buses, and then sold the bus companies to firms that agreed to use only GM products. The first cities that successfully converted to buses were Kalamazoo and Saginaw, Michigan, and Springfield, Ohio. Many others followed, and "in each case, General Motors successfully motorized the city, turned the management over to other interests and liquidated its investment."[111]

GM established two semi-independent holding companies that could be used to pool funds contributed by petroleum-based corporations. The GM-created Omnibus Corporation and the National City Lines systematically dismantled streetcar companies in the nation's largest cities, including New York, Philadelphia, Baltimore, Salt Lake City, and Los Angeles. By 1949, through National City Lines, buses had replaced streetcars in forty-five cities. The capitalization required for all this was large, with GM, Standard Oil of California, Firestone Tire, and some suppliers raising $9 million to purchase streetcars. Most of the new bus systems operated under contractual agreements stipulating that only gasoline or diesel fuel could be used in any of their vehicles. This ensured that the systems could not change back to electric trolleys in the future.[112]

In 1949, GM was convicted in federal court, along with Standard Oil and Firestone, of conspiring to eliminate electric transportation and monopolize the sale of buses and parts. The judge administered a slap on the wrist, levying a fine of $5,000 on the company and convicting and fining one of its executives the sum of $1. Even before this symbolic gesture, the damage to mass transit had already been inflicted. By 1955, Roger M. Keyes, GM's executive in charge of bus sales, pronounced the effort a success: "The motor coach has supplanted the interurban systems and has for all practical purposes eliminated the trolley."[113] Only 5,000 streetcars were still in service, compared to 40,000 in 1936, when National City Lines began its assault on the electric railways.

As its title implies, the 1956 National Defense Highway Act was justified partly on military grounds—part of its stated purpose was to aid the movement of troops and supplies and to help evacuate American cities in case of a nuclear attack. The main rationale, however, was that freeways would stimulate the economy by creating a national system of superhighways linking all the major metropolitan areas in the country. Within urban areas, the new expressways were expected to solve the growing problem of traffic congestion. A committee appointed by President Eisenhower asserted that suburbs were superior to cities and recommended that the new freeway system should be used to decentralize American urban areas.[114] That is exactly what the new freeways eventually did.

The 1956 legislation placed federal gasoline taxes and new excise taxes on tires and heavy vehicles into a Federal Highway Trust Fund. Congress established a grant-in-aid formula of a 90 percent federal and a 10 percent state share for construction. The federal government agreed to distribute the funds for the 42,500-mile system on the basis of need. Since costs in built-up urban areas were greater, urban areas would get the most funds.

In the years leading up to the legislation, urban planners debated with highway engineers about how a national highway system should be built. Urban planners wanted to design highways in the context of larger efforts to shape regional development and revitalize declining central cities. Highway engineers, on the other hand, believed that the new interstate system should be designed with one goal in mind: to move people and goods in the most efficient manner from point A to point B. This meant, in effect, that freeways would go directly from the suburbs to the central cities and that whatever got in the way would have to go. The engineers got their way. The 1956 act was written so that the funds would be administered by state highway departments for projects approved by the federal government. As one historian put it, "Since federal and state road engineers controlled the program, they had few incentives to include urban renewal, social regeneration, and broader transportation objectives in the programming."[115]

It is interesting to note the difference between how federal funds were spent on housing and highways. Public housing was built by local public authorities and local governments were given the power to veto any projects planned for their jurisdiction.[116] By contrast, interstate highways were built by state highway departments, which were given the power of eminent domain to force private owners to sell their property. Local governments could not refuse to participate in the program. Moreover, most city governments favored the program; they thought the new highways would help revitalize central cities by making it easier for suburban residents to commute to jobs in the cities. They could hardly have been more wrong.

Laying wide swaths of concrete had different effects in crowded cities than in the open countryside. As the highway builder Robert Moses said in a speech before the National Highway Users Conference in 1964, "You can draw any kind of picture you like on a clean slate . . . but when you operate in an overbuilt metropolis, you have to hack your way with a meat axe."[117] The meat axe approach turned out to be the method Moses used to build his highways, displacing 250,000 people in the New York City area alone.[118] Since the highway engineers wanted to cause the least disruption to private commercial land values, highways were routed through neighborhoods, especially those with the cheapest housing occupied by poor people and minorities.[119] The program was justified not only as highway building but as slum clearance. According to one estimate, the uncompensated loss to city residents who were displaced averaged 20 to 30 percent of one year's income.[120]

Interstate highways had a destructive impact on cities. They not only took land off the tax roles, but the highways damaged surrounding property and cut cities off from their waterfronts. By separating the South Bronx from the rest of the city, the Cross-Bronx Expressway in New York helped turn the South Bronx into one of the worst ghettos in the country. Scholars estimate that the unsightliness of the Fitzgerald Expressway in Boston reduced surrounding property values by about $300 million.[121] The residents of cities began to protest; "freeway revolts" arose to stop highway construction in cities around the country.[122] One of the first successes came in 1959, when San Franciscans successfully prevented the completion of the Embarcadero Freeway. If they had not succeeded, a freeway would today run along the shores of the San Francisco Bay, thus cutting the bay off from the tourist development that has helped keep San Francisco's economy healthy. Protests forced highway planners to become more sensitive to aesthetic and social considerations, but not until after irreversible harm had been done to hundreds of urban neighborhoods.

By the 1980s the final price tag for building the interstate system was $123 billion.[123] While highway building received huge subsidies year in and year out, urban mass transit was starved. Unlike Europe, where gasoline taxes had always been used to help support mass transit, federal gas taxes in the United States could not be allocated for that purpose until 1975. Funding for urban mass transit gradually increased after that, but remained small. Senator Gaylord Nelson of Wisconsin estimated that up to the 1980s, 75 percent of government expenditures for transportation in the United States in the postwar period had been spent on highways, but only 1 percent went for urban mass transit.[124] The inadequate state of mass transit discourages most people from trying it. Except in the New York region, where 30 percent or more of workers commute by mass transit, for the United States as a whole only 4.2 percent of workers commuted by mass transit in 1996—an actual decline from a 5.4 percentage in 1985.[125]

For a brief period, the new highways seemed to benefit both the suburbs and downtown areas. Suburban land values climbed, and at the same time some central business districts went through a minor retail and office boom. Before long, however, it became clear that freeways had the principal effect of making it easier for commuters to move farther and farther out. At the same time that city officials were using urban renewal to raze slums, in a desperate attempt to make the city attractive to businesses and the middle class, the interstate highway program was making it easier for both businesses and the white middle class to leave. As jobs moved to the suburbs, cross-commuting increased: By 1980 over 40 percent of work trips in the United States were suburb to suburb and only 20 percent were suburb to central city.[126]

In the 1990s concerns about urban air pollution and long commuting patterns finally emerged on the national policy agenda. In 1992 Congress passed the Intermodal Surface Transportation Efficiency Act (ISTEA; commonly referred to as "ice tea").[127] The significance of ISTEA is that it took substantial authority over interstate highway funds from politically insulated state transportation departments, which have always been dominated by highway engineers, and put decisions about urban transportations systems into the hands of Metropolitan Planning Organizations (MPOs). Governed by delegates representing municipal governments within urban regions, MPOs assumed authority over funding categories designed to reduce auto congestion and improve air quality. The ISTEA legislation encouraged regional transportation planning by "flexing" federal highway funds, a process that allowed motor vehicle taxes to be spent not only for highways, but for mass transit and even for bicycle and pedestrian uses. Although federal highway funds were still used overwhelmingly for highways, ISTEA provided much-needed flexibility for regional planning of alternative transportation systems.

THE CONTRADICTORY EFFECTS OF NATIONAL URBAN POLICY

The federal government's urban policies interacted in complex ways to shape the development of metropolitan areas. The FHA/VA programs made it difficult for blacks to leave the city and find adequate housing, but helped affluent white families to buy into the suburbs, and the new expressways made it possible for them to commute. If they were poor, blacks could find safe and adequate housing only by moving into public housing. Demand always exceeded supply;

for the poor families who did not move into housing projects, the big challenge was to keep one step ahead of the bulldozer. For those who outlasted the waiting lists to get into the projects, the reward must have seemed puny indeed: Forced to crowd together into dense clusters of high-rise buildings constructed on land cleared of slum housing, the "projects" often became the worst of slums. For many white Americans, public housing became a cultural symbol for blacks on welfare.

Ironically, racist stereotypes were also encouraged when the black middle class tried to break out of slums. Shut off from the new housing in the suburbs, middle-class black families inherited the housing left by whites fleeing the cities. In the typical scenario, they displaced whites who lived in areas near all-black neighborhoods or bought into neighborhoods targeted by realtors for blockbusting. Because this process was so often repeated, the white middle class developed the habit of associating declining property values with an "invasion" by blacks. By reducing the supply of inner-city housing, clearance projects increased the pressure on the existing housing stock at the margins of all-black areas. One way to understand the effect of this dynamic is to imagine the difference it might have made if middle-class blacks had been as free as the white middle class to leapfrog to suburban housing tracts. No doubt a high degree of racial segregation would have continued to exist. Even if it had, however, some black homeowners would have been able to (1) find affordable and desirable housing by buying new homes, instead of moving into neighborhoods already occupied by whites; (2) benefit from the dynamics of the housing market, just as white homeowners did. With this dynamic in operation, the presence of blacks in a neighborhood would not have become so automatically equated, in the white imagination, with dilapidated housing or with declining property values.

The FHA/VA and interstate highway programs were as expensive as they were influential; over the several decades of their operation, each of them involved more than $100 billion in federal commitments (the value of the insurance covering the FHA/VA loans, on the one hand, and the direct federal expenditures on highways, on the other). It is difficult to imagine that policies of this magnitude would ever be implemented for the purpose of reducing the racial segregation of urban areas. And thus the consequences of past policies linger on.

NOTES

1. Joint Resolution 52–22, 52d Cong. (1892); refer also to U.S. Congress, House, *Your Congress and American Housing—The Actions of Congress on Housing*, 82d Cong., 2d sess., 1952, H. Doc. 82–532, p. 1.
2. Public Law 65–102, 65th Cong. (1918); refer also to Congressional Quarterly Service, *Housing a Nation* (Washington, D.C.: Congressional Quarterly Service, 1966), p. 18; Edith Elmer Wood, *Recent Trends in American Housing* (New York: Macmillan, 1931), p. 79.
3. *Congressional Quarterly Service, Housing a Nation*, pp. v, xiii.
4. Public Laws 65–149 and 65–164, 65th Cong. (1918); refer also to Twentieth Century Fund, *Housing for Defense* (New York: Twentieth Century Fund, 1940), pp. 156–157; Congressional Quarterly Service, *Housing a Nation*, p. 18.

5. Refer to the Emergency Relief and Reconstruction Act, Public Law 72–302, 72d Cong. (1932).
6. The only other loan made under this authorization was $155,000 for rural housing in Ford County, Kansas.
7. Edwin L. Scanton, "Public Housing Trends in New York City" (Ph.D. diss., Graduate School of Banking, Rutgers University, 1952), p. 5.
8. Public Law 73–67, 72d Cong. (1933).
9. From a statement by Harold L. Ickes, Secretary of Interior and Public Works Administrator, quoted in Bert Swanson, "The Public Policy of Urban Renewal: Its Goals, Trends, and Conditions in New York City" (paper delivered at the American Political Science Association Meeting, New York, September 1963), p. 10.
10. *U.S. v. Certain Lands in City of Louisville,* Jefferson County, Ky., et al., 78 F.2d 64 (1935); *U.S. v. Certain Lands in City of Detroit,* et al., 12 F.Supp. 345 (1935).
11. Refer to Glen H. Boyer, *Housing: A Factual Analysis* (New York: Macmillan, 1958), p. 247.
12. Richard D. Bingham, *Public Housing and Urban Renewal: An Analysis of Federal-Local Relations,* Praeger Special Studies in U.S. Economics, Social, and Political Issues (New York: Praeger, 1975), p. 30.
13. Nathaniel S. Keith, *Politics and the Housing Crisis Since 1930* (New York: Universe Books, 1973), p. 29.
14. Public Law 75–412, 75th Cong. (1937). Also found in U.S. Congress, House Committee on Banking and Currency, *Basic Laws and Authorizations on Urban Housing,* 91st Cong., 1st sess., 1969, p. 225.
15. Roscoe Martin, "The Expended Partnership," in *The New Urban Politics: Cities and the Federal Government,* ed. Douglas Fox (Pacific Palisades, Calif.: Goodyear, 1972), p. 51.
16. Keith, *Politics and the Housing Crisis,* p. 33.
17. Speech delivered before the Fourth Annual Meeting of the National Public Housing Conference, New York, December 1935, cited in ibid., pp. 32–33.
18. The restriction limiting participation to low-income families, seen from a comparative perspective, is a root cause of the failure of public housing in America. See Arnold J. Heidenheimer, Hugh Heclo, and Carolyn Teich Adams, *Comparative Public Policy: The Politics of Social Choice in Europe and America* (New York: St. Martin's Press, 1975), pp. 69–96.
19. Public Law 76–671, 76th Cong. (1940), relating to defense housing needs; Public Law 80–301, 80th Cong. (1946), suspended cost limitations for some low-income housing projects.
20. U.S. Housing and Home Finance Agency, *Fourteenth Annual Report* (Washington, D.C.: Government Printing Office, 1961), p. 380.
21. U.S. Congress, Senate Special Committee on Post-War Economic Policy and Planning, *Housing and Urban Development: Hearings Pursuant to S. Res. 102,* Senate, 79th Cong., 1st sess., 1945, pp. 1228–1237.
22. U.S. Congress, Senate Committee on Banking and Currency, *General Housing Act of 1945: Hearings,* 79th Cong., 1st sess., 1945, pp. 837–838.
23. U.S. Congress, Senate Committee on Banking and Currency, *General Housing Act of 1945,* p. 754.
24. Mark Gelfand, *A Nation of Cities: The Federal Government and Urban America, 1933–1965,* Urban Life in America Series (New York: Oxford University Press, 1975), p. 14.
25. U.S. Congress, House Select Committee on Lobbying Activities, Housing Lobby, p. 11; see also Leonard Freedman, *Public Housing: The Politics of Poverty,* (New York: Holt, Rinehart and Winston, 1969), pp. 58–75; Keith, *Politics and the Housing Crisis,* pp. 35–39.
26. International Union, United Automobile, Aircraft, and Agricultural Implement Workers of America, *Memorandum on Post War Urban Housing* (Detroit: International Union, United Automobile, Aircraft, and Agricultural Implement Workers of America, 1944), p. 94.
27. Wilson W. Wyatt, quoted in Congressional Quarterly Service, *Housing a Nation,* p. 6.
28. See Keith, *Politics and the Housing Crisis,* pp. 41–100.
29. Housing Act of 1949, Public Law 81–171, Preamble, sec. 2, 81st Cong. (1949).

30. Martin Meyerson and Edward C. Banfield, *Politics, Planning, and the Public Interest* (New York: Free Press, 1955).

31. Freedman, *Public Housing*, p. 55.

32. Robert H. Salisbury, "The New Convergence of Power in Urban Politics," *Journal of Politics* 26 (November 1964): 775–797.

33. John H. Mollenkopf, "The Post-War Politics of Urban Development," in *Marxism and the Metropolis: New Perspectives in Urban Political Economy*, ed. William Tabb and Larry Sawers (New York: Oxford University Press, 1978), p. 138.

34. Quoted in Institute of Housing, "Proceedings" (University College, Washington University, St. Louis, March 21–22, 1952, Mimeograph), p. 18. For studies of the coalition in other cities, see Harold Kaplan, *Urban Renewal Politics: Slum Clearance in Newark* (New York: Columbia University Press, 1963); Meyerson and Banfield, *Politics, Planning and the Public Interest*; Peter H. Rossi and Robert A. Dentler, *The Politics of Urban Renewal—the Chicago Findings* (New York: Free Press, 1961). Refer also to Jewel Bellush and Murray Hausknecht, "Entrepreneurs and Urban Renewal: The New Mean of Power," *Journal of the American Planning Institute* 32 (September 1961); George S. Duggar, "The Relation of Local Government Structure to Urban Renewal," in *Urban Renewal: People, Politics and Planning*, ed. Jewel Bellush and Murray Hausknecht (Garden City, N.Y.: Doubleday, Anchor Books, 1967), pp. 179–187, 200–208, as reprinted from *Law and Contemporary Problems* 26 (Winter 1961); Herbert Kay, "The Third Force in Urban Renewal," *Fortune,* October 1964.

35. Quoted in Robert A. Dahl, *Who Governs: Democracy and Power in an American City* (New Haven, Conn.: Yale University Press, 1961), p. 136. For another insightful example of the use of urban renewal by political entrepreneurs, see Jewel Bellush and Murray Hausknecht, "Urban Renewal and the Reformer," in *Urban Renewal: People, Politics and Planning*, ed. Jewel Bellush and Murray Hausknecht (Garden City, NY: Doubleday, Anchor Books, 1967), pp. 189–197.

36. Gelfand, *A Nation of Cities*, p. 161.

37. Mollenkopf, "The Post-War Politics of Urban Development," in *Marxism and the Metropolis*, p. 140.

38. Ibid., p. 138.

39. Herbert J. Gans, *The Urban Villagers: Group and Class in the Life of Italian-Americans* (New York: Free Press, 1962), chap. 13.

40. John H. Mollenkopf, "On the Causes and Consequences of Neighborhood Political Mobilization" (paper delivered at the annual meeting of the American Political Science Association, New Orleans, September 4–8, 1973).

41. Quoted in Clarence N. Stone, *Economic Growth and Neighborhood Discontent: System Bias in the Urban Renewal Program of Atlanta* (Chapel Hill: University of North Carolina Press, 1976), pp. 48–49.

42. See Chester Hartman et al., *Yerba Buena: Land Grab and Community Resistance in San Francisco* (San Francisco: Glide, 1974). The following material on the Yerba Buena controversy draws on Chester Hartman's excellent book. In most cases citations are limited to quotations or specific data.

43. Ibid., p. 31.

44. Ibid., p. 19.

45. Ibid., p. 190.

46. Ibid., p. 128.

47. Arthur I. Blaustein and Geoffrey Faux, *The Star-Spangled Hustle*, foreword by Ronald V. Dellums (Garden City, N.Y.: Doubleday, Anchor Books, 1973), p. 71.

48. See Martin Anderson, *The Federal Bulldozer: A Critical Analysis of Urban Renewal, 1949–1962* (Cambridge, Mass.: MIT Press, 1964), p. 65; compare Rossi and Dentler, *The Politics of Urban Renewal*, p. 224.

49. Chester Hartman, "The Housing of Relocated Families," in *Urban Renewal: The Record and the Controversy,* ed. James Q. Wilson (Cambridge, Mass.: MIT Press, 1966), p. 322, as reprinted from *Journal of the American Institute of Planners* 30 (November 1964): 266–286.

50. Anderson, *The Federal Bulldozer,* p. 65.

51. Bernard Frieden and Marshall Kaplan, *The Politics of Neglect: Aid from Model Cities to Revenue Sharing* (Cambridge, Mass.: MIT Press, 1975).

52. Anderson, *The Federal Bulldozer,* pp. 65–66.

53. Mollenkopf, "The Post-War Politics of Urban Development," p. 140.

54. Anderson, *The Federal Bulldozer,* pp. 65–66; see also Bellush and Hausknecht, "Urban Renewal and the Reformer," p. 13.

55. Anderson, *The Federal Bulldozer,* p. 105.

56. Freedman, *Public Housing,* p. 140.

57. Arnold J. Heidenheimer, Hugh Heclo, and Carolyn Teich Adams, *Comparative Public Policy: The Politics of Social Choice in America, Europe, and Japan,* 3rd ed. (New York: St. Martin's Press, 1990), chap. 4.

58. Freedman, *Public Housing,* p. 105. The points in the discussion of public housing that follow borrow from Freedman's treatment at pp. 105–122.

59. Lawrence M. Friedman, *Government and Slum Housing: A Century of Frustration* (Chicago: Rand McNally, 1968), p. 121.

60. Freedman, *Public Housing,* p. 111.

61. Friedman, *Government and Slum Housing,* p. 123.

62. James Baldwin, *Nobody Knows My Name* (New York: Dial Press, 1961), p. 63, quoted in Freedman, *Public Housing,* p. 117.

63. Friedman, *Government and Slum Housing,* p. 121.

64. Lee Rainwater, *Behind Ghetto Walls: Black Families in a Federal Slum* (Chicago: Aldine, 1970).

65. National Commission on Urban Problems, *Building the American City* (New York: Praeger, 1969), p. 153. This commission, appointed by the president, was established in January 1967 and headed by former Illinois senator and longtime urban policy advocate Paul H. Douglas.

66. National Commission on Urban Problems, *Building the American City,* pp. 164–165.

67. Housing and Urban Development Act of 1968, Public Law 90–448, 90th Cong. (1968).

68. John C. Weicher, *Urban Renewal: National Program for Local Problems,* Evaluative Studies Series (Washington, D.C.: American Enterprise Institute for Public Policy Research, 1972), p. 6, citing unpublished HUD statistics: 538,044 housing units had been demolished as a result of urban renewal activities through 1971.

69. U.S. Department of Housing and Urban Development, *1974 Statistical Yearbook of the U.S. Department of Housing and Urban Development* (Washington, D.C.: Government Printing Office, 1976), p. 104.

70. Barry Checkoway, "Large Builders, Federal Housing Programs, and Postwar Suburbanization," in *Marxism and the Metropolis: New Perspectives in Political Economy,* ed. William K. Tabb and Larry Sawers (New York: Oxford University Press), p. 156.

71. Stephen David and Paul Peterson, eds., *Urban Politics and Public Policy: The City in Crisis* (New York: Praeger, 1973), p. 94.

72. Charles Abrams, *The Future of Housing* (New York: HarperCollins, 1946), p. 213.

73. Bureau of National Affairs, *The Housing and Development Reporter* (Washington, D.C.: Bureau of National Affairs, 1976).

74. Ibid.

75. Calculated from data in Congressional Quarterly Service, *Housing a Nation,* p. 6.

76. U.S. Department of Housing and Urban Development, *1974 Statistical Yearbook of the Department of Housing and Urban Development,* pp. 116–117.

77. U.S. Bureau of the Census, *Historical Statistics of the United States, Colonial Times to 1970*, pt. 1, Bicentennial ed. (Washington, D.C.: Government Printing Office, 1975), p. 646.

78. Kenneth T. Jackson, *Crabgrass Frontier: The Suburbanization of the United States* (New York: Oxford University Press, 1985), p. 205.

79. For a discussion of this phenomenon, see Murray Edelman, *The Symbolic Uses of Politics*, 7th ed. (Champaign: University of Illinois Press, 1976), pp. 44–76. We are indebted to Jeffrey Gilbert for several of the ideas contained in this section.

80. Michael Stone, "Reconstructing American Housing" (unpublished manuscript), quoted in Chester W. Hartman, *Housing and Social Policy*, Prentice-Hall Series in Social Policy (Englewood Cliffs, N.J.: Prentice-Hall, 1975), p. 30.

81. Quoted in Brian J. L. Berry, *The Open Housing Question: Race and Housing in Chicago, 1966–1976* (Cambridge, Mass.: Balinger, 1979), p. 9.

82. Quoted in ibid., pp. 9, 11.

83. Luigi M. Laurenti, "Theories of Race and Property Value," in *Urban Analysis: Readings in Housing and Urban Development*, ed. Alfred N. Page and Warren R. Seyfried (Glenview, Ill.: Scott, Foresman, 1970), p. 274.

84. Charles Abrams, quoted in Norman N. Bradburn, Seymour Sudman, and Galen L. Gockel, *Side by Side: Integrated Neighborhoods in America* (Chicago: Quadrangle Books, 1971), p. 104.

85. Gelfand, *A Nation of Cities*, p. 221.

86. Nathan Glazer and David McEntire, eds., *Housing and Minority Groups* (Berkeley: University of California Press, 1960), p. 140.

87. Public Law 90–284, 90th Cong. (1968), Title VIII ("Fair Housing"), sec. 805.

88. D.C. Public Interest Research Group (DCPIRG), Institute for Self-Reliance, and Institute for Policy Studies, *Redlining: Mortgage Disinvestment in the District of Columbia* (Washington, D.C.: DCPIRG, Institute for Local Self-Reliance, and Institute for Policy Studies, 1975), p. 3.

89. U.S. Department of Housing and Urban Development, *1974 Statistical Yearbook of the Department of Housing and Urban Development*, pp. 116–117.

90. Thomas A. Clark, "The Suburbanization Process and Residential Segregation," in *Divided Neighborhoods: Changing Patterns of Racial Segregation*, ed. Gary A. Tobin (Newbury Park, Calif.: Sage, 1987), p. 115; Larry Long and Diane Deare, "The Suburbanization of Blacks," *American Demographics* 3 (1981), cited in Douglas S. Massey and Nancy A. Denton, "Suburbanization and Segregation in U.S. Metropolitan Areas," *American Journal of Sociology* 3 (November 1988): 592–626.

91. Jackson, *Crabgrass Frontier*, p. 205.

92. John R. Logan and Harvey L. Molotch, *Urban Fortunes: The Political Economy of Place* (Berkeley: University of California Press, 1987), p. 195.

93. Clark, "The Suburbanization Process and Residential Segregation," pp. 115–137.

94. Massey and Denton, "Suburbanization and Segregation in U.S. Metropolitan Areas," pp. 592–626.

95. Logan and Molotch, *Urban Fortunes*, p. 194.

96. Douglas S. Massey and Mitchell L. Eggers, "The Spatial Concentration of Affluence and Poverty During the 1970s," *Urban Affairs Quarterly* 29:2 (December). See also S. Roberts, "Shifts in 80's Failed to Ease Segregation," *New York Times*, July 15, 1992, pp. B1–B3.

97. John F. Kain, "Housing Market Discrimination and Black Suburbanization in the 1980's," in *Divided Neighborhoods: Changing Patterns of Racial Segregation*, ed. Gary A. Tobin (Newbury Park, Calif.: Sage, 1987), p. 68.

98. John Farley, *Segregated City, Segregated Suburbs: Are They the Products of Black-White Socioeconomic Differentials?* (Edwardsville: Southern Illinois University, 1983), cited in Joe T. Darden, "Choosing Neighbors and Neighborhoods: The Role of Race in Housing Preference," in *Divided Neighborhoods: Changing Patterns of Racial Segregation*, ed. Gary A. Tobin (Newbury Park, Calif.: Sage, 1987), p. 16.

99. John F. Farley, "Race Still Matters: The Minimal Role of Income and Housing Cost as Causes of Housing Segregation in St. Louis, 1990." *Urban Affairs Review* 31, No. 2 (November 1995).

100. Public Policy Research Centers, University of Missouri-St. Louis, *Analysis of Impediments to Fair Housing: St. Louis County* (St. Louis: Author, 1995).

101. William E. Nelson and Michael S. Bailey, "The Weakening of State Participation in Civil Rights Enforcement," in *Public Policy Across States and Communities,* ed. Dennis R. Judd (Greenwich, Conn.: JAI Press, 1985), p. 160.

102. Public Law 94–200, 94th Cong. (1975), Title III, and Public Law 95–128, 95th Cong. (1977), Title VIII.

103. Calvin Bradford, *Community Reinvestment Agreement Library* (Des Plaines, Ill.: Community Reinvestment Associates, 1992), as cited in *From Redlining to Reinvestment: Community Responses to Urban Disinvestment,* ed. Gregory D. Squires (Philadelphia: Temple University Press, 1992), p. 2.

104. Mitchelle Zuckoff, "Study Shows Racial Bias in Lending," *Boston Globe,* October 9, 1992.

105. Henry Ford, quoted in J. Allen Whitt and Glenn Yago, "Corporate Strategies and the Decline of Transit in U.S. Cities," *Urban Affairs Quarterly* 21, no. 1 (September 1985): 61.

106. James A. Dunn, Jr., *Miles to Go: European and American Transportation Policies* (Cambridge, Mass.: MIT Press, 1981), p. 59.

107. John R. Meyer and Jose A. Gomez-Ibanez, *Autos Transit and Cities* (Cambridge, Mass.: Harvard University Press, 1981), pp. 23, 28, 34.

108. Dunn, *Miles to Go,* p. 116.

109. Whitt and Yago, "Corporate Strategies," p. 52.

110. Dunn, *Miles to Go,* p. 116. Many policy analysts question whether earmarked gasoline taxes pay for the full costs of highways, including the costs of air and noise pollution and the expenses associated with traffic accidents. See Meyer and Gomez-Ibanez, *Autos Transit and Cities;* and Glenn Yago, *The Decline of Transit* (New York: Cambridge University Press, 1984), p. 195.

111. Bradford C. Snell, "American Ground Transport," in *The Urban Scene,* 2nd ed., ed. Joe R. Feagin (New York: Random House, 1979), p. 247.

112. Ibid., p. 248.

113. Quoted in ibid., p. 249.

114. Alan Lupo, Frank Colcord, and Edmund P. Fowler, *Rites of Way: The Politics of Transportation in Boston and the U.S. City* (Boston: Little, Brown, 1971), p. 184.

115. Mark Rose, *Interstate Express Highway Politics, 1941–1956* (Lawrence: The Regents Press of Kansas, 1979), p. 97.

116. A local participation agreement is required before public housing can be built in a jurisdiction. Suburban governments simply refused to negotiate such agreements and therefore excluded all conventional public housing from their locality.

117. Quoted in Leavitt, *Superhighway—Superhoax* (Garden City, N.Y.: Doubleday, 1970), p. 53.

118. Robert A. Caro, *The Power Broker: Robert Moses and the Fall of New York* (New York: Random House, 1974), p. 19.

119. For example, between 1951 and 1974, 89 percent of the 10,000 households displaced by public projects in Baltimore were black. See Anthony Downs, *Urban Problems and Prospects* (Chicago: Marsham, 1970), pp. 204–205.

120. Ibid., p. 223.

121. Meyer and Gomez-Ibanez, *Autos Transit and Cities,* p. 177.

122. By 1970 there were 400 struggles underway by community groups to oppose highway construction. Harry C. Boyte, *The Backyard Revolution: Understanding the New Citizen Movement* (Philadelphia: Temple University Press, 1980), p. 11.

123. H. Josef Hebert, "Billions Needed to Fix Interstates," *Albany Times Union,* April 5, 1987. p. 1.

124. Jackson, *Crabgrass Frontier,* p. 250.

125. U.S. Bureau of the Census, *Statistical Abstract of the United States,* table no. 644 (Employment Status of Civilian Population: 1950 to 1997, September 30, 1998; and table no. 1055, Passenger Transit Industry—Summary, 1985 to 1986, October 2, 1998.

126. Robert Cervero, "Unlocking Suburban Gridlock," *Journal of the American Planning Association* (August 1986): 389.

127. This account of ISTEA relies upon Paul G. Lewis, "The Politics of Structure in Transportation Policy: Resuscitating Metropolitan Planning Organizations under ISTEA" (paper delivered at the Annual Meeting of the Urban Affairs Association, Toronto, Canada, April 17, 1997).

8

THE RISE AND FALL OF NATIONAL URBAN POLICY

THE POLITICS OF NATIONAL URBAN POLICY

In the 1960s the problems of racial segregation, discrimination, and concentrated poverty burst onto the nation's political agenda as the main ingredients of an "urban crisis." The National Commission on Urban Problems (1958); the National Commission on Civil Disorders (1967), called the Kerner Commission after its chairman, Illinois Governor Otto B. Kerner); the President's Task Force on Suburban Problems (1967), President Nixon's Commission on Population Growth and the American Future (1972); and a host of state and city task forces decried the segregation of blacks and the poor in ghetto areas of the central cities. To a considerable extent, the national Democratic party staked its future on solving the problems of race and poverty. The results of the social and urban policies of the 1960s were mixed, but by the mid–1970s there was a growing perception that many of the programs had failed.

From 1969 to 1976, when Republican Presidents Richard Nixon and Gerald Ford occupied the White House, many of the grant programs pushed by the Democrats in the 1960s came under attack. Rather than trying to eliminate them, however, Republicans focused on giving state and local governments broad discretion in spending the money. These reforms were justified by a heavy dose of rhetoric about balancing the federal budget by streamlining government and paring the size and number of programs. Spending for programs, however, continued to rise. By the end of the 1970s Republicans abandoned their efforts to reform federal urban programs, and turned instead to a new objective: eliminating them altogether. Ronald Reagan's presidential victory in the 1980 election signaled the beginning of the end for urban programs. Between 1981 and 1986, most of the urban programs inherited from previous presidential administrations had disappeared.

For decades, the social programs of the Great Society served as useful targets for politicians on the campaign trail. After the Los Angeles riots in 1992,

President George Bush's press secretary, Marlin Fitzwater, declared that the social welfare programs of the 1960s and 1970s were partly to blame.[1] When asked to name the specific programs he had in mind, he replied, "I don't have a list with me," but went on to add, "the basic structures of these communities were formulated in the '60s and '70s on the basis of the social welfare efforts that didn't work." Trying to blame the riots on the Great Society programs struck historian Arthur Schlesinger, Jr., as "pathetic." "What can they be smoking over at the White House these days?" he asked.[2] Whatever it was, it seemed to be extremely addicting. In the first presidential debate of the 1992 campaign, President Bush repeatedly invoked the well-worn slogan "tax and spend." Democratic candidate Bill Clinton retorted, "President Bush is running against Lyndon Johnson, Jimmy Carter, everybody but me in this campaign." In 1992, for the first time in a long time, it was not a winning strategy for the Republicans. Nevertheless, President Bill Clinton did not attempt to revive urban policy. By the 1996 presidential election, neither Republicans nor Democrats spoke about helping the cities or the people living within them. Instead, the talk was about welfare reform, crime, immigration, and balancing the federal budget. Even with the growing budget surpluses in President Clinton's second term, neither candidate in the 2000 presidential election had much to say about the cities. In this chapter we explain why urban policy attracted so much attention in the 1960s and 1970s, and why it fell so far off the agenda after that.

THE FEDERAL ROLE UNDER TWO DEMOCRATIC PRESIDENTS

When President Kennedy was sworn in on January 20, 1961, his administration was already committed to helping the cities. Even before his campaign, Kennedy had concluded that the problem of the cities was "the great unspoken issue in the 1960 election."[3] During the campaign, the Democrats talked about doing something about the urban crisis, while the Republicans tried to avoid such issues. "If you ever let them campaign only on domestic issues," confided presidential nominee Richard M. Nixon to his aides, "they'll beat us."[4] President Kennedy "emerged as an eloquent spokesman for a new political generation. In presidential message after message Kennedy spelled out in more detail than the Congress or the country could easily digest the most complete programs of domestic reforms in a quarter century."[5]

The Kennedy Administration mapped out an ambitious agenda. Widespread poverty, racial segregation, juvenile delinquency and crime, bad schools, and a host of other social problems were discovered in the 1960s only in the sense that they were no longer "out of sight, out of mind." They had existed for a long time and were no worse and little different by the advent of the Kennedy Administration than they had been under presidents Roosevelt, Truman, or Eisenhower. What made them seem worse was their greater visibility. Martin

Luther King, Jr. understood the task of creating visibility during the civil rights demonstrations in 1963: "I saw no way," he later commented, "of dealing with things without bringing the indignation to the attention of the nation."[6] King turned the civil rights issue into a national crisis in Birmingham, Alabama, in the summer of 1963. What started in Birmingham spread across the South and even filtered into northern cities. During the course of the summer, there were 13,786 arrests of demonstrators in seventy-five cities of the eleven major southern states.[7] In the ten weeks that followed Birmingham, the Justice Department counted 758 demonstrations across the nation. It quickly became clear that the administration could no longer avoid dealing with civil rights. The brutal treatment of civil rights demonstrators throughout the South was being televised into the living rooms of millions of American homes. By mid-June 127 civil rights bills had been introduced in the House of Representatives. Whether the Kennedy Administration wanted to or not, it was being drawn into the nation's most significant and divisive internal conflict since the Civil War.

The political pressures applied by the civil rights movement were reinforced by the influence of the black electorate. As John C. Donovan observed in his book *The Politics of Poverty*, "The greatest strength of the Negro communities lies in its voting power, in its numbers, and in their strategic location."[8] In the South the black population was geographically diffused and systematically denied the right to the vote. When they moved to northern cities, blacks gained the franchise. Their votes were concentrated in the cities of the industrial states holding a majority Electoral College votes—Illinois, California, Massachusetts, Ohio, Michigan, New Jersey, New York, Texas, and Pennsylvania. Kennedy targeted his campaign on these key states, and the 68 percent plurality that black voters gave him was crucial to his razor-thin victories in Illinois, Ohio, and other states. In 1956 Adlai Stevenson, the liberal Democratic candidate from Illinois, had received 61 percent of the black vote.[9] If Kennedy had not done better, he would have lost the election: "It is difficult to see how Illinois, New Jersey, Michigan, South Carolina, or Delaware (with 74 electoral votes) could have been won had the Republican-Democratic split of the Negro wards and precincts remained as it was, unchanged from the Eisenhower charm of 1956."[10]

On June 11, 1963, Kennedy overruled his advisers and announced that he would propose a civil rights bill. When Kennedy was assassinated on November 22, the bill had just reached the House Rules Committee. The assassination created an emotionally charged atmosphere that the new president, Lyndon Baines Johnson, adroitly exploited. Opinion polls indicated overwhelming public support for civil rights legislation. Seizing the moment, Johnson added new provisions to the legislation and harried Congress into acting quickly. When Republicans joined with northern Democrats to move the bill out of the House Rules Committee, the bill was sent to the floor, where it passed by a vote of 290 to 130. On June 6, 1964, the Senate mustered the necessary two-thirds vote to overcome a filibuster mounted by southerners, and the legislation passed.

The Civil Rights Act of 1964 was far-reaching. It outlawed discrimination in public accommodations, effectively striking down the South's Jim Crow laws that denied blacks equal access to bus stations, restaurants, lunch counters, theaters, sports arenas, gasoline stations, motels, hotels, and lodging houses. It outlawed racial discrimination in the hiring, firing, training, and promoting of workers. It barred discrimination in the administration of federal grants. A year later, Congress passed the Voting Rights Act, which not only outlawed literacy tests and other discriminatory voting restrictions, but also provided that federal registrars could replace local registrars in counties where there had been a history of discrimination against black voters.

Taking advantage of the post-assassination atmosphere, President Johnson also pressed for a program to redress economic inequalities.[11] Kennedy's advisers had persuaded him that the time had come for his administration to devise a program to attack poverty and unemployment. In June 1963 Kennedy had told Walter Heller, the chairman of his Council of Economic Advisors, to appoint a task force of officials who would be responsible for proposing a program to attack poverty. Although Kennedy's commitment to a program was almost certain by the time of his assassination, it was not clear how prominent it would have been on his legislative agenda.

President Johnson was told about the proposed antipoverty program only two days after assuming office, but he quickly responded, "That's my kind of program. It will help people. I want you to move full speed ahead."[12] The idea of an ambitious, highly visible program appealed to Johnson's desire to be perceived as a second Roosevelt, as a president who would go down in history as the one who completed the social agenda left unfinished in the 1930s. In his first State of the Union address of January 10, 1964, President Johnson announced that he would seek a "total effort" to end poverty in the United States. Using a grandiose military analogy, he said, "This Administration here and now declares unconditional war on poverty in America, and I urge this Congress and all Americans to join me in that effort."[13] When Johnson signed the Economic Opportunity Act on August 8, he had two big legislative victories, the civil rights act and his "war on poverty," to carry into the presidential campaign.

The 1964 campaign provided the setting for an unusually contentious national debate over the federal government's role and responsibilities. The Republican nominee, Barry Goldwater, was one of the few non-southerners to vote against the civil rights act in the Senate. He attacked the welfare programs funded through the Social Security Act of 1935 and even questioned the immensely popular old-age insurance program set up by that legislation. The Republican party platform warned that "individual freedom retreats under the mounting assault of expanding centralized power."[14] Lyndon Johnson, in contrast, called for a Great Society that would eliminate poverty and treat other social ills through federal action on civil rights, the cities, health care, welfare, education, and employment.

Johnson swept the election by a landslide, winning 61 percent of the popular vote and picking up 486 electoral college votes to Goldwater's 53. The president's coattails were long; Democrats commanded a 289 to 146 majority in the House to go along with a 67 to 33 majority in the Senate. The Democrats' overwhelming victory set the stage for a period of legislative activism not seen since Roosevelt's fabled One Hundred Days in 1933. Between 1964 and 1966, Congress authorized 219 new programs, which included some of the most important and enduring social initiatives of the 1960s. In 1965 Congress approved Medicare for the elderly and Medicaid for welfare recipients. The Elementary and Secondary Education Act provided federal grants to schools. Food stamps, an experimental program tried during the Kennedy years, became permanent in 1966. New and expanded educational and job-training assistance was made available for the mentally and physically handicapped. The public housing and urban renewal programs were expanded, and a new "model cities" program to treat the problems of cities was initiated. In 1966, Congress also created a new cabinet-level department, the Department of Housing and Urban Development (HUD), to administer urban programs.

The number and size of federal grants committed to cities and states rose quickly. In 1960, 44 separate grant-in-aid programs were available to state and local governments.[15] Four years later, a Senate subcommittee report identified 115 grant programs and a total of 216 separate authorizations for new spending under these programs.[16] By 1966 there were 399 authorizations.[17] By 1969 the count was approaching 500, and it reached about 530 a year later before leveling off (see Figure 8.1)[18] The number of programs fell in the 1970s, but mainly because many of them were folded into block-grant consolidations and not because funding had declined.[19]

The amount of money spent through federal grants continued to increase exponentially. In 1950 only $2.2 billion in grants were allocated to state and local governments. By 1960 this amount had risen modestly to $7 billion, but by 1970 the national government was spending $24 billion a year for grants-in-aid. When President Nixon left office in 1974, annual funding had climbed to $43.3 billion. Federal grant-in-aid spending continued to rise rapidly, amounting to more than $89 billion by 1980 before beginning a steep decline. The proportion of local budgets that came in the form of grants from federal and state governments also increased sharply in the 1960s and 1970s. In 1950 grants from states and from the federal government accounted for only 10 percent of the revenues making up local budgets, but this proportion rose to over 26 percent of municipal revenues by 1978. In the 1980s, however, sharp cuts in federal grants reduced the cities' reliance on intergovernmental programs. By the end of the decade, cities received less than 10 percent of their income from intergovernmental revenues.

The explosion in federal spending in the 1960s and 1970s was accompanied by an attempt to achieve a large number of national purposes. Not since the closing of the frontier in the 1870s had the federal government attempted so forcefully to set forth a direction for the nation. The Louisiana purchase of 1803, a succession of township and homestead acts, generous land grants to railroad companies, and an aggressive military policy toward the Indians supported the federal government's intention to open up the West in the nineteenth century.[20] In the 1960s the president and Congress once again mapped out a national agenda. This time, the national purpose embraced the goals of eliminating poverty, erasing racial discrimination, providing equal opportunity in education and jobs, and developing cities and communities. The national emphasis on equality and social justice was reflected in especially clear terms in the case of

FIGURE 8.1 Growth of Grants-in-Aid Authorizations, 1962–1986

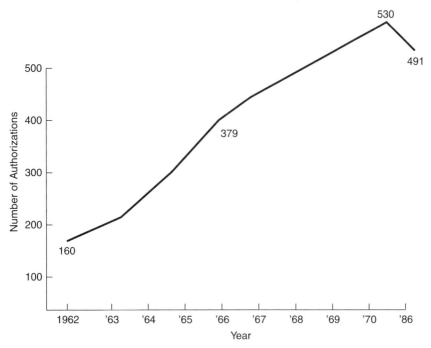

►The number of grants-in-aid programs to state and local governments is somewhat less than the number of authorizations.

Source: Adapted from U.S. Senate, Committee on Governmental Operations, *Intergovernmental Revenue Act of 1971 and Related Legislation,* hearings before the Subcommittee on Intergovernmental Relations, Senate, 92d Cong., 1st Sess., 1971, p. 379; and Michael D. Reagan, *The New Federalism* (New York: Oxford University Press, 1972), p. 55; and the Office of Management and Budget, *Catalog of Federal Domestic Assistance,* 1986 (Washington, D.C.: U.S. Government Printing Office, 1986).

the Civil Rights Act of 1964, when the federal government served notice that its new civil rights statutes would override state and local racial practices. The preambles to the grant programs of Kennedy's New Frontier and Johnson's Great Society articulated a variety of national goals. For example, from the Manpower Development and Training Act of 1962:

> It is in the national interest that current and prospective manpower shortages be identified and that persons who can be qualified for these positions through education and training be sought out and trained, *in order that the nation may meet the staffing requirements of the struggle for freedom.*[21]

Or the Economic Opportunity Act of 1964:

> The United States can achieve its full economic and social potential as a nation only if every individual has the opportunity to contribute the full extent of his capabilities

and to participate in the workings of our society. *It is, therefore, the policy of the United States* to eliminate the paradox of poverty in the midst of plenty in this nation.[22]

And the Demonstration Cities and Metropolitan Development Act of 1966 (the so-called Model Cities legislation):

> The Congress hereby finds and declares that *improving the quality of urban life is the most critical domestic problem facing the United States.*[23]

Imagine these kinds of statements of intention introducing hundreds of pieces of legislation, ranging from rent supplements to federal school aid to crime control, and the complexity of the new system of grants becomes readily apparent. Hardly an economic or a social problem escaped attention, and each program specified its own complicated methods of implementation. Recipient institutions were subjected to close scrutiny and control. After all, it makes no sense to fund a national priority unless the money is going to be used carefully, according to prescribed guidelines and standards.[24]

The Great Society Programs: Between Image and Reality

The War on Poverty and Model Cities programs attracted a great deal of attention because they were sold with grandiose promises about what they would accomplish. In 1964, when Lyndon Johnson proposed the War on Poverty, he announced that his objective was "total victory."[25] Such a promise could not possibly be fulfilled no matter how well the program might be implemented. As it turned out, the War on Poverty became the lightning rod for controversy, as did the Model Cities program, which was implemented through the Demonstration Cities Act of 1966. Under the terms of the War on Poverty, community action agencies were instructed to operate with the "maximum feasible participation" of the poor. Likewise, Model Cities agencies were supposed to galvanize participation by local residents. City Hall and other agencies of local government were cut out of the loop. The idea was to create new institutions in the cities capable of mobilizing the energies of people outside the Establishment. An early program guide distributed by the Office of Economic Opportunity said that to qualify for funding, local antipoverty programs should involve the poor from the very first "in planning, policy-making, and operation."[26]

These programs were, in effect, a means of fomenting a revolution in local power structures. According to two scholars, Frances Fox Piven and Richard A. Cloward, many of the Great Society programs were formulated to preserve and strengthen the Democratic party's electoral advantage in the industrialized states holding the largest blocs of votes in the Electoral College.[27] Rather than work through local politicians who had repeatedly shown an unwillingness to mobilize the votes of inner-city blacks, federal administrators tried to work directly with organizations and leaders in black communities. The expectation was that blacks would vote Democratic in return.

In the 1960s, a multitude of new agencies were established to receive and spend federal dollars. Of all of the community action funds spent by the Office of

Economic Opportunity by 1968, only 25 percent were given to public agencies at all. The remainder went to organizations such as universities, churches, civil rights groups, settlement houses, family services agencies, United Way programs, and newly established nonprofit groups.[28] Likewise, only 10 percent of the funds distributed through programs administered by the Department of Health, Education and Welfare were administered by state and local governments.[29]

A handful of programs received a massive amount of mass media attention when political activists associated with them became embroiled in political fights with mayors and local government officials. In Syracuse, San Francisco, and the state of Mississippi, local administrators of antipoverty programs led protest actions against mayors, welfare departments, and school boards, demanding the implementation of programs that responded to complaints from the black community. Though such protests happened in only a few places, local authorities were upset when they saw federal monies flowing into their jurisdictions to groups and organizations that regularly opposed City Hall. Such organizations encouraged complaints about all sorts of things—police brutality, the hiring of teachers, welfare policies, public housing maintenance; the list could be endless.

Despite such controversies, the War on Poverty and the Model Cities programs continued to receive congressional support mainly because funds flowed into a large number of states and congressional districts. Thus, politicians of both parties were able to take credit for bringing federal spending to their states and districts. This was hardly accidental. To broaden the base of support in Congress, the Johnson Administration abandoned its original intention to restrict the antipoverty effort to a few "demonstration" projects. In the first year 650 projects were funded, but by 1967 the number reached 1,100. The same thing happened with the Model Cities program. Like the War on Poverty, Model Cities was promoted with overblown rhetoric; it was supposed to involve an unprecedented "concentration and coordination of Federal, State, and local public and private efforts" into a few target areas.[30] Initially, the number of cities that would receive money for "demonstration" programs was supposed to be as low as five.[31] By the time powerful congressional leaders were accommodated, the number of cities had gone up to seventy-five, and a year later another seventy-five cities were added in a second round of funding.[32]

Though expanding the number of programs in this fashion effectively guaranteed that there would be enough congressional support for these programs, it also virtually eliminated the possibility that any one program could have much effect. The funding for individual programs did not match the inflated rhetoric. Although it was often portrayed as a massive, radical program, for example,[33] the money appropriated for the War on Poverty was a drop in the bucket compared to the problems it was meant to solve. Model Cities money was likewise very limited, and spread thin.

The combination of political controversy, overblown promises, and limited accomplishments became enduring and damaging legacies of the Great Society. Conservative critics have contended that the social programs of the 1960s and 1970s not only failed to eliminate poverty, but that they made it more intractable by providing incentives for people not to work and support a family.[34] Over the years such claims took on the status of a conventional wisdom, despite the fact that they were mostly wrong. The poverty rate fell by exactly half after the social programs of the 1960s were enacted, from 22.2 percent of the population in 1960 to an all-time low of 11.1 percent by 1973.[35] In the 1980s, when expenditures on programs for the poor were slashed, the poverty rate rose steadily, and by 1992 it had rebounded almost to the pre-1960s level.[36]

Evaluations of specific federal programs to attack urban problems show mixed results. Often the programs were overly complex and administrators ran into severe implementation problems.[37] But some programs worked. Perhaps the best example is Head Start, a federal program to enhance the skills of poor children before they enter school. One study found that children who participated in Head Start were 45 percent less likely to be held back in school than were similar children not enrolled in the program. This produced a substantial savings for local school districts.[38] Medicare and Medicaid improved health care substantially for the elderly and the poor. In 1963, 19 percent of poor persons had never visited a doctor; this fell to only 8 percent by 1970. From 1965 to 1975, the infant mortality rate of the poor fell by 33 percent.[39] Because of such successes, most of the poverty programs became sufficiently popular that they endured despite complaints from conservatives. Two programs—Community Action and Job Corps—took most of the political heat. The first was ended in 1974; the second barely survived as a small program until the 1980s.

To understand the reasons for the backlash against the Great Society programs, it is necessary to examine politics and perceptions. The overwhelming (and erroneous) popular impression was that most of the programs benefited only blacks in the inner cities. This perception dovetailed nicely with the electoral strategy of the national Republican Party, which exploited racial divisions and animosities as a means of winning elections in 1968 and thereafter.

The Backlash Against Urban Programs

The Democratic landslide of 1964 did not lay to rest the debate over the federal government's role. The honeymoon following the election lasted scarcely two years. In the 1966 congressional elections, the Republicans took back many of the seats they had lost to Democrats two years earlier. The Ninetieth Congress, which sat from January 1967 to the end of 1968, was much less willing to approve new programs. By the 1968 presidential election, the Democrats were already on the defensive.

The 1964 landslide had masked a development that would soon undermine the Democrats' ability to win presidential elections. The issue of race was tearing apart the coalition that the Democrats had fashioned in the 1930s. Johnson lost throughout the deep South. Goldwater received 87 percent of the popular vote in Mississippi, almost 70 percent in Alabama, and substantially more than 50 percent in Louisiana, Georgia, and South Carolina. After 1964, Republican candidates began to win elections in the South for the first time since the carpetbagger governments imposed on southern states after the Civil War.

In 1968 the Republicans capitalized on resentment provoked by the successes of the civil rights movement. The Democratic presidential candidate, Hubert Humphrey, carried only one southern state, Texas. Across the South, he won only 31 percent of the vote, running behind both Republican Richard Nixon (34.5 percent) and Alabama governor and third-party candidate George Wallace (34.6 percent), who ran as an avowed segregationist. In 1968 the Nixon campaign adopted law and order as its main theme. This had been Goldwater's campaign slogan too, but he had handled it crudely and ineptly. Goldwater's television ads tried to convey an impression that America's cities were in ruins by showing scenes of blacks rioting. In the scenes meant to portray Goldwater's vision of the American past he would like to restore, blacks were shown picking cotton.[40] The spot ads aired by Nixon four years later were less blatant, though they were not subtle, either. One of his television spots showed scenes of urban riots, with a Nixon voice-over calling for "some honest talk about the problem of order."[41] But at least blacks were not shown in a rendition of a bucolic agricultural past.

The message worked in the North as well as the South. Working-class whites in semiskilled and unskilled occupations gave Humphrey only 38 percent of their votes, less than two-thirds the 61 percent proportion cast for John Kennedy in 1960. Black voters, on the other hand, abandoned the Republicans. Nixon won 32 percent of the black vote in 1960, but his share fell to 12 percent in 1968.[42] One of the president's closest advisers, John Erlichman, told civil rights administrators that "blacks are not where the votes are, so why antagonize the people who can be helpful to us politically?"[43]

The national consensus supporting the Great Society rapidly eroded. The congressional elections of 1966 and the presidential election of 1968 revealed the presence of a powerful backlash. In 1966 the Republicans gained four seats in the Senate, and they raised their proportion of the membership in the House from less than one-third to 43 percent. As the 1968 election made clear, it was impossible to divorce the issue of race from social welfare and urban programs. This had become obvious as early as the 1930s, when southern Democrats in Congress often expressed their concern that New Deal programs might be used to upset traditional racial relationships in the South. In the 1940s and 1950s, they fought to make sure that the public housing programs would not be used to promote racial integration. As long as the programs advanced by Democratic liberals in the North could be divorced from racial politics, southern Democrats were willing to go along. The possibility of doing so ended with the civil rights politics of the 1960s.

The Great Society became identified as a constellation of programs that primarily benefited inner-city blacks. The truth is that very few programs had this character; funds for Head Start and the War on Poverty, for example, were spread broadly across the country, to urban and rural areas alike, and social programs such as Medicare and Medicaid benefited a wide variety of people. This is why so many programs survived the backlash that brought Nixon into office in 1968 and that eventually cost the Democrats the South. A broad base of support for federal spending had been quickly established. Cities had become heavily dependent on federal dollars; thus, Senators and members of Congress from urban districts, and governors, mayors, and other public leaders with ties to cities, wanted the flow of funds to continue. Powerful interest groups rallied behind their favored programs. In addition, both houses of Congress continued to be controlled by the Democratic party. In this circumstance, and after a failed attempt to kill the War on Poverty programs, President Nixon set out to reform rather than to eliminate urban programs.

THE DECENTRALIZATION OF URBAN PROGRAMS

Though the years 1965 and 1966 generally are considered the highwater mark for national urban programs, spending continued to rise for several years through Democratic and Republican administrations alike. From 1969 through 1976, when Republicans held the presidency, aid to state and local governments climbed from $20 billion to $59 billion, staying well ahead of inflation.[44]

What presidents Nixon and Ford did was not to cut federal urban spending but to shift urban aid from categorical grants, which applied complex federal rules specifying how federal funds could be spent, to block grants that gave state and local governments broad discretion in deciding how to use the money. Between 1972 and 1978, the proportion of federal grant-in-aids distributed as block grants to states and local governments rose sharply from just 2.8 percent to 34.5 percent.[45] Block grants—so-called because they bundled several programs into a "block" requiring only a single application —gave the Republicans the opportunity to rewrite legislation so that funds would flow less to the central cities and more to smaller cities and suburbs, where Republican voters lived.

As soon as he became president, Richard Nixon signaled his desire to change how federal programs were administered. He spoke of the grant programs as producing a "gathering of the reins of power in Washington," which he saw as "a radical departure from the vision of federal-state relations the nation's founders had in mind." He proposed a New Federalism, meant to restore "a rightful balance between the state capital and the national capital."[46] This turned out to be a rather modest summary of a theme he was to return to many times, perhaps most concisely in an October 21, 1972, radio address on "The Philosophy of Government":

> Do we want to turn more power over to bureaucrats in Washington in the hope that they will do what is best for all the people? Or do we want to return more power to the people and to their state and local governments so that people can decide what is best for themselves? It is time that good, decent people stopped letting themselves be bulldozed by anybody who presumes to be the self-righteous moral judge of our society. In the next four years, as in the past four, I will continue to direct the flow of power away from Washington and back to the people.[47]

Nixon's call for a New Federalism seemed to have broad appeal to constituencies identified with both parties.[48] The political struggles that broke out over the New Federalism reflected both philosophical disagreements and the different political bases of the two political parties.

Revenue sharing, the first major proposal put forth under the umbrella of the New Federalism, was especially attractive to state and local officials regardless of their partisan affiliation. Under a strict interpretation of revenue sharing, it would mean that the federal government would literally share a proportion of revenues coming into the federal treasury with states and localities. The president's proposal, submitted in January 1971, did not go that far, but it came close: State and local governments would automatically receive federal grants, with no strings attached. Of the $16.1 billion proposed for distribution under revenue sharing for the first year, $5 billion was to come in the form of general revenue sharing and $11.1 billion was to be allocated to state and local governments through so-called "special" revenue sharing in six specified policy areas.[49] Ultimately, only the general revenue-sharing program was implemented.

The Nixon Administration's revenue-sharing proposal received backing from Republican and Democratic mayors, governors, city managers, county executives, and other state and local public officials. The support for the program was centered in a group of organizations, known as the Big Seven, that represented local government officials. The members of this coalition were the National League of Cities (NLC), the U.S. Conference of Mayors (USCM), the National Governors' Conference, the National Legislative Conference, the Council of State Governments, the National Association of Counties, and the International City Management Association (ICMA). City managers had long defined themselves as trained professionals who rejected political activities as beyond their purview. In the fight for revenue sharing, however, they broke with a fifty-year tradition of legislative neutrality.[50]

The Democratic party was deeply split over revenue sharing. On the one hand, social welfare liberals wanted to protect their hard-won social and urban programs and they suspected revenue sharing of being the entering wedge for dismantling their favored policies. On the other hand, Democratic mayors from the big cities strongly supported the proposal. They welcomed the prospect of new dollars that they could spend as they wished. Moreover, the fiscal condition of the cities, where revenues chronically lagged behind expenditures, was sufficiently pressing that no mayor could afford to oppose any proposal that would bring federal dollars. Though sympathetic to the cities' plight, Democrats in Congress resisted the pressure to approve revenue sharing. With the 1972 election only a year away, the Democratic legislative leadership did not want to give Nixon any type of domestic victory. Big-city mayors such as Pittsburgh's Peter Flaherty and Cleveland's Carl Stokes considered this attitude an "ill-advised . . . partisan reflex"[51] to what they considered a nonpartisan issue of urban need.

The tension between the party's congressional leadership and the mayors came to a head in a March 1971 private meeting between the House leadership and the U.S. Conference of Mayors' Legislative Action Committee:

> As one of those in attendance recalls it, New York's Mayor John V. Lindsay had just gotten up to speak, when Majority Leader Hale Boggs (D-La.) suddenly slammed his

fist on the desk and shouted: "You don't need to make any points. Revenue sharing is dead. I'll see that it never passes. So let's get on to something else." Flabbergasted, Lindsay slid back into his seat. There was a moment of embarrassed silence—and then a rolling southern drawl rang out from the back of the room. "Hale," said New Orleans Mayor Moon Landrieu, "that's the rudest treatment I have ever witnessed, and I think you better talk about revenue sharing and you better listen. Because, Hale, if you don't start thinking about helping the cities, I want you to know that you'll never be welcome in the city of New Orleans again." Now it was Boggs' turn to be flabbergasted.[52]

In the aftermath of this heated exchange, the congressional leadership began to reassess its position. Finally, Representative Wilbur Mills, the powerful chair of the House Ways and Means Committee, dropped his opposition to the revenue-sharing idea. Being a back-burner presidential hopeful, he proposed his own version of revenue sharing, a $3.5 billion emergency aid plan for the cities, with few strings attached. His move opened the way for other Democrats to change their minds and support the revenue-sharing concept.[53] After compromises were reached on the tricky issue of how to divide the money between the various levels of government (states, municipalities, counties, and townships), revenue sharing finally passed both houses of Congress and was signed by President Nixon in 1972.

Officials representing every level of the American political system were present in Philadelphia for the outdoor signing ceremony. After the signing, the copy of the new law was inadvertently left behind as everyone scurried off for cocktails. The State and Local Fiscal Assistance Act of 1972 almost suffered the fate of a candy wrapper in the wind as it was left unattended: "[A]fter the great ceremony of signing under the shadow of Independence Hall, nobody picked up the bill. And after everybody else had left, it was still sitting there. One of the policemen picked it up and asked: 'Does anybody want this?'"[54]

Revenue sharing gave local officials extraordinary latitude in deciding how to spend federal money. Unlike the grant-in-aid programs of the 1960s, federal rules were minimal and virtually unenforceable. Because of the lack of detailed federal oversight, revenue-sharing dollars were intermingled with other monies that flowed into the treasuries of the more than 39,000 state, county, township, and municipal governments across the nation. As such, they could not be traced beyond the reports filed with the Treasury Department by local officials. Revenue sharing monies constituted a largely unrestricted, though small, supplement to the tax revenues of state and local governments. In 1974 the $4.5 billion apportioned among 35,077 local governments accounted for an average of 3.1 percent of their revenues for that year.[55] Revenue sharing was used to cover ordinary services already provided by the recipient governments; basically, it allowed them to avoid increasing taxes.

Financially strapped big cities were under the greatest pressure to use revenue sharing funds just to keep things going.[56] While cities of all sizes, on the average, spent 56 percent of their revenue-sharing funds on day-to-day operations and maintenance, cities with populations of more than 250,000 reported spending 79 percent on this category, and because of their intractable fiscal problems, the five largest cities—New York, Chicago, Los Angeles, Philadelphia, and Detroit—reported spending virtually all their revenue-sharing funds (97 percent) for routine operations and maintenance.[57]

The Democratic leadership in Congress continued to feel uneasy about the program, convinced as they were that it threatened to undermine the policy initiatives of the 1960s.[58] Only months after the first checks were sent out by the Revenue Sharing Office, congressional Democrats began to complain about the manner in which the money was being spent. Representative Shirley Chisholm of New York voiced concern "that the program failed to aid the disadvantaged and minority groups."[59] Other members of Congress likewise complained that revenue-sharing funds were not going to people who needed them the most.[60] Despite the offended ideological and political interests of congressional liberals and the Democratic leadership, however, general revenue sharing was extended in 1976. As a concession to liberals, a citizen participation rule was added, requiring public hearings before the money could be spent.[61] Again it was the unrelenting political pressure applied by the Big Seven, with big city mayors taking the lead, that prodded Congress to act. The U.S. Conference of Mayors adopted a resolution "supporting reenactment of the general revenue sharing program and promising to make renewal a key local issue in the Congressional campaigns."[62]

The 1976 extension kept funding at the same level, but because of inflation, the actual amount of funding, measured in constant dollars, dropped by 17 percent between 1972 and 1979.[63] Instead of extending the program for five and three-quarter years as proposed by the Ford Administration, Congress extended revenue sharing for only three and three-quarter years. In 1980 Congress amended the revenue-sharing legislation to eliminate the states as recipients. Through the first half of the 1980s revenue sharing constituted about 1.5 percent of municipal budgets. Even at that level it soon came under attack from President Reagan, who expressed the view that it simply encouraged state and local governments to spend more money. Conservative Republicans wanted to cut government spending at all levels, so revenue sharing had to go. It was dropped at the end of fiscal year 1986.

Streamlining Government: The Housing and Community Development Act

Unlike revenue sharing, the Community Development Block Grant (CDBG) program, enacted in 1974, survived the budget cuts of the 1980s. The most important urban policy initiative enacted in the 1970s, by the 1990s it had become the only significant survivor of the many urban policies enacted since World War II. Although Democrats and Republicans often skirmished over details, the program consistently enjoyed bipartisan support, probably because it offered something for everyone. Liberals liked it because it obligated local governments to fight poverty and urban blight; conservatives liked it because two of its objectives, stated in the original legislation, were "increased private investment and streamlining of all levels of government programming."[64]

The Housing and Community Development Act of 1974 (CDA) was signed into law by President Gerald Ford in August 1974 and took effect in January 1975. Seven major categorical grant programs (for water and sewerage systems, neighborhood facilities, land acquisitions, code enforcement, neighborhood development, urban renewal, and Model Cities) were folded into one Community Development Block Grant (CDBG). Though cities automatically qualified for the program if they met a specified formula, they were required to submit an application that described how the money would be used and were required to submit quarterly reports to the Department of Housing and Urban Development (HUD).

Of the $8.4 billion authorized by Congress for the first three years, 80 percent was to be distributed to cities within Standard Metropolitan Statistical Areas (metropolitan areas with a central city of at least 50,000 population). All cities of at least 50,000 people could qualify to receive funds; thus, all central cities and some larger suburbs qualified. The formula for distributing money to the various entitlement communities (so-called because they were "entitled" to a share of funds if they fit the formula) took into account the population of the city, its poverty level, and its percent of overcrowded housing.

In comparison to the grant-in-aid programs they replaced, the block grants disproportionately benefited bigger cities. The average city of over 100,000 population registered a 1 to 4 percent net increase in federal funding after the block grants became available. By contrast, the annual amounts of aid under HUD-administered programs to cities of smaller size fell sharply, with cities of less than 10,000 persons experiencing an average 38 percent loss.[65] By agreeing to support the CDA legislation, the Republican party penalized its natural base of support in the smaller cities, towns, and suburbs. Balancing this out, however, was the fact that since any city of 50,000 or more people qualified for a Community Development Block Grant, many cities in the Sunbelt, including those that did not have significant urban problems, qualified for federal funds for the first time. This gave Republican congressional representatives from the South and West an incentive to vote for the program.

Unlike general revenue sharing, cities were required to submit an annual application for CDBG funds even though they were automatically eligible. The annual applications asked for statistics and statements so that federal administrators could trace the use of the funds. Entitlement cities also were required to submit a three-year development plan that, among other things, projected "long-range community objectives"(which had to include a housing assistance plan for the poor and elderly), respected equal opportunity and environmental protection guidelines, and, most notably, gave "maximum feasible priority" to low- and moderate-income areas.[66] In addition to the pool of so-called entitlement funds, about 20 percent of the total money authorized for the CDBG program was awarded on a competitive basis and in accordance with detailed applications and performance standards and review procedures.[67]

President Ford had expressed strong opposition to any detailed review of applications by HUD, and thus the Ford Administration did not monitor how cities spent the money. By the end of the program's first year, Secretary Carla Hills reported that HUD had reduced the average review period from two years for the programs that the CDA replaced to forty-nine days, and that applications averaged 50 pages, compared with an average of 1,400 pages for the old urban renewal applications alone.[68]

The lack of HUD oversight became an issue as soon as Democrat Jimmy Carter became president. In HUD's first annual report on the program, issued early in 1976, HUD stated that 71 percent of all community development funds were allocated to low- and moderate-income priority areas.[69] A year later, in its second annual report (and the first issued under Carter), HUD revised its calculation to represent the actual proportion of lower-income residents in such areas, rather than counting the number of areas defined by municipalities, often inaccurately, as "low and moderate income." In the cities, the percentage of funds being spent in low- and moderate-income areas as now defined by HUD (as areas in which the median income was 80 percent or less of the metropolitan average) averaged only 44 percent.[70]

Evidence indicated that southern cities, in particular, were allocating far more money to affluent areas than was intended by Congress. According to the Southern Regional Council, "the very mixed achievements of southern cities had shown that local diversions from national purpose are not just occasional abuses, but rather form a pattern inherent in the implementation of the Act."[71] That community development funds would be spent in affluent areas was hardly a surprising turn of events, since local political elites exerted a controlling voice in the allocation process. In most local communities poorer residents had little influence. As a result of this circumstance, Little Rock, Arkansas, for example, spent $150,000 of the city's block grant funds to construct a tennis court in an affluent section of town. When questioned about this use of funds, the director of the local Department of Human Resources unpersuasively claimed that "ninety-nine percent of this money is going to low and moderate income areas." But he revealingly continued: "You cannot divorce politics from that much money. We remember the needs of the people who vote because they hold us accountable. Poor people don't vote."[72]

One strategy that local communities employed to make it appear that funds were flowing to low- and moderate-income priority areas was to draw their funding district boundaries in such a way as to include affluent and less affluent people within the same program areas. Gulfport, Mississippi, went even further when it declared the entire city to be one big "renewal" area, thus making it impossible to determine who benefited from particular projects. The city built a new central fire station with the money, claiming, "When you expand fire protection, everybody in every census tract benefits from lower insurance rates," including, ostensibly, the primary target population of the legislation, the low- and moderate-income residents.[73] Whatever gimmick or tortured logic a city might employ, the outcome was that federal guidelines were generally ignored. Analyses of a number of individual cities demonstrated higher-than-expected CDBG allocations in more affluent areas. A study by the Brookings Institution examined the distribution of the block grants funds in sixty-two cities and found that only 29 percent of the monies were spent in neighborhoods that had lower-than-median family incomes.[74]

The Carter Administration began to crack down on some communities that flagrantly ignored the congressional intent: "HUD Secretary Patricia R. Harris and Assistant Secretary Robert C. Embry . . . told mayors bluntly that they will have to concentrate their CD [Community Development] programs in poorer areas, instead of scattering projects all over town."[75] In April 1978 HUD issued new regulations that required communities to target 75 percent of their CDBG funds to benefit low- and moderate-income areas.[76] HUD's new policy soon bore fruit. A Brookings Institution study found that the percentage of funds benefiting low- and moderate-income persons increased from 54 percent in 1975 to 62 percent in 1978. In the suburbs, targeting in low- and moderate-income areas increased even more—from 46 percent to 63 percent.[77]

Midway through Carter's term, HUD's goal of targeting funds so that they would reach neighborhoods in need came into conflict with a new approach. New regulations issued by HUD required cities to designate Neighborhood Strategy Areas where public funds could be used to attract private investment. Though federal administrators rarely admitted it, they were now following a "triage" strategy suggested by a consultant, Anthony Downs. Downs proposed that federal money could be used more wisely if it were distributed strategically, like the triage method used to treat wounded French soldiers during World War I.[78] Medical personnel classified the wounded into three groups: (1) those who were so badly wounded that they could not be saved, to whom painkillers were given; (2) those who would die without treatment but would probably live with it, to whom maximum treatment was given; and (3) those who would survive with minimal medical care, to whom treatment was given when time and resources allowed. Based on the triage concept, Downs recommended that areas within cities be divided into three categories: deteriorated, transitional (or deteriorating), and healthy. Pouring money into deteriorated neighborhoods, he said, would be a waste of money because they were too far gone to be salvaged. Transitional neighborhoods would benefit the most from aid because with some visible public improvements, they might attract private investment.[79] Healthy neighborhoods would survive just fine without aid. If distributed on such a basis, the impact of federal money could be maximized. Urban consultant Roger Starr took the triage analogy even further, advocating that public services be pulled out of blighted areas entirely so that resources, both federal and local, could be concentrated in neighborhoods considered still viable.[80]

Local governments generally denied that they used the triage strategy. To admit that such a policy was being followed would surely incite protest from people living in the neighborhoods being written off as hopeless. It is clear, however, that the triage approach was used in a great many cities. In a 1974 report to the city planning commission, a St. Louis consulting firm recommended that the city reduce services and discourage investment in severely blighted areas and allocate most of its resources to neighborhoods it defined as declined but salvageable.[81] Another researcher showed that a similar triage approach underpinned the "Chicago 21" plan for redevelopment of the Loop.[82] Community development funds in Denver were also distributed in conformity with a triage strategy. According to two Denver researchers, it would be surprising indeed if tion, passed in May 1977, dramatically increased the community development entitlement funds flowing to the distressed cities of the North. Under the HUD-sponsored amendments, New York City stood to receive a 50 percent increase in its entitlement for 1978 and about a 42 percent increase ($100 million) in 1980.[95] Several older cities expected to double their entitlements. To win enough support in Congress, Sunbelt cities were offered a guarantee that they would not lose money. To make this possible, overall CDBG funding was increased and a "dual formula" was devised, whereby cities could select the original 1974 formula or the new one, depending on which one they preferred.

To provide additional assistance to distressed cities, in 1978 Congress approved the Urban Development Action Grants (UDAG) program. Unlike the entitlement CDBG grants, these funds required applications to accomplish particular projects, and they were explicitly designed to leverage private investments. Over the years, UDAG grants were used to build festival malls such as Union Station in St. Louis and Harborplace in Baltimore; to expand convention centers; to build public infrastructure (such as improved streets, new lighting, landscaping, and fountains) that might leverage private investment; to repair historic buildings; and to support neighborhood improvements. In July 1977 the community development amendments and the UDAG grants were approved by Congress and sent to the White House for President Carter's signature. As a result of the new legislation, cities in the Northeast received an average 77 percent increase in fiscal year 1980 over the amount of CDBG funds they would have received under the 1974 formula. Cities in the Midwest received 66 percent more in funding. In contrast, cities of the South were held to an 8 percent increase and cities in the West to a 14 percent increase.[96]

The Democrats' bias toward older cities had been revealed when Congress passed the Anti-Recession Fiscal Assistance Act over President Ford's veto in July 1976. The program distributed aid to cities with particularly high unemployment rates and was designed as an emergency measure to help distressed cities avert layoffs, maintain service levels, and avoid tax increases. It was scheduled to end on September 30, 1977, by which time, it was hoped, the recession's impact on these cities would have run its course. But in 1977 the Carter Administration recommended that the act be extended and funds increased. In the Intergovernmental Anti-Recession Act of 1977, $2.25 billion was added and antirecession assistance to city governments was extended to September 30, 1978.[97] These programs were heavily weighted in favor of distressed cities. Five cities—New York, Philadelphia, Detroit, Chicago, and Los Angeles—received 13 percent of the Anti-Recession Fiscal Assistance funds. (Together these cities made up 8 percent of the U.S. population.[98]) By far the smallest allocations went to Sunbelt cities. Dallas, for example, received 4 cents per capita through the program and Houston $1.56; in contrast, Newark's allocation amounted to $39.34 per capita.[99]

The various antirecession and public employment programs reflected the political priorities of a Democratic President and a Democratic Congress; as shown in Table 8.1, between fiscal years 1972 and 1975, federal grants to eight Frostbelt cities increased by an average of 62 percent, while grants to nine Sun-

TABLE 8.1	COMPARATIVE GROWTH OF TOTAL FEDERAL GRANTS TO SELECTED FROSTBELT AND SUNBELT CITIES, 1972–1978		
	Percent Increase		
City	1972–1975	1975–1978	1972–1978
Frostbelt			
Baltimore	146	68	314
Boston	9	81	97
Buffalo	107	154	427
Chicago	75	145	329
Cleveland	184	131	558
Detroit	26	87	136
Philadelphia	59	151	297
St. Louis	123	248	674
Mean for 8 Frostbelt cities	62	133	354
Sunbelt			
Atlanta	269	53	465
Birmingham	346	119	877
Dallas	405	74	777
Houston	267	88	591
Jacksonville	390	34	554
Louisville	68	86	214
New Orleans	209	90	488
Oklahoma City	237	107	599
Phoenix	423	94	689
Mean for 9 Sunbelt cities	238	83	584

Source: Adapted from Paul R. Dommel, "Block Grants for Community Development: Decentralized Decision-Making," in *Fiscal Crisis in American Cities: The Federal Response,* ed. L. Kenneth Hubbell (Cambridge, Mass.: Ballinger, 1979), p. 254. Copyright 1979, Ballinger Publishing Company. By permission.

belt cities rose by 238 percent. This happened because revenue sharing and CDBG grants went to cities on the basis of a formula rather than through an application showing "need." Between 1975 and 1978, however, grants went up faster in the Frostbelt cities (133 percent) than in the Sunbelt cities (83 percent). The federal grants to distressed cities were extremely important to their financial well-being. In 1977, because of new federal funds, revenues in twenty-seven of the largest cities exceeded expenditures by 3.2 percent. In contrast, these cities had accumulated an average per city debt of $28 million in 1975 and $151 million in 1976.[100]

On March 28, 1978, President Carter announced, with great fanfare, a comprehensive new urban policy. Asserting that "the deterioration of urban life in the United States is one of the most complex and deeply rooted problems of our age," the president stated that "the federal government has the clear duty to lead the effort to reverse that deterioration."[101] The centerpiece of the president's proposal was a national development bank, which would be authorized to guarantee loans to businesses in "distressed areas;" in addition, the administration wanted to offer tax credits for businesses hiring ghetto youths, a labor-intensive public works program, and more money for housing rehabilitation. The amount of additional money requested was relatively modest (about $4.4 billion), but this did not deter the president from promising a "new Partnership involving all levels of government, the private sector and neighborhood and voluntary organizations."[102]

Carter's ringing call for a comprehensive urban policy raised hopes in city halls, but it turned into an abject political failure. The only major legislative proposal that was enacted into law was the Targeted Employment Tax Credit. The timing was bad for any new legislative initiative.[103] In 1978 California voters passed Proposition 13, which sharply reduced local property taxes. The gathering strength of a tax revolt across the nation helped shape a mood of fiscal conservatism in Congress and a go-slow approach in the White House.[104] The most innovative proposal in Carter's urban policy was the National Development Bank, which would have made loans and some limited grants available to depressed urban and rural areas. In part because of concerns over cost, this proposal failed to make it out of a conference committee after passing the House and Senate in a much amended form.[105]

Carter's urban policy proposals failed not only because they were ill-timed but also because the president was not willing to fight for them. Perhaps sensing a changing political climate, Carter did an about-face in the last two years of his term, turning his attention away from urban policy toward the problems of the national economy and the cost and availability of energy. A sharp decline in manufacturing jobs and an acceleration in foreign investment by American companies, together with an increase in imports, became the leading domestic issues of the 1980 presidential campaign.

After Carter's election in 1976, Mayor Kenneth A. Gibson of Newark had spoken for many Democratic mayors when he remarked that "we have every reason to believe that this is the beginning of a new relationship between the White House and the nation's mayors."[106] The new relationship, however, proved to be short-lived. Even if Carter had won the 1980 presidential race, it is doubtful that any significant urban programs would have emerged in a second term.

THE REAGAN/BUSH URBAN POLICY: SURVIVAL OF THE FITTEST

In a press conference held in October 1981, President Ronald Reagan suggested that the residents of cities where unemployment was high should "vote with their feet" and move to more prosperous areas of the country.[107] His remark ignited an instant political controversy, but it could well have been (although it probably was not) inspired by the recommendations of a presidential commission appointed by his predecessor, Jimmy Carter. In a report issued in 1980 the Presidential Commission on the National Agenda for the Eighties, which had been appointed by Carter to review urban policy and recommend policy changes, urged that the national government stop helping cities. The commission emphasized that federal policies should be used to promote national economic growth, but that these policies should be neutral about where that growth occurred:

> It may be in the best interest of the nation to commit itself to the promotion of locationally neutral economic and social policies rather than spatially sensitive urban policies that either explicitly or inadvertently seek to preserve cities in their historical roles.[108]

The commission reasoned that economic processes affecting older cities were irreversible:

> The economy of the United States, like that of many of the older industrial societies, has for years now been undergoing a critical transition from being geographically-based to being deconcentrated, decentralized, and service-based. In the process, many cities of the old industrial heartland . . . are losing their status as thriving industrial capitals. . . .
>
> The historical dominance of more central cities will be diminished as certain production, residential, commercial, and cultural functions disperse to places beyond them.[109]

Recommending that the federal government let the process of decay in some areas and growth in others take its natural course, the commission noted that cities adapt and change in response to economic and social forces. This process of adaptation, said the commission, should be facilitated, not altered, by governmental policy:

> Ultimately, the federal government's concern for national economic vitality should take precedence over the competition for advantage among communities and regions.[110]
>
> To attempt to restrict or reverse the processes of change—for whatever noble intentions—is to deny the benefits that the future may hold for us as a nation.[111]

The recommendations by Carter's commission and the policies subsequently pursued by the Reagan Administration constituted a revolutionary change in philosophy: For the first time since national urban policy began to emerge in the 1930s, the judgment was made that individual cities were not valuable cultural, social, or economic entities except to the degree to which they contributed to a healthy national economy. Three University of Delaware researchers characterized the new policies as "a form of Social Darwinism applied to cities as it has been previously applied, with pernicious consequences, to individuals and social classes."[112] Cities would survive if they could manage to regenerate their local economies. Otherwise, they would be allowed to wither away.

The Reagan Administration set about sharply reducing federal urban aid, proclaiming that "the private market is more efficient than federal program administrators in allocating dollars."[113] Cities were instructed to improve their ability to compete in a struggle for survival in which "state and local governments will find it is in their interests to concentrate on increasing their attractiveness to potential investors, residents, and visitors."[114] Thus urban policy was built on the assumption that free enterprise would provide a bounty of jobs, incomes, and neighborhood renewal, and that such local prosperity would make federal programs unnecessary. The Community Development Block Grant (CDBG) and Urban Development Action Grant (UDAG) programs won a reprieve from being drastically reduced in the 1983 budget, and so did revenue sharing. Budget Director David Stockman wanted to kill these programs altogether; he had previously attempted to write them out of the budget in 1981. But the administration, bending to the weakened but still viable urban lobby—represented principally by governors and mayors, quite a few of them Republican—backed off. The groups making up the urban lobby came away relieved that the budget cuts were less drastic than they had feared. Only two years later, however, the administration was able to eliminate most urban programs.

Urban programs gave way to a new priority: tax cuts. On February 18, 1981, President Reagan proposed a massive tax cut to stimulate the economy. This package, which would reduce federal revenues by $54 billion in 1982 alone, called for a 10 percent reduction each year for three years for all individual taxpayers, plus accelerated depreciation of capital assets and other liberalized tax write-offs for corporations. Congress was at first cool to the idea, but it soon became apparent to Democratic lawmakers that they could improve their own reelection prospects if they offered "improvements" that would be appealing to corporate campaign contributors and individual constituents. By the time individual legislators had outbid one another to satisfy their own constituency groups, the revenue losses from the package were so staggering that some White House advisers wanted to kill the bill.[115] Reagan, however, wanted it passed and he lobbied hard for it, even going on television to appeal for expressions of popular support.[116]

Reagan signed the Economic Recovery Tax Act of 1981 on August 13, 1981, asserting that it was "a turnaround of almost a half a century of . . . excessive growth in government bureaucracy, government spending, government taxing."[117] In its final version the act reduced individual tax rates by 25 percent over three years and also substantially reduced business tax liability. The revenue losses were huge. In just the first two years, $128 billion in revenue was lost to the federal treasury, and the total losses by 1987 amounted to more than $1 trillion.[118] The 1981 tax cuts, in combination with massive increases in military spending, created huge budget deficits well into the 1990s that acted like battering rams against domestic social policies. Urban policies suffered the most damage.

The Tax Reform Act of 1986 added to the effects of the legislation adopted five years earlier by further slashing federal revenues and sharply reducing the capacity of governments at all levels to collect increased revenues in step with an improving economy. The 1986 legislation was sold as a fundamental "reform" of the tax code. Most Americans had the impression that the main purpose was to simplify a maddeningly complex tax system. This promise was never fulfilled. Instead, Congress reduced the several tax rates in the code, which increased the rate of taxation as a taxpayer's income went up, to three basic levels: 15 percent, 28 percent, and 32 percent. The tax rates were indexed to inflation, so that over time taxpayers would not slide into a higher tax bracket unless their incomes rose faster than the inflation rate. There were two dramatic effects. First, the new law almost eliminated the feature of the tax code that had historically allowed the federal government to collect increased taxes whenever incomes went up, either in real terms or through inflation. This change had the effect of institutionalizing the tax cuts adopted in 1981 by making it difficult for federal revenues to rise, even in a good economy, to reduce budget deficits. Only cuts in expenditures or increases in tax rates could accomplish that.

The second effect of the Tax Reform Act was that tax rates fell only modestly or not at all for most taxpayers, but they were cut drastically for the rich. In subsequent years the constant talk about rising deficits, the savings and loan scandal, and a general perception that taxes hit the middle class more than anyone else helped fuel a tax revolt. George Bush won the presidency in 1988 partly with the promise, "Read my lips: no new taxes." A political atmosphere that might have maintained federal spending on pressing social problems such as education, housing, health and welfare was thoroughly poisoned. Broad entitlement programs with middle-class recipients, such as the old-age and survivors' benefits funded through the Social Security Act of 1935, veterans' benefits, and Medicare, were affected only marginally. In contrast, deep cuts and new eligibility restrictions were imposed in public assistance programs for the poor. Medicaid, which was available through the states to welfare recipients, was reduced through tighter eligibility requirements at the same time that Medicaid soared because of rising medical costs. Enrollment in Aid to Families with Dependent Children (AFDC) fell by half a million. A million people lost food stamps. It became harder to get unemployment benefits; whereas 75 percent of the unemployed received benefits during the recession of 1975, only 45 percent were able to qualify during the 1982–1983 recession.[119]

President Reagan's cuts were the first reductions of consequence in grants-in-aid expenditures since the 1940s (see Table 8.2). The countercyclical urban aid programs inherited from the 1980s (the Anti-Recession Fiscal Assistance Act of 1976 and the Intergovernmental Anti-Recession Act of 1977) were eliminated early in the Reagan Administration. Several other programs were also killed off by the end of Reagan's first term, including revenue sharing and local public works. The Urban Development Action Grants were cut in 1986, though a trickle of money continued to flow in the administrative pipeline for several years (the total spending fell from an annual level of $400 to $500 million for the first ten years of the program [fiscal years 1978 to 1987] to $200 million in fiscal 1988 and dried up to a nominal $3 million by fiscal 1994).[120] Other budget cuts also affected the cities. Most subsidies for the construction of public housing were eliminated. Only 10,000 new units a year were authorized after 1983, compared with the 111,600 new or rehabilitated units authorized for 1981 alone.[121] Among urban programs, the only real survivor of the Reagan cuts was the Community Development Block Grant program. CBDG spending fell from $4 billion in the

TRENDS IN FEDERAL GRANTS FOR POOR PEOPLE AND POOR CITY GOVERNMENTS OUTLAYS IN CONSTANT 1990 DOLLARS (IN MILLIONS)

	1980	1990	1998	Percent Change 1980–90	1990–98
Benefits Primarily to Individuals					
Medicaid	22,138	41,103	100,960	0.86	1.46
Housing Assistance	7,257	13,561	19,159	0.87	0.41
Welfare payments	10,983	12,246	4,376	0.11	−0.64
Supplemental feeding (WICS)	1,137	2,197	3,889	0.93	0.77
Food stamps	13,808	13,793	3,673	−0.00	−0.73
Child nutrition program	5,363	4,978	8,664	−0.07	0.74
Community services program	868	350	8	−0.60	−0.98
Justice assistance	799	244	3,293	−0.69	12.50
Totals	62,353	88,472	144,022	0.42	0.63
Totals Excluding Medicaid	40,214	47,369	43,062	0.18	−0.09
Benefits Primarily to Governments					
General revenue sharing	10,832	0	0	−1.00	0.00
Public service jobs & job training	9,820	3,042	3,643	−0.69	0.20
Community development block grants	6,189	2,818	4,620	−0.54	0.64
Social service block grants	4,383	2,749	2,443	−0.37	−0.11
Urban mass transit	4,963	3,728	4,068	−0.25	0.09
Compensatory education	5,345	4,437	6,231	−0.17	0.40
Local public works	660	0	0	−1.00	0.00
Economic development assistance[a]	717	160	424	−0.78	1.65
Urban development action grants[b]	357	209	0	−0.41	−1.00
Federal Highway Aid	13,760	13,854	21,423	0.01	0.55
General antirecession assistance[c]	0	0	0	0.00	0.00
Totals	57,026	30,997	42,852	−0.46	0.38

[a]Includes Economic Development Administration, Empowerment Zones and Appalachian Regional Commission.
[b]UDAGS were terminated in 1988 and outlays dropped to zero in the early 1990s.
[c]General antirecession assistance had been 2.664 billion in 1978.

Source: U.S. Office of Management and Budget, *Historical Tables, Budget of the United States Government, FY 99;* U.S. Census Bureau, *Statistical Abstract of the United States, 1998;* and U.S. Dept. of Commerce, Economic and Statistics Administration, *Federal Aid to States for Fiscal Year, April 1998.*

1981 fiscal year to $2.8 billion in fiscal 1990, before rebounding somewhat to $3.1 billion in fiscal 1992, the year the Democrats reclaimed the White House. Under President Clinton CDBG spending rose modestly to $4.6 billion by the 1996 fiscal year.[122]

Cities suffered not only from the cuts, but also from the devolution of policy to the states. Reagan's 1981 budget act reduced spending for grants-in-aid to state and local governments by 30 percent. In 1982 Reagan persuaded Congress to consolidate seventy-six grant programs into nine block grants in health, social services, education, and community development. In the process, overall funding was reduced by 20 percent. Previously, many of these grants went directly to local governments; now all of them went to the states, to be distributed as they saw fit. Because the states tended to spread funds broadly across a great many jurisdictions and to give little priority to distressed communities, the cities were "one of the clearest losers of federal funds" under these block grants.[123] A 1982 study by the Senate Joint Economic Committee showed that distressed cities were losing a larger absolute amount and a higher percentage of federal aid than the cities that were better off.[124] Cities, whose economies were already in trouble before the cuts, were being compelled to endure the highest proportional reductions in federal assistance.

President Reagan also attempted to use the tax code to make it more difficult for states and localities to support activist government. When the tax rates were reduced to three levels as a result of the 1986 Tax Reform Act, most states similarly revised their state income tax laws; this change was irresistible since most state tax forms had been modeled on the federal forms. Thus the states almost automatically reduced their taxes when the federal government did. The cities' ability to borrow was also affected. One of the provisions of the 1986 law was a state-by-state cap on the volume and purposes of tax-exempt municipal bonds. By the early 1990s the effects of federal cutbacks and tax code changes had reverberated throughout the intergovernmental system. State and local governments found themselves deeply in debt, forcing them to slash funding for schools, higher education, and other programs.

Urban Enterprise Zones

Right from the beginning, the Reagan Administration had set out to dismantle federal programs designed to help the cities, and in eight years it largely succeeded. During those same years, however, the administration tried to reap political benefits by proposing (though never enthusiastically backing) urban policies that could be labeled "Republican." Insofar as there was a policy, cities were instructed to cut taxes and offer tax abatements and other incentives to spur local economic growth.

President Reagan promised to push for passage of urban enterprise zones legislation during a special session of Congress in November and December of 1982. In the press of other business, however, the legislation was not even discussed. Finally, on March 7, 1983, the president sent the proposed Urban Enterprise Zone Act to Congress, claiming that the legislation was a clear break from past policy:

> Enterprise zones are a fresh approach for promoting economic growth in the inner cities. The old approach relied on heavy government subsidies and central planning. A prime example was the model cities program in the 1960s, which concentrated government programs, subsidies and regulations in distressed urban areas. The enterprise zone approach is to remove government barriers, bring individuals to create, produce and earn their own wages and profits.[125]

No matter what claims the president made, the legislation was not a "fresh approach" but a logical extension of past policies, Democratic as well as Republican, that stressed the role of government in subsidizing private investment. Throughout the Reagan years, the enterprise zones idea surfaced from time to time, but it was never pushed by the administration. After George Bush's election to the presidency in 1988, the idea continued to receive an occasional nudge from the president or from HUD, but it did not surface as a meaningful item on the president's legislative agenda until after the Los Angeles riot of April 29–May 3, 1992.

Measured by the number of deaths (53), injuries (2,383), property damage (over $700 million), and the response required to reestablish order, the Los Angeles riot was the country's worst episode of civil disorder in the twentieth century.[126] Many people thought that the riot could be used as an opportunity to call attention to the problems of urban America. Two weeks after the riots, 150,000 people descended on Washington for a Save Our Cities/Save Our Children rally. As the crisis atmosphere faded, however, urban issues got lost in election-year politics. Democratic candidate Bill Clinton initially blamed the riots on "twelve years of denial and neglect" by Presidents Bush and Reagan, but fearing that he might be accused of advocating big government spending programs, Clinton soon muted his criticisms.[127] On Monday, May 5, Bush's press spokesman, Marlin Fitzwater, said the Great Society's programs of the 1960s were to blame for the rioting. Nevertheless, in an attempt to look like he was responding positively, President Bush proposed an emergency aid package. In June, Congress passed $1.3 billion in emergency aid that allocated $500 million for summer jobs, $382 million for loans to businesses damaged or destroyed in the riot areas, and some flood relief for the city of Chicago.

Through the summer and early fall of 1992 Congress worked on a larger, permanent urban aid bill. A version was finally approved by the House on October 6 and the Senate on October 8. The legislation would have created twenty-five urban and twenty-five rural enterprise zones and financed "weed and seed" programs that combined enhanced law enforcement with job training and education programs. The bulk of the legislation, however, was made up of an array of items that had nothing to do with cities, including liberalized (tax-free) retirement accounts for upper-income people and a provision for the repeal of luxury taxes on yachts, furs, jewels, and planes (Democrats backed this amendment as enthusiastically as Republicans). It was estimated that of the $30 billion that the bill would cost over five years, about $6 billion would be used to help depressed areas in cities.[128] Congressional leaders delayed sending the urban aid bill to the White House until after the election, hoping that the president would sign it when it could no longer be made an issue in the campaign. They pointed out that the tax increases in the bill were offset by an equal volume of tax reductions. Nevertheless, Bush vetoed the legislation, claiming that it was contaminated by pork-barrel amendments. In the end, even enterprise zones could not pass Republican muster.

URBAN POLICY IN THE CLINTON ERA

In the campaigns of 1980 and 1984, the Republicans virtually wrote off the African-American vote. Richard Wirthlin, Ronald Reagan's campaign strategist, advised before the 1980 election that the "Reagan for President 1980 campaign must convert into Reagan votes the disappointment felt by Southern white and rural voters."[129] Reagan won only 10 percent of the black vote in 1980 and slightly less in 1984. In 1984, however, three out of four southern whites supported him. The Reagan White House actively worked to undo civil rights guarantees, slashing the budgets of civil rights enforcement units and slowing or stopping enforcement.[130] In the 1988 presidential election, the Republican candidate George Bush was also able to successfully use race to mobilize voters. Republicans ran an attack ad that featured a police photograph of Willie Horton, who had raped a woman in Maryland and stabbed her fiancé while on a weekend pass from a Massachusetts prison. The Democratic candidate, Michael Dukakis, had been the governor of Massachusetts at the time. According to Bush's campaign director, Lee Atwater, the fact that Willie Horton was black was the key element explaining the ad's emotional impact.

In 1992, with voters and the media sensitized to racial manipulation, direct racial appeals by the Bush campaign probably would have backfired. Instead, attacks on cities served as a code language for race and welfare-state liberalism. In one of the opening salvos of the campaign, Vice President Dan Quayle attacked New York City by saying, "The liberal vision of a happy, productive and content welfare state hasn't even worked on 22 square miles of the most valuable real estate in the world."[131] A later Quayle attack prompted a *New York Post* headline: "City to Dan Quayle: DON'T DIS' US!"[132] An editorial in the *New York Times* called Quayle's attacks an attempt to make New York City "The Willie Horton of 1992."[133]

As a self-styled "new Democrat" who wanted to project an image as a friend of the "forgotten middle class," Clinton could hardly be expected to place aid to cities or to the poor on the front burner. The Clinton campaign decided to concentrate on appealing to the white suburban middle class and to assume that inner-city voters would support him anyway because they had no place else to go. Clinton's electoral strategy succeeded in making him the first Democrat to be elected to two full terms since Franklin D. Roosevelt.

The logic behind Clinton's suburban strategy was compelling. By the 1990 census, 48 percent of the nation's population lived in suburbs. Because they tended to turn out for elections at a relatively high rate, it seemed certain that they would cast a majority of the votes in the 1992 election.[134] In addition, a large proportion of suburban voters were so-called Reagan Democrats, blue-collar and middle-class voters who had abandoned the party to vote Republican in the three previous presidential elections. They were particularly concentrated in the older suburbs in key states such as New Jersey, Michigan, and California, which could deliver the big blocs of electoral-college votes coveted by any presidential candidate. To bring them back to the fold, Clinton wanted to avoid identifying himself with policies that were targeted to cities, and especially to blacks.

In developing this strategy Clinton followed the advice of a well-known African-American sociologist, William Julius Wilson, whose 1987 book, *The Truly Disadvantaged*, warned against race-specific policies. Wilson, who was a friend and adviser of the president, recommended a "hidden agenda" in which inner-city minorities might be helped "by emphasizing programs to which the more advantaged groups of all races and classes can positively relate."[135] In an interview before the election, Wilson praised Clinton's programs "intended for all low- to moderate-income groups, not just minorities."[136]

Clinton ended up developing what two scholars called a "stealth urban policy" composed of programs that were not specifically targeted to cities, but which would help them.[137] In their campaign book, *Putting People First*, Bill Clinton and Al Gore advocated so-called "cross-cutting" policies designed to help both the middle class and the disadvantaged. Clinton's highly successful campaign bus tours avoided the inner cities and provided the media with ample opportunities to photograph the candidate against small town and rural backdrops. After winning the nomination, Clinton did attend a meeting of the United States Conference of Mayors (USCM) and lent his support to a public works initiative. Clinton stressed, however, that the primary goal was to stimulate the economy and that aiding cities would be a secondary effect.

Clinton succeeded in winning back many of the white suburban voters who had first deserted the party in 1980. Even so, he still lost the overall white vote by a 39 percent to 41 percent margin. He carried huge pluralities in the cities, coming out of New York City, for example, with almost a million-vote lead. His ability to capture 82 percent of the black, mostly urban, vote in a three-way election, was crucial to his victory.

Clinton began his presidency with the intention of rewarding the cities that had voted lopsidedly for him. To accomplish this, he put together a $19.5 billion economic stimulus bill that included $4.4 billion for public works (mostly in cities), $2.5 billion for community development grants, and $735 million for inner-city schools and jobs. Led by Senator Bob Dole (R.-Kansas), Senate Republicans filibustered the bill, refusing to let it come up for a vote. Lacking the sixty votes necessary to end the filibuster, the Democrats were forced to back down. Eventually, all that was passed was a $4 billion extension of unemployment benefits for the chronically unemployed.[138]

If cities benefited at all during Clinton's first term, it was largely because of the indirect effects of policies not targeted to cities. Clinton succeeded in expanding the Earned Income Tax Credit, which gives government payments to full-time workers whose income falls below a minimum standard. Promising to put 100,000 additional police officers on the street to fight crime, in 1998 Clinton narrowly succeeded in persuading Congress to pass a Crime Bill, but only after Republicans removed some of the preventive social programs that were targeted for cities.

The only significant new urban initiative of the Clinton Administration was the Empowerment Zones/Enterprise Communities (EZ/EC) program, which was included as Title XIII of the Omnibus Budget Reconciliation Act of 1993. Though pushed since the early 1980s by both Democrats and Republicans, the idea of enterprise zones tended to appeal to conservatives and Republicans more because they were based on the strategy of cutting taxes and regulations in inner cities, with the intention of stimulating investment in depressed neighborhoods. The Clinton Administration adopted this free-market approach, then grafted onto it some Democratic programs for education, job training, and child care. The result was a hybrid, with the federal government acting as a catalyst to bring together the public, private, and nonprofit sectors in the cause of inner-city revitalization.

The EZ/EC program was composed of four basic components:

1. *Tax incentives:* Within designated Empowerment Zones, employers were eligible for up to $3,000 in tax credits for each new hire. The program also included accelerated depreciation of business property and tax-exempt bond financing for businesses in a zone.
2. *Targeted spending:* Areas chosen as Empowerment Zones were eligible for up to $100 million in flexible grant money to assist zone residents for services such as education, job training, and child care.
3. *Strategic planning:* In order to win designation, cities were required to come up with comprehensive strategies for revitalization that took advantage of the particular "strengths" of the chosen communities.
4. *Partnerships:* The planning process was supposed to be "bottom up," involving the residents of the community. This was to be facilitated by a Community Coordinating Board composed of representatives from government, the private sector, and community groups.

The winning communities were announced on December 21, 1994. Six cities were designated as full Empowerment Zones: Atlanta, Baltimore, Chicago, Detroit, New York, and Philadelphia/Camden. Los Angeles and Cleveland were designated as Supplemental Empowerment Zones with somewhat less than the full complement of resources. Ultimately, 31 Empowerment and Supplemental Empowerment Zones were created, and 74 additional distressed areas (33 in rural areas) also won grants, but these were small in comparison to the full-fledged Empowerment Zones.

The philosophy underlying the Empowerment Zones program proved to be attractive to members of both parties because it emphasized private investment and a decentralized administrative style. Still, Republicans could not call the program their own, so the Republican-dominated Congresses that came in after 1994 failed to appropriate the full amount promised for the program. Even if it had, the program would have remained small, with only about $3.8 billion in grants and tax incentives available over a ten-year period, to be spread over 105 urban and rural areas. In an annual federal budget of more than $1 trillion, the EZ/EC program was a drop in the bucket.

In 1999 President Clinton announced his "New Markets Initiative," which essentially built on the Empowerment Zones program. Perhaps to demonstrate an election-year interest in the urban poor, in the spring of 2000 Republicans reached an agreement with the president to create 40 "renewal communities" and nine new empowerment zones, at a cost of $5 to $7 billion over five years (mostly in estimated taxes lost to the treasury). Republicans gained two concessions dear to their hearts. Though they had not been able to eliminate capital gains taxes generally, they were able to do so for the renewal communities and empowerment zones. Religious groups were also authorized to receive grants to provide drug counseling.[139]

But empowerment zones were the exception to the rule. The mid-term 1994 elections dealt a blow to those who had hoped for more generous urban and social welfare policies. Led rhetorically by House Speaker Newt Gingrich and his Contract with America, the Republicans won control of both houses of Congress for the first time in forty years. The Republicans were openly hostile to what remained of federal urban programs. Speaker Gingrich called for the complete elimination of the Department of Housing and Urban Development, asserting that "You could abolish HUD tomorrow morning and improve life in most of America." He was blunt about why HUD was being singled out for especially harsh treatment: Its "weak constituency," he said, "makes it a prime candidate for cuts."[140]

In a desperate attempt to stave off disaster, HUD Secretary Henry Cisneros proposed to "reinvent" his department in ways satisfying to conservatives. Announced a month and a half after the 1994 election, HUD's *Reinvention Blueprint* called for consolidating HUD's 60 programs into three flexible block grants that would be administered by cities and states, and it proposed converting all public housing aid to vouchers, which would allow recipients to find housing wherever private landlords would take them. Reinventing HUD became the centerpiece of Clinton's National Urban Policy Report, which was issued in July 1995.[141]

The long-term decline in public housing and urban programs predated the Clinton Administration, but having a Democrat in the White House again did not bring about a revival. In the Reagan and Bush years HUD experienced the largest cuts of any cabinet-level department in the federal government. HUD budget authority (what Congress authorizes it to spend) fell from 7.5 percent of the total federal budget in 1978 to only 1.3 percent by 1990. During the Clinton Administration, annual HUD spending recovered slightly, but this only enabled HUD to meet past commitments for housing subsidies. Four programs of special interest to city governments, General Revenue Sharing, Urban Development Action Grants, Local Public Works, and Antirecession Fiscal Assistance, were "zeroed out"—eliminated entirely. As shown by Table 8.2, only four urban programs of any consequence received more funding between 1990 and 1998 than in the past—Community Development Block Grants, local Economic Develop-ment Assistance (the EZ/EC program), Compensatory Education, and Public Service Jobs and job training. Federal highway aid increased, but it is a stretch to call this urban aid.

The welfare reform bill Clinton signed in August 1996 also hurt the cities. Ending the sixty-one-year federal entitlement to welfare, the Personal Responsi-bility Act of 1996 converted Aid to Families with Dependent Children to a block grant run by the states. In addition to a 64 percent decline in welfare spending from 1990 to 1998, food stamps and community services programs were cut sharply. Three programs, child nutrition, supplemental (infant) feeding, and housing assistance, increased somewhat because they were linked to welfare re-form efforts. Medicaid costs went up substantially (by 146 percent), but the big winner was justice assistance, which skyrocketed 1,250 percent in less than a decade! Though most of this money was used by states to build prisons, some of it went to cities. Obviously, crime control trumped any other social purpose.

As shown by Figure 8.2, at the same time that spending for low- and moder-ate-income, government-assisted housing rose modestly, tax breaks for home-owners soared. From 1992 to 1999, congressional outlays for assisted housing rose by 34 percent, from $20.4 billion to $27.6 billion. By far the largest subsidies for housing are given to higher-income families, however. The federal govern-ment permits people who own their own home to deduct from their income taxes what they spend for mortgage interest and property taxes. Monthly rent payments pay for mortgage interest and property taxes for landlords, but renters get no tax breaks. Total homeowner deductions increased from $34 bil-lion in 1978 to $99.9 billion by 1999, almost a 300 percent increase. Homeowner tax deductions are tilted toward higher-income taxpayers; in 1994 almost half (44 percent) of the value of these subsidies went to the top 5 percent of house-holds with incomes over $100,000. In 1996, the wealthiest 20 percent of Ameri-can households received 82 percent of homeowner tax breaks; by contrast, the bottom 60 percent received less than 4 percent of the subsidy.[142] Housing subsi-dies work as a powerful urban policy transferring federal aid to affluent subur-ban homeowners at the expense of lower-income rental households, many of whom are located in central cities.

THE WANING POLITICAL INFLUENCE OF CITIES

Abandoning urban policy made political sense for Republicans and Democrats alike. In the case of the Republicans, party leaders had long sought to capitalize on white suburbanites' disaffection from the Democratically sponsored civil rights and antipoverty policies of the 1960s. What is more interesting is the way that the past friend of the cities, the Democratic party, has shied away from ur-ban issues. In 1968 the Democrats used the word "city" twenty-three times in the party platform adopted at their presidential nominating convention. It did

FIGURE 8.2 **Federal Spending for Housing, 1978–1997, in Billions of Constant 1996 Dollars**

	1978	1980	1982	1984	1986	1988	1990	1992	1994	1996	1997	1998*	1999*
Assisted low income housing budget authority	71.2	52.0	23.0	18.3	15.7	12.3	12.9	21.4	21.9	17.2	16.3	17.2	20.1
Assisted low income housing outlays	8.1	10.5	13.7	16.3	16.7	17.6	18.5	20.5	24.8	26.6	27.6	28.2	27.5

*Note: Figures have been adjusted to 1996 dollars.

Source: National Low Income Housing Coalition, *Housing at a Snail's Pace* (Washington, D.C.: NLIHC 1996), p. 5.

not appear even once in the 1988 platform. The substitute term, clearly a recognition of the power of the suburbs, was "hometown America." In 1992 and 1996, Clinton avoided identification with policies targeted to cities and concentrated his appeals on the suburban middle class. Notably, in the 2000 campaign Democratic candidate Al Gore mentioned urban sprawl as a significant national issue. By the new century, urban policy no longer referred to central cities, but to urban regions.

The simplest explanation of the waning political influence of cities is that central-city voters have declined as an overall percentage of the national electorate. The central cities of the 32 largest metropolitan areas reached a highwater mark of 27 percent of the electorate in 1944, but by 1992 they accounted for just 14 percent of the national vote.[143] In 1940 New York City voters represented 51 percent of the statewide electorate, but by the 1996 presidential election their proportion of the statewide vote had fallen to 31 percent. Chicago claimed 47 percent of the Illinois presidential vote in 1948 but only 21 percent in 1996. Similarly, the share of votes cast by central cities fell in Pennsylvania, Michigan, and Massachusetts, as shown in Figure 8.3.[144]

Cities also lost representation in the U.S. House of Representatives. Between 1963 and 1994, the number of congressional districts with a majority of the population coming from central cities fell from 94 to 84; in the same period, the number of districts with a majority of suburban voters increased from 94 to 214. In 1994, after the Republicans took control of the House, the proportion of leadership positions held by representatives from districts with a sizable proportion of central-city voters fell precipitously, from 30 percent to 10 percent.[145] Similar trends reduced the power of central cities in state governments as well.[146] The

FIGURE 8.3   City Proportion of Actual State Electorate, 1952–1996

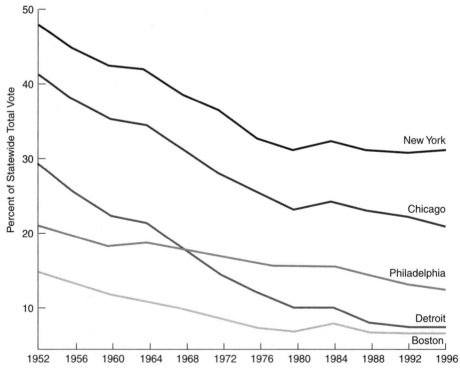

Source: Richard Scammon, *America Votes* (various issues); U.S. Bureau of the Census, *Census of Population and Housing*, various years; and reports of actual city votes from county boards of elections (and newspapers for 1996 election). Data compiled by Richard Sauerzopf.

number of states with suburban electoral majorities increased from three in 1980 to fourteen in 1990, and will surely increase even more when seats are reapportioned as a result of the 2000 census.

The conventional wisdom is that the suburbs now hold the key to winning national elections. Suburban votes were critical to the presidential victories of Presidents Reagan and Bush; Ronald Reagan won huge landslides in 1980 and 1984 even though he only carried about a third of the central-city vote. In the 1988 election, suburban voters gave Bush such a comfortable cushion that he could have carried almost all of the northern industrial states without a single vote from the big cities in those states. By contrast, the central-city electorate was an important part of Clinton's winning coalition in 1992 and 1996. In 1992 New York City provided Clinton with 92 percent of his nearly one-million statewide vote margin, and Clinton lost to Bush in suburban Long Island (Nassau and Suffolk counties). In 1996 Clinton did even better in the cities, winning 67 percent of the vote in Milwaukee, 74 percent in Boston, 76 percent in St. Louis and New York, and 80 percent in Chicago. Clinton came out of New York City with over a million-vote margin.

Although President Clinton owed a great deal to central-city voters for his two election victories, he did not make urban issues a high priority. During his presidency, federal spending for the cities continued to fall. Clearly, Clinton felt that he could take his urban base for granted; there was no place else for city voters to go. This strategy did impose a potential cost on the Democrats, however: As the federal government turned away from the cities, voter turnout in them went into a steep slide. Indeed, in the past half-century, 40 percent of the loss in the proportion of votes cast in the thirty-two largest cities can be traced to falling turnout, and not to shrinking population. As Figure 8.4 shows, turnout by city residents reached a peak in 1944 of 13 percent above the national average, and fell steadily. For some time it has lagged significantly behind the suburban propensity to vote. By 1992 the large central cities had fallen 18 percent below the national average. In 1996 the turnout rate in New York City was only 33 percent, compared to 44 percent for the state of New York as a whole.

Any statistics contrasting the voting behavior of city and suburban residents requires a strict—and somewhat artificial—distinction between cities and suburbs. The suburban voting thesis assumes that suburbanites constitute a unified constituency, with distinct interests separate from central-city residents. In fact, however, suburbs are extremely varied; older, inner-ring suburbs have more in common with their central cities than with wealthy suburbs on the fringe. Inner-ring suburbs suffer from declining job bases, high rates of poverty, high crime, declining tax bases, and fiscal stress. Inner-ring suburbs, such as Harvey, Illinois, Compton, California, and East Cleveland, Ohio, resemble their central cities more than they resemble wealthy outer suburbs. But even if the inner-ring suburban voters were to make common cause with their cousins in the central cities, it is unlikely that a new round of urban policies would be forthcoming. And even if federal budget surpluses continue to be generated, it is hard to imagine that urban policies would ever again occupy a significant place on the national policy agenda. Those days are over.

FIGURE 8.4   **Relative Propensity to Vote, 1944–1992**

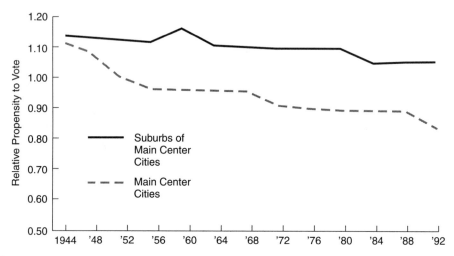

Source: Peter F. Nardulli, Jon K. Dalager, and Donald E. Greco, "Voter Turnout in President Elections: An Historical View and Some Speculation," *PS: Political Science and Politics* (September 1996): 486.

NOTES

1. Quoted in Bob Adams, "The Great Society Programs of the '60s and '70s Under Attack," *St. Louis Post-Dispatch,* May 10, 1992, p. 1B.
2. Quoted in "Schlesinger Accepts Award, Attacks Bush," *St. Louis Post-Dispatch,* May 10, 1992, p. 13C.
3. Reported in the *New York Times,* December 1, 1959, p. 27, quoted in Mark I. Gelfand, *A Nation of Cities: The Federal Government and Urban America,* Urban Life in America Series (New York: Oxford University Press, 1975), p. 295. See also John F. Kennedy, "The Great Unspoken Issue," *Proceedings, American Municipal Congress 1959* (Washington, D.C.: American Municipal League, n.d.), pp. 23–28; John F. Kennedy, "The Shame of the States," *New York Times Magazine,* May 18, 1958.
4. Quoted in Theodore H. White, *The Making of the President, 1960* (New York: Atheneum, 1961), p. 206. Nixon's strategy, which White contends was no strategy at all, was a "national" one, in which he committed himself to visit all fifty states; Kennedy, on the other hand, used an urban strategy centered on the industrial states with large blocs of electoral votes (see pp. 267–352).
5. John C. Donovan, *The Politics of Poverty,* 2nd. ed. (New York: Bobbs-Merrill, Pegasus, 1973), p. 19.
6. Quoted in White, *The Making of the President 1960,* p. 165.
7. Donovan, *The Politics of Poverty,* p. 225.
8. Ibid., p. 104.
9. Nelson W. Polsby and Aaron Wildavsky, *Presidential Elections: Contemporary Strategies of American Electoral Politics,* 7th ed. (New York: Free Press, 1988). The statistics given are for "nonwhite" voters.
10. White, *The Making of the President, 1960,* p. 354.

11. For good recent summary accounts, see ibid.; also James A. Morone, *The Democratic Wish: Popular Participation and the Limits of American Government* (New York: Basic Books, 1990), chap. 6.

12. Quoted In Richard Blumenthal, "The Bureaucracy: Antipoverty and the Community Action Programs," in *American Political Institutions and Public Policy*, ed. Allan P. Sindler (Boston: Little, Brown, 1969), p. 149.

13. *Message of the President to Congress*, reprinted in *Congressional Quarterly Weekly Report* 32, No. 2 (January 11, 1964).

14. *Congress and the Nation, 1945–1964* (Washington, D.C.: Congressional Quarterly Service, 1965), p. 1379.

15. U.S. Advisory Commission on Intergovernmental Relations, *Eleventh Annual Report* (Washington, D.C.: Government Printing Office, 1970), p. 2.

16. U.S. Congress, Senate Committee on Government Operations, *Catalogue of Federal Aid to State and Local Governments*, 88th Cong., 2d sess., April 15, 1964.

17. U.S. Congress, Library of Congress, *Number of Authorizations for Federal Assistance to State and Local Governments*, by I. M. Labovitz (Washington, D.C.: Legislative Reference Service, 1966).

18. Michael Reagan, *The New Federalism* (New York: Oxford University Press, 1972), p. 55. In 1971 and 1972, there was virtually no growth in the number of grant programs, largely because of presidential vetoes. Nixon vetoed sixteen bills in 1972. See U.S. Advisory Commission on Intergovernmental Relations, *Fourteenth Annual Report: Striking a Better Balance* (Washington, D.C.: Government Printing Office, 1973), p. 12.

19. U.S. Office of Management and Budget, *1979 Catalog of Federal Domestic Assistance* (Washington, D.C.: Government Printing Office, 1980).

20. Refer to Daniel J. Elazar, *The American Partnership: Intergovernmental Cooperation in the Nineteenth Century United States* (Chicago: University of Chicago Press, 1962).

21. Manpower Development and Training Act of 1962, Public Law 87-415, 87th Cong. (1962); emphasis added.

22. Economic Opportunity Act of 1964, Public Law 88-452, 88th Cong. (1964); emphasis added.

23. Demonstration Cities and Metropolitan Development Act of 1966, Public Law 89-754, 89th Cong. (1966); emphasis added.

24. See James L. Sundquist and David W. Davis, *Making Federalism Work: A Study of Program Coordination at the Community Level* (Washington, D.C.: Brookings Institution, 1969), pp. 3–5.

25. Lyndon B. Johnson, "Total Victory Over Poverty," Message to Congress, March 15, 1964, reprinted in *The Failure of American Liberalism: After the Great Society*, ed. Marvin E. Gettleman and David Mermelstein (New York: Vintage Books, 1970), p. 181.

26. U.S. Office of Economic Opportunity, *Community Action Program Guide* (Washington, D.C.: Government Printing Office, 1965).

27. Frances Fox Piven and Richard A. Cloward, *Regulating the Poor: The Functions of Public Welfare* (New York: Pantheon, 1971).

28. Ibid., p. 295.

29. U.S. Advisory Commission on Intergovernmental Relations, *Fiscal Balance in the American Federal System*, vol. 1 (Washington, D.C.: Government Printing Office, 1967), p. 169.

30. Demonstration Cities and Metropolitan Development Act of 1966, Public Law 89-754.

31. R. Douglas Arnold, *Congress and the Bureaucracy: A Theory of Influence* (New Haven: Yale University Press, 1979), p. 160.

32. Ibid., p. 168.

33. See Stuart Butler and Anna Kondratas, *Out of the Poverty Trap: A Conservative Strategy for Welfare Reform* (New York: Free Press, 1987), pp. 7–25.

34. See George Gilder, *Wealth and Poverty* (New York: Basic Books, 1981); Charles Murray, *Losing Ground: American Social Policy, 1950–1980* (New York: Basic Books, 1984).

35. U.S. Department of Commerce, Bureau of the Census, *Statistical Abstract of the United States, 1980* (Washington, D.C.: Government Printing Office, 1980), p. 464.

36. John E. Schwarz, *America's Hidden Success: A Reassessment of Public Policy from Kennedy to Reagan,* rev. ed. (New York: Norton, 1988), p. 24.

37. Jeffrey L. Pressman and Aaron Wildvasky, *How Great Expectations in Washington Are Dashed in Oakland: Or, Why It's Amazing That Federal Programs Work at All,* 3rd ed. (Berkeley: University of California Press, 1984).

38. Irving Lazar, *Summary: The Persistence of Preschool Effects,* Community Services Laboratory, New York State University College of Human Ecology at Cornell University, October 1977, quoted in Schwarz, *America's Hidden Success,* pp. 217–218.

39. Schwarz, *America's Hidden Success,* pp. 38–39.

40. Kathleen Hall Jamieson, *Packaging the Presidency: A History and Criticism of Presidential Campaign Advertising* (New York: Oxford University Press, 1984), pp. 202–203.

41. Joseph McGinniss, *Selling the President, 1968* (New York: Trident Press, 1969).

42. Numan V. Barley and Hugh D. Graham, *Southern Politics and the Second Reconstruction* (Baltimore: Johns Hopkins University Press, 1975), pp. 126–127; Everett Carl Ladd, Jr., "The Shifting Party Coalitions—1932–1976," in *Emerging Coalitions in American Politics,* ed. Seymour Martin Lipset (San Fransciso: Institute for Contemporary Studies, 1978), p. 98; A. James Reichley, *Conservatives in an Age of Change: The Nixon and Ford Administrations* (Washington, D.C.: Brookings Institution, 1981), p. 145.

43. Quoted in Reichley, *Conservatives in an Age of Change,* p. 186. For a general discussion, see David B. Robertson and Dennis R. Judd, *The Development of American Public Policy: The Structure of Policy Restraint* (Glenview, Ill.: Scott, Foresman, 1989), pp. 190–197.

44. U.S. Office of Management and Budget, *Special Analyses: Budget of the United States Government: Fiscal Year 1981* (Washington, D.C.: Government Printing Office, 1982), p. 254.

45. U.S. Office of Management and Budget, *Special Analyses, Budget of the United States Government: Fiscal Year 1978* (Washington, D.C.: Government Printing Office, 1979), p. 276.

46. Reagan, *The New Federalism,* p. 97.

47. Quoted in Timothy B. Clark, John K. Iglehart, and William Lilley III, "New Federalism 1: Return of Power to States and Cities Looms as Theme of Nixon's Second-Term Domestic Policy," *National Journal,* December 16, 1972, p. 1911.

48. Timothy Conlan, *New Federalism: Intergovernmental Reform from Nixon to Reagan* (Washington, D.C.: Brookings Institution, 1988), p. 9.

49. U.S. Office of Management and Budget, *Special Analyses, Budget of the United States Government: Fiscal Year 1972* (Washington, D.C.: Government Printing Office, 1973), p. 237.

50. Ibid., pp. 4, 45. For discussions of the politics of passing the legislation, see also Paul R. Dommel, *The Politics of Revenue Sharing* (Bloomington and London: Indiana University Press, 1974); Richard P. Nathan, Allen D. Manvel, Susannah E. Caulkins et al., *Monitoring Revenue Sharing* (Washington, D.C.: Brookings Institution, 1975).

51. *Washington Post,* March 22, 1971, cited in Richard E. Thompson, *Revenue Sharing, A New Era in Federalism* (Washington, D.C.: Revenue Sharing Advisory Service, 1973), p. 69.

52. *Newsweek,* May 24, 1971, p. 94.

53. Thompson, *Revenue Sharing,* p. 72.

54. Senator Howard Baker (Republican from Tennessee), quoted in Thompson, *Revenue Sharing,* p. 120.

55. U.S. Department of the Treasury, Office of Revenue Sharing, *Reported Uses of General Revenue Sharing Funds, 1974–1975: A Tabulation and Analysis of Data from Actual Use,* Report 5 (Washington, D.C.: Government Printing Office, 1966), p. 5.

56. U.S. Department of the Treasury, Office of Revenue Sharing, *Revenue Sharing: The First Actual Use Reports,* by David A. Caputo and Richard L. Cole (Washington, D.C.: Government Printing Office, 1974), pp. 10, 12, 29.

57. Ibid., p. 25.

58. For a discussion of this topic, see Richard P. Nathan, Charles F. Adams, Jr., et al., with the assistance of Andre Juneau and James W. Fossett, *Revenue Sharing: The Second Round* (Washington, D.C.: Brookings Institution, 1977), pp. 1–23.

59. *Congressional Record*, February 20, 1973, p. 746, cited in ibid., p. 2.

60. For example, see *Congressional Record*, February 22, 1973, p. 987; Congressional Record, March 1, 1973, p. 1160.

61. Advisory Commission on Intergovernmental Relations (ACIR), *Citizen Participation in the American Federal System* (Washington, D.C.: ACIR, 1979), p. 18.

62. *Revenue Sharing Bulletin*, July 1973, p. 2.

63. Nathan, Adams et al., *Revenue Sharing*, p. 171.

64. Housing and Community Development Act of 1974, sec. 101.

65. U.S. Department of Housing and Urban Development, Office of Community Planning and Development, Office of Evaluation, Housing and Community Development Act of 1974, *Community Development Block Grant Program: First Annual Report* (Washington, D.C.: Government Printing Office, 1975), p. 142.

66. Housing and Community Development Act of 1974, sec. 104(a).

67. Most of the funds were allocated to entitlement cities with populations of 50,000 or more, SMSA central cities, and certain urban counties. Jurisdictions that participated in the previous categorical programs folded into the Housing and Community Development Act also received "hold-harmless" grants under which their level of funding could not decline for a three-year period. About 20 percent of the monies were distributed without regard to the entitlement formulas. These funds represent the competitive portion of the program.

68. "New Directions Cited in First Annual Block Grant Reports," *Housing and Development Reporter*, January 12, 1976, p. 761.

69. U.S. Department of Housing and Urban Development, *Community Development Block Grant Program*, p. 38.

70. Reported in *Housing and Development Reporter*, January 10, 1977, p. 684.

71. Quoted from the *Report of the Southern Regional Council in Housing and Development Reporter*, April 5, 1976, p. 1051.

72. Interview by Sharon Cribbs (investigator for the Southern Governmental Monitoring Project) with Nathaniel Hill, Director, Department of Human Resources, Little Rock, Arkansas (Summer 1975), quoted in Southern Governmental Monitoring Project, *A Time for Accounting: The Housing and Community Development Act in the South: A Monitoring Report* by Raymond Brown with Ann Coil and Carol Rose (Atlanta: Southern Regional Council, 1976), p. 53.

73. Ibid., p. 51.

74. For a review of the Brookings report and other studies, see Carl E. Van Horn, "Decentralized Policy Delivery" (paper delivered at the Workshop on Policy Analysis in State and Local Government, State University of New York-Stonybrook, May 22–24, 1977); Carl E. Van Horn, *Policy Implementation in the Federal System* (Lexington, Mass.: Lexington Books, 1979).

75. "Grants with Strings Attached," *St. Louis Post-Dispatch*, August 6, 1977, p. 4A; reprinted from the *Washington Post*.

76. *Code of Federal Regulations, Title 24, Part 570* (Washington, D.C.: U.S. Government Printing Office, April 1, 1978), pp. 36–157.

77. Cited in Michael J. Rich, *Federal Policymaking and the Poor: National Goals, Local Choices, and Distributional Outcomes* (Princeton, N.J.: Princeton University Press, 1993), p. 41.

78. Anthony Downs, *Recommendation for Community Development Planning*, monograph based on a study for HUD (Chicago: Real Estate Research Corporation, 1975).

79. See M. Leanne Lachman, "Planning for Community Development: A Proposed Approach," *Journal of Housing* 32, No. 2 (February 1975): 58.

80. Roger Starr, "Making New York Smaller," in *Revitalizing the Northeast,* ed. George Stern-lieb and James W. Hughes (New Brunswick, N.J.: Rutgers University Press, 1978).

81. Jerome Pratter, "How Cities Can Grow Old Gracefully," *House Committee on Banking, Finance, and Urban Affairs Report* (Washington, D.C.: Government Printing Office, 1978).

82. James L. Greer, "Urban Planning and Redevelopment in Chicago: The Political Economy of the Chicago 21 Plan" (paper delivered at the Annual Meeting of the Midwest Political Science Association, Chicago, April 19–21, 1979).

83. Alvin H. Mushkatel and Howard Lasus, "Geographic Targeting of Community Development Funds in Denver: Who Benefits?" (paper delivered at the Annual Meeting of the Western Social Science Association, Albuquerque, N.M., April 23–26, 1980).

84. Quoted in Robert L. Joller, "HUD Secretary Quiets Critics," *St. Louis Post-Dispatch,* April 18, 1977, p. 38.

85. Reprinted in Roy Bahl, ed., *The Fiscal Outlook for Cities: Implications of a National Urban Policy* (Syracuse, N.Y.: Syracuse University Press, 1978), pp. 111–127.

86. Ibid., p. 112.

87. Ann R. Markusen and David Wilmoth, "The Political Economy of National Urban Policy in the U.S.A.: 1976–81," *Canadian Journal of Regional Science* (Summer 1982): 145–163.

88. State of Illinois, Bureau of the Budget, Federal Relations Unit, *Equity in Federal Funding: A First Step* (Springfield: State of Illinois, Bureau of the Budget, 1976), p. 2.

89. Rochelle L. Stansfield, "Federalism Report: Government Seeks the Right Formula for Community Development Funds," *National Journal,* February 12, 1977, p. 242.

90. See State of Illinois, Bureau of the Budget, *Federal Relations Unit, Equity in Federal Funding,* p. 32.

91. Refer to Stansfield, "Federalism Report."

92. Ann R. Markusen, "The Urban Impact Analysis: A Critical Forecast," in *The Urban Impact of Federal Policies,* ed. Norman Glickman (Baltimore: Johns Hopkins University Press, 1979); see also discussion by Ann R. Markusen, Annalee Saxenian, and Marc A. Weiss, "Who Benefits from Intergovernmental Transfers?," in *Cities Under Stress: The Fiscal Crises of Urban America,* ed. Robert W. Burchell and David Listokin (New Brunswick, N.J.: Center for Urban Research, 1981), p. 656; Stansfield, "Federalism Report."

93. Quoted in Rich, *Federal Policymaking and the Poor,* p. 78.

94. See Stansfield, "Federalism Report"; Joel Havemann, Rochelle L. Stansfield, and Neal R. Pierce, "Federal Spending: The North's Loss Is the Sunbelt's Gain," *National Journal,* June 1976, p. 1031.

95. Robert Reinhold, "More Aid on Way for Older Cities," *St. Louis Post-Dispatch,* May 9, 1977, p. 3C, reprinted from the *New York Times.*

96. Calculated from Richard DeLeon and Richard LeGates, "Beyond Cybernetic Federalism in Community Development," *Urban Law Annual* 15 (1978): 31; see also Paul R. Dommel, "Block Grants for Community Development: Decentralized Decision-Making," in *Fiscal Crisis in American Cities: The Federal Response,* ed. L. Kenneth Hubbell (Cambridge, Mass.: Ballinger, 1979), pp. 236–241.

97. John P. Ross, "Countercyclical Revenue Sharing," in *Fiscal Crisis in American Cities: The Federal Response,* ed. L. Kenneth Hubbell (Cambridge, Mass.: Ballinger, 1979), pp. 256–261.

98. Ibid., p. 266.

99. Ibid., pp. 266–267.

100. U.S. Department of Housing and Urban Development, "The Urban Fiscal Crisis: Fact or Fantasy (A Reply)," in *Cities Under Stress: The Fiscal Crises of Urban America,* ed. Robert W. Burchell and David Listokin (New Brunswick, N.J.: Center for Urban Research, 1981), p. 151.

101. Quoted in Robert Reihold, "President Proposes a Broad New Policy for Urban Recovery," *New York Times,* March 28, 1978.

102. "Excerpts from the President's Message to Congress Outlining His Urban Policy," *New York Times,* March 28, 1978.

103. F. J. James, "President Carter's Comprehensive National Urban Policy: Achievements and Lessons Learned," Environment and Planning C: Government and Policy 8 (199): 34.

104. Markusen and Wilmoth, "The Political Economy of National Urban Policy," p. 15.

105. Ibid., p. 15.

106. "Washington Update: Administration Officials, Mayors Have Love Fest," *National Journal,* January 29, 1977, p. 189.

107. *New York Times,* October 23, 1981.

108. President's Commission for a National Agenda for the Eighties, *A National Agenda for the Eighties* (Washington, D.C.: Government Printing Office, 1980), p. 66.

109. Ibid., pp. 66–67.

110. Ibid., p. 4.

111. Ibid., p. 66.

112. Timothy K. Barnekov, Daniel Rich, and Robert Warren, "The New Privatism, Federalism, and the Future of Urban Governance: National Urban Policy in the 1980s," *Journal of Urban Affairs* 3, No. 4 (Fall 1981): 3.

113. U.S. Department of Housing and Urban Development, *The President's National Urban Policy Report* (Washington, D.C.: Government Printing Office, 1982), pp. 2, 23.

114. Ibid., p. 14.

115. Conlan, *New Federalism,* p. 137.

116. Ibid.

117. Ibid., p. 135.

118. Ibid., p. 138.

119. Robertson and Judd, *The Development of American Public Policy,* p. 233.

120. U.S. Office of Management and Budget, *Budget of the United States Government, Historical Tables, Fiscal Year 1996* (Washington, D.C.: Government Printing Office, 1996), table 12.3.

121. Henry J. Aaron and Associates, "Nondefense Programs," in *Setting National Priorities: The 1983 Budget,* ed. Joseph A. Pechman (Washington, D.C.: Brookings Institution, 1982), p. 119.

122. U.S. Office of Management and Budget, *Budget of the United States Government, Historical Tables, Fiscal Year 1996* (Washington, D.C.: Government Printing Office, 1996), table 12.3.

123. George E. Peterson et al., *The Reagan Block Grants: What Have We Learned* (Washington, D.C.: Urban Institute, 1986), p. 21.

124. U.S. Congress, Joint Economic Committee, *Emergency Interim Survey: Fiscal Condition of Forty-eight Large Cities* (Washington, D.C.: Government Printing Office, 1982), p. 6.

125. White House press release, March 7, 1983.

126. James H. Johnson, Jr., Cloyzelle K. Jones, Walter C. Farrell, Jr., and Melvin L. Oliver, "The Los Angeles Rebellion: A Retrospective View," *Economic Development Quarterly* 6, No. 4 (November 1992): 356–372.

127. Robert Pear, "Clinton, in Attack on President, Ties Riots to 'Neglect,'" *New York Times,* May 6, 1992.

128. Clifford Krauss, "Congress Passes Aid to Cities," *New York Times,* June 9, 1992, p. A20.

129. Quoted in Theodore H. White, *America in Search of Itself: The Making of the President, 1956–1980* (New York: Harper and Row, 1982), p. 381.

130. D. Lee Bawden and John L. Palmer, "Social Policy: Challenging the Welfare State," in *The Reagan Record,* ed. John L. Palmer and Isabel V. Sawhill (Cambridge, Mass.: Ballinger), p. 200.

131. Quoted in Robert Pear, "Quayle Criticizes New York as Proof of Welfare's Ills," *New York Times,* February 28, 1992.

132. *New York Post,* April 28, 1992, p. 1.

133. "The Willie Horton of 1992," *New York Times,* March 3, 1992.

134. William Schneider, "The Suburban Century Begins," *Atlantic Monthly,* July 1992, pp. 33–44.

135. William Julius Wilson, *The Truly Disadvantaged: The Inner City, the Underclass, and Public Policy* (Chicago: University of Chicago Press, 1987), p. 155.

136. "A Visit with Bill Clinton," *Atlantic Monthly,* October 1992 and William Julius Wilson, "The Right Message," *New York Times,* March 17, 1992.

137. Bernard H. Ross and Myron A. Levine, *Urban Politics: Power in Metropolitan America,* 5th ed. (Itasca, Ill.: F. E. Peacock, 1996), p. 434.

138. Adam Clymer, "G.O.P. Senators Prevail, Sinking Clinton's Economic Stimulus Bill," *New York Times,* April 22, 1993.

139. Deirdre Shesgreen, "Anti-poverty Plan Pushed by Talent Win Bipartisan Support at White House," *St. Louis Post-Dispatch,* April 24, 2000, p. A8.

140. Quoted in Kenneth J. Cooper, "Gingrich Pledges a Major Package of Spending Cuts Early Next Year," *Washington Post,* December 13, 1994.

141. U.S. Department of Housing and Urban Development, *Empowerment: A New Covenant with America's Communities* (Rockville, Md.: HUD USER, July 1995).

142. National Law Income Housing Coalition, *Housing at a Snail's Pace: The Federal Housing Budget: 1978–1987* (Washington, D.C.: NLIHC, 1996), p. 75.

143. Peter F. Nardulli, Jon K. Dalager, and Donald E. Greco, "Voter Turnout in U.S. Presidential Elections: An Historical View and Some Speculation," *PS: Political Science and Politics* (September 1996): 484.

144. Calculations are from Richard Sauerzopf and Todd Swanstrom, "The Urban Electorate in Presidential Elections, 1920–1992: Challenging the Conventional Wisdom" (paper delivered at the Annual Meeting of the Urban Affairs Association, Indianapolis, Indiana, April 22–25, 1993). Updated by authors.

145. Hal Wolman and Lisa Marckini, "Changes in Central City Representation and Influence in Congress" (paper prepared for delivery at the Annual Meeting of the Urban Affairs Association, Toronto, Canada, April 17, 1997). See also Demetrios Caraley, "Washington Abandons the Cities," *Political Science Quarterly* 107, No. 1 (1992): 20.

146. 146 Margaret Weir, "Central Cities' Loss of Power in State Politics," *Cityscape: A Journal of Policy Development and Research* 2, No. 2 (May 1996): 23–40.

CHAPTER
9

THE RISE OF THE SUNBELT CITIES

THE CONCEPT OF THE SUNBELT

The term Sunbelt was popularized as recently as the mid-1970s, but it quickly became almost indispensable in everyday discourse about national development and politics. Even though the geographic boundaries of the Sunbelt are rather vague in most people's minds, the term conveys a distinctly positive image of a part of the country that is prosperous and growing: "When a person hears the term on radio or on television, or reads it in a magazine or book, or sees it in the telephone book or on a firm's letterhead, it is likely to conjure up an image of growing cities and booming economies in Southern or Southwestern cities with pleasant climates."[1] It would be possible to regard the term as merely a "rhetorical ruse," as one scholar called it,[2] or a "public relations coup," as the president of a corporation helping other companies move to the Sunbelt labeled it,[3] were it not for the fact that the long-term population growth in the region has resulted in a fundamental realignment of political power in the nation. Six of the last seven presidents came from the South or the West. (The exception is Gerald Ford, who came from Michigan; however, he succeeded to the presidency with the resignation of Richard Nixon.) Over the past half-century, the reapportionment that follows each decennial census has shifted the balance of power in Congress decisively toward the delegations that represent southern and western states. Without doubt, this realignment of power helps to account for the decline in federal aid to the cities since the late 1970s.

Kevin Phillips, the chief political analyst for the 1968 Republican presidential campaign, is generally credited as the person who coined the term *Sunbelt*. In his book, *The Emerging Republican Majority*, published in 1969, Phillips asserted that the United States was going through an electoral realignment that was transforming the Republican party into the nation's majority party. The basis of this national political realignment, he said, was the movement of millions of Americans out of the old industrial cities of the North to the suburbs and to the South and West. Phillips sometimes lumped the South and the West into an area he called the Sunbelt, though he never actually defined its boundaries; indeed, of forty-seven maps in his book, none portrays such a region.[4]

Phillips's prediction that regionalism would become an ascendant influence in national politics turned out to be correct. In 1973 an embargo on the sale of oil organized by the Arab oil-producing nations drove the world price of oil sharply upward. The economies of oil-producing states such as Texas, Louisiana, Oklahoma, and Colorado boomed, and new jobs were created throughout the southern and western states. At the same time, energy-dependent industries and consumers in the northern states were hit hard. In 1974 and 1975 northern states went through an economic depression that saw hundreds of thousands of layoffs in industrial jobs. In the winter of 1975, the mood turned ugly. By the spring of 1975, New York City was facing bankruptcy and had to ask the federal government for loan guarantees. President Gerald Ford initially refused to help.[5] Congressional legislative battles began to reflect sharply divided regional politics pitting a prosperous South and West against a declining North.

In this atmosphere, *Power Shift,* a book published by Kirkpatrick Sale in 1975, quickly became a national bestseller.[6] Sale wrote that the states of the South and West—a region he called the Southern Rim—were gaining national political power at the expense of the older industrial states. Trying to find a way to report on the political issues raised by the new regional antagonisms, the media revived Phillips's notion of the Sunbelt, and the term soon came into common use. In February 1976 the *New York Times* published a five-part series documenting the demographic and political trends favoring the Sunbelt. In May *Business Week* devoted its feature article to "The Second War Between the States."[7] The regional war became one of the hot topics helping to sell newspapers and magazines in 1976 and 1977.

Though the concept of the Sunbelt has entered the everyday language of Americans (the term has been included in dictionaries since the late 1970s), the precise boundaries of the region are hard to pin down. In a letter to a scholar researching the politics of the Sunbelt, Kevin Phillips defined it as the "territory stretching from the eastern Carolina lowlands down around (and excluding) Appalachia, picking up only the great Memphis area of Tennessee, omitting the Ozarks and moving west to Oklahoma, thence virtually due west," possibly also including Colorado.[8] It is understandable that Phillips would want to draw his boundaries to exclude pockets of poverty in the border states, but his description is extremely imprecise. For our purposes in this chapter, we adopt Sale's definition, as shown in Figure 9.1. Sale's Sunbelt encompasses the entire portion of the United States below the thirty-seventh parallel (what he called the Southern Rim), extending across the country from North Carolina to the West Coast, including southern California and part of southern Nevada.[9] (For statistical purposes, we will include all of California and Nevada.) Thus there are fifteen states in the Sunbelt. The fourteen states of the Northeast and the upper Midwest constitute the so-called Frostbelt.

A significant number of scholars are troubled by the concept of the Sunbelt. For one thing, the huge area encompassed by Sale's definition is far from uniformly prosperous. The most rapid economic and population growth has oc-

FIGURE 9.1   **The American Sunbelt and Frostbelt**

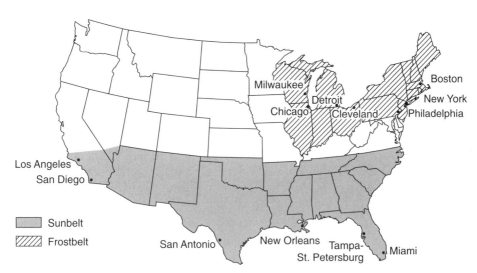

Source: Adapted from Richard M. Bernard and Bradley R. Rice, eds., *Sunbelt Cities: Politics and Growth Since World War II* (Austin: University of Texas Press, 1985), p. 7.

curred in Florida, parts of Texas, Arizona, southern Nevada, and southern California. Rural areas all across the Sunbelt and many urban areas of the South have remained untouched by the prosperity that is proclaimed as the Sunbelt's principal defining feature, a fact that led two scholars to note that the Sunbelt "has collapsed into only a few 'sunspots.'"[10]

A second problem with the Sunbelt concept is that it assumes that the South and the Southwest are similar enough that they can be lumped together under a single label. Until its image was refurbished by its inclusion in the prosperous Sunbelt, the South was often thought of as a backward, poverty-ridden, violent region with a peculiar caste system. Most political studies of the South focused on issues of race, the enduring effects of the Civil War and Reconstruction, and the dominance of a single, authoritarian party—the elements that made up a conservative political culture that had changed little since the Civil War. The main industries that had located in the South were those associated with low-wage labor. In the 1930s, Franklin Roosevelt and the New Deal administrators looked at federal programs as a way to bring economic development to this backward region.[11]

The image of the West, in contrast, tended to be "urban, opulent, energetic, mobile, and individualistic, a region of economic growth and openness to continual change which matched America's self-image."[12] If the image of perpetual sunshine gave the Sunbelt its name, then certainly this image fit the West better than the South. Since Los Angeles was the home of the movie and television industries, America's popular culture became increasingly identified with western images. Los Angeles served as a vision of America's future, with its sprawling suburbs, freeways, shopping centers, and even its smog.

Some observers claimed that the idea of the Sunbelt was nearly dead and that its brief existence was overplayed anyway. Nicholas Lehmann, who edited the *Texas Monthly* in the 1980s, observed that "millions of people were living in the Sunbelt without one of them realizing it. They thought of themselves as Southerners or Texans, or Los Angelenos."[13] The concept of the Sunbelt was regarded with suspicion not only because there were so many differences within it but also because all regions of the United States seemed to be becoming more alike. The old industrial states were becoming less industrial, urban populations were spreading out into suburbs in all parts of the country, and a media-based national culture was replacing regional cultural differences: "Just try to find a town anywhere in the United States without a McDonald's or a television happy-news format featuring an anchorperson with an unidentifiable accent."[14]

Despite the shortcomings of the Sunbelt concept, it remains useful because it sheds light on issues connected to regional rivalries, population movements, a continuing process of economic restructuring, and disputes over governmental policy. The Sunbelt may be somewhat ambiguous, but the effects of regional conflicts linger.

THE RISE OF THE SUNBELT

For the past half-century population and economic activities in the United States have been moving away from older urban areas. There can be no doubt that this dispersal constitutes a historic shift. In the hundred years leading up to the 1930s, the cities of the North had acted as magnets drawing millions of immigrants and migrants to their industrial economies. The North was the most heavily urbanized and prosperous region of the country. With the economic prosperity in the years after World War II, it appeared that northern metropolitan areas—though not necessarily the central cities—would enjoy another sustained period of growth and prosperity. All through the 1950s and 1960s the manufacturing economies of these regions did well. In 1950, 65 percent of the nation's metropolitan population lived in or near the industrial belt that reached from Boston and New York in the Northeast across to the Great Lakes and down to St. Louis.[15] More than two-thirds of the manufacturing jobs and ten of the nation's fourteen urban areas of more than one million people were stretched across this industrial zone.[16] Over the next half century, however, a historic shift in the national population occurred.

After World War II, the population losses that had begun to affect the older central cities in the 1930s continued and even accelerated, but the suburbs surrounding them boomed. In the 1970s, however, this situation changed abruptly. Even the suburbs began to stagnate, and those outside Boston and Pittsburgh actually lost population. In contrast, most metropolitan areas in the Sunbelt were growing so rapidly that it was hard to build infrastructure fast enough. Table 9.1 shows these trends. In almost all of the ten Sunbelt metropolitan areas shown in Table 9.1, population increases from 1950 to 1990 ranged from 20 percent to 40 percent per decade, and sometimes much more. From 1990 to 1997, the rate of growth has slowed for many of these Sunbelt regions, with Los Angeles growing

| TABLE 9.1 | POPULATION GROWTH OF SELECTED METROPOLITAN AREAS OF 1 MILLION OR MORE, 1950–1997 |

| | Percent Increase in Population | | | | |
Metropolitan Area (Ranked by Growth in 1970s)	1950–1960	1960–1970	1970–1980	1980–1990	1990–1997
Phoenix (MSA)[a]	100	46	55	40	27
Houston (PMSA)	52	40	45	21	15
San Diego (MSA)	85.5	32	37	34	9
Anaheim (Orange County) (PMSA)	226	102	36	24	11
Denver-Boulder (CMSA)	52	32	31	44	17
Miami (PMSA)	89	36	28	20	5.5
Atlanta (MSA)	40	37	27	32.5	23
Dallas-Fort Worth (CMSA)	43	39	25	32.5	16
Los Angeles-Long Beach (PMSA)	45.5	16	6	18.5	3
San Francisco-Oakland (CMSA)	24	17	5	16	7
Chicago (PMSA)	20	12	2	0.2	5
Detroit (PMSA)	28	12	−2	−2	5
St. Louis (MSA)	20	12	−2	3	3
New York City (PMSA)	12	8	−4.5	3	1
Boston (NECMA)	7.5	6	−5	6.5	2.5
Pittsburgh (PMSA)	9	−0.2	−5	−7	−1

[a]Abbreviations refer to different statistical types of metropolitan areas, as defined by the Census Bureau in 1990 census.

Source: U.S. Bureau of the Census. *1970 Census of Population,* vol. 1, *Characteristics of the Population,* pt. A (Washington, D.C.: Government Printing Office, 1973), p. 171, table 32; *1980 Census of the Population, Supplementary Reports, Standard Metropolitan Statistical Areas and Standard Consolidated Statistical Areas,* p. 3, table 1; U.S. Bureau of the Census, *State and Metropolitan Area Data Book: 1991* (Washington, D.C.: Government Printing Office, 1991), table A; U.S. Bureau of the Census, *Standard Metropolitan Area Data Book: 1997–98* (Washington, D.C.: Government Printing Office, 1999), table B-1, pp. 60–65.

by just over 3 percent, for example. The six Frostbelt metropolitan areas listed in Table 9.1 grew much more slowly than any of the Sunbelt regions, and indeed, all but one of them lost population in the 1970s. They subsequently rebounded somewhat, with the Pittsburgh region slowing its rate of population loss in the 1990s and Detroit and Chicago showing solid growth after two troubled decades.

The regional redistribution of the national population that had begun with the wartime boom of the 1940s gathered speed in the 1950s. In the five decades between 1940 and 1990, the population of the fifteen Sunbelt states increased 163 percent (to 103,868,000), compared to a population gain in the fourteen Frostbelt states of 48 percent (to 92,818,000).[17] In the 1980s the gap quickly widened; the fifteen Sunbelt states grew overall by 19 percent, compared with 2 percent for the fourteen Frostbelt states. The fastest-growing states were Nevada (+50 percent), Arizona (+35 percent), Florida (+33 percent), and California (+26 percent). The only Frostbelt state to show a significant gain was New Hampshire (+20.5

percent), which was attracting commuters from elsewhere in the Northeast urban corridor.[18]

Census Bureau population estimates showed that these trends continued in the 1990s. Between 1990 and 1995 the population of the Sunbelt states increased 8 percent, while the Frostbelt states gained only 2 percent in population. None of the states in the Frostbelt achieved double-digit growth in the first half of the 1990s, but four Sunbelt states did: Nevada (27 percent), Arizona (15.5 percent), Georgia (11 percent), New Mexico (11 percent), and Texas (10 percent). Many of the fastest growing states, however, were located outside the Sunbelt, in the Rocky Mountains (Colorado, Utah, and Idaho) and the Pacific Northwest (Washington and Oregon).[19]

People moved to the Sunbelt mainly to find jobs. In the 1930s the South was considered the nation's economic basket case. In subsequent decades conditions changed dramatically, however, as the older industrial cities lost business and jobs to the Sunbelt. Table 9.2 shows that in the 1960s the Northeast gained 18 percent of the nation's new jobs and the Midwest region gained 26 percent. In the 1970s, the Northeast's share of job growth increased to 31 percent, but the Midwest's fortunes fell through the bottom, with that region creating only 3 percent of the nation's jobs. From 1980 to 1998, 21 percent of the nation's jobs were generated in the Northeast, and just 11 percent in the Midwest. The big winners were located in the Sunbelt, with the South accounting for 42 percent of job growth from 1980 to 1998. Clearly, the regional economic shift was still occurring in the United States in the 1990s.

The rate of growth in some southern and western regions has been phenomenal in recent decades. Table 9.3 shows that all of the fastest-growing metropolitan areas in the nation in the 1970s were located in the South and West, five of them in Florida. In the 1980s, Florida had seven of the ten regions on the top-ten list. By the 1990s, however, only one Florida region made it onto the list. The fastest-growing regions were widely distributed. With the exceptions of Las Vegas and Phoenix, they were relatively small urban areas. Several, including Boise, Idaho, Austin, Texas, and Provo, Utah, were booming because of an influx of high-tech industries.

The central cities of the Sunbelt are usually not as isolated within their metropolitan areas as are those in the Frostbelt. David Rusk has categorized cities according to their degree of "elasticity," their ability to grow either by filling in undeveloped land or by annexing new territory. Of the fifty-two metropolitan areas having more than 200,000 population that Rusk rated as having "high" or "hyper" elasticity in 1990, forty-nine of them were located in the Sunbelt. No Frostbelt city was ranked in these categories.[20] Older central cities all over the country, including in the Sunbelt, found it impossible to change their boundaries, mostly because they became surrounded by independent suburban municipalities long ago, and suburban governments were able to prevent annexation or merger attempts. Atlanta, for instance, lost 14 percent of its population during the 1970s, but its regional population grew by 46 percent. Denver likewise lost population (–4.5 percent) while its suburbs grew (+60 percent). For the most part, however, Sunbelt cities have had a high degree of elasticity, mainly

TABLE
9.2

COMPARISON OF REGIONAL SHARES OF U.S. EMPLOYMENT AND SHARES OF U.S. JOB GROWTH 1960–1998 (IN PERCENTAGES)

Region*	1960 Share of Employment	1970 Share of Employment	1980 Share of Employment	1998 Share of Employment	1960–1970 Share of Job Growth	1970–1980 Share of Job Growth	1980–1990 Share of Job Growth
Northeast	29	26	27	26	18	31	2
Midwest	29	28	22	19	25.5	3	1
South	26.5	29	31	34	35	39	4
West	15	17	19	21	21	26.5	2

*Regions defined according to Bureau of the Census definition; North Central changed to Midwest in 1989.

Source: U.S. Department of Labor, Bureau of Labor Statistics, *Employment and Earnings,* Statistics for March 1960 (vol. 6, no. 9), and U.S. Bureau of the Census, *Statistical Abstract of the United States, 1999,* Employees in Nonfarm Establishments-States: 1980–1998 (Washington, D.C.: Government Printing Office, 1999) p. 435, table 689.

TABLE 9.3	THE TEN FASTEST GROWING METROPOLITAN AREAS IN 1970–1980, 1980–1990, AND 1990–1997

Metropolitan Area	Percent Increase in Population
1970–1980	
Fort Meyers-Cape Coral, FL	95
Ocala, FL	77
Las Vegas, NV	69
Sarasota, FL	68
Fort Collins, CO	66
West Palm Beach-Boca Raton, FL	64
Ft. Lauderdale-Hollywood, FL	64
Olympia, WA	62
Bryan-College Station, TX	61
Reno, NV	60
1980–1990	
Naples, FL	77
Riverside-San Bernardino, CA	66
Fort Pierce, FL	66
Fort Myers-Cape Coral, FL	63
Las Vegas, NV	61
Ocala, FL	59
Orlando, FL	53
West Palm Beach-Boca Raton, FL	50
Melbourne-Titusville-Palm Bay, FL	46
Austin-San Marcos, TX	46
1990–1997	
Las Vegas, NV	48
Laredo, TX	38
McAllen-Edinburg-Mission, TX	33
Boise City, ID	30
Naples, FL	29
Phoenix-Mesa, AZ	27
Fayetteville-Springdale-Rogers, AR	27
Austin-San Marcos, TX	27
Wilmington, NC	25
Provo-Orem, UT	25

Source: U.S. Bureau of the Census, *1980 Census of the Population, Supplementary Reports, Standard Metropolitan Statistical Areas and Standard Consolidated Statistical Areas* (Washington, D.C.: Government Printing Office, 1981), p. 2, table C; *Urban News* 5, No. 1 (Spring 1991): 5, as reported by the U.S. Bureau of the Census: *State and Metropolitan Data Book 1997–98* (Washington, D.C.: Government Printing Office, 1999), table B-1, pp. 60–65.

because they annexed huge amounts of new territory to keep themselves from becoming surrounded by independent suburbs. Oklahoma City, for example, grew from about 51 square miles in 1950 to 636 square miles in 1970. Much of its territory is semirural land waiting for new housing tracts. Phoenix expanded from just 17 square miles in 1950 to 469 square miles in 1996.[21] Most Sunbelt cities added substantial territory in the 1950s and 1960s and at least some additional territory since then.[22]

THE CHANGING POLITICAL BALANCE

The growth of the Sunbelt has undermined policies intended to help older cities. Urban policy was essentially invented during the New Deal. President Roosevelt was not personally inclined toward cities and in the early years of his presidency supported the back-to-the-land movement.[23] He realized, however, that the urban working class was the key to his electoral success and this is why he supported programs like public housing and public works employment. The big city vote was decisive in every one of FDR's four presidential election campaigns. The nation's eleven largest cities provided 27 percent of his national vote in 1932 and a much larger proportion of the vote in the industrial states.[24]

The urban vote continued to be essential to the Democrats for decades. Time after time an overwhelming Democratic vote in the big cities balanced out Republican pluralities in the suburbs and small towns, providing the margin of victory in key states with large blocs of electoral votes. The Democrats would have lost the presidency in 1940, 1944, and 1948 without the overwhelming margins delivered in twelve big cities.[25] The urban electorate was essential to John F. Kennedy's victory in the close election of 1960. Kennedy beat Nixon by 112,000 votes, a margin of less than one-tenth of 1 percent, but he carried 27 out of the 39 largest cities.[26] In 1964 Lyndon Johnson won by an unprecedented landslide, with the cities topping the national Democratic margins by 10 percent or more.

Democratic successes in presidential elections were bound to end eventually because the Democrats were strongest in the industrial cities, which were losing population. In contrast, the Republicans were strongest in the suburbs, the West, and, after 1964, the South, all of which were booming. Each decennial census was followed by a reapportionment of seats in the House of Representatives, which, together with the two senators from each state, determines the number of electoral votes each state gets. As Figure 9.2 shows, the Sunbelt states increased their number of congressional representatives and presidential electoral votes every time the country was reapportioned after 1928, and the Frostbelt states lost congressional and electoral votes. The number of representatives from six older industrial cities—Boston, New York, Philadelphia, Baltimore, Detroit, and Chicago—fell from 52 in 1923 to only 33 by 1983.[27]

The changing distribution of population and votes has transformed American national politics. Historically, the South and West have been governed by political elites that have been able to keep political participation low. In the

FIGURE 9.2   **Electoral Votes and Congressional Representation: Sunbelt and Frostbelt States, 1928–1992**

Source: U.S. Bureau of the Census, *Historical Statistics of the United States, Colonial Times to 1970,* Bicentennial edition, pt. 1 (Washington, D.C.: Government Printing Office, 1975), p. 1015; U.S. Bureau of the Census, *Statistical Abstract of the United States, 1989* (Washington, D.C.: Government Printing Office, 1989), p. 241; Felicity Barringer, "Census Bureau Places Population at 249.6 Million," *New York Times,* December 27, 1990.

South, business elites defined a good economy as one in which labor was quiescent and cheap. In the West, business elites tended to define the role of government in narrow terms: It was all right to promote business investment and general prosperity through water and dam projects, but otherwise government was to remain out of sight. In short, the political culture of the Sunbelt was, and is, highly individualistic and generally hostile to governmental action, unless that action is geared toward helping business and expanding the private economy. Peter Lupsha and William Siembieda sum up the political orientation in the Sunbelt this way: "The critical elements shaping political forms in the Sunbelt were the values of privatism, individualism, religious fundamentalism, fiscal conservatism, laissez faire, and a view of good government as good business."[28]

In contrast, political participation in Frostbelt cities has historically been more broad-based. Labor unions, blacks, and ethnic groups fought for and expected governments to help ordinary citizens. As a consequence, local expenditures on social welfare tended to be much higher in Frostbelt than in Sunbelt cities. In 1970, fifteen Sunbelt cities averaged only $3.77 per capita for public welfare expenditures, compared with $26.45 in fifteen northern cities.[29]

A generation ago, central-city voters gave the Democratic party an edge in presidential elections. Between 1932 and 1964 the Republicans lost seven out of nine presidential elections. In the 1960s the Republican party found a geopolitical counterweight to the Democrats' urban strategy when Sunbelt and suburban voters put Richard Nixon into the White House. Nixon scorned the eastern establishment that had dominated the Republican party for a century. Born in California and elected congressman and senator from that state, Nixon's roots reached into the expanding electorate of the Sunbelt and in the new corporate wealth located there. In the 1968 election, Nixon appealed to the white, Protestant and Catholic, white- and blue-collar ethnics of the northern suburbs by promising "law and order," a code phrase for cracking down on inner-city civil disorders; the same message appealed to middle-class whites living in the Sunbelt.[30] Though Nixon did not reduce federal spending, his policies shifted resources to the Sunbelt and the suburbs.[31]

The Republican strategy paid off. From the 1968 through 1988 elections, the Republicans won five out of six presidential contests. By 1980 the coming of age of the suburban middle class and the Sunbelt gave the Republicans a decisive advantage in presidential elections.[32] Ronald Reagan won the presidency easily in 1980 even though he carried only 35 percent of the big city vote.[33] A large portion of his campaign funds came from independent oil producers in several Sunbelt states.[34] Once in office, Reagan sharply cut programs targeted to older central cities.[35]

By the 1988 presidential election, the Democrats also began to abandon the strategy of appealing to central-city voters. The Democratic nominee, Michael Dukakis, made little effort to appeal to the central-city vote. Instead, Dukakis crafted a southern strategy. He selected a Sunbelt politician, Lloyd Bentsen of Texas, as his running mate and attempted to lure the suburban blue-collar Democrats back to the party by avoiding the word "liberal" and its connotations. According to Democratic pollster Peter Hart, political analysts had determined that there were not enough votes in the major cities to enable Dukakis to win enough states.[36] George Bush won the presidency, though he did poorly in the central cities and carried only 8 percent of the African-American vote.[37] By the 1988 presidential election, the central cities with populations larger than 500,000 accounted for less than 12 percent of the national vote, and by the 1996 election less than 10 percent of the vote was cast in those cities.

WHY THE SUNBELT BOOMED

The causes of the rise of the Sunbelt are many and complex. Economic and technological factors played a major role.[38] The infrastructure of the older Frostbelt cities was geared to the high-density patterns of production and consumption characteristic of the industrial period. Sunbelt cities had an advantage because they could start afresh to build infrastructure suited to the postindustrial economy. The building of a freeway network throughout the nation provided the foundation for a national economy that favored the decentralization of economic activities. The adoption of air conditioning made the Sunbelt more attractive both for living and for white-collar work.[39] The materials used in manufacturing shifted from heavy metals such as iron and steel to lighter materials such as aluminum and plastic, and the newer manufacturing plants could be located on relatively cheap, easily available land in Sunbelt metropolitan areas. Most importantly, the source of energy for industry and for homes shifted from Frostbelt coal to Sunbelt oil. Oil jumped from meeting less than half of the nation's energy needs in 1940 to almost 78 percent by 1975. By the mid-1970s, coal met no more than 17 percent of the nation's energy needs.[40]

Changing demographics and lifestyles favored the Sunbelt as well. Increased leisure time and more emphasis on recreation lured people to warmer climates. After World War II, tourism became a major component of the national economy. Major recreational and tourist facilities developed in Florida and California (homes of Disney theme parks) and in New Orleans and Las Vegas. Whole communities, such as Lake Havasu, Arizona, arose to serve the needs of an expanding class of retired people who preferred Sunbelt lifestyles and the lower cost of living found there.

Demographic and economic trends do not, however, explain the Sunbelt boom. Governmental policies were also important. The crucial role of governments can be appreciated by looking at the experience of other advanced industrial countries that have their "sunbelts": in Britain, employment has shifted from the industrial north to the south of England, where a high-technology economy has emerged along the M-4 motorway between London and Bristol; in Germany, economic growth has shifted from the traditional centers of industry in the Ruhr and Saar regions to new centers of high-technology engineering and electronics in the southern states of Hesse, Baden-Wurttemberg, and Bavaria. However, no European country has experienced the extraordinary degree of redistribution of population and production that the United States has undergone since World War II.

Populations have moved around less in Europe partly because the European countries have enacted explicit regional development policies designed to counteract uneven development. Britain adopted regional policies in the 1930s to restrain the growth of London and to aid the economies of the industrial north to employ laid-off miners and industrial workers. Britain's regional policies were supported by both Labour and Conservative governments, until the accession of Margaret Thatcher in 1979.[41] Support for regional development policies was even stronger in continental Europe, where programs to move jobs to declining regions were inaugurated in Italy (1950), West Germany (1951), the Netherlands (1951), Ireland (1952), France (mid-1950s), Denmark (1958), and Belgium (1959).[42] The effects of these policies are difficult to evaluate, but in a country like France, which made regional development policy an integral part of national economic planning, there is little doubt that national planners wielding construction controls and powerful incentives were able to disperse jobs and population from Paris to "growth poles" in languishing regions.

The United States has always lagged far behind European social democracies in enacting national growth policies. Some regional development policies were begun in the 1960s (such as the Appalachian Regional Commission in 1962), but these policies did nothing but provide some federal assistance for local economic development efforts. Overall, the United States has never enacted comprehensive regional development policies; "Indeed, in treating the geographical distribution of economic activity and population as a matter of market forces, rather than national planning . . . the United States stands alone among advanced democratic countries."[43]

Though regional development planning has been absent in the United States, public spending has exerted a powerful impact. In particular, the Pentagon budget has induced military-dependent sectors to migrate to the Sunbelt. No other major industrialized nation used military spending so forcefully to relocate economic activity from one region to another.[44]

The Great Depression ended in the United States when government spending for military procurement climbed sharply in 1940 in response to the stunning success of the Nazi blitzkrieg in Europe. As military contracting soared, the War Production Board made a policy decision to spread out defense installations and productive capacity to make bombing and a potential invasion more difficult. The South and West possessed the advantage of favorable weather for aircraft training facilities. Overall, it is estimated that 60 percent of the $74 billion wartime expenditures went into the fifteen states of the Sunbelt at a time when those states contained less than 40 percent of the national population.[45] The metropolitan areas of the South experienced the most rapid growth of any region. World War II pulled the rural poor into the cities in search of relatively well-paid industrial employment, contributing to the rapid urbanization of the South, which had heretofore lagged behind the rest of the country. Between 1940 and 1943, the population of the metropolitan counties of the South grew by 3.9 percent and those of the West by 2.7 percent. By contrast, the metropolitan counties in the upper Midwest grew by only 2.0 percent and the northeastern metropolitan areas contracted by 0.6 percent.[46]

Some cities, most of them located in the South and West, experienced phenomenal growth when people migrated in search of jobs in booming defense plants. Between April 1940 and October 1941, 150,000 people poured into Los Angeles, increasing the city's population by about a third. During the war years, San Diego grew by 27 percent and Wichita, Kansas, by 20 percent.[47] The wartime boom taxed the housing stock, infrastructure, and public services in these cities to the breaking point.

Near the end of World War II, war production began to shift from heavy industry (tanks and guns) to high-technology electronic weapons (missiles, jet airplanes, sophisticated communications systems). The high-tech trend in military weaponry accelerated the shift from older industrial cities to newer Sunbelt cities. The federal government continued its decentralization strategy during the Korean War. In a nine-month period, $15 billion worth of "certificates of necessity" were issued that allowed new plants to be built, largely in the Sunbelt, out of untaxed profits.[48] During the Cold War, military spending remained high and most of it went to the Sunbelt. One study showed a "definite regional shift" from the Northeast to the Sunbelt between 1950 and 1976 in the awarding of defense contracts.[49]

During that period, the number of defense employees in the nation increased by more than 35 percent but fell by 3 percent in the sixteen northeastern and upper midwestern states.[50] By 1975 the defense budget contributed only 3.8 percent to personal incomes in the Northeast, compared to 8.8 percent in the Sunbelt.[51]

Defense spending shifted to the Sunbelt not only because the region was an efficient location for some kinds of military production. For a long time Democratic senators and representatives from the South were so secure in their seats because of uncontested one-party elections that they were able to control key committees in Congress through the seniority system. The southerners used their powerful positions as committee chairs to steer defense spending and major infrastructure investments, such as dams and water projects, to their states and districts. Perhaps the best example is Mendell Rivers, who represented Charleston, South Carolina, for forty years, from 1930 to 1970. As chair of the powerful House Armed Services Committee, Rivers succeeded in getting the federal government to build in his hometown "an Army depot, a Marine Corps air base, a Marine boot camp, two Navy hospitals, a Navy shipyard, a Navy base, a Navy supply center, a Navy weapons center, a Navy submarine base, a Polaris missile base, two Air Force bases, and a federal housing development."[52] Because senators and representatives from more pluralistic and diverse Frostbelt districts usually served fewer terms in Congress before being defeated for reelection, they were not able to accumulate comparable seniority and congressional clout.[53]

Other federal spending programs also disproportionately benefited the Sunbelt. Extensive federal subsidies for highways favored Sunbelt growth over the Frostbelt, which relied more heavily on railroads and mass transit. Federal grants for new sewer and water systems and for large dams and water projects tended to favor the Sunbelt. Of course, some federal spending programs were biased toward the older industrial cities, such as public employment programs and social welfare spending. The difference is that federal spending oriented to the Frostbelt often came in the form of infusions of urban aid or welfare grants that did little to create sustained economic development. In contrast, federal spending in the Sunbelt created permanent federal payrolls and infrastructure to support whole new industries such as microelectronics. One of the most important ingredients of economic growth is a skilled labor force. The military actively recruited highly trained white-collar workers, engineers, and scientists to areas near Sunbelt military installations: "Every year the Department of Defense pays a number of companies a large sum of money to move college-educated (often at the public expense) engineers and scientists from the Midwest and other regions to the Southwest."[54]

Besides spending, provisions in the federal tax code benefited the Sunbelt over the Frostbelt. In 1954, accelerated depreciation allowances deducted from corporate income taxes provided tax breaks for constructing new commercial and industrial structures but not for rehabilitating old buildings. Accelerated depreciation thus speeded up the flow of capital out of older industrial cities to suburban and Sunbelt locations.[55] Between 1954 and 1980, this subsidy was worth $30 billion in reduced taxes. The Investment Tax Credit, introduced by President Kennedy in 1962, gave a dollar-for-dollar reduction on corporate taxes for new investment in plant and equipment. Thus the federal tax code encouraged companies to abandon older plants in the Frostbelt and build new plants in the Sunbelt. Between 1962 and 1981, this subsidy was worth $90 billion,[56] and in 1982 alone it was worth $20 billion.[57]

The federal tax code has served as a powerful counterbalance to national policies designed to help older cities. For a long time, the federal government funded policies targeted to distressed central cities, but at the same time, through policies such as those written into the tax code, the national government subsidized the movement of jobs and people away from them.[58] A study conducted in the early 1980s of nine tax subsidies that promoted the mobility of investment (such as accelerated depreciation allowances on old plant and equipment and allowances for new equipment) found that they were worth more than twice the total budget of the U.S. Department of Housing and Urban Development[59]—and this was before the massive cuts in HUD funding imposed during the Reagan and Bush administrations.

REGIONAL CONFLICT: SUNBELT VERSUS FROSTBELT

In the 1970s a new regional conflict erupted that *Business Week* dubbed "The Second War Between the States."[60] The conflict was precipitated in part by President Richard Nixon's efforts to shift urban aid to small cities and the Sunbelt through formulas in block grants, such as the 1974 Community Development Block Grant Act. High-profile articles in the *New York Times, Business Week,* and *National Journal* focused public attention on the issue in 1976.[61] The *Business Week* article offered this warning:

> As long as the migration of industry and population was gradual from what was a relatively rich Northeast to what was a relatively impoverished South and Southwest, it helped unify the nation. But within the past five years the process has burst beyond the bounds that can be accommodated by existing political institutions.[62]

One study calculated "balance of payments" for the regions of the country, comparing how much money each region sent to the federal government in taxes to how much it got back in federal outlays. In fiscal year 1975 the South and West together enjoyed a $22.2 billion surplus, while the Northeast and the Midwest suffered a $30.9 billion deficit.[63]

Regional inequities in federal policy spawned the formation of regional lobbying groups. In June 1976 the Coalition of Northeast Governors was organized, and in September 1976 congressional representatives from sixteen states formed the Northeast-Midwest Economic Advancement Coalition (today called the Northeast-Midwest Institute). To counter the lobbying of the Frostbelt politicians, the Southern Growth Policy Board, which had been formed in 1971, stepped up its efforts.[64] Regional disparities in federal spending narrowed somewhat between 1975 and 1979,[65] but Ronald Reagan's election in 1980 shifted the momentum once again to the Sunbelt.[66] His administration increased spending in programs that benefited the Sunbelt (defense and highways) and re-duced spending for programs that benefited Frostbelt cities (mass transit, public housing, social welfare, job training). Between 1980 and 1987, for example, grant programs of special importance to cities were cut 47 percent, from $45.3 billion to $21.6 billion.[67]

Not all areas of the Frostbelt were hurt by the new federal spending priori-ties. Areas along the east coast, such as Long Island in New York and the sub-urbs of Boston, received military contracts because of the presence there of ma-jor universities and science and computer centers. In fact, the "Massachusetts Miracle," which Michael Dukakis took credit for in his 1988 run for the presi-dency, was, ironically, stimulated by the Reagan defense buildup.[68] When de-fense expenditures began to fall in the 1990s, some urban areas in the Sunbelt were hard hit. Partly because of cuts in defense spending, California suffered a net loss of half a million jobs between 1990 and 1996.[69] On the whole, however, national spending has heavily favored the Sunbelt for some time.

THE CHANGING POLITICS OF SUNBELT CITIES

The politics of the Sunbelt cities has historically been different from politics in the old industrial cities. Before World War II, many Sunbelt cities were dominated by entrenched political machines based on alliances between machine politicians and conservative business leaders. Tampa, Florida, and San Antonio, Texas, for example, were governed by machine politicians until well after World War II. New Orleans was run by a long-time machine, the Regular Democratic Organiza-tion, until de Lesseps S. Morrison was elected mayor in 1946.[70] These old-style machines were ill-prepared for the rapid growth set in motion by the defense buildup during World War II. After the war, a new generation of political ac-tivists appeared on the scene. In city after city there were "G.I. revolts" in which "bright young candidates marched against corrupt or inept city hall cliques un-der the banner of progress."[71] Informal coalitions of white-collar professionals, business leaders, and growth-oriented city managers and bureaucrats came to-gether to form business-dominated governments in cities all across the Sunbelt.

Political reform and economic growth became the two reinforcing goals of the new regimes. The reformers thought that the best way to accomplish "good government" was to put local government in the hands of people who would be reliably sympathetic to the business community. This wave of reform resulted in nonpartisan, at-large, city manager systems. These regimes favored aggressive annexation to acquire the fiscal resources necessary to provide subsidies to un-derwrite growth. Between 1945 and 1955, San Antonio, Houston, Dallas, Okla-homa City, Albuquerque, Phoenix, and San Jose all adopted reform charters or other significant reforms.[72] These movements, led by such organizations as the

Phoenix Charter Government Committee, the Albuquerque Citizens Committee, and San Antonio's Good Government League, were led by middle- and upper-class, Anglo professionals and business leaders. These regimes were oriented toward investment and growth. Voter turnout tended to be low.

San Antonio produced a typical example of the Sunbelt version of municipal reform. In 1949, A. C. "Jack" White won the mayoralty with the support of good government reformers and the business community. It was not until 1951, however, that reformers put aside their disagreements and voted in a council-manager charter. Subsequently, the Good Government League began endorsing candidates. From 1955 to 1971, seventy-seven out of San Antonio's eighty-one members of the city council were recruited and endorsed by the league. The Good Government League became the functional equivalent of a political party, a "sort of upper-middle class political machine, officing not in Tammany Hall, but in a savings and loan association, whose electoral wonders are impressive to behold."[73]

The Good Government League succeeded in passing a series of bond referenda to finance infrastructure improvements to facilitate San Antonio's growth; for example, by 1986 the league had built a massive 98-mile freeway system within the city limits. It also sponsored urban-renewal clearance and revitalization of the central business district and facilitated the construction of the HemisFair tourism and shopping project on 149 acres southeast of the Alamo. The HemisFair was a classic example of civic boosterism, with local government providing subsidies to a project that was largely planned and operated by the private sector.[74]

THE REACTION AGAINST UNCONTROLLED GROWTH

Though the rapid expansion that Sunbelt cities enjoyed in the postwar period benefited many people, it also entailed significant social costs—from air and water pollution to water depletion, land subsidence (due to pumping of groundwater), traffic congestion, and an overburdened infrastructure such as inadequate schools and sewers. Sunbelt cities are classic "spread" cities, with single-purpose downtowns and low-density residential and strip commercial development. Developers generally find it profitable to build on land at the urban fringe, where a bulldozer can make quick work of hundreds of acres at a time.

Houston is the quintessential sprawled-out "free enterprise city."[75] Giving free rein to developers—which translates into minimal land controls or regulations—Houston enjoyed average growth of 66 percent for each decade from 1950 to 1980, "probably the most sustained for any city in North America."[76] Its local economy was built around oil production and equipment, but it also developed a diverse manufacturing base in nonelectrical machinery, chemicals, and fabricated metal products. For a long time Houston prided itself on being the only major city in the country with no zoning code.[77] But the image of a non-interventionist public sector is false. In fact, governments played a major role in

Houston's growth by investing huge amounts in the ship channel and the Johnson Space Center.

Though governments aggressively built infrastructure, they were not willing to deal with the social and environmental costs of growth. The social costs exacted by Houston's boom economy are legion.[78] Toxic waste spewed forth by the petrochemical industry is a major threat to the environment. In the mid-1980s, William Ruckelshaus, the head of the federal Environmental Protection Agency (EPA), described Houston as one of the worst hazardous waste disposal areas in the nation, with nine major toxic waste dumps on the Superfund list. Industrial waste so polluted water in the Houston ship channel that citizens sometimes were cautioned not to let it touch their skin. Houston also became plagued by water pollution problems due to inadequate sewage treatment. Over 200 small sewage treatment plants, many of them meeting only minimal standards, dumped 50 million gallons of effluent daily into Lake Houston in the 1980s. Fecal coliform bacteria counts were so high that an environmental specialist advised residents not to swim in Lake Houston. Nevertheless, in the mid-1980s, 140 to 160 million gallons of water were drawn daily from the lake and treated for drinking water. Houston's sewer capacity was so inadequate that a sewer connection moratorium was placed on three-quarters of the city. Before a developer could build, the developer was required to obtain a special sewer permit to connect into the existing system. Since the number of permits was fixed by the capacity of the system, acquiring the permits was difficult. Reflecting its free-market image, however, the city allowed unused sewer permits to be bought and sold. Locally, this informal trading, called "poop futures," became a thriving business. In the late 1980s, unused permits, even from cemeteries, could be purchased for $3,000 to $5,000 each.[79]

As a classic low-density Sunbelt city, Houston developed severe traffic problems. Since autos increased at more than twice the rate of the population, highway construction was not able to keep pace with traffic volume. The result was congestion and delays. A mid-1980s study by the Federal Highway Administration found that, of the thirty-seven metropolitan areas studied, Houston had the worst traffic problems. At one point traffic delays triggered a rash of violent incidents involving irate motorists wielding knives and guns, the kind of road rage that spread to other metropolitan areas in the 1990s. Not surprisingly, out of ten cities studied, Houston was found to have the highest per capita gasoline consumption in the nation.[80] In recognition of the severity of the traffic problem, Houston voters approved a 1 percent sales tax in 1978 to improve the bus system and build a light rail transit system. It was not until the 1980s that the city adopted modest restrictions on development in an attempt to improve traffic flow. In 1990 Mayor Kathy Whitmire came out in favor of zoning, and the City Council passed Houston's first zoning ordinance.[81] In November 1993, however, the voters disapproved the ordinance in a citywide referendum (52–48 percent).[82]

Out of many Sunbelt cities that might be cited, Houston is only one example that has become increasingly affected by the costs of rapid urban growth. For example, for decades Los Angeles has been famous for its polluted air. Between

1990 and 1995, it averaged 150.8 days of "unhealthful" air per year, according to the Environmental Protection Agency. During the same period, Las Vegas, the most rapidly growing metropolitan area in the country in the 1980s and 1990s, had the second highest average of unhealthful days (10.2).[83] In 1989 regional officials in Southern California voted to impose severe restrictions on everyday activity in order to reduce air pollution. The plan called for a range of measures, some of them quite radical, including limiting the number of cars per family, raising parking fees for cars that carry only one person, banning gasoline-powered lawn mowers, outlawing the use of liquid fire starter, and requiring that all cars be converted to electricity or other "clean" fuels by the year 2007.[84] Whether it is fully implemented or not, the Southern California air quality plan shows that politicians, under pressure from voters, are willing to take strong measures to address some of the problems caused by uncontrolled urban growth.

Such problems have prompted the mobilization of new constituencies unwilling to defer to the old business-dominated regimes. Concerned about the destructive effects of rapid growth on the quality of life, professionals and the middle classes increasingly broke ranks with the business interests. They supported growth control movements that challenged the accepted orthodoxy that growth is good for everybody. In addition, lower-income inner-city residents demanded that city governments respond to local service needs as well as to the imperatives of regional growth. In short, the business-dominated regimes of the postwar period came under pressure from two movements: the growth control movement and the neighborhood movement.

Growth control has become a national movement, but it started in Sunbelt cities where the costs of runaway growth became obvious long ago. Leaders of the movement advocated such measures as caps on new construction, impact fees (imposed on developers as a way of paying some of the public costs of growth), linkage fees (which require developers to help pay for specific needs such as affordable housing, schools, and day care), and moratoria on new public facilities, such as schools and water systems, to new subdivisions. Growth controls spread rapidly in the 1970s; by 1975 they were in effect in over 300 jurisdictions across the country.[85] A 1973 sample survey of 416 suburbs found that 19.5 percent had enacted growth moratoria in the previous two years and 27 percent had enacted growth limitations, such as placing a limit on the number of new housing units that were allowed to be constructed each year.[86]

The growth control movement first gained momentum in California. Between 1971 and 1986 more than 150 growth control measures appeared on local ballots; fifty measures appeared on ballots in 1986 alone, with three-quarters of them winning.[87] Interestingly, growth controls were pushed hardest in politically conservative areas of southern California. In 1986, over the objections of Mayor Tom Bradley, Los Angeles voters passed Proposition U, which effectively ended most new office construction in residential neighborhoods on the West Side and in the San Fernando Valley.[88] In the same election voters in Newport Beach in Orange County, a bastion of conservatism, defeated plans for a $400 million mixed-use complex overlooking the harbor. The no-growth forces won even though they were outspent in the campaign by $500,000 to $10,000.[89]

Support for growth controls has been strongest in rapidly growing cities, in wealthier cities, and among wealthier individuals.[90] Growth controls have been criticized for driving up the cost of housing and limiting job growth, thus favoring middle- and upper-income residents who already own their own homes.[91] One study concluded that growth controls push average housing prices as much as 35 to 40 percent higher than in communities without growth controls.[92] Nevertheless, over time no-growth and slow-growth movements have sprung up all across the country, and by the end of the 1990s urban sprawl had emerged as a national issue. (We discuss urban sprawl in more detail in Chapter 11.)

THE CHANGING ELECTORATE

Along with the growth control movement in the suburbs, inner-city voters have also been challenging the business-dominated regimes of the Sunbelt. Over the past two decades, African Americans and Latinos have been gaining a voice in the politics of Sunbelt cities. Latinos now constitute the largest minority group in many metropolitan areas of the Sunbelt, and thus their potential political influence is enormous. (For a discussion of recent migration and immigration patterns, see Chapter 6.) African Americans also make up a large proportion of the population of Sunbelt cities: more than 25 percent in Dallas-Fort Worth, Houston, Miami, and Tampa and more than 10 percent in Los Angeles and Denver. The racial and ethnic disparities of Sunbelt cities are at least as extreme as in the older industrial cities of the Frostbelt. As a result, the tensions that have existed in older cities for more than a century have emerged in the Sunbelt.[93]

Television series, such as *Dallas, Melrose Place,* and *LA Law,* long conveyed the impression that the Sunbelt was filled with beautiful, wealthy people leading glamorous lifestyles. Although it is true that white residents of Sunbelt metropolitan areas usually make incomes above the national average and that fewer whites are poor than in the nation as a whole,[94] the gap between the rich and the poor has been greater in the southwestern metropolitan areas than in those of the North.[95] For decades corporations moved South and West to escape higher labor costs in the North and to take advantage of a vast pool of low-wage, nonunionized labor in the Sunbelt. Twelve out of fifteen Sunbelt states have right-to-work laws that allow employers to hire workers in a plant even if they refused to join the plant's union. This helped to discourage unionization and to keep wages low.[96] However, even those parts of the Sunbelt that experienced industrial growth due to low wages, low taxes, and few environmental regulations suffered from deindustrialization, as footloose industries fled to even lower-cost production sites in Third World countries.

Sunbelt cities have traditionally spent less on public health, welfare, and basic municipal services than have the older industrial cities.[97] The problems experienced by African Americans, Latinos, and the poor in Sunbelt cities have been difficult to translate into effective political demands because they have tended to turn out for elections at relatively low rates.[98] Over the years, whites used various methods, both legal and extralegal, to keep African Americans and Latinos from voting. One of the most effective devices was the white primary, which excluded blacks from casting ballots in Democratic primaries. In one-party states like Texas and Georgia this was tantamount to disenfranchisement. In 1944 the U.S. Supreme Court struck down the white primary as a violation of the Fifteenth Amendment of the Constitution.[99]

Other devices continued to be used to dilute the voting influence of blacks and Latinos. Many cities used at-large election districts to deny representation to minority neighborhoods whose votes were overwhelmed in citywide totals. The 1965 Voting Rights Act, however, gave federal judges the power to strike down voting systems when they found that they systematically reduced minority representation. In 1975 the act was extended to Latinos. Both Houston and Dallas were forced to modify their at-large systems by adopting wards that would maximize representation for blacks and Latinos. Likewise, Los Angeles was forced to redraw its ward boundaries. Minority voters helped to pass new city charters that provided for ward-based representation in San Antonio, Fort Worth, Albuquerque, San Francisco, Atlanta, Richmond, and other cities.[100]

Such measures led to a dramatic increase in the number of African American and Latino elected officials. Nationwide, the number of black elected officials increased from 1,479 in 1970 to 7,984 in 1993.[101] African Americans were elected mayor in some of the largest Sunbelt cities, such as Los Angeles, New Orleans, Atlanta, and Birmingham. With about 20,000 Latino immigrants gaining citizenship and the right to vote each year, Latino gains were especially dramatic. Nationwide, the number of Latino public officials increased from 3,128 in 1984 to 5,459 in 1994, almost a 75 percent jump in ten years.[102] Latinos were elected mayor in Miami, Denver, San Antonio, and many smaller cities.

THE FUTURE OF URBAN POLITICS IN THE SUNBELT

A number of scholars have predicted a Sunbelt/Frostbelt economic and political convergence.[103] Economic forces are diversifying the economies as well as changing the demographic profiles of cities all over the country. In the Frostbelt, corporate white-collar employment and services and tourism have become increasingly important to downtown economies. As a result the population composition of older cities has been changing to include a significant proportion of affluent households. At the same time many of the characteristics traditionally associated with older industrial cities—rapid immigration, concentrated poverty, and racial and ethnic conflict—have come to the cities of the Sunbelt. Cities all over the country are now multi-racial and multi-ethnic.

Perhaps reflecting a convergence in politics, the public policies of cities are becoming more alike too. Older industrial cities have moved aggressively to become more "entrepreneurial" in their pursuit of business investment.[104] Many Frostbelt cities have shifted resources away from services and toward developmental programs that subsidize investment.[105] Business-dominated coalitions have come to power in many Frostbelt cities. To reduce the influence of the central-city electorate, a variety of governmental activities have been taken over by private/public partnerships and special-district authorities, which generally derive their revenues from bond issues or user fees. In this way, facilities such as sports stadiums, convention centers, and redevelopment districts can be controlled by political and business elites and insulated from the electorate.[106] Thus it appears that an economic and political convergence is occurring. Cities in every region of the country have been building a corporate services sector and developing an infrastructure to support tourism and recreation. In the process, cities seem to be becoming more and more similar, in their politics and in their physical appearance.

NOTES

1. Bradley R. Rice, "Searching for the Sunbelt," in *Searching for the Sunbelt: Historical Perspectives on a Region,* ed. Raymond A. Mohl (Knoxville: University of Tennessee Press, 1990), p. 217.
2. David R. Goldfield, *Cotton Fields and Skyscrapers: Southern City and Region, 1706–1980* (Baton Rouge: Louisiana State University Press, 1982), p. 192, cited in Rice, "Searching for the Sunbelt," p. 218.
3. Sam Allis, "Regions," *Wall Street Journal,* April 14, 1981, cited in Rice, "Searching for the Sunbelt," p. 218.
4. Kevin P. Phillips, *The Emerging Republican Majority* (New Rochelle, N.Y.: Arlington House, 1969).
5. Prompting the famous headline, "Ford to City: Drop Dead!" *New York Daily News* (October 29, 1975).
6. Kirkpatrick Sale, *Power Shift: The Rise of the Southern Rim and Its Challenge to the Eastern Establishment* (New York: Random House, 1975).
7. "The Second War Between the States," *Business Week,* May 17, 1976.
8. Carl Abbott, *The New Urban America: Growth and Politics in Sunbelt Cities* (Chapel Hill: University of North Carolina Press, 1987), p. 6.
9. Sale, *Power Shift,* p. 11.
10. Bernard Weinstein and Harold Gross, interview quoted in Abbott, *The New Urban America,* p. 4.
11. Bruce J. Schulman, *From Cotton Belt to Sunbelt: Federal Policy, Economic Development, and the Transformation of the South, 1938–1980* (New York: Oxford University Press, 1991), chap. 2.
12. Abbott, *The New Urban America,* p. 22.
13. Quoted in David R. Goldfield and Howard N. Rabinowitz, "The Vanishing Sunbelt," in *Searching for the Sunbelt: Historical Perspectives on a Region,* ed. Raymond A. Mohl (Knoxville: University of Tennessee Press, 1990), p. 224.
14. Ibid., p. 231.
15. William H. Frey, "Metropolitan America: Beyond the Transition," *Population Bulletin* 45, No. 2 (July 1990): 14.
16. Ibid.
17. U. S. Bureau of the Census, *Statistical Abstract of the United States, 1980,* 101st ed. (Washington, D.C.: Government Printing Office, 1981), p. 10; U. S. Bureau of the Census, *Statistical Abstract of the United States, 1992,* 112th ed. (Washington, D.C.: Government Printing Office, 1992), p. 22.
18. U.S. Bureau of the Census, *Statistical Abstract of the United States, 1992,* 112th ed. (Washington, D.C.: Government Printing Office, 1992), p. 22.

19. U.S. Bureau of the Census, *Statistical Abstract of the United States, 1996,* 116th ed. (Washington, D.C.: Government Printing Office, 1996), p. 28.

20. David Rusk, *Cities Without Suburbs* (Washington, D.C.: Woodrow Wilson Center Press, 1993).

21. Timothy Egan, "Urban Sprawl Strains Western States," *New York Times,* December 29, 1996.

22. Rusk, *Cities Without Suburbs.*

23. Phillip J. Funigiello, *The Challenge to Urban Liberalism: Federal-City Relations During World War II* (Knoxville: University of Tennessee Press, 1978), pp. xi–xii.

24. Samuel J. Eldersveld, "The Influence of Metropolitan Party Pluralities in Presidential Elections Since 1920: A Study of Twelve Key Cities," *American Political Science Review* 43, No. 6 (December 1949): 1200.

25. Ibid., p. 1201.

26. John Mollenkopf, *The Contested City* (Princeton, N.J.: Princeton University Press, 1983), p. 83.

27. R. Cohen, "Task for Politicians: Keeping Up with the Votes," *National Journal* (1981): 2037, cited in Robert B. Bradley, "The Changing Political Realities for National Urban Policy in the Eighties," in *Transition to the 21st Century: Prospects and Policies for Economic and Urban-Regional Transformation,* ed. Donald A. Hicks and Norman J. Glickman (Greenwich, Conn.: JAI Press, 1983).

28. Peter A. Lupsha and William J. Siembieda, "The Poverty of Public Services in the Land of Plenty: An Analysis and Interpretation," in *The Rise of the Sunbelt Cities,* ed. David C. Perry and Alfred J. Watkins (Beverly Hills, Calif.: Sage, 1977), p. 185.

29. Lupsha and Siembieda, "The Poverty of Public Services," p. 174.

30. Mollenkopf, *The Contested City,* p. 123.

31. Ibid., p. 131.

32. Kevin Phillips predicted this trend in 1968; see his *The Emerging Republican Majority.*

33. New York Times/CBS News Poll; *New York Times,* November 8, 1984, cited in Gerald Pomper, "The Presidential Election," in *The Election of 1984: Reports and Interpretations,* ed. Gerald Pomper (Chatham, N.J.: Chatham House, 1985), pp. 68–69.

34. "It is the convergence of the interests of the Sunbelt business community and the ideological right-wing that has resulted in the sharpest growth for the Republican party, following the shift of the financial heartland of the GOP South from Wall Street and from downtown Chicago to Houston, Dallas, and Tulsa." Thomas Byrne Edsall, *The New Politics of Inequality* (New York: Norton, 1985), p. 101.

35. Harold Wolman, "The Reagan Urban Policy and Its Impacts," *Urban Affairs Quarterly* 21, No. 3 (March 1986): 311–336.

36. Gerald F. Seib and Alex Kotlowitz, "The Urban Poor Feel Generally Neglected in Presidential Race," *Wall Street Journal,* November 4, 1988.

37. Tom Wicker, "White Flight, Again," *New York Times,* November 18, 1988.

38. For a thorough analysis of the growth of the Sunbelt that emphasizes economic and technological factors, see John D. Kasarda, "The Implications of Contemporary Redistribution Trends for National Urban Policy," *Social Science Quarterly* 61, No. 3 (December 1980): 373–400.

39. Raymond Arsenault, "The End of the Long Hot Summer: The Air Conditioner and Southern Culture," in *Searching for the Sunbelt: Historical Perspectives on a Region,* ed. Raymond A. Mohl (Knoxville: University of Tennessee Press, 1990), pp. 176–211.

40. Kirkpatrick Sale, "Six Pillars of the Southern Rim," in *The Fiscal Crisis of American Cities,* ed. Roger E. Alcaly and David Mermelstein (New York: Random House, Vintage Books, 1977), p. 174.

41. For a brief discussion of British regional policies, see James L. Sundquist, *Dispersing Population: What America Can Learn from Europe* (Washington, D.C.: Brookings Institution, 1975), chap. 2.

42. David Pinder, *Regional Economic Development and Policy: Theory and Practice in the European Community* (London: Allen & Unwin, 1983), pp. 13–14.

43. Sundquist, *Dispersing Population*, p. 241.
44. Ann R. Markusen, *Regions: The Economics and Politics of Territory* (Totowa, N.J.: Rowman and Littlefield, 1987), p. 113.
45. Sale, "Six Pillars of the Southern Rim," p. 170.
46. Funigiello, *The Challenge to Urban Liberalism*, pp. 12–13.
47. Abbott, *The New Urban America*, p. 103.
48. Richard O. Boyer and Herbert M. Morais, *Labor's Untold Story* (New York: United Electrical, Radio & Machine Workers of America, 1977), p. 362.
49. Maureen McBreen, "Regional Trends in Federal Defense Expenditures: 1950–76," in *Selected Essays on Patterns of Regional Change: The Changes, the Federal Role, and the Federal Response*, submitted by Senator Henry Bellmon to the Senate Committee on Appropriations (Washington, D.C.: Government Printing Office, 1977), p. 527.
50. A report issued by the Northeast-Midwest Economic Advancement Coalition, cited in Edward C. Burks, "16 Northeast and Midwest States Find Inequities in Defense Outlays," *New York Times*, September 22, 1977.
51. Richard S. Morris, *Bum Rap on America's Cities: The Real Causes of Urban Decline* (Englewood Cliffs, N.J.: Prentice-Hall, 1978), pp. 148–149.
52. Sale, *Power Shift*, p. 149.
53. Since the early 1970s, exceptions to the seniority rule have been permitted by both parties, and the power of committee chairs has been reduced.
54. Ann R. Markusen, "Regional Planning and Policy: An Essay on the American Exception," Working Paper No. 9 (Center for Urban Policy Research, Rutgers—State University, Piscataway, N.J., July 1989).
55. See George Peterson, "Federal Tax Policy and Urban Development," in *Central City Economic Development*, ed. Benjamin Chinitz (Cambridge, Mass.: Abt Books, 1979), pp. 67–78.
56. Michael I. Luger, "Federal Tax Incentives as Industrial and Urban Policy," in *Sunbelt/Snowbelt: Urban Development and Regional Restructuring*, ed. Larry Sawers and William K. Tabb (New York: Oxford University Press, 1984), pp. 204–205.
57. John F. Witte, "The Growth and Distribution of Tax Expenditures," in *The Distributional Impacts of Public Policies*, ed. Sheldon H. Danziger and Kent E. Portney (New York: St. Martin's Press, 1988), p. 179.
58. For further evidence on the regional bias of the federal tax code, see Roger J. Vaughan, *The Urban Impacts of Federal Policies*, vol. 2, *Economic Development* (Santa Monica, Calif.: Rand Corporation, 1977); Morris, *Bum Rap on America's Cities*.
59. Peter Marcuse, "The Targeted Crisis: On the Ideology of the Urban Fiscal Crisis and Its Causes," *International Journal of Urban and Regional Research 5*, No. 3 (1981): 339.
60. "The Second War Between the States," p. 92.
61. See the five-part series in the *New York Times*, February 8, 9, 10, 11, 12, 1976; "The Second War Between the States," *Business Week*, May 17, 1976, pp. 92–113; "Federal Spending: The North's Loss Is the Sunbelt's Gain," *National Journal*, June 26, 1976, pp. 878–890.
62. "The Second War Between the States," p. 92.
63. "Federal Spending," p. 881.
64. See Markusen, *Regions*, chap. 8. The Southern Growth Policy Board relinquished its federal monitoring activities to the Congressional Sunbelt Council in January 1981.
65. "Neutral Federal Policies Are Reducing Frostbelt-Sunbelt Spending Imbalances," *National Journal*, February 7, 1981, pp. 233–236.
66. For evidence on the Sunbelt bias of direct federal military expenditures during the Reagan Administration, see the data compiled in the *New York Times*, December 20, 1983, cited in Michael Peter Smith, *City, State, and Market: The Political Economy of Urban Society* (New York: Blackwell, 1988), p. 57.
67. Peggy L. Cuciti, "A Nonurban Policy: Recent Public Policy Shifts Affecting Cities," in *The Future of National Urban Policy*, ed. Marshall Kaplan and Franklin James (Durham, N.C.: Duke University Press, 1990), p. 243.

68. David L. Warsh, "War Stories: Defense Spending and the Growth of the Massachusetts Economy," in *The Massachusetts Miracle*, ed. David R. Lampe (Cambridge, Mass.: PERMIT Press, 1988).

69. Egan, "Urban Sprawl Strains Western States."

70. See Gary Mormino, "Tampa: From Hell Hole to the Good Life," in *Sunbelt Cities: Politics and Growth Since World War II*, ed. Richard M. Bernard and Bradley R. Rice (Austin: University of Texas Press, 1983), pp. 138–161; Abbott, *The New Urban America*.

71. Abbott, *The New Urban America*, p. 247.

72. Amy Bridges, "Politics and Growth in Sunbelt Cities," in *Searching for the Sunbelt: Historical Perspectives on a Region*, ed. Raymond A. Mohl (Knoxville: University of Tennessee Press, 1990), p. 2.

73. Robert L. Lineberry, *Equality and Urban Policy: The Distribution of Municipal Public Services* (Beverly Hills, Calif.: Sage, 1977), pp. 55–56, quoting Abbott, *The New Urban America*, p. 139.

74. Our account of San Antonio's business-dominated reform movement relies on Abbott, *The New Urban America*.

75. Joe R. Feagin, *Free Enterprise City: Houston in Political and Economic Perspective* (New Brunswick, N.J.: Rutgers University Press, 1988).

76. Ibid., p. 7.

77. For more on the relatively small size of the local public sector in Houston, see Ted Robert Gurr and Desmond S. King, *The State and the City* (Chicago: University of Chicago Press, 1987), chap. 3.

78. Our discussion of the social costs of growth in Houston relies on Feagin, *Free Enterprise City*, chap. 8.

79. Wayne King, "Houston Spawns a Thriving Underground Market in Sewer Rights," *New York Times*, November 26, 1983.

80. Peter W. G. Newman and Jeffrey R. Kenworthy, "Gasoline Consumption and Cities: A Comparison of U.S. Cities with a Global Survey," *Journal of the American Planning Association* (Winter 1989): 26.

81. Lisa Belkin, "Now That City's Grown, They Plan," *New York Times*, February 10, 1991.

82. Richard Murray, "Houston Rejects Zoning Yet Again," *Urban News* 7, No. 4 (Spring 1994): 1.

83. As reported in Egan, "Urban Sprawl Strains Western States."

84. Robert Reinhold, "Southern California Takes Steps to Curb Its Urban Air Pollution," *New York Times*, March 18, 1989.

85. D'vera Cohn, "Big Is No Longer Beautiful for Many U.S. Communities," *Santa Barbara News-Press*, March 4, 1979, cited in John R. Logan and Harvey L. Molotch, *Urban Fortunes: The Political Economy of Place* (Berkeley: University of California Press, 1987), p. 159.

86. John R. Logan and Min Zhou, "The Adoption of Growth Controls in Suburban Communities," *Social Science Quarterly* 71, No. 1 (March 1990): 122.

87. Mark Baldassare, "Suburban Support for No-Growth Policies: Implications for the Growth Revolt," *Journal of Urban Affairs* 12, No. 2 (1990): 198.

88. Robert Reinhold, "Growth in Los Angeles Poses Threat to Bradley," *New York Times*, September 22, 1987.

89. Charles Lockwood and Christopher B. Leinberger, "Los Angeles Comes of Age," *Atlantic Monthly* (January 1988): 48.

90. See David E. Dowell, "An Examination of Population-Growth-Management Communities," *Policy Studies Journal* 9 (1980): 414–427; Richard Maurer and James Christenson, "Growth and Nongrowth Orientations of Urban, Suburban, and Rural Mayors: Reflections on the City as a Growth Machine," *Urban Affairs Quarterly* 17 (1982): 350–358; William Protash and Mark Baldassare, "Growth Policies and Community Satisfaction: A Test and Modification of Logan's Theory," *Urban Affairs Quarterly* 18 (1983): 397–412.

91. See Bernard J. Frieden, *The Environmental Protection Hustle* (Cambridge, Mass.: PERMIT Press, 1979).

92. Jane H. Lillydahl and Larry D. Singell, "The Effects of Growth Management on the Housing Market: A Review of the Theoretical and Empirical Evidence," *Journal of Urban Affairs* 9, No. 1 (1987): 71; see also M. Bruce Johnson, ed., *Resolving the Housing Crisis: Government Policy, Decontrol, and the Public Interest* (Cambridge, Mass.: Ballinger, 1982).

93. James H. Johnson, Jr., Cloyzelle K. Jones, Walter C. Farrell, and Melvin L. Oliver, "The Los Angeles Rebellion," *Economic Development Quarterly* 6, No. 4 (November 1992): 356–372.

94. U.S. Bureau of the Census, Census of Population, *Supplementary Reports, General Social and Economic Characteristics by Race and Spanish Origin: 1980* (Washington, D.C.: Government Printing Office, 1981), p. 2.

95. Mollenkopf, *The Contested City*, p. 247.

96. Robert Goodman, *The Last Entrepreneurs: America's Regional Wars for Jobs and Dollars* (New York: Simon and Schuster, 1979), p. 42. None of the fourteen Frostbelt states has a right-to-work law.

97. Lupsha and Siembieda, "The Poverty of Public Services in the Land of Plenty."

98. Clifton McCleskey and Bruce Merrill, "Mexican American Political Behavior in Texas," *Social Science Quarterly* 53 (March 1973): 785–798; Susan Welch, John Comer, and Michael Steinman, "Political Participation Among Mexican Americans: An Exploratory Examination," *Social Science Quarterly* 53 (March 1973): 799–813.

99. *Smith v. Allwright*, 321 U.S. 649 (1944). See the discussion in V. O. Key, *Politics, Parties, and Pressure Groups*, 5th ed. (New York: Crowell, 1964), p. 607.

100. Abbott, *The New Urban America*, p. 217.

101. U.S. Bureau of the Census, *Statistical Abstract of the United States, 1996*, 116th ed. (Washington, D.C.: Government Printing Office, 1996), p. 284.

102. Ibid.

103. Theodore J. Lowi, "The State of Cities in the Second Republic," *Fiscal Retrenchment and Urban Policy*, ed. J. P. Blair and D. Nachmias (Beverly Hills: Sage Publications, 1979), pp. 43–54; John H. Mollenkopf, *The Contested City*; Paul Kantor, *The Dependent City Revisited: The Political Economy of Urban Development and Social Policy* (Boulder, Colo.: Westview Press, 1995).

104. Peter K. Eisinger, *The Rise of the Entrepreneurial State: State and Local Economic Development Policy in the United States* (Madison: University of Wisconsin Press, 1988).

105. For evidence of this shift, see Kenneth K. Wong, *City Choices: Education and Housing* (Albany: State University of New York Press, 1990), p. 16.

106. See Roger Friedland, Frances Fox Piven, and Robert R. Alford, "Political Conflict, Urban Structure, and the Fiscal Crisis," in *Comparing Public Policies*, ed. Douglas E. Ashford (Beverly Hills, Calif.: Sage, 1978), pp. 197–225; Todd Swanstrom, "The Limits of Strategic Planning for Cities," *Journal of Urban Affairs* 9, No. 2 (1987): 139–157.

PART III

URBAN POLITICS AND THE FRACTURING OF THE AMERICAN POLITICAL COMMUNITY

C H A P T E R

10

THE POLITICS OF SECESSION: THE SUBURBS

THE GOVERNMENTAL FRAGMENTATION OF AMERICA'S URBAN AREAS

Population movement outward from the urban core is a feature of urban development all over the world. With transportation breakthroughs such as automated rail systems and the automobile, urban areas in the advanced Western countries have been spreading out for at least a century.[1] There are, however, several characteristics that set the experience in the United States apart. Virtually all of America's metropolitan areas contain vast tracts of detached, single-family homes with large yards. No other nation matches the United States in the degree of urban sprawl—even in Canada, for example, which has experienced extensive suburbanization, population densities are about twice that of American cities.[2] Americans drive further to work than people in other countries, and commuting distances have steadily increased.[3] Urban commuters in the United States consume about four times as much gasoline per capita as do commuters in European cities.[4]

In the United States, high-rise, multiunit buildings are equated with the central city, and only recently have townhouses and apartment buildings become common in the suburbs. Partially reflecting housing styles and the cost of housing, the incomes of urban dwellers tend to rise as the distance from the central city increases. A disproportionate number of poor people are clustered in older, decayed neighborhoods, while more affluent people tend to live farther out in newer subdivisions. This is not the case in most other countries, where the wealthiest people continue to live in fashionable neighborhoods in the historic cities, with middle-class areas often located nearby. In Paris, Rome, Barcelona, Vienna, Rio de Janeiro, Mexico City, and Tokyo, for example, the most exclusive residential areas are near the center; the suburbs tend to be reserved for middle-class families that cannot afford to live in the most exclusive areas, and for the working-class and the poor.

The differences between core cities and suburbs are often more extreme in the United States than elsewhere. Even in Britain, whose settlement pattern most closely resembles that of the United States, central cities tend to hold both the poor and a significant number of affluent people. The contrast between New York and London is revealing: "In contrast to New York the emergent pattern [in London] was not one of a succession of waves of immigrants arriving at the center and driving the previous ethnically distinct waves outwards, but, rather, a continuous process of inflow from around Britain, into available space both in the inner areas and newly developing suburbs."[5] In comparison to other nations, it would be accurate to regard the American pattern as not only exceptional but even peculiar.

Clearly, however, what makes the United States unique is not only the extent of its urban sprawl, but the fact that most of its urban population lives within jurisdictions that are separate from the central cities. In other countries, central cities are generally much larger. In addition, suburbs are usually components of regional governmental authorities that distribute resources and services to all urban residents within a region. In contrast, American suburbs are autonomous governmental units that make taxation, spending, and land use decisions independently from one another. Throughout the twentieth century, local governments have proliferated outside the older central cities. By 1992, there were 85,006 local governments in the United States.[6] This made the "degree of governmental fragmentation in the United States . . . unique among the urban-industrial societies."[7]

Governmental fragmentation is central to the character of American urban politics because it helps to stratify people by class, status, ethnicity, and race. The fact that income, ethnic, and racial groups are segregated is certainly not unique to the United States. What makes the U.S. pattern different is the close relationship between patterns of residential segregation and political boundaries. Governmental fragmentation has nurtured an "enclave consciousness" that is expressed in efforts by the affluent to withdraw from the rest of the urban community.[8]

Even before the suburbanization of the twentieth century, the better-off native-born Americans tried to separate themselves from recently arrived immigrants. Residence became a primary indicator of social status. The habit of creating social status by residence bred fears that status would be compromised if "undesirable" racial and ethnic groups invaded the "better" neighborhoods. Spatial separation accentuated class and racial differences. The squabbles among neighborhoods of the nineteenth century translated into conflicts among suburbs and between central cities and suburbs in the twentieth century. Political separation in the form of independent suburban municipalities became a way for the privileged to protect their wealth and status by walling themselves off in their own enclaves. When race became a dominant feature of the political and social life of cities in the twentieth century, the suburbs became even more defensive of their separate status.

THE MOTIVE TO SEPARATE FROM THE CITIES

For wealthy people who fled the industrial cities at the turn of the century, political separation promised an escape from the alleged corruption, anarchy, and immorality of the political machines and their immigrant constituents. Those who fought for the incorporation of suburban towns from late nineteenth-century Boston, for example, based their cause on "the ideal of small town life: the simple informal community, the town meeting, the maintenance of the traditions of rural New England. They held out to their constituents the idea of the suburban town as a refuge from the pressures of the new industrial metropolis." Suburban life could be free from "Boston's waves of incoming poor immigrants."[9]

At the edges of all the big cities municipalities proceeded rapidly to incorporate from the 1890s to the Great Depression. In 1890, Cook County, whose principal city is Chicago, had 55 governments; by 1920 there were 109. Similarly, the number of general-purpose governments in the New York City area grew from 127 in 1900 to 204 by 1920. There were 91 incorporated municipalities in the Pittsburgh area in 1890, but 107 in 1920.[10] During the 1920s, new suburbs were created by the score.

In the first three decades of the century, popular literature exuded an intellectual and sentimental reaction against the city. Cities had few defenders and a host of critics. Academic writers promoted the idea that "our great cities, as those who have studied them have learned, are full of junk, much of it human."[11] A Boston University professor called city life "a self-chosen enslavement" and indicated that "the psychological causes of urban drift are socially most sinister."[12] Cities were thought to nurture every conceivable sort of evil, as evidenced by such titles of sociological research as *The Social Evil in Chicago; Five Hundred Criminal Careers; The City Where Crime Is Play; Family Disorganization; Sex, Freedom and Social Control;* and *The Ghetto*.[13]

A "back to nature" movement, built on a romanticized version of rural and semirural environments, swept the country. Boy Scouts, Campfire Girls, Woodcraft Indians, and other organizations sought to expose children to the healthy influence of nature study. Children's literature was filled with stories of adventure in "natural" settings. Adults, too, were thought to be purified and rejuvenated by visits to the countryside. Bird watching and nature photography became major pastimes. Tourism to national parks boomed, especially after automobiles became more widely available to the middle classes.

Inevitably, the yearning for nature became linked to suburban images. Wealthy urban residents had no intention of giving up the amenities and advantages of urban life. Instead, they attempted a fusion of both worlds—the urban and the rural—in the suburbs. Magazines and newspapers of the day were filled with articles on the advantages of suburban life as an amalgam of city conveniences and rural charm. In 1902, one magazine writer claimed that suburban living could "offer the best of chances for individualism and social cooperation."[14] The next year *Cosmopolitan* carried an article hailing the "new era" of suburban living:

The woeful inadequacy of facilities of communication and transportation which formerly rendered every suburbanite a martyr to his faith have, in great measure, been remedied; and moreover, residents in the environs have now reached the happy point where they consider as necessities the innumerable modern conveniences of the city house which were little short of luxuries in the suburban residence of yesterday.[15]

Advertisements for suburban property just after the turn of the century stressed the presence of springs, orchards, and forests; activities such as bathing, fishing, and shooting; the healthfulness of the environment; and houses that had such modern conveniences as hot water, gas lighting, and telephones.[16] "A Country Home with All City Comforts," promised one advertisement, alongside another that talked of crops of oats and hay, orchards, trees and shrubbery, fruit trees, and other accompaniments of the rural environment.[17] Most of the advertisements carried drawings or photographs of wide expanses of lawn, trees, and meticulously tended gardens.

The shaping of a suburban ideal was closely linked to efforts to form suburban governments that were independent of the core cities. Political separation from the industrial cities, however, was not always easy. Local governments are not mentioned in the U.S. Constitution; legally, they are creatures of the states. In the early part of the nineteenth century, the incorporation of a local government was viewed as a privilege bestowed by state legislatures. In their fights to persuade state legislators to allow them to incorporate their own governments, people who had moved beyond the limits of the industrial cities claimed that smaller governments were closer to the people and were therefore the best possible expressions of democracy.[18]

Gradually, over the nineteenth century, state legislatures made it so much easier for suburbanites to incorporate new towns and cities that incorporation shifted from a privilege to a right.[19] Through general incorporation laws, any group of suburbanites who had migrated beyond the boundaries of the city could, if a majority of them approved, form a separate local government. "By the early twentieth century suburbanites had begun carving up the metropolis, and the states had handed them the knife."[20] By 1930, every state legislature in the country had adopted liberalized incorporation laws which put the decision of whether suburbanites would or would not be annexed by the central city firmly into the hands of those who had already fled the city.

Through much of the nineteenth century, even though many people who moved beyond city boundaries had the option to create new suburbs, they usually sought annexation rather than separation. Some chose annexation in order to receive public services that otherwise were hard to get; others were coerced into joining by the city. Los Angeles, for example, used its monopoly over water supply to force consolidation on neighboring communities, including Hollywood, Venice, Lordsburg, Sawtelle, Watts, Eagle Rock, Hyde Park, Tujunga, and Barnes City. After the Metropolitan Water District was formed in 1927, however, Los Angeles lost its monopoly over water and the courts ruled it could no longer force its thirsty neighbors to agree to annexation.[21] Subsequently, Los Angeles, now the archetype of the fragmented metropolis, led the way in the proliferation of suburban governments through the Lakewood Plan, which enabled suburbs west of downtown Kansas City, where he intended to build and sell top-market residences.

Nichols was different from the typical small-time real estate operator, or "curbstoner," who bought a few small parcels of land on the edge of the city, divided them into lots, and hoped to make a speculative profit. Nichols believed in a scientific approach to land development. In a speech before a real estate convention in 1912, Nichols attracted national attention by criticizing those land developers who went for the fast sale and the quick profit. Instead, he advocated a long-term approach. He shocked his contemporaries by arguing that planning was not only compatible with private profit but could actually increase profits over the long run. As he later put it in a landmark article on suburban shopping centers, "good planning is good business."[33]

Nichols put his principles into practice by developing the Country Club District outside of Kansas City, considered by many at the time the most beautiful suburb in the nation. Nichols appealed to his wealthy clientele with extraordinary aesthetics—he modeled the suburb's shopping center, the first in the nation, on the architecture of Seville, Spain. Nichols also applied the latest in household technology, such as piped gas and electric service, in a period when servants were becoming less common. Nichols's suburban houses promised to provide a secure haven far from the stresses and tensions of city life. Husbands could go off to work in the city secure in the knowledge that their wives and children were safe in the idyllic environment of the Country Club District.

To shape his developments far into the future, Nichols devised the self-perpetuating deed restriction, which required owners to follow requirements laid down by the developer.[34] The deed restrictions specified minimum-lot sizes, minimum cost for houses, setbacks from the street, and even the color and style of houses. And the deeds specified that the houses could only be bought or sold to whites.[35]

Nichols became a prominent national advocate for planned suburban development. He was a leader in the National Association of Real Estate Boards (NAREB), and in 1935 he founded the Urban Land Institute (ULI), which is influential in the housing industry to this day. In his lifetime he saw the private planning he pioneered become public policy through local subdivision regulations, zoning laws, and federal loan guarantee programs.

Nichols' projects were limited to the upper classes. Privately planned suburban development became affordable to typical middle- and working-class families only after World War II. The Levitt family of Long Island in New York pioneered the production of standardized tract housing offered at the lowest possible price. In the late 1930s, Levitt & Sons succeeded as a medium-sized developer of plain tract housing for upper-middle-class families leaving New York City for Long Island, but the company's big break came during World War II when it won contracts to build thousands of houses for the U.S. Navy around Norfolk, Virginia. It is here that the Levitts worked on the mass production techniques that revolutionized home building. Within a few years after the war, William J. Levitt, along with his father Abraham and his brother Alfred, became the largest home builder in the United States.

Unlike Nichols, William Levitt did not set out to build homes or to build communities; he simply drifted into building houses. Caring little for school, Levitt dropped out of New York University after his third year because, as he put it in a *Time* magazine cover story, "I got itchy. I wanted to make money. I wanted a big car and a lot of clothes."[36] In 1936, after passing through several jobs, Levitt and his father decided to build a house on a Long Island lot they had been unable to sell. They made a profit. From this small beginning, Levitt launched his amazing career.

The Levitts quietly began buying up land from Long Island farmers and mass producing inexpensive but well-designed homes. The basic method was to lay a concrete slab for a foundation on top of which were placed preassembled walls and a roof. The Levitts broke down the complex process of building a house into twenty-six operations, each of which was assigned to a separate contractor. Since each contractor did the same job over and over again, it was possible to achieve incredible speed.[37] Levitt avoided unions and used piecework incentives to speed up the process even more.[38] At the Levitt lumberyard, one man was able to cut parts for ten houses in one day.[39] By 1950, the firm was producing one house every sixteen minutes.[40] By preassembling as many components as possible, Levitt reduced the amount of skilled labor necessary on the job site, and by purchasing directly from the manufacturers, he eliminated middlemen's fees. Overall, Levitt was able to cut costs on each house by about 17 percent, which meant that a typical house could be built for about $6,000 rather than the $7,000 it otherwise would have cost.[41]

Between 1947 and 1951 the Levitts converted 4,000 acres of potato farms in Hempstead, Long Island, into "the biggest private housing project in American history."[42] Ultimately housing 82,000 residents, Levittown, as it came to be known, became a huge success. Because of the huge pent-up demand for inexpensive housing following World War II, in the first years people lined up and camped out for days waiting to purchase one of the homes. The basic Cape Cod model sold for $7,990. With federal guarantees for the loan and no down payment required for veterans, an ex-GI could buy a Levitt house for only $56 a month.[43]

Like Nichols, Levitt believed in controlling the market in order to guarantee rising real estate values. Restrictive covenants required the grass to be cut each week (if not done, one of Levitt's men would cut it and send a bill) and disallowed fences (but allowed hedges). Laundry could not be hung out on an ordinary clothesline. In addition, the covenants barred tenants or homeowners from selling to or even allowing their property to be used by blacks. The standard lease for the first homes in Levittown, in which the tenant had an option to buy, contained this language: "The tenant agrees not to permit the premises to be used or occupied by any person other than members of the Caucasian race. But the employment and maintenance of other than Caucasian domestic servants shall be permitted."[44] Levitt argued that economic realities required him to recognize that "most whites prefer not to live in mixed communities,"[45] but clearly he was motivated by more than mere economics; he evicted two tenants who had allowed black children to play in their homes.[46] In 1960, not a single black family lived in Levittown,[47] and even thirty years later only about one-fourth of one percent of its residents were African American.[48]

Architectural and social critics said that the Levitt projects were little more than mass-produced uniformity and boredom, and some writers even imagined the emergence of a suburban personality that conformed to the housing styles. "Levittown" entered the critics' language as an epithet for all mass-produced subdivisions in the suburbs.

In the mid-1950s, Levitt decided to build two more Levittowns, one in Pennsylvania and one in New Jersey. Opened in October 1958 and finished in 1965, Levittown, New Jersey, provided several new features. Fearing that an unfavorable image of sterile uniformity would damage sales, the company offered several different house styles and floor plans. The idea of mixing styles was offered by William Levitt's wife and was implemented by him over the objections of his executives.[49] Levitt did not offer changes from a standardized model to provide more aesthetically pleasing suburban residential areas. His motives were strictly economic: In order to sell houses, he needed to ensure that the houses would continue to be appealing to the aspiring middle class.

Levitt attracted purchasers by other means as well. Long-term financing with low monthly payments was made possible through the firm. He also offered his clientele a preselected community. His firm attempted to exclude people who did not conform to certain middle-class attributes. Prospective customers would be screened, for example, by clothing and appearance. All homes were expressly designed for families with young children. Advertisements stressed that it was a planned community with schools, churches, swimming pools, and parks. In all of these respects, the Levitt company carefully selected the residents of its communities.

Levitt's fortunes began to change in 1968 when he sold his development company to the International Telephone and Telegraph Corporation (ITT) for $60 million in ITT stock. The stock, which he used as collateral for loans, plunged in value. Because of a clause in his sales contract, Levitt was forbidden to renew his building activities for ten years, except in cities where ITT had no interest. Levitt invested $20 million in a project in Iran, but the new government took it over after the 1979 revolution. In 1987, at the age of 80, Levitt was forced to declare bankruptcy and was evicted from his New York City offices.[50]

The careers of Nichols and Levitt demonstrate the power of private developers in shaping the suburbs. Entrepreneurs did not try to satisfy consumer tastes so much as they helped to mold those tastes. Because developers were constrained to specialize, and thus limit, their housing alternatives, segregation on the basis of incomes and lifestyles was a natural result of subdivision development. These observations hold for contemporary suburbs as well. Whether a developer builds luxury single-family homes, townhouses for young middle-class home buyers, or condominiums for singles, the character of the community that results will have already been determined before the first person moves in. Suburbanites can choose their environment before they move, but once they have decided where they are going to live, they "are very largely prisoners of that environment with but little opportunity of changing it."[51]

Selling the American Dream

For some time after World War II, the suburban home, complete with a patio, barbecue grill, and a tree in the yard, occupied center stage in the American Dream. An advertisement typical of the 1950s read:

> Babylon—An early American Waterside Village—Recreated! For the person who has reached that position in life where they desire complete comfort and relaxation. . . .[52]

Most advertisements in the 1950s promised exclusion, social class segregation, and residential status. A "success" theme, designed to appeal to the striving middle class, appears repeatedly in the advertisements, as in this appeal for upward climbers to settle in Birchwood Park, a Long Island suburb:

> When you settle at East Hempstead you are "on the right side of the tracks" in more ways than one. It's the hub of Long Island's most desirable residential section.[53]

Another advertisement labeled one of its home models, "The Cadillac—Split Level Plus. . . . A most worthy addition to the 'Bluebloods of Distinctive Homes.'" For "living on a higher plane," said the builder, "you must get a 'Cadillac'!!"[54] Still another builder pleaded to "Let us show you how to make your most elite dreams come true."[55] Developers touted the features of new developments that would appeal to family-oriented, status-seeking, upward-striving young executives. For example, one subdivision made this appeal to prospective buyers:

> The Cedar Hill Ranch Home, frankly, wasn't designed for the man in the street. There are many homes costing less that ably satisfy his needs. The size and appointments of Cedar Hill were fashioned for the family who considers anything less than the best inadequate . . . Yes, Cedar Hill was definitely designed for the family accustomed to finer things.[56]

The intertwining of social status and racial segregation was often suggested by code phrases, such as "get out of the jungle" of the city.[57]

Starting in the late 1960s, some developers began to promote projects designed for clientele groups other than young, family-centered couples. Around many cities, and especially in Florida, Arizona, and southern California, developers began to construct condominiums and apartments for the growing market of retired and older adults. Naturally, suitable images were required to sell these projects. The following are typical:

> Jefferson Village: The first totally-electric condominium community for people 52 or over. Now that the children have moved out, is your house too large for you? Then consider the comfort of living in a full country apartment, provided for by a full staff of electric servants.[58]

Or,

> Retirement: Where you live it determines how you live it. The "second lifetime" of retirement can be a delight or a delusion. It often depends on where you decide to live it.[59]

By the late 1970s, young singles had joined the elderly as a group targeted for special attention by suburban builders. Over the past two decades, the proportion of the population that is young and unmarried has increased dramatically (just as it has for those over 65). Anyone who has seen television ads for beer would be able to anticipate how builders would attempt to tap into this new market:

> Your move—make it to Woodhollow—pick of the young professionals ... great word association: Woodhollow and Young Professionals. Lawyers ... nurses ... teachers ... engineers ... anyone with success in mind.[60]

And,

> ... for smart young pace setters who like being together ... for professionals who enjoy being adult and young at the same time. It's Cypress Village, where you share much more in common with your neighbors."[61]

The promise often made to young singles, with varied shades of explicitness, was sex and companionship:

> Today's young people are constantly seeking to fill their needs, whether working, playing or relaxing with a special kind of excitement. The Village gives you the opportunity to fill these needs.[62]

Developers took no chances that young people might miss the point of their advertisements, which was the promise of sex and companionship:

> A play pen for kids. Big Kids. It's our clubhouse. Top of the knoll. Sort of an adult playground. The kind of place you go with that certain someone. It's roomy and comfortable. A lounge for relaxing ... cocktails and snapping logs in the fireplace. The games we play are rated M.[63]

Enforcing Segregation

Through advertising, home styles, and sales and lending practices, builders, realtors, developers, and financial institutions encouraged racial, social class, and age segregation in the suburbs. They did not trust market forces to sort out various groups into distinct communities. Instead, they took strong measures to ensure that segregation would be the norm.

For the first half of the twentieth century, restrictive covenants were commonly attached to mortgage deeds. When a buyer purchased a house, the deed might come with a covenant that restricted its subsequent sale. Typically, blacks were the chief target, although sometimes Jews and "consumptives" (anyone with tuberculosis) might also be named. By the 1920s, the suburban subdivisions of most major metropolitan areas were blanketed with restrictive-covenant deeds.

The real estate industry accepted as a fundamental law of economics the principle that the value of property was connected to the homogeneity of neighborhoods. From 1924 until 1950, Article 34 of the realtors' national code (circulated to realtors everywhere by the National Association of Real Estate Boards) read: "A Realtor should never be instrumental in introducing into a neighborhood a character of property or occupancy, members of any race or nationality, or any individual whose presence will clearly be detrimental to property values in the neighborhood."[64] In addition, most local real estate boards were guided by written codes of ethics prohibiting members from introducing "detrimental" minorities into white neighborhoods. The textbooks and training materials used in real estate training courses were careful to point out that realtors were ethically bound to promote homogeneous neighborhoods. The leading textbook used in such courses in the 1940s compared some ethnic groups to termites eating away at sound structures:

> The tendency of certain racial and cultural groups to stick together, making it almost impossible to assimilate them in the normal social organism, is too well known to need much comment. But in some cases the result is less detrimental than in others. The Germans, for example, are a clean and thrifty people. . . . Unfortunately this cannot be said of all the other nations which have sent their immigrants to our country. Some of them have brought standards and customs far below our own levels. . . . Like termites, they undermine the structure of any neighborhood into which they creep.[65]

Any realtor found breaking the code by selling to members of the wrong groups was subject to expulsion from the local real estate board. Even brokers who were not affiliated with the national association felt compelled to accept the realtors' guidelines because most of their business depended on referrals.

In 1948, in the case of *Shelly v. Kraemer,* the U.S. Supreme Court ruled that racially restrictive covenants could not be enforced in the courts.[66] Realtors and developers sought a means of continuing their practice of encouraging homogeneous neighborhoods. The device that eventually replaced restrictive covenants was the common interest development (CID), wherein residents not only own their own home but also share in the cost and maintenance of services and amenities held "in common" with other residents. After buying a condominium or home in a CID, the "community" of homeowners are legally bound by a variety of covenants, contracts, and restrictions (CC&Rs). Such rules can be used to enforce the homogeneity of neighborhoods even more effectively than restrictive covenants, with one principal exception—they cannot be used to explicitly sort out buyers on the basis of race, ethnicity, or gender. The incredible number of CC&Rs, however, almost certainly exerts that effect.

The number of CIDs, which include cooperative apartments, condominiums, and single-family housing developments, exploded from fewer than 500 in 1964 to 10,000 by 1970 and to 150,000 by 1992, when 32 million Americans lived within them.[67] CIDs were concentrated especially in the Sunbelt, with California, Florida, and Texas leading the way. All through the Sunbelt, retired people moved in big numbers into gated communities. By 2000 it was estimated that 225,000 homeowner associations would be administering CIDs.[68] In many metropolitan areas they have become so common that new home buyers who do not want to live in one may find their housing options to be severely limited.

In the 1940s and 1950s developers were able to enforce income and social class segregation in the suburbs by building subdivisions of uniform lot sizes and housing cost. Suburbia was virtually synonymous with low-density tract housing, an equation that reflected the developers' success in marketing the suburbs as an escape from the cities. But by the 1960s, this version of the suburban dream began to yield lower profits. Builders found that the market for single houses constructed on individual lots was diminishing. Huge demographic and income groups, such as retirees and young singles and married couples without children, remained as vast untapped markets. The constantly rising price of suburban land meant that developers could only build lower-priced homes if they could achieve much higher densities. Accordingly, the housing industry initiated a campaign to market a revised version of the suburban dream that would include rowhouses and apartment buildings. By the late 1960s the American Society of Planning Officials, the Urban Land Institute, developers, and the Federal Housing Administration (FHA) became sudden critics of the "gridiron" housing tracts and large-lot, low-density development that they had promoted for so long. The CID idea anchored a campaign to convince local governments and consumers that higher density development was compatible with the maintenance of property values and exclusion.[69]

For more than half a century, the housing industry peddled the idea that exclusion was synonymous with low-density development. It is interesting how fast the same principle was pressed into service on behalf of high-density development. In a report published in 1963, the Urban Land Institute pointed out that CIDs could achieve exclusion better than any alternative form of development: "Existing as private or semi-private areas they may exclude undesirable elements or trouble-makers drifting in."[70] The FHA agreed to insure loans for condominiums in multiunit buildings in 1961. Two years later the FHA released its first manual explicitly encouraging developers to build planned units that would be governed by homeowner associations. In 1964 the FHA and the Urban Land Institute copublished a 400-page volume describing the history of CIDs and setting forth detailed directions on how to establish CC&Rs and the homeowner associations to enforce them.[71]

Developers, mortgage lenders, and the federal government promoted CIDs as a way to stabilize land uses and property values. Since the early 1970s, the two biggest secondary mortgage purchasers, the Federal National Mortgage Association and the Federal Home Loan Corporation, have insisted on formulating and reviewing guidelines for residential associations before purchasing the loans on properties that will be governed by them. In only two decades the institutional pressures applied by the housing industry and the federal government changed the face of the suburbs.

CIDs are often referred to as the "new walled communities" or "gated communities."[72] For developers, the construction of physical walls and guard-gates allows them to play up themes of security, seclusion, exclusivity—even when these developments contain apartments and condominiums on small lots. Developers establish the rules and regulations and even set up the homeowners' association, before the first property is sold. In this way they are able to promise that all residents will follow closely prescribed norms of behavior and decorum. The covenants and restrictions enforced by residents' associations may dictate minimum and maximum ages of residents, hours and frequency of visitors, color of paint on a house, style and color of draperies hung in windows, size of pets and number of children (if either is allowed), parking rules, patios and landscaping—the list can be staggering in length and detail. Many CID residents no doubt find such regulations comforting. For others, the restrictions become intolerable, as evidenced by the high number of lawsuits filed against community associations.

The walled communities are carefully planned as remarkably segregated environments. Many of them are developed and marketed to appeal to people on the basis of particular shared interests or life conditions. There are, for example, communities that exist exclusively for retirees, golfers, singles, even nudists. Green Valley, Nevada, a massive gated community just outside Las Vegas, is sectioned not only by different architectural styles, but by the cost and size of houses.[73] Each of these "villages" (as the developer calls them), carries the accoutrements of community: a name (Silver Springs or Valle Verde, for example), a community center, a school, a recreational center, and sometimes a park.[74] The segregation between this private city and the outside world is, in effect, embellished by layers of segregation within.

The new gated communities, like the walled cities of medieval Europe, are constructed to keep out those who are regarded as dangerous and different. The promotional literature promises exclusivity, security, and, very often, an extreme segregation. Here, for example, are two ads from an advertising supplement to the *New York Times Magazine*:

> The new Southwinds Ocean House offers apartments of 3,000 sq. ft. with all the advantages of a single family home. A resident manager and security gate ensure carefree living. You may laze by the pool/gazebo, exercise in the lap pool, or stroll the miles of sandy beaches at your doorstep.[75]

> Sailfish Point is an idyll celebrating your achievements. Its numbers add up to a lifestyle without compromise. . . . Jack Nicklaus designed our par 72 membership only golf course to stimulate and challenge but not intimidate. . . . Yachtsmen delight in our private sea-walled marina. . . . The St. Lucie Inlet puts boaters minutes from deep-sea fishing and blue-water sailing. . . . Natural seclusion and security are augmented by a guarded gate and 24-hour security patrols.[76]

It is illegal for housing developers to discriminate overtly on the basis of race. Other kinds of exclusions are, however, legal, and they often enforce a homogeneity that goes beyond that which is stated as the developer's goal. Gated communities have thus achieved a high level of racial segregation. These defended enclaves serve as an efficient mechanism that developers can use to enforce a level of segregation that the housing market itself, if left to operate freely, might never achieve.

SUBURBAN GOVERNMENTS AND ZONING

Developers and the housing industry encouraged and often even required those who moved to the suburbs to participate in a politics of segregation and secession. This style of politics has also been molded by suburban governments. Over the past half century, suburban governments have sprung up literally by the thousands. As we noted earlier, a desire to escape the problems of urban life provided much of the motive for political separation. Zoning became the primary instrument for making the escape. The history of zoning shows that it was born as an exclusionary instrument, and it became popular because it was a subtle, though effective, method of segregating on the basis of income and race. Through zoning, communities have been able to regulate the uses of land within their jurisdictions, making it difficult or impossible for less affluent people to cross community boundaries.

The nation's first zoning law was enacted in New York City on July 25, 1916. By the end of the 1920s, 768 municipalities with 60 percent of the nation's urban population had enacted zoning ordinances.[77] Quick adoption was made possible when real estate interests discovered what a useful tool zoning could be for protecting valuable land from uses deemed less desirable. As promoters of New York's ordinance explained it to audiences around the nation, "The small homeowner and the little shopkeeper were now protected against destructive uses next door. Land in the lower Fifth Avenue section, which had been a drag on the market when zoning arrived, was now undergoing so successful a residential improvement that rents were on the rise. 'Blighted districts are no longer produced in New York City.'"[78] The main claim made for zoning was that it kept land values high by segregating "better" from "inferior" land uses. In state after state, real estate groups and politicians lobbied for state laws enabling cities to zone their property.

New York City's zoning ordinance arose from the fears that fashionable sections of Fifth Avenue might be invaded by loft buildings from the Garment District on the West Side. Indeed, there was abundant evidence that such an invasion was likely to occur. From 1850 to 1900, New York's population increased from 661,000 to 3,437,000. Such growth rewarded speculators and entrepreneurs who had been discerning enough to predict the path of the city's expansion. But it was bothersome, too, for the upper-class residents who had repeatedly established themselves at the city's periphery, only to be pushed out again by encroaching waves of immigrants and businesses.

By the turn of the century the upper class had established a mansion district and an exclusive shopping area on upper Fifth Avenue. They felt threatened by the teeming masses only a few blocks away. The Garment District, characterized by tall loft buildings in which thousands of poorly paid immigrant seamstresses and carters worked, threatened to destroy the exclusive shopping district. A way—a legal way—had to be found to protect Fifth Avenue, which was often described (by the rich) as the cultural fulcrum of New York, "a unique place" in "the traditions of this city and in the imagination of its citizens," "probably the most important thoroughfare in this city, perhaps any city in the New World," an area with a "history and associations rich in memories," "the common pride, of all citizens, rich and poor alike, their chief promenading avenue, and their principal shopping thoroughfare."[79] The Fifth Avenue Association, which employed lawyers to invent this kind of rhetoric, pleaded in 1916 that Fifth Avenue was a special area that should be protected from encroachment. Fifty-four years later, the rationale behind zoning had changed little: "We moved out here . . . to escape the city. I don't want the city following me here," explained a Long Island resident.[80]

Between 1913 and 1916, the Fifth Avenue Association, composed of wealthy retail merchants and landowners, lobbied to exclude tall loft buildings from their district. At first they tried to limit the height of buildings, but soon hit on a more ambitious scheme. In 1916, the Buildings Heights Commission, first appointed in 1913 to investigate the problems of tall buildings in New York City, proposed carving Manhattan into distinct zoned areas to ensure a "place for everything and everything in its place."[81] According to the commission, "the purpose of zoning was to stabilize and protect lawful investment and not to injure assessed valuations or existing uses."[82]

New York's law specified five zones based on different uses and values of land. In the zoning pecking order residential uses assumed first place, even though commercial and industrial land was often more valuable. Next in the hierarchy were commercial business districts, differentiated on the basis of building height (the higher the buildings, the lower the place in the zoning hierarchy). Warehouses and industries were allotted last place.

New York City officials set out to publicize their law, in part to ensure that it would be widely adopted before courts could challenge its constitutionality. "By the spring of 1918 New York had become a Mecca for pilgrimages of citizens and officials" who wanted to enact a similar ordinance. Within a year after passage of the legislation, more than twenty cities had initiated "one of the most remarkable legislative campaigns in American history."[83] Zoning was literally mass produced; most cities copied the New York ordinance and adopted it with few changes. Zoning soon became the chief weapon used by urban real estate interests to protect land prices. By 1924, the federal government had given zoning its seal of approval. A committee of the Department of Commerce drafted the Standard State Zoning Enabling Act, which served as a model zoning law for all the nation's cities.

In 1926, the U.S. Supreme Court reviewed a case from Ohio, *Village of Euclid v. Ambler Realty Co.*, and in a landmark decision declared that zoning was a proper use of the police power of municipal authority.[84] One interesting facet of the case revealed how zoning would be used in the future. Ambler Realty had purchased property in the village of Euclid in hopes that it would become valuable as commercial property. In 1922 the village zoned Ambler's property as residential, which had the effect of instantly lowering its market value. In bringing suit against the village, Ambler argued that Euclid's zoning law had lowered its property values without due process of law. In its decision the Court set forth a classic statement in defense of restrictive zoning, arguing that the presence of apartment, commercial, and industrial buildings undermined residential neighborhoods. There was an assumed hierarchy of uses, which the Court itself enunciated:

> With particular reference to apartment houses, it is pointed out that the development of detached house sections is greatly retarded by the coming of apartment houses . . . the coming of one apartment house is followed by others, interfering by their height and bulk with the free circulation of air and monopolizing the rays of the sun which

otherwise would fall upon the smaller homes, and bringing, as their necessary accompaniments, the disturbing noises incident to increased traffic and business, and the occupation, by means of moving and parked automobiles, of larger portions of the streets, thus detracting from their safety and depriving children of the quiet and open spaces and play, enjoyed by those in more favored localities—until, finally the residential character of the neighborhood and its desirability as a place of detached residences is utterly destroyed.[85]

In its decision the court ruled that separating residential from other land uses was a legitimate use of the city's police power to promote the order, safety, and well-being of its citizens.

Zoning became popular at the same time that well-to-do suburbs proliferated around the large cities—Beverly Hills, Glendale, and a multitude of other communities outside Los Angeles; Cleveland Heights, Shaker Heights, Garfield Heights outside Cleveland; and Oak Park, Elmwood Park, and Park Ridge outside Chicago. It is easy to understand why such communities liked the zoning concept. The possibility that the poor might disperse throughout metropolitan areas threatened people living in exclusive neighborhoods, both in central cities and in suburbs. From its inception, zoning became the legal means to ensure what informal social class barriers or the housing market might not have been able to achieve—the exclusion of the inner-city Great Unwashed.

To accomplish this separation, restrictive residential zoning attempted to exclude apartments, to set minimum lot sizes, or to stop new construction altogether. Apartments in the suburbs represented the possibility of class, lifestyle, or racial changes. The residential character of a tree-lined, curved-street subdivision with individual homes set well back seemed to be threatened by apartment buildings. "We don't want this kind of trash in our neighborhood" was an attitude applied even to luxury apartments. Apartments symbolized the coming to suburbia of city problems:

> The apartment in general, and the high-rise apartment in particular, are seen as harbingers of urbanization, and their visibly higher densities appear to undermine the rationale for the development of the suburbs, which includes a reaction against the city and everything for which its stands. This is particularly significant, since the association is strong in suburbia between the visual characteristics of the city and what are perceived to be its social characteristics.[86]

The residents of many suburban communities became deeply concerned when apartment projects were proposed. For example, an executive living in Westport, an exclusive suburb in Connecticut, exclaimed, "Thank god we still have a system that rewards accomplishment, and that we can live in places where we want to live, without having apartments and the scum of the city pushed on us."[87] Most suburbs excluded the building of apartments entirely. In the 1970s, over 99 percent of undeveloped land zoned residential in the New York region excluded apartments.[88] Although this did not mean apartments could not be constructed, it did require apartment builders to secure zoning variances, which maximized the chances for opposition.[89]

Suburban governments also attempted, in effect, to regulate the social class and incomes of people who occupied single-family homes. Subdivision regulations and building codes made developers go through a costly review process that artificially increased the cost of new houses and gave local residents an opportunity to oppose new developments. But the most common device for raising the minimum cost of new construction was (and is) large-lot zoning. Sometimes the regulations requiring large lots also specified minimum floor-space requirements, the use of particular building materials, and minimum street setbacks. These kinds of regulations raised the cost for the home buyer, and thus helped to protect an exclusive area.

Large-lot zoning is a device to keep out people with lower incomes. In some upper-class communities this means keeping out the middle class; in some middle-class communities it means excluding the working class. A defender of four-acre lot minimums in Greenwich, Connecticut, said that large-lot zoning is "just economics. It's like going into Tiffany and demanding a ring for $12.50. Tiffany doesn't have rings for $12.50. Well, Greenwich is like Tiffany." Large-lot zoning was defended by a New Jersey legislator as a means of making sure "that you can't buy a Cadillac at Chevrolet prices." An official of St. Louis County, where 90,000 acres were zoned for three-acre lots in 1965, indicated that his suburban county welcomed anyone "who had the economic capacity [to enjoy] the quality of life that we think our county represents . . . be they black or white."[90]

Exclusionary zoning often makes room for industrial and commercial investment that will provide more in taxes than it consumes in services. Of course, communities only want certain kinds of industry—industry that does not produce bothersome pollution and traffic. Sy Schulman, a Westchester County (New York) Planning Commissioner, wryly noted that the ideal industry "is a new campus-type headquarters that smells like Chanel No. 5, sounds like a Stradivarius, has the visual attributes of Sophia Loren, employs only executives with no children and produces items that can be transported away in white station wagons once a month."[91] Since the demand for such clean industry exceeds the supply, there is a fierce competition for it. As with other aspects of suburban development, it is the wealthier suburbs that usually win.

THE NATIONAL CHALLENGE TO EXCLUSIONARY ZONING

The essence of zoning is its ability to manipulate the value of land. Thus it cannot be neutral, for it protects some people's investments and costs other people money and opportunity. One measure of its importance is that it is frequently the subject of litigation in the courts. From 1948 to 1963, for example, 52 percent of all litigation in the local courts of suburban New York City involved zoning and land use issues.[92]

As a tool for creating and perpetuating exclusion and privilege, zoning went largely unchallenged in the state and federal courts for nearly half a century.[93] In the 1970s it was challenged in the federal courts, on the ground that it violated the equal protection clause of the Fourteenth Amendment to the U.S. Constitution. Zoning survived, but local governments learned that they could not be too blatant about using it as a tool to preserve racial segregation. Black Jack, Missouri, found this out when the federal courts overturned their city's zoning ordinance after years of litigation.[94]

On June 5, 1970, the Federal Housing Administration (FHA) granted approval to a federally subsidized housing project to be built near the unincorporated Black Jack subdivision in St. Louis County, just north of the city of St. Louis. The project, to be sponsored by St. Mark's United Methodist Church of Florissant and the United Methodist Metro Ministry of St. Louis, was to contain 210 two- and three-story townhouses for middle-income residents. The application for federal funding stated that the project would fill a need in St. Louis County for integrated, moderately priced housing.

On hearing of the proposed project, the residents of the Black Jack area held neighborhood meetings, circulated petitions against the project, and contacted political figures, going so far as to send a delegation to Washington to present petitions to federal officials. They complained that the apartment project would overload their schools, crowd their highways, and threaten the value of their homes. Although cautious about saying so in Washington, the delegates and their constituents were mainly concerned that low-income blacks would move into their community. Before they learned to be wary of reporters, residents freely expressed racist sentiments in their first discussions of the housing project. After attending a Black Jack meeting in 1971, a *St. Louis Post-Dispatch* reporter wrote, "The most common statement we heard during the meeting in Black Jack was, 'We don't want those people, we don't want another Pruitt-Igoe in North St. Louis County.'"[95] Pruitt-Igoe was the nationally infamous public housing project built in St. Louis during the 1950s, noted for its crime, broken windows, and urine-stained hallways.

Black Jack residents perceived that they could keep blacks out if they incorporated their own suburban jurisdiction. As an unincorporated area of St. Louis County, they were subject to the county's zoning laws, which made sixty-seven acres available for apartment construction within the Black Jack area. In late June 1970, the Black Jack Improvement Association presented petitions to the St. Louis County Council requesting the incorporation of a new city, to be called Black Jack. The proposed boundaries were to include about 2,900 residents, most of them living in recently constructed middle-income housing tracts. On August 6, 1970, incorporation was approved by the county council, thus terminating the county's zoning authority and passing it to the new Black Jack City Council.

The county's decision to allow incorporation reveals much about the fears not only of Black Jack residents but of suburbanites elsewhere in St. Louis County. The Black Jack Improvement Association lobbied throughout the North

County area, linking the fate of Black Jack with that of other communities. Allowing the project to be built, said the association, "could open the door to similar projects being located almost anywhere in the North County area. By stopping this project, you would lessen the chance of one perhaps appearing in your neighborhood."[96] In the face of overwhelming pressure, the county council decided to beat a retreat from a messy situation by approving incorporation, thus washing its hands of the whole issue.

The Black Jack incorporation ignited a national controversy over zoning. In September 1970, the Park View Heights Corporation (the nonprofit housing corporation formed by the original sponsors of the housing project) filed suit in federal court against the new city of Black Jack, alleging that both the city's incorporation and its proposed zoning ordinance constituted an attempt to use its zoning power to circumvent the Civil Rights Acts of 1866 and 1964, the National Housing Act of 1937, and the Fair Housing Act of 1968. In a brief hearing, Judge Roy W. Harper dismissed the suit and on October 20, 1970, the Black Jack City Council adopted a zoning ordinance that excluded multiunit residential buildings. Judge Harper's decision was appealed.

In the months following the Black Jack incorporation, it seemed unlikely that its zoning ordinance would be allowed to stand. Lawton, Oklahoma, southwest of Oklahoma City, had attempted to use its zoning ordinance to exclude apartments, but the federal appellate court for its circuit ruled that municipalities could not use zoning to exclude minorities or the poor unless they could show a nondiscriminatory intent concerning land-use objectives.[97] In the case of Black Jack, this would be extremely difficult. In April 1971 another case gave even more hope to proponents of suburban integration. The U.S. Court of Appeals for the Second Circuit rejected an attempt by the city officials of Lackawanna, New York, to block the building of a black housing subdivision in a white neighborhood.[98] Comments in the editorials of the *St. Louis Post-Dispatch* compared the Lackawanna suit favorably with the Black Jack suit: "The unanimous action indicates that local governments will have legal difficulties if they try to zone out Negroes from white areas. The Lackawanna decision clarifies the fact that misuse of political powers to keep out minority groups is unconstitutional."[99]

The Eighth Circuit Court of Appeals reversed Judge Harper's decision in September 1974. Surprisingly, the court threw out the argument that the Black Jack zoning ordinance was intentionally discriminatory. The court did, however, rule that the ordinance had a discriminatory effect. This ruling appeared to have the potential to overturn zoning laws all over the country. If zoning could be invalidated in every case where the courts found that it had a discriminatory *effect* (even if not a discriminatory *intent*), zoning laws across the country might be invalidated. In June 1975 the Supreme Court refused to review the circuit court's decision, thereby upholding it.

As it turned out, the Black Jack ruling was not much of a victory for the Park View Heights Corporation. By the time the litigation was concluded, the housing program that funded the project had lapsed. Worse, the inflated costs of housing materials made the project infeasible for moderate-income families.

Black Jack eventually paid a $450,000 settlement to the corporation, but the townhouses were never built.

The Black Jack case seemed to be a turning point because the court ruled that plaintiffs were not required to prove that a municipality had adopted zoning with the overt intention of engaging in racial discrimination. Just two years later, however, the Supreme Court backed away from this constitutional standard. In reviewing the zoning ordinance of Arlington Heights, Illinois, which barred a federally subsidized townhouse project from being built, the Court declared that the impact of zoning laws could not be used as the only argument against them; rather, they had to be shown to have been enacted with the intent to discriminate: "Disproportionate impact is not irrelevant, but it is not the sole touchstone of an invidious racial discrimination."[100] The Supreme Court had already made it much more difficult for litigants to challenge zoning ordinances by requiring them to show a "distinct and palpable injury."[101] By 1977, then, the courts had gotten out of the business of reviewing zoning laws, except in the rare case when a community was careless or overly blatant in applying them against blacks or other minorities.

The courts have consistently held that discrimination on the basis of income or class is not prohibited by the Constitution. If suburbs can show that their zoning laws are designed to protect the tax base and the exclusive residential character of the community, even though they discriminate against poor people, the laws will not be declared unconstitutional. In 1971, for example, the Supreme Court upheld an amendment to the California Constitution, passed in 1950, which required that low-rent housing could not be built without prior approval by a referendum of the voters of the city. While clearly biased against those seeking low-income housing, the Court ruled that discrimination on the basis of income was not unconstitutional under the equal protection clause of the Fourteenth Amendment.[102]

NEW JERSEY'S CHALLENGE TO EXCLUSIONARY ZONING

Federal courts have been unwilling to use the U.S. Constitution to break down the walls of suburban exclusion. The states, therefore, are left as the main avenue of action for those who want to challenge local zoning laws. Since a large proportion of state legislators answer to suburban voters, it is unlikely that state laws will be changed to limit what local governments can do. Clearly, any challenges to zoning would have to go through state courts. New Jersey is the best example of both the promise and the pitfalls of such an approach.

In 1970, Mount Laurel, located not far from Camden and Philadelphia, was a mostly rural community. The area contained a small African-American community that had been there since before the Civil War. Quakers had made

Mount Laurel a sanctuary for runaway slaves on the Underground Railroad, and their descendants still resided in the area. Many of them lived in small shacks and converted chicken coops, and when these were condemned by the city of Mount Laurel, the residents feared that they would be forced to move to the slums of Camden. They formed an action committee and applied for federal funds to build a subsidized housing project. In 1970 the committee's proposal was turned down by the local planning and zoning board.

The residents then turned to the courts. They found three idealistic lawyers working for the Camden Region Legal Services who agreed to pursue a case to strike down Mount Laurel's zoning laws, which allowed only single-family homes and specified large lots, large building sizes (a minimum of four bedrooms), and substantial setbacks from the street. In 1972 a trial court found that Mount Laurel's zoning laws excluded housing for poor people and therefore violated language in the New Jersey Constitution that guaranteed equal protection of the law for all persons. On appeal, the New Jersey Supreme Court upheld the decision in 1975, ruling that exclusionary zoning violated the state constitution even when its main intent was economic; thus, it was not necessary for the litigants to prove racial intent.[103] In an important advance, the Jersey court ruled that, in order to meet the constitutional standard, cities had an obligation to meet not just the housing needs of city residents, but, as the court put it, "the municipality's fair share of the present and prospective regional housing need."[104] Further, the court ruled that not only Mount Laurel but all of New Jersey's 567 municipalities had an obligation to provide land uses that would meet regional housing needs. The U.S. Supreme Court subsequently refused to hear an appeal of this decision.

The Mount Laurel decision had ruled that suburbs must provide the opportunity for low-income housing, but they were not required to provide the resources for it. If low-income housing was not profitable, builders would not construct it. It is hardly surprising that little low-income housing was built, even in the communities whose zoning laws had been declared invalid by the courts. In 1982 the new Chief Justice of the New Jersey Supreme Court, Robert N. Wilentz, heard six cases showing that the city of Mount Laurel was ignoring the original trial court's decision.[105] He combined the six cases into one proceeding, and in 1983 the court issued a pathbreaking, unanimous 270-page decision, widely known as Mount Laurel II. The court noted that the town of Mount Laurel had made no real attempt to comply with the original judicial decision: It had simply rezoned 33 of its 14,176 acres, and none of the 515 low-income housing units required to meet the dictates of the decision had been built.[106] In the words of the court, "After all this time, ten years after the trial court's initial order invalidating its zoning ordinance, Mount Laurel remains afflicted with a blatantly exclusionary ordinance. Papered over with studies, rationalized by hired experts, the ordinance at its core is true to nothing but Mount Laurel's determination to exclude the poor."[107]

The justices in Mount Laurel II stated that they would have preferred that the legislature address the problem, but "enforcement of constitutional rights cannot await a supporting political consensus."[108] In order to speed up compliance with its original decision, Mount Laurel II required that municipalities not only rezone land for low-income housing, but also make low-income housing attractive to developers through such devices as tax incentives and subsidies. Second, to encourage builders to pursue lawsuits against exclusionary zoning, the court established "builder's remedies," which allowed developers of low- and moderate-income housing to sue cities that tried to keep them out.

As a result of Mount Laurel II, New Jersey's suburban municipalities were besieged with lawsuits and politicians were increasingly pressured to do something about it. Republican Governor Thomas H. Kean, who won office in 1981, came out strongly against what he called an "undesirable intrusion on the home rule principle." In a 1984 interview Kean stated, "I don't believe that every municipality has got to be a carbon copy of another. That's a socialistic country, a Communistic country, a dictatorship."[109] Kean advocated an amendment to the New Jersey Constitution that places local zoning policy beyond review by state courts. Meanwhile, on July 2, 1985, Kean signed the Fair Share Housing Act, which was designed to move exclusionary zoning cases (at the time there were more than a hundred pending) out of the courts and into arbitration before a nine-member Council on Affordable Housing (COAH), which was appointed by the governor.[110] Cities and towns were given a grace period to achieve their "fair share" housing goals. In actuality, most communities were let off the hook completely. Municipalities were allowed, for example, to allot up to 25 percent of their "fair share" to the elderly, and any city was allowed to transfer up to 50 percent of its fair share obligation to another city in the region (if the receiving city approved), along with the funds to help the receiving town pay for the housing. Older central cities were put in the position of competing against one another for subsidies from suburbs so they could obtain funds to meet the pressing housing needs of their low-income residents. What had begun as an effort to open up the suburbs ended up doing exactly the opposite.

Despite all of the political thunder and lightning, the payoff from the long, drawn-out Mount Laurel process was meager. The New Jersey Supreme Court estimated that the state needed 277,808 units to meet the Mount Laurel guidelines. By May 1990 only about 8,000 housing units had been built,[111] and most of these were moderate-income, not low-income, units. In the town of Mount Laurel, only twelve families had moved into low-cost mobile homes and twelve more had put down deposits on similar units by the late 1980s, and by May 1988, 20 low-cost subsidized condominiums were nearing completion. This was the grand total of low-income housing after seventeen years of litigation and political controversy.[112]

The New Jersey case illustrates the difficulty of changing local land-use practices by using the courts when a political consensus is lacking. Mount Laurel represents the clash between two deeply held American values: equal protection of the law and local home rule. Americans are reluctant to support policies that force powerful middle-class suburban interests to give up their privileges. In an era when the federal government has cut housing subsidies drastically, even if local zoning laws could be successfully challenged, it is doubtful that much low-income housing would be built in the suburbs. If the New Jersey experience offers a lesson, it is that exclusionary zoning is here to stay.

THE COSTS OF EXCLUSION

The governmental fragmentation of America's urban areas imposes costs as well as benefits. For affluent people, the benefits have been substantial. Those living in suburbs with high property values and plenty of business investment have been able to pay lower taxes but at the same time enjoy higher levels of public services than the residents of poorer municipalities. Central cities are consistently disadvantaged in comparison to suburbs, but within suburbs there are substantial variations as well, with the older suburbs bordering the central cities generally being at the bottom. Because wealthier suburbs can be selective about who and what they let in, "the central city becomes the receptacle for all the functions the suburbs does not care to support."[113] These functions range from public hospitals serving primarily the poor to shelters for the homeless. Suburbanites are able to escape the burdens of paying for the infrastructure of the central city even when they use it. Studies in the 1950s and 1960s showed that although suburban commuters used the streets, police, parks, utilities, water, and sewer services of the central cities, these services cost more than suburbanites contributed in user fees, sales taxes, and earnings taxes.[114] A study of the Detroit area concluded that, in 1970, suburban commuters enjoyed a net subsidy of between $7 and $50 per year for a family of four.[115] If services were available in Detroit, suburbanites were less willing to pay for them in their own communities.[116] A 1986 case study of the Pittsburgh area concluded that nonresident commuters cost the city of Pittsburgh 74 percent more than they contributed in tax revenues.[117] These findings seemed to hold for most urban areas: A study conducted in the early 1970s revealed that for 168 metropolitan areas, the cost of central-city services was explained more by the suburban population level than by any other factor.[118]

The fiscal problems of central cities are also made worse by the disproportionate amount of tax-exempt property located within them, a consequence of the fact that cultural and governmental institutions used by all metropolitan residents—churches, hospitals, parks, symphony halls, state office complexes, and historic landmarks—are disproportionately located in them. Because of the regional role of such institutions, the proportion of tax-exempt property in the central cities is about twice as high as in the suburbs.[119] Research such as this reveals the suburbs are dependent on the central cities. They take a large proportion of jobs and they use many of the amenities and services of the central cities. In the symbiotic relationship between cities and suburbs, the city often acts as the host and the suburbs as parasites: "Suburbanites are suburbanites precisely because they desire to be near enough to the city to enjoy its benefits but not near enough to have to shoulder its burdens."[120]

In analyzing the effects of governmental fragmentation, it would be misleading to focus solely on the inequalities between core cities and suburbs. There is a great deal of variation among suburbs as well. The conventional image of suburbia as a homogeneous collection of upper-middle-class white residential enclaves is not accurate. American suburbs are heterogeneous, though that heterogeneity is generally greater among suburbs than it is within any one suburban jurisdiction. There are working-class, middle-class, and upper-class suburbs. Separate suburban governments are advantageous for the rich, but they can become a liability for small jurisdictions that lack a sufficient tax base to finance adequate services. For example, Kinloch, a predominantly black suburb of St. Louis, incorporated in 1948 to gain control of its local schools and to escape harassment from white county police. Since then, the community has been plagued by inadequate streets, sewers, schools, and law enforcement.[121] Similar cases can be found in virtually all large metropolitan areas. The pattern for suburbs surrounding St. Louis is quite typical. The most populous county in the St. Louis urban region, St. Louis County, has ninety-two municipalities. For the six cities shown in Table 10.1, the 1989 median household income ranged from a high of $139,331, in Westwood, to a low of $12,300 in Wellston. Westwood is a community with large-lot zoning and wealthy homes, and more than 99 percent of its residents are white. African-American families make up almost all of Wellston's population. As one would expect, poverty rates, average assessed value of property, and property tax rates are closely related to the wealth of all five communities shown in the table. When property values are low, however, high tax rates do not necessarily buy adequate services.

As the data from the St. Louis area would suggest, the fiscal resources of municipalities are matched closely to patterns of social class and racial segregation. African Americans are systematically disadvantaged because they reside within poorer jurisdictions. A study of Philadelphia's suburbs for the period 1977 to 1982 found that predominantly black suburbs had a per capita tax base that was 30 percent less than the average for white and mixed suburbs; in addition, municipal debt per capita in Philadelphia's black suburbs was almost twice that in mixed and white suburbs. In general, predominantly black suburbs tend to have lower tax bases, higher debts, poorer municipal services, lower socioeconomic status, and higher population densities than suburbs that house white families.[122] A study of 374 suburbs in the New York metropolitan area found that blacks and Latinos of the same socioeconomic class as non-Latino whites typically lived in suburbs that had less tax wealth, lower rates of home ownership, and higher property crime rates.[123]

It could be argued that the differences among suburbs occur simply because of economic forces. According to this logic, the wealth of neighborhoods and of suburbs vary simply because lot size and the size of homes, the age of housing, and the bundle of services and amenities reflect what people can afford. This argument makes sense, however, only if one ignores the complex interaction between housing values and the fiscal health of local government. Obviously, when wealthier

TABLE 10.1

SIX CITIES IN ST. LOUIS COUNTY

City	1989 Median Household Income	Percent of Population			Assessed Valuation per Capita	1993 Poverty Tax Rate[a]
		White	Black	Below Poverty		
Clayton	$44,218	91	3	5	$29,051	.81
Normandy	24,804	46	50	9	5,254	.30
Pagedale	19,985	13	86	23		1.07
University City	32,150	49	48	13	7,369	1.07
Wellston	12,300	7	93	47	3,486	.60
Westwood	139,331	99	1	1	37,050	.06

[a]Dollars per $100 assessed valuation.

Source: St. Louis County, Missouri: *1994 Fact Book* (St. Louis: St. Louis County Department of Planning), pp. 114–116, 120–122.

residents are able to isolate themselves within a governmental jurisdiction, with modest tax efforts they are able to support superior schools and other governmental services that make one area a more desirable place than another. It would be extremely difficult for the fragmentation of governments to persist in metropolitan areas if it disadvantaged wealthier, politically influential people. It continues to exist precisely because fragmentation benefits the privileged. Accordingly, it would be accurate to consider the metropolitan fragmentation of America's urban areas to be a redistribution scheme from the poor to the middle-class and the rich.

NOTES

1. For a comparative analysis of suburbanization in advanced industrial countries, see Donald N. Rothblatt and Daniel J. Garr, *Surburbia: An International Assessment* (New York: St. Martin's Press, 1986); Christopher M. Law, *The Uncertain Future of the Urban Core* (London: Routledge, 1988).
2. Barry Edmonton, Michael A. Goldberg, and John Mercer, "Urban Form in Canada and the United States: An Examination of Urban Density Gradients," *Urban Studies* (1985): 213.
3. According to the 1980 census, the typical American worker traveled 9.2 miles and expended 22 minutes each way in reaching his or her place of employment, at an annual cost of more than $1,270 per employee. See Kenneth T. Jackson, *Crabgrass Frontier: The Suburbanization of the United States* (New York: Oxford University Press, 1985), p. 10. Between 1970 and 1990 commuting distances increased in the United States by 50 percent. See Matthew L. Wald, "How Dreams of Clean Air Get Stuck in Traffic," *New York Times*, March 11, 1990, p. 1.
4. Wald, "How Dreams of Clean Air Get Stuck in Traffic."
5. Nick Buck and Norman Fainstein, "A Comparative History, 1880–1973," in *Divided Cities: New York and London in the Contemporary World,* ed. Susan S. Fainstein, Ian Gordon, and Michael Harloe (Cambridge, Mass.: Blackwell, 1992), p. 37.
6. Bureau of the Census, *Statistical Abstract of the United States, 1996.* 116th ed. (Washington, D.C.: U.S. Government Printing Office, 1996) (Washington, D.C.: U.S. Government Printing Office, 1996), p. 295.
7. Kenneth Newton, "American Urban Politics: Social Class, Political Structure, and Public Goods," in *Readings in Urban Politics: Past, Present and Future,* 2nd ed., ed. Harlan Hahn and Charles H. Levine (New York: Longman, 1984).
8. Sidney Plotkin, "Community and Alienation: Enclave Consciousness and Urban Movements," in *Breaking Chains: Social Movements and Collective Action,* vol. 3, *Comparative Urban and Community Research,* ed. Michael Peter Smith (New Brunswick, N.J.: Transaction Publishers, 1991), pp. 5–26.
9. Sam Bass Warner, *Streetcar Suburbs: The Process of Growth in Boston, 1870–1900* (Cambridge, Mass.: Harvard University Press, 1962), pp. 164–165.
10. Data cited in Robert C. Wood, *Suburbia: Its People and Their Politics* (Boston: Houghton Mifflin, 1958), p. 69, and in National Municipal League, Committee on Metropolitan Government, *The Government of Metropolitan Areas in the United States,* prepared by Paul Studenski with the assistance of the Committee on Metropolitan Government (New York: National Municipal League, 1930), p. 26.
11. Robert Park, Ernest W. Burgess, and Roderick D. McKenzie, *The City* (Chicago: University of Chicago Press, 1925), p. 109.
12. Quoted in Peter J. Schmitt, *Back to Nature: The Arcadian Myth in Urban America* (New York: Oxford University Press, 1969), p. 180; original quotation found in Ernest Groves, "The Urban Complex," *Sociological Review* 12 (Fall 1920): 74, 76.
13. A more complete list of titles can be found in Schmitt, *Back to Nature.*

14. Editorial, *Independent,* February 27, 1902, p. 52.

15. Weldon Fawcett, "Suburban Life in America," *Cosmopolitan* (July 1903): 309.

16. Advertisement in *Country Life in America* (November 1906): 3.

17. Advertisement in *Country Life in America* (March 1908): 474.

18. See Anwar Syed, *The Political Theory of American Local Government* (Clinton, Mass.: Random House, 1966).

19. Jon C. Teaford, *City and Suburb: The Political Fragmentation of Metropolitan America, 1850–1970* (Baltimore: Johns Hopkins University Press, 1979), p. 6.

20. Ibid., p. 31.

21. Gary J. Miller, *Cities by Contract: The Politics of Municipal Incorporation* (Cambridge, Mass.: MIT Press, 1981), p. 12.

22. Ibid.

23. Teaford, *City and Suburb,* p. 18.

24. C. B. Glasscock, *Lucky Baldwin: The Story of an Unconventional Success* (Indianapolis, Ind.: Bobbs-Merrill, 1933), p. 140.

25. Teaford, *City and Suburb,* pp. 18–19.

26. Charles Hoch, "City Limits: Municipal Boundary Formation and Class Segregation," in *Marxism and the Metropolis: New Perspectives in Urban Political Economy,* 2nd ed., ed. William K. Tabb and Larry Sawers (New York: Oxford University Press, 1984), pp. 101–119.

27. Miller, *Cities by Contract,* pp. 49–50. Another good example of an industrial suburb is Teterboro, New Jersey, which in 1977 had only 24 residents, but employed 24,000 nonresidents. Michael N. Danielson and Jameson W. Doig, *New York: The Politics of Urban Regional Development* (Berkeley: University of California Press, 1982), p. 92.

28. Ann R. Markusen, "Class and Urban Social Expenditure: A Marxist Theory of Metropolitan Government," in *Marxism and the Metropolis: New Perspectives in Urban Political Economy,* 2nd ed., ed. William K. Tabb and Larry Sawers (New York: Oxford University Press, 1984), p. 92. The American system contrasts with that of Britain where the central government retained control over the organization of local government. "English law did not allow every race track promoter, tax evading industrialist, or community of teetotalers to create its own community." Teaford, *City and Suburb,* p. 70.

29. Reynolds Farley, "Suburban Persistence," in *North American Suburbs: Politics, Diversity, and Change,* ed. John Kramer (Berkeley, Calif.: Glendessary Press, 1972), pp. 82–96.

30. Robert Wood, "Suburban Politics and Policies: Retrospect and Prospect," *Publius, The Journal of Federalism* (Winter 1975): 51.

31. See Mark Gottdiener, *Planned Sprawl: Private and Public Interests in Suburbia* (Beverly Hills, Calif.: Sage, 1977).

32. The term is taken from Mark Weiss, *The Rise of the Community Builders* (New York: Columbia University Press, 1987).

33. J. C. Nichols, "The Planning and Control of Outlying Shopping Center," *Journal of Land and Public Utility Economics* 2 (January 1926): 22. By concentrating in one location and using leasing policy to determine store "mix," "Nichols created the idea of the planned regional shopping center," Jackson, *Crabgrass Frontier,* p. 258.

34. Gwendolyn Wright, *Building the Dream: A Social History of Housing in America* (Cambridge, Mass.: MIT Press, 1981), p. 202.

35. Mark H. Rose, "'There Is Less Smoke in the District,' J. C. Nichols, Urban Change and Technological Systems," *Journal of the West* (January 1986): 48. Rose adds, "As late as 1917, no more than five Jewish families resided in the district, the result of resales."

36. "Up from the Potato Fields," *Time,* July 3, 1950, p. 70.

37. Ibid.

38. "The Most House for the Money," *Fortune* (October 1952): 156.

39. Jackson, *Crabgrass Frontier,* p. 234.

40. Wright, *Building the Dream,* p. 252.

41. "Up from the Potato Fields," p. 68.

42. Jackson, *Crabgrass Frontier*, p. 234.

43. "Up from the Potato Fields," p. 68.

44. Bruce Lambert, "Levittown Anniversary Stirs Memories of Bias," *New York Times* (December 28, 1997): 14.

45. Quoted in Gans, *The Levittowners*, p. 372.

46. Lambert, "Levittown Anniversary," op. cit.

47. Jackson, *Crabgrass Frontier*, p. 241.

48. Lambert, "Levittown Anniversary," op. cit.

49. Gans, *The Levittowners*, pp. 8–9.

50. Joe R. Feagin and Robert Parker, *Building American Cities: The Urban Real Estate Game*, 2nd ed. (Englewood Cliffs, N.J.: Prentice-Hall, 1990), p. 211.

51. Robert Goldston, *Suburbia: Civic Denial* (New York: Macmillan, 1970), p. 68.

52. *New York Times*, March 22, 1953.

53. *New York Times*, March 22, 1953.

54. Ibid.

55. *New York Times*, January 6, 1962.

56. *New York Times*, October 26, 1952; emphasis in the original.

57. Ibid.

58. *New York Times*, May 26, 1968.

59. Ibid.

60. *St. Louis Post-Dispatch*, April 16, 1972.

61. *St. Louis Post-Dispatch*, August 18, 1974.

62. *St. Louis Post-Dispatch*, July 5, 1970.

63. Ibid.

64. National Association of Real Estate Boards, *Code of Ethics* (1924), art. 34.

65. Harry Grant Atkinson and L. E. Frailey, *Fundamentals of Real Estate Practice* (Englewood Cliffs, N.J.: Prentice-Hall, 1946), p. 34, quoted in Evan McKenzie, *Privatopia: Homeowner Associations and the Rise of Residential Private Government* (New Haven: Yale University Press, 1994), pp. 61–62.

66. *Shelly v. Kraemer*, 334 U.S. 1 (1948). The Court had struck down racial zoning some thirty years earlier in *Buchanan v. Warley*, 245 U.S. 60 (1917).

67. Evan McKenzie, *Privatopia*, p. 11.

68. Ibid.

69. McKenzie, *Privatopia*, pp. 158–164.

70. Ibid., p. 158.

71. Ibid., pp. 163–164.

72. Dennis R. Judd, "The Rise of the New Walled Cities," in Helen Liggett and David C. Perry, ed., *Spatial Practices* (Thousand Oaks, Calif.: Sage Publication, 1995), pp. 144–166.

73. David Guterson, "No Place Like Home: On the Manicured Streets of a Master-planned Community," *Harper's* (November 1992), pp. 55–64.

74. Ibid., pp. 60–61.

75. From a *New York Times* advertising supplement, November 18, 1990, p. 13.

76. Ibid.

77. Seymour I. Toll, *Zoned America* (New York: Grossman, 1969), p. 193.

78. Ibid., p. 197.

79. Ibid., p. 159.

80. Quoted in Michael N. Danielson, *The Politics of Exclusion* (New York: Columbia University Press, 1976), p. 54.

81. Toll, *Zoned America*, p. 183.

82. Ibid., pp. 182–183.

83. Ibid., p. 187.

84. "Police power" refers to the implied powers of government to adopt and enforce laws necessary for preserving and protecting the immediate health and welfare of citizens. The meaning of this is, of course, subject to a wide variety of interpretations.

85. *Village of Euclid v. Ambler Realty Co.*, 272 U.S. 365, 47 S.Ct. 114, 71 L. Ed. 303 (1926).

86. Quoted in Danielson, *The Politics of Exclusion*, pp. 53–54.

87. "The End of the Exurban Dream," *New York Times*, December 13, 1976.

88. Danielson, *The Politics of Exclusion*, p. 53.

89. Because of the fears concerning apartment developments, the planning process involving their construction was complicated, requiring petitions for zoning variances, public hearings, and lengthy review proceedings. For an excellent account of these complexities, see Daniel R. Mandelker, *The Zoning Dilemma: A Legal Strategy for Urban Change* (Indianapolis, Ind.: Bobbs-Merrill, 1971).

90. Quoted in Danielson, *The Politics of Exclusion*, p. 60.

91. Quoted in Merrill Folson, "Westchester Finds Influx of Business a Worry," *New York Times*, April 18, 1967; cited in Danielson and Doig, *New York*, p. 90.

92. Kenneth M. Dolbeare, "Who Uses the State Trial Courts?" in *The Politics of Local Justice*, ed. James R. Klonoski and Robert I. Mendelsohn (Boston: Little, Brown, 1970), p. 69.

93. A detailed discussion of the legal status of zoning is not included in this section. For further information, the following sources are especially useful: Danielson, *The Politics of Exclusion;* Richard F. Babcock, *The Zoning Game* (Madison: University of Wisconsin Press, 1969); Richard F. Babcock and Fred P. Bosselman, *Exclusionary Zoning: Land Use Regulation and Housing in the 1970s* (New York: Praeger, 1973); Daniel R. Mandelker, *Managing Our Urban Environment* (Indianapolis, Ind.: Bobbs-Merrill, 1971); Randall W. Scott, ed., *Management and Control of Growth*, vol. 1 (New York: Urban Land Institute, 1975); and David Listokin, ed., *Land Use Controls, Present Problems and Future Reform* (New Brunswick, N.J.: Rutgers University, Center for Urban Policy Research, 1975).

94. This account draws on many sources, including articles in the *St. Louis Globe-Democrat* and *St. Louis Post-Dispatch;* Donald F. Kirby, Frank deLeeuw, and William Silverman, *Residential Zoning and Equal Housing Opportunities: A Case Study in Black Jack, Missouri* (Washington, D.C.: Urban Institute, 1972); *Park View Heights Corp. v. City of Black Jack*, 467 F.2d (1972), reversing: 335 F.Supp. 899 (1971); *U.S. v. City of Black Jack*, Civ. Action No. 71; "Confrontation in Black Jack," in *Land-Use Controls Annual* (Chicago: American Society of Planning Officials, 1972); Danielson, *The Politics of Exclusion.*

95. Jack Quigley, *St. Louis Post-Dispatch*, June 15, 1971.

96. Quoted in William K. Reilly, ed., *The Use of Land: A Citizen's Guide for Urban Growth* (New York: Crowell, 1973), p. 90.

97. *Dailey v. City of Lawton*, 425 F.2d 1037 (1970).

98. *Kennedy Park Homes v. City of Lackawanna*, 436 F.2d 108 (1971).

99. Editorial, *St. Louis Post-Dispatch*, April 5, 1971.

100. Quoted in *St. Louis Globe-Democrat*, January 11, 1977.

101. In 1975 the Supreme Court made it more difficult to challenge exclusionary zoning in federal courts by "refusing standing"—dismissing a case on the grounds that the plaintiffs had no right to sue. Those who want to challenge an exclusionary ordinance must prove "distinct and palpable injury"; a suit cannot be based on general injury to those who do not live in the town, but want to live there; see *Warth v. Seldin*, 442 U.S. 490, 1975.

102. See *James v. Valtierra*, 91 S.Ct. 133 (1971) and *Shaffer v. Valtierra*, 402 U.S. 137 (1971).

103. *Southern Burlington County NAACP v. Township of Mount Laurel*, 67 N.J. 151, 336 A.2d 713, cert. denied, 423 U.S. 808 (1975).

104. Quoted in Ronald Sullivan, "Jersey's Zoning Laws Are Upset," *New York Times*, March 25, 1975.

105. Joseph F. Sullivan, "Restless Seeker for Justice," *New York Times*, January 22, 1983; Anthony DePalma, "N.J. Housing Woes Are All Over the Map," *New York Times*, April 17, 1983.

106. Robert Hanley, "After 7 Years, Town Remains Under Fire for Its Zoning Code," *New York Times,* January 22, 1983.
107. *Southern Burlington County NAACP v. Township of Mount Laurel,* 92 N.J. 158, 456 A.2d 390, 410 (1983).
108. Quoted in DePalma, "N.J. Housing Woes."
109. Robert Hanley, "Some Jersey Towns, Yielding to Courts, Let in Modest Homes," *New York Times,* February 29, 1984.
110. 1985 N.J. Sess. Law Serv. 222 (West).
111. Anthony DePalma, "Subsidized Housing Hurt in Ailing Market," *New York Times,* May 15, 1990.
112. DePalma, "Mount Laurel."
113. Wood, *Suburbia,* p. 106.
114. For analyses of the "suburban exploitation" hypothesis, see Amos Hawley, "Metropolitan Population and Municipal Government Expenditures in Central Cities," *Journal of Social Issues* 7 (1951); Harvey Brazer, *City Expenditures in the United States* (New York: National Bureau of Economic Research, 1959); Julius Margolis, "Metropolitian Finance Problems: Territories, Functions, and Growth," in *Public Finances: Needs, Sources, and Utilization,* ed. James Buchanan (Princeton, N.J.: Princeton University Press, 1961), pp. 229–293.
115. William B. Neenan, "Suburban-Central City Exploitation Thesis: One City's Tale," *National Tax Journal* (June 1970): 117–139; Kenneth Green, William Neenan, and Claudia Scott, *Fiscal Interactions in a Metropolitan Area* (Lexington, Mass.: Lexington Books, 1974), pp. 147–206.
116. William B. Neenan, *The Political Economy of Urban Areas* (Chicago: Markham, 1972), pp. 137–138.
117. David Hamilton and Jim Turner, "Fiscal Implications of Suburbanites on the Central City: A Case Study" (paper delivered at the annual meeting of the Urban Affairs Association, Fort Worth, Texas, March 7, 1986).
118. John D. Kasarda, "The Impact of Suburban Population Growth on Central City Service Functions," *American Journal of Sociology* 77, No. 6 (May 1972): 1111–1124.
119. John M. Quigley and Debra Stinson, *Levels of Property Tax Exemption* (Monticello, Ill.: Council of Planning Librarians, 1975), p. 31; see also Gregory H. Wassall, *Tax-Exempt Property: A Case Study of Hartford, Connecticut* (Hartford, Conn.: John C. Lincoln Institute, 1974), pp. 62–64.
120. Robert Goldston, *Suburbia: Civic Denial* (New York: Macmillan, 1970), p. 22.
121. John Kramer, "The Other Mayor Lee," in *North American Suburbs: Politics, Diversity, and Change,* ed. John Kramer (Berkeley, Calif.: Glendessary Press, 1972), pp. 192–198.
122. For citations to this and a substantial quantity of additional literature, see Douglas S. Massey and Nancy A. Denton, "Suburbanization and Segregation in U.S. Metropolitan Areas," *American Journal of Sociology* 94, No. 3 (November 1988): 592–626.
123. John Logan and Richard Alba, "Locational Return to Human Capital," unpublished manuscript, State University of New York at Albany (April 1990).

CHAPTER

11

URBAN SPRAWL AND THE GOVERNANCE OF METROPOLITAN REGIONS

POST-SUBURBIA

Today most urban residents rarely visit the historic city nestled at the geographic center of their region except to play tourist by (for example) going to a ball game or restaurant, the zoo or museum, or hanging out in a festival mall. The edge cities with their office towers, hotels, and restaurants, the megamalls located at freeway interchanges, the subdivisions springing up where fields and forests had recently been—these supply the backdrop for most people's everyday lives. The old urban form, which found a big city surrounded by rank on rank of spreading suburbs, has given way to a new urban form in which "the periphery [is] no longer a subordinate dependent of the center and thus no longer a candidate for the prefix *sub*."[1] The age of suburbia has given way to *post-suburbia*, a metropolitan form characterized by several nodes of activity. In any given day the members of an urban family might commute, shop, and play by going in any conceivable direction from their home. Even at the very edge of an urban area, a new office park or shopping center might spring up, with every service and amenity—even, perhaps, a Starbuck's—found anywhere else. In short, the old concepts of center and periphery have lost much of their meaning.

The post-suburban metropolis has spawned a set of chronic and sometimes vexing problems. For most suburbanites (the term *post-suburbanites* might be justified, but seems awkward), traffic congestion and gridlock are the most irritating consequences of sprawl, followed by a concern about the sheer ugliness of uncontrolled development. But there are other problems as well. Air pollution, the loss of open space and farmland, and a host of other environmental consequences have accompanied sprawl. Though it does not generally register on the radar of most suburbanites, the decline and abandonment of central cities and older neighborhoods necessarily accompanies the relentless spread to the edge.

316

Poorer residents generally inherit older infrastructure and lower tax bases, and in the bargain they unknowingly help to support the infrastructure required for new development. Finally, there is evidence that the economic health of the suburbs may be linked to the economic condition of the central cities. In other words, full-scale abandonment of the urban core may rebound to the disadvantage of all the residents of an urban region, rich and poor alike.

In the late 1990s all of these concerns converged, and urban sprawl blossomed as an important public issue. Scholars, environmentalists, and advocates of the central cities had been trying to sound the alarm for decades, but mostly they played to a deaf audience. Only rarely did the public seem to care about the incredible pace at which new housing subdivisions gobbled up farmland, forest, and open space. Suburbia, after all, seemed to express the American Dream of prosperity and progress. Critics such as the urban specialist, Neal Peirce, called Americans "the champion land hogs of history" because the country's urban areas were growing in land area at a rate four to eight times faster than the growth of the national population. The cost of sprawl, he said, was "frightening" because it brought "despair in the inner cities, environmental degradation, undermining of old neighborhoods and suburbs."[2] For a long time such critics were generally ignored or even greeted with derision, like the deranged prophets carrying signs with the inscription, "The end is near!" Late in the twentieth century, however, several things happened to cause the public to begin to heed some of the alarums.

THE GROWING CONCERNS ABOUT SPRAWL

For sprawl to emerge onto the political agenda, large segments of the public had to experience its effects first-hand and close-up. That began to happen when highway congestion increased to the point that the daily commute ceased to be a mere inconvenience and a headache, and began to become a nightmare. In November 1999, *USA Today*, in a special report on "National Gridlock," offered up one horror story after another. The average commuter's daily experience seemed to be summed up by a Chicago driver's description of a stretch of interstate highway called "the Strangler": "It's not even a traffic jam. It's my enemy. It's my daytime bad dream."[3]

If commuters think that urban highways have become more crowded in the last few years, they are right. In the 1970s there were 61 yards of roadway per vehicle in the United States, but by 1986 this space had shrunk by more than one-third, to 39 yards.[4] The number of vehicles on the roads has increased dramatically. Trucks by the dozen fill rear-view mirrors because they have substantially eclipsed trains for the movement of goods. The number of licensed drivers jumped 65 percent between 1970 and 1997, but registered vehicles increased even more, by 87 percent. Demographic changes accounted for the higher traffic volumes. Though the U.S. population only rose by 32 percent between 1970 and

1997, the number of women in the workplace jumped by 240 percent.[5] As more women entered the workforce and recreational vehicles joined the family car in the garage, two-and three-car families became the norm.

At the same time, cross-commuting gradually replaced trips to the center. By 1980 over 40 percent of all work trips were suburb to suburb, and only 20 percent were from suburb to the central city in the average metropolitan region.[6] Reverse commuting—travel by central city residents to jobs in edge cities or elsewhere in the suburbs—also increased.[7] Because urban transportation networks had not been constructed to facilitate this pattern, gridlock set in, especially around bottlenecks connecting major highways. Traffic engineers define traffic congestion as an average flow below 35 miles per hour. In the decade from 1975 to 1985, the percentage of urban traffic that could thus be classified as congested increased from 41 percent to 56 percent[8]—and this was before the incredible traffic volume of the 1990s. In the fifteen years leading up to 1997, congestion on America's roadways grew by 235 percent. What does this mean for the average commuter? By 1998 a typical motorist could expect to spend 434 hours, or 18 full days, on the road—11 percent more than in 1990.[9] Can it occasion any surprise that incidents of road rage have become a widespread public concern, prompting many state legislatures to enact road rage legislation?

In the first six months of 2000, rising gasoline prices made long commutes an even more pressing issue when prices for a gallon of regular unleaded ratcheted up from about a dollar to close to two dollars. Though most people pointed the finger of blame squarely at the oil cartel, OPEC, or to regulations requiring cleaner-burning gasoline, to a considerable extent commuters had mainly themselves to blame for creating the mismatch between demand and supply. Because of the growing popularity of four-wheel-drive sport utility vehicles (SUVs) and light trucks, the average fuel economy of new vehicles had fallen from 26 miles per gallon in 1987 to 24 in 1999, despite dramatic advances in engine fuel-management technology.[10] The reason for the declining average was that sales of small cars had sagged from one-third of all new-car sales in 1985 to less than one-fourth by 1999.[11] In the place of small cars the highways were clogged by 2 ½-ton sports-utility vehicles, their four-wheel-drive systems destined never to experience a dirt road.

Despite the overwhelming evidence that most people prefer low-density suburbs,[12] a growing popular concern about sprawl became evident by the mid–1990s, and politicians and the media began to jump on the bandwagon. In May 1995, *Newsweek* magazine devoted its cover story to the problems of urban sprawl in New York, Memphis, Miami, Los Angeles, San Francisco, and Washington, D.C. In all of these regions, said the *Newsweek* reporters, sprawl had created "blighted metropolitan landscapes" of strip malls, traffic, and monotonous sameness. In reference to California, they observed that "No wonder they're so sterile—sterility is designed into them! They wrote about "the new American phenomenon, the suburban slum," with aging tract housing interspersed with strip development.[13]

Four years later, in its July 19, 1999 issue, *Newsweek* featured sprawl again, this time declaring that it had become an urgent public issue, part of a "livability" agenda being promoted by affluent suburbanites, suburban politicians, and Vice President Al Gore. The key elements of this agenda, according to *Newsweek*, included "the triple evils of sprawl: air pollution, traffic congestion, and visual blight."[14] Even the conservative *Wall Street Journal* chimed in when it profiled the battle between community groups and developers in the suburbs surrounding Colorado Springs, Colorado. According to the *Journal*, the conflicts in Colorado Springs merely illustrated similar battles occurring in all of the rapidly growing metropolitan areas of the Rocky Mountain West, such as Denver, Salt Lake City, and Boise, Idaho. Always an advocate of an unfettered market, the *Journal* nevertheless noted Boulder, Colorado's efforts to slow growth by the adoption of new regulations.[15] A couple of months later, in January 2000, the *Journal* reported that campaigns against sprawl had set off a political revolution that was toppling pro-growth politicians.[16] Apparently trying to change public sentiment in its urban area, only months before the *St. Louis Post-Dispatch* ran one of a series of articles on sprawl, under the headline, "Urban sprawl is a hot topic." The paper seemed puzzled by the attitude of its readers, observing that "But Missouri's attitude seems to be: What us worry?"[17]

Some politicians joined the media by making sprawl into a big issue. In 1999 *Governing*, a magazine widely read by state and local public officials, devoted two issues and several other articles to the issue of urban sprawl.[18] In January 1997 Democratic Governor Paris Glendening of Maryland promised to fight for a proposed Smart Growth initiative to curb sprawl, and the next year Republican Governer of New Jersey, Christine Todd Whitman shepherded an even stronger bill through her legislature. In the latter half of the 1990s more than half the nation's governors took on sprawl issues.

The heightened interest shown by public officials could be traced, in part, to the mood of the voters. Approximately 200 state and local sprawl initiatives were placed on state and local ballots for the November, 1998 elections. In Ventura County, California, voters overwhelmingly approved several local initiatives creating urban growth boundaries, which were designed to limit new development at the edges of the county's cities and towns. The new regulations were quite tough, specifying that land outside the boundaries of the specified cities could not be rezoned for development until 2020. To ensure that their will would not be overridden by public officials, these laws even took the power to rezone protected land out of the hands of the county's board of supervisors.[19] In New Jersey, voters approved $1 billion to protect about half of the state's undeveloped open land from urban development.[20]

Overall, voters passed 70 percent of the 240 local measures placed on ballots in 1998.[21] For the first time in history, the sprawl issue even began to become incorporated, however tentatively, into national political debates. In January 1999, Vice President Al Gore announced a proposal by the Clinton Administration to spend $9.5 billion to preserve open space, build roads, and public transit, and encourage local communities to plan new schools.[22] In the fall of 1999, as part of its continuing Challenge to Sprawl Campaign, the Sierra Club released its annual ratings of how effectively the states were regulating sprawl.[23] News stories about the report were carried in national and numerous local newspapers. Vice

President Al Gore promised to make urban sprawl a central issue in his campaign. Calling it his "livability agenda," Gore said that the sprawl issue would appeal to people caught in "tidal flows of traffic" who spent too much time trying to get to work and back, at the cost to their family life. According to Gore, "There have been races for governor and mayor all over this country where the voters have made it very clear that this is an issue about which they feel passionately, and I plan in the next 13 months to take this issue to the voters of America."[24] When challenged on the question of whether such a complex issue could be turned into a hot political item, Gore answered, "Give me time." In fact, the issue played no role at all in his presidential campaign. For his part, Republican presidential candidate George W. Bush refused to talk about it, saying that it should be left to state and local governments.[25]

THE CONSEQUENCES OF SPRAWL

The term urban sprawl is often used loosely to refer to low-density residential development at the periphery of urban areas. One leading study published in 1974 defined it as residential density of two dwellings per acre, but a late 1980's study and another conducted by the Environmental Protection Agency in the early 1990s defined it as residential density of three dwellings per acre or less.[26] By such a definition, sprawl is rare in Europe and Asia, where land is more scarce than in the United States and where land-use controls are the norm. In such contexts, urban areas may be expanding outward, but not in such a way as to create the social and political dynamic that characterizes sprawl in the United States: low-density development at the edge of metropolitan regions that consumes huge tracts of land and entails the abandonment of older areas at the urban core.

Because densities are generally low in the suburbs, land is gobbled up at a rate all out of proportion to the population growth of urban regions—indeed, sprawl occurs even in metropolitan areas with steady-state or declining populations! For example, though the New York region's population grew by only 5 percent between 1964 and 1989, the amount of developed land increased by 61 percent.[27] Similarly, from 1950 to 1995 the population of the St. Louis region increased by just 35 percent, but the area of developed land exploded by more than ten times that much, by 355 percent.[28] Why does land disappear so fast even in slow-growth regions? First, families have become smaller and smaller in recent decades because of the increasing number of single-parent families, childless and unmarried couples, and singles. The decline of the "typical" suburban family requires more dwellings for a given population size, and makes many of the single-family houses built only a couple of decades ago obsolete. Second, and despite the declining size of the average family, the size of homes has steadily increased, in step with a desire for more luxuries and amenities. And third, when people move within metropolitan areas, they tend to leave high-

density neighborhoods nearer the urban core for lower-density subdivisions farther out; only a small percentage move in the other direction. In a study conducted in the early 1990s, more than two-thirds of respondents said that they
preferred to live in low-density, single-family neighborhoods than in denser
neighborhoods closer to the central city.[29]

Urban sprawl is associated with a wide variety of serious problems. First,
the infrastructure to support sprawl—new highways, streets, and bridges;
schools; sewer and water systems; street lighting; gas, electric, and telephone
hookups; libraries and parks; the list is long—cost huge volumes of money. Second, sprawl is regarded by many suburbanites as a form of urban blight brought
too close to home. When they moved to the suburbs they thought they would
find less density and more open space, but in recent years many of them have
found it impossible to stay ahead of the subdivision bulldozer. Third, sprawl
has brought with it the decline of the central cities and the abandonment of
neighborhoods in the cities and older suburbs. The concentration of poverty,
racial and ethnic segregation, and the physical dilapidation at the urban core
contrasts sharply with more affluent, newer suburban housing developments
and edge cities. Finally, sprawl is associated with numerous environmental
problems. Thousands of acres of farmland, wetlands, and open space disappear
each year. Runoff from highways, parking lots, and lawns pollutes streams and
rivers; auto and truck traffic spews ozone-depleting and greenhouse gases into
the atmosphere.

Excess energy consumption and air pollution are implicated in global environmental problems. The United States consumes an extraordinarily high percentage of the world's energy and produces a disproportionate share of the
world's pollution. In 1990, with 5 percent of the world's population, the United
States produced an estimated 25 percent of the carbon dioxide emissions in the
world,[30] a principal cause of the greenhouse effect. High energy consumption in
the United States is not due solely to a prosperous economy. European countries
that are as prosperous as the United States consume far less energy per capita.[31]
Unplanned urban sprawl and an overwhelming reliance on the automobile and
truck are major causes of high energy consumption and air pollution. In 1994, 42
metropolitan areas failed to meet national ambient air quality standards for
ozone.[32]

Urban residents in the United States consume about four times as much
gasoline per capita as do urban residents in Europe. Urban sprawl is the basic
reason for this difference. It is instructive to note that in 1995, consumption in
sprawled-out Houston was 567 gallons per capita, compared to 335 gallons per
capita in New York City, where high population density facilitates the use of
mass transit. (In Manhattan, gasoline consumption was only 90 gallons per
capita.)[33] A study conducted for the federal government compared a typical low-
density pattern of suburban development with a high-density planned community composed of a combination of apartments, townhouses, and clustered single-family homes.[34] The authors concluded that the planned community saved
up to 44 percent in energy consumption and reduced automobile pollution by 20
to 30 percent.[35]

The heightened concerns about sprawl does not necessarily mean that effective solutions will be forthcoming. Suburbanites may be troubled by gridlock, the disappearance of open space, and the endless proliferation of new subdivisions, but they are also reluctant to give up their dependence on the automobile or their loyalty to a suburban Republic-in-miniature. Yet it is clear that urban sprawl cannot be curbed without fundamental changes in public policies and governance arrangements. In light of this contradiction, what, if anything, can be done?

The leaders of the Smart Growth movement contend that planned development is the answer to urban sprawl: Growth must occur, but it should be balanced growth, or "quality development" that improves blighted areas, promotes environmental quality, lowers energy consumption through better transportation systems and improved urban design, assesses the cost and need for new public infrastructure, and preserves agricultural, rural and open space.[36] At the heart of the Smart Growth movement is an understanding that all urban development must be seen in a metropolitan perspective. A study of sprawl in California sponsored by the Bank of America as well as by citizens' and environmental groups concluded that "we continue to abandon people and investments in older communities as development leap-frogs out to fringe areas to accommodate another generation of low-density living."[37]

The New Urbanists promote Smart Growth principles such as regional land-use planning but their passion seems focused on the question of how design and architecture can be used to revive community and to reduce reliance on the automobile. Thus, "individual architectural projects should be seamlessly linked to their surroundings"; "the economic health and harmonious evolution of neighborhoods, districts, and corridors can be improved through graphic design codes"; "civic buildings and public gathering places require important sites to reinforce community identity and the culture of democracy."[38]

The third prescription for solving the problem of urban sprawl derives from a movement that is at least eighty years old. The advocates of metropolitan reform have long fought to eliminate the governmental fragmentation of metropolitan areas. In their view, few problems of the suburbs or of the central cities can be solved in the absence of regional governments. Though most of the efforts to achieve metropolitan government have failed, in recent decades cooperative arrangements among suburban governments have been forged to improve service delivery in the suburbs. These modest governmental arrangements preserve local political autonomy, but they make it possible for one of the main characteristics of sprawl—the proliferation of governments—to be partially overcome.

Americans are wedded to the ideals of local government and suspicious of any attempts to interfere in the workings of the marketplace. The culture of privatism favors individual actions over community and cooperation. Even so, history shows that when problems seem serious enough, urban residents are willing to support governmental action. Does this mean that the three movements—Smart Growth, the New Urbanism, and metropolitan reform—will attract political support sufficient to solve the problem of urban sprawl? We try to answer that question in the remainder of this chapter.

SMART GROWTH

Like "sustainable development," Smart Growth has become a popular slogan used to refer to responsible or balanced growth, and like its companion term it rarely is precisely defined. Although it means different things to different people, it is useful to note that to a considerable degree it grew from the concerns of wealthier suburbanites who began to worry that the things they most valued about suburban living were being compromised. As a slogan, Smart Growth was coined to distance its proponents from antigrowth environmentalists. Indeed, Smart Growth advocates increasingly include conservative constituencies that only recently have been won over to the idea that urban development should be directed and planned.

In November 1999, developer John Andrews ran into furious opposition in Loudoun County, Virginia, when he sought approval for his plans to subdivide a cornfield into 69 one-acre lots. He intended to build an upscale housing development so he anticipated no problems, especially in a county dominated by Republican voters. But in the November elections, a new group calling itself "Voters to Stop Sprawl" swept all eight seats on the county's Board of Supervisors. Reading the tea leaves, the planning commission of the tiny town of Hamilton, which held zoning jurisdiction over the new development, did the unthinkable. It voted against it.

This revolt of the affluent against the affluent grew its roots in the same fertile soil found on the margins of every metropolitan area in America. Located 16 miles from Washington, D.C., until the 1980s Loudoun County was dotted with farms and horse barns. By the turn of the century its population had quadrupled, and even though the new residents were prosperous, they brought with them traffic congestion, overcrowded schools, and new subdivisions. Explaining the sudden success of the revolt against sprawl, the newly elected Republican chair of the county board observed, "This wasn't a Republican or a Democrat thing. They did everything out there that the Republican Party should have done, but failed to do."[39]

Even in Loudoun County, Smart Growth carried different meanings. In the part of the county that was already developing, the major issues included the costs of infrastructure and the quality and aesthetics of new development. In the sections of the county that were still mostly rural, the preservation of open space and the character of the landscape dominated the discussion.[40] The issues raised in Loudoun County highlight two impulses of the Smart Growth movement. On the one hand, some of those who first led the suburban invasion into uncharted territory want to pull up the drawbridge. And on the other hand, many of them want to regulate the kind of development that takes place.

Despite the broad support for different versions of Smart Growth, its application across the country is extremely uneven, and is likely to remain so. Unlike European countries, in the United States there is no national land-use policy—nor is there likely to be one in the future. In 1971 Henry M. Jackson, a Democratic Senator from Washington, proposed the Land Use Policy and Planning Assistance Act. It passed the Senate, but narrowly failed in the House. Under its provisions, states would have been required to develop statewide plans intended to direct urban development, influence the location of new communities, and protect the environment.[41] Though the legislation was remarkably vague about what the states should do to accomplish these objectives, the federal government would have picked up 90 percent of the tab. Presumably, the process would have encouraged discussion and built some administrative capacity for overseeing urban development.

When the Jackson bill legislation failed, it guaranteed that in subsequent decades, planned urban development would follow a highly variable course across the country. Nevertheless, advocates of land-use planning continued to hope that some urban areas would require regulated growth. In a 1972 case from Ramapo, New Jersey, that state's high court upheld a town plan that required an 18-year planned sequence of development. Developers appealed the decision to the U.S. Supreme Court, but the justices refused to hear the case; in doing so, the justices established, in effect, that local governments everywhere could regulate development.[42]

Smart Growth goes beyond the municipal and county zoning, building, and subdivision regulations in effect in all urban areas. Planning requirements that add up the usual definition of Smart Growth are metropolitan in scope, and necessarily include such policies as greenbelts and urban development corridors. For example, in Boulder, Colorado, the city and county have taken steps to reduce growth by designating a greenbelt around the city, establishing scenic areas, and refusing to supply public infrastructure or improvements except in areas targeted for growth.[43] Montgomery County, Maryland, has designated three corridors that distinguish between existing communities, fringe growth areas, and rural and agricultural areas, and a timed growth plan has been recommended that would control the rate of development in each area.[44] The idea of different corridors or "tiers" has been adopted in several metropolitan areas, and is being pushed by the land-use specialists of the American Bar Association.[45]

Urban sprawl is encouraged by the fragmentation of governments in metropolitan areas. To keep their bases low and property values high, municipalities adopt restrictive zoning requirements and fight with one another for shopping malls, businesses, and high-end residential areas. Suburbanites are encouraged to move in search of a favored status in school quality, taxes, and zoning regulations. For Smart Growth to work, it must reduce the ability of some municipalities to preserve themselves as islands of affluence. The Minnesota legislature has entertained perhaps more proposals than any other state for curbing the tendency toward polarization among jurisdictions. Bills have been considered that would require all municipalities to accept a "fair share" of affordable housing, pool their tax bases, give up local land-use decisions to a regional planning authority, and regionalize critical public services. The Minnesota case is mostly interesting, however, for what it reveals about the political reaction to proposals to regulate growth through such policies.

In 1967 the Minnesota legislature approved the creation of a Metropolitan Council for the Minneapolis urban region. Originally the council was merely given the authority to review the master plans of local communities, with no authority to penalize local governments that did not cooperate. However, in 1994 a coalition of struggling suburbs joined representatives from Minneapolis and St. Paul in pushing a Metropolitan Reorganization Act through the legislature. The Metropolitan Council for the Twin Cities suddenly became a $600-million regional government that operated sewers and transit and supervised the regional airport.[46] In the same year, the legislature also took a step toward regional land-use planning, when it passed the Metropolitan Land Use Reform Act. The legislation did little—it only protected farmers from public assessments and tax increases that often forced them to sell to developers—but it provided a framework for the future. That future has not been realized, however, in large part because of the passions ignited by proposals that might curb the autonomy of local governments and the activities of developers.

In 1993 a fair-share housing bill passed the Minnesota legislature, but was vetoed by Republican governor Arne Carlson. In its original form the legislation would have allowed the Metropolitan Council to penalize local communities that used their zoning and regulatory powers to stop affordable housing (these communities would lose funds from a local revenue-sharing pool and would be barred from using tax abatements or increment financing for development). Even after all the penalties were removed in an attempt to placate the governor and his allies, Carlson still exercised his veto. As it happens, the governor would not have had to take such action after the 1994 elections, because Republicans won majority control of the legislature and this doomed fair-share housing legislation.

Since the 1970s cities in the Minneapolis region had participated in a regional tax-sharing pool that required each city to place the taxes gained from an increase in the value of commercial industrial growth into a common pool. This tax-sharing arrangement helped curb beggar-thy-neighbor policies (such as tax abatements) that municipalities typically used to lure shopping centers and other businesses. In 1995, new legislation was introduced which would have pooled all municipal taxes collected on homes valued above $150,000. The legislation was defeated. Another much weaker tax-sharing bill, this one completely voluntary, became the lightning rod for a vicious partisan battle. Jesse "The Body" Ventura, the Brooklyn Park mayor and pro-wrestler who would become Minnesota's governor in 1996, tuned up for his future political career by attacking Myron Orfield, the Democratic state representative who had introduced the legislation. Ventura's rhetoric harkened back to the Communist-hunting days of the 1950s: "Representative Myron 'the Communist' Orfield, his latest wealth-sharing strategy, I mean this guy really needs to go to China. I mean I think he'd be most happy there . . . Oh Myron, Myron, Myron. You never realized the communists folded for a reason. You didn't figure it out, did you Myron?"[47] The tax-sharing legislation went down to defeat.

Policies that would reduce inequality between suburbs often provoke an intense reaction like Ventura's. Most battles over such policies have been fought out on local terms, but in years ahead it seems likely that the battle lines will become hardened into national partisan divisions because measures to control sprawl inevitably involve an expansion of governmental authority. The St. Louis region may be a harbinger of things to come. There, Republicans in suburban St. Charles County have objected to the term "urban sprawl," and have asserted that they were simply exercising their "urban choice" when they moved to the suburbs. In this formulation, sprawl is equated with freedom.

Because they require metropolitan-wide cooperation, urban growth boundaries are rare in the United States—only in Portland, Oregon, does one exist that is enforceable by a regional planning agency—but they constitute the purest expression of the Smart Growth movement. In European nations, urban growth boundaries or greenbelts that preserve land from development exist in most urban areas.[48] In England, greenbelts provide a guarantee that new urban development beyond some cities will be clustered at some distance from the major city, like planets around a star. Without such regulations, European urban areas would still be less sprawled than those in the United States, simply because gasoline prices are much higher (in 2000, a gallon of gas cost $5.00 in England and more than $4.00 in France), and mass transit systems are well developed. Even taking these differences into account, however, without land-use controls a significant degree of sprawl would have occurred.

The Portland, Oregon metropolitan region has the only European-style growth boundary in the United States. Because it is drawn around a rapidly growing city, the boundary is easy to see either from the air or from the ground—on one side, there are townhouse developments and subdivisions; on the other, cows graze, grapevines leaf out, and wheat fields ripen. The growth boundary came about as a result of legislation passed by the Oregon state legislature in 1973, which required all local governments in the state to prepare a comprehensive land-use plan and submit its plan to the State Land Conservation and Development Commission for approval. Unlike other metropolitan areas in the state, Portland's spanned several counties. Control over Portland's urban growth boundary was given over to an elected regional government, the Metropolitan Service District, which had been established in 1970. Portlanders soon labeled the new entity "Metro," and in 1992 the name was made official when voters gave it expanded powers.[49]

In most states and metropolitan areas, an effective urban growth boundary would be unthinkable because business organizations, developers, and local governments possess the power to stop the necessary state legislation. Oregon is the only state to approve a growth boundary. Environmental organizations and farmers supplied critical support for drawing a growth boundary around the state's largest city, Portland. Over time, the coalition supporting Portland's boundary has broadened its appeal with the argument that planned growth actually helps to promote local prosperity.[50] The governmental organization that regulates the boundary—Metro—has evolved so that local governments receive its support for valuable public services and improvements. After losing three attempts to overturn the growth boundary (in 1976, 1978, and 1982), even businesses and developers have learned how to accept the boundary because they "know what the rules are."[51]

Since its adoption, no subdivisions or shopping centers have been built in areas outside of Portland's growth boundary. As a result, Portland's urban

growth stops suddenly at the boundary line; on one side of the road new developments fill in the remaining gaps, but on the other, cows graze in meadows,
vineyards sweep across hillsides, and forests crown the hilltops. The subdivisions that normally speckle the landscape at the edges of urban areas are notably
absent. The state government's willingness to override municipal governments
is the key to preserving this kind of pattern. Historically, municipalities in all
states have vigorously resisted attempts to control their land-use decisions, and
most state legislatures and administrative agencies have been reluctant to step
into the fray. Oregon is exceptional in its attitude that "We've had some problems with them [municipalities] and had to whip them into line."[52]

Even in the face of a growing popular reaction against sprawl, in most states
the municipal free-for-all will continue for some time to come. Smart Growth
will spread only if suburbanites can be persuaded that it substantially improves
the quality of life in urban areas. Smart-growth advocates claim that planned
growth would lower the cost of urban infrastructure, that it would improve the
physical environment of the suburbs, and that it would bring economic prosperity to central cities and urban regions. In most urban areas suburbanites will, in
all probability, be persuaded only slowly, but it is important to evaluate the accuracy of these claims.

Several studies have shown that unplanned urban growth requires substantially higher investment in public infrastructure than if there were planned
growth.[53] In general, when infrastructure such as highways, sewers, water lines,
and utilities are supplied in areas with low-density development, costs are much
higher than in high-density areas. In addition, infrastructure costs are driven up
when the existing public facilities in older areas are abandoned. A Smart
Growth advocate has pointed out that in the twenty years between 1970 and
1990, a Maryland county spent $500 million to close 60 schools while opening 60
more, just to keep the schools located in areas where people had moved. He also
cited a study estimating that by 2020 Maryland residents would spend $10 bil-
lion on new roads, sewers, and water systems in newly developed areas. From
this evidence, he concluded that comprehensive planning was necessary to stop
the twin processes of abandonment and new investment.[54]

For most suburbanites, the argument that sprawl drives up the cost of infrastructure is not likely to carry much weight, especially since those costs are
widely distributed, hard to measure, and paid, in large part, by the states and
the federal government. Because financing is so complex, it is difficult to document the often-asserted argument that people in older areas help subsidize the
cost of new development.[55] It is even less likely that suburban residents will
suddenly be struck with remorse that by moving out, they have contributed to
the decay of older cities and neighborhoods. It is possible, however, that suburban residents may pay some attention if an effective case can be made that decay
at the urban center threatens the economic viability of the regions they live
within. Accordingly, this argument has gained much currency in debates over
urban sprawl.

Recently, some analysts have turned the familiar refrain that sprawl brings
"despair to the inner cities,"[56] on its head by claiming that it may ultimately bring

despair to the suburbs. Of thirteen studies conducted between 1989 and 1996, all but one showed that central-city economic performance was associated with the economic performance of suburbs and of metropolitan areas; in addition, studies showed a relationship between greater interjurisdictional inequality and regional economic performance.[57] However, no connection was shown between the degree of concentrated poverty within metropolitan areas and the economic health of suburbs. Aside from the rather technical nature of such studies, it is hard to imagine that most suburban residents will buy into abstract arguments about how their own fate is linked to that of their poorer neighbors. Self-interest tends to be immediate—a lower tax bill, a better school, rising property values—but concern for others tends to be more distant. For this reason, as the Minnesota case illustrates, attempts to implement fair-share housing and tax equalization are likely to become intensely partisan issues wherever they are proposed. But some measures will prove more popular. The revolt against uncontrolled growth in Loudoun County, Virginia, was prompted by a concern that unchecked development was ruining the environment that people had moved to the suburbs to enjoy. Perhaps it is the sheer ugliness of sprawl that provokes intense reaction from affluent suburbanites—a feeling that paradise is being lost. Advocates of the New Urbanism think they have the solution to that concern.

THE NEW URBANISM

The New Urbanism is energized by a diagnosis of a terrible disease—"blighted metropolitan landscapes," "banal places with the souls of shopping malls, affording nowhere to mingle except traffic jams, nowhere to walk except in the health club."[58] The proposed antidote is made up of new transportation networks that would reduce reliance on the automobile, and carefully designed urban communities with harmonious streetscapes and pleasing design features (such as buildings with dormers, gables, and porticos) that integrate home, business, recreation, and community life. By fostering a sense of community in the suburbs, the New Urbanists hope to calm the restlessness that makes people constantly move on to the next subdivision in their search for a suburban Eden.

The alleged disease of the American suburb has long been the subject of commentary. The writer James Howard Kunstler begins his book *The Geography of Nowhere,* with this vivid summary:

> Eighty percent of everything ever built in America has been built in the last fifty years, and most of it is depressing, brutal, ugly, unhealthy, and spiritually degrading—the jive-plastic commuter tract home wastelands, the Potemkin village shopping plazas with their vast parking lagoons, the Lego-block hotel complexes, the 'gourmet mansardic' junk-food joints, the Orwellian office 'parks' featuring buildings sheathed in the same reflective glass as the sunglasses worn by chain-gang guards, the particle-board garden apartments rising up in every little meadow and cornfield, the freeway loops around every big and little city with their clusters of

discount merchandise marts, the whole destructive, wasteful, toxic, agoraphobia-inducing spectacle that politicians call 'growth.'"[59]

In Kunstler's account, suburban residents have learned to live "in places where nothing relates to anything else," a landscape in which daily activities — home, work, shopping, recreation—are pulled apart into large-scale, segregated developments accessible only by automobiles: "The houses are all in their respective income pods, the shopping is miles away from the houses," and schools, malls, and office parks are also set apart, together with their seas of cars glistening on massive parking lots.[60] This version of suburbia might present the image and possibility of open space, but in actuality (in this narrative) human beings are forced to sit in their cars, gridlocked, or find themselves in the embrace of a gated community, school, or shopping mall.

There is an intimate connection between urban decline in older areas and large-scale development elsewhere. Like clear-cutting a forest, a parking lot, mall, or a housing subdivision can most efficiently be built by means of industrial methods; the first step is a bulldozer that removes everything for the sake of progress. Such methods link efficiency and wastefulness in an intimate dance. Urged on by advertising, constant changes in product lines and styles, and the proliferation of disposable packaging, "most consumer goods are destined for a one-night stand."[61] Applied to land and places, such a consumer habit has far-reaching social consequences—"cycling of people through places," a mobility and rootlessness that replaces community with the hope of renewal that comes from moving, "a kind of magic that keeps expectations high."[62] If the new place disappoints, the answer will be found in another move, and still another one after that.

How can suburbs be designed to overcome suburban blight and discourage this constant restlessness? *Newsweek* distilled the lessons of the New Urbanism into a 15-item list: give up big lawns ("the goal of making a walkable community is defeated when houses are spread out on huge lots"), bring back the corner store ("It should still be possible to provide some of the necessities of life within walking distance of many people"), make the streets skinny ("Force cars to slow down"), drop the cul-de-sac ("streets . . . can follow predictable routes and interconnect"), draw boundaries ("imagine how Los Angeles would look today if it had done this [adopt an urban growth boundary] 20 years ago"), hide the garage ("the blank and desolate face of a garage door"), mix housing types ("in Harbor Town . . . the leading recreational activity would be chatting with neighbors . . . ; "set the houses close together"), plant trees curbside ("a canopy over the roadway"), put new life into old malls ("the land they occupy can . . . become the nucleus of a real neighborhood"), plan for mass transit ("Is there any way to get Americans out of their cars and into buses and trains?"), link work to home ("If companies don't want to be downtown, they should . . . integrate their offices— or factories, for that matter—into communities"), make a town center ("a plaza, square or green that is a geographical reference point and a focus of civic life"), shrink parking lots ("Only in the United States does the humblest copy-shop or pizzeria boast as much space for cars as the average city hall"), turn down the lights ("why not use . . . smaller lamps that cast a gentler glow and let you see the stars?"), and think green ("before lawn meets lawn and asphalt meets asphalt, covering the land in a seamless carpet of sprawl").[63]

The problem with a list such as *Newsweek's* is that it mixes nostalgia for a past that probably never existed with some complex policies and distills them into empty homilies about community and family. The list begs the question of whether suburbanites actually care about community, as opposed to some of its quaint architectural signifiers. But the New Urbanism offers a somewhat more systematic analysis than the *Newsweek* article might indicate.

The Congress for the New Urbanism, organized in 1994, announces in its founding charter that it "views divestment in central cities, the spread of placeless sprawl, increasing separation by race and income, environmental deterioration, loss of agricultural lands and wilderness, and the erosion of society's built heritage as one interrelated community-building challenge."[64] Though the congress goes to some pains to point out that "we recognize that physical solutions by themselves will not solve social and economic problems," the approach of the New Urbanism is almost entirely oriented to the physical redesign of urban space. The twenty-seven principles endorsed by the congress emphasize "the neighborhood, the district, and the corridor as the essential elements of development." These principles stand in opposition to the style of urban development that has relied on the bulldozing of vast spaces for single uses such as subdivisions, shopping centers, and office parks. Such segmentation has created an urban pattern that favors cars over human beings, forcing people to spend time on the highway that might be spent at home or in a community setting.

Three advocates of the New Urbanism have distilled these precepts into a simple refrain:

> *No more housing subdivisions!*
> *No more shopping centers!*
> *No more office parks!*
> *No more highways!*
> *Neighborhoods or nothing!*[65]

In place of monotonous subdivisions of look-alike houses, "the goal of the New Urbanism is to promote diverse and livable communities with a greater variety of housing types, land uses, and building densities—in other words, to develop and maintain a melting pot of neighborhood homes serving a wide range of household family sizes, cultures, and incomes."[66] To replace the shopping centers, the New Urbanists urge the building of pedestrian-friendly shopping areas on streets and squares, within walking distances to nearby residences. Office parks are to be banned because they segregate work from home and shopping; like shopping centers, they entail the proliferation of huge parking lots and maximize reliance on the automobile.[67] The New Urbanists recognize that "automobiles are a fact of modern life," but they urge that the grid of high-speed streets and highways that intersect urban areas be replaced by highway corridors clearly separated from neighborhoods. Within neighborhoods, they want to slow traffic by narrowing streets and creating traffic circles and other "traffic calming" devices. They also promote the idea that bicycle paths and sidewalks should be built along all streets, and that mass transit must be made convenient.[68] For the New Urbanists, everything hinges on land-use planning and an urban design that facilitates neighborhood and community.

Suburbanites may be tired of freeway congestion and gridlock and they may sometimes revolt against the ugliness of large-scale development—especially when it is in their backyard—but without a political strategy, the New Urbanism is likely to become little more than a recipe for design features that developers can use to sell new developments. Just outside Disney World near Orlando, Florida, the Disney Corporation has built Celebration, a gated community built according to some of the principles of the New Urbanism. All houses have front porches, a touch from the past designed to encourage people to visit with their neighbors (though, as it happens, it is too hot in Florida for this to work). The houses also have other design features meant to signify a happy, wholesome suburban life—gables, elaborate trim, picket fences. One suspects that Celebration is much like the Frontier Village or Main Street in Disneyland—"authentic reproductions" based on an idealized version of the real thing. If affluent suburbanites come to prefer the design features of the New Urbanism, developers will be happy to accommodate. Affluent home buyers will be able to afford the New Urbanism, leaving less fortunate urban residents to neighborhoods that fail the New Urbanists' standards for aesthetics and community.

To serve as an effective remedy for urban sprawl, the New Urbanism must gain support from a coalition of political interests capable of achieving metropolitan planning. Only in that manner can goals of improved transportation networks, mixed-use housing, and social equity be accomplished. In the Minneapolis region, a coalition composed of representatives of the central city, inner-ring suburbs, and affluent suburbs wishing to rein in developers, came together in the 1970s behind the cause of regional governance. Though comprehensive reform has not been accomplished in Minneapolis, this alliance has succeeded in implementing a modest tax-sharing plan, the regionalization of some services, and the creation of a Metropolitan Council capable of carrying out some planning.[69] If it stays together, this alliance will probably win important victories in tax and school-district equalization, and it may eventually achieve regional planning with enforceable land-use controls. Without such coalitions, the New Urbanism cannot hope to accomplish a regional agenda. The task is formidable. Are suburbanites ready to give up their single-family homes, lawns, and multiple cars? Do they really care about community? Are they willing to share tax bases or support other measures to reduce disparities within urban regions? Judging from past history, the answers to these questions are not likely to be positive.

REFORMING METROPOLITAN GOVERNANCE

In principle, a comprehensive consolidation of governments would seem to be the most obvious, and perhaps the only, effective way to solve the problems of sprawled-out metropolitan areas. A single regional government would, in principle, be able to represent the many voices that make up the metropolis. At the same time, such a government could plan transportation systems, balance investment in older communities and in new infrastructure, impose land-use and environmental controls, and provide efficient services in an equitable fashion to all urban residents. In fact, however, urban areas are made up of a multitude of governments with widely varying taxation levels that provide services ranging from the excellent to the abysmal. These governments compete fiercely with one another for a piece of the economic pie, and generally get in the way of regional planning.

Convinced that such a state of affairs was inefficient and inequitable, for many decades reformers focused their energies on the goal of eliminating governmental fragmentation in urban areas. Time after time they have met with failure, despite the fact that the benefits sounded (to their own ears, at least) irresistible. The metropolitan government reformers were cut from the same cloth, and indeed they were often the same people, as the municipal reformers we profiled in Chapter 4. And their remedies were similar. They maintained that a single government should exercise all public authority within each metropolitan area. They believed that only a few of its officials should be elected, with a sharp distinction drawn between politics and public administration.[70] The proliferation of municipalities within urban regions could be compared to the wards in cities—to the reformer, wards were nothing but hotbeds of parochial politics, with their representatives lacking the capacity or the perspective to attend to the overall problems of the city. Likewise, the multitude of suburban governments made it impossible to attend to the problems facing urban regions. Thus, writing in 1912, one reformer said: "Here [in metropolitan Boston] are thirty-eight towns and cities as intimately related to everything that concerns daily life as the wards of an American city, but with no power or means . . . of constructing, or improving public works or of taking public action that is for the metropolitan district as a whole."[71]

Nearly twenty years later, an influential reformer picked up the same themes when he described what he saw as the parochialism and chaos arising from the fragmentation of local government: "They [the many governments] tend to divert attention of the inhabitants from the fact that they are members of one large community and lead them to act as members of separate units. They result in great variation in municipal regulations . . . and in standards of services, in sectional treatment of problems which are essentially metropolitan . . ."[72] Just like the municipal reformers, those pressing for single-government urban regions thought that economy and efficiency would be found only in streamlined governmental arrangements and hierarchical administrative structures. As a leading reformer argued in 1953: "Only a government with community-wide jurisdiction can plan and provide the services, physical facilities, guidance, and controls necessary to relate functional plans with areal plans. None of the metropolitan areas has such a government today."[73]

The reformers were convinced that truth and virtue were on their side. Such confidence fueled the bitter disappointment they felt when voters repeatedly rejected their proposals, in metropolitan areas all across the country, campaign after campaign, decade after decade. Between 1921 and 1979, reformers went to voters 83 times in an attempt to gain approval of city-county consolidations. They succeeded only 17 times, and only three of those successes came in metropolitan areas of 250,000 or more (Nashville-Davidson County, 1962; Jacksonville-Duval County, 1967; Indianapolis-Marion County, 1969). (The consolidation of Indianapolis with its county was imposed by the state legislature, and not by a popular referendum.)[74] Many other reform attempts were made to consolidate governments by creating two-tier systems (a metropolitan district with specific service responsibilities, but with municipalities and counties possessing important powers). The most notable success came with the creation of Metropolitan Dade County (Miami) in 1957. Under this reform, the county assumed many of the responsibilities (such as fire and police protection, traffic control, parks and recreation, health and welfare programs, air pollution control, and some other activities) formerly assumed by municipal governments.

The ambitious schemes to impose metropolitan governments have usually gone down in flames because both suburban and central-city voters have generally wanted to preserve their control over local powers and services. The experience in the St. Louis metropolitan area has been typical, except there the reformers tried, and failed, more times than anywhere else: in 1926, 1930, 1959, 1962, 1989, and 1990. In 1926 the voters in St. Louis County defeated a proposal to consolidate the city of St. Louis with the county. Four years later the county's voters vetoed a somewhat ambitious proposal, which would have placed the city and county under a regional government, except for a few services and public functions.[75] In 1959 the reformers gave it another try. This time they proposed a Greater Saint Louis City-County District, which would have assumed responsibility for forging a regional plan and for promoting economic development, managing regional mass transit and traffic control on major streets and highways, administering all sewage facilities, and supervising all police training, communications, and civil defense. Municipalities would have been left with the responsibility of regulating local street traffic and providing police and fire protection and garbage pickup. Local officials in the county reacted with a furious campaign of opposition, and voters soundly defeated the plan.[76] But even before tempers cooled down from this attempt, reformers were at it again. This time, in 1962, the "borough plan" would have placed the city and county under a single government and divided the county into twenty-two boroughs, each exercising some limited powers. This plan would have eliminated all existing municipalities. The plan was defeated by a 4-to-1 landslide, an even more lopsided margin than in 1959.

In 1989 an elected Board of Freeholders placed a consolidation plan before the voters of St. Louis County (language in the Missouri Constitution empowered such a board of "freeholders"—property owners—to make such proposals). In addition to reducing the number of municipalities in the county from 90 to 37, the plan would have transferred most land-use, zoning, and building inspections to the county, and also created a county commission to oversee fire and emergency services. It quickly became obvious that the opposition to reform had not died down in the nearly three decades that had passed since the previous reform try. An acrimonious campaign ensued, and both sides readied for the scheduled June 20, 1989 vote. Before election day, however, the U.S. Supreme Court declared the Board of Freeholders illegal because it denied equal protection of the law to nonproperty holders.[77]

The successive generations of reformers in St. Louis showed remarkable resolve because they felt that righteousness and truth was on their side. It was not difficult for them to demonstrate that tax burdens and service levels varied wildly among municipalities. It was also easy to show that the city of St. Louis was in economic decline, and had been since the 1920s. Patterns of racial and social-class segregation between the city and county, and between cities in the county, was a defining feature of the St. Louis region, and the many municipality's zoning ordinances demonstrably helped to establish and preserve such segregation. But such evidence could not overcome the deep attachment that people felt to their local communities. Indeed, some of the things that the reformers saw as problems affecting everyone—such as varying taxing levels and service provisions—others saw as solutions. Many suburbanites had long felt this way, and in the 1980s they began to find support for their point of view in academic quarters. In September 1988, just a few months before the vote on the freeholders' plan, the influential Advisory Commission on Intergovernmental Relations proclaimed that urban residents benefited when they were given the ability to shop around for different bundles of taxes, services, and amenities offered by municipalities.[78] This and similar studies have fundamentally undermined the metropolitan reform movement. Rather than appearing to defend parochial self-interests, it became possible for the defenders of local autonomy to evoke scholarly approval for the view that they were doing nothing but exercising their free choice to live wherever they wished.

Though suburbanites resisted regional governance, they have embraced cooperative arrangements when, as a practical matter, it has seemed in their interest to do so. Cooperative agreements exist among local governments almost everywhere in the United States when they have seemed to be mutually advantageous. These agreements have typically arisen when an urban county has agreed to collect taxes to provide services for small municipalities. They have also evolved as interlocal agreements among two or more governments, as a way of providing common services or sharing tax collection and assessments, data processing, and the like. For the most part they are mundane, boring, everyday administrative undertakings—the exact opposite of the bitterly contested fights over metropolitan reform.

Some examples of cooperation within metropolitan areas reveal both the accomplishments and the limitations of piecemeal reform. In the 1940s, voters agreed to a new charter for St. Louis County (then the principal suburban county in the St. Louis region) that allowed the county to expand its service and administrative responsibilities. The county soon adopted a building code, and in the next few years it began to conduct electrical inspections of new construction in unincorporated areas, and also contracted with municipalities for this service. By 1964 the county was running thirty-two parks and an extensive library system. Following a charter revision in 1954, the county formed its own police department. Over the years, the county police have contracted with numerous cities for police enforcement (these arrangements are often referred to as "rent-a-cop"). In 1971, voters approved another charter amendment, this one giving the county control over waste disposal and authorizing it to set minimum training and educational standards for firefighters. Today, the county also administers 911 emergency services, runs a system of health clinics, builds roads and coordinates transportation, and runs a system of jails and courts.[79]

A similar gradual evolution of urban counties has occurred in metropolitan areas elsewhere. DuPage County, west of Chicago, ran an extensive parks system by the mid–1980s and it coordinated municipal services for those cities that volunteered to participate. Through a regional planning commission it provided planning expertise and advice to cities and applied for federal grants on behalf of municipalities and special districts.[80] Oakland County, Michigan, north of Detroit, also slowly expanded its responsibilities, finally running an airport, providing contracted services to municipalities, and running a public library system and emergency services. Over time it has become, in effect, a regional government that coordinates public works projects.[81] In urban regions elsewhere, counties have likewise evolved into quasi-regional authorities. In particular, their control over key state and federal grants has allowed them to flex their political muscle. By the early 1970s Orange County, California, had evolved into an administrative structure sufficient to provoke repeated protests from local officials. Like other urban counties, it had grown less through big reform than by a gradual accumulation of responsibilities.

Urban areas have also been able to overcome many of the effects of governmental fragmentation through special districts. In 1992, there were 86,692 local governments in the United States; less than one in four—19,296—were municipalities. The fastest-growing form of local government is the special district—an authority granted taxing and spending powers for the purpose of accomplishing special purposes, such as administering sewer systems, running toll tunnels and bridges, and providing mass transit services. Special districts are generally run more like private corporations than like governments, and most of them are unknown to everyone except to their taxpayers.[82] Though most of them come into existence to supply services to new developments (they are often organized, in fact, by developers for the purpose of providing public services), others are truly metropolitan-wide in scope. Without the larger ones, some essential metropolitan services might well degenerate into chaos—hardly a happy prospect when effluents and transportation are involved.

Stronger urban counties, interlocal agreements, and special districts have facilitated improved service delivery while at the same time they have preserved municipal autonomy. Without them, governmental fragmentation would give rise to irresolvable problems; precisely because they exist, fragmentation can be sustained. They are not an antidote to sprawl; indeed, they help to support it. They provide a flexible means by which developers and urban residents moving still farther out can obtain necessary public infrastructure and services. For this reason they are not a substitute for regional government, and they do not help to slow down urban sprawl.

WHITHER SPRAWL?

Municipalities tend to guard their land-use authority jealously—and of course this is precisely the power that must be regionalized if urban sprawl is to be reined in. Except for Portland, Oregon, no regional body in the United States holds the authority to regularly countermand local land-use regulations. Because resistance to regional land-use planning has been so difficult to overcome, states and regions have opted instead for land-trust programs that replace regulations with positive attempts to preserve farmland and open space. From 1988 to 1998, 4.7 million acres of open space were protected from development, an increase of 135 percent. Several states have attempted to curb sprawl by buying up open space. In 1998, voters in New Jersey agreed to spend $98 million in state and local taxes and issue $1 billion in bonds to protect land from the developers. In the same year the Florida legislature established a $3 billion bond program and Illinois committed $160 million for the acquisition of open space. New York's governor has launched a task force to study ways to favor redevelopment over new development, and Connecticut's governor has set a goal of tripling the amount of land preserved from sprawl.[83] In May of 2000, Congress authorized $42 billion to be spent over 15 years to preserve land from development.[84] Does such activity signal an antisprawl revolution?

If New Jersey's experience is a guide, land trusts will not curb urban sprawl. In 1998 Governor Christine Todd Whitman announced that New Jersey's program—with its goal of acquiring more than one million acres of open space— could serve as a national model. But like other states, New Jersey is reluctant to place environmental concerns ahead of economic development. In 2000, when Merrill Lynch announced that it would leave the state unless it was granted permission to build in a rural area, politicians quickly caved. An assistant in the governor's policy office, explained, "They wanted a suburban-style campus, so it was either here or Pennsylvania."[85] Even in the unlikely event that politics did not interfere, land trusts can only preserve islands in the stream. Open lands will simply be surrounded by the ceaseless flow of development.

Suburban residents are caught in a bind, and the way out is likely to be painful. On the one hand, they are fed up with gridlock and the bulldozer. On the other, they are keen to preserve the privileges guaranteed by municipal autonomy. If they forsake local control for the goal of curbing urban sprawl, they may find an affordable housing project sprouting up in the next block, or may discover that some of their tax dollars are being used to help support cities with lower tax bases. So far, suburbanites have not had any trouble in choosing between the alternatives.

NOTES

1. Jon C. Teaford, *Post-Suburbia: Government and Politics in the Edge Cities* (Baltimore: The Johns Hopkins University Press, 1997), p. 1.
2. National Journal, "The Senselessness of Urban Sprawl," September 25, 1993, p. 2326.

3. Scott Bowles, "National Gridlock," *USA Today*, November 23, 1999, p. 2A.

4. Matthew L. Wald, "How Dreams of Clean Air Get Stuck in Traffic," *New York Times*, March 11, 1990.

5. Bowles, "National Gridlock."

6. Robert Cervero, "Unlocking Suburban Gridlock," *Journal of the American Planning Association*, August 1986, p. 389.

7. H. V. Savitch and Ronald K. Vogel, *Regional Politics: America in a Post-City Age* (Thousand Oaks, CA: Sage Publications, 1996), p. 18.

8. J. A. Lindsey, "Urban Freeway Congestion: Quantification of the Problem and Effectiveness of Potential Solutions," *ITE Journal* 57 (1987): 27–32, cited in Robert Cervero, "Jobs-Housing Balancing and Regional Mobility," *Journal of the American Planning Association* (Spring 1989): 136.

9. Ibid.

10. Keith Bradsher, "With Sport Utility Vehicles More Popular, Overall Automobile Fuel Economy Continues to Fall," *New York Times*, October 5, 1999, p. A17.

11. Warren Brown, "We Like to Think Big," *Washington Post National Weekly Edition*, March 1, 2000, p. 19.

12. Real Estate Research Corporation, *The Costs of Sprawl* (Washington, D.C.: Government Printing Office, 1974), p. 2.

13. Jerry Adler, "Paved Paradise," *Newsweek*, May 15, 1995.

14. Daniel Pederson, Vern E. Smith, and Jerry Adler, "Sprawling, Sprawling . . . ", *Newsweek*, July 19, 1999, pp. 23–27.

15. Vicki Lee Parker, "Western Cities Grapple with Rapid Growth," *Wall Street Journal*, September 22, 1999, p. B16.

16. John J. Fialka, "Campaign Against Sprawl Overruns a County in Virginia, and Soon Perhaps Much of Nation," *Wall Street Journal*, January 4, 2000, p. A24.

17. Bill Lambrecht, "Urban Sprawl Is a Hot Topic," *St. Louis Post-Dispatch*, February 7, 1999, p. A6.

18. *Governing: The Magazine of States and Localities*, January 1999 and August 1999 issues.

19. William Booth, "For Voters, the Target Is Sprawl," *Washington Post National*, December 7, 1998, pp. 30, 31.

20. Ibid., p. 31.

21. Sierra Club, *Solving Sprawl: The Sierra Club Rates the States* (Washington, D.C.: Sierra Club, 1999), p. 2.

22. Terence Samuel, "Gore Pushes a Plan to Help Curb Problems Related to Urban Sprawl," *St. Louis Post-Dispatch*, January 12, 1999, p. A8.

23. Ibid.

24. Terence Samuel, "Al Gore Makes Sprawl central to his campaign," *St. Louis Post-Dispatch*, www.postnet.com, October 12, 1999.

25. Fialka, "Campaign Against Sprawl," p. A24.

26. Office of Technology Assessment, Congress of the United States," The Technological Reshaping of Metropolitan America," Ch. 8, at http://www.sustainable.org/SGN/org (1998).

27. Real Estate Research Corporation, *The Costs of Sprawl*, p. 2.

28. "A Call to Action," *St. Louis Post-Dispatch*, March 16, 1997.

29. Office of Technology Assessessment, Ch. 8.

30. Craig R. Whitney, "Scientists Warn of Dangers in a Warming Earth," *New York Times*, May 26, 1990.

31. James A. Dunn, Jr., *Miles to Go: European and American Transportation Policies* (Cambridge, Mass.: MIT Press, 1981), p. 150.

32. U.S. Bureau of the Census, *Statistical Abstract of the United States* (Washington, D.C.: Government Printing Office, 1996), p. 235.

33. Peter G. Newman and Jeffrey R. Kenworthy, "Gasoline Consumption and Cities," *Journal of the American Planning Association* (Winter 1989): 26–27.

34. Real Estate Research Corporation, *The Costs of Sprawl*, p. 2.
35. Ibid., pp. 4, 5.
36. Robert H. Freilich, *From Sprawl to Smart Growth: Successful Legal, Planning, and Environmental Systems* (Washington, D.C.: American Bar Association, 1999), p. 323.
37. Bank of America, "Beyond Sprawl: New Patterns of Growth to Fit the New California," http://seafirst.com/community/comm_env_urban1.html.
38. Congress for the New Urbanism, *Charter of the New Urbanism* (New York, McGraw-Hill, 2000).
39. Fialka, "Campaign Against Sprawl," p. A24.
40. Ibid.
41. Jayne E. Daly, "A Glimpse of the Past, A Vision for the Future, Senator Henry M. Jackson and National Land Use Legislation," *Urban Law* 27, No. 1 (1996).
42. For a full description of the case and its importance, see Robert H. Freilich, *From Sprawl to Smart Growth.*
43. Ibid., pp. 195–196.
44. Ibid., pp. 131–132.
45. Ibid.
46. Myron Orfield, *Metropolitics: A Regional Agenda for Community and Stability* (Washington, D.C.: Brookings Institution Press and Cambridge, Mass.: Lincoln Institute for Land Policy, 1997), p. 13.
47. Quoted in ibid., p. 149.
48. Arnold J. Heidenheimer, Hugh Heclo, and Carolyn Teich Adams, *Comparative Public Policy: The Politics of Choice in Europe and America*, 2nd ed (New York: St. Martin's Press, 1993), chap. 8.
49. Paul G. Lewis, *Shaping Suburbia: How Political Institutions Organize Urban Development* (Pittsburgh: University of Pittsburgh Press, 1996), pp. 105–107.
50. Christopher Leo, *Journal of Urban Affairs*, "Regional Growth Management Regime: The Case of Portland, Oregon", 20, No. 4, 1998: 363–394.
51. Lewis, *Shaping Suburbia*, p. 115.
52. John DeGrove, *Land, Growth, and Politics* (Chicago: APA Planners' Press, 1984), pp. 249–250.
53. For a comprehensive review, see Office of Technology Assessment, Congress of the United States, "The Technological Reshaping of Metropolitan America," ch. 8, at http://www.sustainable.org/SGN/org (1998).
54. Edward T. McMahon, "Stopping Sprawl by Growing Smarter," *Planning Commissioners Journal* 26, (Spring 1997): 4–7.
55. Office of Technology Assessment, "The Technological Reshaping of Metropolitan America."
56. Neal Peirce, "A Call to Action," *St. Louis Post-Dispatch.*
57. Rosalind Greenstein and Wim Wiewel (ed.), *Urban-Suburban Interdependencies* (Cambridge, Mass.: Lincoln Land Institute, 2000), pp. 25–28.
58. Jerry Adler, "Paved Paradise."
59. James Howard Kunstler, *The Geography of Nowhere* (New York: Touchstone, 1993), p. 10.
60. Ibid., p. 118.
61. John A. Jakle and David Wilson, *Derelict Landscapes: The Wasting of America's Built Environment* (Savage, Maryland: Rowman & Littlefield, 1992), p. 182.
62. Ibid., p. 40.
63. Adler, "Paved Paradise."
64. Congress for the New Urbanism, *Charter of the New Urbanism.*
65. Andres Duany, Elizabeth Plater-Zyberk, and Jeff Speck, *Suburban Nation: The Rise of Sprawl and the Decline of the American Dream* (New York: North Point Press, 2000), p. 243.
66. March A. Weiss, in Congress for the New Urbanism, p. 91.
67. Elizabeth Moule, in Congress for the New Urbanism, pp. 105–108.

68. Douglas Farr, in Congress for the New Urbanism, pp.141–146.
69. Orfield, *Metropolitics*.
70. G. Ross Stephens and Nelson Wikstrom, *Metropolitan Government and Governance: Theoretical Perspectives, Empirical Analysis, and the Future* (New York: Oxford University Press, 2000), pp. 31–32.
71. Quoted in ibid., p. 33.
72. Paul Studenski, *The Government of Metropolitan Areas in the United States* (New York: National Municipal League, 1930), p. 29.
73. Victor Jones, "Local Government Organization in Metropolitan Areas: Its Relation to Urban Redevelopment," in Coleman Woodbury (ed.), *The Future of Cities and Urban Redevelopment* (Chicago: University of Chicago Press, 1953), pp. 604–605.
74. Vincent Marando, "City-County Consolidation: Reform, Regionalism, Referenda, and Requiem," *Western Political Quarterly* 32:4 (December 1979): 409–422.
75. Jon C. Teaford, *Post-Suburbia: Government and Politics in the Edge Cities* (Baltimore: The Johns Hopkins University Press, 1997), p. 110.
76. Ibid., pp. 110–112.
77. Ibid., p. 195.
78. Ibid., p. 194.
79. Ibid., pp. 136–138.
80. Ibid., pp. 145–146.
81. Ibid., p. 152.
82. Nancy Burns, *The Formation of American Local Governments: Private Values in Public Institutions* (New York: Oxford University Press, 1994).
83. "Suburban Communities Grab up Land to Keep Developers at Bay," *St. Louis Post-Dispatch*, May 14, 2000, p. A8.
84. Ibid.
85. Iver Peterson, "In New Jersey, Sprawl Keeps Outflanking Its Foes," *New York Times*, March 17, 2000, pp. A1, A19.

12

FISCAL CRISIS AND THE PROBLEMS OF GOVERNANCE

THE ROOTS OF THE URBAN FISCAL CRISIS

In 1975, when the nation's largest city, New York, teetered on the edge of bankruptcy, news of urban fiscal crises splashed across the headlines of newspapers around the country. In the mid-1990s, after a period of continuous economic expansion and low inflation, urban fiscal crises, with a few exceptions, disappeared from public view. New York, Los Angeles, and Washington never stopped struggling to close huge budget deficits but many more cities, including Chicago, Miami, Denver, Detroit, San Francisco, and Cleveland, made stunning comebacks, moving from repeated budget deficits to healthy budget surpluses. Municipal budget deficits should be very rare because they are illegal. City governments in 99 out of the 100 largest cities in the country are, by law, required to balance their budgets.[1] Unlike the federal government, cities cannot run deficits year after year and then cover them by going deeper and deeper into debt. One consequence of this fact is cities cannot easily adjust to swings in the economic pendulum or to adverse social and demographic trends. For decades, these trends seemed to undermine the best efforts of people who wanted to turn the cities around. As Helen Ladd, an expert on urban fiscal health, put it: "Social and economic trends *outside the control of city officials* have led to a significant deterioration in the fiscal health of many big cities."[2] The flight of the middle class and business to the suburbs, the concentration of immigrants in cities, the high rate of poverty among central-city residents—these and other circumstances made it more difficult for cities to balance their budgets. Cities with impoverished populations and declining economies often face unpalatable choices. If cities increase taxes, they may drive business and the middle class out of the city. If they cut expenditures, the loss of services may only have the same effect. All too often, cities have found themselves in a catch-22.

The most fiscally stressed cities find themselves the victims of a process of decline that may be adapted to, but not necessarily reversed. Consider the case of East St. Louis, a depressed city with about 40,000 residents located in Illinois across the river from St. Louis, Missouri. In the 1980s East St. Louis combined the highest property tax rates in the state of Illinois with the state's worst municipal services. Garbage collection ceased in October 1987. Unable to pay for private garbage collection, residents began to pile it up in their backyards or dump it in the streets, making some streets impassable. Rats thrived on the garbage. The odor of burning garbage filled the air. The city's decrepit sewer system seeped raw sewage into streets, homes, and even schools. Police officers were forced to patrol the cities in their own cars because the city's patrol cars had broken down. The city was so mired in debt that its budget was taken over by a state-appointed financial control board. Clearly, neither raising taxes nor cutting expenditures was a viable option for East St. Louis.[3] A few years later, by 1996, the city had restored basic services. Revenue from a riverboat casino moored on the Mississippi River had supplied the necessary revenue to supply an acceptable level of services, but nothing more. An important question remained: What if the quick fix of casino gaming had not been available?

Cities may be fiscally unhealthy even if they are balancing their budgets. When the economic expansion of the 1990s and early century ended and the economy slowed, the retreating economic tide began to reveal the rocks of fiscal stress that can threaten to sink cities. In this chapter we examine city expenditures, revenues, and borrowing, focusing on the structural trends that create fiscal stress for cities. There are many things cities can do to improve their fiscal health, but unless the underlying structural characteristics change, urban fiscal crises will never go away completely.

CITY EXPENDITURES

Collectively, cities spend huge sums of money. In fiscal year 1993, for example, they spent $228 billion, which was one-third of all local government expenditures in the United States. School districts, at 41 percent, accounted for the largest proportion of local government expenditures.[4] In fiscal year 1993 the leading municipal budget by far was New York City's, an astonishing $39.4 billion. Three other cities spent more than $3 billion: Washington, D.C. ($4.8 billion), Chicago ($3.6 billion), and Los Angeles ($3.5 billion).[5]

City expenditures are driven by powerful forces that are largely beyond the control of local officials and voters. City governments are not sovereign entities. Higher levels of government (state and federal) allocate responsibilities to city governments within the intergovernmental system. Equally important, cities must respond to political demands. There is a limit to the cuts that city officials can make, since public services are necessary for maintaining the physical well-being of city residents and the viability of a city. City governments provide a wide range of services that people take for granted as essential to everyday life: police and fire protection, education, water distribution, sewage collection, parks, highways, museums, and libraries. The relative distribution of municipal expenditures among various functional areas for a year typical of the early 1990s is shown in Table 12.1. In 1996 America's six cities of over one million population devoted a combined 38 percent of their expenditures to education, public welfare, health and hospitals, and police. Education and public welfare led the list.

The largest 38 cities (and even most big cities) do not run the schools within their boundaries; normally, education is financed through independent school districts. The exceptions include some older cities, such as New York, Boston, San Francisco, and Baltimore, that built schools before it had become the usual practice to finance education through special districts, in addition, Chicago has also recently taken over its schools. Smaller cities spend much less on public welfare and public health than do big central cities. Thus, since they do not finance education, welfare, and public health services, a few basic services such as police, sewers, highways, parks and recreation, and fire protection account for a larger share of expenditures. Put simply, larger cities spend more for social services.

Per capita expenditures of cities are closely related to city size. Big cities spend more than smaller cities for a variety of reasons: They support a wider array of services, often provide service of better quality (for example, well-trained police officers and firefighters), pay higher salaries to their public employees, and experience the high service costs made necessary by high-density populations, aging buildings and infrastructure, and high rates of poverty and unemployment. On average, the cities with populations exceeding one million people spend about twice as much for each citizen as the average U.S. city, and many times more than most small cities.

City expenditures have risen sharply in the second half of the twentieth century, not only in total amount but also relative to the economy as a whole, increasing from 5 percent of the gross national product (GNP) in 1949–1950 to a high of 9 percent in 1975–1976. Municipal expenditures rose sharply throughout the 1960s and up to the recession of 1974–1975. As indicated in Table 12.2, after the recession of 1974–1975, the brakes were applied to municipal budgets. The six biggest cities lost almost 10 percent in spending power from 1975 to 1980, when inflation is taken into account. After adjusting for inflation, cities of all sizes, on the average, did not increase spending at all over the same years. From 1980 to 1996, spending declined somewhat for cities of all sizes (after adjustments for inflation).

Inflation is a main cause of rising local government expenditures, affecting local governments more than the private sector. The cost of state and local government services has consistently risen at a more rapid rate than prices in general over the past twenty-five years. From 1965 to 1982, prices in the economy as a whole increased 196 percent, while state and local government costs increased 247 percent. In the 1980s inflation slowed down in both the private and public

TABLE 12.1 DISTRIBUTION OF REVENUES AND DIRECT EXPENDITURES FOR SELECTED URBAN GOVERNMENTS[a], IN 1996 (IN PERCENTAGES)

	Total of 38 Largest Cities	Cities of 1,000,000+ Population	Cities of 999,999 to 400,000 Population
Revenues			
Intergovernmental	33.8	35.5	30.6
state aid	25.1	28.4	18.6
federal aid	7.3	6.2	9.7
Local source revenues	66.2	64.5	69.4
Total local taxes	42.7	43.5	41.0
Property taxes	17.5	16.6	19.3
Sales taxes	6.8	6.7	7.1
Income and other taxes	15.8	17.7	11.8
Current charges	16.3	14.9	19.1
Other	7.2	6.1	9.3
Expenditures by Function			
Education	11.1	12.3	9.0
Community development and housing	4.4	4.9	3.6
Public welfare	9.0	11.0	5.2
Health and hospitals	7.0	7.0	6.9
Police protection	8.3	8.1	8.8
Corrections	1.8	1.8	1.9
Fire protection	3.5	3.0	4.5
Highways	3.5	3.4	3.7
Parks and recreation	2.8	1.8	4.7
Sewerage and solid waste	6.7	6.3	7.5
Governmental administration	3.4	2.7	4.6
General public buildings	2.4	0.1	0.0
Interest on debt	5.5	4.9	6.6
Other[b]	30.6	32.7	33.0

[a]38 Cities with estimated populations in 1996 of 400,000 or more.
[b]Includes all expenses relating to outstanding debt, utilities, and pension systems.

Source: U.S. Bureau of the Census, *Statistical Abstract of the United States, 1999* (Washington , D.C.: Government Printing Office, 1999), pp. 334–335, tables 530–531.

TABLE 12.2 CHANGES IN PER CAPITA SPENDING FOR CITIES, 1970–1996 (ADJUSTED FOR INFLATION)[a]

	Growth Rate (percentage)				
	1970–1975	1975–1980	1980–1984	1985–1990	1990–1996
38 Largest municipal governments	21.6	0.02	0.0	−3.2	−3.0
Cities of 500,000 to 999,999[b]	21.6	0.01	−3.8	−0.7	−0.8
Big Six cities	19.2	−9.7	3.4	−1.7	−2.6

[a]Using GNP implicit price deflator for state and local government purchases, U.S. Bureau of the Census, *Statistical Abstract of the United States: 1986* (Washington, D.C.: Government Printing Office, 1986), p. 470.
[b]Population in 1982.

Sources: U.S. Bureau of the Census, *Local Government Finances in Selected Metropolitan Areas and Large Counties: 1969–70,* GF 70, no. 6 (Washington, D.C.: Government Printing Office, 1971), table 4; *Local Government Finances: 1974–75,* GF 75, no. 6 (1976); *City Government Finances: 1974–75,* GF 75, no. 5, table D; *Local Government Finances: 1979–80,* GF 80, no. 5, (1981), table D; *City Government Finances 1983–84,* no. 4 (1985), table 3. U.S. Advisory Commission on Intergovernmental Relations, *Significant Features of Fiscal Federalism, 1980–81* (Washington, D.C.: Government Printing Office, 1981), p. 19; *City Government Finances: 1989–90,* series GP/90-4, (Washington, D.C.: Government Printing Office, 1991), table 3; *City Government Finances 1984–85,* series GF 85, no. 7, (Washington, D.C.: Government Printing Office, 1986), table 3, and U.S. Bureau of the Census, *Statistical Abstract of the United States, 1999* (Washington, D.C.: Government Printing Office, 1999), p. 331, table 525; p. 335, table 531.

sectors, but the inflation rate for public services still ran ahead of inflation for private sector services. Between 1982 and 1990, the costs of government rose 41 percent, but costs in the economy as a whole increased only 31.5 percent.[6]

The high rate of inflation for city governments can be explained in part by the fact that most municipal services are labor intensive. Wages of city workers tend to keep pace with wages in the private sector.[7] However, while labor costs in the private sector can be reduced over time through mechanization and computers, such technologies have limited applications for many public services. The need for police officers and building inspectors, for instance, cannot be reduced to any appreciable extent by the use of computers. Between 1960 and 1975, wages paid to state and local government employees rose from 89 to 98 percent of the earnings of private sector workers,[8] but during the second half of the 1970s, the ratio fell back to 93 percent. After 1975, for the first time since 1955, wage gains in the public sector consistently lagged behind earnings in the private sector,[9] but because of the labor-intensive nature of municipal services, this did not help cities enough to avert layoffs and service reductions.

Public employee unions were instrumental in securing better wages for local government workers. In the 1960s, labor organizations such as the American Federation of State, County, and Municipal Employees (AFSCME) and the American Federation of Government Employees, both affiliated with the AFL-CIO, grew rapidly. Union membership rose from 1.1 million in 1960 to 2.3 million by 1970. At the same time, the unions became more militant. Worker-days lost through work stoppages by state and local employees escalated from 58,000 in 1960 to 1.4 million in 1970 to 2.3 million by 1973.[10] Unionization of city workers, which was more widespread in the older northern cities than elsewhere, brought a 10 to 15 percent higher pay to public employees, which thus generated higher expenditures in the bigger cities.[11]

Few people realize that local governments employ more workers than any other level of government in the United States. In 1993, for example, local governments, including school districts, employed 11.2 million people, far more than the combined total for state governments (4.7 million) and the federal government (3.0 million civilian employees).[12] Since 1970 the rate of growth of local government employment has exceeded state and federal employment growth. Between 1970 and 1993, local government employment rose 51 percent, a sharp contrast to the 4 percent increase in the "growing federal bureaucracy" so often decried by vote-seeking politicians. Employment by city governments (municipalities) grew by 18 percent during this same twenty-three-year period.[13]

The local public sector is an important job creator in cities. In the five major cities listed in Table 12.3, for instance, almost 33,000 new public-service jobs were created between 1967 and 1972, which helped to offset a decline of 73,000 private-sector jobs. Budget cutbacks after the mid-1970s reversed this effect, however. Between 1977 and 1983, more than 15,000 public service jobs were lost in these five cities, in addition to the more than 20,000 private sector jobs that disappeared. Cutbacks in federal and state programs aggravated the recession that began in 1980. Even the economic upturn of the 1990s did not stem the job losses. New Orleans added both public- and private-sector jobs and

TABLE 12.3 CHANGE IN NUMBER OF JOBS IN PRIVATE AND PUBLIC SECTORS IN FIVE CENTRAL CITIES, 1967–1972, 1977–1983, AND 1990–1997

	1967–1972		1977–1983		1990–1997	
	Private Sector[a]	Public Sector[b]	Private Sector[a]	Public Sector[b]	Private Sector[a]	Public Sector[b]
Baltimore	−7,000	+3,900	−13,342	−4,617	−13,991	−500
New Orleans	+7,000	+2,500	+5,349	−2,542	−7,122	+800
Philadelphia	−53,000	+18,400	−19,705	−4,445	−33,684	−2,500
St. Louis	−23,000	+2,300	−29,508	−3,854	−24,064	+500
San Francisco	+6,000	+5,700	+37,000	+7	−1,000	+1,600
Total	−73,000	+32,800	−20,206	−15,451	−65,617	−100

[a]Jobs covered by Social Security only.
[b]Includes city school districts.

Source: Adapted from George E. Peterson, "Finance," in *The Urban Predicament*, ed. William Gorham and Nathan Glazer (Washington, D.C.: Urban Institute, 1976), p. 112; and U.S. Bureau of the Census, *Statistical Abstract of the United States, 1986* (Washington, D.C.: Government Printing Office, 1984), p. 310, table 497, and U.S. Bureau of the Census, *Statistical Abstract of the United States, 1999* (Washington, D.C.: Government Printing Office, 1999), p. 343, table 540, and *County Business Patterns, 1990 and 1997*, table 2 (Washington, D.C.: Government Printing Office).

San Francisco was able to offset its jobs in the private sector with new public-sector employment. The other cities, however, continued to lose jobs in both categories.

The ability of cities to maintain expenditure levels is closely related to local economic vitality. All of the four cities that reduced expenditures between 1975 and 1992, as shown in Table 12.4, are located in the Frostbelt. Five of the cities that increased their budgets, however, were also older industrial cities in the Frostbelt, showing that special circumstances (such as ability to raise taxes or find new tax sources) can be important. Seven of the fourteen cities that increased expenditures were located in the Sunbelt. This mixed pattern continued in the 1991–1996 period, though most of the cities increasing their expenditures were Sunbelt cities.

The economic vitality of cities varies tremendously, and the differences are particularly sharp between central cities and their suburbs. In a 1960 sample of sixty-two cities, the per capita income of central-city residents was 105 percent that of people living in the suburbs; in other words, people living in central cities earned, on the average, slightly more than suburbanites. Clearly, many affluent people still lived in the cities, even after more than a decade of suburban flight. By 1989 the income ratio had fallen drastically to 84 percent. In 1989 the poverty rate in central cities was 18 percent, but in the metropolitan areas outside central cities it was only 8 percent.[14]

High rates of poverty boost the cost and the need for city services. Central cities and older suburbs, therefore, are particularly vulnerable to fiscal stress. Poverty and unemployment are basically national problems, but they are concentrated in central cities and older suburbs, a result of historical patterns of population immigration and of exclusionary policies that keep poor people out of wealthier suburban jurisdictions. The governments of central cities and older suburbs are in no position to reduce poverty and unemployment, but they are disproportionately saddled with these problems. And, sometimes with tragic results, they are the least able of all governments to generate the resources necessary to provide the basic public services that help to ameliorate the problems faced by the poor.

Poverty boosts public spending not only for welfare and social services, but also for a broad range of other services. Central-city governments spend money on lead paint poisoning prevention (a problem prevalent in older homes), rat control, and housing demolition. In the 1980s the problems of AIDS, homelessness, and crack cocaine soared in central cities. Courts have ordered cities to provide shelter for the homeless at significant expense to local governments. In 1987, for example, New York City, as required by court order, spent $274 million to provide emergency shelter to its homeless population.[15] Increased violence associated with substance abuse and other aspects of concentrated poverty strains the ability of police to protect the safety of citizens.[16]

Poverty also drives up the cost of other services. Children from culturally and educationally deprived homes are more difficult to educate than middle-class youngsters. Street cleanliness is more difficult to maintain in ghetto neighborhoods where the streets are used heavily for recreation but infrequently

TOTAL EXPENDITURES FOR SELECTED LARGE CITIES, 1975–1996 (IN MILLIONS OF 1996 DOLLARS[a])

	Fiscal Year 1975 Expenditures	Fiscal Year 1991 Expenditures	Percent Change 1975–1991	Fiscal Year 1996 Expenditures	Percent Change 1991–1996
Frostbelt Cities					
Baltimore	$2,811	$1,795	−36	$1,802	00
Boston	2,080	1,868	−10	1,890	01
Chicago	2,880	3,471	20	3,890	12
Cleveland	764	630	−17	644	02
Detroit	1,749	1,786	02	1,653	−07
Indianapolis	714	947	32	1,346	42
Milwaukee	564	629	11	705	12
New York	34,292	37,871	10	38,753	02
St. Louis	670	564	−15	487	−14
Sunbelt Cities					
Dallas	614	907	47	1,197	32
Denver	934	1,161	24	1,716	48
El Paso	159	308	94	344	12
Houston	1,010	1,514	50	1,777	18
Jacksonville	671	854	27	1,075	26
New Orleans	661	768	16	652	−15
Phoenix	567	1,155	103	1,221	06
San Jose	376	753	100	790	05
Washington, D.C.	4,115	4,896	19	4,368	−11

[a]Adjustments for inflation are calculated using GNP Price Index for state and local government purchases, U.S. Bureau of Economic Analysis, *Survey of Current Business, Dec. 1999*, p. 141, Table 3.

Sources: U.S. Bureau of the Census, *City Government Finances: 1975–76, GF 76, No. 4* (Washington, D.C.: Government Printing Office, 1977), table 5; U.S. Bureau of the Census, *Statistical Abstract of the United States, 1995*, table 493, (Washington, D.C.: Government Printing Office, 1995) and U.S. Bureau of the Census, *Statistical Abstract of the United States, 1999* (Washington, D.C.: Government Printing Office, 1999), p. 335, table 531.

repaired. Costs of fire protection are higher than elsewhere because of deteriorating housing, the high density of building, old and outdated wiring, and a concentration of flammable materials.

Almost all older cities have experienced significant population losses due to the flight of the middle class to the suburbs. As a city's population falls, the cost of providing infrastructure and basic services, such as police and fire, does not decline correspondingly.[17] Cities still have the same sewer and water lines— often old and in need of frequent repair—and the same miles of streets to plow and patrol. Once the middle class has fled, however, there are fewer taxpayers to pay for these services and the taxpayers who are left make less taxable income and own less valuable property than those in surrounding jurisdictions.

Another factor that drives up the cost of city services is the panoply of expensive mandates forced on cities by higher levels of government. Cities are not mentioned in the U.S. Constitution; legally, city governments are the creatures of state legislatures. Though many cities have home rule charters that allow them to govern themselves internally within broad guidelines, municipal corporations are not fully sovereign. The scope of a city's service responsibilities is beyond its control. State and federal governments can, and frequently do, order cities to provide particular services or meet minimum standards of service provision. Rarely do the cities receive more money to cover the costs of the mandated standards and services.

New York State, for example, is one of the few states in the nation that requires local governments to pay a portion of the costs of Medicaid. New York City must pick up 20 percent of Medicaid bills for city residents; this program alone costs local taxpayers over a billion dollars each year. New York City is an extreme example, but many cities across the country are forced to pay a share of welfare costs. Over the past two decades several states have made an effort to reduce their cities' welfare costs, but the problem still is significant. Cities still have expensive welfare burdens, despite state and federal welfare programs, even after adoption of the Personal Responsibility Act of 1995.

Unfunded federal mandates imposed on cities have proliferated since the 1960s. In the case of concurrent powers shared by the federal and state governments, Congress has the power to preempt (override) state and local laws. According to the Supremacy Clause (Article VI) of the Constitution, when there is a conflict between a national law and a state (or local) law, the national law prevails. Since 1965, Congress has used its powers of preemption to force city governments to address pressing problems without members of Congress having to take the politically unpopular action of appropriating money. Thus Congress has been able to take credit for solving problems while foisting the costs of these solutions onto lower levels of government.

The Supreme Court upheld federal preemption in the 1985 Garcia decision.[18] In Garcia the Court upheld the constitutionality of the 1974 amendments to the Fair Labor Standards Act, which applied minimum-wage and overtime pay provisions to public transit workers in San Antonio. This decision made it clear that state and local governments are not protected from federal preemption statutes by the Tenth Amendment (which reserves powers not granted to the federal government to the states). Their only protection comes from political pressures they can put on Congress. In 1986 the U.S. Department of Labor estimated that the cost to state and local governments of complying with the new labor standards exceeded $1.1 billion.[19]

Federal mandates to preserve environmental quality have been enormously expensive. The Clean Air Act of 1990, for example, required 100 cities to install antipollution devices on their garbage incinerators, at an estimated average cost of $20 million per incinerator.[20] The U.S. Environmental Protection Agency estimated that the total cost of environmental mandates for local governments increased from $7.7 billion in 1972 to $19.2 billion in 1987. In March 1995 Congress passed, and President Clinton signed, the Unfunded Mandates bill that requires Congress to weigh the costs and benefits of new rules costing over $50 million and to help pay the costs if state and local governments are forced to implement them, but this legislation came rather late in the day for most cities.

It is easy to say that city officials should limit the soaring costs of local government. As we have seen, however, a variety of economic and political forces beyond the control of local officials drive up the costs of government: inflation in labor-intensive city services, concentrated poverty, and unfunded mandates by higher levels of government. In the next section, we examine the other side of the ledger, revenue. Just as external factors limit the ability of local officials to reduce costs, they also limit the cities' ability to raise money to meet the demands on municipal budgets.

CITY REVENUES

Historically, the property tax has been the principal source of revenue for local governments. The most important and widely used form of property tax is the ad valorem real property tax, a levy imposed as a percent of the value of land and its improvements. From colonial times through the early years of the republic, real property was taken to be the best indicator of both wealth and the ability to pay taxes. Indeed, this was generally true. Most of the wealth of the era was tied to the land, and fortunes were made in land speculation. A person's wealth was roughly proportional to landholdings. The real property tax, therefore, was relied on to finance state and local governmental services.[21]

Taxation of personal (or nonreal) property—that is, assets other than real estate and improvements—evolved steadily as the cities became more complex. As trade and manufacturing grew in importance, more and more wealth became represented in bank accounts, merchandise, patent rights, machinery, capital stock, and corporate assets. Cities (and states) began to levy taxes on such sources of wealth in order to maintain a reliable relationship between individual tax burdens and personal wealth. Such assets were often hard to find and assess, however. Because of this, although the numbers of people with significant personal assets mushroomed after the Civil War, the proportion of the property tax attributable to personal property actually fell.[22]

In 1902 personal and real property taxes accounted for 73 percent of all municipal revenues, with license and franchise fees accounting for most of the rest. These taxes continued to provide approximately three-fourths of all local receipts until the late 1930s and early 1940s, when the proportion began to decline in favor of other revenue sources, especially new municipal sales and income taxes.[23] By 1962 property taxes accounted for barely 50 percent of municipal revenues in the seventy-two largest metropolitan areas (even though the property tax continued to generate almost all the revenue for school districts). In the 1960s, intergovernmental transfers contributed such large amounts to local revenues that the proportion of the revenues derived from property taxes necessarily fell. By fiscal 1975, property taxes accounted for little more than a third (35 percent) of the revenues in the largest metropolitan areas, despite a 130 percent increase in the average per capita levy since the early 1960s.[24] Other sources of local and intergovernmental revenue had increased faster.

Reliance on the property tax dropped to 23 percent of local revenues for municipalities in metropolitan areas by 1991–1992 (refer to Table 12.1); as recently as 1970, this tax had generated 39 percent of all municipal revenues.[25] By the end of the century, property taxes accounted for less than 10 percent of the budget in several big cities. Property taxes have remained more important for other local governments than for cities. In 1990–1991, school districts raised 97.4 percent of their tax revenues from the property tax.[26]

Only in rapidly growing cities of the Sunbelt has the property tax been used as an important source of revenue growth since the 1960s. This has been possible because of the sharply escalating value of property in those cities. In Phoenix the value of taxable property rose 251 percent from 1965 to 1973; in Newark it increased only 2 percent and in Detroit 14 percent during the same period.[27] But stagnant property values in the industrial cities were only part of the problem. Antiquated assessment procedures in many cities failed to keep the assessed valuations of property in line with their market values in periods of inflation.[28]

The property tax has a number of weaknesses, which has prompted cities to search for alternatives. One weakness is the high proportion of tax-exempt property. According to one study, almost one-third of all real property in the United States is subject to some kind of exemption.[29] In 1982, in just twenty-three states and the District of Columbia, there were $15 billion in exempt property for religious institutions, $22 billion for educational institutions, $15 billion for charitable institutions, and $128 billion for government property.[30] Cities must provide services for these properties, including police and fire protection, but the owners pay no taxes. Unfortunately, the burden of tax-exempt property falls most heavily on those cities that are least able to afford it, since "the percentage of property exempt in the central city is generally at least twice the percentage found in the respective suburbs."[31] In 1985, for example, over 51 percent of the real property in Boston was tax exempt, up from 41 percent in 1972.[32] A 1983 article traced a 3.2-mile route through Boston where a walker would not set foot on a single parcel of taxable property.[33] The situation in New York so incensed one taxpayer that he sued the city tax commission over the "subsidy of religion," going all the way to the U.S. Supreme Court before finally losing the case.[34]

In recent decades the proportion of tax-exempt property has increased. Many cities have provided tax relief for the aged or the poor ("circuit breaker" laws). States and cities have tried to attract or retain businesses and investors by forgiving or reducing their property taxes. Many states have exempted various forms of business property, such as machines and inventory, from taxation without consulting local governments.[35] Another weakness of the property tax as a revenue generator for central cities is that it does not touch suburban commuters and visitors who work and play in the city but do not live there. Commuters cost cities money. Researchers have found that cities with higher proportions of suburban commuters "must spend more per capita on crime protection, traffic control, parking, parks, and other general services to keep up with the flow of people into and through the central city."[36]

One method cities have used to deal with this problem is to levy earnings taxes to be paid by anyone working in the city. Although Charleston, South Carolina, is reported to have levied a tax on income prior to the Civil War, the modern municipal income tax movement began in Philadelphia in 1939. That levy, a flat-rate payroll tax on all earnings of persons who lived or worked in the city, was adopted to relieve financial pressures during the Great Depression. Since that time it has been adopted in thousands of communities, more than 3,500 by 1970. It "was not adopted because cities thought it was in some sense a 'fairer' tax than the property tax, but solely because it was a tax that could generate large amounts of revenue."[37]

The big advantage of the income tax is that it enables cities to tax nonresident commuters. Research demonstrates that the export ratio (proportion of taxes paid by nonresidents) is higher for local income taxes than for sales taxes or property taxes.[38] Not surprisingly, except for Ohio and Pennsylvania, where virtually all cities can levy such taxes, suburban-dominated state legislatures have been reluctant to grant cities the power to impose income taxes: Only fifteen out of eighty-six major central cities have the power to impose an earnings tax.[39] As Table 12.1 demonstrates, the income tax provides about from 15 to 19 percent of revenues for cities, depending on size—about the same proportion as property taxes. Sales taxes account for about 7 percent, on the average.

The revenue source that saved the cities during the 1960s, allowing them to expand both the level and scope of services, was intergovernmental aid. At that time, the federal government established a direct partnership with city governments that helped to relieve their fiscal stress. Between 1965 and 1974, intergovernmental transfers to all cities rose 370 percent, more than twice the 153 percent increase in municipal expenditures.[40] Direct federal aid to cities peaked in 1978 at 25.8 percent of cities' own-source revenue. Federal aid began to decline during the Carter Administration, and the bottom fell out in the 1980s. By 1991, federal aid had bottomed out at 6.5 percent of city revenues. Subsequently it climbed again to just over 10 percent by 1994, and it is stabilizing at about that level. Most of the new aid came for law enforcement activities.

The Reagan Administration effectively ended the special relationship that had been forged between the federal government and cities in the 1960s. Overall, nine grants-in-aid programs of special importance to urban governments were cut 47

FIGURE 12.1   **Direct Aid to Cities as a Percentage of Own-Source Revenue, 1965–1992**

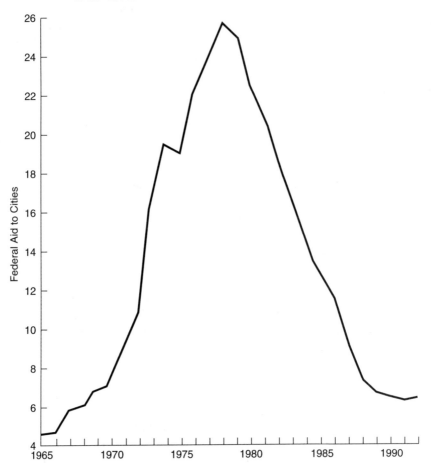

Source: Helen F. Ladd and John Yinger, *America's Ailing Cities: Fiscal Health and the Design of Urban Policy,* updated ed. (Baltimore: Johns Hopkins University Press, 1989), p. 270. Updated using U.S. Bureau of the Census, *City Government Finances 1991–92* (Washington, D.C.: Government Printing Office, 1994), table 4.

percent between 1980 and 1987. General revenue sharing for cities was eliminated in 1986 and the Community Development Block Grant was reduced by 20 percent between 1980 and 1987. Moreover, the targeting of federal grants shifted from distressed to relatively prosperous urban areas.[41] Few cities emerged unscathed, but the most distressed cities lost the most. Direct federal aid to Chicago fell from $472 million in 1981 to $151 million in 1986. Baltimore's grant volume fell from $220 million to $124 million, Indianapolis's from $125 million to $65 million. Detroit lost $305 million annually, falling from $456 million in 1981 to $151 million by 1986.[42]

Although federal assistance grew at a faster rate than state government aid in the 1960s and 1970s, more intergovernmental assistance still came from the states. In 1974, cities as a whole received nearly $2 in state revenue for each $1 in federal revenue. By 1980 the ratio of state to federal dollars had declined to $1.47 in state funding for each federal dollar.[43] In the 1980s, some state governments, such as New York, Florida, and Oklahoma, stepped in aggressively to compensate for the federal cuts, but others, such as California, responded minimally.[44] In any case, no state stepped in to completely replace the federal programs.

Not surprisingly, cities responded to cuts in aid from higher levels of government by raising taxes. Between 1980 and 1993, city governments' tax revenues increased 152 percent, but many city governments still had trouble balancing their budgets.[45] Moreover, many found it difficult to respond to cuts in grants by increasing taxes, for they had not escaped the taxpayers' revolts started in the 1970s. During that period, at least fourteen state legislatures enacted laws that limited property tax rates or spending by local governments.[46] Even more far-reaching, however, were the citizen initiatives. The first well-publicized of these was Proposition 13 in California, which was passed by popular referendum in June 1978. From March to November 1978, sixteen states held initiatives or referenda to limit taxes or spending, though not all were binding on public officials.[47] Thirteen of the citizen initiatives passed. More such proposals were approved after 1978. Consequently, even though cities faced severe fiscal problems, their budgetary options were drastically constricted.

Cities imposed a variety of user fees in lieu of new taxes. In 1991, 73 percent of cities increased user fees and 40 percent adopted new user fees for at least one city service.[48] Fees for museums, public parking, ice rinks, and swimming pools were increased. In many cities garbage collection became a private service for which each household pays instead of being a public service paid for out of general tax revenues. User fees and sales taxes take a larger proportion of income for low-income households than for better-off households. To the degree that these taxes replace property and income taxes, therefore, the municipal tax structure becomes steadily more regressive.[49]

MUNICIPAL BONDS

If cities had always relied on taxation alone, they would never have been able to build the permanent infrastructure on which all city life depends. From the mid-nineteenth century to the present, cities have issued bonds to private investors as a way of borrowing money. Cities are authorized by state legislation to issue long-term bonds to pay for capital improvements, such as schools, highways, bridges, and hospitals, that will benefit city residents over a long period of time. Cities in most states can borrow short term, using tax anticipation notes (TANS) repaid in 30 to 120 days, to cover temporary budget shortages or to time their entry into the long-term bond market. Unlike the federal government, cities cannot use bond funds to cover long-term operating deficits.

Given the continuing need to build and maintain public infrastructure, access to the municipal bond market is essential for the well-being of cities. Cities are directly dependent on the willingness of private sector individuals and institutions to buy their bonds. The municipal bond market is a significant sector of the economy. Borrowings typically represent 20 to 25 percent of all state and local spending.[50] In 1995 cities and towns issued $28 billion in new long-term debt, with total debt outstanding by all local governments amounting to $626 billion.[51]

The most important fact about municipal bonds is that they are tax exempt. Because the interest income derived from municipal bonds is not subject to taxation, investors are willing to buy municipal bonds at a lower interest rate than they would pay for corporate bonds. In effect, the federal government provides cities with a subsidy by exempting municipal bonds from taxation. In 1988 the Supreme Court ruled that state and local governments had no constitutional right to borrow at tax-exempt rates; Congress has the power to take away this subsidy to state and local governments.[52] The municipal bond market is dominated by corporations and wealthy individuals because the minimum bond size is typically $25,000 or greater. Municipal bonds are purchased by commercial banks, casualty insurance companies, and, increasingly, wealthy individual investors, who find the federal tax exemption especially attractive.[53] Unlike other corporations, commercial banks are taxed at the full corporate tax rate, and therefore they have invested heavily in tax-exempt municipal debt. Because the banks control such a large portion of the outstanding bonds (32 percent in 1984), city finances are heavily dependent on their investment decisions.[54]

The federal subsidy to cities through the bond market is relatively inefficient because only part of it, in the form of lower interest rates paid to investors, goes to cities. The rest of the federal subsidy is siphoned off to wealthy taxpayers who avoid paying federal taxes by buying the tax-exempt municipal bonds. Legislation was proposed, but never passed, to allow municipalities to float bonds at normal interest rates in exchange for a direct subsidy by the federal government.[55] In this way, the subsidy would go entirely to cities and not, indirectly, to investors.

Cities issue two types of long-term bonds: general obligation bonds and revenue bonds. General obligation bonds pledge the "full faith and credit" of the city's taxing powers behind the bonds, generally require voter approval, and are used to build public infrastructure like bridges and parks. Revenue bonds are not guaranteed by the issuing government and do not require voter approval; anticipated future revenues from the facilities that are constructed with the bond monies are committed to pay back the bonds. Revenue bonds are usually issued by public authorities set up by local governments. Run by appointed boards, authorities are free from democratic controls.[56] Cities use revenue bonds, basically, to avoid having to go before the voters and to evade borrowing limits placed on them by state governments. States do not require voter approval for revenue bonds because, in theory, the voters' tax dollars are not at risk. However, when revenues are not sufficient to pay bond premiums (and they often are not), local governments must make up the difference. Sports stadiums (such as the Superdome in New Orleans) often lose millions of dollars a year, and taxpayers pay these debts.

By the mid-1990s state and local governments had established between 6,000 and 7,000 authorities,[57] and in 1995 alone, these authorities issued $75.3 billion in new long-term debt.[58] Almost any facilities that can charge user fees—sports stadiums, convention centers, museums, aquariums—are financed through revenue bonds. Local government borrowing through revenue bonds rose sharply in the 1970s. In the 1960s and through much of the 1970s, general obligation bonds represented about 60 percent of outstanding local long-term debt.[59] By 1985 nonguaranteed revenue-bond debt represented 62.8 percent of all outstanding debt issued by city governments and their dependent agencies.[60]

Revenue bonds permit cities to use their tax-exempt borrowing privileges to support private programs and activities. In the late 1970s, cities began issuing mortgage revenue bonds to subsidize interest rates for middle-income home buyers, although in 1980 Congress restricted this practice with the passage of the Mortgage Subsidy Act. In an attempt to stimulate economic growth, in the 1970s and 1980s cities increasingly issued industrial revenue bonds to subsidize a broad assortment of businesses, including K-Marts, McDonalds, liquor stores, and law offices. Critics charged that the tax-exempt borrowing was being used for private purposes that did not serve any public interest. Examples of flagrant abuses abounded. Chester County, Pennsylvania, for example, issued revenue bonds for an "adult" bookstore and topless go-go bar in downtown Philadelphia. Congress, noting the hemorrhage of federal tax revenues, restricted the use of revenue bonds by passing the Tax Equity and Fiscal Responsibility Act of 1982 and the Deficit Reduction Act of 1984.[61] The Tax Reform Act of 1986 placed state-by-state limits on what it termed governmentally subsidized "private-activity bonds."[62]

Besides being used for questionable private purposes, municipal bonds have been subject to a number of other abuses. Some local governments have borrowed money in the tax-exempt market and then put that money into risky investments, hoping to make substantial profits. Unwilling to raise taxes, Orange County, California, attempted to maintain services by putting the proceeds of bond sales into risky investments called "derivatives" that were essentially gambling on the direction of interest rates. When interest rates plunged, Orange County lost $1.6 billion. In April 1994 Orange County became the largest municipal government in history to file for federal bankruptcy protection under Chapter 9. More than 180 other governments lost money in similar high-risk investment pools.

In recent years, the municipal bond market has been rocked by charges that bond underwriters, in order to obtain lucrative government bond business, kicked back profits to public officials in the form of campaign contributions.[63] In April 1994 the Securities and Exchange Commission (SEC) enacted Rule G–37, which barred campaign contributions by municipal bankers. To get around this ban, municipal finance companies provided funding for lavish receptions at the 1996 Democratic and Republican conventions where bond underwriters could mingle with top state and local officials. At the Republican convention in San Diego this included golf and tennis parties, a fishing expedition, and a luncheon honoring House Speaker Newt Gingrich.[64] A 1996 lawsuit alleged that bond underwriters overcharged municipalities for escrow accounts by as much as $1 billion.[65] Such abuses have led to repeated demands that the municipal bond industry be more closely regulated.[66]

THE RATINGS GAME

A city's cost of borrowing is basically determined by its bond rating. A bond rating purports to represent the relative credit quality of the issuing municipality and thus determines the rate of interest a city must pay. A high rating means a lower interest rate, on the theory that there is less risk for the investor. When a city's bond rating is lowered due to fiscal problems, a bond may be more difficult to sell, and the additional interest paid over the amortized life of the bond can amount to millions of dollars.

Bond ratings are published by two national rating firms: Moody's Investors Service and Standard and Poor's Corporation. Until the late 1960s, both firms routinely rated most bond issues. Since that time, however, the firms have rated municipal bonds only for an annual fee, ranging from $500 to $2,500 or more.[67] Cities have no choice but to seek a rating if they want to be able to market their bonds.

Ratings represent a combination of subjective and objective evaluations. The exact formulas and procedures for making the ratings are unknown, and the rating agencies do not reveal the factors determining bond ratings.[68] The system almost certainly is basically arbitrary. One commentator on the rating system noted, "Instead of using systematic and objective measurements, both municipal bond rating agencies emphasize the importance of careful study and [subjective] decisions made by experienced municipal bond analysts and committees."[69] If the amount of time spent is in any way indicative of the quality of analysis, it is interesting to note that though initial ratings typically take a few days, "ratings on subsequent sales of outstanding bonds take only a couple of hours" or less.[70] The rating of municipal bonds has been very inconsistent over time. Using objective data about a city's financial condition it is possible to duplicate the ratings only 50 to 70 percent of the time. So-called hidden factors known only to the ratings firms must therefore account for the discrepancies in ratings between otherwise similar communities.[71]

Nevertheless, distinct patterns in ratings can be identified. Cities that were downgraded in their ratings between 1975 and 1980 lost population in the 1970s, while cities whose bonds were upgraded grew. The downgraded cities also experienced slower growth in per capita income.[72] Fiscal factors correlate closely with bond ratings. The cities that became most dependent on intergovernmental resources in the 1960s and 1970s were the most frequently downgraded.[73] All these factors are associated with older cities of the Northeast and Midwest. Table 12.5 makes this relationship obvious, as does a study of larger cities published in 1980.[74] Each of the seven cities listed in the table as being downgraded between 1965 and 1978 was an older industrial city noted for its social and eco-

TABLE 12.5	CHANGES IN RATINGS ON GENERAL OBLIGATION BONDS (MOODY'S RATINGS)		
Rating Downgraded 1965–1978	Rating Downgraded 1978–1986	Rating Downgraded 1986–1995	Rating Downgraded 1995–1998
Buffalo	Chicago	Dallas	Los Angeles
Cleveland	Cincinnati	Fort Worth	Miami
Newark	Cleveland	Houston	Norfolk, VA
Philadelphia	Columbus	Los Angeles	San Diego
Pittsburgh	Detroit	Miami	Sacramento
	Houston	Newark	
	Louisville	New Orleans	
	Milwaukee	Oakland	
	San Francisco	Philadelphia	
	St. Louis	Toledo	
	Toledo	Tulsa	
		Washington, D.C.	

Sources: Moody's Municipal and Government Manual, 2 vols. (New York: Moody's Investors Service, 1986); *The Municipal Yearbook 1987* (Washington, D.C.: International City Management Association, 1987), pp. 178–213; U.S. Bureau of the Census, *Statistical Abstract of the United States 1996,* 116th edition (Washington, D.C.: Government Printing Office, 1996), p. 305; and U.S. Bureau of the Census, *Statistical Abstract of the United States, 1999* (Washington, D.C.: Government Printing Office, 1999), p. 332, table 519.

nomic problems. Of eleven cities downgraded from 1978 to 1986, nine were older industrial cities in the Northwest or Midwest. The situation changed between 1986 and 1995 when fiscal stress spread to some Sunbelt cities. Between 1995 and 1998, none of the five major cities that had their bonds downgraded were older industrial cities. Clearly, fiscal risk had become spread around.

Bond ratings are totally unrelated to the likelihood of default. (Default does not mean that the loan was not repaid; it simply means that the payments were not made on time.) The discrepancy in the interest rates between the highest and lowest investment grade bonds is inexplicable on the basis of relative risk.[75] From 1929 to 1933, when 77 percent of all municipal defaults of the twentieth century occurred, the highest-rated bonds recorded the highest incidence of default.[76]

Major cities simply do not fail to pay their debts. True, from the first recorded default in 1838 (Mobile, Alabama) through 1969 there were more than 6,000 recorded bond defaults by local governments. Fewer than a third of these, however, involved incorporated municipalities (cities); most of the rest were special districts that provided particular services such as irrigation. Seventy-five percent of all such failures occurred between 1930 and 1939. Less than 10 percent occurred after the depression.[77] During the worst period for municipal bonds, 1929 through 1937, only 8 percent of all cities and 19.9 percent of their bonded debt were ever in default.[78] Almost all of the debts were eventually paid.

From World War II through early 1970, a total of 431 state and local units defaulted on their obligations. The total principal involved was $450 million, approximately 0.4 percent of the outstanding state and local debt. Three noncity units, the West Virginia Turnpike Commission, the Calumet Skyway Toll Bridge, and the Chesapeake Bay Bridge and Tunnel Commission, accounted for over 74 percent of this amount. Only two of twenty-four major default situations ($1 million or more) were related to general obligation bonds.[79] Of 114 defaults by cities during the 1960s, almost all were temporary or technical defaults. Only thirty-four involved general obligation bonds, and in all these cases the cities had populations under 5,000 and the amount in default was less than $1 million.[80]

An analysis of cases filed in federal district courts between 1938 and 1971 reveals that nine cities took advantage of federal municipal bankruptcy legislation. With one exception (Saluda, North Carolina), all the cases came from small, rather obscure cities in Texas (Ranger, Talco, Benevides) or Florida (Manatee, Medley, Center Hill, Webster, Wanchula). Only in the case of Benevides (population 2,500) were general obligation bonds of post–World War II origin involved. In all other cases, the defaulted debt was of prewar origin, related to revenue bonds, or unrelated to bonds altogether.[81]

In the rare cases when a city defaulted on its obligations, it has invariably involved only a technical failure to pay on time, and the failure has been temporary. Bondholders have always recovered their money, even though it may have taken longer than they liked. On December 15, 1978, Cleveland became the first major city to default, even in a technical sense, since 1933. On that day the city failed to make payments on $14 million in short-term notes; the city renewed payments a few months later and officially ended default in 1980.[82] There would appear to be little justification for differential rating of city bonds, especially general obligation bonds: "Where the full faith and credit has been pledged . . . there simply has been no record of meaningful risk for forty years."[83]

A USEFUL COMPARISON: NEW YORK AND CHICAGO

Why do some cities experience fiscal crises while others avoid them? A good way to answer this question is to examine two cities with sharply contrasting experiences: New York City and Chicago. Since its 1975 fiscal crisis, New York has been continually ensnared in fiscal crises. Chicago, on the other hand, known as "the city that works," has largely avoided them. An examination of the contrasting experiences of these two cities helps to identify the structural factors that lead to urban fiscal crises.

New York and Chicago are quite similar, in that they have shared the basic characteristics of urban decline. In the two decades between 1960 and 1980, for example, New York's population fell 9 percent, and Chicago's dropped 15 percent. In both cases the main cause of the population loss was a massive white flight to the suburbs. In twenty years the nonwhite percentage of the total population increased from 15 percent to 39 percent in New York and from 24 percent to 50 percent in Chicago.[84] Both cities suffered substantial job losses in the postwar period, especially in manufacturing. In the ten-year period from 1967 to 1977, New York lost 287,000 manufacturing jobs and Chicago lost 181,000.[85] Both suffered from high unemployment rates, welfare dependency, and concentrated poverty.[86] Clearly, in the 1960s and 1970s New York and Chicago were both cities in decline. Various attempts to measure urban decline all ranked New York and Chicago in the "distressed" category.[87] One study rated cities according to "standardized fiscal health," which was measured as the difference between a city's revenue-raising capacity and its expenditure needs based on economic and social trends. In 1972, out of seventy-one cities, Chicago ranked sixty-eighth and New York ranked dead last.[88]

Though the underlying socioeconomic profiles of New York and Chicago looked quite similar, their fiscal conditions diverged dramatically. In the mid-1970s, while New York approached financial collapse, Chicago managed to restrain expenditure growth and avoid going deeply into debt. Chicago did not use short-term debt to cover operating expenses the way New York did. In 1975 New York's per capita short-term debt was $618, compared with only $72 for Chicago. That same year Chicago's long-term per capita debt was about a fourth of New York's.[89] During the 1970s, when New York's bond ratings plummeted and the city lost access to the bond market, Chicago retained high ratings and access to credit. Mayor Daley was viewed almost as a hero by the business community. Why did the financial histories of two cities with similar conditions diverge so greatly, and what can their differences tell us about the politics of urban fiscal stress?

In the case of New York, blame can be apportioned to both politicians and bankers. For years New York spent more than it took in, and by 1975 it had accumulated a $3 billion operating deficit.[90] Politicians tried to avoid the painful remedies that could reduce the debt—namely, lowering spending or raising taxes. Instead, they engaged in creative accounting. One method of making each year's budget appear balanced when it actually was not, was to count projected revenue instead of actual revenue received. The flaw in this method was that not all revenue was collectible even in the distant future. From 1970 to 1976, between $2 and $3 billion in city taxes, fees, and fines went uncollected, $1 billion in 1976 alone. Between 1970 and 1975, the delinquency rate for real property taxes rose from 4 percent to 7 percent, totaling $571 million by June 30, 1975.[91] By treating all taxes, fees, and fines as collectible, and therefore as projected income, millions of dollars were added, on paper, to the revenue side of the ledger.

Other creative techniques moved funds around and put off the day of reckoning. The last payday of the year was advanced into the next fiscal year. Some current operating expenses, such as planning and engineering operations, were dumped into the capital expenditures budget, where deficits could be covered by long-term bonds. In 1975–1976 alone, $600 million was thus transferred to long-term debt.[92] Vendors and other creditors were held off until a new fiscal year arrived. Contributions to the city's pension funds were delayed and underfinanced, while the interest on those accounts above the statutory minimum was "borrowed" for the city's current general fund.[93] Present expenses were shifted onto future taxpayers by calling borrowed funds "income" and issuing Revenue Anticipation Notes (RANs) and Tax Anticipation Notes (TANs). These were short-term bonds against which future intergovernmental receipts and taxes were pledged.

All these gimmicks simply papered over the underlying problem: Each year expenditures exceeded revenues. New York's accumulated debt continued to rise. The deficits were rolled over from year to year by issuing new short-term bonds to cover debt service on last year's bonds coming due. Short-term debt, which represented the bulk of this accumulated rolled-over debt, grew by over 400 percent in ten years. (On a personal level, this is like charging living expenses on one credit card, then using a second credit card to cover payments on the first, a third to cover the second, ad infinitum—and never coming up with the cash.)

The politicians could not have resorted to such clever shell games without cooperation and even enthusiastic encouragement from bankers and lenders. The bankers were making an enormous amount of money underwriting and marketing New York's securities. Between 1965 and 1975, New York issued nearly $58 billion in bonds. Of this total, $48.5 billion was in short-term, high-interest notes used to roll over the accumulating deficit and rectify the cash flow problems of the city. Bankers and brokers made commissions on every bond sale and were able to promote the bonds to investors because of the high interest rates they carried.

The banks and bond brokers were direct participants in the financial processes of the city through the Bond Counsel and the Comptroller's Technical Debt Advisory Committee. The latter body, which was composed of both public officials and bankers, existed to advise the city on its borrowing strategy. It implicitly endorsed the city's practices by approving the continuous stream of bonds. William E. Simon, one of the nation's biggest bond brokers, was a member of the committee in 1971 and 1972. As a senior partner in the firm of Salomon Brothers, he "was personally in charge of Salomon's [substantial] municipal and governmental bond sales."[94] One participant in the committee's meetings remarked that "all Simon and some of the other bankers wanted to do was sell bonds, make their profits, and look the other way."[95] This was the same William E. Simon who, as President Gerald Ford's Secretary of the Treasury, advocated a policy of punitive measures against New York when the city asked for a federal loan to avoid default on its debts in 1975. His own culpability in New York's problems did not deter him from observing, when the city asked for help, "We're going to sell New York to the Shah of Iran. It's a hell of an investment."[96]

The deteriorating economy in the mid-1970s and the troubles of many private businesses (such as the failure of the retail chain W. T. Grant, which left banks holding $640 million in debts[97]) led banks to reevaluate their holdings. New York's bonds were doubly threatening. Not only were they deemed marginal, but should the city default, the banks could not avoid a possible bankruptcy action that might result in a write-down in the value of the bonds. A rapid write-down would translate into huge losses for the banks[98] and would reverberate through the national and world economies. A near panic about the financial viability of the city ensued.

As described in a report issued by a committee of the New York State legislature, the banks scrambled to save their own profits at the city's expense:

> They began to rapidly and quietly (and perhaps improperly and illegally) unload their New York City bonds and thus saturated the market. You recall, they claimed the market was saturated and hence they could not sell their bonds. This seems to be untrue. In fact it appears that Chase [Manhattan Bank] unloaded two billion dollars' worth of bonds in a very short time!
>
> . . . Here is where the problem gets sticky for the banks. They had knowledge of the problems ahead, but they kept this knowledge to themselves while unloading their portfolios on others. They created the panic by their heavy sales.[99]

The culpability of the banks in precipitating the fiscal crisis was subsequently documented in a 10-pound, 800-page investigative report issued by the U.S. Securities and Exchange Commission.[100]

New York City's fiscal crisis came to a head in May 1975 when the banks publicly refused to market the city's securities. To resolve the crisis, the state legislature of New York, in response to pressure from the city's banking and business elite, established the Municipal Assistance Corporation (MAC) and the Emergency Financial Control Board (EFCB), both of which essentially took control of city government away from the city's elected officials. Members of the financial community firmly controlled both agencies and through them wielded the power to review annual budgets and borrowing requests.

The bankers were still not satisfied. To get the taxpayers to ensure the safety of their investments, they asked the federal government to guarantee MAC bonds issued to cover the city's debts. Initially, President Ford refused to consider any special aid for New York, prompting a *New York Daily News* headline, "FORD TO CITY: DROP DEAD" (October 29, 1975). Eventually, the Ford Administration did support a modified bailout bill that enabled the city to borrow funds at 1 percent above the U.S. Treasury borrowing rate. Summing up the federal bailout, one scholar remarked, "Not only did the federal government make money on New York's fiscal crisis but the 'aid' package to the city was actually much less than the Chrysler Corporation bailout and aid given to many Third World nations."[101]

The fiscal retrenchment that followed the crisis had a profound impact on New York. Immediately, 25,000 city workers were fired, with African-American and Latino workers disproportionately losing their jobs. Between 1975 and 1980, city expenditures declined by 21 percent (in constant dollars).[102] Municipal services declined in quantity and quality. Within a year of the crisis, the century-old tradition of free tuition at the City University ended. Subway fares were increased three times in the next six years.[103] As New York gradually regained access to the bond market, tax subsidies for economic development were accorded highest priority and social services were pared.[104] Poor people bore most of the burdens of retrenchment.[105]

The 1975 fiscal crisis transformed the politics of New York City. Led by Mayor Edward Koch (1978 to 1989), New York formed a "fiscal crisis" regime in which priorities shifted from services for the poor and middle class to tax breaks and other incentives for corporate investors and real estate developers. Koch effectively used the threat of another fiscal crisis to limit demands for public spending.[106] After the 1975 crisis, New York enjoyed a decade-long economic boom that enabled the city to balance its budget once again. Between 1978 and 1987 the city's economy gained over 300,000 jobs and tax revenues soared.[107] Even with Mayor Koch's skillful use of the rhetoric of urban fiscal crisis, however, the city failed to restrain its expenditure growth adequately and with the economic downturn that began in 1989 found itself, once again, on the brink of fiscal disaster. Despite a healthy national economy, Mayor Giuliani's preliminary budget for 1998 projected a $1.9 billion deficit.[108]

Chicago's experience provides an instructive contrast to New York's. Following the death of Richard J. Daley in 1976, Chicago experienced a period of political turbulence that threatened the ruling regime and its budgetary policy. In the early 1980s, Chicago, like other cities, had fiscal problems. Its bonds were downgraded in 1984. However, the city was able to control spending growth and by 1987 Moody's had returned the city's bond rating to an A level.[109] Mayor Daley's son, Richard M. Daley, was elected mayor in 1989 and largely reconstituted the governing coalition that his father ran so effectively for many years. An editorial in the *Wall Street Journal* praised Daley's responsible management of city government and cited Chicago as an example for other cities, like New York, to emulate.[110]

Though some of the differences between New York and Chicago can be attributed to styles of leadership, it is clear that political leaders in the two cities worked in different institutional contexts. The fragmentation of New York's Democratic party, among other factors, led to a unique situation: By the 1960s, the only way a citywide governing coalition could be held together was for the mayor to spend more than the city took in. In the absence of party loyalty, politicians had to buy electoral loyalty from individual interest groups with expensive programs. Various groups and constituencies expected concrete programs in exchange for their support.[111] By contrast, because Chicago's machine was able to deliver votes "through its ward-based organization, the machine either suppressed or absorbed most interest group activity in the city."[112]

New York's per capita tax burden was more than three times higher than Chicago's in 1996 (see Table 12.6). New York's high tax rates can be traced to several causes. The fragmented nature of its politics is one cause, but to blame everything on "liberal" politicians who caved in to demands from interest groups is simplistic. New York City was forced to fund a whole series of functions that in Chicago were funded by other governments. A study of sixty-two cities found that New York's functional responsibilities were broader than any other city's.[113] Chicago concentrated on basic housekeeping services, such as police, fire, and street cleaning. In 1975, Chicago spent only $12.18 per capita on public welfare, while New York City spent $365.78.[114] In Chicago most public welfare functions were the responsibility of Cook County, thus saving Chicago city taxpayers considerable money. To cite another example, in 1974 Chicago formed the Regional Transportation Authority (RTA) that spread funding for mass transit over a six-county area.[115]

TABLE 12.6	PER CAPITA MUNICIPAL TAX BURDEN AND PER CAPITA BONDED DEBT, 1965–1996			
	Tax Burden		Debt Burden	
	New York	Chicago	New York	Chicago
1965	$285.93	$83.99	$959.00	$281.43
1970	$382.90	$122.76	$1,101.00	$497.00
1975	$614.61	$176.63	$1,874.00	$616.00
1980	$948.50	$245.00	$1,505.00	$716.00
1989	$2,052.79	$478.12	$2,486.00	$1,848.00
1996	$3,333.56	$1,069.43	$6,232.49	$2,902.28

Sources: Adapted from tables in Esther Fuchs, *Mayors and Money: Fiscal Policy in New York and Chicago* (Chicago: University of Chicago Press, 1992); and U.S. Bureau of the Census, *Statistical Abstract of the United States, 1999* (Washington, D.C.: Government Printing Office, 1999) pp. 334–335, tables 530–531; U.S. Bureau of the Census, *Statistical Abstract of the United States, 1998* (Washington, D.C.: Government Printing Office, 1998), p. 47, table 48.

New York, on the other hand, had costly responsibilities in welfare, health care, education (including an expensive city university system), public hospitals, public housing, and mass transit. In 1968 New York created the Metropolitan Transit Authority (MTA) to coordinate mass transit policy for the city and seven suburban counties, but the city still carried a substantial financial burden for mass transit.[116] In most cases, there was little the city could do about the added burden of all these responsibilities because it was New York State that determined the city's responsibilities. For example, New York City paid 23 percent of the Medicaid bill for recipients in the city.[117] Because such social programs relied on federal grants, New York became dependent on intergovernmental grants. In 1975, 50 percent of its total revenue came in the form of intergovernmental grants, compared with only 29 percent for Chicago. This left New York far more vulnerable than Chicago to the federal cuts of the 1980s.

The comparison between New York and Chicago shows that leadership can make a difference in avoiding fiscal crises. However, leaders are constrained by the setting within which they work. New York's mayors lacked the political authority to control spending. Indeed, the costs of many of the social programs the city helped fund were driven by the number of eligible recipients, and thus the city could not really control their costs. Chicago's solution, which was to move such programs into special districts or county or regional authorities, could not be implemented in New York. The suburban-dominated state legislature would never allow it. The lesson is that cities rarely control, to any significant degree, the causes of their fiscal difficulties. The social problems besetting central cities are related to national economic and social conditions. When cities try to manage the problems caused by such conditions, they find themselves locked into institutional and political arrangements that leave them little flexibility.

THE POLITICAL SOURCES OF URBAN FISCAL STRESS

Cities are subject to the actions of the federal and state governments and of private economic institutions in ways that severely restrict their ability to cope:

> A city's fiscal health . . . depends on economic, social, and institutional factors that are largely outside the city's control. Poor fiscal health is not caused by poor management, corruption, or profligate spending, and a city government's ability to alter the city's fiscal health is severely limited.[118]

City officials under fiscal stress find themselves confronted with a dilemma: They can either raise taxes or cut services, but either alternative can have a negative impact on the long-term fiscal viability of a city. When cities raise taxes, they run the danger of losing the investors and middle-class taxpayers that are so essential to urban revival. Already, by 1981, the tax burdens of central cities, as a percentage of personal income, exceeded suburban tax burdens by more than 50 percent.[119] Alternatively, when cities reduce the level of services and fail to build and maintain infrastructure, they become less attractive places to live and work. For cities in severe fiscal crisis, a vicious cycle of decline may set in: Deteriorating services chase away business and residents, the tax base sags as a result and revenues decline and services must be cut further, and so on.

Urban fiscal crises are not inevitable. They result from the structure of America's intergovernmental system, which makes each city an autonomous fiscal unit but also subject to the whims and demands of higher levels of government. Western European cities have had no general tendency toward fiscal crisis.[120] A major reason for this is that central governments provide a substantial portion of local revenues. In 1984, for example, when intergovernmental transfers provided only about 20 percent of local revenues in the United States, they provided 40 percent in Japan, 54 percent in Britain, and 80 percent in the Netherlands.[121] Most Western European city governments do not have to rely on private lenders to raise money for capital projects; those are generally financed by national governments. The U.S. arrangement is peculiar: "By not providing capital resources to subnational governments from the central government, the United States stands apart from almost every other advanced capitalist state, even other federal states."[122] All across the country, urban residents must live, often very uncomfortably, with this peculiar arrangement.

NOTES

1. Carol W. Lewis, "Budgetary Balance: The Norm, Concept, and Practice in Large U.S. Cities," *Public Administration Review* 54 (November/December 1994): 517–518.
2. Helen F. Ladd, "Big-City Finances," in *Big City Politics, Governance, and Fiscal Constraints,* ed. George E. Peterson (Washington, D.C.: Urban Institute Press, 1994), p. 202. Emphasis added.

3. Jonathan Kozol, *Savage Inequalities: Children in America's Schools* (New York: Harper-Collins, 1991); Isabel Wilkerson, "Ravaged City on Mississippi Floundering at Rock Bottom," *New York Times*, April 4, 1991, p. 4A.

4. U.S. Bureau of the Census, *Statistical Abstract of the United States*, 1996, 116th ed. (Washington, D.C.: Government Printing Office, 1996), pp. 153, 298, 315.

5. Ibid., p. 318.

6. Inflation is measured by the GNP Implicit Deflator. *Business Statistics: 1961–88, Survey of Current Business*, March 1991, cited in Roy Bahl et al., "The Fiscal Conditions of U.S. Cities at the Beginning of the 1990s" (paper delivered at the Urban Institute Conference on Big City Governance and Fiscal Choices, Los Angeles, June 6–7, 1991), table 12.

7. This is known as "Baumol's disease," after the economist who first fully analyzed the problem. William Baumol, "The Microeconomics of Unbalanced Growth," *American Economic Review* 57 (June 1967): 415–526.

8. U.S. Advisory Commission on Intergovernmental Relations, *Significant Features of Fiscal Federalism, 1985–86* (Washington, D.C.: Government Printing Office, 1986), p. 71. These data exclude school district employees. If they were included, public employee earnings would be 104.7 percent of private wages in 1975.

9. U.S. Advisory Commission, *Significant Features of Fiscal Federalism, 1980–81* (Washington, D.C.: Government Printing Office, 1981), p. 71.

10. Ibid., p. 19.

11. See Roger W. Schmenner, "The Determination of Municipal Employee Wages," *Review of Economics and Statistics* 60 (February 1973): 83–90; Orley Ashenfetter, "The Effect of Unions on Wages in the Public Sector: The Case of Fire Fighters," *Industrial and Labor Relations Review* 24 (January 1971): 191–202; George E. Peterson, "Finance," in *The Urban Predicament*, ed. William Gorham and Nathan Glazer (Washington, D.C.: The Urban Institute, 1976), pp. 108–109.

12. U.S. Bureau of the Census, *Statistical Abstract of the United States, 1996*, p. 319.

13. Ibid. and U.S. Bureau of the Census, *Statistical Abstract of the United States, 1992*, 112th edition (Washington, D.C.: Government Printing Office, 1992), p. 304.

14. Larry C. Ledebur and William R. Barnes, *City Distress: Metropolitan Disparities and Economic Growth* (Washington, D.C.: National League of Cities, 1991), pp. 2, 6. Figures based on the 85 largest metropolitan areas.

15. Jonathan Kozol, *Rachel and Her Children: Homeless Families in America* (New York: Crown, 1988), p. 14.

16. "Homicide Records Set in 3 Big Cities," *New York Times*, January 3, 1992.

17. Bahl et al., "The Fiscal Conditions of U.S. Cities," pp. 5–6.

18. *Garcia v. San Antonio Metropolitan Transit Authority*, 469 U.S. 528 (1985).

19. Employment Standards Administration, *Minimum Wage and Maximum Hours Standards Under the Fair Labor Standards Act* (Washington, D.C.: U.S. Environmental Protection Agency, 1986), pp. 110–111; U.S. Congress, House Committee on Education and Labor, *Report to Accompany H.R. 3530*, 99th Cong., 1st sess., 1985. H. Rept. 99–331, p. 30; both cited in Joseph F. Zimmerman, "Federally Induced State and Local Governmental Costs" (paper delivered at the Annual Meeting of the American Political Science Association, Washington, D.C., August 29–September 1, 1991), p. 14.

20. Todd Sloane, "Clean Air Act Likely to Burn Many Municipalities," *City & State*, November 19, 1990, p. 2, cited in Zimmerman, "Federally Induced State and Local Government Costs," p. 12.

21. Refer to Richard T. Ely, *Taxation in American States and Cities* (New York: Crowell, 1888), pp. 109–113; Sumner Benson, "A History of the General Property Tax," in *The American Property Tax: Its History, Administration, and Economic Impact*, ed. C. G. Benson, S. Benson, H. McClelland, and P. Thompson (Claremont, Calif.: College Press, 1965), p. 24.

22. E. R. A. Seligman, *Essays in Taxation*, 9th ed. (New York: Macmillan, 1923), p. 24.

23. U.S. Bureau of the Census, *Historical Statistics of the United States: Colonial Times to 1970*, Bicentennial ed. pt 2 (Washington, D.C.: Government Printing Office, 1975), p. 1133.

24. Calculated from the data in U.S. Bureau of the Census, *Local Government Finances in Selected Metropolitan Areas and Large Counties: 1969–70*, GF 70, No. 6 (Washington, D.C.: Government Printing Office, 1970), p. 7; U.S. Bureau of the Census, *Local Government Finances in Selected Metropolitan Areas and Large Counties: 1974–75*, GF 75, No. 6 (Washington, D.C.: Government Printing Office, 1976), p. 7.

25. U.S. Bureau of the Census, *Government Finances in 1978–79*, GF 79, No. 5 (Washington, D.C.: Government Printing Office, 1980), p. 64.

26. U.S. Bureau of the Census, *Statistical Abstract of the United States, 1996*, p. 169.

27. Peterson, "Finance," p. 52.

28. Ibid., p. 53.

29. Alfred Balk, *The Free List—Property Without Taxes* (New York: Russell Sage Foundation, 1971), pp. 10–12.

30. J. Richard Aronson and John L. Hilley, *Financing State and Local Governments*, 4th ed. (Washington, D.C.: Brookings Institution, 1986), p. 136.

31. Gregory H. Wassall, *Tax-Exempt Property: A Case Study of Hartford, Connecticut* (Hartford, Conn.: John C. Lincoln Institute, 1974), p. 27.

32. Todd Swanstrom, *Capital Cities: Challenges and Opportunities* (Albany, N.Y.: Rockefeller Institute of Government), p. 17.

33. Michael J. Barrett, "The Out-of-Towners," *Boston Globe Magazine*, August 7, 1983.

34. *Walz v. Tax Commission of the City of New York*, 397 U.S. 664. See also Boris I. Bittker, "Churches, Taxes and the Constitution" *Yale Law Review* 78 (July 1969): 1285–1310.

35. Helen F. Ladd and John Yinger, *America's Ailing Cities: Fiscal Health and the Design of Urban Policy*, updated ed. (Baltimore: Johns Hopkins University Press, 1989), pp. 129–130, 180. See also Michael Wolkoff, Municipal Tax Abatement: A Two-Edged Sword, *New York Case Studies in Public Management* no. 4 (Albany, N.Y.: Rockefeller Institute of Government, 1984).

36. Ladd and Yinger, *America's Ailing Cities*, p. 87.

37. Christopher H. Gadsen and Roger W. Schmenner, "Municipal Income Taxation," in *Local Public Finance and the Fiscal Squeeze: A Case Study*, ed. John R. Meyer and John M. Quigley (New York: Ballinger, 1977), p. 70.

38. Ladd and Yinger, *America's Ailing Cities*, p. 54. Surprisingly, local sales taxes have an even worse export ratio than property taxes.

39. Ibid., p. 293.

40. Eric A. Anderson, "Changing Municipal Finances," *Urban Data Services Reports 7*, No. 12 (Washington, D.C.: International City Manager Association, December 1975), p. 2.

41. Peggy L. Cuciti, "A Nonurban Policy: Recent Public Policy Shifts Affecting Cities," in *The Future of National Urban Policy*, ed. Marshall Kaplan and Franklin James (Durham, N.C.: Duke University Press, 1990), pp. 243–244. See also Hal Wolman, "The Reagan Urban Policy and Its Impacts," *Urban Affairs Quarterly* 21, No. 3 (1986): 311–335.

42. Richard L. Cole, Delbert A. Taebel, and Rodney V. Hissong, "America's Cities and the 1980s: The Legacy of the Reagan Years," *Journal of Urban Affairs* 12 No. 4 (1990): 348.

43. U.S. Advisory Commission, *Significant Features, 1980–81*, p. 59.

44. Richard P. Nathan and Fred C. Doolittle, *Reagan and the States* (Princeton, N.J.: Princeton University Press, 1987), p. 19.

45. U.S. Bureau of the Census, *Statistical Abstract of the United States, 1996*, p. 315.

46. John L. Mikesell, "The Season of Tax Revolt," in *Fiscal Retrenchment and Urban Policy*, ed. John P. Blair and David Nachmias (Beverly Hills, Calif.: Sage, 1979), p. 109.

47. Ibid., p. 109.

48. Pagano, *City Fiscal Conditions in 1991: A Research Report of the National League of Cities* (Washington, D.C.: National League of Cities, 1991), p. 24.

49. Cole, Taebel, and Hissong, "America's Cities and the 1980s," p. 352.

50. Twentieth Century Fund Task Force on Municipal Bond Credit Ratings, *The Rating Game*, with a background paper by John E. Peterson (New York: Twentieth Century Fund, 1974), p. 25.

51. U.S. Bureau of the Census, *Statistical Abstract of the United States, 1996*, p. 304. Amounts are estimates subject to sampling variation.

52. *South Carolina v. Baker*, 108 S.Ct. 1935 (1988).

53. Alberta Sbragia, "Finance Capital and the City," in *Cities in Stress: A New Look at the Urban Crisis*, ed. M. Gottdiener (Beverly Hills, Calif.: Sage, 1986), p. 210.

54. Aronson and Hilley, *Financing State and Local Governments*, p. 174.

55. See Robert Huefner, *Taxable Alternatives to Municipal Bonds, Research Report No. 53* (Boston: Federal Reserve Bank of Boston, 1972); *Building a Broader Market: Report of the Twentieth Century Fund Task Force on the Municipal Bond Market*, with a background paper by Ronald W. Forbes and John E. Peterson (New York: McGraw-Hill, 1976).

56. For insightful discussions of the powerful role of local authorities, see Ann Marie Hauck Walsh, *The Public's Business: The Politics and Practices of Government Corporations* (Cambridge, Mass.: MIT Press, 1978); and Alberta M. Sbragia, *Debt Wish: Entrepreneurial Cities, U.S. Federalism, and Economic Development* (Pittsburgh, Pa.: University of Pittsburgh Press, 1996).

57. Sbragia, *Debt Wish*, p. 144.

58. U.S. Bureau of the Census, *Statistical Abstract of the United States, 1996*, p. 304.

59. Elaine B. Sharp, "The Politics and Economics of the New City Debt," *American Political Science Review* 80, No. 4 (December 1986): 1271–1288.

60. U.S. Bureau of the Census, *Statistical Abstract of the United States, 1992*, p. 285.

61. Thomas A. Pascarella and Richard D. Raymond, "Buying Bonds for Business: An Evaluation of the Industrial Revenue Bond Program," *Urban Affairs Quarterly* 18 (September 1982): 73–89.

62. Daphne A. Kenyon and Dennis Zimmerman, "Private-Activity Bonds and the Volume Cap in 1990," *Intergovernmental Perspective* (Summer 1991): 35–37.

63. For citations on municipal bond corruption, see Sbragia, *Debt Wish*, pp. 224–225.

64. Leslie Wayne, "Ban on Political Contributions Considered for Bond Lawyers," *New York Times*, August 15, 1996.

65. Peter Truell, "Municipal Bond Dealers Face Scrutiny," *New York Times*, December 17, 1996, p. 1; Michael R. Lissack, "A Giant Shell Game Snares Taxpayers," *Albany Times Union*, August 1, 1996.

66. "Shine the Light on Muni Deals," *Business Week*, August 26, 1996.

67. Twentieth Century Fund Task Force, *The Rating Game*, p. 55.

68. Ibid., p. 78.

69. George H. Hempel, *Measures of Municipal Bond Quality*, Michigan Reports No. 53 (Ann Arbor: Bureau of Business Research, Graduate School of Business Administration, University of Michigan, 1967), p. 124.

70. Twentieth Century Fund Task Force, *The Rating Game*, p. 83.

71. Ibid., p. 107; Allen J. Michel, "Municipal Bond Ratings: A Discriminant Analysis Approach," *Journal of Financial and Quantitative Analysis* 12 (November 1977): 587–598; W. T. Carleton and E. M. Lerner, "Statistical Credit Scoring and Municipal Bonds," *Journal of Money, Credit and Banking* 1 (November 1969): 750–764; Larry K. Hastie, "Determinants of Municipal Bond Yields," *Journal of Financial and Quantitative Analysis* 7 (June 1972): 1729–1748.

72. Jesse F. Marquette, R. Penny Marquette, and Katherine A. Hinkley, "Bond Rating Changes and Urban Fiscal Stress: Linkage and Prediction," *Journal of Urban Affairs* 4 (Winter 1982): 92.

73. Ibid., p. 93.

74. John E. Peterson, "Changing Fiscal Structure and Credit Quality: Large U.S. Cities," in *Fiscal Stress and Public Policy*, ed. Charles H. Levine and Irene Rubin (Beverly Hills, Calif.: Sage, 1980), pp. 179–202.

75. Thomas Geis, "Municipal Credit and Bond Rating System" (paper delivered at the Municipal Officers Association Meeting, Denver, May 31, 1972), pp. 5–6.
76. Ibid.
77. U.S. Advisory Commission on Intergovernmental Relations, *City Financial Emergencies* (Washington, D.C: Government Printing Office, 1971), p. 10.
78. Ibid., p. 12.
79. Ibid., p. 16.
80. Ibid., p. 17.
81. Ibid., pp. 81–82.
82. Todd Swanstrom, *The Crisis of Growth Politics: Cleveland, Kucinich, and the Challenge of Urban Populism* (Philadelphia: Temple University Press, 1985), chap. 7.
83. Twentieth Century Fund Task Force, *The Rating Game*, p. 117. See also Geis, "Municipal Credit and Bond Rating System"; Hempel, *Measures of Municipal Bond Quality*, p. 74.
84. U.S. Bureau of the Census figures as compiled by Ester R. Fuchs, *Mayors and Money: Fiscal Policy in New York and Chicago* (Chicago: University of Chicago Press, 1992), pp. 22–23. For our comparison of New York and Chicago, we rely heavily on Fuchs's insightful account.
85. U.S. Bureau of the Census, *Census of Manufacturing*, selected years (Washington, D.C.: Government Printing Office, 1950 and 1981), as compiled by John D. Kasarda, "Urban Change and Minority Opportunities," in *The New Urban Reality*, ed. Paul Peterson (Washington, D.C.: Brookings Institution, 1985), p. 44.
86. See William Julius Wilson, *The Truly Disadvantaged: The Inner City, the Underclass, and Public Policy* (Chicago: University of Chicago Press, 1987).
87. See Robert W. Burchell et al., "Measuring Urban Distress: A Summary of the Major Urban Hardship Indices and Resource Allocation Systems," in *Cities Under Stress: The Fiscal Crises of Urban America*, ed. Robert W. Burchell and David Listokin (Piscataway, N.J.: Center for Urban Policy Research, 1981), p. 219; Katherine L. Bradbury, "Urban Decline and Distress: An Update," *New England Economic Review* (July–August 1984): 43.
88. Ladd and Yinger, *America's Ailing Cities*, p. 121.
89. Ester R. Fuchs, *Mayors and Money: Fiscal Policy in New York and Chicago* (Chicago: University of Chicago Press, 1992), pp. 30, 32.
90. Martin Shefter, *Political Crisis/Fiscal Crisis: The Collapse and Revival of New York City* (New York: Basic Books, 1985), p. 106.
91. Jack Newfield and Paul DuBrul, *The Abuse of Power: The Permanent Government and the Fall of New York* (New York: Viking, 1977), p. 31.
92. Fred Ferretti, *The Year the Big Apple Went Bust* (New York: Putnam, 1976), p. 46.
93. George E. Peterson, "Finance," in *The Urban Predicament*, p. 65.
94. Ferretti, *The Year the Big Apple Went Bust*, p. 45.
95. Roger E. Alcaly and Helen Bodian, "New York's Fiscal Crisis and the Economy," in *The Fiscal Crisis of American Cities*, ed. Roger E. Alcaly and David Mermelstein (New York: Random House, 1977), p. 288.
96. Quoted in Ferretti, *The Year the Big Apple Went Bust*, p. 6.
97. Alcaly and Bodian, "New York's Fiscal Crisis and the Economy," p. 53.
98. Edward J. Kane, "Why 'Bad Paper' Worries Economic Policies," *Bulletin of Business Research* (July 1975), cited in ibid., pp 53–54.
99. From a confidential memorandum from William Haddad, director of the Office of Legislative Oversight and Analysis, to George Cincotta, chairman of the New York Assembly Banking Committee, July 7, 1976; quoted in Newfield and DuBrul, *The Abuse of Power*, p. 42.
100. *CBS Evening News*, August 26, 1977.
101. Fuchs, *Mayors and Money*, p. 91.
102. Raymond D. Horton and Mary McCormick, "Services," in *Setting Municipal Priorities, 1981*, ed. Charles Brecher and Raymond D. Horton (Montclair, N.J.: Allanheld Osmun, 1980), p. 89.

103. Shefter, *Political Crisis/Fiscal Crisis,* p. 135.
104. Charles Brecher and Raymond D. Horton, "Retrenchment and Recovery: American Cities and the New York Experience," *Public Administration Review* 45 (March–April 1985): 270.
105. Shefter, *Political Crisis/Fiscal Crisis,* p. 148.
106. Fuchs, *Mayors and Money,* p. 10.
107. Robert F. Wagner, Jr., *New York Ascendant: The Report of the Commission on the Year 2000* (New York: HarperCollins, 1987), p. 1.
108. Clifford J. Levy, "Mayor Rebuts Criticism of Budget Plan," *New York Times,* February 1, 1997, p. 1.
109. Fuchs, *Mayors and Money,* p. 8.
110. *Wall Street Journal,* May 15, 1991, cited in ibid.
111. Shefter, *Political Crisis/Fiscal Crisis,* p. 105.
112. Fuchs, *Mayors and Money,* p. 275.
113. Terry N. Clark, Lorna Ferguson, and Robert Shapiro, "Functional Performance Analysis: A New Approach to the Study of Municipal Expenditures and Debt," *Political Methodology* 8, No. 2 (1982): 87–123.
114. Fuchs, *Mayors and Money,* pp. 112, 119.
115. Ibid., pp. 194–196.
116. Ibid., p. 205.
117. Wagner, *New York Ascendant,* pp. 93–94.
118. Ladd and Yinger, *America's Ailing Cities,* p. 291.
119. U.S. Advisory Commission on Intergovernmental Relations, *Fiscal Disparities: Central Cities and Suburbs, 1981* (Washington, D.C.: Government Printing Office, 1984), cited in ibid., p. 297. See also James Heilbrun, *Urban Economics and Public Policy* (New York: St. Martin's Press, 1974), p. 484.
120. L. J. Sharpe, "Is There a Fiscal Crisis in Western European Local Government? A First Appraisal," in *The Local Fiscal Crisis in Western Europe,* ed. L. J. Sharpe (London: Sage, 1981), pp. 5–28.
121. Arnold J. Heidenheimer, Hugh Heclo, and Carolyn Teich Adams, *Comparative Public Policy: The Politics of Social Choice in America, Europe, and Japan,* 3rd ed. (New York: St. Martin's Press, 1990), p. 278.
122. Thomas H. Boast, "A Political Economy of Urban Capital Finance in the United States" (Ph.D. dissertation, Cornell University, 1977), p. 114.

13

REVITALIZING THE CITIES: THE GROWTH IMPERATIVE

AN URBAN RENAISSANCE

On August 26, 1976, Boston's Mayor Kevin White presided over opening day ceremonies for Quincy Market in downtown Boston. The brainchild of developer James Rouse, who made a fortune developing suburban shopping malls, Quincy Market was housed in three 150-year-old market buildings that were creatively renovated, at a cost of more than $40 million, into a collection of boutiques, gourmet food shops, and restaurants.[1] Few expected Quincy Market—located as it was, in the center of a declining central city with inadequate parking and no big-ticket items to sell—to succeed. Indeed, six weeks before opening day, the retail complex was less than 50 percent leased. In order to hide the empty stores, Rouse came up with the idea of pushcarts, leased to artists and craftspeople for $50.00 a day, plus a percentage of the sales. On opening day forty-three pushcarts contributed to a carnival-like atmosphere.

By eleven o'clock only a modest crowd had gathered for the ceremonies. After the speeches were over, Mayor White cut the ribbon and developer Rouse and a company of kilted highland bagpipers led the crowd inside for a champagne reception. At lunchtime, the crowd swelled as curious workers poured out of nearby office buildings. By mid-afternoon it was clear that opening day would be a huge success, with police estimating the crowd at 100,000.

Opening day was not a fluke; people never stopped coming to Quincy Market. In its second year of operation the market drew 12 million visitors—more than Disneyland that year. Newspapers reported the market's "instant acceptance" by the public, which delighted in the colorful sights, sounds, and smells of the food and imaginatively displayed merchandise and the festival air created by a liberal sprinkling of magicians, acrobats, and puppeteers. The banks that financed the project were originally highly skeptical; they calculated that Quincy Market would have to produce retail sales comparable to the most successful suburban shopping malls ($150 per square foot) to justify its unusually high development costs. Quincy Market shocked the experts by producing sales of $233 per square foot in its first year, with the pushcarts doing best of all. The opening of Quincy Market was hailed by the media as a sign of an "urban renaissance." It seemed to disprove the conventional wisdom that the downtowns of American cities were doomed to obsolescence and decline.

Other cities built sprawling indoor complexes connected by pedestrian bridges and tubes. Architect John Portman pioneered such "bubble cities" when he opened the Peachtree Plaza in downtown Atlanta in 1967. The hotel lobbies and vaulted atriums that make up the complex are dazzling, filled with flowing water and pools, ascending ranks of balconies vanishing toward a skylight, corridors rigged with lights and mirrors, glass elevators outlined in lights. Peachtree Plaza replaced the old downtown Atlanta, which was almost completely razed, with a new, gleaming, enclosed city-within-a-city. Portman built several other complexes, lesser in scale but aspiring to a similar grandeur, in several other cities—the Renaissance Center in Detroit, the Hyatt at Embarcadero Center in San Francisco, the Bonaventure Hotel in Los Angeles, and the Marriott Marquis in Times Square, New York City.

Downtown malls helped to boost a downtown retailing boom that began in the mid-1970s. There was also a renaissance in a whole range of downtown real estate developments: corporate offices, hotels, convention centers, sports stadiums, concert halls, and museums. By the mid-1980s every mayor's downtown "trophy collection" included at least one luxury hotel (preferably one with a multistory atrium), a new sports stadium (usually domed), a downtown shopping mall, a redeveloped waterfront, and a new convention center.[2] The real estate development boom occurred when central business districts became centers of corporate white-collar employment, entertainment, culture, and a burgeoning tourism and convention trade.

The revival of downtown real estate was connected to a change in the methods used by city governments to spur development. The urban renewal and slum clearance programs of the 1950s and 1960s had been based on a massive infusion of federal funds. Urban renewal was replaced by the Community Development Block Grant (CDBG) and the Urban Development Action Grant (UDAG) programs, which gave cities greater discretion over how federal funds were spent. But as the rules changed, the pipeline for federal aid earmarked for urban development gradually dried up, falling by almost 80 percent in the 1980s. The Reagan Administration instructed cities to promote local economic growth as a way to make up for declining federal grants.

Cities began to experiment with partnerships between the public and private sectors to promote investment in the local economy. They devoted CBDG and UDAG funds to big downtown projects, floated bonds, offered property tax abatements, built utilities tunnels, constructed sewer lines and water mains, and rerouted and resurfaced streets. In these and other ways cities provided public subsidies to encourage private investment in office towers, malls, and cultural and tourist facilities. The melding of public subsidies and private dollars took place through newly created incorporated entities that oversaw specific projects—a sports authority to build a stadium, for example, or a public development corporation run like a private corporation, established specifically to receive both public subsidies and private investment funds.[3]

As cities aggressively pursued new strategies to replace disappearing federal funds, the dividing line between the public and private sectors became blurred. Public-private partnerships became the talisman of urban economic development. More cities began cutting complex deals with private developers. In exchange for subsidies, some cities took profit-sharing positions in development projects. In the case of Quincy Market, for example, the city of Boston provided $12 million—almost 30 percent of the total cost of the project—and gave the Rouse Corporation a ninety-nine-year lease on the property. In exchange, the city was guaranteed a minimum annual cash payment plus a portion of income from store rents above that minimum.

The skylines of American cities were transformed by forests of new skyscrapers constructed to house the thousands of corporate employees working downtown. Most cities experienced at least some degree of gentrification, the movement of young professionals and businesspeople into older urban neighborhoods. In some cities—Boston, Chicago, Washington, Philadelphia, San Francisco—there was a massive displacement of the poor and aged from older residential areas. Metropolitan newspapers and city magazines loved to feature the renovation of historic architecture in such neighborhoods as Society Hill in Philadelphia, Park Slope in Brooklyn, and Lincoln Park in Chicago. An entire generation of "messiah mayors" led the efforts and took much of the credit for the revival of downtown. As noted by the historian Jon Teaford, "if nothing else the messiah mayors . . . boosted the spirits of many urban dwellers and made them proud of their cities."[4]

It is important to be cautious, however, when evaluating the urban renaissance. Local boosters and media have invariably overstated the extent of the revival. Though central city economies undoubtedly improved in the 1980s compared with the 1970s, they still lagged behind the nation as a whole. Suburban job growth far outpaced job growth in the central cities.[5] In the first half of the 1980s the glitter of new development could not be missed in Baltimore, Philadelphia, and St. Louis and other cities, yet most cities experienced job losses and continued decline in many areas. Was the renaissance in such cases a mere "political sleight-of-hand" or an "illusion of success"?[6] The answer to that question depends on one's point of view and, crucially, on whether one was a beneficiary or a loser in the most recent round of revival.

WHY CITIES PURSUE GROWTH

From the very beginning, European settlement in North America was founded on town promotion and growth. The first colony, Jamestown, founded in 1607, was the risky venture of a group of English entrepreneurs who organized themselves into a joint stock company. Shares sold in London for about $62 in gold. If the colony was successful, investors hoped to make a profit on their investment. Though Jamestown failed, town promotion and civic boosterism became a way of life in the New World as cities competed for the settlers and investors who swept across the continent.

Government subsidies to aid business expansion are as old as the Republic. Alexander Hamilton, Secretary of the Treasury under President Washington, justified subsidies for private businesses as an effective way of promoting growth:

> This has been found to be one of the most efficacious means of encouraging manufactures, and is, in some views, the best. . . . It is a species of encouragement more positive and direct than any other, and for that reason, has a more immediate tendency to stimulate and uphold new enterprises, increasing the chance for profit, and diminishing the risk of loss. . . . [7]

The popular notion that nineteenth-century capitalism developed without government intervention is false. Governments heavily subsidized private turnpike, canal, and railroad companies. Railroads, especially, enjoyed huge subsidies from city governments. Railroad connections were the key to urban growth in the nineteenth century, and consequently, civic boosters did everything in their power to attract railroads to their towns.

Today, although the objects of civic largesse have changed from railroads to highways, airports, corporate towers, and the tourism and entertainment infrastructure, the nature of local boosterism has remained remarkably similar. Public and private leaders still promote local growth, and they do it by claiming that growth brings prosperity to everyone. Because the political coalitions promoting growth are so similar from city to city, two urban scholars have called them "growth machines" made up of local public officials and influential business leaders, plus, usually, real estate developers, local media, labor leaders, and others who have a stake in the value of local real estate and economic performance.[8]

Most supporters of public subsidies sincerely believe that redevelopment will ultimately benefit everyone living in the city. Politicians and civic elites are convinced that the city's survival depends on local economic vitality. The logic of their argument is as follows: A healthy tax base is necessary to maintain the public services and infrastructure that the local economy and residents rely on; a healthy tax base, in turn, requires rising land values and business prosperity; in order to attract private investment, a city must offer a good business climate and special incentives that make it less expensive for mobile investors to locate there than in other cities; an increasing volume of private investment begins the cycle all over again, resulting in rising land values, a healthy tax base, better services, and a better business climate.[9] Built into the logic underlying this argument, it should be noted, is the assumption that cities must be actively involved in creating the conditions for growth. This argument, and the assumptions on which it rests, are shown in Figure 13.1.

The reverse of the logic of growth is a presumed downward spiral linking economic decline and fiscal impoverishment, wherein a poor business climate leads to disinvestment, which in turn causes land values to fall. Consequently,

FIGURE 13.1 **The Logic of Growth Politics**

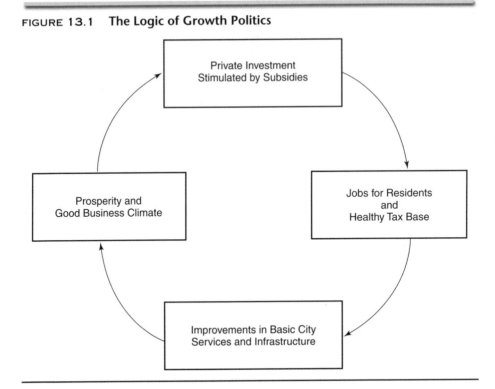

the property tax and other sources of revenue arguably decline, causing deterioration in city services. The city then finds it more difficult to borrow funds to improve its public infrastructure. Many people would recognize this downward spiral as an all-too-familiar experience for older cities over the past several decades.

Considering the degree to which business leaders believe that their own success undergirds everyone else's, it is not surprising that they become infuriated when opponents question their motives and accuse them of feeding at the public trough. Members of local growth coalitions tend to be intolerant of opposition. Appeals to unity are frequent, as exemplified by the slogan adopted by a midwestern city in the 1920s:

> United we stick, divided we're stuck.
> United we boost, divided we bust.[10]

Few people would prefer economic decline over prosperity. It is not always clear, however, that growth brings the benefits that the proponents of business subsidies claim. Development projects often displace small businesses. Neighborhood gentrification typically drives up rents and housing costs. Growth can also impose what economists call "negative externalities," such as air pollution, water pollution, and traffic congestion. Finally, new investment does not necessarily provide more in tax revenues than it costs in subsidies and additional city services. As we discuss in the next section, economic change is inevitable in cities. The role that governments assume in promoting growth, however, is not.

THE CHANGING ECONOMIC FORTUNES OF THE CENTRAL CITIES

The distribution of economic activities in the nation has changed fundamentally over the past hundred years. In the late nineteenth and early twentieth centuries, cities prospered as centers of manufacturing production. Railroad connections made it possible to transport raw materials into industrial cities and ship the finished products around the country. Large factories, employing the new energy sources of steam and electricity, reaped the benefits of economies of scale as the new techniques of mass production were perfected. Large factories required thousands of workers. As the center of the nation's economic production, cities, with their growing concentrations of immigrant workers, burst at the seams.

In the 1920s, American cities began to lose their status as centers of goods production, wholesale trade, and retail sales, and in the next several decades they began a slow recovery by emphasizing services, culture, entertainment, and tourism. These trends accelerated after World War II. After 1950, cities lost a large proportion of their manufacturing jobs. One reason is that manufacturing employment everywhere declined as a percentage of the overall workforce. Technological advances in production processes, such as the use of robots for assembly, made it possible to produce goods with far fewer workers than in the past. Between 1970 and 1988, though the volume of production increased, the nation's manufacturing employment remained stable at 19 million jobs. During the same period, however, the number of service jobs increased rapidly. There were two distinct tiers of service employment. The upper tier included jobs in business and financial services (white-collar professionals such as lawyers, accountants, investment brokers, and computer and communications specialists). The lower tier was employment in food, retail, and personal services (such as those provided in restaurants, stores, laundromats, and barbershops). From 1975 to 1990, 30 million new jobs were created in service industries, so that by the end of the 1980s, 84 million people were employed in services, as compared to 25 million in goods production.[11] Almost 80 percent of employment growth in the 1980s came in the form of service jobs.[12] These changes thoroughly restructured urban economies. As shown by Table 13.1, in seven northeastern and midwestern metropolitan areas, the percentage of jobs in the manufacturing sector fell from 30 percent to 12.5 percent in the twenty-seven years from 1970 to 1997. The largest gains came in services, which grew from 18.4 percent of local employment to 35.6 percent over the same period. Though it remained a relatively small proportion of the economy in many cities, the only other sector to show an increase in jobs in these cities was finance, insurance, and real estate, which grew from 6.4 percent to 9.9 percent.

TABLE 13.1 **CHANGE IN JOB CATEGORIES IN SEVEN NORTHEASTERN AND MIDWESTERN METROPOLITAN AREAS, 1970–1997**

	Percent Employed in Each Category					
	1970	1975	1982	1986	1991	1997
Manufacturing	30.1	25.8	22.4	18.5	15.6	12.5
Transportation, communications and public utilities	6.4	6.3	5.9	5.8	5.8	5.2
Wholesale and retail trade	20.8	21.6	21.9	22.5	21.9	20.2
Finance, insurance and real estate	6.4	6.7	7.4	9.1	9.2	9.9
Services	18.4	20.6	24.6	27.4	30.6	35.6
Government	13.6	15.1	14.5	13.4	13.5	11.3

Source: U.S. Department of Labor, Bureau of Labor Statistics, *Earnings and Employment* (Washington, D.C.: Government Printing Office, 1970, 1975, 1982, 1986, 1991 and 1997).

Another reason the economies of cities changed was that factories left them. The development of highways and truck transportation, heavily subsidized by government policies, enabled factories to move to the periphery of metropolitan areas and beyond, especially to locations with convenient connections to interstate highways. Modern mass production requires large amounts of inexpensive land for one-story, assembly-line production methods. With the range of commuting made possible by the automobile, factories could locate at a distance from residential centers and still be accessible to workers. Manufacturers also moved out of older metropolitan areas to such places as the Caribbean, Latin America, and Asia, where wages were much lower and environmental regulations were lax.[13] Within metropolitan areas, a spatial restructuring was also occurring. Manufacturing, retailing, and wholesaling activities moved out of the central cities to the suburbs. If the lost jobs were replaced, they were replaced by services connected to the downtown office sector and a tourist economy.

Until the 1950s, cities were the centers of retail and wholesale trade within urban areas. The large downtown department stores offered the best selection and prices, and middle-class shoppers took mass transit downtown to shop. Downtown shopping was killed in the 1950s by suburbanization and the automobile. By the 1960s, suburban shopping centers had begun to eclipse central business districts. With big parking lots and freeway interchanges nearby, the shopping centers and their later incarnation, the malls, were more convenient for shoppers, who had by now completely abandoned mass transit for the automobile.

In 1956, the first enclosed, climate-controlled mall, Southdale, was opened in the Minneapolis suburb of Edina. By making shopping comfortable all year round it was an instant success.[14] Mall owners created a leisurely atmosphere conducive to consumption, including common hours for stores, directories and uniform signs, and benches and landscaping. In comparison, downtown shopping seemed chaotic and inconvenient, and sometimes even menacing. By 1974,

15,000 shopping centers had captured more than 44 percent of the nation's retail sales.[15] Downtown department stores began to close for good. Hudson's, a long-time landmark in downtown Detroit, finally closed its doors in 1981.[16] Few downtowns now are sites for major consumer purchases, such as appliances or furniture. Instead, the most that can be expected of central business districts is that they capture a portion of specialty niche and entertainment shopping that appeals to downtown workers and tourists.

In only three decades the central business districts of cities were transformed from centers of wholesale and retail trade to centers of high-level corporate services. Corporations prefer to concentrate a variety of interdependent activities within small geographic areas, whether those areas are within central cities or in the new edge cities on the periphery of metropolitan areas where light manufacturing, retail, service, and residential functions cluster.[17] By concentrating a mass of skilled service specialists in a geographic area close to restaurants and entertainment, central business districts provide rich hosting environments for corporations. Corporate decision makers have quick access to skilled professionals. Small firms clustered around and in the corporate skyscrapers provide basic secretarial, reproducing, office supply, and maintenance and janitorial services. The bigger and more concentrated the downtown, the more specialized services can become, providing access, for example, to patent-law lawyers and accountants who are experts in the intricacies of corporate taxes. Downtowns also provide the face-to-face contacts that are essential for effective relationships with key clients and customers.

The skyscrapers that sprout from the downtowns of American cities are the physical manifestation of the new economic functions of central cities. From the 1920s to the 1950s, few office towers were built in downtowns. Between 1950 and 1984, over 40 percent of the nation's gain in office employment and construction was concentrated in the downtowns of the thirty largest urban areas.[18] In the 1980s office boom, cities even increased their share—a significant feat given the simultaneous boom in suburban office construction.[19]

The phenomenon of service sector expansion in cities has taken place within a changing international division of labor. Corporate headquarters cluster most densely in a few global cities such as San Francisco, New York, Paris, London, Hong Kong, Sidney, and Tokyo. Sitting atop the urban hierarchy, these cities house corporate command and control functions that manage production and distribution networks that are truly global. Second-level cities, such as Chicago, Atlanta, Montreal, and Hamburg, may lay claim to a few international firms, but for the most part they house national and regional corporate systems. Further down the hierarchy, medium-sized cities such as Cleveland and St. Louis are the hubs of regional corporate networks. Down the pyramid further still, there are cities that depend upon quite specialized economies. The higher a city is in the urban hierarchy, the more pulling power it has for jobs and investment and the more control it potentially has to shape its economic future.[20]

The changing economic complexion of central cities presents opportunities as well as dangers for downtown economies. Corporations tend to pull highly specialized, well-paid professionals into downtown office districts. A study of fourteen large metropolitan areas in 1987 found that wages of central city jobs averaged 20 percent higher than suburban jobs, and that gap was increasing.[21] These corporations and professionals drive up the cost of housing, sometimes to fantastic levels, and they support amenities such as expensive restaurants, exclusive shopping districts, and the arts. On the other hand, much of the services economy is composed of low-paying jobs in personal services (cleaning and laundering, haircutting, waitressing and bartending, and the like). At either end of the services spectrum, central city residents are not generally the chief job-takers. The cities that led the nation in office employment growth from 1950 to 1984 did not, thereby, appreciably reduce their levels of unemployment.[22] The main problem was that most of the jobs went to suburban commuters. In 1984 commuters held 60 percent of the jobs in San Francisco and 70 percent in Boston.[23]

THE CORPORATE CENTER STRATEGY:
THE BALTIMORE EXAMPLE

Mayors and development officials in central cities realize that the cities will never regain their dominant position in manufacturing. They accept as well that it is pointless for cities to compete head-to-head with suburbs for certain kinds of wholesaling and retailing. Cities must carve out a niche. The special mix that central cities try to nurture today has been labeled the "corporate center strategy," a stew of financial, administrative, and professional services and "an orientation toward luxury consumption that is appealing to young corporate managers, educated professionals, convention goers, and the tourist trade."[24]

Baltimore is an excellent test case of the corporate center strategy because it is there that the strategy was applied consistently over an extended period of time to revitalize a depressed downtown. Writing in *Fortune* magazine, journalist Gurney Breckenfeld praised the close collaboration between government and business in Baltimore: "Their [public and private sector] strategy, established at the outset, has been to convert the heart of the city into a culturally rich, architecturally exciting magnet where both affluent and middle-class families will choose to work, shop, and live."[25] Dubbed the "Cinderella city of the 1980s," Baltimore is one of the nation's most successful examples of the corporate center strategy.[26]

Downtown redevelopment in Baltimore is closely identified with an extraordinary politician, William Donald Schaefer. As the leader of a coalition of government and business, Schaefer served as the energizing force behind redevelopment in Baltimore during his four terms as mayor from 1971 to 1987. Fiercely loyal to Baltimore, Schaefer continued to live with his mother in the same West Side house where he was born. Baltimore was Schaefer's love, politics his obsession. On weekends he would cruise the city in his 1975 Pontiac jotting down the location of uncollected garbage, faulty street lights, and abandoned cars. On Monday morning, department heads would find "mayor's action memos" on their desks, and a few days later mayoral aides would follow up to make sure the problem was solved. Known for his showmanship, Schaefer demonstrated his devotion to Baltimore in sometimes eccentric ways:

> When the new National Aquarium failed to open by the July 4 deadline he (Schaefer) had guaranteed, Willie Don, as they call him, demonstrated his contrition by plunging into the seal pool (temperature 79 degrees) in striped Victorian swimsuit and straw boater, clutching a yellow duck (he is also affectionately known as Donald Duck). His penitential immersion was shared by a voluptuous model done up as a mermaid.[27]

As the head of a strong-mayor system of government in a city characterized by machine politics, Schaefer modeled himself on Chicago's Mayor Daley and, like Daley, he knew how to exercise power. After spending nineteen years on the city council, Schaefer was elected mayor in 1971 and quickly became one of the shrewdest, most powerful mayors in the country. Realizing he wanted to redevelop the downtown as fast as possible, Schaefer devised a strategy that circumvented the slow-moving bureaucratic and democratic processes of city government at the same time that he won the confidence of corporate investors. Schaefer relied on a network of twenty-four quasi-public development corporations that contracted with the city government to direct and implement downtown redevelopment. Schaefer's model for these corporations was the Charles Center Management Office, a development corporation that contracted with the city, beginning in 1959, to implement a $180 million, 33-acre urban renewal project in the middle of downtown. Charles Center became a bustling complex of offices, apartments, and retail shops that convinced investors that downtown could succeed.

In 1964 the city unveiled an even more ambitious $270 million plan for rehabilitating Baltimore's decaying waterfront. When Schaefer was elected mayor in 1971, he enthusiastically embraced a plan to rehabilitate 240 acres in Baltimore's Inner Harbor and staked his political future on aggressive implementation of the plan. Charles Center–Inner Harbor Management, Inc. (CCIHM) was at the center of the network of quasi-public corporations used to redevelop the harbor. The city contracted with CCIHM to plan and implement the Inner Harbor project. More specialized development corporations were established to implement other parts of the plan, such as housing. Though they contracted for public projects (and thus could be called quasi-public), as private entities the development corporations were able to pay higher salaries than public agencies to attract talented executives and could circumvent public regulations concerning such requirements as competitive bidding and affirmative action. Proponents viewed them as "apolitical means for improving the city's development potential by infusing speed, flexibility, and technical expertise into the policy-making process."[28]

The Inner Harbor project was daunting. In an earlier period, the harbor had been a bustling center of commerce, but by the 1960s it was an eyesore, composed of rotting, rat-infested piers, abandoned buildings, and desolate parking lots, perched on a harbor that smelled, in H. L. Mencken's words, "like a million polecats."[29] The audacious idea was to transform the area into a national tourist attraction.

The linchpin of the Inner Harbor plan was Harborplace, two block-long, translucent pavilions situated right on the harbor. Designed by James Rouse, the designer of Boston's Quincy Market, Harborplace offered a dazzling array of specialty shops, ethnic foods, and, above all, sights and sounds, including dancers, clowns, and magicians. Harborplace was designed to be a marketplace that would make the inner city, in Rouse's words, "a warm and human place, with diversity of choice, full of festival and delight."[30] Completed in 1980, Harborplace succeeded beyond anyone's expectations, attracting 18 million visitors the first year (like Quincy Market, it outpulled Disneyland), earning $42 million, and creating 2,300 jobs. In 1981 the National Aquarium was completed, giving the Inner Harbor a major tourist attraction. By 1992 more than 15 million visitors had toured the aquarium's exhibits, including a 64-foot glass pyramid housing a reproduction of a South American rain forest.[31]

The success of Harborplace and the National Aquarium established the Inner Harbor as a tourism and convention center, unleashing a surge of private investment throughout the entire Inner Harbor area. Between 1980 and 1986 the number of tourists and the amount of money they spent tripled; in order to accommodate the increased demand, the number of hotel rooms also tripled. The benefits to the city seemed obvious. The city's manpower programs succeeded in placing 1,300 persons in jobs at Harborplace.[32] More than 40 percent of the Harborplace workforce was drawn from minorities.[33] By 1984 a revived convention business was pumping an estimated $52 million annually into Baltimore's economy.[34] Tax revenues from Baltimore's central business district soared from $13.8 million in 1976 to $44.3 million in 1987.[35]

Inner Harbor was a big political winner for Schaefer. The press hailed him as "The Best Mayor in America"; Howard Cosell dubbed him "the genius mayor."[36] Schaefer won reelection three times in succession by overwhelming margins. In November 1986 Schaefer rode the wave of positive publicity about Baltimore's renaissance into the Maryland governor's mansion.

Amidst the hoopla over Baltimore's highly visible downtown revival, however, conditions in the city's deteriorating neighborhoods were generally overlooked. Kurt Schmoke, who succeeded Schaefer as Baltimore's first black mayor in 1987, observed, "If you were revisiting Baltimore today after a twenty-year absence, you would find us much prettier and much poorer."[37] Though Baltimore's rate of population loss slowed in the 1980s, its population still fell by 50,000 people during the decade. In a comparison with eleven Frostbelt cities of similar size in 1979, the per capita income growth of Baltimore residents lagged behind nine of them, and Baltimore showed the highest poverty rate.[38] On an index of urban hardship that ranked fifty-five cities, Baltimore improved only three places between 1970 and 1980, moving from the sixth worst to the ninth worst.[39] Between 1970 and 1980 the poverty rate increased in 90 percent of Baltimore's predominantly black neighborhoods.[40]

How can the apparent paradox between the stunning commercial success of Baltimore's corporate center strategy and the declining conditions in nearby neighborhoods be explained? Studies indicate that in most cities the downtown corporate economy has been largely irrelevant to the success of small businesses and the creation of jobs for inner-city residents.[41] Central city residents often lack the skills and education to qualify for the knowledge-intensive jobs that locate in central business districts.[42] In 1979 a majority of the employees working in central business districts lived outside the central cities. And the better the jobs paid, the more likely they were to be held by suburbanites; 71 percent of those working downtown and making over $50,000 in 1979 lived in the suburbs.[43] Many of the jobs in the tourist industry that do go to central city dwellers are unpleasant, low-skilled jobs, with little or no prospects for advancement. Hence, the overall skill level of the resident workforce does not necessarily improve even if the downtown is new and glittering.[44]

In addition to its failure to bring material benefits to most city residents, Baltimore's corporate center strategy was criticized for sidestepping the democratic process. Because they were private-sector institutions that received public funds, the development corporations were not required to give information to the public or to consult with the citizens in making decisions. They operated just as private corporations do, with their files locked and meetings closed.

Baltimore's redevelopment projects involved conflicts and tradeoffs that are the legitimate subject of democratic debate. The Inner Harbor development did not induce middle- and upper-income residents to move into the city despite the fact that significant amounts of money were used to build middle-income housing. Area residents adjacent to the Inner Harbor found their tax assessments rising rapidly. Those living on fixed incomes were forced to sell their suddenly valuable homes or seek tax relief from the city. Though downtown development expanded tax revenues, it also absorbed additional city services. Indeed, according to one scholar, "Downtown redevelopment in Baltimore annually absorbs around $17 million more in city expenditures than it generates in municipal revenues."[45]

The development corporations constituted a kind of shadow government that made key decisions about Baltimore's future and yet remained outside the democratic process. The most important of these corporations was the Baltimore City Trustee Loan and Guarantee Program, which between 1976 and 1986 used public funds to loan or guarantee loans worth $500 million in 239 projects.[46] The trustees were appointed by the mayor, but as a private entity the corporation that ran the program was not required even to provide information to the city council. Numerous loans were awarded to political contributors to Mayor Schaefer's campaigns. Perhaps sensing that the loan program could become an issue in his upcoming gubernatorial campaign, Schaefer abolished the trustees in 1986 and moved the loan portfolio to the City Finance Department, where it would be subject to public scrutiny.[47]

The corporate center strategy in Baltimore was a great commercial success. However, instead of "a rising tide lifts all boats," the appropriate metaphor to describe Baltimore's renaissance is a "leaky bucket," with most of the benefits leaking out to developers and to suburban residents who took the best white-collar jobs in the Inner Harbor. Relatively few benefits trickled down to the residents of the city. Baltimore became, in essence, two cities. One city was populated by office workers, executives, and tourists, who passed the residents of the other city on their commute from the suburbs or on the expressway to the airport. In this regard, the Inner Harbor development made Baltimore much like other American cities that have successfully implemented a corporate center strategy.

THE DEVELOPMENT OF URBAN TOURISM

Tourism, entertainment, and culture have been pivotal to the corporate center strategy in all cities. It is generally assumed that tourists spend money without taking anything out of the local economy. Tourism frequently has been described as "the industry without a smokestack." As a consequence, there is keen competition among cities for a share of the nation's tourist and entertainment business. To remake themselves into places that tourists want to visit, cities have invested heavily in such facilities as convention centers, sports arenas, community centers, festival malls, urban entertainment districts, and performing arts halls. The reconstruction of the urban core can be compared to the building of the industrial city a century ago, when cities invested heavily in streetcars, paved streets, and parks. These undertakings laid the foundation of the industrial cities of the twentieth century. The recent era of city-building can be compared, as well, with the restructuring of downtown economies and land use wrought by the massive urban renewal clearance projects of the 1950s and 1960s.[48] Truly, the physical environment of cities has been transformed in only a few years.

Though tourist venues often are constructed on a site that was once devoted to primary production, such places are normally rebuilt to project a contrived, nostalgic, and idealized version of city life. The "entertainment cities" such as South Street Seaport in New York try to create an ambience evoked by "authentic reproductions" of a working harbor, a Main Street, frontier town, or colonial village[49]—not unlike an urban miniversion of Disneyland, with its Main Street, U.S.A., and Frontier Village. The examples abound: the Wharf and Ghirardelli Square in San Francisco, and the renovated Union Stations everywhere (while the actual train stations are relegated to a shed well out of sight and sound).

The facilities and amenities devoted to leisure activities and the tourist trade are often clustered within a well-defined space separated from the rest of the city. Where crime, poverty, and urban decay make parts of a city inhospitable to visitors, specialized areas must be established as virtual tourist reservations. The 30 million visitors who come to Harborplace each year are conveniently protected from seeing the Baltimore beyond the tourist enclave, the other part of what has been labeled "the two Baltimores."[50] Likewise, Greektown, a two-block-square renovated district in downtown Detroit anchored by an enclosed mall, is an island in a sea of decay. Such areas exist in most cities and constitute, in effect, tourist "bubbles" that "envelope the traveler so that he/she only moves inside secured, protected and normalized environments."[51] Some of the facilities that make up the tourist bubble include convention centers, sports stadiums, festival malls, and gaming casinos, which we discuss in the remainder of this chapter.[52]

Convention Centers

If cities in the United States only recently began to compete intensely for tourists, it is only because tourism was not, in the past, the primary focus of local boosters. After the turn of the century tourism promotion to the masses expanded with a growing middle class, entering the modern era in the 1920s when improved roads and the mass ownership of automobiles made travel cheaper and more convenient. Although tourism was originally promoted by owners of hotels and tourist attractions who advertised through pamphlets, books, and newspapers, civic boosters soon joined private promoters in extolling the virtues of individual cities. An early twentieth-century British traveler found himself "regaled everywhere with inspiring statistics concerning the population of 'our city,' the seating capacity of the auditorium, the number of banks, the amount of their clearings, and the quantity of belt buckles annually manufactured."[53] On the whole, the promotion of tourism was left to entrepreneurs in the business community.

For the most part, town halls doubled as assembly facilities, if any were needed. In the 1920s some cities helped construct the first generation of sports stadiums and arenas; St. Louis, for example, built the St. Louis Arena in 1929 to accommodate an agricultural exhibit. During the Great Depression, a flurry of more ambitious public assembly and exhibition facilities were financed by the Public Works Administration. This generation of halls often contained one or more auditoriums as well as exhibition space under one roof, and in many cities these structures were not replaced until the 1980s or 1990s. These all-purpose facilities were expensive to operate and virtually always lost money, but they had the effect of attracting and even helping to create an array of traveling shows and exhibitions. The benefits to the local economy were quickly comprehended by civic boosters and entrepreneurs, who then pushed for public subsidies.

Beginning in the 1950s, larger cities began constructing a second generation of meeting halls in the form of convention centers built specifically for professional meetings and trade shows. Since the mid-1970s, the competition has heated up. Between 1970 and 1985 more than 100 convention centers were constructed in the United States; in 1970 there was a total of 6.7 million square feet of convention space in the nation, but this almost tripled, to 18 million square feet, by 1990.[54] In the 1980s cities began a virtual arms race for the convention trade, with even small towns and cities joining the competition. From 1980 to 1987 the number of convention centers increased by 37 percent, but the square feet of exhibition space rose even faster, by 60 percent.[55] By July 1998, 409 convention centers with exhibition space were operating in U.S. cities, and more than 70 percent of them had opened since 1970.[56]

All convention centers require yearly subsidies for the payment of construction bonds and for operating costs, but escalating construction, maintenance, and promotion costs have not deterred cities from investing in larger and more elaborate convention facilities. Much is at stake. The 25,000-plus associations in the nation spent $32 billion for meetings in 1992, and corporations spent an additional $29 billion on off-premises meetings and conventions.[57] Associations meet about three times a year, on average. Tourism-related organizations alone had 1.4 million members in 1998, and the meetings industry produced $81 billion in economic output.[58] The average attendance at new exhibition shows nearly quadrupled from 1990 to 1997.[59] Although only from 4 to 5 percent of meetings are held in convention centers,[60] the size of the meetings and convention business has been large enough to prompt hundreds of cities to build or expand their existing convention centers. In 2000, 41 convention centers were being built or renovated, and 66 were slated for expansion or renovation.[61]

The convention business is extraordinarily competitive. Table 13.2 ranks the top thirty-three convention cities by their share of meetings with exhibits in 1981, when there were far fewer convention centers than there are currently. New York and Chicago easily led the nation as magnets for conventions, accounting for more than 17 percent of the total convention trade between them. The share of the convention trade captured by individual cities rapidly falls as one goes down the list. The top ten cities accounted for 44 percent of total attendance, with all the other cities listed in the table contending for a 25 percent share. Those cities outside of the top thirty-three received about 31 percent of the nation's convention business in 1981.

As the number of cities competing for conventions increases, it becomes difficult for a particular city to increase its share of the country's convention business. Nevertheless, as revealed by Table 13.3, by 1992 New York City had fallen from first to seventh place, Anaheim had dropped from seventh to eighteenth place, but Orlando had shot up from twenty-seventh to second place. The volatility expressed by these changes is shown by the fact that Orlando slipped from second in 1990 to fifth in 1991, then rebounded to second again in 1992.

The construction of a convention facility may provide a foundation, but obviously a lot of other factors determine a city's ability to successfully compete for meetings. In Orlando's case, obviously, Disney World is the entire story. For other cities, such a singular magnet is rarely, if ever, available. Convention centers do not exist in isolation from the cities they are located within. Large cities, with their abundance of entertainment, cultural, and commercial attractions, remain the primary drawing cards for national and international conventions. A combination of things is essential: There must be available hotel space, cultural and entertainment opportunities, sightseeing, restaurants, and other amenities.[62] The one major advantage smaller cities have is lower cost.[63] Even for those cities, however, something besides a meetings space is necessary. According to a meetings planner, "If we're going to use a second-tier city and promote it as an attraction, then we have to make it an attraction. We bill it as a tourist destination and give that equal billing with the technical [meeting] program."[64]

By the 1980s virtually every major city in the United States had formed a convention and visitors bureau, and throughout that decade these increased rapidly in size. Convention bureaus construct lists of international, national, regional, and local associations that regularly sponsor or organize conventions. The bureaus send them promotional literature and frequently attend the meetings of these organizations, where they may stage rather elaborate promotional presentations or exhibits. Cities often invite representatives of the tourist industry and of important business and professional groups for a complimentary visit. In November 1975, for instance, the St. Louis Convention and Visitors Bureau hosted representatives of 227 associations for a weekend tour in an effort to promote the city's new convention center, which was then under construction.[65]

TABLE 13.2	CONVENTION TRADE/MEETINGS WITH EXHIBITS IN TOP 33 U.S. CITIES, 1981
	Percent of Total Attendance
1. New York	10.6
2. Chicago	6.7
3. Atlanta	4.4
4. Las Vegas	3.8
5. Dallas	3.8
6. Los Angeles	3.7
7. Anaheim, CA	3.5
8. San Francisco	2.9
9. New Orleans	2.6
10. Boston	2.3
11. Detroit	2.0
12. Kansas City	2.0
13. Philadelphia	1.7
14. Indianapolis	1.7
15. Houston	1.5
16. St. Louis	1.4
17. Atlantic City	1.3
18. Columbus	1.2
19. Minneapolis	1.2
20. San Antonio	1.1
21. Louisville	1.1
22. Miami Beach	1.1
23. Seattle	1.1
24. San Diego	1.0
25. Denver	1.0
26. Cleveland	0.8
27. Orlando	0.8
28. Phoenix	0.6
29. Cincinnati	0.6
30. Oklahoma City	0.6
31. Memphis	0.5
32. Pittsburgh	0.5
33. Tulsa	0.3

Source: Successful Meetings magazine, *Convention and Exhibit Market Profile*, 1983.

City[a]	1992 Rank	1991 Rank	1990 Rank
Chicago	1	1	1
Orlando	2	5	2
Dallas	3	2	3
Atlanta	4	3	6
Los Angeles	5	4	5
San Diego	5	7	9
New York	7	8	6
Boston	8	9	8
New Orleans	9	14	14
Phoenix	10	12	13
San Francisco	10	6	4
Houston	12	10	10
Las Vegas	13	13	10
Washington, D.C.	14	11	18
Nashville	15	—	—
Denver	16	16	18
Philadelphia	17	20	15
Anaheim	18	14	31
Miami	18	—	—
St. Louis	18	—	—

TABLE 13.3   TOP U.S. CITIES BOOKED, 1990–1992

[a]Duplicate rankings indicate ties.

Source: *Successful Meetings* magazine, July 1983, p. 62.

The intense competition among cities makes it possible for groups of professional and trade associations to strike a hard bargain. The biggest associations already assume that they can persuade cities to give them convention space rent-free, and the bargaining position of these organizations will only improve. In 1993 the Future Farmers of America (FFA), a youth organization that had traditionally met in Kansas City, demanded that the city give it cash subsidies, lower hotel rates, and other incentives. Since their annual convention brought 28,000 visitors to the city, the city's Convention and Visitors Bureau chair thought it was worth it to spend "whatever it takes" to keep the group from going elsewhere.[66] Such an approach will become more common as groups become more adept at playing cities off against one another. (Ultimately, Kansas City lost the FFA.)

Sports Stadiums

Professional sports franchises occupy an important place in the corporate center strategy. Cities compete vigorously for sports teams, often financing the construction of stadiums and offering subsidies such as guaranteed attendance and revenues. Because teams have moved more and more frequently in recent years, the concessions that cities must offer are constantly on the rise—but cities are willing to pay them. Civic boosters consider professional sports franchises as pivotal to the economic revitalization of central cities, and it is doubtful that arguments showing the limited economic contributions of sports to local economies will much deter their often desperate efforts to get or keep professional teams. Sports teams have long been central to the civic and cultural life of American cities. Oddly, the assumption that a team expresses a city's essence, spirit, and sense of community has not been much eroded since teams became highly mobile. Part of the reason for this is that local boosters consider professional sports teams to be an absolutely essential signifier of "big league" status. Sports teams carry a substantial emotional charge, so that their worth is rarely, if ever, calculated in simple economic terms. Through the national and international publicity accompanying network broadcasts of games and playoffs, professional sports teams are a powerful vehicle for conveying a city's image. For all of these reasons, cities fight hard to keep and attract teams.

Professional sports is a big business. In 1992 there were 102 North American franchises in four major sports worth almost $9.5 billion (two new National Football League franchises have been awarded since then). In 1992 major league baseball franchises were valued from $75 million dollars for the Montreal Expos to $200 million for the New York Yankees. National Football League teams ranged in value from $103 million for the New England Patriots to $150 million for the Miami Dolphins and the New York Giants. Some National Basketball Association franchises could be bought for smaller sums; the Indiana Pacers, for example, cost only $43 million dollars. However, the Detroit Pistons were valued at $120 million, while the Los Angeles Lakers were the most valuable professional basketball team at $150 million. Professional hockey teams went for less, with values ranging from $30 million for the Winnipeg Jets to $70 million for the Detroit Red Wings.[67]

Professional baseball franchises had their origins in amusement parks. Just as streetcar companies tended to lay track to drive up the value of land, team owners were often real estate speculators who used the teams to attract buyers to their subdivisions.[68] For decades, teams identified so closely with their cities of origin that moving would have been unthinkable. The first baseball franchise relocation occurred in 1953, when the Boston Braves relocated to Milwaukee. The baseball franchise relocation game began in earnest in 1957 when owner Walter O'Malley moved the Brooklyn Dodgers to Los Angeles. The Brooklyn Dodgers were one of the most lucrative franchises in baseball, with fanatically loyal fans who packed the seats at Ebbetts Field. At first O'Malley wanted to build a new stadium with public assistance, but he was thwarted by Robert Moses, who controlled the public authorities in the New York region. To lure the Dodgers out of New York, Los Angeles agreed to renovate its minor league stadium at Chavez Ravine, install 22,000 more seats than Ebbetts field, and then give the stadium to O'Malley. As the clincher, they offered him 300 acres of downtown Los Angeles real estate. O'Malley jumped at the chance to add to his personal fortune.[69]

It did not take long for other owners to follow O'Malley's lead. Threats to move became potent weapons for prying more subsidies out of cities. Between 1953 and 1982 there were 78 franchise relocations in the four major professional sports: 11 in baseball, 40 in basketball, 14 in hockey, and 13 in football.[70] In just six years, from 1980 to 1986, more than half the cities with major league sports franchises were confronted with demands for increased subsidies, with relocation an implied if not always explicit threat hanging over negotiations.[71]

Cities have been willing to go to extraordinary lengths to get and keep a professional sports team, and owners realize that public subsidies are theirs for the asking. From 1953 to 1986, 67 of the 94 stadiums used by professional sports teams were publicly owned.[72] For the last several years the two most important new revenue sources for sports teams have been network broadcasting and local and state subsidies.[73] By the end of the 1980s, it could be safely assumed that it would be an exception when an owner agrees to build a stadium with private dollars. Owners have come to expect other subsidies as well, in the form of guaranteed attendance minimums, the construction of luxury boxes, and control of stadium merchandising.

Since the early 1980s, the relocation game has become extremely fast-paced. From 1980 to June 1992 there was an incredible amount of activity involving baseball and football teams. During this period, twenty cities sought baseball and twenty-four cities tried to attract football teams, an interesting statistic considering that there were, at that time, a total of twenty-eight major league baseball and twenty-eight professional football franchises (two new expansion football franchises were added in 1993, with several cities competing for them). Eleven cities had completed or were building stadiums, and twenty-eight more considered building or had plans to build stadiums. Eleven teams threatened to move in the 1980s and early 1990s, and six actually did so.

As teams became more and more footloose, cities found themselves at a disadvantage. In an attempt to improve their poor bargaining positions, cities began the practice of building stadiums even when they did not have teams. In the 1980s Indianapolis built a football stadium, then persuaded the owner of the Baltimore Colts, Robert Isray, to move. After the Maryland legislature passed an eminent domain law to make it possible for Baltimore to seize the Colts for public use, Isray moved the team in the middle of the night.

St. Petersburg, Florida, built a $139 million domed stadium in 1988 in the hopes of attracting a major-league baseball team. Called "heaven's waiting room," boosters justified the Florida Suncoast Dome as a way of changing the city's image as a conservative retirement community.[74] For years the stadium remained the site of tractor pulls and concerts. In the 1990s St. Petersburg tried to lure several major league baseball teams, including the Seattle Mariners, the San Francisco Giants, and a National League expansion team. When Florida won a baseball team in 1991, it was awarded to Miami. In October 1993 an expansion team of the National Football League was awarded to Jacksonville; St. Petersburg's stadium was purpose-built for baseball and would not have been suitable for football. St. Louis, which also put in a bid for one of the NFL expansion teams, lost out. St. Louis undertook the construction of a domed stadium anyway, many months before the negotiations that eventually brought the Los Angeles Rams to the city.

Stadiums require generous land, infrastructure, and direct public subsidies because almost all of them lose money. Annual operating deficits are generally considerable; the New Orleans Superdome lost about $3 million a year during the 1980s, for example, compared to the annual $1 million loss for the Pontiac, Michigan, Silverdome. In its first year, the Florida Suncoast Dome lost $1.3 million, plus $7.7 million in debt payments.[75] Modern domed stadiums cost so much to build that they cannot conceivably schedule enough events or charge enough for them to avoid large operating deficits. Toronto ended up paying $400 million for its domed stadium, while Baltimore spent $200 million for its new open stadium. St. Louis's domed stadium, completed in 1995, cost $301 million.[76]

Do stadiums justify their enormous costs by bringing gobs of money into local economies? Studies of the economic effects of stadiums concluded that they may have an extremely limited economic impact—and that some may even have a negative effect by replacing some local spending with expenditures that exit the local economy quickly.[77] Claims that spending on sports stadiums will have a multiplier effect by introducing a stream of new economic activity into a local economy is, therefore, suspect. It is undoubtedly true, as civic boosters argue, that the most important benefits of a major sports franchise is intangible and therefore impossible to measure solely in economic terms. However, as teams become more mobile and owners more insatiably greedy, such arguments may be wearing thin. In December 1996 the owners of the Seattle Mariners baseball team put the team up for sale, even though the city had earlier bought land and made plans to construct a new ballpark. Just a few months earlier, Seattle's football team, the Seahawks, had already threatened to leave town, and it too, demanded a new stadium. Together, the two stadiums would cost an estimated $760 million. Many Seattle sports fans called the threats "blackmail," amidst a public controversy about whether anything should be done to keep the teams. A group called "Citizens for More Important Things" initiated an opposition campaign behind the slogan, "Just say no to welfare for the wealthy." Though the owners of the teams in Seattle got their stadiums, in the next few years such "just say no" campaigns may become more common.

Festival Malls and Urban Entertainment Centers

Enclosed malls have become a principal weapon used by cities in the competition for recreational shopping and tourism. Cities typically have subsidized the construction of downtown malls heavily. To support mall development, they have devoted Community Development Block Grant and Urban Development Action Grant funds, floated bonds to finance site acquisition and loans to developers, offered property tax abatements, created tax increment districts, built utilities tunnels, constructed sewer lines and water mains, and rerouted and repaved streets. When malls are successful—as Quincy Market has been in Boston—the city may make money. When malls fail, however, cities can end up saddled with debt.

Malls are important not only because they can help reverse the long-term decline of downtown retailing but also because they are a means of creating defended space even in the midst of urban crime and decay. Malls built by the developers John Portman and James Rouse and their imitators have become such common features of American downtowns that it is hard to keep in mind how recently they have been constructed. The malls increasingly engulf and centralize activities that were formerly spread through the urban community-at-large. Such complexes are easily criticized as "fortified cells of affluence,"[78] but there can be little doubt that as locations for tourism and recreation, these spaces are extremely successful. In 1992, for example, Atlanta ranked fourth among cities in the United States for convention business. Without doubt, Portman's Peachtree Center is much of the reason.

The Peachtree complex dates back to the original cylindrical towers that distinguished Portman's first atrium hotel, which opened in downtown Atlanta in 1967. It was an instant hit with architectural critics, the media, and the public. By the late 1980s Peachtree Plaza had swallowed up Atlanta's historic downtown. Sixteen buildings clustered around the aluminum cylinder that housed the Marriott Hotel, anchoring a constantly expanding, enclosed downtown business district. Atlanta moved indoors, its city streets left almost deserted to pedestrian traffic. Shops, hotels and their lobbies, offices, food courts, and atriums are connected by a maze of escalators, skytubes, and arcades forming glassed-in skyways that isolate inhabitants from the streets below. Pedestrians can gain access to the center only through a few grand porticos, usually the entrance to hotel lobbies. The fortresslike walls of the buildings give the streets a menacing feeling, and the public sidewalks are often deserted.

Since opening his first mall in Boston, Rouse has designed festival malls for cities all across the country. What made Rouse's developments so unique and newsworthy was the artful combining of play and shopping. Rouse's formula was to create a carnival-like atmosphere, accomplished through a mixture of specialty shops, clothing stores, restaurants and food stands, with musicians, jugglers, acrobats, and mimes to entertain shoppers. There soon were Rouse malls at the Gallery of Market Street East in Philadelphia, Grand Avenue in Milwaukee, Pike Street Market in Seattle, Horton Plaza in San Diego, Trolley Square in Salt Lake City, Union Station in St. Louis, Harborplace in Baltimore, South Street Seaport in New York, and on and on.

Like Peachtree Center, many of the enclosed malls began modestly and then accreted block-by-block over many years, with tubes and skyways connecting the various components. In Minneapolis a sprawling mall complex has grown by eating away the interiors of the downtown buildings, leaving their historic facades intact. In Kansas City, the Crown Center has inexorably spread from its beginnings as a luxury hotel; by the mid-1990s it occupied several city blocks. In Montreal and Dallas veritable underground cities have been formed through a network of molelike tunnels. The mall's assault on Atlanta has been much more direct: The huge Peachtree complex has been built on the rubble of the historic downtown.

Because they are an aspect of leisure and tourism, the kinds of malls built in downtown areas do not revitalize retailing in the urban core per se. Rather, they rely on a style of shopping that is most effectively promoted within a controlled environment. The malls' mix of gift and souvenir shops, specialty food stores, bars, and fast-food or franchise restaurants mimic tourist villages such as Jackson Hole, Wyoming, and Estes Park, Colorado. Malls give developers the control over a contiguous space sufficient to accomplish a totally planned combination of shopping and entertainment. In the West Edmonton Mall in Alberta, Canada, for example, leisure facilities take up about 10 percent of the total floor space, but their presence is essential to an ambience of leisure that permeates the entire mall.[79] The West Edmonton Mall copies Disney World in the theming of particular areas, such as (for example) an imitation Parisian street, Bourbon Street in New Orleans, Hollywood, and Polynesia. The combination of shopping and leisure in this way encourages a "shop 'til you drop" approach to buying.

Urban entertainment centers are more recent, comprehensive versions of the festival mall. These complexes commonly house one or more malls, but they also spread out to portions of the surrounding city. Because they offer a way to build a defended space even in a seemingly hostile environment, entertainment centers provide even the most dilapidated cities with a strategy for reintroducing a vital culture and street life to the urban core. Recreational or entertainment districts have sprung up in virtually all central cities, usually in historic areas and often in connection with revitalized waterfronts. Contained within these districts are restaurants, coffeehouses, sports bars, jazz clubs, dinner theatres, and other entertainment venues, plus an array of corporate tenants providing a standardized assortment of clothes, shoes, electronic goods, jewelry, and so forth.[80] New York City's Times Square and San Francisco's Yerba Buena Center both anchor urban entertainment centers, but smaller versions have sprung up in many cities.

Malls and themed shopping-leisure environments are making downtowns into places of specialized consumption segregated from the rest of the city. In these environments, out-of-town visitors mingle with local residents because in them, local consumers are prompted to act as if they are, in effect, in a dreamscape far removed from the city that surrounds them. The similarity between Disney theme parks and these environments is not accidental. Thirteen years before James Rouse built Quincy Market he asserted that Walt Disney was the most influential urban planner ever. And so he was. Probably more than any other component of the standardized tourism space, malls establish the atmosphere and the context that potentially makes every city, whatever its past function or present condition, a tourist attraction.

Casino Gaming

Until the 1980s there were few casinos in any major city in the world, but in the space of less than two decades casino gaming has spread rapidly. Since the mid-1980s, gaming casinos have become established as a component of tourism promotion in many cities throughout the world—notably, in Adelaide, Perth, Sydney, and Brisbane; in Montreal, Winnipeg, and Windsor; in Christchurch and Auckland; in Amsterdam and Rotterdam; and in several cities on the Mediterranean, such as Athens, Istanbul, and Cairo.[81] In the United States, Atlantic City, New Jersey, broke Nevada's monopoly in 1978, but it took until 1992 for New Orleans to open the first casino in a major U.S. city. Within a year Kansas City and St. Louis, Missouri, joined the list, and Chicago's mayor announced his intention to seek state legislative approval for the construction of casinos in his city.

As with other components of the tourist infrastructure, urban leaders feel that they are forced by the logic of competition to seek gaming. The commission that recommended to Chicago's mayor that four casinos be opened in the city reasoned that it would "prevent other cities from using the attraction of casinos to siphon off visitors from Chicago."[82] In making his pitch for casinos in his city, the mayor of Philadelphia predicted that by the end of the decade "almost every urban area will have some form of gambling . . . if people are going to gamble away their paychecks better they do it here than in Atlantic City."[83] As expressed by the general counsel of the St. Louis Redevelopment Corporation, for that city casino gaming was viewed as the latest essential feature of the city's tourist infrastructure: "In a city that has recently built a new convention center, dome (sic) stadium, indoor sports arena and light rail system, gaming was the element needed to provide the necessary critical mass to draw visitors to St. Louis and enhance the city experience for residents."[84] Driven by such a logic, most mayors will try to add casinos to their trophy collection, but, as we shall see, only some of them will succeed.

Historically, Nevada served as the casino gambling mecca for most of the United States, making it possible for the state to keep its property taxes low and to avoid a state income tax altogether. In 1967 New Jersey adopted a lottery and in 1978 Atlantic City, New Jersey, broke Nevada's monopoly on casino gaming. All through the 1970s and 1980s states adopted lotteries either through legislative action or referenda; by 1994 thirty-eight states ran lotteries. Following the spread of state lotteries, gambling became legitimated as a source of tax revenues. By 1996, twenty-six states allowed or had approved casino gaming in some form.[85] In 1988 as a means of promoting economic development on Indian reservations, Congress passed the Indian Gaming Regulatory Act. The legislation permitted tribes to negotiate with states to run gaming operations, and, notably, required the states to negotiate with the tribes that wanted to open casinos. Since then, casinos have been opened on Indian lands in twenty-two states.

In 1990 Iowa became the first state to approve riverboat gaming. After the opening of the first boat in Iowa in April 1991, six riverboats generated $12 million in state income taxes within eight months, prompting neighboring states to begin steps to join the competition.[86] In 1992 riverboats began operating in Illinois, two near St. Louis (one in East St. Louis, Illinois, directly across from St. Louis and the Gateway Arch). Mississippi began operating boats in 1993. Missouri, Louisiana, and Indiana all approved riverboat gaming soon after, with operations beginning in 1994.[87]

Despite the promises proffered by the industry and the eagerness of public officials to get a piece of the action, the initial euphoria about gambling abated rather quickly. Though the majority of Americans have come to accept gambling, in general, as a legitimate activity over the past thirty years,[88] a Harris Poll conducted in 1992 still found that 51 percent of the public opposed casino gaming in their own state, and 56 percent opposed it in their own communities.[89] The media find gambling to be a convenient topic, much like crime, for "controversy" and "analysis." For example, in its April 1, 1996 issue *Time* magazine carried a feature story that purported to document a national backlash against gaming. Proposals to allow gaming typically are accompanied by a considerable amount of controversy. In 1992 Colorado voters soundly defeated a constitutional amendment that would have allowed gaming to spread past the three communities named in an earlier referendum. On April 5, 1994, Missouri's voters turned down gaming, despite being subjected to a campaign in which proponents outspent opponents by $3 million to $100,000. A couple of weeks later the Missouri legislature amended the gaming statute that had been rejected by voters to allow games of "skill" rather than "chance" on riverboats. On April 27 and 28 riverboats opened for business in Missouri but without slot machines and roulette.[90] Thus the stage was set for another statewide referendum in November, when, given another opportunity, voters approved "games of chance."

Three issues are often raised by opponents of casino gambling. Though concerns about its social and moral effects once came mainly from religious groups, now a diverse array of people have raised that alarm. Substantial research has demonstrated that teenagers have about twice the rate of addiction to gambling as do adults, and that lotteries have contributed to the problem.[91] Perhaps as part of a public relations effort, the industry has acknowledged that there are gambling addicts, and it finances research on the problem (providing the financing, for example, for the National Council on Problem Gambling). In 1996 the Missouri Gaming Commission, with industry support, proposed legislation that would allow gambling addicts to put themselves on a list that would bar them from entering any of the state's casinos.[92]

The second issue is related to the economic effects of casino gaming on local communities, the argument being that casinos cannibalize other businesses by locating restaurants, bars, and shops on premises, thereby drawing business away from local enterprises. Research is also accumulating that demonstrates a spending substitution effect, in which gamblers spend less on goods and services to make up for what they lose on the lotteries and in the casinos.[93]

A third often-discussed issue is the concern that the gaming industry brings with it crime, organized crime, and political corruption. Virtually all efforts to legalize casino gambling are accompanied by well-publicized reports of political corruption. For instance: Just weeks before the April 1994 vote in Missouri, the state's governor asked the members of the St. Louis Election Board to resign because all of them had financial ties to gaming companies. The governor's action followed weeks of newspaper stories detailing how politicians had become investors in the companies competing for gaming franchises. In Louisiana, the relationship between gambling and politicians seemed to be even closer, a circumstance that prompted a segment on ABC's *60 Minutes.* A grand jury investigating the gaming industry in 1994 found that friends and relatives of Governor Edwin Edwards had been paid large amounts of money for consulting, legal advice, or as "returns" on investments. Governor Edwards, a notorious gambler for years, liked to host high-stakes poker games in the governor's mansion.

Industry projections of the potential contributions of gaming to local treasuries often make it appear that gaming would constitute a magic elixir for ailing central city economies. Despite this promise, casino gaming is likely to spread somewhat more slowly than was anticipated only a few years ago. In 1996 ten state legislatures refused to pass laws to legalize casinos or slot machines,[94] and Congress passed legislation to initiate a two-year study of gaming. When completed in 1999, the study urged states and localities to be cautious about pursuing gaming.

THE NEW DOWNTOWN ECONOMIES

As in the railroad era of the nineteenth century, there has been fierce economic competition among cities in the last two decades. The successful cities have undergone downtown redevelopment, characterized by corporate towers, waterfront recreational development, enclosed shopping malls, new convention centers, and stadiums. Mirroring the tendency of suburbanites to separate themselves into enclaves, many of the affluent workers and residents of inner cities have retreated into these protected spaces.[95] Projects like the Peachtree Center in Atlanta, Renaissance Center in Detroit, Water Tower Place in Chicago, and the IDS Center in Minneapolis bring recreation, shopping, and work into enclosed environments. These multiuse structures make it possible for suburbanites to drive into the city, park in an underground garage, work in an attached office tower, shop in a mall connected by skyways, and perhaps attend a ball game in a domed stadium or attend a concert—all without setting foot on a city street. Whether located in suburbs or in central cities, whether corporate headquarters, a convention center, or a domed stadium, the new megastructures enclose and segment space.

Critics often note that sports stadiums, convention centers, and other components of the recreation and tourist infrastructure rarely pay for themselves. Public officials and civic boosters do not, on the whole, care much if they do. This apparently cavalier attitude toward taxpayers' money can be explained by noting the general irrelevance—to city officials and civic boosters—of cost-benefit analyses of tourism infrastructure. The attitudes of public officials toward development projects have "little do with the . . . profitability . . . of a project," and far more to do with the vision officials share about the overall direction a city is taking.[96] Such a stance often means that cities become driven by a vision of regeneration that is not entirely of their own invention. Cities exist in a complex political environment shaped by economic changes, national policies, the actions of other cities, and, in the case of tourism, a well-organized industry. The manner in which interurban competition in the United States is conducted, however, dictates that cities must compete, that they must be as generous as their competitors in providing subsidies, and that they must try to adopt every new variation on a theme that comes along. The competition imposes a logic of its own that is hard to resist.

For public officials tempted to proceed on blind faith alone, it is useful to keep in mind that abject, total, even humiliating failure is possible. In the 1970s Flint, Michigan, tried to make itself into a tourist city, and the unanticipated result was that its often sad and sometimes pathetic efforts were subsequently portrayed in a low-budget but popular movie, *Roger and Me*.[97] After the closing of its General Motors plant had devastated the local economy, public officials in Flint launched an effort at regeneration behind the motto, "Our New Spark Will Surprise You." The city committed $13 million in subsidies to the construction of a luxury hotel, the Hyatt Regency. Within a year it closed its doors. Approximately $100 million in public money was used to build AutoWorld, a museum that contained, among other items, the "world's largest car engine" and a scale model that portrayed downtown Flint in its more prosperous days. AutoWorld closed within six months. Still more public subsidies were committed to the construction of the Water Street Pavilion, a theme park/festival market built by the developer of the South Street Seaport in New York City. Most of its shops closed within the first year. Commenting on Flint's failure to become a magnet for tourism, the former director of AutoWorld said, "You can't make Palm Beach out of the Bowery. If you want to make Palm Beach, you have to go to Palm Beach."

Perhaps one lesson from the Flint story is that it did not do the right things to become more like Palm Beach. Virtually all cities of consequential size must take some steps to promote tourism, recreation, and culture. Now that the basic infrastructure is in place in many cities, public support for the arts and culture has become common. Every one of the nation's fifty largest cities provides public support for the arts. Some smaller cities are also offering subsidies. From the big cities (New York, with the Kennedy and Lincoln Centers, and more recently, the Ford Center on 42nd Street) to villages (Riverhead, a hamlet outside New York, which is building an arts and historic district), from the downtowns in need of a boost (Newark, with its $180 million New Jersey Center, opened in October 1997), to the already prosperous (San Francisco, with a newly renovated opera house and several other performance halls), the development of local culture has become a leading formula for urban revival.[98] The text for a major exhibit in 1998 sponsored by the National Building Museum in Washington, D.C., noted that culture has replaced both the urban renewal bulldozer and the preservation movements that followed in its destructive wake as the main focus for downtown revitalization.

Collectively, cities of all sizes support an almost unimaginable variety of events that carry the signature of local culture and community. Jazz and blues festivals, strawberry and garlic festivals, jumping frogs and gold rush days, rodeos and fireworks—such activities help define and sometimes knit together local communities.[99] These activities usually take place in or near the new tourism infrastructure (in smaller towns this may mean at local parks, bandstands, waterfronts, or ball diamonds). Every city must go through debates about how much the public purse should be devoted to these activities. But no city can afford to forego these debates altogether.

NOTES

1. This account of Quincy Market is based on Bernard J. Frieden and Lynn B. Sagalyn, *Downtown, Inc.: How America Builds Cities* (Cambridge, Mass.: MIT Press, 1989), and Jon C. Teaford, *The Rough Road to Renaissance: Urban Revitalization in America, 1940–1985* (Baltimore: Johns Hopkins University Press, 1990).
2. Frieden and Sagalyn, *Downtown, Inc.*, p. 43.
3. These arrangements are described in Peter K. Eisenger, *The Rise of the Entrepreneurial State: State and Local Economic Development Policy in the United States* (Madison: University of Wisconsin Press, 1988).
4. Teaford, *The Rough Road to Renaissance*, p. 307.
5. Ibid., p. 296.
6. Ibid., p. 307.
7. Alexander Hamilton, *The Works of Alexander Hamilton*, vol. 3, ed. John C. Hamilton (New York: Trow, 1950), p. 246, quoted in Norman Krumholz, "Recovery in Cities: An Alternative View," in *Rebuilding America's Cities: Roads to Recovery*, ed. Paul R. Porter and David C. Sweet (New Brunswick, N.J.: Center for Urban Policy Research, 1984), p. 182.
8. John R. Logan and Harvey L. Molotch, *Urban Fortunes: The Political Economy of Place* (Berkeley: University of California Press, 1987).
9. For an influential defense of the logic of growth politics, see Paul E. Peterson, *City Limits* (Chicago: University of Chicago Press, 1981).
10. Quoted in Robert S. Lynd and Helen Merrill Lynd, *Middletown* (New York: Harcourt Brace and World, 1929), p. 487. The Lynds' monumental study of Muncie, Indiana, is a classic sociological analysis of local booster culture.
11. U.S. Bureau of the Census, *Statistical Abstract of the United States, 1992,* 112th edition (Washington, D.C.: Government Printing Office, 1992), p. 397.
12. Robert B. Reich, *The Work of Nations* (New York: Random House, Vintage Books, 1991), p. 86.
13. Barry Bluestone and Bennett Harrison, *The Deindustrialization of America* (New York: Basic Books, 1982).
14. Ibid., p. 65.
15. Ibid., p. 69.
16. Kenneth T. Jackson, *Crabgrass Frontier: The Suburbanization of the United States* (New York: Oxford University Press, 1985), p. 261.
17. Joel Garreau, *Edge City: Life on the New Frontier* (Garden City, N.Y.: Doubleday, 1991).
18. Alexander Ganz, "Where Has the Urban Crisis Gone?," *Urban Affairs Quarterly* 20, No. 4 (June 1985): 456.
19. Frieden and Sagalyn, *Downtown, Inc.*, pp. 256–266.
20. Norman J. Glickman, "Cities and the International Division of Labor," in *Enduring Tensions in Urban Politics*, ed. Dennis Judd and Paul Kantor (New York: Macmillan, 1992), pp. 493–513.
21. Joseph Persky, Elliot Sclar, and Wim Wiewel, *Does America Need Cities?* (Washington, D.C.: Economic Policy Institute, 1991), p. 12; Thomas M. Stanback, Jr., *The New Suburbanization: Challenge to the Central City* (Boulder, Colo.: Westview Press, 1991), p. 45.
22. Frieden and Sagalyn, *Downtown, Inc.*, p. 288.

23. Ibid., pp. 288–289.
24. Richard Child Hill, "Crisis in the Motor City: The Politics of Economic Development in Detroit," in Norman Fainstein, Susan S. Fainstein, Richard Child Hill, Dennis Judd, and Michael Peter Smith, *Restructuring the City: The Political Economy of Urban Redevelopment* (New York: Longman, 1983), p. 105.
25. Gurney Breckenfield, "It's Up to the Cities to Save Themselves," *Fortune*, March 1977, p. 196.
26. Neal R. Peirce, Robert Guskind, and John Gardner, "Politics Is Not the Only Thing That Is Changing America's Big Cities," *National Journal* (November 26, 1983): 2480.
27. "He Digs Downtown," *Time*, August 24, 1981, p. 47.
28. Robert P. Stoker, "Baltimore: The Self-Evaluating City?" in *The Politics of Urban Development*, ed. Clarence N. Stone and Heywood T. Sanders (Lawrence: University Press of Kansas, 1987), p. 248.
29. Quoted in Tony Hiss, "Annals of Place: Reinventing Baltimore," *New Yorker*, April 29, 1991, p. 62.
30. Quoted in "He Digs Downtown," p. 42.
31. Christopher Corbett, "What's Doing in Baltimore," *New York Times*, February 23, 1992.
32. Bernard L. Berkowitz, "Rejoinder to Downtown Redevelopment as an Urban Growth Strategy: A Critical Appraisal of the Baltimore Renaissance," *Journal of Urban Affairs* 9, No. 2 (1987): 129.
33. "He Digs Downtown," p. 47.
34. Marc V. Levine, "Downtown Development as an Urban Growth Strategy," *Journal of Urban Affairs* 9, No. 2 (1987): 110.
35. Berkowitz, "Rejoinder to Downtown Redevelopment," p. 130.
36. Richard Ben Cramer, "Can the Best Mayor Win?" *Esquire*, October 1984, p. 58.
37. Quoted in Hiss, "Annals of Place," p. 41.
38. Levine, "Downtown Redevelopment," pp. 111–112.
39. Richard P. Nathan and Charles F. Adams, "Four Perspectives on Urban Hardship," *Political Science Quarterly* 104, No. 3 (Fall 1989): 488.
40. Levine, "Downtown Redevelopment," p. 112.
41. Ibid., p. 116.
42. John D. Kasarda, "Urban Change and Minority Opportunities," in *The New Urban Reality*, ed. Paul E. Peterson (Washington, D.C.: Brookings Institution, 1985); William Julius Wilson, *The Truly Disadvantaged: The Inner City, the Underclass, and Public Policy* (Chicago: University of Chicago Press, 1987); William Julius Wilson, *When Work Disappears: The World of the New Urban Poor* (New York: Alfred A. Knopf, 1996).
43. Levine, "Downtown Redevelopment," pp. 113–114.
44. Dennis R. Judd, *The Politics of American Cities: Private Power and Public Policy*, 3rd ed. (New York: HarperCollins, 1988), p. 393.
45. Marc V. Levine, "Response to Berkowitz," *Journal of Urban Affairs* 9, No. 2 (1987): 136.
46. Levine, "Downtown Redevelopment," p. 108.
47. Richard C. Hula, "The Two Baltimores," in *Leadership and Urban Regeneration: Cities in North America and Europe*, ed. Dennis Judd and Michael Parkinson (Newbury Park, Calif.: Sage, 1990), pp. 199–200.
48. Fainstein, Fainstein, Hill, Judd, and Smith, *Restructuring the City*.
49. Christine Boyer, "Cities for Sale: Merchandising History at South Street Seaport," in *Variations on a Theme Park: The New American City and the End of Public Space*, ed. Michael Sorkin (New York: Hill and Wang, 1992), pp. 189–190.
50. Hula, "The Two Baltimores."
51. G. J. Ashworth and J. E. Tunbridge, *The Tourist-Historic City* (London and New York: Belhaven Press, 1990), p. 153.
52. See also Dennis R. Judd, "Constructing the Tourist Bubble," in Dennis R. Judd and Susan S. Fainstein, eds., *The Tourist City* (New Haven: Yale University Press, 1999).

53. John A. Jackle, *The Tourist: Travel in Twentieth Century North America* (Lincoln: University of Nebraska Press, 1985).

54. Heywood T. Sanders, "Building the Convention City: Politics, Finance and Public Investment in Urban America." *Journal of Urban Affairs* 14 (1992): 135–159.

55. Ibid.

56. David H. Laslo, *Proliferating Convention Centers: The Political Economy of Regenerating Cities and the St. Louis Convention Center Expansion*, Ph.D. dissertation, University of Missouri-St. Louis, May 1999.

57. George G. Fenich, "The Dollars and Sense of Convention Centers" (Ph.D. dissertation, Rutgers University, 1992), p. 34.

58. Laslo, *Proliferating Convention Centers*, p. 67.

59. *Tradeshow Week Data Book, 1998* (Bill Communications, 1998).

60. *Successful Meetings* magazine, "State of the Industry 1993" (New York: Bill Communications, July 1993), pp. 32–33.

61. *Convene Magazine* website http://www.pcma.org/convene, accessed April 2000.

62. *Successful Meetings* magazine, p. 11.

63. Ibid., pp. 60–61.

64. Amy Teibel, "The Pros and Cons of Second-Tier Cities," *Convene* 9, No. 1 (Birmingham, Professional Convention Management Association, February 1994): 33–37.

65. *Sunday Magazine, St. Louis Globe Democrat*, November 9, 1975, p. 8.

66. Tabak, "How Much Do We Want Their Money?" p. 62.

67. *New York Times*, 1992.

68. John R. Logan and Harvey L. Molotch, *Urban Fortunes: The Political Economy of Place* (Berkeley: University of California Press, 1987), p. 58.

69. Neil J. Sullivan, *The Dodgers Move West* (New York: Oxford University Press, 1987).

70. Arthur T. Johnson, "The Sports Franchise Relocation Issue and Public Policy Responses," in *Government and Sport: The Public Policy Issues*, ed. Arthur T. Johnson and James H. Frey (Totowa, N.J.: Rowman & Allanheld, 1985), p. 232.

71. Arthur T. Johnson, "Economic and Policy Implications of Hosting Sports Franchises: Some Lessons from Baltimore," *Urban Affairs Quarterly* 21, No. 3 (March 1986): 411.

72. Robert A. Baade and Robert E. Dye, "Sports Stadiums and Area Development: A Critical Review," *Economic Development Quarterly* 2 (1988): 265–275; Robert A. Baade, "Professional Sports and Economic Development," *Journal of Urban Affairs* 18, No. 1 (1996): 1–18.

73. Charles C. Eichner, *Playing the Field: Why Sports Teams Move and Cities Fight to Keep Them* (Baltimore: Johns Hopkins University Press, 1993), pp. 12–13.

74. Ronald Smothers, "No Hits, No Runs, One Error: The Dome," *New York Times*, June 15, 1991.

75. Eichner, *Playing the Field*, p. 67.

76. Donald Phares and Mark S. Rosentraub, "Reviving the Glory of Days Past: St. Louis's Blitz to Save Its Image, Identity, and Teams," in Mark S. Rosentraub, *Major League Losers: The Real Cost of Sports and Who's Paying for It* (New York: Basic Books, 1997).

77. John Zipp, "The Economic Impact of the Baseball Strike of 1994," *Urban Affairs Review* 32, No. 2 (November 1996); see also Baade and Dye, "Sports Stadiums;" Baade, "Professional Sports;" Eichner, *Playing the Field*, p. 71.

78. Mike Davis, "Fortress Los Angeles: The Militarization of Urban Space," in *Variations on a Theme Park*, ed. Sorkin, p. 155.

79. Myriam Jansen-Verbeke, "Leisure+Shopping=Tourism Product Mix," in *Marketing Tourism Places*, ed. Gregory Ashworth and Brian Goodall (London and New York: Routledge, 1990), p. 132.

80. ULI—The Urban Land Institute, *Developing Urban Entertainment Centers* (Washington, D.C.: Urban Land Institute, 1998).

81. William R. Eadington, "The Emergence of Casino Gaming as a Major Factor in Tourism Markets: Policy Issues and Considerations," in *Change in Tourism: People, Places, Processes*, ed. Richard Butler and Douglas Pearce (London and New York: Routledge, 1995).

82. Quoted in Robert Goodman, *Legalized Gambling as a Strategy for Economic Development* (Northampton, Mass.: United States Gambling Study, 1994), p. 29.
83. Quoted in ibid., pp. 26–27.
84. Harrah's Entertainment, Inc., *Harrah's Survey of Casino Entertainment* (1996), p. 13.
85. Ibid., p. 4.
86. Fred Faust, "It Wasn't in the Cards," *St. Louis Post-Dispatch,* April 10, 1994, pp. 1–5E.
87. *Company Analysis* (New York: Donaldson, Lufkin & Jenrette Securities Corporation, June 23, 1993), p. 12.
88. *Company Analysis,* p. 6.
89. Goodman, *Legalized Gambling,* p. 34.
90. Phil Linsalata and Terry Ganey, "Casinos Prepare to Throw the Dice," *St. Louis Post-Dispatch,* April 27, 1994, pp. 1, 12.
91. Goodman, *Legalized Gambling,* pp. 91–94.
92. William C. Lhotka, "Gambling Addict? State May Let You Deal Yourself Out," *St. Louis Post-Dispatch,* June 11, 1996, p. 6A.
93. Sabina Dietrick, Robert A. Beauregard, and Cheryl Zarlenga Kerchis, "Riverboat Gambling, Tourism and Economic Development," in *The Tourist City,* ed. Dennis Judd and Susan S. Fainstein (New Haven: Yale University Press, 1999); Goodman, *Legalized Gambling,* pp. 51–57; Margot Hornblower, "*No* Dice: The Backlash Against Gambling," *Time,* April 1, 1996, pp. 29–33.
94. Ellen Perlman, "The Gambling Glut," *Governing: The Magazine of States and Localities* 9, No. 8 (May 1996): 49–56.
95. Dennis R. Judd, "Enclosure, Community, and Public Life," *Research in Community Sociology* 6 (1996): 217–236; see also Dennis R. Judd, "The Rise of the New Walled Cities," in *Spatial Practices,* ed. Helen Liggett and David C. Perry (Thousand Oaks, Calif.: Sage, 1995), pp. 144–166.
96. Michael A. Pagano and Ann Bowman, *Cityscapes and Capital: The Politics of Urban Development* (Baltimore: Johns Hopkins University Press, 1995), p. 74.
97. A Dog Eat Dog Films Production. Written, produced and directed by Michael Moore (Warner Bros. Pictures).
98. Bruce Weber, "Cities are Fostering the Arts As a Way to Save Downtown," *New York Times,* November 18, 1997.
99. Dennis R. Judd, William Winter, William Barnes, and Emily Stern, *Tourism and Entertainment as a Local Economic Development Strategy: The Report of a NLC Survey* (Washington, D.C.: National League of Cities: A Research Report, 2000).

14

THE CHALLENGE OF URBAN GOVERNANCE

THE DELICATE TASK OF GOVERNANCE

Racial and ethnic conflicts have long served as the fault lines in the politics of America's cities. The successive waves of foreign immigration in the nineteenth and early twentieth centuries were followed by massive internal migrations. In recent decades the flow of foreign immigration has again accelerated. As in earlier periods, immigrants have settled in the cities and as a result, the cities have become places where an intense power struggle is taking place between the newly arrived immigrants, African Americans, and a middle- and upper-income gentry. In such a context, governance becomes an urgent and difficult task. Just as in previous periods of rapid change, can city governments keep the peace among the various contending groups?

It should be noted that sometimes the peace has not been preserved. In the nineteenth century violent clashes sometimes broke out between racial and ethnic groups. The urban riots of the 1960s erupted as expressions of the deep anger and frustrations felt within African-American communities. More recent social disorders—Liberty City in Miami, 1980; Washington, D.C., 1991; and Crown Heights in Brooklyn, 1991—revealed that the tensions persisted. The most serious riot of all occurred in Los Angeles in 1992. With 53 people dead, 2,383 injuries, 16,291 arrests, over 5,500 fires, and over $700 million in property damage, the Los Angeles riot was the most violent urban disturbance of the twentieth century, and unlike previous riots, it was multi-ethnic, involving blacks, Latinos, and Asians.[1] In subsequent years it might have seemed that racial and ethnic tensions had subsided, but in April 2000 fears of rioting ran rampant in Miami the day after federal agents seized Elian Gonzalez and returned him to his father. Cuban-American leaders called for calm, fearful that rioting might break out. This incident showed that the social fabric is held together by tenuous bonds in America's cities.

Keeping the peace and maintaining social order without the use of force is the challenge of urban *governance.* City governments are designed as mechanisms not only for providing services but for managing social and political tensions. They do this—ideally—by incorporating into a democratic politics the various political interests that make up a city. The legitimacy of local government requires that citizens perceive it as sufficiently representative and responsive to their needs. If citizens become convinced that their participation makes no difference, they will demonstrate their alienation from the political system by withholding their vote, refusing to participate in the civic life of organizational politics, and—occasionally—by resorting to violence to vent their frustrations.

Cities are contested arenas within which groups jostle for political influence and advantage. Over the past four decades, these struggles have given rise to three main political movements, which we shall label urban liberalism, populism, and conservatism. The movement that we call urban liberalism sprang forth from the civil rights movements of the 1950s and 1960s. It has been energized, mainly, by concerns for racial equality and social equity. As a political movement, urban populism grew out of neighborhood protests of the 1950s and 1960s, and it has become institutionalized in neighborhood organizations and community development corporations that continue to deliver important urban services. Urban conservatism emerged in the 1980s as a local version of the national conservative movement centered in the Republican party. The mayors that we label as conservatives (an admittedly broad category) have implemented cutbacks in municipal and social services and pursued aggressive law-and-order policies. Above all, they have placed their faith in private economic investment, and thus have offered heavy subsidies to stimulate the local economy. As it turns out, the leaders of all three of these political movements use government to promote investment, but the urban conservatives have done so with particular enthusiasm, and with the purest faith that economic growth solves all problems.

Urban liberalism arose out of the civil rights movement of the 1960s, which broke down the barriers to political participation by African Americans and Latinos. Beginning in the late 1960s, a generation of African-American and Latino leaders entered public office, and they broke ground for those who followed. As would be expected, these public officials were forced to negotiate a political terrain that often pitted blacks, Latinos, and whites against one another. These leaders confronted a central issue in urban governance: how to build electoral and governing coalitions that transcend racial and ethnic divisions.

Urban populism drew energy from the civil rights movement, but its roots were put down in the neighborhood protests against the massive urban renewal and highway projects of the 1950s and 1960s. During these struggles neighborhood leaders learned how to mobilize their constituencies to oppose downtown growth coalitions and the policies that often came at the expense of neighborhoods. Gradually, the neighborhood movement shifted from protest to politics. Neighborhood leaders and associations ran candidates for public office and demanded a voice in administering urban programs. With their requirements for citizen participation, the War on Poverty and the Model Cities programs gave neighborhood advocates the experience and the expectation that some governmental services would be administered through nonprofit groups. Community development corporations (CDCs) became the vehicles for providing such services as job training, educational services, recreational activities, and legal and counseling services.

Urban conservatism emerged in the 1980s. In large part it was motivated by a white working-class and middle-class reaction to the entry of African Americans and Latinos into city politics. Urban conservatives promised to cut taxes by holding down spending, which appealed to businesses and middle-class voters. To bring order to the streets, they promised to get tough with criminals, panhandlers, and the homeless. And they promised to use local government to restart the engine of private investment. This three-part agenda appealed to a broad alliance of voters, but it brought with it the danger that racial and ethnic antagonisms might be reignited. Unlike their counterparts at the national level, however, urban conservatives have generally taken moderate positions on such explosive social issues as affirmative-action hiring and multicultural curriculums in the schools.

URBAN LIBERALISM AND THE DILEMMAS OF COALITION POLITICS

Before the civil rights movement succeeded in mobilizing the African-American electorate, few blacks held public office in the United States. Until 1967 not a single African American had ever been elected mayor of a major American city. In that year, Richard Hatcher was elected mayor of Gary, Indiana, and Carl Stokes became the mayor of Cleveland. In the intervening years the number of black mayors of major cities (over 50,000 population) has increased steadily, reaching 28 by 1988 and 38 five years later.[2] The number of black city and county elected officials increased from 715 in 1970 to 5,669 by 1997 (see Figure 14.1). Likewise, the number of Latino county and municipal public officials grew from 1,316 in 1985 to 2,197 in 1994.[3] With the election of Kurt Schmoke as the first black mayor of Baltimore in 1987, every city of more than 100,000 people that had a majority black population had elected an African-American mayor. At different points in the 1980s African-American candidates won the mayor's office in four of the five largest cities in the country, even though African American voters were in the minority in those cities (David Dinkins in New York, Tom Bradley in Los Angeles, Harold Washington in Chicago, and Wilson Goode in Philadelphia), and in the 1990s African Americans won in several cities where they constituted a minority of voters, including St. Louis, Denver, Kansas City, and Seattle. Latino mayors won office in Denver, Miami, San Antonio, and in many smaller cities. The former mayors of Denver and San Antonio, Frederico Péna and Henry Cisneros, were appointed to Bill Clinton's cabinet in 1993.

How effective have minority officials been at delivering the goods to their constituents? Do coalitions of blacks, Latinos, and white liberals represent the

FIGURE 14.1   Black City and County Elected Officials, 1970–1997

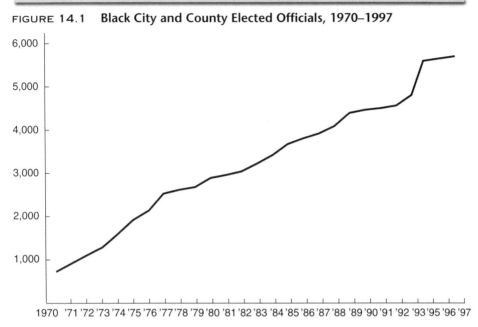

Source: Joint Center for Political and Economic Studies, *Black Elected Officials: A National Roster,* annual; as cited in U.S. Bureau of the Census, *Statistical Abstract of the United States,* various years (Washington, D.C.: U.S. Government Printing Office).

wave of the future, or do the notable defeats of minority candidates in New York, Chicago, and Los Angeles signal the demise of urban liberalism? In order to answer these questions, it is important to examine the dynamics of coalitional politics in central cities.

In the vast majority of the cases where an African American has become mayor in a big city, blacks have not constituted a majority of either the overall population or of the voters. Even in those cases where blacks have made up an electoral majority, African-American candidates have almost always had to win a significant proportion of the votes cast outside of the black neighborhoods to assemble a winning electoral coalition. African-American candidates have been forced to walk a fine line. The more they stress issues such as minority hiring and contracting and cultural curricula in the schools, the more they risk alienating white supporters. Black mayors find that whatever the composition of their electoral coalition, they are unable to do very much unless they forge a good working relationship with the one group that can bring about prosperity in the downtown—the business community. But once in office, if they seem to ignore their constituents in the neighborhoods, black mayors may harm their chances for reelection.

A comparison of electoral politics in the nation's two largest cities, New York and Los Angeles, sheds light on the conditions that can undermine interracial and interethnic coalitions. By 1990 non-Latino whites made up less than half—43 percent—of the population of New York City. Blacks accounted for 25 percent, Latinos 24 percent, and Asians 8 percent.[4] With a large Jewish population (accounting for about half of the non-Latino whites) that was historically sensitive to discrimination and supportive of the civil rights movement, New York City seemed to be an ideal context for forging a multi-racial and multi-ethnic coalition. In fact, however, this context has produced an unstable and fractious politics that first elected a conservative white ethnic politician as mayor (Ed Koch elected and reelected in 1977, 1981, and 1985), then a one-term African-American mayor (David Dinkins, 1989), and then a Republican conservative (Rudolph Giuliani, 1993 and 1997). By contrast, Los Angeles, which is also racially and ethnically diverse, elected an African-American mayor, Tom Bradley, in 1973, and then kept him in office for five consecutive terms. Blacks accounted for just 14 percent of the population of Los Angeles in 1990. We can learn a lot about the nature of coalition politics if we can explain Bradley's success.

Tom Bradley, the son of Texas sharecroppers, moved to Los Angeles with his family at the age of seven. Raised in poverty, Bradley was a star athlete in football and track and an exceptional student. Throughout his life he chose to enter white-dominated institutions and always excelled within them. After attending UCLA, where less than 1 percent of the student body was black, Bradley took a job with the segregated Los Angeles Police Department. Moving his family to a largely white neighborhood, he organized a new community relations unit on the West Side, where he formed close personal contacts with Jewish merchants and civic leaders. Studying at night, he obtained a law degree and quit the force to practice law. Bradley became active in reform Democratic politics at a time when cooperation was being forged among upwardly mobile African Americans, Jews, and liberals—all of them largely excluded from the regular Democratic party.

In 1969 the reform Democrats ran Bradley as a mayoral candidate against the conservative incumbent, Sam Yorty. In the racially polarized atmosphere, which was still influenced by the Watts riot of four years before, Yorty won an overwhelming majority of white votes, and received particularly strong support from upper-middle-class homeowners in the San Fernando Valley. When he ran against Yorty four years later, Bradley broadened his appeal by expressing his support for policies to stimulate the revitalization of the downtown and by promising to keep taxes low. This time Bradley was able to pull enough white and Latino votes to defeat Yorty. Bradley's electoral coalition included African Americans of all income levels, higher-income and especially Jewish white liberals, and Latinos. In subsequent elections Bradley gradually incorporated Asian-Americans into his coalition as well. Bradley succeeded largely because he was able to symbolize different things to different people: "Whites saw Bradley as a symbol of racial harmony, while blacks saw him as a symbol of racial assertion."[5]

Bradley's success was predicated on a long history of collaboration between white liberals and the upwardly mobile black middle class. Both groups had been systematically excluded from governance prior to Bradley's victory, and therefore they did not view each other as competitors but as allies in ousting the

Yorty regime. After his initial victory, Bradley also reached out to business, making the downtown banks and corporations key elements of his regime. As a result, Bradley always had a massive campaign chest at his command when he ran for reelection.

Many of the conditions that allowed an African American to become the mayor of Los Angeles were absent in New York, despite the fact that blacks were already well entrenched in New York City's government by the mid-1960s.[6] By the time blacks entered New York City's political system, liberals and Jews had already established themselves by successfully electing a liberal Republican, John Lindsay, as mayor for two terms (1966–1973). Though New York's blacks, Jews, and white liberals could clearly cooperate, their leaders viewed one another with suspicion. These tensions came to a head in 1968 when the African-American community attempted an experiment in community control in the Ocean Hill–Brownsville schools in Brooklyn. The school board's attempt to transfer nineteen teachers, some of them Jewish, out of the district resulted in a bitter citywide strike by the teachers' union, which divided blacks and Jews in ways that are still being felt in New York today. The same sort of conflicts and suspicions have characterized the political relationships between African Americans and Latinos, 90 percent of whom identify themselves as white (the other 10 percent mostly come from the Caribbean).[7] Conflicts among these groups allowed Ed Koch to assemble a conservative coalition with Jews and Catholics at its center, which became the basis of his mayoral victories in 1977, 1981, and 1985.[8]

In 1989 New York elected a black mayor, David Dinkins. Having come up through the regular Democratic party, Dinkins possessed a dignified, nonconfrontational style that was nonthreatening to whites, though without doubt blacks made up the heart of his electoral coalition. In the early stages of the mayoral contest, Koch miscalculated by attacking Jesse Jackson, who had made a run for the presidency the year before, for expressing support for the Palestine Liberation Organization (PLO). Koch commented that Jews "would have to be crazy" to vote for Jackson. An African-American newspaper, *Amsterdam News,* replied bitterly by reminding Koch to remember that "he is mayor of the city; not just of New York Jewry."[9] In an atmosphere of growing inequality and racial tension, many white voters felt that Dinkins would better be able to keep the peace and he defeated Koch in the 1989 multicandidate Democratic primary by a 51 to 41 percent margin.

The Rewards of Political Incorporation

An ability to elect a mayor is only the first step toward exercising political power. To actually derive substantial benefits, it is also necessary for minorities to seek political incorporation, which can be defined as possessing "an equal or leading role in a dominant coalition that is strongly committed to minority interests."[10] Incorporation entails the ability to influence a city council and the various bureaucracies that deliver important services; otherwise, a mayor can become isolated, unable to deliver on the campaign promises made. In Chicago, for example, Harold Washington, who was mayor from 1983 to 1987, found himself tied down in the so-called "council wars" during his entire first term. The city council—still dominated by white ethnic politicians left over from the Daley organization—overrode Washington's policy proposals. Department administrators and city workers routinely ignored problems in the African-American neighborhoods; instead, they followed orders from aldermen and precinct captains hostile to Washington. Blacks in Chicago had succeeded in electing a mayor, but they had not changed Chicago's government very much.

To govern effectively and deliver benefits to supporters, a mayor must assemble a broad and comprehensive governing coalition. In American cities authority is highly fragmented and dispersed.[11] The mayor's office is a center of power but there are many other centers of power that can act as veto points to frustrate mayoral leadership. In order to produce significant results that can be used to run for reelection, mayors need cooperation from institutions well beyond the city council, including labor unions, the media, independent authorities (such as school boards), the courts, and state and federal officials. To be effective while in office, a mayor must reach out for support from many sectors.

Downtown business leaders are essential partners or deadly adversaries. In his study of governance in Atlanta, Clarence Stone argued that downtown business exercised a "preemptive power" to shape the city's regime because it possessed the institutional resources that enabled mayors to accomplish important public tasks, like building a new stadium, a rapid transit system, or an airport. The day after he was elected Atlanta's mayor in 1981, Andrew Young, a former top aide to Martin Luther King, Jr., confirmed the accuracy of Stone's assessment in a speech before a group of downtown business leaders. "I didn't get elected with your help," Young began, but then quickly added: "I can't govern without you."[12] Mayors must recognize that economic logic requires them to pay close attention to the attitudes of business leaders and investors. This often conflicts with a political logic that tempts them to spread benefits broadly to the major groups that make up their electoral coalition.

Minority mayors and city councils have been successful in rewarding their followers in ways that do not adversely affect the downtown business establishment. Public employment is their most important resource; downtown business does not care, for the most part, if blacks rather than whites pick up their garbage or police their streets. Studies have consistently shown that when blacks are politically incorporated—that is, when they win the mayor's office and become influential throughout the institutions of local government—minority employment in city government increases.[13] From 1973 to 1991, under Mayor Bradley in Los Angeles, black, Latino, and Asian-American municipal employment increased from 36 to 50 percent. Minorities are often concentrated in lower-level jobs but in Los Angeles during this period minority representation in top-level city jobs increased as well.[14]

The urban liberal regimes have also frequently enacted preferential procurement programs requiring that a minimum percentage of city contracts be given to minority business enterprises (MBEs). In 1973, at a time when blacks accounted for a majority of Atlanta's population, black-owned firms received only one-tenth of 1 percent of the city's contracts. As a result of a preferential pro-curement program, by 1988, 35 percent of the city's contracts was awarded to minority firms. Preferential procurement programs have been damaged, how-ever, by evidence that some MBEs have acted as mere fronts for nonminority firms doing most of the work.[15] Moreover, like many affirmative action pro-grams, preferential procurement generally has benefited higher-income and better-educated people within the minority community. Atlanta's first black mayor, Maynard Jackson, boasted that the minority set-asides for Atlanta's air-port expansion created twenty-one African-American millionaires; however, benefits to the low-income community were more difficult to identify.[16]

The U.S. Supreme Court has made it harder for cities and states to use prefer-ential procurement programs. In *City of Richmond v. J. A. Croson Co.* (1989) the Court ruled that the City of Richmond's program requiring that 30 percent of contracts be set aside for MBEs violated the Equal Protection Clause of the Fourteenth Amend-ment.[17] In order to withstand the "strict scrutiny" standard of constitutionality, cities must document past discrimination by city government and demonstrate that race-neutral alternatives will not solve the problem. This case makes preferen-tial procurement programs more difficult but not impossible to implement.[18]

Police reform is another important policy benefit flowing from political in-corporation. Police brutality and inadequate police protection have long been two of the most frequently expressed grievances in minority communities around the country. For many years the police department of Los Angeles was particularly loathed in minority communities. Under Los Angeles' governmen-tal structure, the LAPD operated well beyond the influence of elected officials. Appointed by an independent Police Commission, the Chief of Police had a free hand in running the department. The LAPD had always prided itself on its tough law-and-order approach to law enforcement, and the chief liked to brag about the department's state-of-the-art high-tech weaponry. In Los Angeles, policing relied on helicopters equipped with infrared cameras for night vision and 30-million candlepower spotlights, called "Nightsuns," that could turn night into day. Street numbers painted on rooftops gave police helicopters a navigable street grid from the air. Synchronization with patrol cars was facili-tated by a high-tech communications system conceptualized by Hughes Aircraft and refined by NASA's Jet Propulsion Laboratory.[19] In low-income neighbor-hoods, this strategy meant that the LAPD acted more like an occupying army than as an instrument for preserving public safety.

From 1978 to 1992, Chief Daryl Gates ran the LAPD as his own personal fief-dom. Under operation HAMMER, patrol officers and elite tactical squads de-scended on South Central Los Angeles, arresting thousands of minority youths in each sweep. Young men were brought in for a wide range of infractions—from selling drugs to suspected gang activity to charges of loitering and jay-walking. In the absence of other charges, resisting arrest became a favorite police option. By 1990 as many as 50,000 suspects had been arrested in these sweeps, which is astounding considering there were only about 100,000 African-Ameri-can youths in all of Los Angeles.[20] The LAPD had a practice of using a danger-ous chokehold to control people in custody. In 1982, after frequent use of the chokehold resulted in a rash of deaths among young black men, Chief Gates made the inflammatory statement that the problem could be traced to the anatomy of blacks, rather than to police practices: "We may be finding that in some Blacks when [the carotid chokehold] is applied the veins or arteries do not open up as fast as they do on normal people."[21] The beating of Rodney King, which set off the 1992 riots, came as no surprise to blacks in Los Angeles.

Mayor Bradley, who had the advantage of being a former cop, succeeded in bringing the LAPD under some degree of civilian control but only after twenty years of fierce political battles. The LAPD's share of the city's budget fell from 23 percent in 1972–1973 to 17.6 percent in 1987–1988. Between 1980 and 1988, minority representation in the LAPD increased from 20 to 32 percent, but minority representation in leadership positions still lagged. Most importantly, in June 1992, shortly after the riots, the voters approved Proposition F. Strongly supported by Bradley, Proposition F limited the terms of police chiefs and removed their civil service protection. Having campaigned vigorously against Proposition F, Chief Gates resigned and was succeeded by an African American, Willie Williams, who pledged to implement community-based policing.[22]

What the Los Angeles case shows is that even under adverse conditions, when minorities are incorporated into the political system, they are able to bring about important changes. In the case of Los Angeles, the black community considered it to be essential that more African-American police officers be hired and that the police department be brought under greater civilian control.[23] Racism and police brutality still occur within integrated police forces, but changing the composition of the force is a first step toward reform.

An increasing number of racial and ethnic groups have recently sought incorporation into city politics. When these groups must cooperate to gain access to the political system, they are often able to put aside their differences and support a candidate. But these alliances are hard to keep together. A study of forty-one cities with at least 10 percent blacks and 10 percent Latinos found that, generally, black and Latino municipal employment was associated with the incorporation of both groups into local political systems. The same research showed, however, that as the African-American population increased, the Latino share of municipal employment fell.[24] Tensions arise because it is difficult to satisfy both groups with the limited jobs and other resources available. In New York City, the failure of blacks and Latinos to forge a stable electoral coalition facilitated the election of conservative mayors Ed Koch and Rudolph Giuliani. Similarly, after Bradley retired in Los Angeles, his black and Latino coalition immediately fell apart, which paved the road to the mayor's office for Republican conservative Richard Riordan.

The main weakness of urban liberal regimes, however, has not been their instability but their failure to deliver much-needed social programs. In the 1960s and 1970s, when federal grants were flowing into cities, the first generation of minority mayors were able to fund programs that benefited the poor. Since the withdrawal of federal funds, the subsequent generation of mayors has found it difficult to find the necessary resources to fund housing, health, jobs, recreational, and other initiatives. In an attempt to improve local economics, black mayors have adopted rather conventional pro-growth policies in the hopes that the benefits will trickle down:

> The black mayors operate on the basis of a simple equation: private economic development in the city produces jobs in the private sector and tax money that may be used for jobs and purchases in the public sector. Through the various affirmative action devices . . . a certain proportion of these jobs and purchases may be channeled to the black community.[25]

But public-sector jobs can supply employment to no more than 6 to 8 percent of the black population of central cities—even assuming that no jobs would go to other groups.[26] In any case, a large proportion of public jobs, minority business contracts, and other benefits have gone to middle- and upper-income people and even to suburbanites.[27]

Minority mayors have often subsidized downtown development as a way to turn their cities around. Tom Bradley provides a good example. Early on, he stressed the need to make Los Angeles a "world class" city. He courted Japanese investors, who poured more than $3 billion into Los Angeles real estate in 1988 alone. But the Japanese connection also had a downside: Between 1975 and 1990, Japanese imports wiped out 50,000 high-wage manufacturing jobs in the Los Angeles region.[28] Before Bradley there was almost no downtown in Los Angeles; in 1975 there were only five buildings above thirteen stories. By 1990 there were over fifty such buildings—many of them visible in the dramatic footage that opened the television series *L.A. Law*.[29] To subsidize this expansion, Los Angeles created a huge 255-block downtown Tax Increment Finance (TIF) district. The TIF allowed the city to float bonds to provide public improvements and services to stimulate private investment. But the city was required to use all the additional taxes from the downtown redevelopment to retire the bonds or to support further development; the new taxes could not be used for projects or services elsewhere in the city.[30] The downtown office complex experienced a boom, but the high-level professional jobs generated by corporate investment were taken either by suburbanites or by professionals who moved into gentrified neighborhoods close to the downtown. The overall effect was to displace lower-income residents, to drive up the cost of housing, and to segment urban space into distinct enclaves.

The 1992 riots laid bare the limitations of Bradley's regime. His policies had mainly aided real estate developers and expanded opportunities for white-collar professionals, including some who were black and Latino. Redevelopment did not benefit the poor much. According to the 1990 census, the poverty rate in South Central L.A., where the riots started, was 32.9 percent. The area was seething with tensions between newly arrived Central American immigrants and long-time African-American residents. Competition for housing was fierce. Finally recognizing the depth of the housing crisis, in 1991 Bradley began to push for "linkage" fees that would require developers to allocate funds for low-income housing, in exchange for approval of downtown building projects.

As development spread from downtown to the affluent West Side, Bradley began to encounter stiff opposition from environmentalists who objected to increased air pollution and traffic congestion. Unable to keep up with new development, the sewerage system broke down in 1987, dumping millions of gallons of raw sewage into Santa Monica Bay. Bradley proposed a cap on new sewer construction to slow the pace of new development. The next year, however, Bradley infuriated environmentalists by reversing his long-standing opposition to oil drilling in the Pacific Palisades, an area on the ocean floor extending several miles out from Los Angeles. Under siege from residents in low- as well as high-income neighborhoods, Bradley chose not to run for a sixth term in 1993.

Most African-American mayors have supported a pro-growth, downtown development agenda much like Bradley's.[31] Atlanta's experience shows why. In 1973 Maynard Jackson was elected the first African-American mayor of Atlanta with strong support from the black community and from neighborhood activists in both black and white neighborhoods. Jackson came into office with a strong social reform agenda, explicitly rejecting what he termed "slavish, unquestioning adherence to downtown dicta."[32] What set Jackson apart from previous mayors was that he insisted that business elites "come to City Hall to meet in his office and to ask for his support, rather than simply to inform him of their needs and assume his compliance."[33]

In order to undertake complex projects that he could take credit for when seeking reelection, however, Jackson needed the support of the business community and, over time, he was pulled toward accommodation with downtown business elites. He supported all the major redevelopment projects favored by downtown business, including construction of the MARTA (Metro Atlanta Rapid Transit Authority) system that mainly connected downtown to the Atlanta airport. Jackson's successor, civil rights activist Andrew Young, continued Jackson's unqualified support of downtown development. Commenting on his partnership with the business elite, Young said, "Politics doesn't control the world. Money does."[34]

Jackson and Young were able to increase African-American public employment, government contracts for minority-owned firms, and African-American representation on the police force, but the booming downtown and suburbs did little to help blacks trapped in inner-city low-income neighborhoods. They were left behind.[35] From 1980 to 1985 predominantly white areas in the Atlanta region had job growth fourteen times greater than predominantly black areas. Between 1970 and 1985, while the black professional middle class prospered, the black poor were hurt by a sharp decline in manufacturing employment. Between 1970 and 1982, the percentage of central city households living in poverty doubled. Atlanta's housing and job markets remained highly segregated. After 1980, applications to higher education, especially among Atlanta's black males, fell rapidly. A 1989 study by The Atlanta Constitution found that one black man in six had been imprisoned.[36]

In sum, the payoffs for minority political incorporation have been uneven. Liberal regimes have been quite successful in altering hiring policies and reigning in the police. These are important accomplishments. Studies provide little evidence, however, that the incorporation of blacks into political systems has led to significantly different taxing, spending, and service delivery policies. For the most part, African-American mayors have not significantly altered development trends favoring downtown areas over the neighborhoods. The incorporation of African Americans into politics has had the effect of making people feel better about politics, however. Survey research shows that blacks living in cities with a black mayor expressed more trusting and efficacious attitudes toward politics, paid more attention to political affairs, and participated more in politics.[37] Regardless of its objective limitations, minority incorporation has increased the legitimacy of city governments among a substantial portion of the urban population.

URBAN POPULISM: THE RISE OF THE NEIGHBORHOOD ORGANIZING MOVEMENT

The neighborhood organizing movement of the 1950s and 1960s built the foundation for urban populism. In the first step, clearance projects and highway building catalyzed protests from neighborhoods located in the path of the bulldozers. In the second step, neighborhood organizations began to articulate a variety of issues, and their continued existence was assured by the federal programs of the 1960s. The War on Poverty, Model Cities, and other programs contained citizen participation requirements. Soon federal funds flowed into neighborhood organizations or equivalent institutions such as community action and Model Cities agencies. In the third and final step, neighborhood organizations and community action agencies were transformed into community development corporations (CDCs) relying on a variety of funding sources and administering a complex array of programs. CDCs are major service providers in virtually all large cities today, and in some cities they play a major political role as well.

Between 1956 and 1972, an estimated 3.8 million persons were displaced in cities as a result of two federal programs: urban renewal and interstate highways. Up to one-fifth of the entire population of New Haven was displaced by public projects over roughly the same period.[38] The uncompensated costs equaled 20 or 30 percent of the annual income of families forced to move, a fact that prompted a noted researcher to call it "an injustice on a massive scale."[39] Of course, the costs of displacement were borne not only by individuals. The social networks and community ties making up neighborhoods torn apart by clearance were irretrievably broken.

With inner-city neighborhoods bearing huge uncompensated costs for these projects, it is hardly surprising that residents began to organize to defend themselves. For the most part, the victims of renewal and clearance found elections to be an unsatisfactory means of bringing about change. Most city elected officials accepted the idea that what was good for downtown was good for the city, and they generally succeeded in bringing middle-class voters around to their point of view. Moreover, urban renewal authorities were run by boards dominated by politicians and civic elites, while expressways were being rammed through densely settled urban areas by state highway departments whose engineers regarded local protests with contempt. In New Haven, Mayor Richard Lee (1954–1967) led an executive-centered coalition that, following long-standing plans of business, succeeded in getting more urban renewal money per capita than any city in the country except the nation's capital.[40] The minority community's need for low- and moderate-income replacement housing was largely ignored. Quite the opposite. Urban renewal destroyed more housing than it built in New Haven, resulting in a net loss of 5,636 units by 1972.[41] A similar pattern was replicated in numerous cities.

Neighborhood organizers learned about protest tactics from the civil rights movement, but the community organizing movement also produced its own leaders and teachers. Saul Alinsky, a neighborhood organizer in Chicago, is generally considered the father of the community organizing movement in the United States. In the late 1940s, Alinsky began organizing in the Back of the Yards, a sprawling area of mostly one- and two-story working-class flats, made famous early in the century by Upton Sinclair's novel *The Jungle*. Alinsky had a forceful personality and he was not afraid of antagonizing people. Corporations hired detectives to tail him everywhere he went, and the Oakland, Illinois, city council once passed a resolution barring him from entering the city. In the end, however, it was not Alinsky's personality that irritated the powers-that-be so much as his organizational methods, recognized as effective even by his opponents. Through traveling seminars, demonstrations, and a number of influential books, Alinsky helped to train an entire generation of organizers. As Heather Booth, a national leader in the community organizing movement, put it: "Alinsky is to community organizing as Freud is to psychoanalysis."[42]

Alinsky's method of community organizing can be summarized in three basic principles:

1. *Empowerment:* The goal of organizing is power; the best way to improve American democracy is to empower the powerless, starting where they live in their communities.
2. *Nonideological pragmatism:* Organizers should not impose their values or ideologies but should start with the concrete interests and issues of the community; organizers should be catalysts for empowerment, uniting all the institutions and leaders of the community.
3. *Conflict tactics:* For people without money or political influence, the end justifies the means; any tactics are justified so long as they bring about victories.

Alinsky was famous for inventing creative ways to dramatize his demands—for instance, he once proposed that a group eat voluminous quantities of beans and then pack the 1968 Democratic convention, flatulence at the ready. Controversy followed from Alinsky's dictum that the best tactics are those that confront the powerful and force them to react—resulting in either a victory or, if the establishment counterattacks, an escalation of the conflict with people united in defense of their community. "A People's organization is a conflict group," Alinsky said.[43]

Alinsky-style community organizing against urban renewal and highway projects began in the 1950s. The Embarcadero and Central Freeway projects in San Francisco were stopped in their tracks in the 1950s. Neighborhood organizing really began to take off, however, in the 1960s. By 1970, 400 communities were fighting against highway plans.[44] In 1966 plans for urban renewal in San Francisco's Western Addition, adjacent to downtown, were in progress. As part of the second largest urban renewal project in the country, the San Francisco Redevelopment Agency (SFRA) labeled the Western Addition a blighted area and called for massive demolition that would displace nearly 8,000 individuals. Community residents soon found that promises of replacement housing were hollow. About 60 percent were forced out of the neighborhood even though the vast majority wanted to stay. After attending a conference led by Saul Alinsky in 1966, three white ministers decided to pull together a "people's organization" in the Western Addition. Blacks from the area soon took over leadership and the group, known as the Western Addition Community Organization (WACO), then launched an all-out attack on the SFRA.

In a meeting with San Francisco Mayor Jack Shelley, WACO's leader, Hannibal Williams, articulated the demands of the group:

> We've been misrepresented by a lot of people who don't speak for us. I'm a humble man, but one thing I'm sure of, somewhere in federal law there must be something about self-determination. . . . We're not begging or asking for anything. It's our right, and we want it.[45]

Several times WACO members sat in front of bulldozers in order to halt displacement until satisfactory replacement housing was built. In 1968 a federal judge stopped federal funds for the project until SFRA came up with an acceptable relocation program. WACO negotiated more than a doubling in the number of replacement units, but still these units housed less than a quarter of those who were displaced.

In his 1964 State of the Union Message, President Johnson called for an "unconditional war on poverty," and that summer Congress passed the Economic Opportunity Act, which authorized the establishment of community action agencies (CAAs) funded by the federal government and "developed, conducted, and administered with the maximum feasible participation of residents of the areas and members of the groups served."[46] Two years later Congress approved the Model Cities program, which also contained requirements for citizen participation; in subsequent years similar requirements were inserted into other urban programs. These federal programs gave a tremendous boost to community organizing, especially in inner-city minority communities.

The concept of community action, as implemented in the War on Poverty, was inspired by Alinsky-style community organizing.[47] During the Kennedy Administration, David Hackett, Robert Kennedy's closest friend from prep school, was appointed director of the President's Committee on Juvenile Delinquency.

Through his exposure to community organizing efforts, Hackett became convinced that juvenile delinquency could not be solved by top-down approaches. Instead, he said, young people who were the targets of governmental efforts should be enlisted to identify their own needs. Through the Committee on Juvenile Delinquency, Hackett funded a small number of grassroots community projects. Alinsky's The Woodlawn Organization in Chicago was among them.

Following John Kennedy's assassination in 1963, President Johnson was searching for a bold new program that would bring him out from under the shadow of the dead president. He put the former president's brother-in-law, Sargent Shriver, in charge of devising a war on poverty. Hackett persuaded Shriver to make community action the centerpiece of the federal government's antipoverty effort. Johnson was attracted to the boldness of the idea, partly because he knew that the urban black vote would be crucial in the upcoming election. Community action provided a way for federal administrators to bypass local Democratic party organizations, which had long ignored the needs of African-American communities. By giving grants directly to community action agencies, the federal government could build direct ties with African-American voters, thus improving the electoral prospects of the national Democratic party.[48]

Within a year and a half of the passage of the Economic Opportunity Act, more than a thousand community action agencies (CAAs) were operating in cities around the country. Most of the CAAs received and administered federal funds quietly. About 10 percent of them went further, however, when their staffs organized against such institutions as local housing agencies, welfare offices, school boards, and mayors' offices. These activities nurtured activists and encouraged new neighborhood organizations to form. One study of Cincinnati found a high correlation between War on Poverty involvement in neighborhoods and the development of neighborhood organizations. The Neighborhood Services program, launched by President Johnson in 1967, even paid the salaries of part-time staff working for community organizations. During the first two years of the War on Poverty, twenty new neighborhood organizations formed in Cincinnati, twice as many as there had been in the previous decade.[49] Thus, the War on Poverty especially aided community organizing in low-income neighborhoods, which previously had lacked the financial resources and connections to organize themselves.

The antipoverty program deprived city governments of potential patronage by channeling federal money directly to community associations. More importantly, the federal programs actually encouraged inner-city residents to organize and pressure city governments to pay more attention to low-income black neighborhoods. Tom Wolfe satirized this process in a well-known essay entitled "Mau-Mauing the Flak Catchers:"

> Going downtown to mau-mau the bureaucrats got to be the routine practice in San Francisco. The poverty program *encouraged* you to go in for mau-mauing. . . . If you were outrageous enough, if you could shake up the bureaucrats so bad that their eyes froze into iceballs and their mouths twisted up into smiles of sheer physical panic, into shit-eating grins, so to speak—then they knew you were the real goods.

They knew you were the right studs to give the poverty grants and community organizing jobs to.[50]

Mayors wanted to shift city services to low-income neighborhoods only on their own terms; they certainly did not want to be coerced into doing it. Above all, they were angry that the federal government was now funding their political opponents. "I have a very definite feeling," said San Francisco's Mayor Shelley, "that this program is headed in a direction we don't want . . . it has the potential for setting up a great political organization. Not mine. Because I have had nothing to say about it."[51] Mayors counterattacked by pressuring Congress to give them more control over the program. In 1967 Congress responded by passing an amendment to the appropriations bill for community action agencies, which stipulated that all future grants be routed through state or local governments. The amendment also gave public officials the right to appoint the members of CAAs and lifted the requirement that all board members had to come from the community served by the CAA. Though this amendment gave City Hall leverage over the community action agencies and, indirectly, over the nonprofit organizations and neighborhood organizations receiving funds from the CAAs, there was no turning back the clock. The complexion of city politics had been changed.

From Protest to Politics

Even though local elected officials were able to reassert some influence over many of the federal programs flowing into the cities, community groups continued to flex their muscles. Many federal programs still allocated funds directly to such groups. Federal, state, and local governments contracted with community groups to provide social services such as job training, day care, and housing. Some community organizers agreed with Saul Alinsky's charge that such programs were turning community organizations into mere service providers and diverting them from advocacy and protest.[52] Alinsky had a point. Many organizers were drawn into government employment, and after acquiring professional titles and good incomes, they generally moved out of low-income neighborhoods. Poverty pimps, they were derisively called. On the other hand, many also became active in city politics. Newark's first black mayor, Kenneth Gibson, began his career as a vice president of a local community action agency.

Many Alinsky-style groups, such as the National People's Action, remained skeptical about participation in electoral activity and mainstream politics. Other community organizers, however, began to recognize the limits of protest, especially as it became more and more difficult to maintain the fevered pitch of excitement required to sustain confrontational politics. One of the most effective national coalitions, ACORN (Associated Community Organizations for Reform Now), was founded in 1970 in Little Rock, Arkansas. ACORN claimed 50,000 dues-paying members in twenty-six states by 1982, and it increasingly became involved in local electoral activities. Other national community coalitions such as Citizen Action and Mass Fair Share also pushed an electoral strategy.

Even Saul Alinsky's organization, the Industrial Areas Foundation (IAF), began to move into electoral politics by the end of the 1970s. Following a less confrontational approach than when it was run by Alinsky, the IAF began to emphasize networking and coalition-building. In Texas, the IAF sponsored voter registration projects, get-out-the-vote efforts to help pass bond referendums for improvements in IAF neighborhoods, and held "accountability sessions" to keep politicians in line with IAF objectives. In the 1980s the IAF organization in San Antonio, Communities Organized for Public Service (COPS), became one of the most powerful community organizations in the country. As one IAF organizer boasted, COPS is "now part of the power structure in San Antonio."[53]

The impact of the community organizing movement has reverberated through city politics. Neighborhood organizations became a permanent feature of local politics in cities large and small. These organizations not only administer important programs and services; they also have become basic building blocks for activities that keep social issues on the political agenda. They are essential as well for recruiting new political leadership.

Neighborhood organizations engage in a wide variety of activities, but three main items have dominated the neighborhood agenda:

1. *Neighborhood control:* Neighborhood organizations have lobbied city governments to decentralize the administration of services and infrastructure. A 1990 survey of 161 cities with populations of over 100,000 people found that 60 percent of them had active systems of neighborhood councils, with 70 percent of these being officially recognized by city government.[54] By the early 1990s New York City had instituted a system of moderate decentralization wherein fifty-nine community planning boards appointed by elected officials exercised advisory powers over land use and city services.[55] St. Paul has one of the most extensive systems of neighborhood control in the country. Seventeen District Councils, each elected by district residents, possessed substantial powers over zoning, the distribution of goods and services, and capital expenditures.[56] The degree to which neighborhood organizations are incorporated into local government structures varies greatly from city to city, but these organizations play some role virtually everywhere. For example, in most cities, a substantial portion of the federal government's block grant funds flow through neighborhood and nonprofit organizations.

2. *Housing policies:* Neighborhood groups have pressed city governments to give high priority to neighborhood revitalization, with a special emphasis on housing. A 1991 survey of 133 cities with populations over 100,000 found that 64 percent had formed housing advocacy coalitions.[57] Partly in response to cuts in federal support for housing in the 1980s, state and city governments began to spend more on housing. Cities also began to use their regulatory powers to increase the supply of low and moderate income housing by passing rent control laws, placing moratoriums on the conversion of rental units to more expensive condominiums, and passing inclusionary zoning ordinances that require developers to add units in their projects for low- and moderate-income families. Linkage policies that impose fees on downtown developments have also become more common, with the revenue usually being used to build affordable housing.[58]

3. *Growth control policies:* Neighborhood activists began challenging the assumption that local economic growth is good for everybody. Big downtown projects pushed by mayors and business elites—convention centers, sports stadiums, subsidized mall and entertainment districts—are regularly questioned because of the presence of neighborhood organizations. The incorporation of neighborhoods into city politics has created a political dynamic wherein neighborhood organizations and the leaders articulate issues of equity and social justice, while city hall and downtown business tends to promote an ideology of growth.

Community organizations never succeeded in taking over city governments (and that was rarely their intent), but they did manage to help elect a number of mayors and other public officials. In 1967 Kevin White was elected mayor of Boston in part because of support from neighborhood groups that opposed urban renewal. Once in office, he supported rent control and set up "Little City Halls" around the city to satisfy demands for more community control. Later, White lost neighborhood support when he reversed himself on rent control and supported unbridled downtown growth. In 1972 Neil Goldschmidt won the mayor's office in Portland, Oregon with key backing from neighborhood activists. A veteran of the civil rights movement before being elected to the Portland City Council, Goldschmidt had worked with Legal Services, which provided legal assistance to antipoverty and community groups. In 1971 and 1972 Goldschmidt cast the only dissenting votes on the city council on major urban renewal projects. As mayor, Goldschmidt formalized neighborhood authority over selected land use decisions and the city even provided staff to neighborhood associations so that they could review planning proposals. Between 1974 and 1979 the number of neighborhood groups in Portland doubled to sixty.[59]

Another early success for the neighborhood movement came in Cincinnati. This was notable because the city's reform-style governmental structure—with a city manager and at-large, nonpartisan elections—seemed to discourage decentralization of decision-making. But in 1971 several neighborhood groups came together to propose a slate of council candidates. Enough members of the slate were elected to make up a majority of the new city council. Whereas the previous Republican council had emphasized downtown development, the new council stressed neighborhood revitalization. Soon Cincinnati instituted neighborhood planning and began providing direct assistance to neighborhood associations.[60] From 1969 to 1979 Hartford, Connecticut, operated under a city council whose members had strong roots in the neighborhoods. During these years the city negotiated an equity partnership for neighborhood groups in major downtown developments, thus providing these organizations with a steady source of income and a stake in the downtown's success.[61] In 1981, Santa Monicans for Renters' Rights (SMRR) swept the city council elections in Santa Monica, and then implemented a strong rent control ordinance that reportedly saved renters $1.1 billion between 1987 and 1997.[62]

Such success stories should not be taken as typical, however. The politics of most cities continued to be focused on downtown development, and in many cities—especially Sunbelt cities like Phoenix, Las Vegas, and Houston—neighborhood groups have had relatively little success in organizing or in shaping city government policies. Commenting on Houston, one study called its neighborhood groups "largely invisible." During the 1970s and 1980s, Houston had only one organization representing poor neighborhoods, the Alinsky-style TMO (The Metropolitan Organization).[63] Though TMO won infrastructure improvements for poor neighborhoods, it failed to stop the Hardy Toll Road that, for the convenience of white suburban commuters, destroyed many units of moderate-income housing.[64] Denounced as radical, TMO has been excluded from the governing regime. Compared with cities like Boston and San Francisco, which have hundreds of community-based nonprofit housing developers, Houston had only five in the early 1990s. In 1988 Houston spent only 10 percent of its Community Development Block Grant (CDBG) on housing, compared to 75 percent in Boston and Santa Monica.

Although neighborhood groups have changed the complexion of politics in many cities, it is not surprising that urban populists have usually failed to form stable governing regimes. Racial and ethnic tensions have plagued urban populist mayors. Harold Washington, elected as Chicago's first African-American mayor in 1983 behind a strong neighborhood agenda, was crippled by racial conflict during his entire term in office. Neighborhood groups can be parochial and obstructionist. The NIMBY syndrome (Not In My Backyard) often pits middle-income neighborhood groups against low-income people who need subsidized housing, thus splitting the urban populist coalition along class lines.

Perhaps the biggest problem urban populists face in forming stable coalitions is that they are perceived as anti-business and lacking in a broad program of economic revitalization. The belief that the main purpose of government should be to facilitate the accumulation of private economic wealth is still dominant ideology not only in cities, but in American culture generally. In 1977 Dennis Kucinich was elected mayor of Cleveland with extensive support from neighborhood groups. He carried the confrontational approach of Alinsky-style neighborhood groups into the mayor's office, engaging, for example, in a bitter fight with corporations and banks over tax abatements for downtown. In retaliation, the banks pushed Cleveland into default by refusing to refinance the city's debt. Perceived as anti-business, Kucinich was defeated by Republican George Voinovich after only two years in office.[65] Urban populist mayors cannot govern effectively in the face of widespread business opposition. Somehow, they must bridge the chasm between downtown and neighborhood interests.

Ray Flynn of Boston was probably the nation's most successful urban populist mayor. First elected in 1983, Flynn left office nine years later to become Ambassador to the Vatican. Growing up in South Boston, Flynn's father was an immigrant longshoreman and his mother cleaned downtown office buildings. After serving fifteen years on the city council, Flynn mounted a surprisingly strong campaign in the 1983 mayoral race by building on his support from tenants' groups and neighborhood organizations. He stirred up his poor, largely Roman Catholic followers by pitting them against the Yankee bluebloods and downtown Republicans, and promised to implement linkage policies to force developers to help the neighborhoods.

Once in office, Flynn recognized the importance of forging a governing coalition. Largely abandoning the confrontational rhetoric that had catapulted him into office, Flynn called for an alliance with business based on a program that would pursue downtown development and neighborhood revitalization at the same time. Boston's booming downtown office market allowed developers to make profits even while paying linkage fees. By walking a tightrope between downtown and the neighborhoods, Flynn was able to accomplish an impressive agenda of urban populist reform. He strengthened the city's rent control laws and enacted regulations to limit the conversion of rental units into condominiums. To supplement linkage fees, Flynn enacted an inclusionary housing policy that required developers of projects with ten or more units to set aside 10 percent of the units for low- and moderate-income families. To deal with redlining, Flynn enacted a "linked deposit" policy in which the city would only deposit its funds with banks that demonstrated a commitment to Boston's neighborhoods. The city contributed funds to Boston's nonprofit housing developers and also gave crucial support to one of the most successful comprehensive neighborhood revitalization projects in the country, the so-called Dudley Street Neighborhood Initiative (DSNI). With one-third of the land vacant, DSNI was blocked from assembling desirable parcels by an incredible jigsaw puzzle of private owners. In an unprecedented move, the city gave DSNI, a community-based organization, the power of eminent domain so that it could force owners to sell their properties.[66]

How successful was Flynn in improving the lives of neighborhood residents? By 1993 linkage had raised about $70 million and helped build 10,000 affordable housing units, and by the end of Flynn's second term, community-based housing corporations had built or rehabilitated another 5,000 units. The banks agreed to commit $400 million to a community reinvestment plan for low- and moderate-income neighborhoods. Through Neighborhood Councils and other innovations the Flynn administration gave residents more power over land use decisions. Nevertheless, severe "limits to localism" were encountered.[67] Innovative local housing policies could not compensate for cuts in federal housing assistance imposed by the Reagan Administration. And there was relatively little the Flynn administration could do about the income inequality arising from the combination of a booming corporate services sector and a rapidly declining industrial base.

Neighborhood Nonprofits and City Politics

Beginning in the late 1960s, neighborhood organizations across the country began to spin off community development corporations (CDCs) to deliver services and rehabilitate housing in their neighborhoods. CDCs are nonprofit corporations run by boards composed of area residents, formed for the purpose of delivering services and building infrastructure in neighborhoods or in somewhat larger areas. Federal, state, and city governments contract with CDCs to administer services such as job training, day care, homeless shelters, health clinics, and meals-on-wheels. They also administer funds to rehabilitate housing or fix up playgrounds and other neighborhood facilities. To varying degrees, CDCs have become incorporated into local governmental structures, though they exercise considerable autonomy in deciding how to spend the funds they receive. Because they nurture their own constituencies, in many cities they have become influential political organizations.

The CDC movement began in the 1960s as a variation on the community action agencies funded by the federal government (and many CDCs evolved from community action agencies). They were supposed to arise from and represent the neighborhoods within which they were located. By seeking funding from many sources, they would establish their independence, and thereby be able to represent the neighborhoods. It was expected that, over time, they would evolve into fully fledged service agencies.

The CDC idea was planted when Senator Robert Kennedy toured the Bedford-Stuyvesant section of Brooklyn on a cold, cloudy afternoon in 1966. After seeing the unemployed men lounging on street corners, children playing without coats in thirty-degree cold, and mounds of uncollected garbage, Kennedy attended a meeting with community activists. Angry residents took out their frustrations on the surprised senator. A prominent black politician from the area told Kennedy: "I'm weary of study, Senator. Weary of speeches, weary of promises that aren't kept. . . . The Negro people are angry, Senator."[68] Appalled by the urban decay and the bitterness expressed by the residents, Kennedy vowed to devise a comprehensive strategy that would involve the residents themselves in revitalizing their neighborhood. The result was the Bedford Stuyvesant Restoration Corporation (BSRC). Kennedy used his contacts to persuade corporations to support the project, but it was never very successful in attracting major private investments into the ghetto. Public funds were the key to leveraging private investment. The recipient of $33 million in federal dollars between 1968 and 1974, BSRC succeeded in attracting retail stores and rehabilitating thousands of housing units. In 1966 there were only 36 CDCs funded by the War on Poverty's Equal Opportunity Act's Special Impact Program, with most receiving between $1 million and $3 million.

But by the mid-1970s there were an estimated 200 CDCs, and in the 1980s they proliferated. A 1989 survey of 133 cities with populations of more than 100,000 found CDCs active in 95 percent of them.[69] According to a national survey, by 1994 the number of CDCs in the United States had grown to over 2,000.[70] CDCs were much more common on the west coast and in the Northeast than in the South and the mountain states.[71] With a median staff size of seven, most CDCs were quite small.[72] Ninety percent of CDCs reported engaging in housing production, 23 percent were involved in business development, and 66 percent said they engaged in advocacy and community building.

Over the years a network has evolved to support the work of CDCs. National "intermediaries" have been developed by the Ford Foundation and the Enterprise Foundation, the latter established by the developer James Rouse, who became rich building suburban shopping malls and central-city festival markets.[73] These national institutions market federal Low Income Housing Tax Credits (LIHTCs) to wealthy investors, who are enticed by the tax writeoffs. The investments are then bundled together and allocated to CDCs, which rehabilitate housing units and sell them to individual buyers (who generally qualify for below-market interest loans). The LIHTC program has become the main federal support for low-income housing, with nonprofits receiving in 1994 over one quarter of the subsidies. Foundation support for CDCs expanded from $74 million in 1987 to $179 million in 1991.[74] Housing advocacy coalitions have formed in 85 cities as conduits for low-income tax credits, foundation grants, and local, state, and federal housing funds. By pooling funds from many sources, the advocacy coalitions work with CDCs (and sometimes independently) to build affordable housing.

CDCs receive assistance from private banks, which were goaded into helping by the requirements of the Community Reinvestment Act (CRA) of 1977. Congress passed the CRA in response to intense pressure applied by neighborhood groups, which sent activists from cities around the country to pack the halls of Congress. The protesters argued that banks were engaging in "redlining"—the practice of drawing a red line around certain areas and refusing to grant mortgage loans within those boundaries. The CRA outlaws redlining, specifically stating that "regulated financial institutions have continuing and affirmative obligations to help meet the credit needs of the local communities in which they are chartered."[75] It is almost impossible to define the "affirmative obligations" of banks, and federal regulators have tended to side with the banks, very rarely ruling against them.

Nevertheless, the CRA has given advocacy agencies and CDCs leverage with the banks. Under CRA, a community group can file a formal protest with a relevant federal regulator if it thinks a bank is failing to meet the credit needs of the community. During the time when the protest is under consideration, the bank is forbidden to engage in certain actions, such as buying another bank or opening up a new branch. To avoid such disruptions and to steer clear of negative publicity, banks are usually willing to cut a deal with neighborhood activists. According to one study, by 1992 approximately $18 billion in new investment commitments had been negotiated with private lenders by over three hundred neighborhood groups in seventy cities across the country.[76] Much of this money has been used by CDCs to build or rehabilitate housing.

Although most CDCs are quite small, some have become significant players in local politics. The New Community Corporation (NCC) of Newark, New Jersey, has become one of the country's oldest and most successful CDCs. Formed after the 1968 riots in Newark, by the mid-1990s the NCC had become Newark's largest employer, providing jobs for 1,426 people. NCC's job training centers placed 1,100 graduates each year, operated 2,500 housing units, ran seven day care centers enrolling 500 children, and operated a nursing home, credit union, domestic violence shelter, a supermarket, and a restaurant. Until the late 1990s, when some corporate offices once again began moving into Newark, the NCC filled the vacuum left by the absence of big employers.

Mayors often view CDCs with suspicion, but they must work with them. With the exception of a period of cooperation under Mayor Harold Washington, CDCs in Chicago have been viewed as rivals who might threaten the power and patronage of the Democratic party organization. In contrast, Pittsburgh has brought CDCs directly into its governance structure. In most cities the city council, mayor's office, or an administrative agency of the city government determines how block grants and city funds will be spent, and CDCs compete for a piece of the pie. In Pittsburgh an unusual arrangement exists in which the Partnership for Neighborhood Development (PPND), which is composed of representatives of CDCs, foundations, business, and city government, makes the allocation decisions. As a result, 80 percent of the city's capital budget between 1978 and 1987 went to neighborhoods, compared with only 20 percent at the peak of neighborhood investment in Chicago.[77]

CDCs have steadily increased their capacity, especially in the area of low-income housing. In 1994, for example, they produced an estimated 30,000 to 40,000 units of low- and moderate-income housing. Proponents of CDCs argue that they do more than rehabilitate housing—they rehabilitate communities. At their best, CDCs are expressions of grassroots democracy, run by local residents and not by remote planners in city hall or Washington, D.C. CDCs form grassroots lobbying efforts to press for funding from governments, foundations, and private corporations. The main argument for CDCs is that they knit together the fabric of local community by empowering the residents to solve their own problems.

The problem with the CDC model is that poverty, inequality, and neighborhood decline are brought about by factors well beyond individual neighborhoods. CDC development is highly uneven in different regions of the country and within cities. Neighborhoods that are well organized are represented by CDCs, but as one would expect, neighborhoods with the highest poverty levels are generally those that are the least organized. Even the most successful CDCs cannot address the root causes of poverty, inequality, and urban decline. Critics maintain that these causes can only be addressed by challenges to the larger political system. As CDCs have been pulled into delivering services and developing housing, they have largely given up their advocacy mission.[78] When CDCs rely on corporations, foundations, and governments for funding, they hesitate to confront these same institutions.[79]

There is, however, an opposite view, founded on the recognition that urban populism has always relied on government for its sustenance. CDCs have been able to garner substantial resources from private corporations and foundations, but they are still largely creatures of public funding. A 1992 study of 130 CDCs found that 78 percent received federal funds, and that such funding represented about twice the resources derived from any other public or private source.[80] The biggest danger to urban populism is that federal support could be withdrawn at any time.

URBAN CONSERVATISM

In the 1990s the national conservative movement began to put down roots in local politics, energized in considerable measure by racial, ethnic, and class divisions within the cities. Within a few short years conservative white mayors replaced prominent African-American mayors in several cities. In 1993 Rudolph Giuliani, a white former district attorney, defeated New York's first black mayor, David Dinkins; that same year in Los Angeles, white millionaire financier Richard Riordan defeated Mike Woo, an Asian American who tried unsuccessfully to reconstruct Tom Bradley's coalition. A year earlier, Bret Schundler had become the first Republican in 75 years to be elected mayor of Jersey City, New Jersey, and conservative Republican William Goldsmith became mayor of Indianapolis. Elsewhere, African-American mayors were defeated by Democrats who advocated distinctly downtown-oriented agendas. Richard M. Daley, the son of Democratic machine boss Richard J. Daley, twice defeated African-American opponents, and Edward Rendell replaced Philadelphia's first black mayor, Wilson Goode.

Urban conservativism is not new. The same forces that set in motion urban liberalism and urban populism—the civil rights and neighborhood organizing movements—also provoked a reaction. As a broad political program, urban conservativism was prompted by (1) resentments about minority political demands, especially in the areas of affirmative action and busing; (2) a reaction by downtown business elites against higher taxes and programs with a social-welfare dimension, such as linkage policies; (3) a middle-class reaction against crime and disorder; and (4) increasing support among middle- and upper-income voters for downtown revitalization. Though it may be hazardous to lump all of these elements together into something called a conservative agenda, they do share in common a general understanding that city governments should spend less repairing wrongs and injustices and more on making cities into livable and prosperous places.

Urban conservatives face problems of governance similar to those faced by liberals and populists. One problem is how to appeal to their core middle-class and business constituencies without inciting an electoral backlash from disadvantaged minority and neighborhood groups. More important in the long run, urban conservatives face the task of moving from an electoral coalition to a governing coalition sufficiently broad and cohesive enough to coordinate the efforts of fragmented political structures. The question is whether urban conservatives can deliver tangible benefits to their core constituencies without at the same time provoking unacceptable levels of racial and ethnic animosity.

The first generation of conservative mayors came into office during a period of racial, ethnic, and class tension. In the wake of the Los Angeles riots of 1992, issues connected to social disorder, drugs, and crime became paramount. By playing on such themes, Republican Rudolph Giuliani was able to overcome a 6 to 1 Democratic advantage in party registration in the 1993 mayoral race in New York City. While Giuliani got 78 percent of the white vote, the African-American incumbent, David Dinkins, carried 95 percent of the black vote. Giuliani's campaign slogan, "Taking Back the City," was a not-so-subtle racial appeal, and it also played on a law-and-order theme. Latinos played a crucial role in the election. Giuliani had lost by a narrow margin in 1989, when he received 34 percent of the Latino vote. In the 1993 election Giuliani put a prominent Latino politician, Herman Badillo, on his ticket for the office of City Comptroller. This time, Giuliani got 39 percent of the Latino vote. He also benefited from an unusually high voter turnout on Staten Island, a turnout stimulated by a ballot initiative calling for secession from New York City. Racial tensions provided the main motivation for the controversial proposal to secede.[81]

Latino voters also supplied the swing vote in the 1993 Los Angeles mayoral race. A Republican, Richard Riordan, carried only 14 percent of the African-American vote that year, but he defeated a Democratic candidate, Mike Woo. Riordan won the election by persuading 67 percent of white voters and 43 percent of Latino voters to support him. To achieve the necessary name recognition, Riordan poured $6 million of his own money into the campaign. Riordan had acquired his fortune by financing leveraged buyouts through junk bonds and by speculating in downtown Los Angeles real estate. Riordan had been a frequent contributor to Tom Bradley's campaigns, and by portraying himself as a pragmatic manager "tough enough to turn L.A. around" he was able to win 31 percent of the votes cast by previous Bradley supporters.[82] In April 1997 Riordan won reelection with 61 percent of the vote; he improved his support among Latino voters but lost the black vote by a 3 to 1 ratio.

The conservative mayors have fought hard to reverse policies perceived as unfairly benefiting blacks. At the time Giuliani was elected, 38 percent of New York City's municipal jobs went to blacks, even though they constituted only 29 percent of the city's population.[83] On taking office Giuliani repealed the city's affirmative action policies in hiring and contracting, and he began to reduce city payrolls. Within two years the city's workforce had been trimmed by 17,000 workers.

Concerns about law and order also energized the conservative turn in city politics, and crime became a highly charged symbolic issue, "a shorthand *signal*, to crucial numbers of white voters, of broader issues of social disorder, tapping powerful ideas about authority, status, morality, self-control, and race."[84] Some voters perceived black mayors as being soft on crime because they sometimes advocated more spending on social services instead of police and supported civilian review boards to rein in the police.[85] Conservatives vowed to "get tough" with criminals. As a former federal prosecutor, Giuliani was ideally situated to portray himself as a law-and-order candidate. At the same time, he benefited from the racist perception that his African-American opponent, Dinkins, was soft on crime, notwithstanding the fact that Dinkins had made hiring more police a high priority of his administration.

Giuliani delivered on his promises by cutting budgets for almost every city agency except the police and fire departments. He hired William Bratton as his police commissioner. Bratton instituted three controversial policing strategies. First, officers were allocated to hot spots on daily computer mappings of shootings and drug sales. Second, police began to crack down on minor offenses such as drinking in public, urinating on the street, or hassling motorists by demanding money for cleaning their windshields. This strategy was derived from the so-called "broken windows" theory of urban decline. Stated broadly, it suggested that small signs of decay, such as broken windows or trash on empty lots, served as signs that a neighborhood was dangerous and in decline. As applied to crime control, it suggested that small offenses created an atmosphere of disorder on the streets. Third, officers were encouraged to frisk people who were stopped for minor violations, such as playing loud music or drinking in public, in order to get guns off the street. The new policing strategies appeared to work when New York's crime rate dropped dramatically. The number of murders fell over 50 percent, from a high of 2,245 in 1990 to 983 by 1996. Formerly regarded as one of the most dangerous cities in the country, for the first six months of 1996 New York City ranked 144th out of the largest 189 cities in per capita total crime.[86] Though the media attributed the decline to the new policing strategies, in fact the crime rate had begun to drop in the last year of the Dinkins administration, and the decline in New York City's crime rate followed a national pattern. Nevertheless, Giuliani made the improved crime statistics a major plank in his successful 1997 reelection campaign.

In addition to exploiting racially charged issues, conservative mayors also claimed that they possessed the magic formula for bringing prosperity to the local economy. The formula was made up of a combination of cuts in spending and aggressive policies to stimulate investment. Urban conservatives had initially developed their analysis of the urban condition in response to New York City's fiscal crisis of 1975. When the banks refused to underwrite any more of its loans in April of that year, the city suddenly found itself unable to borrow the money it needed to meet payroll obligations and redeem outstanding notes. Conservatives blamed the crisis on a pattern of profligate spending. The writer Ken Auletta said that the prominent conservative William F. Buckley had been right when he ran for mayor in 1965. As Auletta put it: "We [in New York City] have conducted a noble experiment in local socialism and income redistribution, one clear result of which has been to redistribute much of our tax base and many jobs right out of the city."[87] Ed Koch won the mayoral race in 1977 by emphasizing just such an analysis of the causes of New York's fiscal crisis. Soon after entering city hall, Koch asserted that "the main job of municipal government is to create a climate in which private business can expand in the city to provide jobs and profit. It's not the function of government to create jobs on the public payroll."[88] In subsequent years, Koch would provide billions of dollars of incentives for businesses at the same time that he laid off 60,000 city workers. Koch's policies appealed to homeowners in Brooklyn and Queens, who were sick of high taxes, and to real estate developers and to Wall Street firms, who expressed their gratitude in the form of generous campaign contributions.

The fiscal crisis of cities has not gone away.[89] In the 1990s urban conservatives continued to attack their opponents as representatives of special interests whose free-spending policies would bankrupt cities. At the same time, they maintained that all problems could ultimately be solved if the private sector was unleashed. The rhetoric of fiscal crisis became a useful way of withdrawing the city from a variety of programs and services with a social content.[90] Mayor Giuliani cut city payrolls and services and at the same time reduced income taxes, property taxes on condominiums and co-ops, and slashed the commercial rent tax and the hotel tax on the grounds that reduced taxes would stimulate private investment. His counterpart across the country, Los Angeles Mayor Richard Riordan, took a similar approach. "Economic development is the whole future of the city," Riordan said during his first year in office.[91] Working to reduce the regulatory burden on developers, Riordan pushed generous business subsidies. In one case, he put together a $70 million subsidy package to convince Dreamworks SKG to build its new studio in L.A.[92]

Privatization was another top priority for conservative mayors. As they employed it, the term meant that to reduce costs, city governments should contract out such services as garbage collection or even education (in the form of charter schools). As a way of cutting costs and improving quality, privatization is long-standing and noncontroversial. In the city-building era at the beginning of the twentieth century, all cities contracted for streetcar, telephone, and utilities services, and many also contracted with private firms for water supply. The city of San Francisco contracted out garbage collection to private companies as early as 1932.[93] Partial privatization, which involves contracting out publicly funded services, often saves city governments money. One of the earliest scholarly evaluations concluded that Scottsdale, Arizona, by contracting for fire protection from a private firm, paid about half of what it would have had to pay if it had provided the service itself.[94] A 1982 survey of 1,780 cities found that the average city contracts approximately 26 percent of its services, in whole or part, to private firms.[95]

In the 1980s, however, privatization became a strategy not only to make government more efficient but to reduce the size and scope of government altogether. E. S. Savas, called the "the godfather of privatization," served as Assistant Secretary of Housing and Urban Development (HUD) in the Reagan Administration. In his books, Savas stressed that privatization was a tool not only to make a better government but to make a more limited government: "Limited in its size, scope, and power relative to society's other institutions."[96] Savas later became an advisor to the Giuliani administration, which used privatization mainly as a threat to squeeze concessions out of municipal unions.

Among mayors, Indianapolis mayor William Goldsmith became one of the most ardent proponents of privatization. Elected in 1992, during his first eighteen months in office Goldsmith privatized fourteen services, sold off the municipal golf course, and slashed the city payroll from 5,700 to 4,200, giving Indianapolis the lowest number of employees per capita of any of the nation's fifty largest cities.[97] When Goldsmith attempted to contract with neighborhood groups and churches to maintain local parks, however, he found little interest. And his proposal to privatize two troubled public housing projects was vehemently opposed by the residents themselves.[98] Called a "populist Republican," Goldsmith won support for providing resources to distressed inner-city neighborhoods, but critics argued that he crippled the ability of the city to regulate some of its key services.[99]

It is difficult to assess the political significance of the conservative mayors. Do they represent a permanent realignment of urban voters from liberal or populist Democrats to conservative Republicans? This appears unlikely because cities are still voting overwhelmingly Democratic in national elections and urban conservatives rarely have majorities on city councils. Moreover, demographic trends do not favor the conservative base in big cities. The conservative mayors recognize that they must appeal to distinct racial and ethnic groups.

Accordingly, both Giuliani and Riordan bucked the national Republican agenda and opposed legislation that would deny government benefits to immigrants who have not yet become citizens.

The key to the long-term success of the urban version of conservativism lies in its ability to deliver benefits to its core constituencies—better services and amenities to middle-class voters and a better business climate for corporations. At the same time, other constituencies must remain satisfied enough, or at least not excessively alienated. Economic growth will not solve all problems, and sometimes it can exaggerate inequalities. For example, in the boom years of the 1980s, when Ed Koch promoted policies that subsidized corporate development in Manhattan, the new economic sectors increased the gap between rich and poor, and the resulting social polarization eventually hurt Koch at the polls.[100] Like mayors of all political stripes, conservative mayors find themselves torn between an economic logic that leads them to use public resources to promote economic growth, and a political logic that requires them to build and maintain broad electoral coalitions.

FINDING A CONSENSUS

The three modes of governance that we have discussed in this chapter reflect much more than mere stylistic differences. They reflect basic philosophical positions about the methods and purposes of government. Urban liberalism has drawn its strength from the conviction that particular groups and sectors of society have been denied adequate representation in the political system. Blacks, Latinos, Asians, women, and in some cases gays, have fought for both incorporation into local political structures and the rewards that come from that incorporation. Urban populism overlaps with urban liberalism to some degree, but its central premise is the decentralization of political power down to the neighborhood level. Because urban populism was borne of a struggle against the centralized authority exercised by city hall and downtown business, the commitment has been to process more than to particular outcomes; indeed, populists expect that different neighborhoods will express their own preferences. The last mode of governance, urban conservativism, was spawned by a reaction by business elites and a substantial portion of the electorate to high taxes, crime and disorder, and to the idea that government at any level should attempt to redistribute resources, even modestly. Fiscal austerity and private investment have been its guiding mantras.

In actuality, there is room for some accommodation among these three political tendencies. In the abstract, virtually nobody opposes investment and economic growth. The devil is in the details. When a city government pursues investment regardless of who pays for it, conflict can be expected. Cities are fundamentally dependent on investment, but there are a range of options available for pursuing it. Cities may pursue investment through tax abatements, tax increment districts, or tax-free bonds for investors, but at the same time they can negotiate with developers for impact and linkage fees that can be used for public infrastructure and affordable housing. No matter what a city's needs may be, it can make a commitment to an open, democratic process that gives voice to a wide variety of interests. Neighborhoods can be brought into planning processes in such a way as to reward those neighborhood associations that come forward with creative plans. To create an attractive environment for investment, cities can also focus their energies on improving administrative practices, improving services, and providing amenities such as pedestrian walks, vestpocket parks, bicycle paths, and farmers' markets, all of which which can improve the quality of life for residents and for tourists and visitors. Such measures generate a healthy climate for investment—without pillaging the public treasury. In other words, behind a visionary leadership, fiscal conservatism can be, to some degree, compatible with a decentralized democratic process and with progressive social goals.

NOTES

1. James H. Johnson, Jr., Cloyzelle K. Jones, Walter C. Farrell, Jr., and Melvin L. Oliver, "The Los Angeles Rebellion: A Retrospective View," *Economic Development Quarterly* 6, No. 4 (November 1992): 356–372.
2. U.S. Bureau of the Census, *Statistical Abstract of the United States: 1995* (Washington, D.C.: U.S. Government Printing Office, 1995), p. 287.
3. As reported by the Joint Center of Political and Economic Studies (JCPES), *Black Elected Officials: A National Roster: 1988* (Washington, D.C.: JCPES, 1989), table 12 and *Black Elected Officials: A National Roster: 1993* (Washington, D.C.: JCPES, 1994), table 12.
4. John Mollenkopf, *A Phoenix in the Ashes: The Rise and the Fall of the Koch Coalition in New York City Politics* (Princeton, N.J.: Princeton University Press, 1992), p.12.
5. Raphael J. Sonenshein, *Politics in Black and White: Race and Power in Los Angeles* (Princeton, N.J.: Princeton University Press, 1993), p. 63.
6. Patrick D. Joyce, "A Reversal of Fortunes: Black Empowerment, Political Machines, and City Jobs in New York City and Chicago," *Urban Affairs Review* 32, No. 3 (1997): 291–318.
7. Charles P. Henry, "Urban Politics and Incorporation: The Case of Blacks, Latinos, and Asians in Three Cities," in *Blacks, Latinos, and Asians in Urban America: Status and Prospects for Politics and Activism,* ed. James Jennings (Westport, Conn.: Praeger, 1994), p. 18.
8. Our account of Koch is based on Mollenkopf, *A Phoenix in the Ashes.*
9. Quotes in Ibid., pp. 171–172.
10. Rufus P. Browning, Dale Rogers Marshall, and David H. Tabb, "Minority Mobilization in Ten Cities: Failures and Successes," in *Racial Politics in American Cities,* ed. Rufus P. Browning, Dale Rogers Marshall, and David H. Tabb (New York: Longman, 1995), p. 9.
11. Barbara Ferman, *Governing the Ungovernable City: Political Skill, Leadership, and the Modern Mayor* (Philadelphia: Temple University Press, 1985), chap. 1; Clarence N. Stone, *Regime Politics: Governing Atlanta 1946–1988* (Lawrence: University Press of Kansas, 1989), chap. 1. Urban regime theory stresses that cities are not governed by elected officials but by "informal arrangements by which public bodies and private interests function together in order to be able to make and carry out governing decisions." Ibid., p. 6.
12. Quoted in Stone, *Regime Politics,* p. 110.

13. Rufus P. Browning, Dale Rogers Marshall, and David H. Tabb, *Protest Is Not Enough: The Struggle of Blacks and Hispanics for Equality in Urban Politics* (Berkeley: University of California Press, 1984); Peter K. Eisinger, "Black Mayors and the Politics of Racial Economic Advancement," in *Urban Politics: Past, Present, and Future,* 2nd ed., ed. Harlan Hahn and Charles H. Levine (New York: Longman, 1984), pp. 249–260; Kenneth R. Mladenka, "Blacks and Hispanics in Urban Politics," *American Political Science Review,* 83, No. 1 (March 1989): 165–191. Mladenka concludes that minority mayors have little impact on policy outcomes, but minority council majorities do.

14. Sonenshein, *Politics in Black and White,* p. 152.

15. Timothy Bates and Darrell Williams, "Preferential Procurement Programs and Minority-Owned Businesses," *Journal of Urban Affairs,* 17, No. 1 (1995): 1.

16. Stone, *Regime Politics,* p. 145.

17. *City of Richmond v. J. A. Croson Co.,* 109 S. Ct. 706 (1989).

18. Mitchell F. Rice, "State and Local Government Set-Aside Programs, Disparity Studies, and Minority Business Development in the Post-*Croson* Era," *Journal of Urban Affairs,* 15, No. 6 (1993): 529–553.

19. Mike Davis, *City of Quartz: Excavating the Future in Los Angeles* (London: Verso, 1990), pp. 251–253.

20. Ibid., p. 277.

21. Ibid., p. 272.

22. Sonenshein, *Politics in Black and White,* pp. 155–161.

23. Albert Karnig and Susan Welch, *Black Representation and Urban Policy* (Chicago: University of Chicago Press, 1980); Eisinger, "Black Mayors;" Browning, Marshall, and Tabb, *Protest Is Not Enough;* Mladenka, "Blacks and Hispanics in Urban Politics;" Grace Hall Saltzstein, "Black Mayors and Police Policies," *Journal of Politics* 51, No. 3 (August 1989): 525–544.

24. Paula D. McClain and Albert Karnig, "Black and Hispanic Socioeconomic and Political Competition," *American Political Science Review* 84, No. 2 (June 1990): 535–545; Paula D. McClain, "The Changing Dynamics of Urban Politics: Black and Hispanic Municipal Employment—Is There Competition?" *Journal of Politics* 55, No. 2 (May 1993): 399–414.

25. Eisinger, "Black Mayors," p. 257.

26. Ibid., p. 258.

27. William Julius Wilson, *The Truly Disadvantaged: The Inner City, the Underclass, and Public Policy* (Chicago: University of Chicago Press, 1987), p. 115.

28. Davis, *City of Quartz,* pp. 136–137.

29. Ibid., p. 135.

30. Sonenshein, *Politics in Black and White,* p. 168.

31. See Adolph Reed, "The Black Urban Regime: Structural Origins and Constraints," *Comparative Urban and Community Research* 1, No. 1 (1987): 138–189; and "Demobilization in the New Black Political Regime: Ideological Capitulation and Radical Failure in the Post-segregation Era," in *The Bubbling Cauldron: Race, Ethnicity, and the Urban Crisis,* ed. Michael Peter Smith and Joe R. Feagin (Minneapolis: University of Minnesota Press, 1995), pp. 182–208.

32. Maynard Jackson, quoted in Stone, *Regime Politics,* p. 87.

33. Adolph Reed, Jr., "A Critique of Neo-Progressivism in Theorizing About Local Development Policy: A Case from Atlanta," in *The Politics of Urban Development,* ed. Clarence N. Stone and Heywood T. Sanders (Lawrence: University Press of Kansas, 1987), p. 206.

34. Quoted in Stone, *Regime Politics,* p. 136.

35. The evaluation of black progress in Atlanta that follows is based on Gary Orfield and Carole Ashkinaze, *The Closing Door: Conservative Policy and Black Opportunity* (Chicago: University of Chicago Press, 1991).

36. Cited in ibid., p. 151.

37. Lawrence Bobo and Franklin D. Gilliam, Jr., "Race, Sociopolitical Participation, and Black Empowerment," *American Political Science Review* 84, No. 2 (June 1990): 377–393.

38. Susan S. Fainstein, et al., *Restructuring the City: The Political Economy of Urban Redevelopment*, rev. ed. (New York: Longman, 1986), p. 49.

39. Anthony Downs, *Urban Problems and Prospects* (Chicago: Markham, 1970), chap. 8.

40. Robert Dahl, *Who Governs? Democracy and Power in an American City* (New Haven, Conn.: Yale University Press.) Criticizing Dahl, G. William Domhoff presents convincing evidence that urban renewal was initiated by business, not ordinary citizens, in *Who Really Rules? New Haven and Community Power Reexamined* (Santa Monica, Calif.: Goodyear Publishing, 1978).

41. Fainstein, et al., *Restructuring the City*, p. 47.

42. Quoted in Harry C. Boyte, *The Backyard Revolution: Understanding the New Citizen Movement* (Philadelphia: Temple University Press, 1980), p. 39.

43. Saul D. Alinsky, *Reveille for Radicals* (New York: Vintage Books, 1969), p. 132.

44. Boyte, *The Backyard Revolution*, p. 11.

45. Quoted in Mollenkopf, *Contested City*, p. 187.

46. Economic Opportunity Act of 1964 (P.L. 88–452), title II.

47. The following account of the War on Poverty is taken from Nicholas Lemann, *The Promised Land: The Great Black Migration and How It Changed America* (New York: Alfred A. Knopf, 1991), pp. 109–222.

48. Frances Fox Piven and Richard A. Cloward, *Regulating the Poor: The Functions of Public Welfare*, rev. ed. (New York: Vintage Books, 1993), chap. 9.

49. John Clayton Thomas, *Between Citizen and City: Neighborhood Organizations and Urban Politics in Cincinnati* (Lawrence: University Press of Kansas, 1986), pp. 33, 69.

50. Tom Wolfe, *Radical Chic and Mau-Mauing the Flak Catchers* (New York: Bantam Books, 1971), pp. 117–118.

51. Quoted in Piven and Cloward, *Regulating the Poor*, pp. 271–272.

52. See Saul Alinsky, "The War On Poverty—Political Pornography," *Journal of Social Issues* 21 (January 1965): 42.

53. Quoted in Robert Fisher, *Let the People Decide: Neighborhood Organizing in America*, updated ed. (New York: Twayne, 1994), p. 195.

54. Carmine Scavo, "The Use of Regulative Mechanisms by Large U.S. Cities," *Journal of Urban Affairs* 15, No. 1 (1993): 100.

55. Robert F. Pecorella, *Community Power in a Postreform City* (Armonk, N.Y.: M. E. Sharpe, 1994).

56. Jeffrey M. Berry, Kent E. Portney, and Ken Thomson, *The Rebirth of Urban Democracy* (Washington, D.C.: Brookings Institution, 1993), p. 13.

57. Edward G. Goetz, *Shelter Burden: Local Politics and Progressive Housing Policy* (Philadelphia: Temple University Press, 1993), p. 52.

58. W. Dennis Keating, "Linking Downtown Development with Broader Community Goals: An Analysis of Linkage Policies in Three Cities," *Journal of the American Planning Association* 52, No. 2 (1986): 133–141.

59. Carl Abbott, *Portland: Planning, Politics, and Growth in a Twentieth-Century City* (Lincoln: University of Nebraska Press, 1983), chaps. 8 and 9.

60. Thomas, *Between Citizen and City*, chap. 6.

61. Pierre Clavel, *The Progressive City: Planning and Participation, 1969–1984* (New Brunswick, N.J.: Rutgers University Press, 1986), chap. 2.

62. Stella M. Capek and John I. Gilderbloom, *Community Versus Commodity: Tenants and the American City* (Albany: State University of New York Press, 1992), p. 182.

63. Capek and Gilderbloom, *Community Versus Commodity*, p. 212.

64. Joe R. Feagin, *Free Enterprise City: Houston in Political and Economic Perspective* (New Brunswick, N.J.: Rutgers University Press, 1988), pp. 279–280.

65. Todd Swanstrom, *The Crisis of Growth Politics: Cleveland, Kucinich, and the Challenge of Urban Populism* (Philadelphia: Temple University Press, 1985).

66. Peter Medoff and Holly Sklar, *Streets of Hope: The Fall and Rise of an Urban Neighborhood* (Boston: South End Press, 1994).

67. Peter Dreier and W. Dennis Keating, "The Limits of Localism: Progressive Housing Policies in Boston, 1984–1989," *Urban Affairs Quarterly* 26, No. 2 (December 1990): 191–216.

68. Quoted in Jack Newfield, *Robert Kennedy: A Memoir* (New York: E. P. Dutton, 1969), p. 94.

69. Edward G. Goetz, *Shelter Burden: Local Politics and Progressive Housing Policy* (Philadelphia: Temple University Press, 1993), p. 117.

70. National Congress of Community Economic Development, *Tying It All Together: The Comprehensive Achievements of Community-Based Development Organizations* (Washington, D.C.: NCCED, 1995).

71. U.S. Department of HUD, *Status and Prospects of the Nonprofit Housing Sector* (Washington, D.C.: HUD, June 1995), p. 31.

72. NCCED, *Tying It All Together,* p. 9.

73. James Rouse died on April 9, 1996.

74. Reported in HUD, *Status and Prospects,* p. 46.

75. Community Reinvestment Act of 1977, 12 USC 2901.

76. Calvin Bradford, *Community Reinvestment Agreement Library* (Des Plaines, Ill.: Community Reinvestment Associates, 1992; as reported in *From Redlining to Reinvestment: Community Responses to Urban Disinvestment,* ed. Gregory D. Squires (Philadelphia: Temple University Press, 1992), p. 2.

77. Barbara Ferman, *Challenging the Growth Machine: Neighborhood Politics in Chicago and Pittsburgh* (Lawrence: University Press of Kansas, 1996), p. 99.

78. Randy Stoecker, "Empowering Redevelopment: Toward a Different CDC," *Shelterforce* (May/June 1996).

79. Robert Fisher, "Community Organizing in the Conservative '80s and Beyond," *Social Policy,* 25, No. 1 (Fall 1994): 11–20.

80. Avis C. Vidal, *Rebuilding Communities: A National Study of Urban Community Development Corporations* (New York: New School for Social Research, 1992), p. 54.

81. Karen M. Kaufmann, "A Tale of Two Cities: The Impact of Intergroup Conflict on Mayoral Voting Behavior in Los Angeles and New York" (paper delivered at the American Political Science Association Meeting, San Francisco, August 29–Sept. 1, 1996), p. 18. Giuliani was reelected by a wide margin in 1997.

82. Ibid., p. 22.

83. Institute for Puerto Rican Policy, *The Giuliani Budget Cuts and People of Color: Disproportionate Employment Impact* (New York: Institute for Puerto Rican Policy, 1994), p. 1; as reported in Michael Leo Owens, "Race, Place, and Government Employment" (paper delivered at the New York State Political Science Association Meeting, Ithaca, New York, March 29–30, 1996), p. 12.

84. Thomas Byrne Edsall and Mary D. Edsall, *Chain Reaction: The Impact of Race, Rights, and Taxes on American Politics* (New York: Norton, 1991), p. 224.

85. Grace Hall Saltzstein, "Black Mayors and Police Policies," pp. 525–544.

86. Randy Kennedy, "FBI Report Confirms Drop in New York Crime," *New York Times,* January 6, 1997.

87. Quoted in William E. Simon, *A Time for Truth* (New York: Berkeley Books, 1978), p. 155.

88. Quoted in Martin Shefter, *Political Crisis/Fiscal Crisis: The Collapse and Revival of New York City* (New York: Basic Books, 1985), p. 175.

89. Ester R. Fuchs, "The Permanent Urban Fiscal Crisis," in *Breaking Away: The Future of Cities—Essays in Memory of Robert F. Wagner, Jr.,* ed. Julia Vitullo-Martin (New York: Twentieth Century Fund Press, 1996), pp. 49–73.

90. Ester R. Fuchs, *Mayors and Money: Fiscal Policy in New York and Chicago* (Chicago: University of Chicago Press, 1992).
91. Quoted in Laura Mecoy, "Ain't Too Proud to Beg: Is L.A.'s Businessman Mayor Good for L.A. Business?" *Los Angeles* (July 1996).
92. Ibid.
93. David F. Linowes, *Privatization: Toward More Effective Government. Report of the President's Commission on Privatization* (Urbana: University of Illinois Press, 1988), p. 2.
94. Roger S. Ahlbrandt, Jr., *Municipal Fire Protection Services: Comparison of Alternative Organizational Forms* (Beverly Hills, Calif.: Sage Publications, 1973).
95. Derived from *Rethinking Local Services: Examining Alternative Service Delivery Approaches* (Washington, D.C.: International City Management Association, 1984), table B; as reported in E. S. Savas, *Privatization: The Key to Better Government* (Chatham, N.J.: Chatham House, 1987), p. 72.
96. Ibid., p. 288.
97. Nancy Hass, "Philadelphia Freedom: How Privatization Has Worked Wonders in the City of Brotherly Love and Beyond," *Financial World* (August 3, 1993): 37.
98. William D. Eggers, "Righting City Hall," *National Review* (August 29, 1994): 40.
99. Rob Gurwitt, "Indianapolis and the Republican Future," *Governing* (February 1994): 24–28.
100. Mollenkopf, *A Phoenix in the Ashes*, pp. 188–189.

CHAPTER 15

THE FRAGMENTED SOCIETY

THE RISE OF URBAN ENCLAVES

The racial, ethnic, and class divisions of American society are expressed in its urban landscapes. Ever since the early days of the republic, distinct ethnic and social groups have tended to fragment into different communities. What is striking about geographic avoidance behavior today is the increasingly sophisticated ways that spaces between and *within* cities and suburbs are being physically marked off and privatized. Over the past four decades, the material enclosure of urban space in the United States has been proceeding at an accelerating pace. The urban scholar Peter Marcuse has identified three features that distinguish the divided cities of the late twentieth century from the industrial cities inherited from the nineteenth century: (1) an intensified "turf allegiance," (2) sharply defended "turf barricades and turf battles," and (3) "the subsuming of the public interest under the private."[1] The enclosure of urban space represents a secession from the larger society that is inspired by (and inspires) fear of crime and social disorder,[2] and it signals a withdrawal from public space and public life.[3]

By the mid-1990s, walls or their functionally equivalent barriers had begun to enclose all of the four principal venues and activities that compose urban life: residence, work, consumption, and leisure. A large proportion of urban residents commute from suburban subdivisions, gated communities, or from townhouse developments or high-rise condominium towers to downtown office complexes or suburban office parks; they drive to enclosed malls or mall complexes for shopping, and commute to tourist bubbles to enjoy themselves.[4] For many, the urban experience has turned into a series of enclosures, each connected by a transportation corridor.

The urban historian Kenneth Jackson has observed that, "Throughout history, the treatment and arrangement of shelter have revealed more about a particular people than any other product of the creative arts."[5] Current trends in housing can be regarded as a bellwether of a society that is achieving a remarkably efficient social segregation, even by the standards of the segregated living patterns that have historically characterized urban America. By 1992 an estimated 32 million Americans lived in common interest developments with private governments.[6] The gated housing developments that have sprung up in suburbs make a fine-tuned segregation possible that separates people not only along the traditional dimensions of race, ethnicity, and wealth but also on the basis of age and lifestyle. Perhaps gated communities can be regarded merely as the latest expression of a logic of urban growth that has been unfolding for decades. What makes them different from the typical suburb, however, is that they are privatized and walled, and entry is often strictly regulated.

The downtown office–corporate complex of large cities is becoming increasingly demarcated and defended from surrounding land uses.[7] In many cities a variety of physical barriers protect the downtown corporate enclave. In St. Louis, for example, a huge stadium/convention center complex anchors the north side of the downtown and a baseball stadium and an elevated freeway anchors the south. To the east is a freeway and the grounds of the Gateway Arch. Only the west side is lacking in physical barriers of some sort. For pure defense of downtown corporate enclaves, however, physical walls are more efficient than porous barriers. Atlanta and Detroit have shown the way by moving a large proportion of their downtown office workers into the comprehensive sealed realms of the Peachtree Center and the Renaissance Center. In both these structures, workers drive into parking garages and then enter a city-within-a-city where they can work, shop, eat lunch, and find a variety of diversions after work. They never have to set foot in the city.

After work, people are increasingly able to pursue their consumption activities in walled-off settings. Since the mid-1960s, enclosed shopping malls have sprouted like mushrooms near freeway interchanges, and more recently they have invaded the downtown areas of central cities. Today thousands of enclosed malls are sprinkled across the urban landscape. Despite the superficial resemblance, malls are not town squares. They are privately owned, and their corporate sponsors are not bound to respect the constitutional rights guaranteed in public places. "Undesirable" characters, such as bag ladies, the homeless, or in some cases, teenagers, may be asked to move on or they will be thrown out. The overall effect of malls is to segment rather than bring together people making up the urban community.

Besides residence, work, and shopping, walled-off spaces also embrace leisure and tourism. The facilities composing tourist spaces in cities are enclosed, and frequently a well-defined perimeter surrounds the entire complex. Tourists and visitors who visit central cities now commonly fly into an airport, take a taxi or a light rail to a downtown hotel, and stay within the well-defined tourist area, never seeing or even becoming aware of the larger city around them. This is particularly the case in older port and industrial cities, where urban decay and social problems have made substantial areas inhospitable to visitors.

Even for the affluent middle class who regularly use them, the tourist spaces are unlikely sites for the expression of community spirit or civic solidarity. They are places of consumption, and the activities defined as fun and leisure are organized and managed to keep them that way. The events surrounding the opening of the World Financial Center in New York City in October 1988 provide an example. The advertising agents for the developer, Olympia & York, staged five days of celebrations, all intended to convey (in the advertising firm's language) "a progressive understanding of the uses of public space."[8] As it transpired, the celebrations were tied closely to the marketing needs of the businesses located in the World Financial Center. The activities defined, and strictly limited, the recreation and leisure that those attending the events could "consume."

ARE CITIES OBSOLETE?

The motivations for geographic avoidance behavior are understandable. It is natural that people want to escape the concentrated social problems of central cities and move to safe havens in the suburbs with lower crime rates and better schools. It makes more sense for families to move than to get involved in the long and messy process of political problem-solving. The ability to move freely is a fundamental characteristic of any free society. And middle-class workers and consumers, especially women, feel safer (indeed, often are safer) in walled-off and controlled urban spaces. Having said all this, however, it is important to recognize that geographic avoidance behavior tears at the social fabric.

Some people think that central cities are obsolete and that the suburbs would be better off without them. In 1991 *Newsweek* magazine ran a story entitled, "Are Cities Obsolete?" quoting an expert in urban land use as saying, "The basic problem is that cities are no longer functional. . . . We don't need them anymore."[9] Polls conducted by the *New York Times* showed that residents of the suburban counties outside of New York City no longer felt significantly connected to the city. The percentage of respondents who said that events in the city had "hardly any impact" on their daily lives increased from 39 percent in 1978 to 51 percent by 1991.[10] The implication of this view is that those who secede from the city into the suburbs are deserting a sinking ship whose fate is of little concern to them.

If core cities were somehow to disappear tomorrow, suburbanites might quickly notice interdependencies they had overlooked. Essential economic activities still are located in central cities, and they are pivotal to the health of metropolitan areas. The management and control functions of corporations are disproportionately centralized in a network of cities that occupy strategic places in a global economy. In many cities across the United States, downtowns have been revitalized, for the simple reason that many business concerns find it advantageous to be located next to one another. Especially (but not exclusively) in larger cities, high-level professional operations and information industries have become clustered into "strategic nodes with a hyperconcentration of activities"[11] supporting layer on layer of highly educated, technologically sophisticated professionals offering specialized services—corporate managers, management consultants, legal experts, accountants, computer specialists, financial analysts, media and public relations consultants, and the like. Such jobs are essential for keeping a metropolitan area competitive in the global marketplace; in 1990 central cities in the United States contributed $23 billion more in services to the world economy than they took in.[12] The clustering of highly skilled workers in downtown office buildings explains why the earnings of workers in central cities are higher than the average earnings of those who work in the suburbs.[13]

The central cities are also uniquely positioned to become centers of a metropolitan economy based around leisure, tourism, and culture—the fastest-growing sectors of the American (and world) economies. Few suburbs can conceivably compete in this regard; they lack the historic architecture, public monuments, redeveloped waterfronts, and older neighborhoods—in other words, the ambience—of the older core cities. These cities also contain an expensive infrastructure essential to culture, including symphony halls, parks, zoos, and museums. Convention centers and most sports stadiums tend to be located within the core cities because they benefit from being near amenities such as restaurants, bars, and cultural facilities. Suburban commuters take the lion's share of the jobs in the downtown corporate towers and tourist facilities. In 1989, for example, 46 percent of all earnings of suburban residents of San Francisco were earned in the central city; the figure was 41 percent for the Denver metropolitan area and 39 percent for New Orleans.[14] Without the economic contribution of their central cities, in most metropolitan areas 40 percent or more of suburbanites would find themselves without a job. In short, the economic fate of the suburbs is linked with the central cities, and the cities also supply essential social and political capital to urban regions.

THE URBAN FUTURE

At the beginning of the twenty-first century, it is becoming clear that central cities are on the rebound. Downtown business districts and entertainment/tourist districts draw people from throughout metropolitan areas and from elsewhere. City neighborhoods also seem to be undergoing a renaissance. An informal *New York Times* survey of nine cities (Boston, Chicago, Houston, Los Angeles, Miami, New York, San Antonio, San Diego, and Washington, D.C.) conducted in 2000 found that as crime rates dropped, businesses and new residents began pouring into neighborhoods previously considered off-limits. Displacement of poorer residents was no doubt occurring, but the quality of life for long-term residents had also improved.[15]

But one must be careful about reaching conclusions from a survey of successful downtowns and neighborhoods. It is true that regeneration is occurring—and equally true that gross inequalities persist. Since the 1970s income inequalities in the United States have continued to widen. The bottom 10 percent of income earners are worse off in the United States than in any European country, and their buying power has fallen in recent decades.[16] From 1990 to 1995, the poverty rate increased for cities and in suburbs in all regions of the country,[17] and there is no evidence that these rates have appreciably fallen since then. The minority poor remain concentrated into ghetto neighborhoods, and housing shortages have become progressively worse. In 2000, for example, a full-time minimum-wage worker could not afford the rent for a typical one-bedroom apartment unit; to do so, this worker would have had to work more than 100 hours per week.[18]

Crime rates have dropped not because social inequalities have been reduced, but in part because of draconian policing practices.[19] The relative peace that may have been brought by sharply increasing the prison population in the United States may be difficult to sustain the next few years. Between 2000 and 2010, it is estimated that 3.5 million prisoners will be released into American society, even accounting for lower release rates because of mandatory sentencing requirements.[20] Without ways to integrate that population back into the society, the drop in crime rates may prove to be hard to sustain without seriously compromising civil liberties.

The spatial patterns of urban America can make it appear that all problems have been solved. The increasing tendency for the white middle and upper classes to live, work, shop, and play in virtual reservations set aside for their exclusive use breeds indifference to the inequalities of American society. It is important to consider whether affluent urban residents live, work, and play in "Potempkin cities" like Baltimore or Cleveland, where a thriving downtown and a tourist bubble hide urban problems, or in "boutique cities" like Seattle or Denver where highly paid professionals can sustain a critical mass of expensive restaurants, international boutique and clothing stores, and neighborhoods with stratospheric housing prices.[21]

In recent years, the policies of the federal government have exacerbated the social polarization of urban areas. The end of federal entitlements—in particular, the five-year lifetime limit on welfare—has removed the floor that previously kept the poor from becoming completely desperate. Local governments are not in a position to treat inequality in any consequential way; even if local officials and taxpayers were willing to do so, local governments do not have enough reach or resources to do so. National policies that reduced social and economic inequalities would allow local governments to concentrate on addressing genuinely local problems, rather than the consequences of national problems. Until that happens, the economic, racial, and ethnic tensions of American society are likely to be represented in a style of urban governance that builds walls so that the problems not solved can be swept out of sight.

Notes

1. Peter Marcuse, "What's So New About Divided Cities?" *International Journal of Urban and Regional Research* 17, No. 3 (September 1993): 358.
2. Dennis R. Judd, "The Rise of the New Walled Cities," in *Spatial Practices: Critical Explorations in Social/Spatial Theory*, ed. Helen Liggett and David C. Perry (Thousand Oaks, Calif.: Sage, 1995), pp. 144–166.

3. Michael Sorkin, "See You in Disneyland," in *Variations on a Theme Park: The New American City and the End of Space*, ed. Michael Sorkin (New York: Noonday Press, 1992), pp. 205–232.

4. Dennis R. Judd, "Enclosure, Community, and Public Life," in *Research in Community Sociology: New Communities in a Changing World*, ed. Dan A. Chekki (Greenwich, Conn. and London: JAI Press, 1996), pp. 217–238.

5. Kenneth Jackson, *Crabgrass Frontier: The Suburbanization of the United States* (New York: Oxford University Press, 1985), p. 3.

6. Evan McKenzie, *Privatopias: Homeowner Associations and the Rise of Residential Private Government* (New Haven, Conn.: Yale University Press, 1994).

7. Saskia Sassen, *Cities in a World Economy* (Thousand Oaks, CA: Pine Forge Press, 1994); Sharon Zukin, *Landscapes of Power: From Detroit to Disney World* (Berkeley: University of California Press, 1991).

8. M. Christine Boyer, *The City of Collective Memory: Its Historical Imagery and Architectural Entertainments* (Cambridge, Mass.: The MIT Press, 1994).

9. Quoted in Tom Morgenthau and John McCormack, "Are Cities Obsolete?" *Newsweek*, September 9, 1991, p. 42.

10. Elizabeth Kolbert, "Region Around New York Sees Ties to City Faltering," *New York Times*, December 1, 1991; William Blaberson, "For Many in the New York Region, the City Is Ignored and Irrelevant," *New York Times*, January 2, 1992.

11. Sassen, *Cities in a World Economy*.

12. Joseph Persky, Elliot Sclar, and Wim Wiewel, *Does America Need Cities?* (Washington, D.C.: Economic Policy Institute, 1991), p. 4.

13. "In a sample of fourteen large metropolitan areas, the wages of central city jobs in 1987 averaged 20 percent higher than those of suburban jobs." Ibid., p. 12.

14. Ibid., p. 13.

15. New York Times News Service, "City Neighborhoods Are Undergoing a Renaissance as Crime Rates Drop," *St. Louis Post-Dispatch* (May 29, 2000): A-12.

16. A. B. Atkinson, "Income Distribution in Europe and the United States," Luxembourg Income Study Working Paper No. 133 (Wolferdange, Luxembourg: Centre d'Etudes de Populations, de Pauvreté et des Politiques Socio-Economics/International Networks for Studies in Technology, Environment, Alternatives, Development, 1995).

17. U.S. Bureau of the Census, *USA Counties Database* (www.census.gov-statab-www/county.html).

18. National Low Income Housing Coalition, *Out of Reach: The Gap Between Housing Costs and Income of Poor People in the United States* (Washington, D.C.: Author, 1999).

19. Sophie Body-Gendrot, *The Social Control of Cities? A Comparative Perspective* (Malden, Mass. and Oxford, U.K.: Blackwell, 2000).

20. Ibid., p. 174.

21. Neal R. Peirce, "Business Basic: Rx for All Cities," *Washington Post*, March 5, 1999.

Action for Cities: A Guide for Community Planning, 128
addiction
  drug, 155, 168
  gambling, 393
affirmative action hiring, 72
AFL-CIO (American Federation of Labor–Congress of Industrial Organizations), public housing and, 183–184
African Americans
  blockbusting and, 195
  in Chicago, 64, 140, 144
  discrimination against, 141, 142–143
  electoral representation of, 103–105
  housing discrimination and, 177–182, 194–195, 198–202, 207
  in Levittown, 292–293
  lynchings of, 141
  in machine politics, 64
  in mayoral politics, 402–411
  migration of, 136, 137, 139–145
  in Mount Laurel, New Jersey, 305–307
  population growth of, 140
  poverty and, 152–157, 190–191
  public housing and, 191–193
  in suburbs, 200–201, 207, 309–311
  of Sunbelt, 148, 149, 278–279
  urban adjustment by, 142
  urban renewal effects on, 190–191
  violence against, 141, 142–143, 155–156
  voting patterns of, 216, 222–223, 242
Agricultural Adjustment Act, 121

AIDS (acquired immunodeficiency syndrome),
  poverty and, 155
air pollution
  highways and, 206
  in Los Angeles, 276–277
  sprawl and, 321
Alabama, election rules of, 103
Albany, New York, 63, 113
aldermen
  corruption of, 42, 78
  organizational position of, 55
  saloon ownership by, 54
Alger, Horatio, 36–37
Alinsky, Saul, 412–414, 415, 416
Ambler Realty, 300–301
American Association of Parks Superintendents, 81
American Dream, 290, 294–295
American Municipal Association, public housing support by, 184
American Tragedy, An (Dreiser), 80
Anaheim, California, population growth in, 263
Andrews, John, 323
annexation, 288–289
antipoverty programs
  during Great Depression, 121–122
  of War on Poverty, 414–415
Anti-Recession Fiscal Assistance Act (1976), 233, 238
Anti-Saloon League, 289
anti-urban values, 3, 44–47, 126, 157, 158, 240, 287
apartments, in suburbs, 296, 301
Appalachian migration, 136, 137, 139
Appalachian Regional Commission, 271
Arcadia, California, 289
Arlington Heights, Illinois, 305
Armed Services Committee, 272

Art of Money Getting, The (Barnum), 36
arts and culture, 395–396, 436
Asian-American immigration, 148, 150
Associated Community Organizations for Reform Now, 415
Atlanta, Georgia
  downtown enclave of, 434
  economic development of, 410
  Peachtree Center of, 371, 390
  political regime of, 9–10
  population of, 163, 164, 263, 264
  urban renewal in, 189
Atlanta Real Estate Board, 189
at-large elections, 82, 87–88, 89–90, 103, 105, 279
Atwater, Lee, 242
Auletta, Ken, 425
Austin, Illinois, 289
Australian ballot, 85–86
automobiles. *See also* highways
  municipal spending and, 123
  road rage and, 276
  sprawl and, 316, 317–318
  suburbanization and, 160–162, 202–206
AutoWorld museum, 395
avoidance behavior, 10–11

back to nature movement, 287–288
Baker v. Carr (1962), 46
Baldwin, E. J. "Lucky," 289
Baldwin, James, 193
Baltimore, Maryland
  African-American population of, 144
  corporate center strategy of, 378–381

Baltimore, Maryland (*continued*)
  employment in, 345
  expenditures of, 346, 347
  immigration to, 32
Baltimore City Trustee Loan
  and Guarantee Program,
  381
banks
  during Great Depression, 119,
  120
  urban fiscal crises and,
  360–361
Barnum, P. T., 36
baseball franchises, 387–388
Bedford Stuyvesant Restoration
  Corporation, 420
Bell Telephone Company, in
  Detroit, 70
Bentsen, Lloyd, 269
Birmingham, Alabama, 216
Black Jack, Missouri, 303–305
blacks. *See* African Americans
Black Thursday, 118
blockbusting, 195, 207
block grants, 224, 227–231, 247.
  See also Community Development Block Grants
  reductions in, 240
boards and commissions, 43–44
Boggs, Hale, 225–226
Bond Counsel, in New York
  City, 360
bonds, 353–356
  abuse of, 355
  default on, 357–358
  during Great Depression, 124
  market ratings of, 356–358
  for railroads, 22, 23
boosterism, 4, 373
  sports stadiums and, 387, 388
bosses. *See* machine politics
Boston, Massachusetts
  African-American population
  of, 144
  expenditures of, 346, 347
  immigrant hierarchy of, 34
  immigration to, 32, 63
  Kennedy clan of, 63
  machine politics of, 63
  neighborhood revitalization
  in, 418–419
  population of, 19, 161, 162,
  164, 263
  Quincy Market of, 370–371
  sewer development in, 38–39
  suburbs of, 287
  tax-exempt property of, 350
  urban renewal in, 186, 188
Boston Harbor, 38
Boulder, Colorado
  African-American population
  of, 149
  Hispanic population of, 149

slower growth regulations in,
  319, 324
Bradley, Tom, 277, 402,
  404–405, 406, 407–408,
  409, 424
Bratton, William, 424–425
Breckenfeld, Gurney, 378
Britain
  industrial production in, 270
  settlement pattern of, 286
Brooklyn, New York
  ferry to, 159
  riots in, 151
Bruér, Henry, 92–93
Bryan, William Jennings, 112
Bryce, James, 78–79
Buckley, William F., 425
budgets, municipal
  balanced, 340
  expenditures of, 123–124,
  341–349
  during Great Depression,
  123–126
  New York *vs.* Chicago,
  358–363
  revenues of, 349–356
Building Heights Commission,
  of New York City, 300
Bunyan, John, 81
Bureau of Efficiency, 93–94
buses, 203–204
Bush, George, 215, 238, 241,
  269
business model, for municipal
  reform, 94–96

_____

Cabrini-Green projects, 193
California, growth control
  movement of, 277–278,
  319, 322
Canadian immigration, 31
canal projects, 17, 20
Carlson, Arne, 325
Carnegie, Andrew, 100
Carter, Jimmy
  Community Development
  Block Grant program
  and, 229–230
  new urban policy of, 234–235,
  236
  urban policy decline and,
  231–235
casinos, 341, 391–394
Caudill, Harry, 139
Celebration, Florida, 331
Central Atlanta Improvement
  Association, 189
central business district (CBD).
  service sector of, 167, 375–377
  slum clearance and, 182–183,
  185–188
chain migration, 147

Challenge to Sprawl Campaign,
  319
Charles Center–Inner Harbor
  Management, Inc., 379
charter reform, 42, 82, 88, 95–99
Chester County, Pennsylvania,
  355
Chicago, Illinois
  African-American population
  of, 64, 72, 140, 144,
  153–154
  Cabrini-Green projects of, 193
  casinos and, 392
  community development corporations of, 421
  convention trade of, 384, 385
  election fraud in, 84–85
  expenditures of, 346, 347
  fiscal condition of, 358–363
  immigration to, 32–33
  machine politics of, 10, 56–57,
  64, 102, 186
  per capita tax burden of, 362,
  363
  population of, 18, 19, 161, 164,
  263
  public housing in, 186, 193
  race riots in, 142–143
  railroad investment by, 21,
  22–23
  restrictive covenants in, 143
  Richard J. Daley Jr., machine
  of, 56–57, 102, 186
  saloons in, 54
  suburbs of, 287
  unemployment in, 153–154
Chicago Defender, 140–141
child labor legislation, 8, 46
Childs, Richard S., 98
Chinatown, of New York City,
  150
Chisholm, Shirley, 227
Cincinnati, Ohio
  neighborhood revitalization
  in, 417
  reform in, 67
Cisneros, Henry, 245
Citizen's Action Committee, of
  New Haven, Connecticut,
  187
Citizens for More Important
  Things, 389
city councils
  election to. *See* elections, municipal
  state legislatures *vs.*, 42–43
*City of Richmond v. J.A. Croson
  Co.*, 407
city residency requirements, 72
Civilian Conservation Corps
  (CCC), 121, 127
Civil Rights Act (1964),
  216–217, 218–219

Civil Rights Act (1968), housing and, 200–201
civil rights movement, 215–216
civil service reform, 88, 93–94
Civil Works Administration (CWA), 121, 127
class
    in merchant cities, 25–26
    municipal reform and, 99–100
    political party affiliation and, 110–111, 122–123
    segregation by, 79
Clayton Act, 112–113
Clean Air Act (1990), 349
Cleveland, Ohio
    African-American population of, 140, 144
    default of, 358
    expenditures of, 346, 347
    immigration to, 32
    population of, 161, 162, 164
    reform in, 67
Clinton, Bill (William Jefferson)
    election of, 215, 242–243
    urban policy of, 242–246, 249
Cloward, Richard A., 220
Coalition of Northeast Governors, 273
coalition politics, 401, 402–411
cocaine abuse
    poverty and, 155
    suburban, 168
Colorado Springs, Colorado, 319
Commercial Appeal, 141
commission government, 96–98
Commission on Economy and Efficiency, 93–94
Commission on Population Growth and the American Future, 136, 214
common interest developments (CIDs), 296–298
Communities Organized for Public Service (COPS), 416
Community Action, 222
community action agencies (CAAs), 414
Community Development Block Grants (CDBGs), 194, 227–231, 237, 238, 240, 273
    applications for, 228
    distribution formula for, 231–233
    economic priorities and, 231, 371–372
    funding district boundaries for, 229–230
    geographic distribution of, 233–234

HUD oversight failure and, 228–230
    Neighborhood Strategy Areas for, 230
    triage method for, 230–231
Community Development Corporations (CDCs), 419–422
Community Reinvestment Act (1977), 202, 421
Comprehensive Employment Training Act (CETA), 231
condominiums, 296–297
Conference of City Managers, 81
Conference on Federal Economic Policies (1976), 232
Congress for the New Urbanism, 330
congressional reapportionment, for Voting Rights Act compliance, 104
conservatism, urban, 401, 402, 422–427
consolidation, county-city, 332–334
Contract with America, 245
convention centers, 382–386
Cook County, Illinois, 287
cooperative agreements, between local governments, 334–335
cooperative apartments, 296–297
corporate center strategy, 378–381
corporate services, 377–381
corporations
    community development, 419–422
    development, 378–381
    Hazen S. Pingree's attack on, 68–70
    headquarters of, 167, 377
    limited-risk, 26–27
    in Sunbelt, 278
    tax breaks for, 272–273
corruption, 42–43
    electoral, 83–85
    machine politics and, 42–43, 60–62, 78–79
    in municipal bonds, 355–356
    railroad building and, 24
    reform response to, 78–79, 81–82
    rhetoric of, 88
Council of State Governments, revenue sharing support by, 225
Council on Affordable Housing (New Jersey), 307
Country Club District, Kansas, 291

Cox, George, 62–63
crack cocaine abuse
    poverty and, 155
    suburban, 168
Crack in the Picture Window, The, 166
crime
    in mayoral elections, 424
    media response to, 170
    organized, 393–394
    police force development and, 39–40
    poverty and, 155–156
    public housing and, 192
    rates of, 437
    suburban, 168–169
Crime Bill (1998), 244
Cross-Bronx Expressway, 205
Crump, Ed, 85
Curley, James Michael, 102, 186

Daley Jr., Richard J., 56–57, 102, 186
Daley, Richard M., 64, 72, 362
Dallas, Texas
    African-American population of, 149
    expenditures of, 346, 347
    Hispanic population of, 149
    population growth in, 164, 263
Danger Signals: The Enemies of Youth from the Business Man's Standpoint (Barnum), 36
Danville, Illinois, election rules of, 103–104
Darst, Joseph, 186–187
Dartmouth College case, 44–45
Darwin, Charles, 36
Dawson, William, 64
Dayton, Ohio
    electoral systems of, 89
    government reform in, 98–99
Dayton Plan, 98–99
deeds, restrictive covenants of, 143, 200, 291, 292–293, 295
Deepwater Committee, 96
default, 24, 357–358
    bond rating vs., 357
defense plant workers, public housing for, 178
Deficit Reduction Act (1984), 355
Democracy in America (de Tocqueville), 45
Democratic Party
    community development corporations and, 421–422
    1924 convention of, 116
    Great Depression and, 120–122

Democratic Party (*continued*)
  machine politics and, 10, 113
  political interests of, 111–112,
    220, 246–250
  revenue sharing opposition
    by, 225–226, 227
  urban-rural conflicts in,
    114–115
  urban wing of, 110–111,
    116–117
Demonstration Cities and Metropolitan Development
  Act (1966), 220
Denver, Colorado
  African-American population
    of, 149
  expenditures of, 346, 347
  Hispanic population of, 149
  population of, 164, 263, 264
  railroad investment by, 22
depression. *See also* Great Depression of 1873, 24
Des Moines, Iowa, commission
  government of, 97
Des Moines Plan, 97
Detroit, Michigan
  African-American population
    of, 144
  downtown enclave of, 434
  expenditures of, 346, 347
  during Great Depression,
    124–125
  Mayor Hazen S. Pingree of,
    68–70
  population of, 164, 263
Detroit City Railway Company,
  68–69
Detroit Gas Company, 70
Dickens, Charles, 2
Dillon, John F., 44–45
Dinkins, David, 402, 404, 405, 423
disease
  municipal services develop-
    ment and, 37–39, 41
  poverty and, 154–155
Disney Corporation, 331
Dole, Bob, 243
Donovan, John C., 216
Downs, Anthony, 230
downtown. See also central
  business district
  development of, 29
Dreiser, Theodore, 80
drug addiction, 155, 168
Dukakis, Michael, 242, 269,
  274
dumbbell tenement, 34
DuPage County, Illinois, 335

Earned Income Tax Credit, 244
East St. Louis, Illinois, 289
  fiscal crisis of, 341

economic growth, x–xi, 3–4
  arts and culture and, 395–396,
    436
  boosterism and, 4, 373, 387,
    388
  casinos and, 391–394
  convention centers and,
    382–386
  corporate center strategy for,
    378–381
  costs and benefits of, 7,
    394–396
  culture of privatism and, 1–3
  democratic processes and,
    381
  disparities in, 375–378
  enterprise zones and, 244–245
  entertainment centers and,
    391
  factory system and, 4
  federal initiatives and, 8
  festival malls and, 389–391
  global, 377
  international, 377
  interurban competition for,
    18–24
  national level of, 236, 375–378
  neighborhood neglect and,
    380–381
  opposition to, 373–375, 417
  public-private partnerships
    and, 370–372
  railroads and, 21–24
  rationale for, 372–375
  sports stadiums and, 386–389
  tourism and, 382–396
Economic Opportunity Act
  (1964), 217, 219–220, 413
Economic Recovery Tax Act
  (1981), 237
Edge Cities, 167–168
education
  expenditures for, 341, 342,
    343
  during Great Depression, 125
efficiency movement, 91–94
Eighteenth Amendment,
  114–115
Eisenhower, Dwight, 129
elections
  municipal, 6
    at-large, 82, 87–88, 89–90,
      103, 105, 279
    corruption of, 83–84
    machine politics and, 66
    of merchant cities, 25
    nonpartisan, 85, 86–87,
      88–90
    reforms for, 85–91
    Voting Rights Act compli-
      ance of, 103–105
  presidential. *See* presidential
    election(s)

electricity, Detroit municipal
  plant for, 69–70
Elementary and Secondary Ed-
  ucation Act (1965), 218
El Paso, Texas, expenditures of,
  346, 347
Embarcadero Freeway, 205
Embry, Robert C., 230
Emergency Banking Act (1933),
  120–121
Emergency Financial Control
  Board (EFCB), in New
  York City, 361
Emergency Quota Act (1921),
  115
Emergency Relief and Con-
  struction Act (1933), 119
*Emerging Republican Majority,
  The* (Phillips), 259–260
eminent domain, 180
  in highway development, 205
employment
  manufacturing, 375, 376
  public sector, 344–346, 406,
    408–409
  service, 375, 376
Empowerment Zones/Enter-
  prise Communities
  (EX/EC) program,
  244–245
enclaves
  suburban, 166–169
  urban, 286, 433–435
energy consumption
  Arab oil embargo and, 260
  sprawl and, 321
  in Sunbelt, 270
English immigration, 30, 31
entertainment centers, 391
Equal Credit Opportunity Act
  (1974), 202
Erie Canal, 17, 20
Erlichman, John, 223
ethnic particularism, in machine politics, 64
Europe
  cities of, 2, 3, 285–286
  industrial development in,
    270
  urban growth boundaries in,
    326
exclusionary zoning, 298–302
  challenges to, 302–305
  New Jersey's challenge to,
    305–308
expenditures, 341–349
  categories of, 342, 343
  economic vitality and, 346
  employment, 344–346
  governmental mandates and,
    348–349
  increases in, 342, 344–345
  machine politics and, 60–61

poverty effects on, 346, 348

during 1920's, 123–124

Fair Labor Standards Act, 348–349

Fair Share Housing Act, 307

family structure, poverty and, 154

Farm Credit Administration, 121

Federal Emergency Relief Act (FERA), 121, 122, 127

Federal Farm Loan Act, 113

Federal Highway Trust Fund, 204

Federal Home Loan Bank Act, 119

Federal Home Loan Corporation, 297

Federal Housing Administration (FHA), 195–200, 297

Federal National Mortgage Association, 297

Federal Public Housing Authority, 181

Federal Reserve Act (1913), 112

Federal Savings and Loan Insurance Corporation (FSLIC), 196

Federal Trade Act, 112–113

Federal "Truth in Securities" Act, 121

Fifteenth Amendment, 279

Fifth Avenue Association, 299–300

Financier, The (Dreiser), 80

Firestone Tire Company, highway legislation and, 203–204

First Annual Conference for Good City Government (1894), 81–82, 91

fiscal crises, 340–364, 425–426

banking factors in, 360–361

expenditures and, 341–349

New York *vs.* Chicago, 358–363

origins of, 72, 340–341

political factors in, 359–360, 364

railroad development and, 23–24

revenues and, 349–356

Fitzgerald Expressway (Boston), 205

Fitzwater, Marlin, 215, 241

Flaherty, Peter, 225

Flint, Michigan, 395

Florida, population growth of, 264, 266

Flynn, Ray, 418–419

food stamp program, 218

football franchises, 387, 388

Ford, Gerald, 214, 233, 259, 260, 360, 361

Ford, Henry, 160

Fort Lauderdale, Florida

African-American population of, 149

Hispanic population of, 149

Fort Worth, Texas

African-American population of, 149

Hispanic population of, 149

population growth in, 263

Fourteenth Amendment, 46, 303, 305

fragmentation, governmental, 11, 285–286, 308–311, 332

Frostbelt

Community Development Block Grants for, 231–233

congressional representation of, 268

electorate of, 267–269

expenditures of, 346, 347

federal antirecession aid to, 233–234

population decline in, 163, 164, 262–264

Sunbelt *vs.*, 273–274, 279–280

Fulton, Robert, 159

Future Farmers of America (FFA), 386

Gallatin, Albert, 21

Galveston, Texas

African-American population of, 149

commission government of, 96–97

Hispanic population of, 149

Galveston Plan, 96–97

gaming industry, 391–394

Garcia decision, 348–349

gasoline consumption, sprawl and, 285, 318, 321

gasoline taxes, 204, 205

gated communities, 169, 297–298

General Motors, 395

highway legislation and, 203–204

general obligation bonds, 354

Geography of Nowhere, The (Kunstler), 328–329

German immigration, 30, 31, 33–34, 102

Germany

industrial production in, 270

mass transit in, 203

Gibson, Kenneth, 235, 415

Gingrich, Newt, 245

Giuliani, Rudolph, 404, 422–424

Glendening, Paris, 319

Goldschmidt, Neil, 417

Goldsmith, William, 423, 426

Goldwater, Barry, 217, 223

Goode, Wilson, 402

Good Government League, of San Antonio, 275

Gore, Al, 243

livability agenda of, 319–320

governance, xi, 5–8, 400–428

authority for, 6

community development corporations and, 419–422

consensus and, 427–428

conservatism and, 422–427

context of, 8

economic inequality and, 436–437

economic logic of, 7

policy choices and, 8–10

political incorporation and, 405–411

political logic of, 6–7

populism and, 411–422

reform theory of, 91

regional, 331–335

urban liberalism and, 401, 402–411

Governing, 319

Government of American Cities, The (Munro), 45

Grant, Madison, 115

grants-in-aid programs, 218, 219, 224

reductions in, 238–240, 351–352

Grapes of Wrath, The (Steinbeck), 127

Great Atlantic and Pacific Tea Company, 29

Great Depression, 117–123

Democratic Party and, 120–122

Hoovervilles of, 119

intergovernmental relationships during, 123–127

municipal budgets during, 123–126

public housing during, 179–181

state government expenditures during, 125–126

suburbs during, 162

unemployment during, 118–119

Great Divide, 135–138, 169-170

immigration and, 145–152

migration and, 138–145

poverty and, 152–157

suburban development and, 157–170

Greatest Trust in the World, The,
    80
Great Migration, 139–141
Great Northern Drive, The,
    140–141
Great Society programs,
    217–222
    backlash against, 214–215,
        222–224
    failure of, 214–215
Great Unwashed, 79, 301
Green Valley, Nevada, 168–169,
    298
Greenwich, Connecticut, 302
growth control movement,
    277–278, 322
growth control policies,
    319–320, 417

Hackett, David, 413–414
Hague, Frank, 54–55, 60
Hamilton, Alexander, 373
Harborplace (Baltimore),
    379–380, 382
Harlem, New York
    death rate in, 142
    public housing of, 193
Harper, Roy W., 304
Harris, Patricia R., 230
Hart, Peter, 269
Hart-Cellar Act (1965), 145–146
Hartford, Connecticut, neigh-
    borhood revitalization in,
    417
Hatcher, Richard, 401, 402–411
Head Start, 222, 223
health care, poverty and,
    154–155
Heller, Walter, 217
Hempstead, Long Island, 292
Herman, M. Justin, 190–191
Highway Act (1956), 129
highways
    air pollution and, 206
    design of, 204
    destructive impact of, 205
    state control of, 205
    subsidies for, 203–205
    U.S. legislation on, 128, 129,
        178, 188, 204–205, 206
Hispanics. *See* Latinos
homeless, 156
homeowner associations, 297
Home Owners' Loan Act, 121
Home Owners' Loan Corpora-
    tion, 121
home rule charter, 82, 95–96
Hoover, Herbert, 119–120, 179
Hoovervilles, 119
Horton, Willie, 242
housing
    blockbusting and, 195, 207

corporate production of, 163
federal loan programs for,
    195–200
federal tax deductions for,
    246, 247
during Great Depression, 119
New Jersey zoning laws and,
    305–308
in post–civil rights era,
    200–202
poverty and, 156
public. *See* public housing
redlining and, 202
rent supplement programs
    for, 194
restrictive covenants and,
    143, 200
revitalization of, 416
segregation in, 27, 29,
    177–182, 198–202, 286,
    292–293, 295–298
after World War II, 162–163
Housing Act (1937), 128
Housing Act (1949), 184–185
Housing and Community De-
    velopment Act (1974),
    227–231. *See also* Commu-
    nity Development Block
    Grants
Housing and Home Finance
    Agency (HHFA), 185
Housing and Urban Develop-
    ment Act (1968), 194
Houston, Texas
    African-American population
        of, 149
    business elites of, 9
    expenditures of, 346, 347
    Hispanic population of, 149
    neighborhood organization
        in, 418
    population growth in, 263
    uncontrolled growth of,
        275–276
How I Made Millions (Barnum),
    36
How to Succeed (Barnum), 36
Hoyt, Homer, 199
Huntington, Henry E., 159–160
Huntington, Samuel, 70
hyperpluralism, 10
hypersegregation, 152–153

Illinois, casinos and, 392
illiteracy, voting patterns and,
    86
immigration, 7–8, 9. *See also* spe-
    cific immigrant groups
    assimilation and, 65–67
    city distribution of, 147–150
    community breakdown and,
        30–35

electoral reform and, 85–89
ethnic composition of, 30, 31,
    33–34
history of, 15–18, 30, 31, 110
illegal, 151–152
machine politics and, 102
reaction against, 16, 79, 110
suffrage and, 82–83
upward mobility and, 63–65,
    66
after World War II, 145–152
Immigration Reform and Con-
    trol Act (1986), 151
income tax, 237–238, 240, 351
incorporation, 287–289
    political, 405–411
Indianapolis, Indiana, expendi-
    tures of, 346, 347
Indian Gaming Regulatory Act,
    392
Industrial Areas Foundation
    (IAF), 416
industrialization
    community breakdown and,
        24–27
    employment trends and,
        375–376
    growth in, 26
    Social Darwinism and, 35–37
    standardization and, 27
    suburbanization and, 158, 160
    suburban site of, 167, 289, 302
Industry, California, 289
inequality, 436–437
    in merchant cities, 25–26
infant mortality, 142, 154–155
inflation, 342, 344
Inner Harbor project (Balti-
    more), 379–380, 382
Intergovernmental Anti-Reces-
    sion Act (1977), 233, 238
intergovernmental relation-
    ships, 351
    block grants and, 227–231
    during fiscal crises, 351–353
    during Great Depression,
        119–127
    for housing development,
        179–182, 184–185
    during recessions, 233–234
    revenue sharing and, 225–227
    during War on Poverty,
        218–220
Intermodal Surface Transporta-
    tion Efficiency Act (IS-
    TEA), 206
International City Management
    Association, revenue
    sharing support by, 225
International Telephone and
    Telegraph (ITT) Corpora-
    tion, 293
Investment Tax Credit, 272–273

Iowa, casinos and, 392
Irish immigration, 30, 31, 33, 35, 102
  machine politics and, 63–65
Isray, Robert, 388
Italian immigration, 30, 31, 63–64

Jackson, Andrew, 21–22
Jackson, Henry M., 323–324
Jackson, Kenneth, 433–434
Jackson, Maynard, 410
Jackson, Michigan, reform movement of, 101
Jacksonville, Florida
  expenditures of, 346, 347
  migration from, 141
Jefferson, Thomas, 3, 158
Jersey City, New Jersey, 60, 63, 67
Jewish immigration, 35, 63–64
Jim Crow laws, 216–217
Job Corps, 222
Johnson, Lyndon Baines
  antipoverty policies of, 217–222, 413
  civil rights policies of, 200, 216
  election of, 267
Johnson, Tom L., 67
Jones, Samuel, 67
Journal of Housing, 184
Jungle, The (Sinclair), 80–81, 412
"just say no" campaigns, 389

Kansas City, Kansas
  railroad investment by, 22
  suburban development and, 290–291
Kansas City, Missouri, James Pendergast machine of, 57–59, 84
Kean, Thomas H., 307
Kennedy, John F., 63
  election of, 129, 267
  urban policies of, 215–217
Kennedy, Joseph P., 63
Kennedy, Robert, 420
Kerner Commission, 136, 214
Keyes, Roger M., 204
King, Martin Luther, Jr., 215–216
Kinloch, Missouri, 309
Knickerbocker Village, 179
Koch, Edward, 361–362, 404, 405, 425
Koreatown, 150
Ku Klux Klan, 115
  Democratic Party resolution against, 116
Kunstler, James Howard, 328–329

Lackawanna, New York, 304
Ladd, Helen, 340
LaGuardia, Fiorello, 64, 102
Lake Houston, 276
Lakewood Plan, 288–289
Lampard, Eric, 24
Landrieu, Moon, 226
land trusts, 336
La Puente, 289
large-lot zoning, 302
Latinos
  immigration of, 138–139, 148, 149, 150–151
  municipal employment of, 408
  of Sunbelt, 278–279
Lawton, Oklahoma, 304
League of Kansas Municipalities, 101
Lee, Richard, 187
Lehmann, Nicholas, 262
Leisure World, 169
Levitt, William J., 291–293
Levittown, Long Island, 292–293
Levittown, New Jersey, 293
liberalism, urban, 401, 402–411
limited-risk corporations, 26–27
Lindsay, John V., 3, 225–226, 405
Little Havana, Florida, 150
Little Rock, Arkansas, block grants to, 229
London, England, 2
  population of, 16
  settlement pattern of, 286
Los Angeles, California
  African-American population of, 144, 149
  air pollution of, 276–277
  downtown development in, 409–411
  electoral politics of, 403–405
  Hispanic population of, 149
  police force of, 407–408
  population growth in, 161, 164, 263
  riots in, 214–215, 241, 409
  suburbs of, 288–289
lotteries, 392
Loudoun County, Virginia, 323
Louisiana, state legislature of, 45
Louisiana Purchase (1803), 218
Low Income Housing Tax Credits (LIHTCs), 420–421
Lupsha, Peter, 268

McClure's, 80
McGuffey's Readers, 37

machine politics, 52–67
  of Abraham Reuf, 61, 62
  African-Americans in, 64
  anti-idealism of, 66
  centralized power and, 59–63
  contemporary, 71–73
  corruption and, 42–43, 60–62, 78–79
  decline of, 101–103
  definition of, 52–53
  economic growth and, 102
  hierarchical organization of, 54–56, 65
  immigrant assimilation and, 65–67
  immigrant upward mobility and, 63–65, 66
  Irish domination of, 63–65
  of James Pendergast, 57–59, 84
  national political parties and, 113
  origins of, 53–57
  patronage and, 41, 55–56
  personality and, 54
  public expenditure and, 60
  reform and, 60, 67, 82–91, 101–103
  of Richard J. Daley Jr., 56–57
  saloon culture and, 54
  in Sunbelt, 274
  trade unions and, 66–67
  of William Marcy Tweed, 42–43, 60–61
Macon, Georgia, migration from, 141–142
Maine, state legislature of, 45
malls. *See* shopping centers
manager government, 98–99
Man in the Gray Flannel Suit, The, 166
Manpower Development and Training Act (1962), 219
manufacturing. *See* industrialization
Marcuse, Peter, 433
Maryland
  infrastructure costs in, 327
  slower growth initiatives in, 319, 324
Marzullo, Vito, 56
Massachusetts Miracle, 274
mass transit, 27–29, 203, 362, 363, 410
  funding for, 205–206
mayors
  conservative, 422–427
  election of, 43
  federal revenue sharing and, 225–226
  during Great Depression, 120, 124–125, 127
  of merchant cities, 25
  minority, 72, 402–411

mayors (*continued*)
  state legislature effects on, 43
  strong, 82, 95
Maysville Turnpike bill, 21–22
media
  on casinos, 393
  on crime, 170
  political activists and, 221
  on Quincy Market, 370–371
  reform movement and, 80,
    100
Medicaid, 222, 348
Medicare, 222
Memphis, Tennessee, electoral
  fraud in, 85
merchant cities, 24–27
  class relationships in, 25–26
  inequality of, 25–26
  political system of, 25
  social services of, 35–36
Merrill Lynch, 336
Metro Atlanta Rapid Transit
  Authority, 410
Metropolitan Council for the
  Minneapolis Region,
  324–325
Metropolitan Council for the
  Twin Cities, 325
Metropolitan Dade County, 333
Metropolitan Land Use Reform
  Act, 325
Metropolitan Planning Organi-
  zation (MPO), for trans-
  portation policy, 206
Metropolitan Transit Authority,
  363
Metropolitan Water District
  (Los Angeles), 288
Mexican migration, 136, 137,
  138–145
Miami, Florida
  African-American population
    of, 149
  Hispanic population of,
    149
  population growth in, 164,
    263
  riots in, 151
Michigan-Peninsula Car Com-
  pany, 69
migration
  African-American, 137,
    139–145
  Appalachian, 137, 139
  from farm to city, 138–145
  Mexican, 137, 138–145
  waves of, 136, 137
  after World War II, 143–145
military expenditures, 271–272
Mills, Wilbur, 226
Milwaukee, Wisconsin
  expenditures of, 346, 347
  municipal services of, 40–41

Minneapolis, Minnesota
  population of, 164, 168
  tax-sharing bill for, 325
Minnesota, land use reform in,
  324–325, 331
minority business enterprises
  (MBEs), 406–407
Mississippi, antipoverty pro-
  grams in, 221
Missouri, casinos and, 393
Mitchell, John Purroy, 92–93
Model Cities Program, 218, 220,
  221
Model T, 160
Monsanto Chemical Company,
  289
Moody's Investors Service,
  356–358
Morrison, de Lesseps S., 274
Mortgage Disclosure Act (1975),
  202
mortgage foreclosure, during
  Great Depression, 119
Moses, Robert, 93, 205
Mount Laurel, New Jersey,
  305–308
Mowry, George, 100
muckrakers, 80–81
Municipal Affairs, 83
Municipal Assistance Corporation (MAC), in New York
  City, 361
municipal bonds, 353–356
  abuse of, 355
  defaults on, 357–358
  during Great Depression,
    124
  ratings for, 356–358
Municipal Finance Officers Association, 81
municipal services
  business model of, 94–96
  development of, 37–42
  efficiency and economy in,
    91–94
  growth of, 5
  institutionalization of, 40–42,
    44, 71–72
  in merchant cities, 26, 35–36
  reform of, 88, 91–94
  sprawl and, 327
  suburban use of, 308
Munro, William, 45
Murphy, Frank, 124–125

National Agenda for the Eighties, 236
National Association of Counties, revenue sharing support by, 225
National Association of Home
  Builders (NAHB), 183

National Association of Hous-
  ing Officials, urban de-
  velopment and, 184
National Association of Port
  Authorities, 81
National Association of Real
  Estate Boards, 291
  ethical code of, 295–296
  urban development and,
    182–183, 186
National Child Labor Commit-
  tee (1904), 81
National City, Illinois, 289
National City Lines, 204
National Civic Federation
  (1900), 81
National Commission on Civil
  Disorders, 136, 214
National Commission on Urban
  Problems, 136, 214
National Defense Highway Act
  (1956), 188, 204
National Development Bank,
  235
National Governors' Confer-
  ence, revenue sharing
  support by, 225
National Highway Users Con-
  ference, 203, 205
National Housing Act (1934),
  121, 196–197
  Section 203 of, 196–197
National Housing Association
  (1910), 81
National Industrial Recovery
  Act (1933), 121, 128, 179
National League of Cities
  public housing support by,
    184
  revenue sharing support by,
    225
National Legislative Conference, revenue sharing
  support by, 225
National Municipal League,
  81–82, 88, 98
National Origins Act (1924),
  115, 145
National People's Action, 415
National Public Housing Conference, 183
National Resources Committee,
  128
National Short Ballot Association, 81, 98
negro removal, 190–191
neighborhood control, 416
neighborhood organizing
  movement, 411–422
Neighborhood Services program, 414
Neighborhood Strategy Areas
  (NSAs), 230

Nelson, Gaylord, 206
Nelson, Herbert U., 182–183
Newark, New Jersey, New
    Community Corporation
    of, 421
New Community Corporation,
    421
New Deal, 110–129
New Federalism, 224–227
New Haven, Connecticut, ur-
    ban renewal program of,
    187
New Jersey
    land trusts in, 336
    Smart Growth initiative in, 319
    zoning laws of, 305–308
New Markets Initiative (1999),
    245
New Orleans, 274
    employment in, 345
    expenditures of, 346, 347
    legislative control of, 43
Newport Beach, California, 277
New Urbanism, 328–331
    Congress for, 330
    goals of, 322, 330–331
    media attention to, 329–330
New York Bureau of Municipal
    Research, 92–93, 99–100
New York City, 2–3
    African-American population
        of, 140, 144
    Chinatown of, 150
    civil service reform in, 93–94
    convention trade of, 384, 385
    1924 Democratic Convention
        in, 116
    efficiency movement in,
        92–93
    electoral politics of, 403–405
    expenditures of, 346, 347
    ferry service of, 158
    fiscal condition of, 260,
        358–363, 425
    immigration to, 30, 32, 34–35
    Knickerbocker Village of, 179
    mass transit in, 203
    Medicaid expenditures of,
        348
    per capita expenditures of, 37
    per capita tax burden of, 362,
        363
    police force of, 39–40, 424–425
    population of, 16, 17–18, 19,
        161, 164, 263
    public housing of, 193
    saloons in, 54
    settlement pattern of, 286
    state legislative control of,
        42–43
    suburbs of, 158, 309
    Tammany Hall machine of,
        54, 64, 65–66

    tax-exempt property of,
        350–351
    tenement districts of, 34–35
    zoning law of, 299–300
Nichols, Jessie Clyde, 290–291
Night Comes to the Cumberlands
    (Caudill), 139
NIMBY (not in my backyard)
    syndrome, 418
Nixon, Richard M., 214, 215
    law and order theme of,
        223
    New Federalism of, 224–227
    Sunbelt constituency of, 269,
        273
Northeast-Midwest Economic
    Advancement Coalition,
    273
Northeast-Midwest Institute,
    273

Oakland, California, reform
    movement of, 100–101
Oakland County, Michigan, 335
Oak Park, Illinois, 289
obsolescence, 435–436
oil embargo (1973), 260
Oklahoma City, growth of, 267
O'Malley, Walter, 387
Omnibus Corporation, 204
omnibuses, 27–28
one man–one vote principle,
    46–47
Orange County, California, 335
    bankruptcy of, 355
Orfield, Myron, 325
organized crime, 393–394
Origin of Species, The (Darwin),
    36
Our Cities: Their Role in the Na-
    tional Economy, 128
Our Country (Strong), 79

Pacific Electric Railway Com-
    pany, 159–160
Pacific Railways Acts (1862,
    1864), 21
Paris, France, 2
    population of, 16
Park View Heights Corpora-
    tion, 304
Partnership for Neighborhood
    Development (PPND),
    422
Passing of the Great Race, The
    (Grant), 115
patronage, in machine politics,
    41, 55–56
Patterson, John H., 98–99
Peachtree Center (Atlanta), 371,
    390

Pendergast, James, 57–59, 84
Pentagon budget, Sunbelt
    growth and, 271–272
personal property tax, 349–350
Personal Responsibility Act
    (1996), 151–152, 246
Philadelphia, Pennsylvania
    African-American population
        of, 140, 144
    casinos and, 392
    colonial, 26
    election fraud in, 83–84
    employment in, 345
    immigration to, 32
    income tax in, 351
    population of, 19
    reform in, 67
    suburbs of, 309
    waterworks of, 37–38, 40
    yellow fever in, 37
Phillip, David Graham, 80
Phillips, Kevin, 259–260
Phoenix, Arizona
    African-American population
        of, 149
    elections in, 83
    expenditures of, 346, 347
    growth of, 267
    Hispanic population of, 149
    population growth in, 163,
        164, 263
Pilgrim's Progress, 81
Pingree, Hazen S., 68–70, 101
Pittsburgh, Pennsylvania
    African-American population
        of, 144
    at-large elections in, 89
    commission government of,
        97
    community development cor-
        porations of, 421–422
    electoral fraud in, 85
    immigration to, 32
    nonprofit sector of, 10
    population of, 164, 168, 263
    tax loss in, 308
Piven, Frances Fox, 220
Plunkitt, George Washington,
    78
police force
    cooperative agreements for,
        334–335
    development of, 39–40
    federal aid for, 244
    of Los Angeles, 407–408
    of New York City, 39,
        424–425
    reform of, 407–408
    of San Francisco, 61
political incorporation, 405–511
political leadership, 6
Politics of Poverty, The (Dono-
    van), 216

pollution
air
highways and, 206
of Los Angeles, 276–277
sprawl and, 321
water
in Boston, 38
in Houston, 276
polynucleated metropolis, 167
populism, urban, 401–402,
411–422
Portland, Oregon
growth policy of, 326–327
neighborhood movement in,
417
Portman, John, 371
post-suburbia, 316–317. *See also*
sprawl
poverty
in Baltimore, 380
concentration of, 152–157
crime and, 155–156
family structure and, 154
during Great Depression, 154
growth in, 436–437
housing and, 156
illness and, 154–155
joblessness and, 153–154, 346
President Johnson's war on,
217–222
public expenditures and, 346,
348
rural, 126–127, 139
social disorganization and,
119
substance abuse and, 155
urban renewal and, 190–191
Powers, John, 84
Power Shift (Sale), 260
presidential election(s)
of 1896, 112
of 1900, 112
of 1912, 112
of 1928, 110, 116
of 1932, 110, 120–122, 267
of 1960, 215, 267
of 1964, 217, 222, 267
of 1968, 223, 269
of 1980, 269
of 1988, 238, 269
of 1992, 243, 249
of 1996, 215, 249
of 2000, 247
race and, 222–223
suburban electorate and, 249,
250
Sunbelt and, 269
urban electorate and,
247–250, 267
President's Committee on Juvenile Delinquency, 413–414
President's Emergency Committee for Employment, 119

President's Organization on
Unemployment Relief,
119
President's Task Force on Suburban Problems, 136, 214
*Principles of Scientific Manage-
ment, The*, 91–92
privatism, culture of, x, 1–3
privatization, 426
Progressive Era, 80
Prohibition, 114–115
property taxes, 349, 350–351
during Great Depression,
124
Proposition 13, 353
Pruitt-Igoe project (St. Louis),
193, 303
public authorities, 354–355
public heath system, development of, 41
public housing, 177–182,
206–207
AFL-CIO and, 183–184
African Americans and,
191–193
commercial development *vs.*,
185–188
for defense plant workers,
178
design of, 193
eligibility for, 192
federal legislation for, 178–182
during Great Depression,
179–181
local government support of,
184–185
opposition to, 182–183, 184,
186, 194–195
racial segregation and,
191–195
sites for, 192–193
during World War I, 178–179
after World War II, 182–185
during World War II, 181–182
Public Housing Act (1937),
180–181
Public Housing Administration,
181
public housing authorities,
180
public-private partnerships,
370–371
Public Works Administration
(PWA), 121, 127
Housing Division of, 179–180
Putting People First (Clinton and
Gore), 243

Quayle, Dan, 242
Quayside, Florida, 169
Quincy Market (Boston),
370–371

race
Federal Housing Administration policies and, 198–200
presidential elections and,
222–223
race riots, 142–143
racial segregation, 298
highway programs and, 178
housing policies and,
177–182, 191–193,
198–200
in North, 142–145
in post–civil rights era,
200–202
in South, 140–142
suburban, 201
white flight and, 43–145, 136
railroads
bankruptcy of, 23–24
economic growth and, 20,
21–24
governmental aid to, 23–24
political corruption and, 24,
62
population growth and, 18
public subsidies for, 21–22
steam, 28
suburbanization and, 158–159
Ramapo, New Jersey, 324
Reagan, Ronald
election of, 214, 242, 269
housing policies of, 194
tax cuts of, 237–240
urban enterprise zone proposal of, 240–242
urban policy of, 235–242
Reconstruction Finance Corporation (RFC), 179
recreational shopping, 389–391
redistricting, for Voting Rights
Act compliance, 103–105
redlining, 202
reform
metropolitan, 322, 331–335
municipal, 6, 67–71
bias of, 99–101
business model for, 94–96
class and, 79, 99–100
commission government
and, 96–98
in Detroit, 68–70
for elections, 85–91
electoral consequences of,
103–105
environment of, 80–82
Hazen S. Pingree's ap-
proach to, 68–70, 101
immigrant voting participation and, 85–89
machine politics and, 60,
67, 82–91, 101–103
manager government and,
98–99

motive for, 78–79, 99
opposition to, 100–101
organizations for, 81
in Sunbelt, 274–275
regimes, urban, 9–10
regional development policies, 270–271
regional government, 331–335
regionalism, 260. *See also* Sunbelt
in Europe, 270
Regional Transportation Authority, 362
Reinvention Blueprint (HUD), 245
religious conflict, 101, 114–115
Rendell, Edward, 423
rent supplement programs, 194
Republican Party
machine politics and, 113
political interests of, 111, 217
restrictive covenants, 143, 200, 291, 292–293, 295
Reuf, Abraham, 61, 62
revenue, municipal, 349–356
bonds for, 353–358
from convention centers, 383–384
federal aid and, 351–353
income tax for, 351
personal property tax for, 349–350
property tax for, 349, 350–351
during 1920's, 124
from sports stadiums, 389
state aid and, 353
user fees for, 353
revenue bonds, 354, 355
revenue sharing, 225–227
revitalization, 370–396
casinos and, 391–394
convention centers and, 382–386
corporate center strategy for, 378–381
entertainment centers and, 391
malls and, 389–391
motivation for, 372–375
public-private partnerships and, 370–372
sports stadiums and, 386–389
tourism and, 382–396
Reynolds v. Sims (1964), 46
Richard M. Daley, 423
Riordan, Richard, 423, 424, 425–426
riots, 400
ethnic, 39, 151
during Great Depression, 120
Los Angeles, 214–215, 241, 409
race, 39, 142–143

Rising Tide of Color Against the White World-Supremacy (Stoddard), 115
Rivers, Mendell, 272
road rage, 276
Rockefeller, John D., 36, 80, 100
Roman Catholics
Al Smith's presidential campaign and, 117
fundamentalists opposition to, 114–115
of Jackson, Michigan, 101
Rome, 2
Roosevelt, Franklin Delano
election of, 110–111, 267
housing policies of, 179–180
legislative initiatives of, 120–122, 127
Roosevelt, Theodore, 52, 81, 91
Rouse, James, 370, 379–380, 390, 391
Royal Road to Wealth, The (Barnum), 36
Ruckelshaus, William, 276
Rule G–37, 355–356
rural areas
antiurban sentiment of, 45–46, 126
poverty of, 126–127, 139
Rusk, David, 264
Russian immigration, 30, 31
Rustbelt. *See* Frostbelt

_____

St. Louis, Missouri
African-American population of, 140, 144
consolidation plans for, 333–335
downtown enclave of, 434
electoral systems of, 89, 90
employment in, 345
expenditures of, 346, 347
immigration to, 32
population of, 18, 19, 161, 162, 164, 168, 263
public housing of, 193
railroad investments of, 23
residential segregation in, 201
suburbs of, 309, 310
urban renewal program of, 186–187
St. Petersburg, Florida
African-American population of, 149
Hispanic population of, 149
Sait, Edward, 60
Sale, Kirkpatrick, 260
San Antonio, Texas
African-American population of, 149
Hispanic population of, 149
municipal reform in, 275

San Diego, California
African-American population of, 149
Hispanic population of, 149
population growth in, 263
San Francisco, California
Abraham Reuf machine of, 61, 62
African-American population of, 144
antipoverty programs in, 221
corruption in, 61, 62
employment in, 345
hyperpluralism of, 10
police force of, 61
population growth in, 263
saloons in, 54
urban renewal of, 189–191
Western Addition Community Organization action in, 413
San Jose, California, expenditures of, 346, 347
Santa Anita raceway, 289
Santa Monicans for Renters' Rights, 417
Sartre, Jean-Paul, 3
Sauget, Illinois, 289
Savas, E. S., 426
Save Our Cities/Save Our Children rally, 241
Scandinavian immigration, 30
Schaefer, William Donald, 378–379
Schlesinger, Arthur, Jr., 215
Schmoke, Kurt, 380, 401, 402–411
schools
financing for, 341, 342, 343
during Great Depression, 125
Head Start preparation for, 222, 223
shootings at, 169
Schulman, Sy, 302
Schundler, Bret, 423
scientific management movement, 91–92
Scottsdale, Arizona, 426
secession, politics of, xi, 10–11. *See also* suburbs
Secret of Success, The (Barnum), 36
segregation
class, 79, 152–153, 286
housing, 27, 29, 177–182, 198–202, 286, 292–293, 295–298
racial. See racial segregation
suburbs and, 201, 295–298
service sector employment, 167, 375–377
sewer systems
development of, 38–39, 41
in Houston, 276

Shame of the Cities, The (Steffens), 80
Shelley, Jack, 413, 415
Shelly v. Kraemer, 296–297
shopping centers (malls), 167, 376–377, 389–391
   downtown, 370–371
   downtown department stores *vs.*, 376–377
   enclave nature of, 434
Shriver, Sargent, 414
Siembieda, William, 268
Sierra Club, 319
Simon, William E., 360
Sinclair, Upton, 80–81, 412
Sister Carrie (Dreiser), 80
slum areas, 34–35. *See also* public housing
   clearance of, 178–180
   AFL-CIO and, 183–184
   central business districts and, 182–183, 185–188
   local government support of, 184–185
   protest against, 188–189, 190
Smart Growth movement, 322–328
   in Loudoun County, Virginia, 323
   in Portland, Oregon, 326–327
Smith, Alfred E., 110, 113, 116–117
Social Darwinism, 35–37, 235–236
socialists, 89, 100
Southern Growth Policies Board, 232, 273
Southern Rim, 260. *See also* Sunbelt
special districts, 10–11, 335
Split Level Trap, The, 166
sports stadiums, 386–389
   subsidies for, 389
sport utility vehicles, 318
Sprague, Frank Julian, 28–29
sprawl, 11, 316–336
   air pollution and, 321
   consequences of, 320–322
   energy consumption and, 321
   gasoline consumption and, 285, 318
   governmental fragmentation and, 324
   infrastructure and, 321, 327
   media attention to, 318–319
   political response to, 319–320, 336
   Smart Growth movement and, 322–328
   traffic congestion and, 316, 317–318
Springfield, Illinois, election rules of, 103

Standard and Poor's Corporation, 356–358
Standard Oil Company, 80
   highway legislation and, 203–204
State and Local Fiscal Assistance Act (1972), 226
state governments
   federal funds to, 224–225, 240
   during Great Depression, 120, 125–126
state legislatures
   antiurban sentiment of, 45–46, 126
   city government and, 42–46
   during Great Depression, 125–126
   highway development by, 205
   housing authorities and, 180
   machine politics *vs.*, 113
   municipal aid from, 353
   rural majorities of, 45–46, 126
   suburban incorporation and, 288–289
   tax policy of, 240
Steffens, Lincoln, 80
Steinbeck, John, 127
Stevenson, Adlai, 216
Stoddard, Lothrop, 115
Stokes, Carl, 225, 401, 402–411
Stone, Clarence, 9–10, 406
Story of Life Insurance, The, 80
streetcars, 28–29
   bus replacement of, 204
   suburbanization and, 159–160
Strong, Josiah, 79
strong mayor government, 82, 95
substance abuse
   poverty and, 155
   suburban, 168
suburbs, 157–170, 285–311. *See also* sprawl
   advertising for, 294–295
   African Americans in, 200–201, 207, 309–311
   apartments in, 301
   automobiles and, 160–162
   autonomy of, 286
   back to nature movement and, 287–288
   bedroom (1946–1965), 162–166
   blighted landscapes of, 328–331
   city services used by, 308
   cooperation between, 334
   core city *vs.*, 285–286, 308–309, 328
   cross-commuting between, 167, 318
   diversity of, 168

   during Great Depression, 162
   enclave (1965-present), 166–169
   entrepreneurial shaping of, 290–298
   gated, 169
   growth of, 11, 29, 157–158, 168
   incorporation of, 287–289
   industrialization in, 167, 289, 302
   large-lot zoning in, 302
   low-density development in, 296–297
   middle-class character of, 166
   national housing policies and, 195–202
   national transportation policies and, 202–206
   political leadership of, 9
   population growth in, 161, 162, 163, 168
   promotion of, 290–298
   railroads and, 158–159
   segregation and, 295–298
   stages of, 157–158
   streetcars and, 159–160
   urbanization of, 168–169
   variation among, 309–310
   zoning and, 298–302
   zoning challenges in, 302–305
success
   ideology of, 35–37
   machine politics and, 66
   suburban developments and, 294
Success in Life (Barnum), 36
suffrage, 53, 82–83
Sullivan, Big Tim, 65
Sumner, William Graham, 36
Sunbelt, 259–280
   boundaries of, 260–261
   business elites of, 267–268
   common interest developments in, 296
   concept of, 259–262
   congressional representation of, 267, 268
   economic growth of, 269–273
   elasticity of, 264, 266–267
   electoral systems of, 89–91
   electorate of, 267–269, 278–279
   expenditures of, 346, 347
   federal spending in, 233–234, 270–272
   Frostbelt *vs.*, 273–274, 279–280
   growth control movement of, 277–278
   machine politics in, 274
   manufacturing in, 269–272
   military contracting in, 271–272
   minority elected officials in, 279

municipal reform in, 274–275
national political balance and,
  267–269
politics of, 274–275
population growth of, 148,
  149, 163–166, 262–264
presidential elections and, 269
property tax in, 350
rise of, 262–267
southern portion of, 260–261
tourism in, 270
uncontrolled growth of,
  275–278
western portion of, 261
Suncoast Dome sports stadium,
  388
Supremacy Clause, 348
Susan Lenox (Phillip), 80
Syracuse, New York, anti-
  poverty programs in, 221

Taft, William H., 93–94
Tammany Hall, 54
immigrant assimilation and,
  65–66
patronage workforce of, 64
Tampa, Florida
African-American population
  of, 149
Hispanic population of, 149
Tarbell, Ida, 80
Targeted Employment Tax
  Credit, 235
tax
corporate, 272–273
exemptions from, 350–351, 354
gasoline, 204, 205
homeowner deductions from,
  246
income, 237–238, 240, 351
personal property, 349–350
property, 124, 349, 350–351,
  353
tax anticipation notes, 353
tax code, Sunbelt development
  and, 272–273
tax cuts, of Reagan administration, 237–240
Tax Equity and Fiscal Responsibility Act (1982), 355
tax-exempt property, 350–351
Tax Increment Finance District,
  in Los Angeles, 409
Tax Reform Act (1986), 237–238,
  355
state-level effects of, 240
Taylor, Frederick Winslow,
  91–92
Teaford, Jon, 44
Technical Debt Advisory Committee, in New York City,
  360

technology, economic consequences of, 375
tenements, of New York City,
  34–35
Tennessee Valley Authority,
  121
Thatcher, Margaret, 270
Thornburg v. Gingles, 103
Tilden Commission, 83
Toledo, Ohio, 67, 86–87
tourism, 382–396
enclave spaces for, 434–435
towns, politics of, 9
traffic congestion, 276, 316,
  317–318
transportation. *See also* automobiles; railroads
community breakdown and,
  27–29
mass, 27–29, 203, 205–206,
  362, 363, 410
Metropolitan Planning Organization authority over,
  206
national policies on, 202-
  206
New Urbanism approach to,
  330–331
suburbanization and,
  159–162, 202–206
Treason of the Senate, The, 80
*Treatise on the Law of Municipal
  Corporations* (Dillon), 45
trolley cars, 28–29, 159
Truly Disadvantaged, The
  (Wilson), 243
Tulsa, Oklahoma, 143
Tweed, William Marcy, 42–43

underclass, 153
Underwood-Simmons Act,
  112
unemployment
in Great Depression, 118–119,
  121–122, 124
in high-poverty areas,
  153–154, 346
unions
machine politics and, 66–67
presidential responses to, 112,
  113
public employee, 344–345
public housing and, 183–184
racial discrimination and, 142
United Cities Motor Transit
  Company, 203–204
United States Conference of
  Mayors, 127
Up Ahead, 189
Urban Development Action
  Grant programs, 233, 237,
  238, 371

urban enterprise zones, 240–242
urbanization, 16–24
immigration and, 30–35
industrialization and, 24–27
population changes with,
  16–18
transportation and, 27–29
Urban Land Institute, 291, 297
urban regime, 9–10
urban renewal, 371. *See also* economic growth
coalitions for, 186–188
commercial priorities of,
  185–188
opposition to, 194
poverty and, 190–191
public housing and, 178–185,
  191–193
public-private partnerships
  and, 370–372
racial segregation and,
  191–195
resistance to, 188–191
in Sunbelt, 275
U.S. Conference of Mayors
Legislative Action Committee
  of, 225–226
public housing support by,
  184
revenue sharing support by,
  225
U.S. Congress
antipollution legislation of,
  349
antipoverty legislation of,
  217–220
antirecession legislation of,
  233–234
civil rights legislation of,
  216–217
Community Development
  Act of, 227–231, 232–233
Community Reinvestment
  Act of, 421
enterprise zone legislation of,
  240–242, 244–245
highways legislation of, 128,
  129, 178, 188, 204–205,
  206
housing legislation of, 128,
  178–182, 184–185,
  195–202
housing policies and, 177–185
immigration legislation of,
  115, 145, 147, 151–152
land use legislation of,
  323–324
New Deal legislation of,
  120–123, 127
preemption power of,
  348–349
rent supplement legislation
  of, 194

U.S. Congress (*continued*)
revenue bond legislation of, 355
revenue sharing legislation of, 225–227
tax reduction legislation of, 237–242
tenement investigations of, 178
urban representation in, 248–249
voting rights legislation of, 103, 279
U.S. Constitution
Article VI of, 348
Eighteenth Amendment to, 114–115
Fifteenth Amendment to, 279
Fourteenth Amendment to, 46, 303, 305
income and class discrimination and, 305
U.S. Department of Housing and Urban Development
Community Development Block Grant program and, 228–230
complaints to, 201
opposition to, 245–246
U.S. Emergency Housing Corporation, 180
U.S. Environmental Protection Agency, 349
U.S. Food and Drug Administration, 81
U.S. Housing Administration, 181
U.S. Housing Corporation, 178
U.S. Savings and Loan League, urban development and, 182, 183
U.S. Supreme Court
in *City of Richmond v. J.A. Croson Co.*, 407
Dartmouth College case of, 44
on electoral districts, 104–105
Garcia decision of, 348–349
on restrictive covenants, 200, 296
in *Reynolds v. Sims*, 46
in *Shelly v. Kraemer*, 296
on tax-exempt borrowing, 354
in *Thornburg v. Gingles*, 103
in *Village of Euclid v. Ambler Realty Co.*, 300–301
on zoning laws, 305
user fees, 353

Ventura, Jesse, 325
Ventura County, California, 319
Veterans Administration (VA) loans, 195–196, 197–200
vigilante committees, 39
Village of Euclid v. Ambler Realty Co., 300–301
violence
against African Americans, 141, 142–143, 155–156
police force development and, 39–40
poverty and, 155–156
public housing and, 192
Voinovich, George, 418
volunteers, in merchant cities, 35–36
voting
African American patterns of, 216, 222–223, 242
fraud during, 83–85
one man–one vote principle and, 46–47
restrictions on, 83, 86
southern patterns of, 222–223, 242
suburban patterns of, 243, 249–250
underrepresentation with, 103–105
urban patterns of, 100, 247–250
white primary and, 279
Voting Rights Act (1965), 217, 279
Voting Rights Act (1982), 103–104

Wagner, Robert F., 181
Wagner-Ellender-Taft Act (1949), 184
Wagner Labor Act, 128
Wagner-Steagall Public Housing Act (1937), 127, 180–181
Wallace, George, 223
Warner, Sam Bass, 1–2, 26
War on Poverty, 217–222
War Production Board, 271–272
Washington, D.C., 3
African-American population of, 144
expenditures of, 346, 347
riots in, 151
Washington, Harold, 64, 72, 402, 406, 418

water pollution
in Boston, 38
in Houston, 276
Water Street Pavilion, 395
waterworks, development of, 37–38, 40
Wellston, Missouri, 309, 310
West Edmonton Mall, 391
Western Addition Community Organization (WACO), of San Francisco, 413
Westminster, California, 150
Westport, Connecticut, 301
Westwood, Missouri, 309
White, A. C. "Jack," 275
White, Andrew D., 83
White, Kevin, 370, 417
white flight, 136, 143, 166. *See also* suburbs
white primary, 279
Whitlock, Brand, 67, 86–87
Whitman, Christine Todd, 319, 336
Whitmire, Kathy, 9, 276
Wilentz, Robert N., 306
Williams, Hannibal, 413
Wilson, William Julius, 153, 243
Wilson, Woodrow, 93–94, 112–114
Wirthlin, Richard, 242
Wolfe, Tom, 414–415
Woo, Mike, 423
Woolworth, Frank W., 29
Works Progress Administration, 127
World War I, public housing during, 178–179
World War II
public housing after, 182–185
public housing during, 181–182

yellow fever, 37
Yerba Buena Center, 189–190
Young, Andrew, 406, 410

zoning, 298–302
challenges to, 302–305
New Jersey's challenge to, 305–308